EBRAHIM ALKAZI

Holding Time Captive

ADVANCE PRAISE FOR THE BOOK

'A monumental work about a colossus. Post-Independence Indian theatre undeniably owes everything to the iconic Mr Alkazi. He, in every sense, is the fountainhead of modern Indian theatre. His supreme genius as a director and teacher, his unmatched erudition, his Western sophistication coupled with deep knowledge of ancient Indian theatre traditions, his unfailing vision—all these have permanently radicalized our regional theatres forever. It is not easy to encompass his enormous contribution in one single volume, but Amal Allana stands up to the challenge this task throws up with tremendous elan and confidence. She is objective as only she can be about her subject, and being his daughter, she also brings an unusual warmth and luminosity to her narrative. I hope her narrative is taken up further by others to continue exploring this phenomenon called Alkazi'—**Mahesh Elkunchwar, playwright and screenplay writer**

'As its somewhat Proustian subtitle—*Holding Time Captive*—indicates, Amal Allana's biography of her father, the legendary theatre director Ebrahim Alkazi, develops a richly detailed and much-needed social portraiture of the people, relationships, associations and crises that shaped much of metropolitan Indian culture between the 1940s and the 1990s. With a sure touch backed by meticulous research, Allana reconstructs the linkages between personal and public histories, straddling the domains of theatre, literature, the visual arts, cinema and politics. Allana writes both as daughter and chronicler, shuttling adroitly between these roles; satisfyingly, her narrative is both enthralling and critically astute. While Alkazi emerges as the titanic figure that he was in life—as theatre-maker, painter, cultural impresario, collector, archivist and institution-builder—he also takes his place, in this book, among an ensemble of gifted and original contemporaries. At the heart of this book is a deeply moving account of the author's parents, Roshen and Ebrahim Alkazi, the life they crafted for themselves, their joys and tribulations. Reader, you hold in your hands a superb contribution to modern Indian cultural history'—**Ranjit Hoskote, cultural historian**

'Personal, even intimate, yet expansive and comprehensive. Amal Allana tells the story of Ebrahim Alkazi, her father, a major force shaping modern Indian theatre and the visual arts. She details his roots in the Arab world, his schooling in England, his deep knowledge of both Indian and European culture, his path-breaking work in Bombay and Delhi, and his both Indian and international approach to the arts. Amal Allana's account of Alkazi's sophisticated world view is not only fascinating but also foundational to Alkazi's expansive vision of Indian theatre and art. Alkazi believed in and practised international dialogue and knowledge, an artistic and humanist ecumenicism that is inspirational and generative. Allana also shares and discusses in depth Alkazi's complex private life, which was part and parcel of his extraordinary achievements. Drawing on personal experience, letters, interviews, anecdotes and archives, this book brings Ebrahim Alkazi alive as an epoch-shaping man, unique and inspiring'—**Richard Schechner, editor, *TDR*, and University Professor Emeritus, Tisch School of the Arts, New York University**

EBRAHIM ALKAZI

Holding Time Captive

A Biography by
AMAL ALLANA

VINTAGE
An imprint of Penguin Random House

VINTAGE

USA | Canada | UK | Ireland | Australia
New Zealand | India | South Africa | China | Singapore

Vintage is part of the Penguin Random House group of companies
whose addresses can be found at global.penguinrandomhouse.com

Published by Penguin Random House India Pvt. Ltd
4th Floor, Capital Tower 1, MG Road,
Gurugram 122 002, Haryana, India

First published in Vintage by Penguin Random House India 2024

Copyright © Amal Allana 2024

All rights reserved

10 9 8 7 6 5 4 3 2 1

The views and opinions expressed in this book are the author's own and the
facts are as reported by her which have been verified to the extent possible,
and the publishers are not in any way liable for the same.

ISBN 9780670096381

Typeset in Bembo Std by Manipal Technologies Limited, Manipal
Printed at Thomson Press India Ltd, New Delhi

This book is sold subject to the condition that it shall not, by way of trade
or otherwise, be lent, resold, hired out, or otherwise circulated without the
publisher's prior consent in any form of binding or cover other than that in
which it is published and without a similar condition including this condition
being imposed on the subsequent purchaser.

www.penguin.co.in

*For
Nissar,
and
Zuleikha, Tariq and Rahaab*

CONTENTS

A NOTE ON THE TITLE   xiii
INTRODUCTION   xv

PART ONE: POONA & BOMBAY, 1939–1948

CHAPTER 1
ESCAPE TO ANOTHER WORLD   3

CHAPTER 2
GOD SAVE THE KING!   18

CHAPTER 3
QUIT INDIA   26

CHAPTER 4
THEATRICAL PURSUITS   36

CHAPTER 5
THE THEATRE GROUP @KT   49

CHAPTER 6
LOVE LORN   62

CHAPTER 7
PASSING FROM TIME INTO ETERNITY   79

CHAPTER 8
THE HOUSE OF THE FOOLISH VIRGIN   89

CHAPTER 9
TO BE OR NOT TO BE   97

CHAPTER 10
BOMBAY DANCES WITH DEATH 106

PART TWO: ENGLAND, 1948–1951

CHAPTER 11
THE PARIS OF PICASSO AND THE ENGLAND OF MOORE AND SUTHERLAND BECKONS 121

CHAPTER 12
38, LANSDOWNE CRESCENT 133

CHAPTER 13
40,000 YEARS OF MODERN ART 147

CHAPTER 14
THE ANATOMY OF DRAMA 159

CHAPTER 15
POETRY IN PICTORIAL FORM 172

CHAPTER 16
A MEETING OF WORLD CULTURES AND AU REVOIR 184

PART THREE: THEATRE GROUP, BOMBAY, 1951–1954

CHAPTER 17
'SOCIETY NEEDS BUILDERS—NOT ONLY OF BRIDGES AND BUILDINGS, BUT OF IDEAS AND INSTITUTIONS' 203

CHAPTER 18
'LIFE QUICKENS INTO ART AND IN TURN ENRICHES LIFE' 212

CHAPTER 19
HEADING FOR A SPLIT 232

CHAPTER 20
LULL BEFORE THE STORM 244

CHAPTER 21
THE BREAK-UP 260

PART FOUR: THEATRE UNIT, BOMBAY, 1954–1962

CHAPTER 22
THEATRE AS A WAY OF LIFE 273

CHAPTER 23
HOSTING SPENDER 285

CHAPTER 24
THE SCHOOL OF DRAMATIC ARTS: MODERNITY AND PROFESSIONALISM ON STAGE 297

CHAPTER 25
THE THEATRIC UNIVERSE OF POST-INDEPENDENCE INDIA 312

CHAPTER 26
MADRAS MOTHER: THE NEED FOR ROOTS 330

CHAPTER 27
ALKAZI'S WOMEN: AGENTS OF CHANGE 352

CHAPTER 28
DIFFICULT DECISIONS 368

CHAPTER 29
IN LIMBO 379

PART FIVE: NATIONAL SCHOOL OF DRAMA, NEW DELHI, 1962–1977

CHAPTER 30
AASHAD: PUTTING HINDI THEATRE ON THE MAP 397

CHAPTER 31
ANDHA YUG 411

CHAPTER 32
THE METAMORPHOSIS OF DELHI: THE INDIA TRILOGY 425

CHAPTER 33
THE WAR CYCLE 440

CHAPTER 34
THE EAST-WEST THEATRE SEMINAR 453

CHAPTER 35
NEW NARRATIVE STRATEGIES: BRECHT AND FOLK THEATRE 459

CHAPTER 36
REACHING OUT 470

CHAPTER 37
PURANA QILA: SCALING NEW HEIGHTS 487

CHAPTER 38
ALKAZI OUSTED! 504

PART SIX: ART HERITAGE, CICA, SEPIA, ALKAZI FOUNDATION FOR THE ARTS, NEW DELHI, NEW YORK, 1977...

CHAPTER 39
OPTIONS 517

CHAPTER 40
ART HERITAGE: UNFINISHED BUSINESS 524

CHAPTER 41
BRITAIN: DEVELOPING A SENSE OF HISTORY 539

CHAPTER 42
THE PASSAGE OF TIME 555

CHAPTER 43
CICA: A GLOBAL IDENTITY 569

CHAPTER 44
THE RISE AND FALL OF CICA 586

CHAPTER 45
CIVILIZATIONAL CHRONICLES 596

CHAPTER 46
I DO NOT KNOW, LORD, ARE YOU THERE? 610

CHAPTER 47
DISAPPEARANCE 613

ACKNOWLEDGEMENTS 629
CREDITS 631
NOTES 632

A NOTE ON THE TITLE

The title of this biography, *Ebrahim Alkazi: Holding Time Captive*, arises from a few sentences inscribed by my father on a scrap of paper that fell out of one of his notebooks unannounced, on the day he passed away.

My husband, Nissar, our children and grandchildren, my brother, Feisal, and his wife, Radhika—all of us were sitting around trying to absorb the loss. My father's handwriting on the note was very shaky and his ideas somewhat incoherent, so one assumed it had been written some years earlier. Taking the scrap from my hand, my son, Rahaab, read it out loud, trying to make sense of it . . . The gist of the few lines seemed to suggest that it was difficult to grasp the fleeting quality of time, and my father wondered if 'time' could be held 'captive'. It immediately struck me that these three words evocatively captured the very essence of his desires, his love for life and living . . .

In another sense, the phrase was open-ended enough to also reflect my efforts as his biographer—to 'hold' the essence of his 'time' 'captive' within the pages of this book.

INTRODUCTION

Does Ebrahim Alkazi's story need to be told? It certainly does, especially since he was an inspirational force during the post-Independence period—a time when a new nation was being constructed, both culturally and economically, to keep pace with a fast-changing world. Alkazi's modernist staging of plays, his effective new programme of theatre training, his laying the foundations for the first professionally oriented theatre institution, the National School of Drama (NSD), his inclusive approach in visualizing the relationship of the regions to the centre in the field of culture, and, later, his support and fostering of Indian modernity in the visual arts through the establishment of his own arts institutions. Art Heritage in Delhi, Centre for International Contemporary Art and Sepia International in New York, and, finally, the Alkazi Foundation for the Arts were achievements that contributed to his impact and influence on the course modern Indian culture between the 1940s and 1990s. Such a contribution, coupled with his formidable and charismatic personality, accrued to Alkazi a considerable national and international reputation.

One was therefore surprised to find insufficient material on his life and work, not at all worthy of a polymath of his stature; nothing much other than reviews of his productions, interviews in the media, some television conversations, scattered articles where he is mentioned or the occasional contribution he himself made to a few journals. Why? One possible reason could be that Alkazi was an extremely reserved person, verging on the hermetic. Insistent on exactitude, he was known to dissuade the press and even scholars from interviewing him, as he felt they were not sufficiently conversant with the range of his work to engage in a meaningful dialogue with him. He was also extremely careful that his often blunt and at times controversial views should not be misquoted or pulled out of context, so that Alkazi, towards the latter years, began to request journalists for written questions, which he diligently answered in his own calligraphic hand. I realized then that the considerable cultural impact Alkazi had made, was made by him directly—live, in either one-to-one interactions, or with audiences both large and small. In which case, should Alkazi's inspirational thoughts, ideas and life be allowed to fade away like an ephemeral theatre performance?

As his daughter as well as a theatre practitioner myself, I brought the paucity of material available on him to his notice, reasoning that future generations would want an insight into his life and work as one of the prime movers of the contemporary movement in the arts. 'Why not write yourself?' I repeatedly suggested. He promised but was eventually unable to give this task the priority it deserved.

My mother's passing in 2007 brought the urgent need to put together some material on him. He was already eighty-two by then. Nissar, my husband, and I decided to undertake three projects: an exhibition on his theatre work—*The Theatre of E. Alkazi*, 2016, which we jointly curated and designed; a comprehensive publication—*Ebrahim Alkazi: Directing Art*, edited by Parul Dave Mukherjee—on Alkazi's work in the field of the visual arts; and an exhibition—*The Other Line*, in 2019, curated by Ranjit Hoskote—with over a hundred drawings and paintings by Alkazi that we magically discovered wrapped in a tattered bedcover, in an old tin trunk that belonged to Roshen, my mother.

These projects demanded that we now actively search for more material. We travelled to my father's workspaces and homes in Kuwait, London, New York, Delhi and Bombay. We were thrilled to find my father's notebooks from his student days at RADA, notebooks of theatre productions, sketches for sets and lighting plans, sources of music selected for plays, fragile manila envelopes with old reviews and brochures of productions, copies of the *Theatre Group* and *Theatre Unit Bulletin* that Alkazi had brought out in Bombay between the 1950s and '60s, old family photographs and more. Invitation cards and catalogues of exhibitions provided us with dates and venues. We began creating timelines for Alkazi's theatre work, for major events in his life, a timeline for all the art exhibitions he had curated in the course of his career, the talks he had delivered. Patterns emerged as we corelated his life to his work.

These three projects, then, became an opportunity for me to study and understand where Alkazi's ideas had emerged from, ideas that had led to an enormous range of multidirectional work in the future.

Although we had located scores of letters sent by my father to my mother, to Uma Anand, to my brother, Feisal, and to myself, as well as ours to him, I had only scanned them for references pertaining to his work. From around 2016–17, I began to relook at the private correspondence, especially with the two women in his life, with whom he shared his ideas and plans at length, also discovering that they revealed an intense, youthful, romantic strain in his character that continued over the years, a penchant for humour and wit with wordplay, a gift for poetic expression, and a deeply felt need for constant companionship and the endorsement of his plans by his partners. In addition, I found Alkazi's responses to the changing political scenario, to people and to cultural events.

What the letters revealed on second reviewing was his state of mind at particular junctures. All of a sudden, they began to provide me with an emotional graph of my father's life that had been missing so far. They also presented clues regarding his development as a person, as well as his deep philosophical and spiritual musings, and his quest for the meaning of existence. I was excited. These letters added a new dimension to my store of memories and experiences of my father as I had known him while growing up. It was only then, after years of working with this raw material, that I felt I was ready to embark on a biography.

* * *

It was never my intention to assess Alkazi's work. I was clear from the start that this was going to be a biography of my father written from my perspective of being both his daughter and a theatre person. The documents I have cited will, I hope, enrich and provide authenticity and veracity to his story; however, what remained central to my approach was my *experience* of him as a daughter.

I have tried to bring to this narrative lesser-known aspects of my father's life that have rarely been touched upon—like the fact that he was an Arab by birth. To me, his 'otherness' would reveal itself when I accompanied him on visits to the Middle East to meet his family. There he was totally at ease, speaking Arabic fluently, wearing the Arab dress, following Arab customs and protocol, abiding by the Arab hierarchical family structure codes and Arab gender relations—a side of him rarely glimpsed in our family life together in India. This often bred in him contradictory attitudes that brought into sharp focus the fact that my father was indeed a product of two cultures—an Arab one that he had inherited and an Indian one that he had constructed, resulting in a complex personality, which led him to jokingly refer to himself as a 'Maharashtrian Arab'.

As a daughter, I have experienced my parents tackling their marriage with integrity—neither of them felt compelled to play out their relationship according to some conventional yardstick, making them perhaps one of the earliest generation of Indians who examined the institution of marriage on entirely new terms—as a partnership of equals.

I have also included in my narrative the experience of our lives as a close family of theatre people. I was always actively involved in my father's theatre work—I was cast in several of his plays as a child, and as I grew older I was made responsible for various backstage duties as well. I was privy to my father's rehearsals, as they happened mostly at home, in our Bombay flat; in later years, when they shifted to the Bhulabhai Desai Memorial Institute, I used to slip across there after school, as it was virtually next door. When he built a theatre on the terrace of our building, all I needed to do was walk up a flight of stairs and look on spellbound! My being privy to my father's work continued when we shifted to Delhi in 1963, as well as 1965 onwards, when I joined the NSD, becoming his 'formal' student.

This biography, then, gains a second and parallel perspective arising from the fact that my father was also my 'guru' at the NSD. Now, what I imbibed from him was of a completely different order. For three years at the NSD, I was taught to become a professional director. Part of my education came from observing him direct some of his finest productions at the NSD. My gaze was now different—I began watching him as an aspiring director myself, absorbing his rehearsal process from the first day up to the opening night. Besides my studies, I also had the opportunity of observing him mould the NSD as an institution, as it was still in the making. I saw how he continuously remodelled the curriculum to keep pace with the times, inviting top instructors from across the country and from abroad as guest lecturers.

After the NSD, I spent two years on a scholarship to East Germany to comprehend and imbibe the ideas of Bertolt Brecht. Nissar joined me, and we were exposed to theatre of an international standard. The shift away from home and Delhi allowed me to gain a much-needed distance and objectivity from my father. With my marriage, and the setting up of my own company in Bombay with Nissar, we began to practise theatre with an entirely different approach from my father's. I had now become a 'professional' and began to view my father as part of the 'theatre movement'—I began to assess his contribution in relation to that of his contemporaries with a greater critical perspective.

It is therefore with these two lenses that I look at my father's life—one as being his daughter, which is a more personal view; the other a more detached, objective stance of being his chronicler, where I attempt to see him in context, as being part of the first generation of nation-builders post Independence in the field of culture.

In order to share this vast, rich repository of memories, experiences and facts of my father's life, I hope to provide the reader with a unique glimpse into a powerful and enigmatic personality whose emotionally charged personal life closely reflected and ran parallel to the growth and evolution of his startlingly fresh ideas and vision for a modern cultural movement in India. I hope my dual perspective will add texture and emotion to this biography—which would otherwise have become a dry narration of Alkazi's undoubted achievements—and will thereby provide a more holistic representation of the life of a unique individual.

PART ONE

Poona & Bombay, 1939–1948

Alkazi as a child, 1926

Courtesy: Alkazi Personal Archives (APA)

CHAPTER 1
ESCAPE TO ANOTHER WORLD
1939

Carrying his bicycle, Ebrahim tiptoed across the sandy patch of the compound. Alerted out of her afternoon siesta, Mariam leapt out of bed and, pushing aside the daintily embroidered curtains, anxiously called out, 'Ebrahim! Ebrahim!' Pretending not to hear her, the young lad mounted his bicycle and sped out of the gate, nearly colliding into the Parsi spinster sisters returning from their weekly lunch of dhansak at an Irani restaurant on East Street. '*Arre, arre, gelo gando chokro! Kya kartaye tum? Su karech?!*' (Hey, you silly boy! What are you doing?!) screeched the elder one, moving out of his way and nearly spilling the contents of her closely guarded tiffin box that held the remnants of lunch. Ebrahim hastily acknowledged his mistake. 'So sorry, Aunty!' he called back with a bashful, apologetic smile that totally disarmed Armaity, the younger, plumper one. '*Ketlo naughty boy che! Pan ketlo mitho!*' (Such a naughty boy! But so sweet!)

Peddling as fast as he could down Synagogue Street, Lal Deval was a fiery blur in the afternoon light. Looking over his shoulder continually, he was praying that his mother would not wake up the entire household of six children, get into her Packard car and launch into a full-scale search for her missing son, her favourite Ebrahim! Finally sensing that there was, in fact, no pursuing battalion on his heels, he slowed down to catch his breath. In the dim distance, he heard the Lal Deval clock strike the half hour—1.30 p.m. He had enough time to get back before his father returned from Bombay by the Deccan Queen, getting in at 8 p.m.

It was a Saturday afternoon in Poona in 1939. Ebrahim Alkazi, the second-eldest son of Hamed and Mariam Alkazi, was scarcely fourteen years old. A little shorter than most boys his age, he was dressed in longish cotton shorts and a short-sleeved shirt. Fair-complexioned, without a single pimple to attest to his adolescence, an aquiline Roman nose separated his unusually sharp, deep-set, beady eyes. Slim, well-formed, sensuous lips and deep brown, wavy hair softened the otherwise longish, narrow, sharp jawline, which could perhaps be regarded as his most Arab feature.

His father was, after all, a Saudi Arab from the Nejd region, a central part of Saudi Arabia comprising a mainly rocky plateau. An entirely self-made man, Hamed Alkazi had suffered intense hardship, deprivation and poverty, crossing the Rab-al-Khali desert twenty-five years earlier in 1914 to finally settle in Bombay and build himself up into a state of economic stability. His main attributes were his quietness, piety and scrupulous honesty, rare for a merchant in a strongly competitive market. What Ebrahim, even at this young age, seemed to have inherited from his father was a sense of single-minded purposefulness. The heat of the Poona midday sun was therefore of no consequence to him and his mind sped ahead of him, past Raviwar Peth, past the Deccan Gymkhana, past the 'cantonment' limits to the bustling Poona 'city'. Zig-zagging through the serpentine lanes with their tongas that were jammed on the bridge across the River Mutha, Ebrahim could not wait to enter what he experienced as the hallowed precincts of Poona's International Book Service. He had been waiting for copies of J.R.R. Tolkien's *The Hobbit* and John Steinbeck's *The Grapes of Wrath* to arrive for many weeks now.

Ebrahim paused to inhale the aroma of paper that immediately hit the nostrils. Adjusting his eyes to the dimness of the interior, he deftly made his way to the bookshelf where his books would be awaiting him. His search ended in... naught! Disappointed, he began to turn away when he spotted a book with an intriguing title—*Untouchable*. The author was someone named Mulk Raj Anand. The dust jacket advertised it as one of the first Indian novels in English, a novel about a poor Indian man. Intrigued as to how a 'sweeper' could be the protagonist of a whole novel, he put it down, only to be distracted by a mustard-coloured magazine lying on the bottom-most shelf, the word 'Theatre' glinting through the dust covering it. What thrills there were in store for him today! Ebrahim's heart pounded as he cleared away the dust, gradually revealing the title:

Theatre Arts Monthly
January 1933
The next two lines mentioned the articles it held:

'Theatre Outpost USSR by Mordecai Gorelik; Portrait of a Theatre, America by Edith J.R. Isaacs...' An entire magazine on theatre?

Father Ricklin, his school principal, had cast him in play after play every year since he had enrolled in St Vincent's School at the age of four and acting had become Ebrahim's passion. On stage were the moments when he got to assume another life and another personality. Now, with solemnity and a great sense of reverence, Ebrahim carried the dusty magazine to a nearby wooden table and ceremoniously wiped it clean with his kerchief. He drank in the photographs and advertisements! Page 1 had a photograph of women in white shroud-like garments. The advertisement read, 'Mary Wigman and Group. Opening performances at the New Yorker Theatre.' Next to that was an ad for an Indian company, 'SHANKAR and his Company of Hindu Dancers and Musicians', at the same theatre! Then *Teatro del Piccolo* at Lyric Theatre. An advertisement for a book by Lee Simonson called *The Stage is Set* followed. Another ad announced *New Plays for Little Theatres* was now available at Samuel French's bookstore. These were names that Ebrahim had never heard of before, but so engrossed was he that they were immediately committed to his memory. Each photo was ablaze with vibrant faces, gestures and bodies in motion, all of which began to imprint themselves on his consciousness.

Loud voices abruptly jerked him into the present. An argument appeared to be underway at the back of the store.

Reverting to the theatre magazine, he thought he should certainly buy it! A single copy was 50 cents (approximately Rs 3). He was a little short, but it was enough to reserve the magazine. Maybe he would request Mr Dixit to accept the balance next time.

He made his way to the back of the shop, where Mr Dixit normally sat in a secluded corner shut off by bookshelves. Peering around the shelves, Ebrahim came upon the sight of four people in an acrimonious discussion. Most of them sported their caste marks on the forehead, which Ebrahim recognized only too well. Dressed in quasi-Indo–European attire fashionable among more progressive members of the upper-caste Brahmin community of the Bombay Presidency, the upper part of the torso was encased in a western-style shirt, tie and jacket, the only difference being that the shirt was not tucked into trousers, but its ends flapped loosely over the dhoti, over which was worn a knee-length morning coat of a deep hue. Western-style laced-up shoes were worn with cotton socks held up by garters! The entire look was complemented by a Maharashtrian *pheta*, or turban on the head, while a fashionable European-style walking stick completed the educated Maharashtrian Brahmin look!

'Blasphemy! Total blasphemy!' exclaimed one, emphasizing his words with a firm tap of his walking stick. 'What is the need for this author to always talk about the underdog in our society? Always about the underprivileged! In this new book, it's a poor sepoy', he said, pointing to a copy of *Across the Black Waters*, Mulk Raj Anand's latest. 'But in this one...' he said, triumphantly holding aloft a copy of *Untouchable*, '... it was unpardonable! To show this Bakha, this *untouchable* character, actually *touching* an upper-caste Hindu!'

The youngest in the group shot back, 'There *is* an urgent need to talk about such issues, Mama, don't you see? We have to re-examine our caste system. Embedded in it are the seeds of our present-day problems! Mulk Raj Anand does not mean to overturn society; he wants us to understand and accept all people as *equal*!'

'Exactly, my boy!' agreed Mr Dixit. 'Mr Anand is, for the first time, as far as I know, providing the downtrodden of our country with a *face* by introducing this Bakha character as the *protagonist* of his novel. We should appreciate these books in light of what Gandhiji and Dr Ambedkar are untiringly fighting for—that outcastes be allowed to return to the fold through seat reservation!'*

'Absolutely, Mama! I have read *Annihilation of Caste* by Babasaheb Ambedkar from cover to cover! And I agree that there is absolutely no place for *chu-achut* in our country any longer! That is why books like *Untouchable* must become our new Bible! It is compulsory reading for all right-minded nationalists!'

Great consternation followed. Mr Dixit smiled, more than satisfied that his tiny, unassuming bookshop was one of the *addas* for serious intellectual debate in Poona City! Raising his voice above the hullabaloo, he tried to calm ruffled nerves while simultaneously calling out to an unseen servant.

---

* The historic Poona Pact between B.R. Ambedkar and Gandhi on reserved seats for the Depressed Classes was signed in 1932.

E. Alkazi (second row, seated right), aged eleven years, with his siblings, Poona

'*Aikto kai, Sakha? Panch garam chai paije . . . ani tyacha barobar, taza poha!*' (Are you listening, Sakha? Bring five cups of hot tea . . . and along with it, some fresh poha.)

He stood up from his rotating-cum-rocking chair to repeat the order and as he did so, the chair tilted back, hitting the corner of a framed calendar of Shiva, Parvati and Ganesh, which flew off its unstable nail. Without thinking, Ebrahim flung the *Theatre Arts Journal* to the side and sprang into the room. Six pairs of eyes were now riveted on the calendar, which took a nonchalant somersault in the air to come to rest in Ebrahim's outstretched hands. A beat. Then, as if on cue, a tea cup that had overturned in the ensuing melee slowly rolled to the edge of the table, teetered there momentarily and then daintily fell to the floor. Another held pause as all eyes surveyed the debris.

Noiselessly, Ebrahim put the calendar back on its hinge, adjusting it to hang absolutely straight. Awkwardly, he turned to the group of men and offered an apology for barging in.

'No need to apologize, son! On the contrary, thank you for saving my new calendar! It's a Ravi Verma one from his press in Lonavala!' said Mr Dixit, kindly.

Ebrahim politely nodded to each of the men and walked out of the enclosure, out through the book racks and finally out onto the streets. Hearing the muezzin's call, he realized that he was inordinately late for the early evening prayers. He mounted his bike and slowly peddled off, silhouetted against the pink of the setting sun. It had been an exciting afternoon. *The Theater Arts Journal* lay on the bookshelf, temporarily abandoned.

***

As he entered the courtyard, it was already dark. Ebrahim saw his brothers and sisters file into the house from their table under the trees, laid out for their Arabic classes. Each one was carrying their books in with them when Sulaiman, around nine, plucked Munira's book from under her arm, tweaked at Lulu's hair and began to run. Munira gave chase, while Lulu let out a scream and ran off to complain to Ummi in the kitchen. Ali, Ebrahim's elder brother by barely three years, and the Arab tutor, Shaikh Husain, a young man of not more than eighteen, walked towards Ebrahim.

'Salaam Alaikum,' they greeted one another rather formally and stood in the shadows, conversing in chaste Arabic. Ebrahim politely excused himself for being late to attend the Arabic class, as he had gone in search of a book. Shaikh Husain ignored the excuse. He was always pleased to see Ebrahim, who invariably cracked jokes with him in Arabic.

'We are preparing for the recitation session set up for your parents next week, Ebrahim. What do you plan to recite?'

'If you permit, Sir, I will read a passage from Taha Hussein,' replied Ebrahim without a second thought.

'That will be just excellent!' said the Shaikh, pleased. Undoubtedly, Ebrahim would excel. He had an ear for languages and would be well-prepared enough to reassure Hamed and Mariam, his employers, that their money was being well spent!

Ali and Ebrahim walked away towards the little room at the side of the outhouse, which Ebrahim had only recently been allowed to use as his own private den. The door boasted a handwritten sign: LITERRATI!

Ebrahim was in the process of building up his personal library, which he had carefully arranged on open wooden shelves lining one of the walls. His father had encouraged him in this endeavour, providing him with regular pocket money to buy books. Though Ubba himself was unable to read or write English, he would inspect the room from time to time and make Ebrahim read aloud the titles along with the names of the authors. Charles Dickens was undoubtedly among Ebrahim's favourites, as he had already acquired *David Copperfield* and *A Tale of Two Cities*. Others on the bookshelf were *Robinson Crusoe*, *Gulliver's Travels*, *The Adventures of Tom Sawyer* and *Treasure Island*. Reading about adventures in foreign lands seemed to appeal to the young Ebrahim, who now began to leaf through a colourful booklet of Michelangelo's murals in the Sistine Chapel that he had recently won as a prize for elocution.

Fr Ricklin had taken a personal interest in guiding Ebrahim and selecting books for him to read, awakening the boy's interest not only in the classics but, surprisingly, in writers such as John Steinbeck and Pearl S. Buck. When Ebrahim came in during the holidays to help sort, arrange and cover library books, Fr Ricklin, quite pleased by the young boy's maturing response to literature, suggested that he gather a few like-minded friends and form a small literary circle. And so it was that the LITTERATI Club came to be in an Arab household!

Ummi was not supportive of this venture, as she preferred that her children avoid 'mixing' too much with others, especially not in their home. But Ubba drew a compromise, suggesting that the club could be away from the main house in the outhouse cottage. So, every few weeks, a topic for discussion was initiated by Ebrahim for the LITTERATI members. There would be much excitement among Ebrahim's siblings when his friends were to come over, despite the fact that he had strictly forbidden them from entering his den on such occasions—Ali was the only exception and party to these secret, 'hi-brow' ventures! His younger brothers and sisters would stand outside, their ears glued to the closed doors. To this day, they swear that it was only Ebrahim's voice they heard, holding forth, either giving some kind of speech or lecture or declaiming a poem![1]

Hamed and Mariam had spent long hours in the early days of their marriage sitting on the veranda of their tiny home, discussing the upbringing and education of their children in great detail. It was around 1926 and by then Ali, Fatima and Ebrahim were already born.

'We are so far away from our *watan*, our homeland, Om Ali,"* said Hamed with a deep sigh of reflection. 'We cannot, we must not, allow our children to forget their roots. Hind is changing so fast, right in front of our eyes. If we are not careful, our children will be adrift, without moorings.'

A self-made man, Hamed Ibn Ali Al-Qadi, an orphan, had left his native country, Saudi Arabia, at the age of fifteen, in order to make something of himself. Born in 1898 in the city of Unayzah, one of the two important cities of the Nejd region that stretched from Jabal Shammar, Ha'il, in the north to the Wadi al-Dawasir in the south and from the Al-Dahna sands in

Gateway at Bombay to Commemorate the Landing of Their Imperial Majesties King George V & Queen Mary on 2 December 1911

the east to the inland side of Al-Sarawat Mountain in the west, this region (part of the Al Qassim Province) may have been one of the poorest areas not only in Arabia but also in the entire world until the discovery of oil. In fact, the social and economic lives of this province, and Arabia in general, had not changed since medieval times.†

---

* Mothers in the Arab world are not called by their given names; they are called 'Om Ali' or 'Om Feisal', etc., after their eldest son. So my grandmother was always called Om Ali.

† However, by the twentieth century, through the efforts of the Qusman people, their province rose to be the wealthiest, not just in Nejd, and today it boasts the highest per capita income in Saudi Arabia.

The poor economic conditions of Nejd could be attributed to its hot and dry weather, making agriculture irregular and undependable, often leading to famines; secondly, because of its inland location, Nejd was an isolated region. Thus, trade had become the most appropriate alternative for the people of Arabia since ancient times. However, what prompted Hamed to finally leave his native land were the recent skirmishes between the Al-Saud family and the Ottomans, each fighting to gain control and consolidate their power over the region, making it politically unstable. In such circumstances, Hamed was frequently handed a gun and directed to shoot.

'Shoot whom? Fight for what? Who is the enemy? Why is there fighting?'

'Don't ask so many questions! Just shoot in the direction where the gunfire is coming from!' he was told. Throwing his gun aside, Hamed, both poor and insecure, realized that this kind of existence did not hold the promise of a meaningful future for him.

It was then, in 1913, at the age of fifteen, that Hamed Al-Qadi departed from Nejd with nothing more than a few articles of clothing, a camel and what was supposed to be his tiny inheritance, to begin his epic journey of virtually walking across the desert, a journey that was fraught with uncertainty at every turn. He soon ran through his last penny and even had to sell the camel. Found by some Bedouins in a caravanserai lying in a dusty heap, half dead, he was bought a meal. Hamed plucked up enough courage to ask whether his services could be of any use. Could he tend to their camels en route in return for meals? Travelling with them as far as Basra, they parted ways.[2]

Hamed worked in Al Zubair (Basra, Iraq) for a while as a record keeper in a trading firm, acquainting himself with the trading business before getting in touch with the Al-Bassams, distant relatives of his from Unayzah. Hamed handed over the promissory note that he had safely carried with him from his uncle in Nejd, requesting that the boy be helped, if possible. After some confabulation, the Al-Bassam merchants confirmed that they were leaving for Calcutta in a few weeks and offered Hamed the job of companion to their young son. With little choice, Hamed took up the assignment and they set sail for 'Hind' by dhow. Weeks later, the skyline of Calcutta was spotted!

The Al-Bassams, like other traders in India from the Qassim province, were known as the Qasimi merchants of Arabia. The Al-Bassams had established themselves in Calcutta, the centre of the tea trade, in the early 1900s, as their business mainly involved exporting Indian tea to Gulf countries. Shrewd traders, their business grew exponentially with them establishing offices in Bombay as well, making them amongst the wealthiest and most powerful of Arab business families in India.

The Al-Bassams were well pleased by Hamed's earnestness. They soon discovered his ability to write in a neat, calligraphic hand, a talent not easy to come by in those days. Elevated to the position of a clerk in their Calcutta office, Hamed was quick to learn the administration of trading—how to maintain the shop's financial records, in addition to the shop's storage and goods. When a vacancy came up in the Al-Bassam Bombay office, Hamed was selected to fill it. It was 1914 when he alighted the East Indian Railways train at Bombay.

Hamed soon found his way around the bustling cosmopolitan city. Arabs, Jews, Iranians, Afghanis, Nepali Gurkhas, Sindhis, Chinese and Eurasians, other than the British, of course, had all come to seek their fortune as merchants and traders of one kind or the other. The native languages of Marathi, Hindustani, Gujarati and Konkani became laced with Arabic, Persian, Sindhi and, of course, English words, becoming a new lingo that was alive, racy and part of the spirit of a new cosmopolitan age.

The Al-Fawzan family, the Al-Shaya family, the Al-Bassam family, the Al-Nasser family, the Sultans, the Behbahanis, the Al-Hamdan and Al-Fadil families were some of the oldest and most well-established Arab merchant families to have settled in Bombay. Most of them exported spices, rice, sugar, textiles, tea and Alphonso mangoes, while perfumes, pearls, horses, carpets, gold, currency and dates were imported from the Arab world. Hamed carefully observed how their hard work led many Arabs to grow prosperous, even wealthy. Within a couple of years, he felt confident enough to establish his own trading agency, deciding that Indian spices and textiles were much sought after by the Arab world, making them safe commodities to trade in.

Through their daily interactions with their Indian counterparts—Gujarati sethias, or commission agents—Arab merchants were exposed to the widespread changes sweeping across the vast Indian subcontinent. Hamed observed how Indians, a colonized people, were responding to the

First World War that their rulers, the British, were involved in. He saw that Indians had greeted the event with a show of loyalty and support for the Empire by showering money and men into the war effort. At the same time, he noted a burgeoning sense of nationalism being mobilized through the demand for self-rule by leaders such as Annie Besant and Bal Gangadhar Tilak, who used India's war contributions to demand self-government for India. Gandhiji, on the other hand, felt that 'England's need should not be turned into India's opportunity.'

By 1919, India's massive war contribution had no doubt prompted Britain to declare that 'the progressive realization of responsible self-government would, from now on, be the aim of British rule in India'. Yet, as the war ended, promises were broken. The Rowlatt Act of 1919 carried wartime ordinances into peacetime legislation, giving powers to the British to imprison Indians without trial. This infuriated Indians. Gandhi condemned it as the 'black' act passed by a 'satanic' government. A watershed moment was the Jallianwala Bagh massacre on 13 April 1919 in Amritsar, Punjab. The post-war years saw Gandhi's rise to power in nationalistic politics and he became increasingly visible at rallies and meetings in Bombay.

Besides a rise in nationalist politics, the interwar years (1919–1939) saw a phenomenal transformation of Bombay. Hamed astutely observed how age-old traditions were altering. How interactions with the British had begun to influence not just the feudal class of princely Indians or those working in the Indian Civil Service, but more significantly, led to the emergence of a new Indian middle class primarily composed of merchants. Introduced to modern and progressive ways of thinking, this class of Indians had begun sending their children to Catholic or Protestant schools, where the medium of instruction was English, followed by an education in England, from where they returned as highly proficient barristers, doctors, etc.

Bombay began to offer new lifestyle patterns. Concepts of family entertainment such as going to the cinema and social clubs encouraged mixed gatherings and the socializing of women—a custom that had been frowned upon so far by local Bombay society. Jazz had caught on, making wining, dining and dancing a regular social event; there were dance schools dotted all over Colaba teaching the rumba, samba, salsa, waltz and foxtrot to young enthusiasts. For a more exclusive evening out, affluent Indians and Indian royalty enjoyed playing bridge, rummy or billiards in their clubs.

The major transition in the intellectual landscape of Indians was also reflected in the tremendous alterations in the physical landscape of Bombay. Hamed began to notice an enormous amount of capital being invested in Bombay. The older section of the city, known as the 'Black City', was by and large untouched, while new and attractive multi-storey apartment homes sprung up. These avoided the earlier Indo–Sarasenic or 'Indian–Gothic' style in architecture that had been used for public buildings like the Rajabai Clock Tower, the Bombay High Court and the Victoria Terminus Station, or even the typical colonial style for bungalows, in favour of the new rage—the art deco style popular in France and the US between the 1920s and 1930s.

Appealing to nouveau-riche Indians, whose taste for elaborate swirls and decorative ceilings and flooring was appeased, a large number of flats in posh areas such as the sea face of Marine Drive and opposite the Oval Maidan sprang up in this art deco style. Auditoria for theatre performances of visiting British troupes built in the late nineteenth century, such as Gaiety (later renamed Capitol) and Excelsior, were now joined by new cinema houses like Regal, Eros and Metro, which were specially built as glamorous venues for the latest Hollywood films.

By now, Indians had been exposed to practically 200 years of British rule and were fairly familiar with ideas of modern democracy. Indians were, after all, living in a technologically advanced age, with all manner of reproductive mediums such as photography and print technology in place even before the turn of the century. By 1925, Bombay, with its trams, trains, telegraph systems and its massive dockyards, was regarded as not only a major centre of industry and trade, but one of the most affluent colonial cities worldwide. To be in Bombay was to practically be at the economic hub of the world!

Hamed realized this and it excited him, but he found it difficult to absorb this new westernized culture sweeping across the city. The reconstruction of the old, traditional India was a heady experience for the average Arab merchant, who, by and large, came from small, isolated tribes in the desert. With a clannish mentality, they were totally unlettered in western ways. To them, India appeared 'very advanced and modern'.

This was true of what was happening in Turkey under Kemal Ataturk and in Egypt too, where there was a similar impact of the West on those ancient civilizations. Hamed had made it a point to keep in touch with happenings in the Arab world. He ordered out progressive newspapers like *Al-Ahram*, avidly reading each issue from cover to cover on his weekly train journey back to Poona from Bombay by the Deccan Queen, leaving them neatly stacked in the compact library of Arab and English books he had created in his Poona home. He wanted his children to keep abreast of not only the political news but also to be exposed to Arab poetry and the new Arab literature that was coming out of the Arab world. This was Hamed's small way of countering the full impact of the western tornado.

Hamed was keen that his children imbibe traditional Arab values. From time to time, he would point to a red box on a dresser containing the desert sand of Unayzah that he had carried with him to India so many years ago. Addressing them, Hamed would say in quiet, hallowed tones:

'My beloved children, this is the sand of your country; this is the sand of Nejd, our home. To belong to Nejd is a privilege; never forget that. You belong to a very old and very well-respected Nejdi family, the Al-Qadi family. Being a Nejdi means to always be honourable and truthful, to be gracious, kind and loving to all of God's creatures. People will recognize you as a Nejdi when you behave honorably, never arrogantly. They will respect you. But we are now here, in Hind, as guests, so never betray the hospitality that is being offered to you here. You have been born here. Hind too is an ancient and honourable civilization with many great and forward-looking leaders, so respect and honour them in equal measure.'

During such moments, the child Ebrahim sat silently, mesmerized by the shiny red box, as he took in his father's words. How could the contents of the red box be his land? What did that mean?

Hamed often wondered when and whether he would ever return to his country. It was, however, still in a time warp, unwilling to give up its tribal lifestyle. Hind was a good alternative, but Hamed continued to look out for a progressive Arab country that would be closer to his heart and to his sense of home and belonging. As a kind of gesture of his growing open-mindedness, Hamed began to sport the Egyptian red fez along with western suits rather than the regular Arab *dish-dasha* for formal occasions. He was never of the opinion that the women folk of his family, neither his wife Mariam nor his daughters, needed to wear a burka or even a hijab. But Hamed had no intention of blindly following the West. All he wanted was to somehow keep pace with life around him.

So though the young Arab couple were excited and curious about the transformations they observed in a rapidly changing India, they felt a great sense of unease and uncertainty about how to process all these experiences as Arab migrants. True, their rising incomes now allowed Arabs to set up homes in affluent areas like Marine Drive, Marine Lines, Colaba or Ballard Estate, but their offices still remained in the heart of the commercial district, Nagpada, Chakla Street, Crawford Market and around the Bombay Stock Exchange, where the Khojas, Bohris and Memons, the traditional commercial communities of Bombay, thrived. Here, perhaps was where they felt most at home. Here, the rules of pure 'commerce' dictated the norms of behaviour and social interaction. Though the odd Arab did sometimes become a member of the Radio Club, the Cricket Club of India (CCI) or the Willingdon Sports Club and frequent the restaurants at Bombay's new hotels like the Taj Mahal, the Ambassador or the Grand Hotel, his comfort zone as well as his belly were still appeased by the local Irani restaurant that served Persian fare or by the delicious kebabs at Sarvi, opposite Foras Road, in the red light district of Bombay.

Hamed himself was a very simple and austere man who never flaunted his hard-earned money. He was neither interested in clubs or hotels, nor in living in a posh building or watching films. None of these new ideas shook his faith; in fact, they strengthened it. Hamed strove to understand the Quran in all its dimensions. The repetition of the prayers five times a day were moments he looked forward to. Each time, a new meaning echoed the last, expanding his understanding, like ripples in water. The metaphors drawn from nature allowed him to see new visions of beauty in the everyday, giving a sense of wonder and uniqueness to even the most mundane. A closet poet himself, Hamed was transported by the sheer aesthetic brilliance of Quranic suras. He wanted his children to experience and perceive the world through their understanding and appreciation of the Prophet's words. Studying the Quran was a must for his children, as it would anchor their lives wherever they might finally go.

Having pondered the issue of belonging and home long and hard, one fine morning, Hamed announced to Mariam in low, loving and deliberate tones, 'My dearest wife, I have come to a conclusion; I am going to shop for a tutor.' He and Mariam agreed that bringing an Arab tutor from Saudi Arabia to teach the children the Quran, its meanings, its correct pronunciation and its rhythmic recitation would be quite an expense, but in the end, it would be money well spent. It was a necessity.

Before long, Shaikh Husain was interviewed through a proxy and 'imported', so to speak, into their little Poona home. He was soon absorbed into the Alkazi family, dining with them and living in one of the outhouse rooms in the garden. Always dressed in a cool, white *dish-dasha* made out of pure Egyptian cotton, Shaikh Husain was a pleasant and soft-spoken young man with impeccable manners and a truly melodious voice. He articulated the Quranic verses very becomingly, allowing them to resonate through the rooms of the bungalow punctually, five times a day, the drone of the children's voices accompanying him as closely as possible. It appeared that the neighbours were attentively silent at these hours, and then, as if in response, the Parsi spinster sisters living in the house to their right, would contribute a 'Chopin in C-sharp minor' on the piano at 4 p.m., while the Goans in the opposite building, sipping their cashew feni into the wee hours, shared their soulful jazz music, played off His Master's Voice (HMV) records on their recently acquired gramophone machine, which beckoned the young Khoja girl on the second floor to open her windows, sensuously lift her bare arms, and sway to its rhythms, while the other residents of 10, Synagogue Street secretly watched the performance that was actually meant for the Pathan lurking around the compound gate, till the faint sound of a child's cry made her reluctantly withdraw from centre stage, bringing the sultry night to a close and ultimately satiated, a hushed silence enveloped the compound until the fireflies faded into the early morning light.

This symphony of music of various peoples, experienced as a child, embedded itself in the consciousness of Ebrahim Alkazi, providing him with a template, a module, of how sharing occurs—unobtrusively filtering into his understanding of how different cultures interweave and allow life to continue in perfect harmony. Like the music, Ebrahim carried his pantheon of Poona neighbours within him too, reinventing and bringing them to life in the shape of characters in the theatre productions he would direct thirty, forty and fifty years hence.

CHAPTER 2
GOD SAVE THE KING!
1939

It was Friday, 1 September 1939, a day Ebrahim would not easily forget. He repeatedly came back to this day. What exactly happened? Nothing really. On the surface, all the things they did continued to be done, except that over the sameness loomed a shadow... the shadow of his father's frown, his preoccupied look.

When[1] the church bells announced the eleventh hour, calling the faithful to the last morning mass, the maids in the Alkazi household had more or less finished their daily tasks. Ummi's non-stop flow of talk changed from 'ordering around' and 'scolding', to more pleasant exchanges, always verging on an angry outburst, so that when something moved her to loud laughter, everyone smiled and the tension eased. Nobody took Ummi for granted or counted much on her good humour; she was only as humourous, friendly and interested as a queen! Nobody questioned her or dared to hold an alternate opinion! She even dispensed kindness severely! Like telling the vegetable vendor:

'Why are you carrying that weight from house to house... if you get ill, nobody will look after you! Go, someone make her a cup of tea and give her some bread! You, Abdul, don't touch her tea or bread! You'll desecrate it! Let a Hindu serve her, so she can enjoy her cup with a clear conscience!'

The vegetable vendor, grumbling about life, said something about all men being equal in the eyes of God.

'I believe that too,' said Ummi. 'Is there any real difference between Ram and Rahim?'

Lovingly reminiscing about his mother, my father said: 'My mother slowly came to know some of the Indian languages, such as Marathi, Gujarati, Urdu and Hindustani, all of which she mastered over a period of time, coming to know the choicest of abuses!'[2]

Mariam Alkazi, Poona

Observing his mother with the maids from the corner of his eye, Ebrahim made his way to the library, the script of *The Merchant of Venice* tucked under his arm. Just when he thought he was out of Ummi's eyesight, she called out in Arabic, 'Don't ever leave the house again without telling me, Ebrahim! I get so worried that something will happen to you, *habibti!** You are never to go out alone!'

Ebrahim's grip tightened on the book. He wanted so much to explore the world on his own! Just last week, when he had gone along for a class picnic, Praxy Fernandes, Amjad Ali and he were bringing up the rear when some stray dogs they were teasing suddenly began to bark noisily. Turning back, Ebrahim could not believe his eyes! There was Ummi in their Packard, stealthily following the school group! Were Fr Daschner,

---

* Endearment in Arabic, meaning 'dearest one' or 'darling'.

Fr Oesch and Mr Godbole, the drawing teacher, not enough to control a small contingent of boys on a day trip? Why did she do such things? It embarrassed him![3]

The fire of rebelliousness rose within Ebrahim now, and he was about to respond to his mother's admonishment when he noticed his father on the far side of the veranda. The family had not been unduly surprised when Hamed returned from Bombay a day earlier than he normally did each week, although they were not quite sure why they had been kept from attending school. Now Ubba was sitting on a planter's chair, eyes wide open, concentrating on the news on his prized Marconi radio. On other days, he would be half dozing, his legs resting on the extended arms. Not wanting to stir up a commotion, Ebrahim just said, 'You are right, Ummi,' and made himself scarce, entering his father's library located in the centre of the house.

A quiet, hushed space, the library was lined with bookshelves. Crowding them were English encyclopedias, Arab novels and poetry, the literary magazine *Rauz Al-Yusuf*, and stacks of copies of the *Al-Ahram* newspaper that his father specially ordered from Egypt. All had been neatly arranged by his elder sister, Fatima (also known as Fatty). Ummi's pencil-coloured childlike drawings, mainly of the environs of Poona, decorated one wall, while the other was filled with group photographs of the family taken each year at a photographic studio on East Street! These were mounted in velvet frames that Fatty had patiently embroidered with exquisite cross-stitch patterns. Along with the tastefully embroidered velvet cushions and crocheted lace-trimmed half curtains at the window, Fatty had created a sombre colour scheme that complemented the lush Persian carpets that lined the floor, giving the otherwise austere room a graceful, feminine air.

Fatty herself, around sixteen years old, was a round-faced, pretty girl with alabaster skin and dark, curly hair that fell becomingly around her face. She closely resembled her mother. At the moment, she was wearing a loose, old, rose-coloured cotton kurta and sitting on the maroon, pistachio green and beige-coloured Persian carpet, with a pile of schoolbooks, glue, scissors and labels to one side. She was totally engrossed in covering the books with brown paper and then, in her fine, calligraphic hand, inscribing them in English. Composed next to her was Ebrahim's elder brother, Ali. He stood at his father's desk, intently filling a fountain pen! Ali, in his last year at school, was a strapping lad close to seventeen years old. He already sported a thin moustache and was in a khaki-coloured dish-dasha that he wore at home. It was strange how neither the outside light nor the heat penetrated the library, allowing it to remain bathed, for the better part of the day, in a strange twilight glow.

Reflecting back on scenes such as these from his childhood, Ebrahim saw the close resemblance they bore to the look and feel of old Dutch interiors painted by Johannes Vermeer and Frans van Mieris. It was not just the light, but the fact that their lifestyle had a certain unhurried calm about it, that his parents had created a certain sense of order and had inculcated in them a reverence for things, for never wasting anything whether it was finishing food from the plate, making use of the last pages of an exercise book or even finding use in a little rag. Nothing would just be thrown away; it was always put to some use, always neatly labelled and stored. Habits and discipline were inculcated through repetition, not unlike the repeating of the prayers five times a day. Gaining perfection through repetition—that appeared to be both method and motto. Much, much later, Alkazi recognized that, to some extent, it was this sense of orderliness that motivated him to create a kind of mental or intellectual orderliness for himself that was translated into a love of collecting, of labelling, of storing, so as to ultimately make sense of that which was collected, and put it to use.

'Look Ebrahim! I've redone yours, as the covers were beginning to fray,' Fatty said to him in Arabic. The children were forbidden to speak English at home, though all of them could speak, read and write the language. She handed him a notebook to inspect. 'Does your Highness approve?'

Having removed his sandals at the door, Ebrahim lowered himself on to the floor next to her and taking the new-looking, tightly covered exercise book, he checked for spelling errors. The top right-hand corner bore his name: 'Ebrahim Alkazi, Standard 9, English Composition, St Vincent's School, Poona.' Ebrahim never failed to compliment her. 'Absolutely beautiful! Thanks!'

He then settled down to learning his lines. Leaning against a bolster pillow, he closed his eyes. Fr Ricklin was also the director of the annual school plays. He had suggested that memorizing dialogues together with the gestures one would use was a far easier way than just trying to commit them to memory.[4] Ebrahim began to fling his arms around. He was to play Bassanio, who falls in love and ultimately wins Portia's affections. But how would he speak convincingly when Portia was to be played by Percy Karanjia, the boy with light blue eyes? Every time he looked at Percy and began his dialogues, the entire classroom, full of young boys, was convulsed with laughter! He would have loved to join them, but he knew that it would lead to a sound hiding. All of this made Ebrahim nervous. The Shakespearean lines were difficult enough to master...

'Ali, please take me up in this,' he pleaded, handing his brother the script. 'You read Portia's lines.'

'Go to hell!' snorted Ali.

'Is Ali to be a girl with a moustache?' Fatty dissolved into peals of laughter.

After the midday prayers, lunch, unlike the noisy encounter it usually was, was eaten in stony silence. Ubba barely spoke and Mariam was monosyllabic. The children spent the afternoon with Shaikh Hussein under the tree, busy with Arabic studies. From beyond the high walls of the Lal Deval, they could hear nationalistic slogans being raised, but they had become quite commonplace, so no one except Ubba seemed to pay heed to them today. He crossed the compound, making his way to the green fields belonging to a Maharashtrian farmer, from whom they sometimes bought their vegetables. He was one of Ubba's closest friends, despite the two men not having a common language in which to communicate. The farmer spoke only Marathi, while Ubba managed with his smattering of Hindustani. Both men seemed engrossed in deep conversation till 4 p.m. when Ubba returned to the children, announcing it was time to go to the Bund Gardens. There was much silent scuttling around as hair was brushed and shoes were worn. Then Ubba directed Mariam, Sulaiman, Munira, Lulu, Noora and Fatty to go ahead in the Packard, a second-hand seven-seater that Ubba had recently bought from Sir Karimbhoy Ibrahim. This was Ubba's special gift to Mariam and the children for their comfort and safety. Ubba never used the car himself; he was a simple man, never given to luxury. Putting on his fez cap and collecting his walking stick, Ubba, Ali and Ebrahim followed on foot.

Ebrahim, always a good walker, loved the bristling energy that Poona exuded with its mix of cultures, a fact that he often spoke about nostalgically in later life.

There was an extraordinary cosmopolitan feeling about Poona. It was a very richly textured kind of life that one experienced. And the feeling between communities and the distinction between communities did not arise.

Moharram always convulsed us with fervour and an almost emotional kind of catharsis. And on the very last day of Moharram, when you had the hearses going around, simulating the deaths of Hassan and Hussein and the beating of the chests of hundreds of people who were participating in this, it was a terrifying experience.

At the same time, you had the experience of a Maharashtrian culture. It was vivid . . . during Ganesh Chathurthi, Diwali and Dusshera. Then there was the Pateti of the Parsis—musicians came around and played at your doorstep, whether you were a Parsi or not! Songs like 'Isle of Capri' . . . There was the celebration of Christmas by the Christian families, which surrounded you and they sent trays of fruits and so there was constantly a kind of sharing of experiences among these families . . . It was largely the womenfolk that saw to it.

At the same time, you must remember that Poona was not merely a military station; it was also the capital of the Bombay Presidency, particularly during what is known as 'the Season', when the government was shifted from Bombay to Poona . . . So you became very aware because the Governor of Bombay would come to Poona . . . would be taken in state, along with his bodyguard and so on . . . and to see on a Saturday certain types of society in Poona dressed up in their flowing gowns and straw hats, with feathers . . . and with parasols and going in Victorias . . . was something extraordinary, something out of the twenties, something so Edwardian . . . that was literally there in front of you . . . that was a time of an extraordinary mixture of cultures that lived side-by-side.[5]

For quite a while, the three Alkazi men walked in silence, with Ubba a few paces ahead of the boys. Slowing down, he put his arm around Ebrahim's shoulder and, in a commiserative undertone, spilled out his anxieties. With his eyes on the road and never once making eye contact with his sons, Ubba made them aware of the potentially difficult times ahead.

'Today is a very important day . . . World War II has been declared! No need to get alarmed, but as my sons, you should know that whatever happens in the world will eventually affect us too. For example, my weekly trips to Bombay have come to the attention of the authorities. I have been told to report to the police station in Poona every week when I come here. I have to carry my papers with me at all times.'

'But why, Ubba? You have done no wrong!'

'No, I haven't . . . but today we are all under suspicion . . . they are worried about spies!'

Ebrahim looked terrified.

'These are new rules, my boys. They are ominous and may not bode well for our family. I must share with you that we may not always be welcome here. Another matter of concern to me is: in this war, who is going to be recruited to the British Army? Are they to be Indians? I hear that there is no consensus on this matter. Gandhiji and Jinnah seem to hold very different opinions. Subhas Bose has his own ideas. I have not mentioned this to you before, but there have been a lot of lathi charges in Bombay lately, especially near our office. The jails are full. Everyone is waiting for Gandhiji to make a statement. Because of the war, there will be shortages. But a lot of black marketeering too, as people will want to continue their affluent lifestyles at any cost. In the middle of all this, I don't know what they have in store for Musalmans. We have to think of ourselves. We do not belong to Hind . . . we may get caught in the crossfire. I want you to understand that we must always be very careful . . . steer clear of politics . . . I may need to travel . . . We must have options. Ali, I don't want the business to be in jeopardy. I want you to stop school right away and come with me to Bombay. You must begin to learn the ropes. And you, Ebrahim, must stay here and look after your mother, brothers and sisters. You are the next eldest son. Finish your studies. Now don't let your mother know what I have told you. Life has to go on and it will.'

Ubba fell abruptly silent and then picking up pace, he resumed his position as head of the small group. The boys had not completely grasped the import of their father's words, but Ebrahim sensed Ali's withdrawal—a steely, glazed look coming up on his face. They neared the Bund Gardens. As usual, there were the British women in their crinoline dresses with parasols looking very grand, followed by their Indian ayahs with the

Certificate of Naturalization, Hamed Alkazi

Hamed Alkazi

'baba-log' in their prams. There, in the distance, they saw Ummi fanning herself on a bench, close to the bandstand. The military band was playing a boisterous march and the little children were imitating the marching of soldiers that they regularly saw in the early mornings and late evenings returning to the barracks in neat rows. Poona, after all, was a garrison town, with the British Army in station. Finding it difficult to join in the merriment, Ali and Ebrahim shifted to the further end of the gardens, overlooking the bund, or dam. The gushing water falling from a height reflected the tumultuous confusion they were experiencing. It seemed as if a whole new future was about to unravel before them. Ali was going to shift to Bombay? Ebrahim felt quite anxious to be the one looking after his mother and siblings, week after week...

As Ubba moved on towards Ummi and the children, the band struck up 'God Save the King'. The boys turned around to see their father immediately stop in his tracks and stand to attention, ramrod straight. This gesture suddenly and sharply brought home to them the intensity of their father's fear and it hit home that they were indeed aliens in a foreign land who were required to toe the line!

CHAPTER 3
QUIT INDIA
1942

Hurtling down the steps two at a time, Ebrahim rushed out of the Gobhai Karanjia Building and made his way through the labyrinthine back lanes, pushing past a sea of humanity comprising Bohras, Banias, Memons, Khojas, Marwaris, Sindhis, Parsis, Moplahs, Goans and Pathans. In doing so, he encountered a virtual babel of different languages that, in some incomprehensible way, embedded itself into his consciousness. Several years later, when he became a much-lauded cultural icon and some self-appointed custodians of the 'Indian identity' presumed to ask him what India was from his 'westernized' perspective, it was to this experience of his youth and to these sounds, smells and visuals that Alkazi would repeatedly return, laying claim to their intensity as vital to the formation of his 'Indian' identity. 'I am a local Bombay boy,' he would thunder. 'We are, all of us, of one bastard stock or another!'

Ebrahim suddenly remembered that he had forgotten his Duckback raincoat* in the hurry to get out unnoticed. Mercifully, the rain gods were holding out today, he thought, as he glanced up towards the darkening sky filled with huge, billowing clouds. Finally, the lane spilled onto Mohammed Ali Road, where he saw the shining red BEST bus turning around the corner. He made a dash for it, somehow managing to hang on to the handrail just as the conductor rang the bell for the bus to take off.

He had not accounted for such a rush. It was not nearly 9 a.m., and he had to reach Sophia College at Warden Road by 11 a.m. for his debate competition. Then to St Xavier's to meet Fr Duhr by 2 p.m. He was auditioning for a tiny role in the new Shakespeare play. Today's was a tight

---

* The famous Duckback brand comes from Bengal Waterproof Ltd., which was founded in 1920 and is said to be India's first waterproofing company. Like Bengal Chemicals, this enterprise, too, was born of Swadeshi fervour.

schedule, indeed! The bus was jam-packed with mill workers, it seemed. Where were they off to in white kurtas and dhotis? The bus seemed to be crawling through the mohallas of Kalbadevi, Bhuleshwar and Girgaon. Although he had started well in time, it was going to be difficult to make it. No point in getting tense, he thought, deciding instead to ponder the positives. It was so exciting just being in Bombay, sitting on a bus and taking off on his own! The Jesuit priests at St Xavier's, like those at St Vincent's, were most encouraging about his acting and debating skills, what with him winning many a debate for the college. These activities had already won Ebrahim some amount of acclaim, not to mention popularity, among his peers.

On the flip side, the last six months spent living with his father had been a strained experience. Hamed Alkazi had rented two flats in the Gobhai Karanjia Building, both on the fifth floor. One was used as the office, from where he conducted his small import–export business and alongside was the flat where he lived with Ebrahim and a few other young Arab assistants. Located in the heart of the business centre of Bombay's Crawford Market, the locality was noisy and crowded.

Ebrahim had never lived alone with his father for an extended period of time. A man of a few words, Ubba believed in spartan living and high morals, which could best be inculcated through strict Arab discipline. A red-haired cook called Gulab, a eunuch, joined the all-male residents at Gobhai Karanjia and together, they lived a near monastic existence. The general monotony was broken with the noisy arrival of Ummi and the children from Poona at least twice or thrice a year, often coinciding with the school holidays. These visits were sometimes planned along with those of their Arab relatives from Saudi Arabia who lodged with them and brought dates, nuts and Arabic sweets as gifts for the Alkazi family. In turn, Ummi would reciprocate with Kashmiri shawls and the best-quality Alphonso mangoes, gifts that most Arabs prized and relished. But for the rest of the year, it was mainly Gulab's incessant chatter and gossip that brought some light and laughter into the otherwise grey flat.

As soon as the 'Bada Sahib' left the flat, Gulab would roll up his greasy wide pyjamas with great theatrical flourish, lower himself onto his haunches and begin grinding the spices on the *masala ka patthar* (grinding stone) clenched between his two feet, while a stream of stories would gush forth.

Gulab had an innate flair for storytelling, laced with the choicest of abuses and many a licentious sexual innuendo. As he proceeded breathlessly, he was able to transform the most trivial incident into a highly potent and pungent melodrama! His bloodshot eyes would widen into great round orbs while his red, henna-stained fingers and palms shot through the air like flames, all of which kept his listeners enthralled. The extreme heat and smoke emanating from the coal fire, the fumes of the spices and the effort of working and talking at the same time caused him to sweat copiously through the entire performance, which came to an abrupt, suspenseful halt when he heard the lift halting and its cage-like doors opening. Peering towards the entrance, Gulab's red betel-stained tongue would shoot out of his mouth as he bit it, his eyes would squint and he would bring his fingers to his pursed lips. '*Saheb aa gaye!*' he would whisper, '*Shh! Baad mein bataunga!*' (Sir has returned. Shh! I will tell you later.)

Silence would descend once again as father and son partook of their meal, with barely a few polite, formal words of exchange. The cacophony of the crowded streets below barely penetrated the walls, allowing the chasm to appear palpable and looming. There was never a question of Ebrahim opening up a topic of conversation with his father. It was deemed impolite for a young man to have anything at all to share with his elders, much less an opinion!

But there were times when the silence was deafening for Ebrahim. This was not the silence of deference, obedience or respect. It was the silence of things left unspoken and denied. This was the silence that had come to stay after Ali's departure.

No one referred to Ali; no one explained what had happened, why Ali had run away, left, vanished. His parents, though immeasurably bereaved, never acknowledged Ali's absence in words; it was a wound that was left to ooze in silence.

Ebrahim had been looking forward to being in Bombay with Ali. In fact, the two brothers had often discussed what they would do together once Ebrahim finally moved there! The day Ebrahim arrived from Poona, his father was there to receive him at Victoria Terminus Station. They rode to Crawford Market in a Victoria carriage. His father dropped him off at Gobhai Karanjia, saying he was going to be busy that day and that Ebrahim should carry on upstairs.

Gulab met Ebrahim effusively. Throwing open the door, he passed his hands over Ebrahim's face, cracking his knuckles on either side of his head! *'Masha Allah! Dekho kitna bada ho gaya hai mera Munna! Mera Lal! Tu sahi salamat pohonch gaya! Allah ka lakh, lakh shukar hai!'* (Allah be praised! Look how big you've grown, my boy! Thank God you've reached safely!) Ebrahim entered the flat with great excitement. Passing through the rooms, he noticed that none of Ali's belongings seemed to be around.

'Where's Ali?'

A pause. Then Gulab began to whimper, to cry and finally to sob uncontrollably.

'Mat pooch, Beta, mat pooch, mein nahin bata sakta!' (Don't ask, son, I cannot tell you!)

Ebrahim was quite perturbed by this sudden response. He got Gulab a glass of water from the *matka* (earthen pot) and made him sit down.

'*Lagta hai ki mujh badnaseeb ki kismet mein likha hai ki tujhe yeh kissa sunaoon. Sun Beta, yoon hua ki* (It seems I'm the unfortunate one who's meant to tell you the tale.) . . . That day, your father had gone to Poona. I was cooking when your elder brother suddenly barged into the kitchen and asked me for the keys to the *tijori* (safe). I said I did not know where they were. He then caught me by the neck and dragged me to the bedroom. He pulled out a gun . . . yes, a gun, and held it to my head. I was so afraid, I began to cry and piss in my pants! Hamed Sahib had told me where he kept the keys. I was so scared, I pointed to the cupboard. Like a madman, your brother grabbed them, opened the tijori and in front of my very eyes, God curse me if I tell a lie, he wiped the tijori clean! Took everything! Threw it in a sack. I was so scared . . . because of the gun, you know! Still, I said, "Don't do this, Baba! Where are you going?" He screamed, "I'm leaving! Tell them I'm going to join the army! Don't you know there is a war going on? One can't sit around while everything is going to hell!"'

Ebrahim walked out, numb, on to the balcony. Yes, his elder brother, Ali, was full of a spirit of adventure, and true, there was a certain rebelliousness about him, but why did he have to leave without telling the family? He had often spoken about the need to defend the country, that Gandhi had urged every able-bodied young man to join the British in their fight against Nazi Germany. Maybe he left because he felt his father would stop him, saying that this was not their country, not their business.

When Hamed returned that night, he knew that Ebrahim knew. They avoided eye contact. The incident was never referred to. Ever.

Ebrahim was jolted out of his reverie. The bus had now come to a complete halt because of the severe traffic jam caused by thousands of people on the streets. They were carrying banners that said 'Boycott British Goods' and 'Quit India'; slogans were being shouted. People on the bus joined in full-throatedly and began to scramble off the bus en masse.

'What's happening?' Ebrahim asked one of the white khadi-clad passengers in Hindustani. 'Where are all these people headed?'

'*Arre*! Young man, don't you know? Today is the eighth of August. Mahatmaji will be addressing a rally at Gowalia Tank in a while . . . A historic AICC meeting is happening. We are all headed there to hear what the resolution is. Come along!' He held out his hand; it was as rough as a labourer's. 'Come along! Come along! You won't regret it!'

Ebrahim looked doubtful. How would he make it in time for the debate? Sophia College was still a long way off.

'Have you ever seen Mahatmaji in person?' Ebrahim shook his head. 'Good! Then this is your chance. Otherwise, how will you tell your children in later years that you actually saw a mahatma (great soul)? Come along!'

The man's advice was so persuasive that Ebrahim could hardly refuse. He clasped the large, calloused hand and was led into the thick of the crowd.

Massive crowds were converging from all directions onto the Opera House intersection, where the bus had eventually been stalled—from Chowpatty, from Charni Road, from Grant Road. The sea of humanity narrowed itself into a rope-like stream and made its way over French Bridge. Caught up in the frenzy of the moment, he joined in, shouting slogans: 'Boycott British Goods!' Suddenly, there was a surge in the movement of the massive crowd. Screams rent the air as the crowd turned back in an attempt to flee in the opposite direction. It was not clear why. British Tommies appeared out of the mist, many of them on horseback. Menacingly, one of them galloped in Ebrahim's direction. Trying to get out of the way of the officer's swaying truncheon, Ebrahim stumbled and fell, hitting his head on the sidewalk, his debate papers scattering in all directions.

A few passersby rushed forward to help him up. 'He's bleeding!' said someone. Incensed, a Parsi gentleman in a *pheta* screamed after the officer, 'Go home! *Ghere jao,* mother fuckers! *Suna tumne,* we want Home Rule!' Then, turning to Ebrahim, he dabbed the wound with his kerchief and began tying it like a bandage across his forehead. "Don't worry! Not a deep wound, *Dikra! Aisa hota hai . . . Azadi ke leye, buddha, baccha, sab ko khoon bahana padta hai! Shaheed hona padta hai! Aaj tumhari baari thi! Aaj tum asli desh bhakt ho! Jao! Mummy Daddy ko dikhao! Woh itna khush hone wale hai!'* (Son, such incidents happen! In order to win freedom, young and old alike must be prepared to shed their blood! Become martyrs! Today, it was your turn! From today onwards, you will be counted as a true patriot! Go! Show your wounds to your parents! They will be proud of you!)

Ebrahim swelled with pride. For the first time, he was mistaken for a Hindustani, not a Parsi or a Jew! He was thrilled! 'Thank you, Uncle, thank you!' stuttered Ebrahim, overcome with emotion. Forgetting his head injury, he was at once energized and forged ahead.

For the first time, the thought momentarily flashed through his mind—how desperately he wanted to belong, to feel part of a larger movement, a cause like this one! The cosy comfort and pristine world of contentment that his family had always provided him with had indeed given him a sense of security, but he had always sensed that they lived isolated lives. As children, they were constantly reminded not to mingle, not to participate in any kind of politics . . . because that would implicate them and complicate their lives. Ebrahim had never really been able to understand what exactly it was that they should fear. Yes, he did remember the great transformation that took place while they were in school after World War II began in 1939. Many of the Jesuit priests at St Vincent's High School were foreigners—Italian, American, Swiss and German. All of a sudden, one day, the German priests were picked up and taken off to internment camps! As children, they had watched this happen with almost a sense of bereavement and, of course, fear.

But today, at Gowalia Tank, people's spirits were uplifted, they appeared undaunted. Their multiple voices merged into a full-throated, unified and defiant call! Ebrahim was elated, his spirits buoyed. He had lost track of time. What time was it? He looked in vain for his wristwatch, but it was gone! It must have been snitched in the chaos. It was long past the time for the debate, long past the time he was to meet Fr Duhr at Xaviers'. After hectically trying to find a way out of this avalanche of humanity, he finally succumbed, allowing himself to fully experience these glorious moments, where it was not about him but something much, much larger, something beyond himself or his immediate family.

And then miraculously, through the mist of white clothing, there in the distance, sitting calmly on the dais, was the iconic Mahatma Gandhi—sacred, still, silent, composed. He was carefully spinning his *charkha* (wheel) with complete focus, unperturbed by the commotion around. No one disturbed him from his sadhana, the spinning wheel creating the movement of life, yet steady on its fulcrum. Ebrahim was quite close now and totally transfixed. The sea of white around the Mahatma was like a shining light, a halo—pure and undiluted. Aruna Asaf Ali sat quietly to one side, not betraying her steely determination to make today's rally a meaningful event in their journey towards freedom.

The microphone was tapped and the Mahatma was asked to address the gathering. The raucousness and sloganeering died down and a hush descended over the entire maidan.

'My brothers and sisters', Gandhiji began, 'Occasions like the present one do not occur in everybody's, and but rarely in anybody's, life. I want you to know and feel that there is nothing but the purest ahimsa in all that I am saying and doing today. The Draft Resolution of the Working Committee is based on ahimsa, the contemplated struggle similarly has its roots in ahimsa. If, therefore, there is anyone among you who has lost faith in ahimsa or is weary of it, let him not vote for this resolution.'

The crowd responded that they were 100 per cent with him. He continued, 'Ours is not a drive for power but purely a non-violent fight for India's independence. In a violent struggle, a successful general has often been known to effect a military coup and set up a dictatorship. But under the Congress scheme of things, essentially non-violent as it is, there can be no room for dictatorship . . . The Congress is unconcerned as to who will rule when freedom is attained. The power, when it comes, will belong to the people of India, and it will be for them to decide in whom they will place their trust.

'It may be the reins will be placed in the hands of the Parsis, for instance, as I would love to see happen—or they may be handed to some others whose names are not heard of in the Congress today ... Ever since its inception, the Congress has kept itself meticulously free of communal taint. It has thought always in terms of the whole nation and has acted accordingly ...

'I believe that in the history of the world, there has not been a more genuinely democratic struggle for freedom than ours. I read Thomas Carlyle's book, *The French Revolution*, while I was in prison and Pandit Jawaharlal has told me something about the Russian Revolution. But it is my conviction that, inasmuch as these struggles were fought with the weapon of violence, they failed to realize the democratic ideal. In the democracy that I have envisaged, a democracy established by non-violence, there will be equal freedom for all. Everybody will be their own master. It is to join a struggle for such a democracy that I invite you today. Once you realize this, you will forget the differences between the Hindus and Muslims and only think of yourselves as Indians, engaged in the common struggle for independence.'

Gandhi's stirring speech continued in this vein. In conclusion, he said, 'There is a mantra, a short one, that I give you. You should imprint it on your heart and let every breath of yours give an expression to it. The mantra is "Do or Die".' The crowd was ecstatic ... 'Do or Die! Do or Die!' they chanted in unison ... surging towards the stage ... 'From now on, there are only two words to offer by way of resistance,' said Gandhiji. 'Quit India!'

By now, it was past midnight, and, the entire Congress, to the man, returned to headquarters and passed the famous 'Quit India' Resolution. The young Aruna Asaf Ali remained at the site. Unknown to the others, she hoisted the Congress flag, marking the commencement of the nationwide mass movement. The crowd went berserk, as this was the first time the Indian tricolour was being hoisted. Lathi charge was used by the police to disperse the crowds. The crowd refused to budge. Finally, the police began firing tear gas at the assembly. The national flag was pulled down and volunteers who went to its rescue were beaten off mercilessly.

Ebrahim was shaken to the core. Each word Gandhiji had uttered was imprinted in his consciousness. They were so simple, so effective so unpretentious, spoken without any histrionics because truth, he realized, did not require a loud or strident voice. And it was so magical—the manner in which Gandhiji was able to reach out to each and every person in that huge audience. He not only captured their imagination, but more importantly, encouraged them to take action—not just passively applaud him but use their energies positively to transform ideas into words and words into actions.

Isn't that what was meant to happen in theatre too? Theatre was the field he felt more and more drawn to. It was a field where one could make a difference, where one could directly affect the lives of others and bring people together. That certainly appeared to be the need of the hour. The films he had begun to watch were also filled with a sense of purpose, a spirit of sacrifice and of serving one's country. He had read about the selfless work of missionaries in remote parts of Africa with much interest! For Ebrahim, these were examples of what it meant to serve a community—to devote oneself with passion and a tremendous feeling of commitment so that the society around you benefited from your presence, your knowledge, your expertise. On the one hand, there were these stirrings of the Independence movement taking place, while on the other, there was this kind of idealism, all of which made Bombay such an exhilarating place to be in!

With such thoughts crowding his mind, Ebrahim made his way back home, walking through streets that were emptied out by now. There was a lightness in his step—he felt he was shedding his old life and was being nourished, not by the ideals and ideas of his parents and teachers, but directly by participating through his own experiences. This feeling was entirely new to him. His step quickened and he broke into a run, with street after street passing him by in a blur. 'I love you, Bombay! I just love you!' he belted out. The exhaustion of the long day simply vanished and he was filled with renewed vigour.

When he returned home, it was practically dawn. Sighing with relief, the young Alkazi tiptoed to the veranda. 'This city never sleeps,' he thought, as he watched the metropolis still active. *Pattiwallahs* were gathering around Crawford Market with their carts full of fruits and vegetables that were being offloaded to be taken in by urchin boys. The Byculla factories were sounding the early morning alarm for the next shift, which was followed by the distant whistle of a departing train. Exhausted, Ebrahim finally withdrew and, undressing noiselessly, he crept into bed, which was

Alkazi with his college friends at a railway station en route to Karla Caves, 1943

a small wooden cot placed to one side of the single room he shared with Ubba. It seemed barely a few minutes since he had dozed off when he was awakened by the strains of the azaan. It was already bright; the rays of the sun shot into the room, piercing his unprotected eyes. Ebrahim was filled with guilt from the previous night's late return home. He hurriedly stowed away his cot, did *wazu* and laid out his prayer mat, conscious of his father's eyes following him. There was never a word of reprimand. But the sense of guilt it evoked in the young man was immense.

CHAPTER 4
THEATRICAL PURSUITS
1943

Hamed Alkazi, Ebrahim and Gulab were standing at the top of the staircase, waiting for the lift to bring the Al-Bassams to the fifth floor. Fourteen-year-old Sulaiman had been sent down to receive them. All four men were wearing brand-new clothes. The only problem was that they were all made from the same fabric! Ebrahim could never understand his father's logic—that it was far more economical to purchase an entire bolt of forty or more yards of fabric to fulfil everyone's needs! As a result, the boss, his sons and the cook's clothes were all made of identical fabric! *'Isse bahut bachat hota hai'* (This is very economical), Gulab would say, no doubt thrilled to look part of the family! The new dish-dashas were delivered by the *darzi* this morning and Ubba looked pleased with the results. The fact that the four of them ended up looking like quadruplets or bearers in uniform never occurred to Ubba! Ebrahim and Sulaiman's vehement protestations to their mother had been of no avail. Ummi was adamant that they simply 'do as they were told and not fuss, as today was a busy day!'

True, today was very special. Ummi had come down from Poona with the children and Ebrahim was relieved that, for a few days at least, their bachelor existence would give way to greater maternal domesticity and a lot more opportunities for him to abscond in the continuous confusion of comings and goings—but not, of course, before the arrival of their guests. The Al-Bassam family was coming to formally meet with the Al-Qadi family for the engagement of Fatima and Noorie to the two Al-Bassam brothers—Abdur Rehman and Abdulla, two fine young lads who were not only good-looking with a great sense of humour but were hard-working to boot. Their father, Mohammadali Al-Bassam, was a distant relative and the merchant who had helped Hamed establish himself independently. Over the years, the two families had grown close until finally, when their children came of age, they felt that this dual marriage alliance—God willing—was the practical and right thing to do.

Today, both couples were to be engaged, followed by the *nikah* a few days later. Ummi and Gulab had been ensconced in the kitchen since early morning, making biryani, tashreeb, jeeresh and kebabs, to which Ummi was adding a special desert—her own version of flaky pastry with cream, that they had named 'Om Ali', or 'Mother of Ali', after her!

While putting the finishing touches to the aromatic meal, Mariam happily chatted with Gulab about her childhood days in Bombay, complaining that she missed the hubbub of the city where she had been born. Her father, of the Al-Nassar family, was a well-known horse dealer whose office was next to the Arab stables in Bhendi Bazaar.[*] Dealing in top-quality stallions required for the Bombay, Poona and Bangalore races was a highly specialized and lucrative trade, more so because Arab mares were not allowed to be exported out of Arabia, making each pedigreed Arab stallion worth several thousand rupees. A large number of horses were also required by the British Army. This led to an increase in their price and, along with the fact that horses were exempt from import duties, this immensely benefited Arab horses dealers.

Though Ummi loved horses,[†] she had been brought up to excel as a homemaker. But like other women of her generation whose children were being educated,[‡] she secretly nursed a desire to know more about the world, its politics and the great changes that were taking place.

---

[*] Horses in Arabia had always been considered precious, especially those of Nejd, whose horses were considered among the best. With the British colonization of India, Bombay became a major centre for horse trading. An article that appeared in the *Times of India* in 1894 proudly states that 'the greatest foreign market for Arab horses is, and has for the last hundred years been, Bombay'. The most famous market in Bombay for Arabian horses was the market of Byculla.—M., Alsharidah, *Merchants without Borders: Qusman Traders in the Arabian Gulf and Indian Ocean, c. 1850-1950*, 2020, retrieved from https://scholarworks.uark.edu/etd/3719

[†] When asked about his mother, Alkazi would jokingly respond, 'My mother was a bareback rider in the circus!'

[‡] Ummi agreed with her husband that the time had come for their daughters to be educated. All five girls had initially been sent to a Parsi kindergarten school near their home, and then for a few years to Convent of Jesus and Mary in Poona. However, with the arrival of their tutor, Shaikh Husain, their formal English education had been abandoned in favour of learning to read and write Arabic, though English continued with the help of a private Anglo-Indian teacher.

Her dreams became a reality when Ummi happened to visit a young Muslim neighbour, Khatija, who lived across the compound from them in Poona.

Confiding in Gulab, Ummi began to recount the story of the day Khatija had welcomed her, escorted by little Lulu,[1] into her dainty parlour, respectfully uttering the word *'Bandagi'* as she salaamed Ummi. She went on to describe Khatija's drawing room—scattered around were a number of women's magazines in Urdu. Interested in looking at the picture of the fashionably dressed young woman on the cover of one, Ummi picked up the magazine and, glancing at the text, was surprised to find that she was able to read the magazine's name—*Musarrat*! Turning the pages, she discovered to her delight that she could read everything with ease, as Urdu and Arabic had the same script. Besides, she could actually understand the words as well, being fluent in Urdu! Ummi was so engrossed in reading that she barely noticed Khatija returning from the kitchen with a tray of tea and snacks. Flustered, Ummi hastily put down the magazine.

'Please Mariam Appa, you are most welcome to borrow the magazines. They are really so interesting and I spend many hours reading about my sisters from across the world! Please, take as many as you like . . .'

'No, no . . . I was just looking . . .'

'No please, I insist, don't be formal . . . You will enjoy learning new recipes as well . . . And look! Aren't these lovely designs for children's dresses?'

Thereafter, there was a lot of toing and froing between Khatija's home and their own, as magazines were borrowed and returned, binding the women in a new kind of conspiratorial sisterhood that led to news and views from across the world being discussed!

Women's magazines in Urdu, such as *Musarrat, Shama, Tehzeeb-un-Niswan* (Refinement of Women), *Payam-i-Niswan, Shareef Bibiyan* and *Zebu Nissa*, had gained much popularity from the mid-1930s onwards, some even earlier, since women began to be educated. These magazines covered a wide variety of topics, such as home management, recipes, homemade medicines, health and beauty tips, duties of women, the need for and the means to becoming better wives, conjugal fidelity, women's dress codes and suitable literature, how a woman could be successful—stressing the need to keep her husband and his extended family happy.*

However, women also began to be exposed to current affairs, from world news to details of the proceedings of the All-India Muslim Women's Conference, demand for political representation in state institutions, women and economic development, stressing the need for opening the doors of industries to women, women's right to vote, etc. They also came to know of enlightened women of bygone eras through biographical sketches of Mughal begums, highlighting their educational backgrounds, essays on Muslim mystics, women's poetry, etc.

Suddenly, the doors to a wider experience of the world had been flung open. Ummi could now converse with her daughters about how they would need to be independent-minded and acquire skills that went beyond cooking and darning. Ubba soon got wind of this new-found afternoon hobby Ummi was indulging in—reading! Giving up her afternoon nap, she was to be found tucked comfortably in an easy chair, adrift into another world. Rather than questioning or reprimanding her, Ubba, without mentioning it, began to subscribe to her favourite magazines himself! Ummi, emboldened by her husband's silent concurrence, now began to ask Ebrahim if he could pick up some Urdu novels for her whenever he happened to visit a bookshop next!

Through all this, Ebrahim could not help noticing that it was really poetry that Ummi was responding to favourably. One day, he casually mentioned that there was a mushaira to be held in the city, where many poets would be reciting their new verses. 'If you like, Mother, I can take you there.' Ummi was thrilled. Several years later, Lulu recollected, 'Yes, I remember Ebrahim accompanying Mummy to mushairas that usually began only after 8 p.m. Off they went in a tonga! It seemed so exciting and special! Ebrahim was Mummy's favourite! He did things like that for her ... that made her feel loved and special!'†2

---

* The journals included articles on the position of women in Islam; biographical accounts of famous Muslim and European women; heroic deeds of women; advertisements of books for women; education in Germany; the plight of widows and the support for widow remarriage; famous women poets of Hyderabad; the need for women's education to be based on the values of Eastern culture rather than of the West; and the role of women in modern democracy.

† Ubba, a closet poet himself, was totally supportive of Ummi attending mushairas and was eager to accompany her whenever he was in town. For Ubba, it is clear that he regarded the Quran as *the* most beautiful poem ever written—one meant to uplift the soul and allow

Sultan and Kulsum Padamsee, on their return from England, 1940

* * *

Lulu ran excitedly into the kitchen, 'Mummy, come, hurry up; they are all here!'

The Bassams alighted from the lift and greeted Hamed with full respect, lifting his right hand to their eyes and then kissing it. The younger men embraced one another thrice, as is the Arab custom. All were dressed in traditional Saudi full-length *bishts* (ankle-length cloaks) over the long *thwab* or dish-dasha. They wore the keffiyeh with the black corded rope

---

the spirit to soar. Ebrahim's love for poetry undoubtedly stems from these early exposures to Urdu poetry, and Lulu, in later years, became a scholar, writing a modern and updated commentary on the Quran.

wound around to hold the head scarf in place. All in all, they made a splendid and dignified entry, which the neighbours came out in full force to observe with excitement.

The younger Arab boys came laden with gifts in trays covered with embroidered napkins. These were carried into the house and left unobtrusively aside for the Alkazi family to enjoy later. As Hamed led the male contingent into the *diwaniya*, Ebrahim noticed that his father's stoop had become more prominent. He appeared happy, but all the same, a certain weariness had taken over. All said and done, his father was an optimist and believed that after Ali's departure, Ebrahim, the next in line, would eventually continue the business that he had painstakingly built. Over this last year, he had done his best to see that Ebrahim spent a lot of time each day learning the intricacies of the trade from the Gujarati accountant, Mehtaji. This meant accounting, getting to know the market and who the customers were. 'Our work is with Arab countries; all the correspondence is in Arabic; all the statements of accounts are in Arabic; all the books are kept in Arabic. So, Ebrahim, please give more time to Arabic and not just your college work,' he would cautiously advise.

Ebrahim understood his father's anxiety, but at the moment he had other, more interesting things on his mind that compelled him to make excuses to stay out beyond college hours. This was especially after he became acquainted with the unbelievably charismatic Sultan Padamsee. After a brilliant but incomplete college education at Christ Church College in Oxford, Sultan had been forced to return to India at the outbreak of World War II and had enrolled at St Xavier's College to complete his graduation.

Reminiscing about his arrival in college, Fr Duhr, his English professor, remarked that Sultan Padamsee (nicknamed Bobby) with his 'Oxonian drawl and his highfalutin mannerisms and his high-brow interests in hyper-modern verse and original poetry innovations and artistic fads and novelties burst on to the placid world of Xaverian jog-trot and solid but rather remote admiration and pursuit of things of the mind. It is astounding how much this irrepressible single active being set the waters astir. The peace of the professors of English was at an end. Not only did Sultan's first term Intermediate Arts examination papers show astounding maturity, they were followed, in his Junior and BA College Examinations by a brilliant analysis on British Civilization.'[3]

However, Fr Duhr wrote in large, red letters across the front page of his answer paper that this was personal stuff, showing infinite promise but not likely to curry favour with the Bombay University examiners! But Padamsee did not seem to care excessively for academic success of the conventional order.

In fact, what Sultan Padamsee cared most about were the special Friday and Saturday afternoon readings of poetry by young, budding writers that he began to organize in college. Revamping the loosely coordinated activities of the so-called Shakespeare Group, along the lines of the drama society he had been a part of in Oxford, the Oxford Union Drama Society (OUDS), Sultan now included literary discussions on surrealism or 'the latest manias of super-intellectual coteries', or even talks on new and innovative techniques of staging Shakespeare. 'There was no peace for the wicked and even the fathers/professors were dragged into all kinds of sudden, "unhallowed" student activities.'[4]

Not always resorting to staging entire plays, Padamsee initiated the idea of a theatre workshop, as it were. He asked for small scenes from plays to be enacted on stage, which were then opened up for critiquing by the rest of the members of the group. Ebrahim thought this to be a fine way of learning more about theatre. Before long, Sultan noticed Ebrahim in these small, improvised enactments and invited him to join the Shakespeare Group on a regular basis. For Ebrahim, these afternoons had become absolutely sacrosanct—he felt he could not miss a single session. Sisters' engagements or not, he had to find a way to arrive in time for Padamsee's rehearsal.

Thankfully, the engagement ceremony was simple and brief, concluding by noon. Lunch partaken, the men were sitting in the diwaniya of the fifth-floor office, puffing at their hookahs, chatting about politics and enjoying their kahwa and dates. Meanwhile, the women were crowded into a tiny bedroom, with Ummi looking exhausted but utterly radiant and happy in her pink, flowing dress and diaphanous head scarf. The Al-Bassam women, the wives of Ali Hameed and Saleh Al-Shaya, the Al-Fawzan women, the wife of Husain bin Isa, the wife of Sulaiman Mussalam and her daughters Ayesha, Hind and Laila, were all pressed around the brides-to-be, discussing the latest wedding fashions in Riyadh and what pearl jewellery could be ordered from Basra. Ebrahim, finding all guests and the family

Shakespeare's *Twelfth Night*, Theatre Group, 1944

Sultan Padamsee and Mary Sethna in Shakespeare's *Macbeth*, St Xavier's College, Bombay, 1943

happily engaged, took the opportunity to steal out and catch a tram to VT station from where it was but a stone's throw to Xavier's.

Looking over the sea of heads in the canteen at Xavier's, Ebrahim tried to spot Sultan Padamsee. It was still a little before 2 p.m., and the popular college canteen was overflowing with young students queuing up for the keema-roti rolls! A knot of priests occupied one of the tables. 'Oye, Alkazi!' one of the students called out. 'Rehearsal's in the auditorium today! Padamsee gave no lunch break!'

By now, Ebrahim himself was pretty well-known around college. He had a coterie of admirers struck by his singularly prepossessing presence on stage, totally unlike his off-stage persona, which was soft-spoken and rather retiring. Adding undoubtedly to his charm were his fair, aquiline good looks that made the flirtatious Anglo–Indian and Parsi girls titter in the corridors, if by chance he made eye contact with them—which was never his intention, but it did seem to happen quite often.

'Alkazi! Please say that line from *Romeo and Juliet*, the way you did in class!'

Most times, Alkazi walked on, pretending not to hear, but when he was in a playful mood, he would stop dead in his tracks, strike a theatrical pose and declaim the romantic lines, dreamily looking into the girls' eyes.

Alarmed, the girls would dissolve into peals of laughter and scatter down the corridor in different directions!

What! Was the rehearsal already underway? He was quite sure that it was to begin at 2 p.m.! He would surely be given a dressing down despite the fact that he was only playing a tiny walk-on role of a guard— there was only a week left to opening night! Crossing the quadrangle in the blazing heat, he entered the dark orifice of the Xavier's auditorium. It took him some time to adjust to the darkness. It was empty except for a couple of girls practising a dance on stage. He recognized Manik Servai, the Parsi girl who, despite the fact that she was still in college, had made quite a reputation for herself by acting in a number of productions by Adi Marzban for the Amateur Dramatic Company. Now Sultan Padamsee had cast her in the titular role of Oscar Wilde's *Salome*, opposite himself as Herod.

Mary Sethna, a rather big-made girl with a large, well-cut face, rather like Katherine Hepburn, stole up to Ebrahim and taking him aside, muttered under her breath, 'This has been going on since morning, Alkazi! Manik just can't seem to pick up the steps! How can she play Salome if she can't manage the Dance of the Seven Veils?'

'Where is Mr Padamsee?' asked Ebrahim.

'Up there! On the balcony! He's in a foul mood! We can't move forward! The whole rehearsal has been stalled!'

Ebrahim glanced up in the direction Mary had indicated. There was Sultan Padamsee, lit by the glow of a lamp installed on a small table. His head bowed, he was impatiently running his hands through his wavy hair. He crossed one leg over the other, looked at the stage, then turned away in despair. Jean Bhownagry, his close friend who was sitting next to him, whispered something into his ear. Bobby stood up abruptly.

'One, two, three, four! One, two, three, four,' he shouted, clapping to keep the rhythm. 'Manik! For heaven's sake! Why can't you get it? It's pretty simple! Watch me.' And he demonstrated the steps.

'Roshen! Darling! Improvise! Think of something even simpler for Manik! We can't keep waiting like this! Dammit! This can't go on . . .'

The slight young girl, Roshen, waved assent to Bobby. She was a slim, slip of a girl in trendy, wide trousers and a printed silk blouse that was tucked in. She daintily tripped up onto the stage in her open sandals, which revealed her delicate feet, her shoulder-length tresses bobbing up and down. Manik had lost confidence, it was clear. Roshen appeared to say some comforting words and began to demonstrate another, simpler step. Breaking it into units of movements, her hips swayed most becomingly.

'Who is that,' asked Ebrahim, 'the girl who is teaching Manik?'

'Oh! That's Roshen . . . Bobby's sister. Haven't you met her?'

A cry of anguish and agony rent the air! It was more like the howl of a wounded animal. Roshen and Manik ceased moving on stage . . .

'HOW CAN THIS BE HAPPENING TO US?' bellowed Bobby.

In a trice, Bobby had leapt from his chair, raced down the circular steps from the balcony and was striding across the auditorium in a state resembling the torment of some tragic Shakespearean character! Suddenly, Zarine, Jean Bhownagry, Hamid Sayani, Deryck Jefferies, Yasin Vazir Ali, Ashraf Jairazbhoy, Karsan Shroff, Khorshed Wadia, Katie Umrigar and several other people appeared from nowhere, becoming natural spectators to the ensuing scene.

'I think we cannot, in all fairness to our audience, allow them to see us in this *shoddy*, unrehearsed state! This is the first production of this bloody group and we need it to be either a brilliant success or there is no point in continuing! No half measures!'

Manik, of course, had by now crumpled into an inconsequential blob of nothingness. Tears were streaming down her face.

'Manik! For heaven's sake, I will not be emotionally blackmailed! That will not help! Let us just decide that you will put in whatever hours are necessary and perfect this bloody dance! PERFECT IT! It's the central climax of the entire production! Roshen and I will stay back. I'm willing to stay all night, every night until the show, if necessary!'

There was now a vocal exhibition of Manik's distress!

'Why don't you understand, Bobby?' she wailed, 'I would love to stay on late, but I can't! My parents received a stern warning from the Parsi Panchayat just a few days ago! From now on, Parsi girls will not be allowed to act with boys from other communities! They insist that Parsis can only act with Parsis!'

There was major consternation among the bystanders! 'What nonsense!'

'We can't allow religion to be involved in our daily affairs!'

This was becoming a more complex situation than Bobby had bargained for. Multiple problems were already piling up since they had begun rehearsals. To begin with, the Jesuit priests were extremely uncomfortable with the students performing the work of an author as controversial as Oscar Wilde, who had been imprisoned because he was a homosexual. Besides, this script was too risqué for the college to present. They objected, saying parents would find it immoral! Bobby was unrelenting. He was determined that it was going to be *Salome* or nothing! There was a deadlock. Finally, they arrived at a compromise that the play could be *rehearsed* in college but not *performed* there. Bobby's solution was to do it outside the college, at the Cowasji Jehangir Hall under the auspices of a new group that he had formed—the Theatre Group.

Deryck, the most experienced stagehand among them, a young man who had done some amount of professional theatre in the city with a number of British theatre groups,[5] reminded Bobby that the acoustics at the CJ Hall were atrocious![6] It wasn't really meant for plays. Besides, the stage set with a long ramp that Bobby had designed, though spectacular, was so large that it would not fit on the CJ Hall stage! In fact, if it did have to be installed there, it would need to sweep off the stage and swerve into the auditorium, requiring the first few rows of seats to be removed! This idea immensely appealed to Bobby! Special permission was sought for the same and ultimately granted, for no other reason than Bobby's theatrical persuasiveness!

Then there was the question of a sizeable budget required for the historical costumes, which was significantly reduced by Kulsumbai Padamsee (mother of Bobby and Roshen) loaning her beautiful brocade and lamé saris for the production as long as Roshen, the costume designer, did not cut them up! As the director, producer and main actor of *Salome*, Bobby certainly had his hands full!

A pall of gloom descended. This new situation was, of course, of an entirely different order—it was a sensitive issue, a communal problem, a gender problem. Bobby was about to leave the auditorium, thinking this was the last straw, when he suddenly stopped dead in his tracks and turned back.

'Wait a minute! Roshen, please go back on the stage and stand next to Manik!'

Roshen Padamsee, 1943

Roshen did so, feeling rather self-conscious!

'I knew it!' exclaimed Bobby. 'I have the solution! Roshen, *you* will do the Dance of the Seven Veils. You and Manik are the same size and height. I will see to it that she exits from the stage, the lights will dim and you will come on, in her place, in her costume and do the Dance of the Seven Veils.'

'But Bobby,' Roshen tried to intervene, 'How can I change into her costume so quickly?'

'Don't be an ass, Roshen! You will be totally ready in the wings—in a *duplicate* one! Manik, there's no need for you to stay late. Everything is sorted!'

Thunderous applause rent the air! Manik ran down and hugged Bobby. 'Bobby, you're a genius!' she gushed. 'I will act! I will! Don't worry! I will tell these Panchayati babas to go take a walk! Don't worry Bobby . . .'

'That's the spirit, my girl! The show must go on!'

Ebrahim had witnessed and experienced his first real moment of theatre life . . . how artistic solutions are magically found, how life in the theatre is so full of the unexpected and how people bond so closely. Bobby was walking towards him.

'Hello, Alkazi, old chap! Come along with us. We are going to need all the help we can get to put this production on the road!' Calling out to everyone in general, Bobby loudly announced, 'Dress rehearsals begin at Cowasji tomorrow! Roshen, please inform everyone! Tomorrow at 2 p.m. sharp!'

The entire gang of technical helpers was following Bobby out of Xavier's for Cowasji Jehangir Hall. Ebrahim was too embarrassed to beg off. He slowed down, trying to disappear into the shadows.

'Aren't you joining us, Mr Alkazi?' a soft, mellow voice interrupted his thoughts. He turned and there, bathed in the soft light of the street lamps, was the young woman, Roshen. It had just stopped raining and the streets were wet and sparkling. All Ebrahim could think of was that she looked so beautiful . . . like a sea nymph! Lowering his eyes bashfully, he shook his head, unable to utter a single word. The beautiful, young nymph shrugged her shoulders.

'All right then, good night!'

Before he could say anything, she skipped across the road to the bus stop.

'Bobby! Wait! I'm coming!'

Ebrahim didn't know why he felt so light-hearted. The beautiful girl had actually spoken to him! He remained hidden in the shadows, watching her until a bus arrived and carried her and the other troubadours off into the night.

CHAPTER 5
THE THEATRE GROUP @KT 1944-45

'No, we are not going to completely withdraw from the Shakespeare Society! We are just in the process of formalizing the Theatre Group. We need a logo. Without a logo, our organization has no identity.'

Bobby held up the very art deco-looking design of intertwined letters of 'T' and 'G' he had sketched out. Taking the small sketch from Bobby, Ebrahim examined it carefully. 'I like the little crown on the T . . . Looks rather regal! Like a coat of arms emblem! Very elegant!'

What appealed to Ebrahim was the elongation of the letters and the V shape they formed. They held snugly together, making the logo look like a seal—regal, formal, professional.

Meanwhile, the others reverted to the discussion on whether their newly formed group, under whose banner they had just completed their second production, *Macbeth*, should be linked to the Xavier's Shakespeare Society.

'Bobby, let's be honest here! One can't say the Shakespeare Society actually did a darn thing for the success of either *Salome* or *Macbeth* . . . It's us, the people in this room, who did all the donkey work! We are the Theatre Group!'

'Yes, Bobby! From filling the houses by virtually begging our friends and relatives to come to the shows to . . .'

'Who designed the sets? The props? The costumes? Roshen and Bobby! Who else? And Deryck Jefferies slogged day and night to create the sets! Let's be fair! It's all us . . . just us . . . So why should Xavier's get the kudos?'

'Because that's how it is to begin with, my darlings! That's how any decent, new, experimental theatre company has to make a start . . . With a lot of *sacrifice*, a lot of *hard work*! A lot less ego!'

Bobby Padamsee at home in Bombay with his trophies, 1944

Bobby walked across to the bookshelf and pointed to the stacks of *Theatre Arts* journals piled up in a corner.

'Read what Harold Clurman has to say! Read what Hallie Flanagan has to say! They are talking about theatre being meaningful, not just entertainment. We need to think along those lines as well. And in order for that to happen, we *have* to have a *base* . . . we must have a *mass* base! We can either get that in a *college* with young students or build a strong *proletarian* base among *factory workers*! We need an *audience*! Who is our audience? *These* students who are being *educated* . . . they are impressionable . . . we can guide them . . . make them see the kind of serious yet very exciting work we are doing and wish to continue doing!'

Not understanding the point Bobby was making, Yasin Vaziralli offered, 'Everyone loved the plays, Bobby! I don't think that Bombay has seen the likes of it before! The audience just loved the sets of *Salome*! The way the circular ramp swept down . . .'

'Yes! And what about Roshen's costumes? All your mother's gorgeous saris draped in various styles . . . So original!'

'And did you see how they responded to the idea of an "after dinner performance"? A genius stroke on your part, Bobby! The college authorities said it would *never* work!'

Bobby cut them short.

'Shut up for a moment, all of you! Try to understand what I'm saying! My suggestion is that we should have the best of both worlds—continue to do the plays we *want* to do the *way* we want to do them, AND keep drawing talent and audiences from the college! So, in an *informal* way, the Theatre Group and the Xavier's Group are linked; we continue side-by-side. This is hardly the time for break-ups; we have barely even begun! Don't you see? *Macbeth* did very well on the Xavier's stage, didn't it?'

'True, true, but next time let's do a comedy, Bobby! Something a little lighter! What about those tongue-in-cheek farces that Adi Marzban is known for?' suggested Homi.

Bobby appeared as if a blood vessel might burst. Just then, Lame Boy, the Padamsee cook, walked in with a tray of steaming hot tea and some chiwda. Bobby stood up, his speech over. He had lost interest.

Bobby was in the process of introducing his young college friends to the new ideas he had been exposed to abroad, where the avant-garde theatre movement was reorienting itself to talking to a war-torn audience. Rejecting the crass commercialism of the fare offered on Broadway and the West End, serious-minded amateurs began developing topical plays and playlets and evolving a new aesthetic of theatrical expression. From America to England, this movement gathered momentum and began to be known as the 'group theatre movement' and later, the 'little theatre movement'. In fact, the very name Bobby gave his group—*Theatre Group*—was inspired by the Group Theatre of the US founded by Harold Clurman.

However, Bobby's ideas appeared too idealistic and lofty to many of these youngsters, who came from anglicized backgrounds and were happy to engage with theatre as a light hobby.

Observing Bobby's frustration, Ebrahim retired to one corner of the room with a cup of tea and a copy of *Theatre Arts Monthly*. This was Bobby's den-cum-bedroom. Located in the centre of a sprawling terrace, which occupied at least half the fourth floor, Bobby's room had a private entrance from the main stairwell, allowing his friends to come and go unnoticed.

The room was simple enough. Furnished like a student's pad, there was a low divan to one side with some cushions strewn across it. This doubled up as his bed. A rolltop desk and a rotating chair in the art deco style were the only additional bits of furniture. The front and side walls were pierced with glass-panelled doors that led to the terrace on three sides, allowing the room to be both breezy and bright. The remaining wall was partially covered with a floor-to-ceiling bookcase, with Shakespeare, Auden, Eliot, Ezra Pound, Chaucer, the Bible and books in Greek and Latin all crammed in, while a few open shelves were adorned with trophies and cups that Bobby had won at school and college. Several oil paintings by Bobby, most of which featured bare-bodied men, filled the remaining space on the wall. One even noticed a kind of abstract portrait of a young man resembling Ebrahim among them. A radiogram was precariously perched on a pile of books rising up from the floor.

It was from this tiny room on the terrace of his parents' Colaba Causeway flat that Bobby functioned. It was here, at Kulsum Terrace, that Theatre Group meetings and rehearsals were held, where he entertained his friends until the wee hours of the morning, moving at times to the open terrace under the stars. Here he sprawled across the two-seater swing, declaiming his poetry to a small coterie of his intimate friends who listened mesmerized by his haunting voice.

Jean was now keeping the others amused, showing them his magic tricks. Hamid looked on interestedly. Bobby walked across the room and stood, arms up, holding the doorway, his back to the others, looking out through an open door. Alkazi's eyes followed him. Bobby glanced back and, a moment later, walked out onto the terrace. Turning to the left, he disappeared around the corner and began ascending a narrow staircase leading to another terrace, and then up another flight of steps that led to yet another third terrace! Alkazi quietly slipped out and followed Bobby up.

It was around 6.30 p.m. From where Alkazi stood at the base of the second terrace, he could see Bobby majestically silhouetted against a flaming red sky . . . Whenever Bobby was still, he assumed and held a kind of heightened pose that one might use on the stage. It was very

Dancer by Sultan Padamsee, 1944–45

theatrical, very sculptural and imbued with a kind of contained physical and emotional energy. Bobby had assumed a thoughtful pose, one hand to his head and the other on his hip. His hair needed a trim—it had grown rather wild and the tendrils curled around his face and the back of his neck. Alkazi held his breath. Bobby standing there was like a painting, an apparition of a Romantic poet—a kind of Keats or Shelley figure!

Then, all in an instant, Bobby began to tear his clothes off—his jacket, his shirt, his vest. He was about to strip down to his underpants when he sensed another presence.

'Who's there?'

'Excuse me, Bobby. I'm sorry if I'm interrupting...'

'Oh, it's you, Alkazi! No, no, not at all! Come on up!'

Portrait of E. Alkazi by Sultan Padamsee, 1945–46

Alkazi moved forward hesitantly. He noticed that Bobby was perspiring, his chest covered in droplets. He was breathing quite heavily.

After a pause, he said, 'I don't know why, but I can't take it, really! The others, I mean! They're such knuckleheads and I'm impatient! They are always so petty. So infantile! They don't seem to see the larger picture. It's not an 'us' and 'them' situation. Why don't they understand? We have barely begun building a theatre group and the last thing one wants is to be another 'British Wives Association' doing revues and sketches. If we are not careful, we are going to be compared to them one of these days!'

Bobby then leaned over the terrace parapet. 'Just think, Alkazi, there is no other really *new* kind of theatre work happening in English in Bombay. Ours will be one of the first serious efforts!'

Bobby's face was lit by the last embers of the dying sun. His gaze was now distant; it encompassed the vast islands of Bombay that were spread out around them. His tone became low, base, guttural.

'In no time at all, Alkazi, we could be *the* top company! I want us to be like Diaghilev and the Ballets Russes! Look at the man's vision! He got artists like Matisse and Picasso to design his sets! The greatest dancers of Russia—Anna Pavlova and Nijinsky—worked with him! Choreographers like Michel Fokine! What flair, what boldness, what vision—so modern, so wild. Encompassing all the arts—poetry, music, dance! Simply superlative!* That's what I want us to achieve. Just the three of us can take the country by storm. I know we can do it. Just you, me . . . and Roshenara!'

Alkazi's heart missed a beat. Had Bobby invoked the name of Roshen? The name he had repeated at least a thousand times a day to himself ever since their meeting outside Xavier's! Alkazi was at a loss for words.

'Why yes, of course. Of course, I will do all I can, whatever is necessary . . . we shall work hard . . . make it happen . . .'

He found it impossible to regain his calm.

'But do you mind terribly, Bobby, may I borrow some of these TAJs? You're quite right; one has to keep abreast of what's happening!'

Bobby gently took Alkazi's hand and placed it on his bare chest.

'Can you feel my heart beat?' It was thudding. 'Our hearts have to beat in unison.'

The two young men just stood there.

Then suddenly.

'Bob . . . bby! I say, Bobby! Could you send Mr Alkazi down, please! I have to do his costume trial!'

The strangely intoxicating moment evaporated . . . only to be overtaken by another that was equally heady. Alkazi couldn't get himself to budge.

'You have heard the command of Roshenara Begum, have you not?! You must comply forthwith! Attend to her wishes or else . . . ! Go! Go! Off with you, old chap!'

Alkazi leapt down the staircase as if he had heard a fire alarm! About to rush into the drawing room, he halted. He was greeted by the view of

---

* 'I suppose he had been sort of stimulated by the readings that he had made of persons like Diagilev, forming his own ballet company and so on and so forth. Ballet was very much in the air at the time. People like Leonide Massine and George Balanchine, stimulated people in the performing arts'—E. Alkazi in an interview with Amal Allana, NYC, 1999.

a bevy of beauties framed in the doorway—all at sewing machines. It was amazing how the formal KT drawing room, with its life-size portraits of the family, had been converted into an improvised wardrobe-cum-fitting room. The large, pink-upholstered sofas had been pushed aside to accommodate two hand-manipulated sewing machines. Khorshed Wadia and Katie Umrigar were spinning away, while Zarine and Shiraz, Roshen's younger sisters, were attaching trimmings. It looked like they had set up a regular sewing 'bee'. And there was Roshen standing in their midst, measuring out fabric while politely giving instructions. Yards and yards of fabric surrounded her, creating a kind of multi-hued aura around her slim, elegant frame. Today she looked even more intriguing to Alkazi as she was dressed in a pair of khaki breeches, an open-necked shirt and a pair of riding boots—her riding crop and round black velvet cap were lying beside her on a tall boy. This kind of boyish attire suited Roshen's slim frame admirably, he thought! None of his sisters would dare wear such an outfit. He had only seen actresses in American and British movies in this kind of riding gear.

He was still at the door, taking in the scene, when Roshen turned around and spotted him.

'It's about time, I would have thought, Mr Alkazi! Didn't I say your costume would be ready for a fitting at 6 p.m.? It's half past!'

Alkazi was absorbed in gawking at her. The girls giggled, except Katie who snorted.

'Maybe he had better things to do!' Katie flashed him a wide smile.

Roshen gave her a sharp look and, picking up huge wads of cotton wool, went forward to Alkazi.

'Mr Alkazi, please remove your shirt and put this tunic on!' Taking the loose tunic she held out, Alkazi looked around for the bathroom.

'Just take it off here, for heaven's sake! We won't look!'

This was greeted with another peal of laughter, which Alkazi now decided to join in as he was quite enjoying the attention of so many young women. Moving to a corner, he unbuttoned and removed his shirt. Katie helpfully went forward.

'Pass it here, Mr Alkazi; I'll hang it up for you!'

Katie squeezed his hand as she took his shirt and slipped him a note.

'Hide it! Read it later!' she whispered under her breath.

Kulsum Padamsee, with Roshen (left), Bobby (right), Bubbles (seated on stool), Zarine (seated on carpet), in Oswestry, England, 1940

Katie Umrigar was acting opposite Ebrahim in *Gods and Kings** as one of the women Napoleon calls to his room, asking her to sleep with him! It is then not difficult to understand why Katie fell head over heels in love

---

*   'Bobby did a thing called *Gods and Kings*, which was five one-act plays, and this was done in a little hall near the Scots Kirk opposite the Lion Gate. And I remember the thing that caused a scandal was when a girl called Ariadne Karanjia appeared on stage in a bathing suit. You know, in those days, for a girl to appear in a bathing suit was courting excommunication as it were. And she appeared in one of the short plays, opposite Jean Bhownagry, who was the funniest man this side of anywhere.'—Cedric Santos, 'Suddenly Last Summer', *BOMBAY* magazine, 22 August–6 September 1983.

with Alkazi while rehearsing and began writing him interminably long love letters! For Ebrahim, this may have been very embarrassing because he was an Arab and had never before moved in circles of such liberated and outspoken young women.*

Glancing furtively to see whether Roshen had noticed this activity, Ebrahim hurriedly pushed the note into his pocket and, pulling the unbleached cotton tunic over his head, he stepped forward towards the centre of the room. Roshen then began the process of laying wads of cotton across his stomach and patting them down to create the paunch he was to sport as Napoleon Bonaparte!

Alkazi was feeling quite foolish with this strange, manual way of being dressed. But he gradually began to relax, finding that it was rather pleasant being attended to exclusively by Roshen. Everyone in the room fell silent, conscious of the proximity of the young couple. Just to break the awkward silence from time to time, Ebrahim pretended to feel ticklish and started jitterbugging around. The girls sniggered.

'Oh, do stand still, Mr Alkazi! Can't you see I'm working?' said Roshen in mock irritation.

'What can I do? You're really tickling me!'

'Rubbish!'

Roshen glanced up over the top of her rimless spectacles, trying to look stern while trying to stifle a smile at the same time.

'Roshen, it's not working! He's not looking at all like Napoleon with a paunch!' said Khorshed critically.

'He looks more like a pregnant woman, I'd say!'

'Shut up, Katie! Why don't you try?'

'If you gave me half a chance, Roshen darling, and stop occupying all of Mr Alkazi's time, I'd certainly be in his arms by now!'

Alkazi turned a beetroot red. He lowered his eyes, fixing them firmly on his toes! Was Roshen upset? He cast a furtive glance in her direction. She gave a final pat to the paunch and didn't let on. Handing him his Napoleon

---

* 'So this must have been very stimulating for him because it was a life he had never known and probably one of the things that drew him to me was, to a certain extent . . . I was this more modern woman. His family women at that time were not observing the purdah . . . but were not really socializing . . . and I don't think he had mixed around with women much . . .'—Roshen Alkazi in an interview with Amal Allana, August 2000.

shirt and uniform, she gestured towards a full-length standing mirror that had been brought into the formal drawing room for the costume trials.

'There!' said Roshen. 'What do you think? Does the costume help you feel like Napoleon?'

Before he could lavish praise on her for her strenuous efforts, Kulsumbai Padamsee walked in from an inner room with Bobby. He had his arm around his mother's shoulders.

Glancing at them reflected in the mirror, Ebrahim was quite taken aback by the older woman's attire. She, like her daughter Roshen, was wearing breeches and boots! He immediately averted his gaze at the sight of an older woman dressed so. Sensing his embarrassment, Roshen quickly explained, 'Mummy and I have just come from riding! At the Gymkhana! We have a few horses, you know!'

'My mother is such a sport! There's no one quite like her! I'm so proud of you, Mummy darling! Truly!'

Mrs P, as everyone called her, chuckled.

Roshen ran up to Bobby, putting her arm around his waist.

'What do you think, Bobby? Does Mr Alkazi look the part?'

'Turn around at once, Alkazi! I, the director, will decide if you look like Napoleon or not! Come on, Alkazi, strike a Napoleonesque pose!'

Complying with equal elan and panache, Alkazi beheld his reflection in the mirror. He then spat on his fingers, slicked some of his front hair onto his forehead in little peaks, thrust the thumb of his left hand into his cummerbund, the other behind his back, paunch jutting out. He turned around with a flourish and struck a pose. Everyone applauded!

'Splendid! Spitting image of Napoleon! Roshenara Begum, you have utterly transformed this young whippersnapper into the lunatic Emperor Napoleon himself! Leon Bakst* himself could not have done better. What do you say, Mummy?'

Mrs P, of course, had no idea who Leon Bakst was, nor was it important to her as long as her children were happy. She smiled indulgently.

A thought flashed through Ebrahim's mind—this kind of camaraderie between Mrs P and her children, their informality towards one another,

---

* Major costume designer of the Ballets Russes.

the embracing of a new age, of modern ideas—could this ever be possible in his family?

'I beg your pardon; I forgot to introduce you. Mummy, this is one of the founder members of our new Theatre Group.'

'*Salam Alaikum*! Ma'am, I hope I am not disturbing you?'

'I am never disturbed, young man! My house is for my children. Whatever they like to do, we do! By the way, what is your name?'

'Ebrahim Alkazi, Ma'am.'

'Ebrahim... that, of course, is a common name. But Alkazi? Where are you from, hunh?'

'We are from here, Ma'am. My father is an Arab businessman, settled here.'

'An Arab? Well, as they say, *Arab ka baccha! Kabhi nahi saccha*!' (The son of an Arab can never be trusted!) Mrs P looked quite pleased with herself, chuckling rather loudly!

Alkazi was taken aback! He did not quite comprehend what Mrs P meant by that. Wasn't it a bit rude? Kulsumbai continued laughing at her own snide remark!

'Bobby, who's staying for dinner? Let me know, so we can get the table laid.'

'About five or six people, Mama! Girls, you'll be staying, won't you? It's really no trouble at all.'

They were clearing up. Alkazi was changing.

Roshen moved closer to Bobby on the sofa.

'Bobby, how high are the stools on which the "gods" will stand? I need to know so that we have enough fabric.'

'Eight or nine feet at least! The gods must seem towering! As the curtain goes up, you just see these enormous giants. Deryck is going to create smoke from dry ice. It will be floating around the stools they will be standing on, so that the gods look like they are up in the clouds, in heaven! Your costumes have to flow over the stools and, even longer, drape over the floor.'

'But Bobby, all this fabric is going to be pretty expensive.'

'Money will come, Roshenara Begum! Don't worry! It's ideas we need! Dreams! Let yourself go... be poetic! Did I tell you? Our next production after *Gods and Kings* is to be *Othello*. Listen! I have a great idea. Everything will be extremely stark... everything... The colour scheme of the sets and costumes will be restricted to only purple and yellow.'

Bobby stood up and began gesticulating...

'The play opens with Desdemona's death and then goes into a flashback. I'm rewriting the scenes. The whole story is going to be seen from Iago's point of view! I, of course, am going to play the Turk!'

He swept up some of the fabric from the floor and swung it around himself like a cape.

'The entire production is going to be very Oriental, very dark and brooding, very sensuous... like a deep, musky perfume, like heady wine... attar!'

Alkazi was so caught up listening to the ideas and thoughts that just tumbled out of Bobby. He was on to his next production without completing this one first! He was in such a hurry... always. All Ebrahim could think was that this friend of his was so greedy for life, so eager...

Energized, Alkazi bounded out of the KT lift, not quite sure what the outcome of his engagement with these anglicized Khojas might turn out to be. Whatever it was, Bobby and his family appeared to hold the promise of offering him what he was in search of—a new path.

As he caught the BEST bus from across the street, Ebrahim glanced up. Maybe he was mistaken, but was that his nymph, Roshen, silhouetted against the curtains?

CHAPTER 6
LOVE LORN
1945

There's drama in everyday life. It was barely two months since World War II had ended. A Friday. Ubba was visiting the family in Poona and Gulab had excused himself, saying he had to visit his relatives. Ebrahim was alone in the flat. The doorbell rang. Ebrahim looked out through the peephole. There was a British man with a rucksack in a tattered military uniform. A bit puzzled, Ebrahim opened the door.

'Good evening. I am Alex Turner. Are you Ebrahim Alkazi?'

Ebrahim nodded. The man looked as if he was about to collapse on the landing. Taken aback, Ebrahim helped to steady him.

'I have come from Burma. Rather a long journey . . . I have a message for you.'

'Please, please . . . do come in.'

'Thanks! I'm grateful.'

Water was offered and drunk. The stranger looked disoriented.

'I don't wish to intrude, but I was with your brother, Ali Alkazi, in the army, and he asked me to stop by. He asked me to look you up. To tell you . . . To tell your family . . . that he's fine.'

Ebrahim was stunned. His brother Ali was alive! This was unbelievable! After a gap of nearly two years, there was news of Ali!

'Where's Ali?' Overwhelmed, Ebrahim could barely get himself to utter the name.

'Can't say. The last time I saw him was a couple of months ago in Rangoon. Spirited! Tough! A good soldier, your brother, if ever there was one!'

Saying so, the stranger threw down the rucksack he was carrying and began to carefully unwrap the string that held it together! It was unbelievable! Penguin publications tumbled onto the floor! The plays of

Shakespeare! All of them . . . in paperback! Play after play, the whole series emerged like treasures from the torn rucksack!

'A gift for you! From your brother! He mentioned you were something of a theatre buff! This was the collection you always wanted! I carried them for you . . . all the bloody way from Burma!'

Ebrahim could no longer contain himself. He sank to his knees, drinking in the sight of the books. They seemed to unleash a whole lifetime of pent-up emotions. He sobbed uncontrollably!

'I cannot thank you enough! It's incredible that you carried them all this way. The sheer weight! I cannot . . . You are to go nowhere! Please . . . you must stay here! With me! This is your house.'

'Thanks, I won't say no to that! I have no place for the night. I catch the ship back home tomorrow to England.'

That night, out of sheer excitement, Ebrahim could not stop talking. He asked Alex so many details about his brother. Was he alright? Had he been wounded? Who were his friends? Was he cheerful? Did he eat enough? Did he mention when he would return? The stranger, though exhausted, complied, answering each query with detailed, thoughtful responses that were full of compassion. The young soldier's patience, earnestness and sympathy allowed the conversation to extend deep into the night. In the darkness, Ali became present and alive, till at last Ebrahim laughed out aloud, as if Ali were right there with them in the room. The prodigal had returned with gifts and love and that was all that mattered! Most importantly, his mother, whose sweet, soft Madonna-like face, easily animated by laughter, had over the last two years become more shadowed and set—now, her grieving would be over! Her wonderful boy, her eldest, had got in touch!

Throughout, the Penguin paperback series lay mutely there, Ebrahim having arranged them sequentially in a neat row. As they spoke, he glanced at the books every now and then, involving them in the conversation. Ebrahim knew at that instant that these were going to be among his most precious possessions and he would always carry them, wherever he went. And he did.

That night, the strands of a strange brotherhood and filial bond enmeshed Ebrahim with the stranger Alex, wrapping them in a collusive conspiracy of knowing that Ali was *not* missing. Through a serendipitous quirk of fate, about twenty or thirty years later, the two were destined to meet again! By then, the young messenger from Ali had gone on to become one of the top officials in the Delhi branch of the British Council, while Alkazi had risen to become the director of the National School of Drama! It was at an official dinner that Alex came up to Alkazi and said, 'Don't you remember me, Mr Alkazi? I've stayed at your house!'

Ebrahim had not forgotten. He could never forget, and the bonds of friendship between the two men were instantly re-established. Ali never returned, but Alkazi and Alex Turner stayed in touch thereafter for several years.

* * *

It was Saturday, and Ebrahim was supposed to be at rehearsals at 2 p.m. at Cama Hall at Lion's Gate, near the Town Hall. A cool sea breeze drifted across the Gulmohar trees, causing their delicate leaves to quiver. Ebrahim was in high spirits. Lately, he had taken to wearing Indian outfits occasionally, which had met with approving remarks from some of the young women in college!

'Alkajee! Are you a prince or what? *Ketlo charming lagech*! *Baap re baap*! (You look so charming, by God!) I could easily fall in love with you ... except my parents would kill me! I'm a Parsi, no? And you are a Musalman! *Hai Khoda*! My hard luck!'

'Yes, this is it,' Alkazi mumbled under his breath, pulling on a light mauve kurta with a side opening, Bengali style. This, along with a pair of wide, white pyjamas and open sandals, completed the casual, arty look he wished to affect today. Sprinkling his father's 4711 eau de cologne on to his handkerchief and dabbing a bit behind his ears and on his wrists, Ebrahim inhaled its refreshing fragrance. He had begun to appreciate good perfumes and soaps. Finally, he crunched his front locks into a highish 'puff' and critically appraised the results in the bathroom mirror. 'Something's missing,' he thought. 'Ah, yes!' He reached for his new round sun goggles and whipped them on with a flourish.

'Perfect!'

Ebrahim loved exploring Bombay on foot. It was a city on the move—a youthful city. It had energy and drive, with a spirit of nationalism in the air. It was now only a question of time before freedom became a reality.

With Gandhiji in and out of Bombay often, his stay at Laburnum Road and his prayer meetings at Chowpatty transformed the city into a vast political arena, giving it a sense of being in the vanguard of the nation's affairs. Despite the shortages caused by the war, despite the fact that thousands were courting arrest, despite the fact that man-made famines were still raging in parts of the country and despite the fact that there were communal riots, Alkazi sensed the energy of the city as it fiercely began to assert its national and secular ideals through its artistic achievements.

Ever since he left the provincial garrison town of Poona, Alkazi had rapidly begun to acquaint himself with Bombay's theatre legacy. He learned that the lavish commercial entertainment offered by Natak companies in Urdu, Marathi and Gujarati had once brought in massive audiences, with theatrical routes running across not only India but Southeast Asia as well. Conversely, enterprising impresarios like Maurice Bandman regarded Bombay as an important destination, bringing in a repertoire of popular operas, musical comedies and dramas from London that were performed at the western-styled proscenium theatres built across the city. Again, Bombay had been privy to great performances by internationally acclaimed dancers, such as Anna Pavlova and the Denishawn Dance Company from the US, both performing at the Royal Opera House in 1926 and 1927. Bombay was also the port from which Uday Shankar set sail for Europe with Simkie, Zohra Segal and Uzra Butt in tow in the 1940s.

A significant change towards a more serious kind of theatre came with the intensifying of the political situation. The presence of the Communist Party of India (CPI) headquarters in Bombay since 1943 was largely responsible for the foundation of the Indian People's Theatre Association (IPTA),[*] the cultural wing of the CPI. Radical writers, poets, musicians and actors had spontaneously come together to form the organization, protesting against fascism and colonialism. They performed in working-class districts for factory workers and travelled to smaller towns and villages where folk-performing traditions were remodelled to serve as effective tools for arousing mass audiences to political awareness. Regarded as a 'people's theatre', IPTA appeared to be finally ringing the death knell on Parsi theatre with its historical and mythological blockbusters, in favour of

---

[*] IPTA drew on ideas from the Little Theatre Movement and the Federal Theatre Project.

experimental playlets, such as *Laboratory*, based on topical issues and K.A. Abbas's *Yeh Amrit Hai*. IPTA's Central Squad had also produced a ballet, *The Spirit of India* (1944), which Alkazi had watched, where classical and folk forms were sought to be fused.

From the late 1930s, Bombay had also become home to most of the writers belonging to the Progressive Writers Association,* such as Ismat Chughtai, Krishan Chander, Majrooh Sultanpuri, Ali Sardar Jafri, Kaifi Azmi and Sahir Ludhianvi. Though Alkazi did not know these writers personally, he was becoming aware of their work. Many were IPTA members upholding leftist ideas, but not all of them were Party members, nor were they necessarily pushing towards a socialist realist aesthetic. Instead, what defined them as a group was their commitment to engage with the 'real', choosing to uncover the oppression of both capitalism and colonialism. With the rise of communalism, these writers were repelled by religious divisions and dogma and openly criticized caste, gender and class inequalities. For their unabashed forthrightness, the short stories of Ismat Chugtai (*Lihaaf/The Quilt*) and Saadat Hasan Manto (*Boo/Odour*) had been charged with obscenity the previous year. The writers were finally exonerated on grounds of artistic freedom, after a much publicized and humiliating trial.

Another theatre company was Prithvi Theatres, established in 1942 by actor–manager Prithviraj Kapoor, who launched *Shakuntala*, a spectacular production with massive sets and a huge cast, at Bombay's Royal Opera House. Carrying several nineteenth-century ideas into the twentieth century, the script was based on Kalidasa's classic by Pandit Narayan Prasad 'Betaab', one of the leading playwrights of the Parsi theatre. Alkazi had watched both *Shakuntala* as well as Prithviraj's most recent, *Deewar*. Finding the latter relevant to the unfolding communal tensions and impressed by Prithviraj's charisma as an actor, Alkazi was nonetheless unable to relate to the four-and-a-half-hour-long spectacle that Prithviraj produced and delivered in highly charged melodramatic tones. Coupled with large casts and elaborate sets, Alkazi found that there was a certain unwieldiness in these efforts of Prithviraj that needed to be trimmed

---

* The origin of the All India Progressive Writers' Association lay in an organization formed in England in 1934 under the leadership of Sajjad Zaheer and Mulk Raj Anand. Its first meeting in India was in 1936 in Lucknow and was endorsed by Jawaharlal Nehru.

down, if for no other reason than the financial and logistical sustainability of theatre on a long-term basis.

IPTA and Prithvi Theatres were among the first groups to begin working in Hindi, Hindustani and Urdu in Bombay and, to an extent, helped to dislodge the large, unwieldy commercial Parsi Natak companies that worked in Urdu. However, it was the arrival of the Talkies in the 1930s that finally brought the commercial theatre industry to its knees, with theatre actors, writers, composers and technicians moving towards the more lucrative enterprise. While Bombay's Marathi and Gujarati-speaking audiences showed signs of moving with the times and becoming more experimental in nature, English-speaking audiences had little on offer—the odd J.B. Priestley like *Blithe Spirit* performed by amateurs at the Cowasji Jehangir Hall or students tackling an annual Shakespeare play. It was to capture, enthuse and expand this 'English-speaking' and 'educated' Indian audience that Bobby Padamsee directed his efforts by offering a range of modern, exciting fare.

Contemplating his good fortune, Alkazi's footsteps led him to the Sir J.J. School of Arts. Inspired by Bobby, Ebrahim had begun sketching and had been dropping in at JJ, where he had made a few acquaintants. Passing classrooms where the doors were flung wide open, he could see easel painting classes underway. He ventured to peep in through a closed door—a life study class was in progress. An old Maharashtrian woman with sagging breasts was seated on a platform; young student artists were grouped around her at their pedestals. He often wondered what it would have been like to join an art school rather than a regular college like Xavier's. After all, the principal of JJ, Charles Gerard, had actively involved the students in creating stupendous forty-foot frescoes for the interior of the new Metro cinema. 'How exciting to be involved in painting frescoes for such a magnificent public building, designed on such a scale!' thought Alkazi.

Entering the life study class, Ebrahim cast his eye around. Young students were intent on capturing the likeness of an old Maharashtrian woman who was seated on a stool in the centre of the room. All of a sudden he experienced a sense of déjà vu. He felt he had seen this scene before. Trying hard to recollect where, it dawned on him that he had seen photographs of JJ's life study class in an old issue of the *Illustrated Weekly*!

Years later, when Alkazi himself was in his eighties, he met and befriended Homai Vyarawalla, and recognized her JJ work immediately. He instinctively responded to Homai's work because he was able to identify closely with the Bombay she depicted; it was the Bombay of his youth. In fact, many of the photos taken by Homai around this time now lie in Alkazi's private collection of photography.

Ebrahim looked at his watch as he was walking out of the JJ gate. Unbelievable! It was only 11 a.m.! Still hours to kill before the rehearsal!

'Oye! Alkazi! Wait!'

There was Francis Newton Souza racing towards him!

'Listen, Alkazi! I've got to tell you the bloody good news! I'm free at last! Liberated! Can you believe it? I've just been *expelled*! These rotten bastards just can't take me! They can't bear my work! It's too goddam modern for them!'

'Expelled? But Francis, why? Who expelled you?'

'The college authorities! Who else?'

'Why?'

'Who the hell knows, "why"? It's because I'm on the warpath against academic realism and the "syrupy" work that is showcased year after year at the Bombay Art Society Salons that have actually become occasions for hen parties because the amateur efforts of memsahibs are included! Frankly, I don't give a rat's ass, I can tell you! They're just so screwed up, the bunch of them . . . This place is a bloody mausoleum! No "art" happening here . . . it's all fart . . . with a capital "F". It's mediocre! Uninspiring!'

'But they can't just do that, Souza. What will your mother say?'

'My mother doesn't know anything about what I'm up to in any case . . . she's too busy keeping heart and soul together!'

They walked in silence for a while. Ebrahim was taken aback by this news. He had known Newton for about a year now; they had been introduced at a Bombay Art Society show and had struck up a kind of distant friendship. Thereafter, Souza had taken Alkazi to his tiny Crawford Market flat a couple of times, where he lived with his mother, a graceful Goan lady who supported him through her efforts as a seamstress. It was here that Alkazi first saw Souza's sketches and some watercolours. True, Souza was loud, foul-mouthed and totally reckless, but Alkazi somehow felt drawn to him. There was something true and unpretentious about him.

Indian Family by F.N. Souza, 1947, seen along with other works displayed on a bridge in Goa

What appealed to Alkazi was that this man's work was directly inspired by his Goan background—the villagers, the landscape and the sea. His robust colours and the sureness of his line gave his work a primitive strength that reminded Alkazi of Gauguin and Rouault. At the same time, Souza was so connected to Catholicism. One sensed an inextricable bond between man, nature and religion in his work that was compelling and somehow rung true. For Alkazi, Souza represented everything that he could not be, as a person and as an artist. Souza was, simply put, emphatic, bold and rebellious. At the moment, he was a rebel in search of a cause!

'So what are you going to do then?' They were passing the Victoria Terminus station.

'To begin with, I'm going to celebrate... I'm going to down a full bottle of feni, then go and have it out with some whores. Coming?'

Alkazi was too taken aback to even respond, and nor was Souza really looking for a response.

'That will help to wash off this JJ bullshit! Then I'll be as clean and innocent as a baby lamb! I'll be *me*! You understand, man?... I want to be *me*! Who am I? Not some patched together, ass-licking "gentleman" artist!'

'You're right; one must be true to oneself. No great art is possible without...'

'Spare me the lecture, Alkazi! Listen, my plan is, after that . . . *after* I've become who I *really* am . . . I will have my own show. My first one-man show! It will be called a "salon". It will be *my* salon—"Souza's Salon"! And I'll have it in front of their noses! At the Bombay Art Society! I'll show these bastards! I'll show them who Francis Newton Souza is! My name will be there! Up there! You wait and see, Alkazi . . . These buggers are *nothing*!'

Alkazi couldn't take Souza's diatribe much longer. He was beginning to wallow. As soon as Alkazi spotted a pavement bookstall, he halted. Squatting on his haunches, he began to carefully scan the wares. In fact, it was at such pavement bookstalls in Flora Fountain that he had picked up unbelievable bargains and had been able to build up quite an enviable little library of his own.

Ah, here was the 1941 January–March issue of *Art and Culture*, a quarterly published from Calcutta. He had always wanted to subscribe. He went down the list of contents—an article by Uday Shankar, *The Need for an India Culture Centre*, *An Analysis of Kathakali Dance* by Padmanabhan Thampy, *Contemporary Indian Art Examined* by R.V. Leyden, *Poems* by Rabindranath Tagore, etc. He handed the magazine to the seller.

'*Kitna?*' (How much?)

'*Doh anna*, Sahib.' (Two annas, Sir.)

'*Theek hai. Aur hain?*' (Ok, do you have any more?)

'*Ek aur hai*, Sahib.' (I have one more, Sir.)

He handed Alkazi the January–March 1944 issue.

'Alkazi! Are you going to be here all day?' Souza was getting impatient.

'Well. I thought . . . I have some time to spare and my rehearsal is at 2 p.m. It's just around the corner actually, at Cama Hall . . . The show's in a few weeks . . .'

'Which one?'

'*Othello,* produced by Sultan Padamsee . . . 19 November! I'm playing Roderigo.'

'Yes, ok . . . I'll try and come . . .'

Souza disappeared into the crowd.

Alkazi bought the other issue as well. It had some more articles by Tagore, then others by Dr Maria Montessori, Nicholas Roerich, Hannah Sen on *Women's Education at Lady Irwin School*, Comola Dutt Paranjoti on *Can Indian Music Be Harmonized?* There was a photograph of Comola with Anna Pavlova! Comola and Victor Paranjoti were close friends of Bobby, and here she was—with Pavlova!

It was still only 12 p.m. Why was today inching forward? Normally, days, weeks and months were just swallowed up without him being aware of time, but today, the wait to see Roshen seemed simply interminable. He decided to wait at the steps of the Town Hall. From here, he could keep an eye on who was entering Cama Hall. He felt a wreck; it was by now hot and muggy. His efforts to look good today were put paid to by the suffocating humidity.

Would Roshen arrive early to the rehearsal? The cast had been asked to get into costumes and parade before Bobby today. He was praying that if this happened, perhaps Roshen and he could possibly, even for a brief moment, be alone. Then he could *maybe, maybe, maybe* . . . say something to her!

But was it even dimly possible that this girl, who was always surrounded by people and unfortunately, too many were *boys*—friends of Bobby . . . *asses* actually!—would this girl who was so comfortable with boys, who discussed books with them, who wrote poetry, who was such a graceful ballroom dancer, so well-dressed, who flashed her beautiful smile so carelessly, who was dainty and pretty and always so willing to help, especially her brother Bobby, would this goddess give him even the time of day? Would she entertain the deep feelings he had grown to have for her? Or would she simply laugh him off?

And then, to top it all, she belonged to this huge Padamsee family—a 'clan' actually! True, there were only seven siblings, but they were a prominent Bombay family who had begun to dominate a certain young, intelligent circle that Ebrahim was slowly becoming a part of. Undoubtedly, the Padamsee prestige arose from the formidable reputation that Bobby had begun to acquire for himself. His intellectual brilliance as a speaker and his theatrical flair both off stage and on as a young director and actor, when coupled with his skills as a painter and poet, made Sultan Padamsee the toast of the town. Savouring his solitude but equally enjoying company, Bobby loved opulence, high living and parties. In this, he was wholeheartedly supported by his mother, who simply doted on him. Bobby had more than repaid his mother for her strenuous efforts at giving not only him but all her children a 'proper English education', commensurate with her father's social standing. All her children, especially Bobby, were highly accomplished and able to move in the highest social circles.

It had not been easy for Kulsumbai, in the early years of her marriage, to forget that she had been married off to an unlettered Jafferbhai Padamsee, whose only claim to fame was that his family had been granted a licence to carry on an extremely lucrative opium business in Taloja. Once the Padamsees migrated to Bombay, Jafferbhai, along with his brothers, began to hold a monopoly over the glassware business in Bombay. Jafferbhai was also part of the building boom in Bombay during the 1920s and 1930s, and before long, had acquired and built more than ten properties along the stretch between the Colaba Causeway and the Sassoon Docks.

Kulsumbai had no complaints about Jafferbhai's business skills as it allowed them to shift out of Padamseewadi in Dongri to the posh art deco-style terrace flat in the building Jafferbhai had built that bore her very name, Kulsum Terrace, on Colaba Causeway, soon after their marriage. This was Phase One of Kulsum's plan—to distance herself and her children from the rest of the 'lesser educated' Padamsees who continued to live cheek-by-jowl in tenement-like chawls in Dongri, despite their growing affluence.

Having ensured a presentable location from which to conduct her affairs, Kulsumbai set about handcrafting a 'more than presentable' future for her children. She devised a scheme whereby, as each child turned about four years old, he or she was enrolled in a private boarding school on Altamount Road run by two Irish spinsters, Miss Murphy and Miss Delaney. Highly exclusive, Miss Murphy's School was meant for children of royalty like the Rajpiplas. It was here that the Padamsee children not only learned to read, write and speak English fluently, they learned table manners, had an Anglo–Indian governess, wore only western clothes, and had their names appropriately anglicized into jaunty British nicknames. So Sultan became 'Bobby', Zarine became 'Jerry', Bapsy became 'Bee', Roshan Ali became 'Alyque', Chotu Ahmed became 'Chotu', Aziz became 'Bubbles' and Dilshad became 'Candy'! To top it all, Miss Murphy gave them a taste for 'theatricals', encouraging them to do little playlets every evening or sing or read poetry to her and Miss Delaney.

By all accounts, Miss Murphy was truly a great lover of fine literature and drama and was the first to spot that Bobby was unique in many ways. Not only were his expressive powers through acting and recitation quite remarkable, but his intellectual grasp of complex thoughts was far beyond his years. By the age of twelve, Bobby was transferred to a Jesuit institution in the Kumaon Hills, where he began writing poetry and studied Latin. This later led him to study the Greek language, its thought and philosophy, which was perhaps the strongest influence felt in his poetry. At fourteen, with a brilliant scholastic record, he sat for his Senior Cambridge exams. Miss Murphy suggested to Kulsumbai that Bobby be taken to England, where the boy must remain for further studies.

Promptly, Kulsumbai whipped her brood out of school and set sail for the British Isles in 1937. Jafferbhai, undoubtedly, was taken aback but declined from joining them. Not in the least deterred, Kulsumbai boarded the ship with seven children (Candy was not yet born), twenty-four trunks, but more importantly, with thirty *barnis* (pickle jars) of her own homemade mango pickle, which would help her survive the inedible English cuisine for the next few years!

Accordingly, the girls were enrolled at Ellesmere College, while Bobby was accepted at Christ Church College, Oxford, where he excelled. Always level-headed, Mrs P (which she began to be called in England) set up house halfway between both schools in Oswestry, Shropshire, so that the children could visit her on weekends. Here, she learned to adapt to British ways and the extreme weather, while also undertaking gruelling domestic chores that she was unused to in her own land.

The outbreak of the war in 1939 caused them to unexpectedly return to India before Bobby completed his graduation.

It was an entirely new, well-travelled Kulsumbai who returned home. In two long years in Great Britain, she had learned to speak and read English fluently, acquiring a taste for detective novels, with Agatha Christie's Miss Marple and Hercule Poirot, Erle Stanley Gardner's detective Perry Mason and Arthur Conan Doyle's Sherlock Homes becoming her favourites. She was determined that the Padamsee lifestyle be brought up-to-date so as to be commensurate with their newly acquired educational status.

One of the first things Kulsumbai did was commission several larger-than-life size tinted photographic portraits of herself posing with various members of her offspring, chiefly Bobby. These majestically adorned the high-ceilinged walls of their huge chandeliered flat in Kulsum Terrace.

Enormous pink-upholstered sofa sets with 'skirts', an elaborate love seat, a chiming grandfather clock and two huge, exquisitely carved 'showcase' cupboards were ordered. These teak wood showcases were the centre of attraction, with their bevelled glass sides and ornate cut-glass handles, which housed a variety of cut-glass knick-knacks like frolicking horses, lovebirds beak to beak, a nude marble Venus de Milo, a porcelain shepherd and shepherdess and many, many more such delights that guests and their children could admire. Venturing beyond the stately drawing room, one encountered pink marble bathrooms and a unique horseshoe-shaped dining table made of solid teak.

But what truly dominated the house was the presence of Kulsumbai—either in person or symbols of her in the shape of her initials 'KJP', which were designed to become the family crest. An elaborate KJP was embossed on each exquisite stained-glass ventilator that encircled not just the formal drawing room, but the KJP monogram enlivened all the window panes of the entire house. The entire dinner service and cutlery, all of which Jafferbhai specially ordered from Czechoslovakia, were monogrammed with gold and pink KJPs. Likewise, it was Kulsum who sat at the head of the dining table, dominating the conversation during all meals for years. She was the Queen Mother who ruled over Kulsum Terrace and

New Year's celebration, 1946; top row: (extreme right) Zarine; bottom row: (L–R) Sultan Padamsee, Bapsy and Roshen

Jafferbhai, though supporting her empire financially, was relegated to the veranda space to live in whatever regal splendour he could muster! He had a capacious sofa swing; he had a bell; he had a servant who passed him his spittoon and attended to the needs of his guests; he had a barber who visited him twice a day; he had his own toilet; his clothes were washed and well-starched, his shoes polished. But otherwise, he was an outsider to the world of Kulsumbai and her brood, who took over the rest of the house to do what they wished—hold rehearsals, practice sword fights, roll up the carpets for dance parties and entertain whomever they wished. What Jafferbhai, the Dongri businessman, thought of all this would only gradually become apparent later; for the moment, he was patient—terribly patient.

These were the stories—grown into myths—surrounding the Padamsees that Ebrahim had heard of. And, to say the least, it was this daunting family whom he would have to ultimately confront before he could even dream of Roshen! Was he up to the task? Did he fit in? What would his parents think?

'Ah! There you are, old boy! We thought we had lost you! What are you doing here? We had costume trials at home today! Don't you remember?'

Bobby arrived like an emperor with his entire entourage of the *Othello* cast. Laughing and chattering, they tumbled into Cama Hall. Ebrahim wanted to kick himself. He had totally forgotten that they were to meet at KT and he had been waiting here at Cama Hall all this while like an ass!

'Do you think Roshen will be bringing my costume here, by any chance?' he whispered to Mary Sethna as they settled down.

'Are you crazy . . . She's got her hands full with 'The Hunt'* this evening. You should see what Bobby's got Roshen and Khorshed to do! The entire house is being turned upside down—it's going to look like a film set from the *Arabian Nights*. Can't wait to see it. It's a fancy dress party. Now, Alkazi, no excuses . . . you *have* to come this evening. Everyone's going to be there.'

---

* 'We used to watch a lot of movies about England, you know, the countryside, the Fox Hunt and after every Fox Hunt, every night there used to be a ball, it was called the Fox-Hunt Ball. And all the men would get into their fineries, beautiful tuxedos and so on. I think that fascinated Bobby and then he decided that every Saturday we would have a party after the rehearsals and it would be a "pound-party" . . . people would bring things. So that's how it came to be known as The Hunt.'—Alyque Padamsee in an interview with Amal Allana, Mumbai, 2011.

The fact that Roshen was not coming made Alkazi's entire afternoon completely meaningless. The rehearsal passed in a blur—Alkazi just went through his part like a zombie. For one, he was, by now, quite faint with not having eaten since morning. Besides, there was the heat and, of course, his mind was elsewhere.

'What's the matter? You're looking quite faint, Alkazi! Come along, rehearsal's done!' Mary tucked her arm into his. '*Chalo ni!* Now for the fun! Off to KT for "The Hunt".'

Alkazi had no idea what happened next . . . no idea how he found himself lying on a carpet in Mrs P's bedroom, of all places! It must have been around 7 p.m. He was awoken by the sound of dance music. He got up shakily and looked for the way out, in the direction of the music and lights. He opened the door and was bedazzled by the sight. Stretching from Kulsumbai's room across the entire drawing room, many, many carpets and mattresses were strewn around, covered in brocade cloth. People were lounging against bolster pillows, talking, laughing, flirting. Many of them were in fancy dress, some with party hats, others with gaily coloured party masks. All the lights were off and the entire area was lit with thousands of candles.

Ebrahim groggily tried to navigate a path between costumed and masked people—though they greeted him, he couldn't recognize any of them. As he moved onto the terrace, there were Chotu and Alyque, aged about twelve and sixteen years, respectively, hidden behind a trellis, watching the grown-ups. The dancing couples obviously intrigued them the most.

Ebrahim's sole aim was to locate Roshen, but she was nowhere to be seen. Finally, on climbing up to the first-floor terrace, Ebrahim spotted Bobby. He was surrounded by a group of mostly foreigners. They, too, were lounging on carpets and playing the 'spinning the knife' game.*

---

* A game of 'suicide', where a group of five or six sit in a circle around a pocketknife. They spin the knife and whoever the blade faces has to place one slit on his or her wrist. It just keeps going until a person dies; the first person to die is a winner. It continues until one person is left.
NB: This is the first time I have found out about this game! I think Bobby changed the rules. Whoever the blade stopped at had to do a forfeit of some kind. The fact that this is a game related to suicide is, in this context, quite bizarre. It appears that Bobby was playing with the idea of death even here!

'Ah! Are you finally up, Alkazi, old chap?' Bobby called out, signalling for Ebrahim to join them.

'Come on, let me add you to the players. Homi, add Alkazi's name . . . Just a short form, man."

Homi wrote ELK, instead of ALK! He thought the surname was spelled 'Elkazi'.

'Great! That's a genius stroke, Homi. I was always wondering what nickname we should give Alkazi!' exclaimed Bobby, 'From today I baptize thee "ELK" . . . Isn't that just so dandy? "Elk"!'

'Fine by me,' said Ebrahim.

They continued spinning the knife for some more time, and then Bobby insisted they play the game where they all tumble on one another. There was much excitement, much horsing around. The young men were crashing on to one another—Ebrahim stood apart watching. He noticed that Bobby kept throwing himself on a particular young man, a foreigner, and the two were laughing uproariously. All of a sudden, Katie Umrigar's voice rang out.

'The new moon! The new moon is out.'

Everyone rushed out onto the terrace. Everything was bathed in shimmering blue light. It was a commonly held superstition that if one first looked at the new moon and then at the person one loved, one's love would be reciprocated. Ebrahim looked at the new moon and prayed desperately from within himself. He then looked away from the moon and, as if by magic, there was Roshen directly in his line of vision, across the terrace, dressed in a blue chiffon sari, like an *apsara*, a celestial being! She was looking at the moon, too. Slowly, she shifted her gaze and their eyes met! A sea of people separated them. Without flinching, Alkazi walked across the terrace in silence. A hush descended and like in the movies, the revellers parted, like the waves before Moses, giving the determined young man right of way. Then, with utmost devotion, Elk knelt in front of Roshen and, taking her hand in his, he lifted it to his lips, closed his eyes and kissed her hand ever so gently. For that moment, everyone and everything around the lovers evaporated. Stunned and mesmerized, the revellers would remember this scene for years as among the most simple and pure declarations of love they had ever witnessed.

'Of course, after that, we realized that we were considered to be, sort of, going together!' my mother told me when she was well into her seventies. We were sitting in her bedroom one Sunday afternoon in Greater Kailash Part II, New Delhi. I had the tape recorder on and she continued:

'Occasionally, after rehearsals, Elk and I would secretly go for a quiet walk by ourselves because Mummy never allowed us to go out alone. Even in the house, Mummy would circulate from room to room, keeping an eye on these three daughters of hers, who were all being courted! Deryck was courting Bee, and Hamid was courting Jerry . . . It all happened simultaneously . . .

'Mummy allowed all three young men to visit the house. So they would be there practically morning, noon and night and Mummy would be circulating through the rooms to make sure we were not up to any hanky-panky! Then, one day, Daddy put his foot down. I think he got really worried that what are these three men doing in the house. "There's been no talk of marriage; there's been no talk of engagement. Why are they here? They're just spoiling the reputation of our girls. Who will propose to them and how will we marry them off?" That was always the big question in Indian families: "Will there be any proposals?"

'So we were still thinking, in traditional terms, of a proposal. And there *were* proposals that came, but none of them was *suitable* according to Mummy and Daddy. Finally, one day, Daddy just lost his temper and came into the drawing room, pointed to the door and told the three boys, "You! Get it out of my house! And don't come ever again to see my daughters!" He said it so forcefully that even Mummy couldn't say anything!

'I think all three of them realized that if they wanted to see us girls again, they would have to actually broach the subject of marriage! Although we were banned from meeting, the three suitors would come to this bus stop opposite the house—particularly Elk, who was practically there the whole day! People would wait for him to get onto a bus and he would say, "No please; you go along, I'll come later." He would just be standing there . . . and I would have to bribe Alyque and Chotu to carry notes to and fro between us! And little gifts would come up to us. Finally, Elk summoned the courage to speak to his family and tell them that he wanted to get married and I think his parents said, "No!"'

CHAPTER 7
PASSING FROM TIME INTO ETERNITY
1946

It was 8 January 1946, a rather overcast day. Bobby, Roshen and Jerry were on their way to the hospital to visit Elk, who had undergone an emergency operation for appendicitis. Bobby was currently directing *Chitra*,* a dance drama by Rabindranath Tagore, for which Guru Panikkar had especially been engaged to train the actors in Kathakali. During a rather strenuous class, Ebrahim suddenly developed excruciating pains in the abdomen and was rushed to the hospital.

Quite a few members of the Theatre Group were taken aback at Bobby's suggestion of an Indian play. Were there any *Indian* plays in English? Anyway, Tagore was a poet, not a playwright, they argued, and *Chitra* was hardly a play; it was more like an abstract poem—difficult to follow. But Bobby was adamant. His ideas appeared to be undergoing a sea change day by day. Leaving Shakespeare and Oscar Wilde aside, of late he had begun to speak feverishly about the need to forge an Indian approach to theatre, believing that Tagore was right in creating dance dramas, combining poetry with movement, which felt truer to Indian expression.

Bobby was aware of the serious experiments in the field of dance by Uday Shankar, who had spent considerable time in Europe and worked with the great Anna Pavlova for a year in 1923 in Paris. He established a dance centre in Almora in 1939, where he attempted to integrate different classical and folk traditions of Indian dance into a new idiom, choreographing startling new 'Indian ballets', such as *Labour and Machinery*

---

* '...to move towards the Indian theatre. In the sense that Bobby Padamsee had already started it by working with a very eminent Kathakali dancer who would train us. The training was very intensive and there was no nonsense about it at all. He was very harsh and aggressive in his approach and we began bringing that quality into the production.'—E. Alkazi in an interview with Samik Bandyopadhyay, Natya Shodh Sansthan, Kolkata, 15 March 1988.

Sultan Padamsee, 1945

(1939). Shankar was currently working on a film, *Kalpana*, conceived completely in dance.

Absorbing these new ideas like a sponge, Roshen was encouraged to pursue her love of dancing under the guidance of the Vajifdar sisters—Shirin (who later married Mulk Raj Anand), Roshan and Khurshid—who had begun the Nritya Darpana Society along with Krishna Kutty. Now Roshen was daintily perched on the hospital bed next to Ebrahim—they were in the habit of holding hands—while Jerry sat at the foot of the bed. Bobby was pacing up and down agitatedly.*

'Elk, let's face it, behind every Indian artist (Hindu predominantly), the *inner* vision is reality and the outer world is *maya* or illusion. That is why, despite the fact that modern Indian artists have begun to appreciate realism in art and may even master the technique of *trompe l'œil*, unfortunately, their work remains an *exposition*; it does not become a detached, *objective* view of reality.'

---

* All Sultan's ideas that follow regarding the comparison of Indian aesthetics to western ones are in his article (unpublished) in one of his notebooks.

'I wouldn't say that is entirely true', Elk interjected, 'we have a whole generation today sitting in art schools like JJ, being taught how to paint in the western academic realistic style. Would you say they are being misled?'

'Yes! To an extent, I would! You must understand, Elk, that under the influence of the West, a few Indian artists think they have adopted an entirely western approach, like easel painting and the like. More often than not, the work is a holy mess because the Indian artist naturally comes back to ornament and detail. Here, the Indian *craftsman* comes into his own and produces, according to western standards, excellent stuff that is precise and detailed. That's exactly why I say that the Oriental artist is incapable, both temperamentally and otherwise, of producing an exact copy! Mass production of replicas is abhorrent even to the meanest Indian artisan!'

The conversation continued animatedly for some time until Jerry noticed that a group of four or five extremely well-dressed people had entered the room. An elderly gentleman in a red fez cap and two young couples. Roshen sprang off the bed, realizing at once that this must be Elk's family.

'May I introduce my respected father, Mr Hamed Alkazi ... Ubba, this is Mr Sultan Padamsee.'

Bobby immediately extended his hand for a handshake, while Ubba automatically raised his in salutation.

'Salam Alaikum! *Aapse milke khushi hui.*' (I'm glad to meet you.)

Bobby withdrew his outstretched hand and tried a weak, amateurish *adab*.

'My two brothers-in-law, Mr Abdulla Al-Bassam and Mr Abdur Rehman Al-Bassam ... and my two sisters, Fatima and Noora. And this is Roshen and Zarine, her sister.'

The young men bowed respectfully, while Fatima and Noora embraced the two girls with beaming smiles, kissing Roshen and Jerry on both cheeks, fumes of French perfume enveloping them.

'Mashallah! How beautiful Roshen is, Ebrahim! *Mabrook!*' whispered Fatty in Ebrahim's ear as she kissed him.

Both sisters then took their place on either side of Ebrahim, kissing their brother several times ... on his cheeks, his forehead, his hands. They laughed a lot, making light of his condition. It was obvious to Roshen that they doted on him. The father sat apart, not uttering a word.

After a few polite niceties and some stilted pauses, the Padamsees excused themselves. This had been the very first interaction between members of both families. Roshen looked totally crestfallen.

'I suppose that was a disaster. Elk's father didn't even acknowledge my presence! God! And his sisters are so good-looking! I look like a "Plain Jane" compared to them! What am I going to do?'

'Rubbish, Roshenara Begum,' said Bobby, 'stop undermining yourself! You are the most beautiful, most intelligent, most loving . . . What more can I say? Cheer up! I predict everything will be fine once it becomes official! I was actually going to keep it as a surprise, but I might as well tell you. I've planned to officially announce the impending weddings of my three sisters next month. On my twenty-fourth birthday. So what do you think? Good idea?'

Roshen and Jerry squealed with delight.

'Bobby! You are absolutely the best brother any girl can ever have! I love you so, so, so much,' exclaimed Jerry.

'I agree! Let's go tell Mummy and Bee as soon as we get back!' Roshen said sagely over her rimless glasses.

That night, the girls were too excited to sleep. They kept talking about their engagements and whether 25 February was actually going to be the day of the *engagements* or the day the *announcements* would be made. There was so much planning to do. Roshen and Jerry talked about this late into the night, waiting to discuss plans with Bobby, but Bobby seemed unusually preoccupied and withdrawn this evening and asked not to be disturbed. Timothy, a sailor Bobby had befriended and with whom he spent a lot of time when the latter was in town, had dropped in that evening. Bobby was holed up with him.

Bobby was an insomniac at the best of times. He would either write or paint at night or go for long walks. Bombay, as Gyan Prakash vividly describes in his book, was where one could go to 'the Taj Hotel, where "advanced" Indian girls and Russian and German tarts [could be observed] dancing to what they believed to be the latest American songs'. Later still, in the wee hours, Bobby would hop into a Victoria and have it drive past the bleak chawls and brothels of Kamathipura, where 'the flesh trade was brisk and sordid. Once a neighborhood where European prostitutes were concentrated,

Kamathipura had become the city's Red Light district that catered to mill workers and the underclasses. Like the rest of the city, the brothels too were cosmopolitan—with Greek, East European, Levantine and Arab women described as belonging to the "Jewesses" caste, often ending up in *Safed Gulli* (White Street), servicing European sailors and soldiers'.[1]

Lately, Roshen had noticed, while tidying up Bobby's room, that there were a few portraits by Bobby resembling Timothy. A blond-haired young man with soulful blue eyes looking out of the canvases. Bobby had never shown these to Roshen. He usually shared all his work with her—paintings, poems and essays. In fact, these paintings appeared to have been hidden away, tucked away under the bed. Under these, Roshen discovered some more paintings of nude men. She had never seen these either. The paintings did not offend her in any way, so she did not give her 'discovery' of them a second thought.

Finally, around 11.30 p.m., Jerry yawned and said she was off to bed. Roshen lingered a little longer, waiting to chat with her brother.

Reminiscing many years later, my mother said to me:

> When Bobby was alone and was studying Latin and other things for his exams, I had this habit of going to the terrace at night. I liked to be out when it was dark, sit on the terrace and swing. And he would bring his chair and sit in front of me and read out long chapters in Latin to me or recite a new poem he had just written. He shared a lot of that with me or if he'd written something new, he would tell me about it. Of course, I couldn't react in a very brilliant way because I was not well-read and all, but I must have been a very sympathetic listener because he always wanted to share. He wanted to share with a lot of people and not just me; he shared things with all his friends. So in that way, he was a very generous and warm person.

Finally, Roshen noticed Timothy leaving. She walked out onto the terrace. Bobby's lights were still on, but the opaque glass doors of the room were shut. Roshen tapped gently. There was no response. Maybe Bobby had fallen asleep with the lights on. She then decided to sit on the swing for a few more moments and wait. Her mind moved to the future. What would it be like to be married? Elk was only twenty years old and she was a year older—just twenty-one! A hundred questions came tumbling out. What would it be like to move away from this home? How could she stay away from Bobby? She was his right hand; he depended on her. Where would she and Elk live? She had never really thought of all this. So far, she had been in a cloud of being 'in love'! She was sure Bobby would help. Yes, she was going to talk to him about all this in the morning. Bobby had often told her, 'I am so glad you are marrying Elk and not anyone else. True, he's a bit of a dark horse, but he has it in him—he has a passion and a quest! If there's anyone in this group who is going to take theatre seriously, it's Elk.'

Roshen was getting tired. She stood up to leave when Bobby's door swung open—and there he stood in his underwear, framed in the doorway. He seemed groggy with sleep. In his hands were some sheets of paper.

'Roshenara Begum, tarry a moment, my love, and listen to this . . . my latest literary attempt . . .' Then he stopped.

Roshen was about to ask him to continue when Bobby took a step back, lurching slightly, shut the door and bolted it from within. Roshen stood there for a moment, then thinking that Bobby was extremely tired, she slipped silently back into her room, the unanswered questions still buzzing in her head.

That was the last anyone saw of Sultan Padamsee, alive. The next morning, he was found by Jerry, lifeless, in his room, with a whole lot of handwritten papers scattered around him like fallen leaves. It was later discovered that these constituted his Last Will and Testament. Sultan Padamsee, aged 24, had died of an overdose, it was declared.

His body lay in state, as it were, in the vast Kulsum Terrace drawing room. For two whole days, an unending stream of mourners filed past. The shroud that Bobby was wrapped in seemed to envelop the near-lifeless bodies of all those who ever knew him: members of the Theatre Group, professors and students of Xavier's, intellectuals of Bombay, close family members of Padamseewadi and Dongri, distant relatives from Taloja, the tenants of all Jafferbhai's buildings—Kulsum Terrace, Chotu Terrace, Candy Castle, etc.—the business community of Chakla Street, the fruit

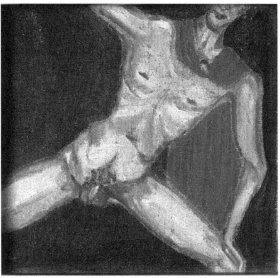

Nude by Sultan Padamsee, 1944–45

wallas and paan wallas from downstairs, the *mehtars* and *mehtaranis* of the building, the pimps and prostitutes of Colaba Causeway, in general, and Walton Road in particular, Parsi friends from Cusrow Baug, across the road, the Russian émigré, Miss Hurley, the Anglo–Indian woman on the second floor who had a sign on her door for years saying 'Marge's Bargain Sale', and even complete strangers—all respectfully made the pilgrimage up the narrow staircase, undoubtedly an arduous journey up four flights, making it look like a religious yatra was underway. Old and young alike, rich and poor, friends and strangers, strained onwards and upwards for a cherished, last glimpse of Bobby Padamsee.

Despite Roshen's best efforts to keep the news from Elk, as it might have a detrimental effect on his weakened condition*—Roshen ensured that even the newspapers were not delivered to him that day—the news did somehow reach him. Waving aside the doctor's orders, he arrived in time for the funeral, becoming one of the pall-bearers. For Elk, it was a

---

* 'I remember I had an appendicitis operation and I was in hospital. Roshen couldn't bring herself to give me this news, so I didn't know that he had committed suicide. Roshen felt that I shouldn't be informed because it might affect me. She showed an enormous amount of courage and endurance, not to share this with me at that time.'—E. Alkazi in an interview with Samik Bandyopadhyay, Natya Shodh Sansthan, Kolkata, 15 March 1988.

brutal blow. He felt he had now lost a second elder brother in Bobby, Ali being the first.

An extremely touching memorial service was held for Sultan Padamsee at St Xavier's College Quadrangle, where, among others, Fr Duhr, Bobby's English professor, read out a moving obituary:

> A couple of days after he had sat for his BA, Sultan surprised me by a visit that eventually evolved into a three hours' tense discussion on the most serious problems the mind of man is ever struggling with . . . From that day, I took him seriously and I began to believe in his really surpassing gifts and ideals. I studiously avoid the word genius, which too readily obtrudes itself whenever we come across abilities out of the ordinary . . . Yet, there was something genial in more senses than one about Sultan Padamsee: his struggle to try his hand at all manner of literary forms, his over-ambitious poetry, his many-sided intellectual artistic and social interests, his gift of friendship and of leadership. And, whatever friend or foe may say, his pursuits, interests and ideals were far removed from the mundane frivolities into which his easy circumstances and the example of the 'gilded youth' of this city might have entangled him.
>
> With my unhesitating faith in man's immortal soul, I am ever haunted by the thought, what was Padamsee's exclamation when he stepped from Time into Eternity and I seem almost to hear him cry out:
>
> *How unlike my superficial fancies!*
> *How like my deepmost yearnings!*

Fr Duhr's obituary was followed by Katie Umrigar reciting a poem she had penned herself:

From Shadows unto Light
To the memory of the late Sultan Padamsee

> That we should thus be doomed to fall
> By Death's untimely ruthless blow . . . !

> That Body fair and sacred Soul
> These Twain-in-One should strangers grow ...!
>
> Hence, ere we helpless sink to sleep
> Enshrouded in the silent Earth,
> 'Mother of mothers!'—her we ask—
> 'Wherefore, pray, didst thou give us birth!' ...
>
> Just when the Rose's hues unfold
> And with all bloom's her perfumes blend
> And springs their magic tissues weave,
> Why must Death's scythe the fabric rend ...?
>
> What Thou didst give, may'st rightly take;
> What Thou didst make, may'st fondly keep:
> Unto Thy Heart his soul unfold
> Thy Heart, all Beauty's Fountain deep ...
>
> For us there lives his memory—
> A silent call, a sign-post bright.
> It ever calls, it ever points:
> *Through Art—the Shadow—to The Light!*

The evening ended with the Theatre Group staging *Music at Night** by J.B. Priestley as a solemn tribute to Sultan Padamsee. Adi Marzban, Bobby's close friend, took over the direction, while Deryck Jefferies produced and stage-managed it. The action took place in the darkness of a drawing room, with the characters slowly coming to life to relate incidents from the life of a boy who had passed on. This struck all concerned as rather ironic, given the circumstances. It was perhaps the first time that a western play in English had been adapted to India with Indian names for the characters. So, for example, the Mother (played by Bapsy Sabawalla, mother of the artist to be, Jehangir Sabawalla), was called Peru Umrigar. An important part of the *mise en scène* consisted of a piece of concert music

---

* Bobby Padamsee had already begun rehearsing *Music at Night*, which was slated to be performed in January 1946, while *Chitra* by Tagore was to follow in February 1946.

playing off-stage for the entire duration of the performance. Deryck had chosen Sibelius' 'Violin Concerto'. Alkazi played the violinist, who appears on stage only at the end of the performance.[2]

A few days later, on 20 January 1946, Kamaladevi Chattopadhyay organized a memorial service for Sultan Padamsee at the Merchant Chambers, where it is reported that there was massive attendance.

The one person conspicuous by her absence on all these occasions was Kulsumbai Padamsee. Bobby was her son, her world. She decided to stay away from the prying eyes of those who wanted to share in her loss and console her. She neither wanted the tears and condolences of others, nor their advice. The loss was hers, and hers alone to bear. She blanked out on 9 January 1946 and retired to her room, where she remained virtually incarcerated for more than a year. All the doors and windows of her room were kept tightly shut. A year of mourning, not eating much, not sleeping much and not speaking much. What Kulsumbai went through during that year was unimaginable. A zero year, they said. Time eked out imperceptibly until it came to a grinding halt. What Kulsumbai's extended mourning ensured for Bobby Padamsee was immortality—an afterlife. Bobby had been deified by his mother and thus became a myth.

CHAPTER 8
THE HOUSE OF THE FOOLISH VIRGIN
1946

The tragic death of Sultan Padamsee had a lasting and complex effect on both Roshen and Elk. The impact of him taking his own life would manifest itself in different ways in their own lives later, becoming a touchstone that invisibly altered their perception of the very nature of existence.

Bobby may have died, but he continued to live as part of their consciousness. He was the reason for them being together; he was the one who mentored their creativity; it was his unbounded energy that unfurled through them, connecting their actions to his. The brief years spent together as a threesome had been intense.

Roshen, of course, had been the recipient of her brother's unrivalled attention from a young age. Her siblings, especially the next in line, Jerry, had always been envious about Roshen being by Bobby's side when he discussed ideas with his friends or read his poems and that her advice and response to his work were always sought after, valued and heeded. Roshen doubled up as Bobby's companion and confidant long before Alkazi came onto the scene.

Bobby wanted his sister Roshen to be a liberated and intellectually alive modern woman and he encouraged her to become one. Roshen flowered under Bobby's watchful eye. To begin with, he addressed her as 'The Lady Roshenara'! He nurtured her talent as a poetess. He developed her sartorial taste—he told her what sari to wear, what kind of blouse to wear with it, its colour, texture and design. He wrote to her frequently while in England, introducing her to the latest fashions as well as guiding her to study the work of the greatest costume designers of the time, such as Leon Bakst and Natalia Goncharova of the Diaghilev company. From Bobby, Roshen learned of great literature, great art, great filmmakers and great modern poets. No school could have instilled in her a love of all the arts more than Bobby did.

Alkazi arrived in their midst as if on an Arabian steed. His arresting looks were not lost on Bobby, who appreciated the Grecian nose, the aquiline, sharply etched features and the taut muscular body of this aspiring young Arab actor who, though he craved attention, was shy and retiring.

However, Roshen has said that for a long time she never noticed Elk and was unaware of his eyes following her. Of course, everyone, including Bobby, did! Bobby noticed and possibly calculated that it would be better for Alkazi to be the object of his *sister's* desire rather than his own! Perhaps he would have liked to develop a relationship with this attractive young man himself, whom he began painting in a variety of guises. Drawn into the ambit of Bobby's personal attentions, Roshen, Elk and Bobby soon became a threesome, connected by physical attraction as well as intellectual pursuits.

With Bobby gone, a sense of gloom and despair descended on Kulsum Terrace. Piecing together his last actions and words over and over again in order that they might find some rational meaning in an otherwise incomprehensible act, Roshen and Elk came up with only one reason... that by taking his own life, Bobby had asserted that it was *his* choice and his alone, to live or to die.

Was his suicide the result of the rapidly changing times they were living through?

On the one hand, the massive destruction wrought by the two World Wars had bred an overall sense of insecurity and anxiety in young people across the world. At the same time, advancements in the fields of science and technology had awakened the individual to a greater sense of his own agency and self-worth. Bobby had been raised in an era where the ideas of democracy had gained currency, leading to a utopian dream where a classless, egalitarian society was a very palpable and achievable goal. Thus empowered, the individual sought to free himself from all types of dogma and enslavement, ready to revolt against all forms of hierarchy—of class, religion and sexuality. Practically for the first time in history, the individual was asserting his own will and was clearly determined to be master of his own fate.

Sultan Padamsee, in fact, epitomized this free-spiritedness. Everything he did was the gesture of throwing off shackles and liberating himself—his flamboyance, his very individualistically conceived theatre productions, his theatrical parties, his original way of subjecting even sacrosanct authors, such as Shakespeare, to his own, very individual treatment. The very fact that he insisted on producing a controversial text like Oscar Wilde's *Salome*, based on a Biblical theme, in a well-established Jesuit educational institution like St Xavier's College was proof that Sultan Padamsee believed in fighting for artistic freedom of expression and wished to challenge any kind of censorship in the garb of moral self-righteousness.

In Bobby's Last Will and Testament, it is startling to read how he unambiguously stated that he was well aware of his own 'exceptional talents', conscious of his 'genius' in so many spheres and very conscious that these gifts could be of benefit to the 'living', to the 'lives of others'. But then he goes on to analyse that he is not part of such a coterie of persons who wish 'to live' and spread such riches; his focus lies elsewhere. His idea of fulfilment is not so much to be involved in a love affair with Life, but to be in an eternal love affair with Eternity! It was this remarkable sentiment, coming from one so young, merely twenty-four years old at the time, that Fr Duhr grasped so accurately when he spoke of Bobby's wish to step from 'Time into Eternity'; of his need to experience something beyond what Life had to offer, he intuited the only way to achieve that was 'to embrace Death'.

Perhaps without him even being aware of it, Bobby had spent the past few years before he died in an amazing effort to, in fact, bestow and share the bounty of his talents with more and more friends, gathering great numbers of people around him and enthusing and infecting them with his passion for and knowledge of the arts. It was amazing that in a span of barely two or three years, Sultan Padamsee, through his persuasive charm, wit, humour, penchant for fun, energy and exuberance, had attracted more than 150 young men and women as members of the Theatre Group.

Alongside, he had also built up an inner core of trusted lieutenants, three of whom would marry his three sisters. In hindsight, one cannot help but think that Bobby practically masterminded these marriages, making this group of six individuals—his three sisters and their husbands-to-be—a core group of excellent theatre workers, around whom other members of the Theatre Group would gravitate in future. Bobby did not forget to bestow 'the theatre bug' even on his youngest brothers—Alyque and Chotu, mere teenagers at the time. By involving his mother Kulsumbai and centring the activities of the Theatre Group in their own home, Bobby, with considerable foresight, had looked into the future, paving the way for the continuance of the theatre that he loved so much, well beyond his own lifetime. Thus, by passing on his knowledge, as well as his worldly possessions, to others, Bobby had finally cleansed and prepared himself for the final journey to join his maker. 'Death is my Lover and I embrace him.' As Roshen, my mother, often said, 'Bobby always made a dramatic entry into a room so that his presence was seen, heard and acknowledged.' Similarly, Bobby made his final exit unforgettable. It was orchestrated to the last detail by Bobby himself, with nothing left to chance.

Today, some seventy years later, theatre history bears witness to the fact that Sultan Padamsee was the fiery initiator of a new theatre movement in Bombay. Working primarily in English, as it was the language he was familiar with, Bobby Padamsee was a catalyst who lit up and energized the theatrical firmament by finding ways and means of making modernity work in contemporary urban theatre. His legacy was carried forward not only by my parents, Roshen and Ebrahim, but also by Bobby's other brothers and sisters and their respective spouses and children. Today, many, many members of our vast Padamsee/Alkazi/Allana/Jefferies/Sayani 'clan' remain engaged, in one way or another, with theatre activity across the globe.

Between January 1946, when Bobby died, and October 1946, when my parents got married, it was left to Alkazi to take over the reins of the Theatre Group. He was a stunned young man of barely twenty-one years, bemused and confused that such an onerous task had landed on his frail shoulders! This was the second time in his young life that a responsibility of such import had, without warning, descended on him. Ali's sudden departure and now Bobby's had left him feeling abandoned, left to shoulder the responsibility of a family, an institution and a number of younger siblings, all at a time when he himself was still indecisive as to whether he wanted to take up theatre seriously at all. And now, all of a sudden, he was asked to fill the shoes of his mentor and be the leader of a theatre group. Ebrahim felt totally inadequate. He was not a Bobby; he could never be. To begin with, he did not have Bobby's self-confidence.

Political events were becoming more and more unstable and volatile, with Bombay increasingly under curfew. Stalling for time in making long-term decisions, Alkazi hastily put together a production of *Richard III* within a month of Bobby's passing, with himself directing and playing the lead. All TG members rallied around in support, only to be shaken by the unexpected news of the Naval Mutiny in the same month, February 1946. A curfew was imposed on Bombay and the evening show timings of *Richard III* were altered to matinees. Being so close to the Gateway of India at Colaba, the group felt particularly vulnerable.

'Rosh, my love, I am appalled and terrified that Bobby's mantle has fallen on me. How can I possibly manage all this? How does everyone assume that I will be capable of carrying on his work?'

It was a quiet evening after the *Richard III* shows. He and Roshen were sitting on the swing on the terrace of KT.

'Elk, it's funny, you know, but looking back, I remember Bobby mentioning to me several times that if anyone could carry on his work, it would be you.'

'What? Did he really say that?'

'Yes!'

'But how could he? What did he see in me?'

'It's not just Bobby who saw it; it's all of us, Elk! We all see how serious you are about theatre! You read so much! You know a lot!'

'That's not true. I know nothing—nothing at all!

'Nothing at all?' Roshen asked coquettishly, glancing at him sideways. She wanted to lift him out of this morose mood. He was quick to respond.

'No, you're right! There is this one thing that I *do* know, and that is . . . that I love you!'

He looked deep into Roshen's eyes and whispered one of his favourite verses from the 'Song of Solomon' into her ear:

> Set me as a seal upon thine heart
> As a seal upon thine arm
> For Love is as strong as Death . . .

Richard III by Shakespeare, dir. E. Alkazi; Alkazi as Richard, Nargis Cowasji as Lady Ann, Theatre Group, Bombay, 1946

He kissed her long and tenderly, with great passion. Alyque[*] and Chotu were playing cricket nearby on the terrace. They stopped dead in their tracks, shocked to see what the young couple were up to, exchanged mischievous looks and ran off chuckling!

With their entire world shattered, Kulsum and Jafferbhai were probably so overwrought that they were indifferent to the fact that their daughters were not marrying within the Khoja community. My parents were the first couple to tie the knot in October 1946. They decided that the celebrations would be low-key and simple. Kulsumbai continued to be in mourning, making a brief, silent appearance, draped in a black and red *bandhini pacheri,* a scarf worn on special occasions, over her long, Khoja *farak.* Ummi, Ebrahim's mother, was conspicuous by her absence, a painful

---

[*] Alyque, by this time, was probably sixteen or seventeen years old and was in his last year at Cathedral School. He loved cricket and was the captain of the house cricket team.

Alkazi weds Roshen, October 1946

fact that was only partially smoothed over by the entry of Ebrahim's father and his two glamorous sisters, Fatima and Noora, along with their spouses. The five of them were the sole representatives of the groom's family. It was a simple nikah.*

However, the surviving photographs and a five-minute 16mm film of the wedding shot by Deryck show the young couple as very much in love and surrounded by their theatre friends. The short film appears to have been taken after the nikah and shows the wedding group on the terrace. Alkazi, dapper and handsome in a suit, slips a ring onto the slim finger of his bride, Roshen, who is dressed in a silver lamé sari with sprinkles of delicate flowers embroidered across it. Ebrahim's sisters, along with Jerry, Bee and Candy are flanked by Khorshed Wadia and Freni Lala, as well as Hamid Sayani and Deryck Jefferies. A few other women friends who are recognizable as young members of the Theatre Group crowd around the couple, smiling. Elk is holding aloft the six-year-old Candy. He cracks a joke and looks debonair, yet self-conscious.

---

* Though both were Muslims, my father was a Sunni and my mother a Khoja Shia.

Another photograph taken on the same occasion is a portrait of my mother. She looks at the camera with a shy yet radiant smile that comes alive each time one looks at it. In 2007, when my mother passed away, my father 'seated' this framed photograph of my mother on a chair opposite the one he normally occupied in his drawing room. None of us ever felt the need to shift this photograph from the place he had installed her. It was touching to see the way he occasionally stole a glance at Roshen's photograph, comforted by his beloved's proximity.

'*What I miss most about her, is her presence.*'[1]

The young couple went off to Matheran for their honeymoon and fell in love with a *mali*'s small cottage there. Renting it for next to nothing, they began to spend more time in Matheran over the next few months. My father enjoyed hiking up from Neral, while Roshen came up on a *tattoo* (pony). They furnished the rather run-down rooms with odds and ends. Soon Alkazi brought his books and canvasses up and was determined to spend more time on his painting. One bright morning in December, Alkazi, in a fit of inspiration, picked up his brush and, instead of working on a canvas, began to feverishly paint the walls of the cottage, covering both the inner and outer surfaces with his murals! It was an idyllic time, with Roshen reading, pottering around the kitchen and doing a spot of gardening. Soon they discovered she was pregnant (with me!), so to mark the occasion, Elk playfully named their little cottage 'The House of the Foolish Virgin'!*

---

* Why this name? I'm not exactly sure. Either Alkazi was punning on 'virgin' suggesting that Roshen, the virgin, was foolish enough to be deflowered. Or it is somehow related to 'The Wise and Foolish Virgins', which is a biblical parable of five wise virgins and five foolish ones who await the Lord (Juliet Margaret Cameron of the Bloomsbury Group created a staged photograph of the five foolish and five wise virgins in the mid-nineteenth century). The foolish ones are not in readiness for the arrival of the Lord; their lamps don't have oil. The wise ones are in readiness with their lamps lit. By that reading, does it mean that this is the house of those who are foolish and unprepared? Does it mean that the house belongs to 'artists' who are innocent and unprepared? The name seems open to several interpretations.

CHAPTER 9
TO BE OR NOT TO BE
1947

Those were the early days of their marriage, when they were getting to know one another. Roshen had never experienced living with such a quiet person! Her family was loud, talkative and boisterous. Elk, on the other hand, was generally monosyllabic. So there were long stretches of silence when he was reading, writing or painting, all with complete concentration. At times when Candy, Roshen's youngest sister, came down to their flat to play, Rosh would immediately say, 'Shush! Don't make a noise, Candy! Elk is listening to music!'[1] It was clear that it was neither family nor friends, but work and work alone, that assumed priority in Elk's life. True, she did believe that he had given his heart to her, but she began to sense that it was only a partial surrender and never a complete one.

The problem lay, thought Rosh, in Elk not being able to fully express himself emotionally. He seemed to always hold back a bit—not just with her but with everyone else too, which prevented him from developing deep or abiding friendships. Was it just his natural reserve, she wondered, or a kind of formality, so much a part of Arab etiquette, that had been ingrained in him since childhood? Was it this that prevented Elk from giving himself to her completely? What had actually drawn them to one another? These were questions that the young Roshen carelessly flirted with in the early days of her marriage, but they were the very thoughts that lay dormant within her, developing deep roots over the years, assuming huge proportions that would finally rise to the surface at critical junctures, demanding answers in unequivocal terms.

On the rare occasion when Roshen brought up such matters, Elk confessed that though formality was very much part of his Arab upbringing, he, in fact, was seen as an extrovert, a kind of rebel, by his siblings. After all, he was the only one among them who had actually crossed the boundaries of what lay beyond their limited, circumscribed lives in India. Elk had always longed to travel in the country, to see more, do more. More than anything, he first wanted desperately to know India—like an Indian, he said. Rosh began to see how it must have taken guts and determination on his part to transition from being part of an expat, closely knit Arab family and push himself to integrate into a wider, more cosmopolitan urban circle. Elk frequently struggled with doubts and severe mood swings, oscillating between clowning around and withdrawing into a small, dark space. He wasn't sure if he was doing the right thing by distancing himself from his family. Filled with a sense of guilt and 'self-loathing', Elk castigated himself for somehow betraying the ideals and values of his parents. The process of integrating the two divergent worlds— one, which Alkazi belonged to, and the other, which he aspired to be a part of—was not always easy. Roshen observed that at times the conflict was so intense that it created a deep schism within him, cleaving him in two. Writing to Rosh years later, he was able to articulate these feelings more clearly: 'For myself, I have all along felt guilty about my whole life. Since my childhood, it has been one based on deception and my self-loathing and self-hatred are not things I can continue to live with.'[2]

However, the young couple pushed these more personal issues onto the back burner for the moment and tried to address the immediate concern—problems that had arisen as a result of Bobby's death, namely, future plans of the Theatre Group. Elk, whom all TG members looked up to for guidance, didn't seem to have a clear idea of how to take the fledgling group forward. Disappearing to Matheran from time to time to clear his mind in solitude, Elk vacillated between wholeheartedly committing himself to the theatre or pursuing painting, which he increasingly found creatively fulfilling. The idea of going abroad to study art was attractive, an option that he did not want to dismiss without careful consideration.

It was early 1947. The Bombay art scene since the War had been enlivened by a fair amount of exposure to European modernity in the arts, giving the city a distinct international flavour of its own. This had primarily happened through the presence of refugee artists from different parts of the world settling in Bombay, making it one of the

> hubs of globalizing modernism . . . a city . . . of entrance, transition and creativity for people fleeing their native countries

due to changes in political systems, dictatorships and wars, repression, persecution and violence.

> ... it was a group of German-speaking emigrants who exerted the most sustained influence on Bombay's cultural scene: Walter Langhammer, painter and art director at the *Times of India*, Rudy von Leyden, art critic for the *Times of India* and illustrator for the *Illustrated Weekly* and Emmanuel Schlesinger, an entrepreneur and art collector who reportedly brought works by Oskar Kokoschka and Egon Schiele with him to Bombay ... in addition the Polish painter and illustrator Stefan Norblin, the Hungarian photographer Ferenc Brenko and the Russian painter Magda Nachman (Acharya) ...[3]

These were among the migrant artists, intellectuals and art connoisseurs in Bombay who actively sought institutional spaces for discourse—teaching and lecturing at a variety of universities, while giving public talks in which they innovatively addressed and challenged issues such as 'nationalism' in art and in a way began to guide the trajectory that modern Indian art was taking. They were especially instrumental in

> catalyzing the emergence and popular reception of the Progressive Artists' Group (the Progressives), which included Indian artists such as Francis Newton (F.N.) Souza and Krishnaji Howlaji (K.H.) Ara. In addition, von Leyden was a regular contributor to *MARG: A Magazine of Architecture and Art*, co-founded in Bombay in 1946 by a group of artists, architects and intellectuals led by Mulk Raj Anand and including the German architect Otto Koenigsberger, who was exiled in princely Mysore State and regularly visited Bombay. Similarly, the exiled art historian Ernst Cohn–Wiener was employed in the princely state of Baroda, as was Hermann Goetz, a specialist in Mughal art history. Both lectured at the University of Bombay.[4]

Alkazi and Roshen made it a point to attend art-related events at Bombay University, the Town Hall or the Cowasji Jehangir Public Hall, venues not far from Colaba Causeway, where they lived.

Alkazi and Roshen, 1947

In order to stay abreast of trends in modernism worldwide, Elk eagerly began to devour literature from Europe, England, the US and the Soviet Union through magazines, periodicals and publications freely available in Bombay's bookshops and public libraries. Rosh and Elk's circle of friends now expanded beyond the theatre crowd to include writers, painters and art critics. Besides Souza, there were youngsters like M.F. Husain, K.H. Ara, H.A. Gade, Sadanand Bakre and, of course, Akbar Padamsee, Rosh's first cousin—all of whom were at the forefront of evolving a modernist idiom for contemporary Indian art.

* * *

Elk was seeing off his college friend, George Coelho, at VT Station.[5] Nissim Ezekiel, also a friend of George's, was there too, and both young men were introduced to one another for the first time. By the time the train chugged out of the station, Nissim and Elk were embroiled in a heated literary discussion that continued over lunch at Alkazi's home. The fact that Nissim was registered for his master's in English literature at Bombay's Wilson College, that his parents were academics and that the family were

Marathi-speaking Bene Israeli Jews,* were details that Alkazi responded to favourably. Most importantly, Nissim's favourite authors included James Joyce, Ezra Pound, W.B. Yeats and T.S. Eliot—Alkazi's own favourites!

Theirs was an instant meeting of minds. Elk was taken by Nissim's love of modern English prose and verse, while for Nissim, over the next few years, Elk became a kind of mentor–friend, guiding him into a deeper understanding and appreciation of theatre and painting. As Nissim listened to Alkazi speak knowledgeably and unpretentiously about art, he began to realize the importance of the public being introduced to the language of modernity.

* * *

On a pleasant evening towards the end of January 1947, Nissim, Rosh and Elk made their way down Colaba Causeway towards Chetna restaurant at Kala Ghoda for a cup of tea and vegetarian samosas. A lively discussion on Bombay theatre was underway.

'I mean, can we actually build a new theatre movement on the foundations of the commercial Natak company type of theatre? Absolutely not! We have to ask ourselves, Is there a new way to function?' Elk asked in all earnestness.

'Well, what do you say about the efforts of Prithviraj? He is seeking to strike a balance between commercial fare and serious theatre. Take *Deewar* and *Pathan,* for instance. He seems to have touched a nerve. He speaks to the common people. He has a growing following in both cities and smaller towns.'

'Sorry, Nissim, but I find the scripts too propagandist and melodramatic for my taste.'

Always wanting to see the efforts of others in a positive light, Rosh objected. She was in her second month of pregnancy and somewhat out of breath.

'Don't be so harsh, Elk. Prithviraj has an agenda. He is using theatre to build a nationalistic spirit. His theatre is for the masses—to stem

---

* The Bene Israeli Jews had settled in India centuries earlier, in cities such as Poona and Bombay. Ebrahim, in fact, had had many Bene Israeli Jewish friends in school and since they had virtually lived opposite the Jewish synagogue in Poona, the Lal Deval, Elk was familiar with Jewish rituals and observances.

this terrible tide of hatred between Hindus and Muslims that continues unabated. Every production cannot be judged on its artistic merits alone!'

'I'm not talking of artistic merits, Rosh. I'm talking about new experiments that are happening. Did you know that Marathi adaptations of Ibsen, Shaw, Odets and Priestley have already been presented in Marathi and Gujarati? These are plays with themes drawn from modern, urban life. That's what we need. Nissim, go on, please tell Rosh about the *A Doll's House* experiment!'

'You see, Rosh, a few years ago, this Maharashtrian director–writer Rangnekar, opened his new play called *Kulavadhu* (Bride of a Respectable Family) at the Royal Opera House (not a normal venue for Marathi theatre). It had obvious references to Ibsen's *A Doll's House*. Rangnekar created history by allowing his heroine to walk out of her marriage and earn a living for her family by becoming a film actress. It was a non-musical play and with its bold theme, it was hailed as a critical success, ushering in a new era!'

'Oh! That's interesting!' said Rosh.

'Yes! And what about Damu Jhaveri? His Indian National Theatre, which performs both in Gujarati and Marathi, was expressly set up to initiate a *non-political*, "national" theatre movement to counter the blatantly propagandist efforts of IPTA.[*] You see, Rosh, these are efforts in the vernacular theatre that we are totally unaware of, sitting in our cushy drawing rooms.'

They passed Regal Cinema and the Prince of Wales Museum and were nearing the Artist Aid Centre, which had recently been set up on the suggestion of Walter Langhammer, the Jewish émigré, as an alternative to the Bombay Art Society as a venue where younger artists could be exhibited.[†] Next to the Artist's Aid Centre was the Institute of Foreign Languages and alongside that were India Coffee House and The Wayside

---

[*] The INT was established in Bombay in 1944 with a broad agenda to perform in different Indian languages, such as Marathi and Gujarati, reach back to folk traditions in theatre and dance as well as encourage new playwrighting. It did not support any political ideology as IPTA did and was, in that sense, apolitical.

[†] The Bombay Art Society, which had been in place for almost a century to support the arts, was well-established but was now being lambasted by the younger generation for being a bastion of conservatism and supporting either western academic art or showing revivalist tendencies.

Inn. Bombay was certainly developing a café culture around the Kala Ghoda area where young writers, painters, actors and cinema directors would fill ashtrays with cigarette stubs while fervently discussing their latest projects over steaming cups of tea. Chetna was yet another addition to this busy art district, transforming the Fort area into a desi version of the 'Quartier Latin' of Paris.

In fact, it was precisely with this idea of nurturing an artist's quarter that Raja Rama Rao,[*] a writer and staunch believer in Shri Ramana Maharishi, who had recently returned from Paris, rented the lower floor of a building and converted it into a unique vegetarian café, which he appropriately called Chetna, meaning 'awareness'.

On one side of the restaurant was a bookshop with a range of books on yoga, spiritualism, literature and the arts. A large number of intellectuals began to frequent Chetna, with young students working there as dishwashers and waiters, as they did in Paris, as a way of paying their own way through university. Young artists were encouraged to display their works on the walls of the cafe, so currently Ara's magnificent and incredibly forceful work, 'The Maratha Battle Scene', drew everyone's attention.

Finding the place smoke-filled and overflowing, Nissim, Elk and Rosh were about to depart when Elk spotted an empty table tucked away in a corner. Wending their way through the crowd, they managed to seat Roshen.

'So what we are saying is that if theatre has to function as a real collective, it needs to be based on democratic principles...' Nissim picked up the threads of the conversation that had been temporarily abandoned.

'Exactly!' countered Alkazi, adding, 'you cannot say "I do plays on the themes of secularism and socialism" when in your films you actually function like a capitalist and promote a "star system"! I find this highly problematic. Creating a democratic work ethic is central to the new culture we are creating...'

'As is the freedom of expression,' added Nissim.

'Absolutely! Creative artists need space . . . they need air to breathe; they cannot conform to diktats. No artist worth his salt is going to tolerate the "Big Brother is Watching You" syndrome. Isn't that exactly why a

---

[*] Fluent in French, Raja Rao had moved among the highest intellectual circles in Paris. Now in Bombay, besides the artists, he befriended the Consular Corps, for whom he frequently threw dinner parties at Chetna, to which artists and art patrons were invited.

E. Alkazi, F.N. Souza and Nissim Ezekiel

significant production like *Nabanna* based on the Bengal Famine shut down? Sombhu Mitra, the director, couldn't take the Party's interference any longer. He simply walked out!'

'Sounds like a repeat of the Newton story,' interjected Nissim.

Suddenly, a voice from above them slurred: 'Did I hear my name being taken in vain?'

There was Newton Souza, with his pencil-thin moustache, towering above them. All this while, he had his back to them and they hadn't noticed! Lurching a bit . . . they helped him sit down . . .

'Now, tell me why my dearest Roshen wants to know about me?' He peered into her eyes, smiling vacantly.

'Oh, nothing really! I was about to tell her the story of your tiff with the Commies!' Nissim was somewhat apologetic.

'Oh, *that* story? That's old hat! Ancient history, actually! It's public knowledge by now . . . But Rosh, darling, if you don't know it, I'll tell you myself!'

Lighting a cigarette, he settled down to brag . . .

'You see, after my solo show in 1945 at the Bombay Art Society, I joined the Communist Party. Soon after that, the Party denounced my work. He said my work was "a manifestation of bourgeois aesthetics"! Can you believe that? He said they had decided to purge me out.'

By now, Newton's voice was rising.

'My rejoinder to them was, "Damn you! I'm a true artist. I don't paint for the proletariat, nor do I paint for select coteries! I paint for myself! I paint in order to exist!' Souza said, thumping his chest.

'Newton, did you really say that?' Roshen was thrilled.

'Bloody hell, I did! Now let me tell you the latest news, Elk, and that is that our native artists, some of whom are sitting around here right now, lack direction! And the only solution for us is to band together . . . to form some kind of a group . . . a 'progressive' group. I've spoken to people like Ara and Husain . . . and they are actually seriously considering the idea of joining me! And guess what? Leyden, Schlesinger and Langhammer are supporting us!'

Elk had been listening to Souza's slightly drunken but important diatribe very carefully.

'That's wonderful, Newton. It will surely shake things up. Something like this is so necessary in the *theatre* world too . . . The way I see it, from the performing arts, only Uday Shankar's efforts have been significant. He is the only person interested in culling out a *new form* . . . It's not just about *content*, but a new *language* . . . combining theatre and dance, the modern and the traditional. Shankar's dance school in Almora was such a far-sighted idea—brilliant! It was truly a laboratory to try out new ideas and . . .'

All of a sudden, Nissim exploded, 'Well, frankly, Elk, let's stop talking about what *other* people are doing or not doing! The point is, what are *you* doing? *Who* are you waiting for? A messiah in the field of theatre? Who is that going to be? Why are you procrastinating? You've inherited something, dammit! Can't you see that? A whole theatre company! The Theatre Group. Without even asking for it! You have *ready-made* followers who don't even need to be convinced. Aren't you going to make something of *that*?'

Nissim was obviously very agitated. He was usually quite soft-spoken, so this was unlike him. The way he threw the words out, it was like a challenge to Alkazi. For some time, the words just hung there, suspended, awaiting an answer, a response—anything!

A long pause. It didn't look like anything was forthcoming from Alkazi. They were walking back. Then, after about half an hour, Elk muttered, 'Give me time, Nissim! I must think this through carefully.'

No one said a word. The three young people were preoccupied with thoughts of their futures crowding in on them.

CHAPTER 10
BOMBAY DANCES WITH DEATH
1948

I was sitting on the swing with Roshen at Kulsum Terrace when we suddenly heard the patter of thousands of feet in the streets below, the banging shut and the pulling of shutters and the slamming of the doors of shops and establishments. Suddenly, all the streets of Colaba—there was the BEST tram terminus opposite the house—became completely empty... and then the news... coming to us on the radio... that Mahatma Gandhi had been assassinated! It was an electrifying moment. It was a feeling you felt that your life could never be the same again. From that moment onwards, something devastating had happened... not only to the country but to one personally, in your own life and it could never really be the same again.[1]

The entire nation was in a state of shock over the assassination of Mahatma Gandhi on 30 January 1948, with life virtually coming to a standstill.

Gandhiji was part of the air that you breathe; there's nothing that you could have done from day to day, literally from moment to moment in Bombay, without the presence of Gandhiji, without the face of Gandhiji in front of you. Whether it was on the posters or in calendars, in photographs. His movement had already been there for the last twenty-five or thirty years, before the 1940s. And he was not merely a household name; people hung on his every word. So, his presence was all over... we felt lost...[2]

Gandhiji's assassination came as a climactic response to the Partition of the country and the communal frenzy that followed. In Bombay, the communal riots never reached the scale of other areas, yet the politics of Partition and Independence cast a pall over the city's multicultural world.

> The city was divided into 'Hindu Bombay' and 'Muslim Bombay'. No Muslim ventured into a Hindu area, and no Hindu would stray into a Muslim area . . . The intellectuals and artists of the city . . . (Saadat Hasan Manto, Ismat Chughtai, K.A. Abbas, etc.) who had dreamed of a cosmopolitan nation of justice and freedom were left reeling in the blood soaked birth of India and Pakistan . . . Chughtai wrote, 'Communal violence and freedom became so muddled that it became difficult to distinguish between the two' . . . PWA and IPTA mobilized several theatre groups and cultural organizations in a unity procession that marched through the city . . . Prithviraj Kapoor, Raj and Shammi Kapoor, Balraj Sahani, Chetan Anand, Dev Anand, Prem Dhawan . . . spread the message of communal harmony from an IPTA truck. The Urdu writers Sajjad Zaheer, Ali Sardar Jafri, Kaifi Azmi, Sahir Ludhianavi and Majnooh Sultanpuri, joined the procession for peace. Abbas wrote a play titled 'Main Kaun Hoon' drawing on his experience of 'mistaken killings'.[3]

In such a situation, Ebrahim's father seriously feared for the safety of his family, making preparations to move out of India.

Ebrahim felt trapped. He was well aware of his father's anxiety about remaining in India but was constrained to break the news to them of his growing interest in the arts. How could he tell his father that working in the family business was no longer a viable option for him? The tension had been further exacerbated by his marriage to Roshen, whom his parents did not appear to have accepted wholeheartedly. After all, Ebrahim thought, they may be resenting the fact that it was *she* and *her* family who were actively responsible for furthering Ebrahim's interest in theatre, and it was *her* family whom he seemed to be drawn to.

Ebrahim was in turmoil. On the one hand, his family was dependent on him and, on the other, the members of the Theatre Group were looking to him for leadership. And finally, he was still unclear whether he wanted to opt for painting or theatre! He needed time on his own to help clear his mind.

After their wedding, Ebrahim had moved out of the Gobhai Karanjia Building, where he had lived and worked with his father, into Kulsum Terrace, where the young couple were given the use of a tiny, one-bedroom flat on the third floor. The Theatre Group rehearsals had to relocate from Kulsumbai's spacious drawing room on the fourth floor to Roshen and Elk's minuscule ten-by-ten-foot drawing room. Their daily routine consisted of pushing their solid Burma teak sofa set, received as a wedding gift, into the passage outside and, when rehearsals got over, moving it back in.[4] As Roshen said, her mother was not as generous with her son-in-law as she had been with her son. Kulsumbai, it was felt, held a lurking yet unspoken resentment against Elk, who she thought might replace Bobby, who, in her mind, was irreplaceable and never to be forgotten.

Alkazi was restless for the next few months. He had been reading quite a bit about Shri Ramana Maharishi from books he had acquired at the Chetna bookshop. He was taken by the idea of undergoing a spiritual experience and, on the spur of the moment, went off to Tiruvannamalai on his own for a week. There, in the gentle aura of the Maharishi's presence, he did sense a loosening up and a calm.[*] Returning to Bombay, he now began to face the realities of life. To begin with, he needed an income in order to have financial independence. He was lucky to get a job as a teacher of English at the Urdu-medium Ismail Beg Mohammed High School on Mohammed Ali Road.

* * *

I, Amal, had already been born in September 1947—a Midnight's Child! Born free, I was given another appropriate name by my parents—'Uma', whose meaning—tranquility, splendour or fame—perhaps matched the mood of liberation. The fact that it was the name of a Hindu

---

[*] 'I went to Tiruvannamalai myself in order to find out what was really meant by the spiritual experience. And so I did go there on my own, entirely alone, and was there for about a week. It had a very gentle aura and was not flamboyant; it was very low-key and, at the time, Sri Ramana Maharishi was extremely ill and about to die.'—E. Alkazi in an interview with Amal Allana, NYC, 1999.

goddess seemed to matter little to my parents, who were secular-minded to the core. 'Amal', which means hope or good deeds, is my Arab given name and one that I would begin to use many years later, possibly because another 'Uma' made an entry into our lives! But for the moment, we are in 1947.

Suddenly, with a baby in their arms, it looked like it was time to start making concrete decisions regarding their future. In March 1948, Rosh and Elk returned to Matheran with baby Uma. Undoubtedly inspired by reading about great French artists like Cezanne, Picasso, Matisse and Gauguin, who expressed the need to regularly return to the land for creative rejuvenation, spiritual sustenance and inspiration, the young Alkazis extended invitations to their artist friends to visit them, making The House of the Foolish Virgin a kind of retreat for pursuing artistic work in relative peace and solitude, 'away from the madding crowd' of the city.

Elk felt the urgent need to talk things over with Nissim. Receiving Elk's missive to join them in Matheran as soon as possible, as there were important matters to discuss, Nissim dropped everything and arrived there post-haste.

Early the next day, over their morning cup of tea, the three young friends gathered under the shade of the mango grove in their tiny patch of garden. It had drizzled the previous night and the damp red earth emitted a peculiar clayey odour common to this part of the Deccan Plateau. Not yet 8 a.m., Rosh sat cross-legged on a durrie. Looking pristine in a white cotton salwar kameez with a large floppy straw hat and Uma in her lap, she was a picture of contented motherhood. Elk was tensely perched against a fallen tree trunk. Nissim sat in a battered cane chair, erect and in anticipation. After a slight pause, Elk began to speak. Slowly and precisely, he articulated his thoughts about his future plans, perhaps for the first time. Nissim and Rosh listened intently.

'Nissim, Rosh, I will get straight to the point. The question you put to me some months ago, Nissim, as to whether I was going to do anything about the opportunity to lead the Theatre Group, has been rankling in my mind. I have finally realized that, in fact, I really have no option. I have already, in a sense, taken on a very responsible position as head of a prestigious theatre group. It would not be honourable for me to back down now.

Alkazi and Roshen in Matheran, 1947

'I feel I have to prepare myself to be equal to the task and have decided that the most practical and feasible step for me is to go abroad to study and equip myself and then return to build the organization.'

Rosh and Nissim let off yelps of agreement. 'Rosh! This calls for a celebration! I can't believe my ears! The Sphinx has spoken at last! A decision! We have a decision!' exclaimed Nissim.

Elk raised one hand to silence them. 'But, but, but... hold on a minute! Not just me, but *both of you* have to come too! All *three* of us must go to London! We must do this together, as a *team*!'

Nissim was so shocked that the cup of tea nearly slipped out of his hand!

'What? Everyone leave?' They started talking at once.

'Please, wait; let me finish! We will get to the details and solve them one by one. Please! Quiet!'

They got up, excitedly chattering while moving inside for some breakfast. Elk made a second announcement while frying the eggs.

'It's not an *omelette* today, my friends! It's *Hamlet*... It's to be *Hamlet, the Prince of Denmark*! Before we go anywhere, we are going to do an absolutely brilliant production for TG that will make a mark. We will leave something memorable behind so we won't be forgotten while we are away.'

'Elk, you are so full of surprises today!'

'Nissim, you and I are getting down to work on the script of *Hamlet* today. We will perform in June or July and then leave soon after—term opens in September in London, doesn't it?'

'Elk, it's difficult for me to say this, but it's going to be really problematic for me to put together the money for the travel, not to mention my living expenses!'

'Everything in good time, my friend! For the moment, Rosh, my love, my sweetheart, my angel, please cook us a glorious meal today. I'm absolutely famished. I feel like I haven't eaten for weeks. Nissim, we will have to start work at once. I'm really worried, but let's take the plunge!'

Elk was suddenly animated, elated and moved with a sense of purpose. Something had fallen into place! When referring to this moment in his life many years later, my father said, 'I suddenly felt a very strong sense of conviction about the importance of theatre. When you are a young person, I think you have this kind of, what shall we say, passion, determination, self-confidence and so on, bubbling inside you.'[5]

***

For the next few weeks, Elk and Nissim worked ceaselessly on editing the script of *Hamlet*.

We are very fortunate that the very first notes of an Alkazi production discovered so far are of this very early directorial venture of *Hamlet* in 1948. They show a remarkable level of sophistication in his understanding of not just the text but also of its rendering in theatrical terms. It is all the more surprising because Alkazi has not yet been schooled in the complexities and conventions of modern theatre practice.

Reading these jottings, it is clear that the young Alkazi was educating himself on the 'constructional' aspects of theatre. Additionally, he was becoming aware of the significance of 'lighting' and 'colours'; he often indicated the use of 'gestures' and 'body movements' for characters, suggesting an awareness of the potency of physical expression; how mood could be created through 'tempo'; the meaning of 'silence' and 'pause'. What is remarkable is that he was discovering all this for himself by studying the work of a great master like Shakespeare.

Nissim awakened Alkazi's sensibilities to appreciate Shakespeare's poetry in a more nuanced manner—its metre, syntax, associations, how

Alkazi in his studio, Matheran, 1947

words conjure up images and how they create emotions. Nissim's sharp, analytical mind, together with his sensitivity to poetry, complemented Elk's acute sense of visualizing effectively for the stage. Collaborating with Alkazi on later productions as well, Nissim remarked that his association with Alkazi on these projects provoked him to experiment with 'dramatic dialogue' in his poetry.[6]

With mornings spent working on the script, it was in the evenings that the three friends, along with baby Uma, took long walks, often ending up at Panorama Point, from where they enjoyed a sweeping view of the surrounding Western Ghats. These meanderings became occasions for animated discussion, especially about the books they were avidly reading. Sharing his literary interests with me in later years, my father said:

> On the one hand, we were reading Arthur Koestler's *Darkness at Noon*—Koestler himself descended on Bombay a few years later—as it was he who brought in the ideas of the Existentialists like Sartre and Camus that were so much in the air at that time, as well as Andre Malraux...

And on the other hand, there was Penguin Painters series. You would come across the work of the great Sutherland, John Piper, Paul Nash, Edward Burrough and so on . . . and these were the people who really stimulated you. Then you read about Epstein, his sculpture, his struggle to express himself and have his work accepted by the public who were rather resentful of his ideas and his association with Oscar Wilde . . . . . . So it was these people, I suppose, the rebels, the outsiders . . . who stimulated one.

. . . and there was the Penguin War Poets, whose poems were vividly illustrated by some of the most important British painters of the day. So all that kind of activity that seemed to surround you, as it were, one found extremely exciting; therefore, one wanted to go to the source of it. I thought if I went to London and then found my way to Paris, I'd lead the bohemian life of a Parisian artist in Montmartre and so on.[7]

A few weeks later, they returned to Bombay and rehearsals began. Elk cast Mary Sethna as Gertrude, Hamid Sayani played a brilliant Claudius, while he himself played Hamlet. With Roshen designing the costumes and providing a sense of continuity in the role of the loyal, steadfast and level-headed lieutenant, friend and companion to the play's director, TG members were reassured that the Theatre Group would fare well under Elk's stewardship.[*]

*　*　*

For Rosh, Nissim and Elk, the relative success of the production established their bona fides in the theatre world. The production over, the friends were extremely excited about their forthcoming plans to go abroad, but finances still remained a concern.

---

[*] D.G. Nadkarni, later a close friend and associate of the Alkazis' and a renowned art and theatre critic, happened to see the production of *Hamlet*. Fifty years later, in 1998, when Alkazi received the Time and Talents Lifetime Achievement Award in Bombay, Nadkarni, sitting amongst the audience, referred to the high calibre of the performance and said that though this production was staged by youngsters, it compared very favourably with the *Hamlet* done in Marathi by professionals.

Poster of *Hamlet* by Shakespeare, dir. E. Alkazi; Alkazi as Hamlet, Theatre Group, Bombay, 1947

Finally, Alkazi mustered the courage to ask his father for a one-way passage to England and a small stipend to support himself over the next few years of his studies. He would, of course, not be attending to the family business during this time. He added that there was a brilliant but needy friend of his who also wished to expand his horizons and that they had decided to work together in the future as well. Could his friend Nissim Ezekiel's fare also be met by his father? Back then, it cost Rs 627 for a one-way steamer ticket to England.

Hamed Alkazi had to think long and hard before making a financial commitment to his son. He was extremely doubtful of Ebrahim's choice of career in either theatre or painting, both fields that Hamed knew nothing about and it filled him with great anxiety. Sitting down on his cot that night, Hamed's mind sped back to that eventful day when Ebrahim was barely twelve years old.[8] Little Lulu had run up to her parents, brandishing a whole bunch of handwritten papers, saying, 'Look what I found!' Ebrahim was in hot pursuit demanding their return. Calming the children down, Ubba inquired what they were. Ebrahim kept quiet. Finally, Ubba suggested that Ebrahim read out the contents to them.

In a slightly shaky voice, Ebrahim slowly read the title: 'How I am Going To Lead My Life'. With utmost earnestness, he laid out the founding principles on which he would base his actions, the values he regarded as sacred and inviolable and how he wished to help people. The substance of the contents was written in point form and in both Arabic and English. Ummi, Ubba and by now the rest of the family stood around listening to Ebrahim, transfixed. The younger siblings looked from Ebrahim to their two parents, who seemed to pay close attention to their son's words. When Ebrahim concluded, Ubba asked if he could see the papers and he reread them aloud in Arabic. The children were sent to bed. That night, Ubba said to Ummi, 'Ebrahim seems to be a very special child . . . Very different from the rest. We have to see what becomes of him, Ummi. I am somehow reassured to hear his intentions.'

'He sounds like you,' said Ummi, turning away to sleep.

From that day on Ubba began to give Ebrahim an allowance to buy himself books and for his thirteenth birthday, Ebrahim was also given an Olivetti typewriter!

Recollecting this incident reaffirmed Hamed's faith in his son. Ebrahim would do well in whatever he took up, God willing, as beneath it all, he had sound values and was extremely hard-working.

Calling Ebrahim to the office the next day, Hamed Alkazi agreed to Ebrahim's request for support during his education in England, as well as the request for a passage to England for his friend, Nissim Ezekiel. Hamed Alkazi knew exactly what it meant to be needy and recalled the kindness he had received from so many strangers when he himself was struggling. It is also a fact that Hamed Alkazi was a devout Muslim and believed in zakat. One can only surmise that this was the reason my grandfather extended this very generous offer to a complete stranger.

Hamed himself had finally decided to move to Karachi with the entire family, as they were unsure what fate would befall them as Muslims in India. Their already tenuous status as expats had been made more fragile by the uncertainties of communal tensions in post-Partition India.

Hamed Alkazi left with a heavy heart. India had been kind and hospitable to him. What also bothered him was that he was emigrating to another country without being able to set up Ebrahim, who was married and already had one child, in a business where he could support himself.

Then suddenly, as if his prayers had been answered, Hamed had a flash of inspiration. He would not shut down his export–import company. Instead, he would rename it Ebrahim Alkazi and Sons and leave it for Ebrahim to earn a comfortable income from. The entire infrastructure had been in place for years. In Ebrahim's absence, Hamed decided to appoint his very capable nephew, Ahmed Alkazi, to be Ebrahim's working partner.

This was the best Hamed could do for his son, who wanted to pursue a career in the arts. Hamed was a closet poet himself, of no mean order and, placing his faith in his son's strong desire to excel, he recalled the sura from the Quran that positions the creative artist in close proximity to the Creator himself. Without further ado, the Arab family silently boarded the *Sabarmati* steamer at Mandvi, setting sail for Karachi, where a new destiny awaited them. Ebrahim consoled his sisters, Fatima and Noora, who, like him, stayed back in India with their spouses.

Alkazi and Roshen, 1948

PART TWO

England, 1948–1951

Alkazi

CHAPTER 11

THE PARIS OF PICASSO AND THE ENGLAND OF MOORE AND SUTHERLAND BECKONS
1948

There had barely been enough time to pack. Having just wrapped up the last performance of *Hamlet* the week before, Alkazi's head was spinning. Accolades and criticism had hit him in turn. Francis Newton Souza declared, 'It's unbelievable, Elk, how you've managed to perform *Hamlet* with histrionic ability never seen before in Bombay!'[1]

A few months earlier, a small advertisement in *Art News* had caught his attention. It stated that the Anglo–French Art Centre in London was offering courses in art, with a visiting faculty of great modernist painters such as Henri Matisse and Fernand Léger. Alkazi was beside himself with excitement—*to be taught by the great modernists themselves*! This became the decisive factor for him to depart at the very earliest.

And now, finally, here he was aboard the SS *Stratheden* on his way to London on 23 September 1948! His first journey out of the country! Looking dapper in a casual jacket with a camera slung over one arm and a portfolio of his recent drawings under the other, Elk tried to focus his entire attention on the luggage attendant, who was weaving through the milling crowds up the gangplank with his trunks at such a lick that Alkazi found it practically impossible to keep up.

Rosh, Nissim and George Coelho were bringing up the rear. They had come to see Elk off and were chatting animatedly among themselves.

'I'm not entirely convinced,' Nissim was saying, 'there were too many loose ends in the production. The editing, for one, should have been tighter, crisper.'

Visibly irritated by Nissim's lack of attention in helping with the luggage, Elk abruptly cut him short, 'Leave that for later, Nissim. No need for a post-mortem right this minute! Honestly, this is hardly the time

New Theatres for Old by Mordecai Gorelick

Courtesy: Dennis Dobson, London

or place.' And then, swiftly turning on Rosh, Elk admonished her in an undertone. 'Rosh, really! Let's concentrate on important matters. I may forget to tell you things. It's vital that you inform me about the *Hamlet* gate receipts. Also, the audience's response to the questionnaire.[*] Most importantly, post me all the cuttings and photographs!'

Rosh nodded solemnly. Elk always made such instructions sound terribly important. An edge of tension crept over the small group, resulting in momentary silence. Coelho fidgeted, turning away to observe other passengers bidding farewell to their loved ones, while Nissim looked at his watch. Alkazi, having made his point and regained control of the conversation, now disarmed them with a boyish grin.

> Let's savour the moment, my dearest, dearest, confreres! I'm so thrilled that it's not just me, but our entire group who will soon be abroad together! Nissim, this trip has to be a collective education for all of us! You, Rosh, myself and Newton Souza, too. Yes, I think he will definitely join us. We must experience new art together, we shall discuss it threadbare, thrash out our understanding of it, sift what is of consequence to us. It will be an exciting time![2]

Elk's animation and ebullient mood were contagious and they all chimed in in agreement. A gust of breeze tousled Alkazi's hair, making the youthful twenty-three-year-old look so artistically dishevelled, thought Roshen. Handsome! A veritable 'Sheikh of Araby'!

The first hoot of the ship's siren sounded, signalling that it was time to say their final goodbyes. A woman was engaged in performing *arati* for her son, garlanding him and applying the customary vermilion *teeka* to his forehead. Other families lined up for family portraits. Disappointed that he had not loaded his camera, Elk debated whether he should engage the services of the professional photographer who was hanging around when the ship's siren blasted for the final time. Taking Rosh aside, Elk looked deep into her eyes for a long, long time and said,

---

[*] There was a questionnaire for the audience, where the Theatre Group would request responses to the production.

Now don't look so woebegone, Rosh. Time will fly, you'll see . . . We will be meeting in barely a couple of months from now, in March! Remember, darling, we are so lucky to have the opportunity to transform our dreams into reality. Together! I have an earnest longing to make our lives fuller, more intimate, more *one*, because I love you, my darling and because I want us to live not merely our own lives but each other's too and I want us to be conscious of it and make Uma—when she is a little bigger—conscious, too. Isn't all this extraordinary? This is a moment for us to celebrate!'[3]

Rosh nodded, and said, 'I know all that, but I'm going to miss you terribly!' She hastily looked away, not wanting him to see the teardrop descend on to her cheek.

'Promise me you will be cheerful for Uma's sake! Kiss her for me every night and every morning!'

Rosh nodded without turning back. Then, moving on to Nissim and shaking his hand, Elk said, 'Though it may seem niggardly, Nissim, I wish to tell you how grateful I am for your tremendous effort in making *Hamlet* a success and for your unstinted assistance throughout the production. And if there were moments where I was rude or harsh, please do forgive me.'[4]

Embarrassed at this sudden outburst of emotion, Nissim hastily shoved a brown paper packet into Elk's hand, and said, 'Bon voyage, Elk. Just a little something to relieve the tedium of the long journey!'

'There was no need, Nissim. But thanks, anyway.'

They embraced.

'I leave it to you, Nissim, to take care of my beautiful bride!'

Feelings of loss, coupled with great elation, overwhelmed Elk as the SS *Stratheden* pulled out of the Bombay dockyard. He waved goodbye for a good fifteen minutes as Rosh, Nissim and George gradually blurred out of sight.

'The Paris of Picasso, Braque, Matisse and Leger and the England of Moore, Nicholson and Sutherland beckoned.'[5]

***

Kicking off his shoes, Elk lay down in his cabin. Absentmindedly removing the wrapper from the book that Nissim had gifted him, he glimpsed at the intriguing title—*New Theatres for Old* by Mordecai Gorelik. Within a few minutes, he was absorbed in the book, the idea of a nap evaporating. Gorelik, the blurb read, was an American of Russian descent who had travelled across Europe in 1936–37, putting on record the basic realities of contemporary European theatre.

His fluency in French, German and Russian allowed him to gain an insight into post-war problems in theatre. He stressed how both world wars had deeply affected European theatre, sensitizing it to its social and political responsibility. Alkazi found the book an eye-opener as it foregrounded a new role for contemporary theatre.

An inveterate loner, it was not in Elk's nature to strike up conversations with strangers. Never allowing an exchange to go beyond the initial niceties, he would politely excuse himself and disappear into a quiet corner of the deck, where he would bury himself in the Gorelik book. From time to time, he would take a short stroll, looking intense and preoccupied. On other occasions, oblivious to his surroundings, he would gaze intently at the oceanic landscape for hours together, the sea breeze curling his hair into soft, wavy tendrils.

The nature of Alkazi's meditations was not solely tied up with the contents of the Gorelik book alone; these were soon disclosed in a long letter he penned to Nissim a week after his departure, on 1 October. He laid bare his concerns regarding his future, both immediate and long-term. He confessed that he was anxious to make the right decisions regarding where he should study art—Paris or London. He rationalized that though Paris was undoubtedly the centre of the art world, London, though more conservative, would probably furnish him with a more solid foundation, besides which he was at home with the English language. Then again, he seemed to be in conflict as to what kind of course he should apply for. He concluded by returning to his fundamental dilemma—whether, in fact, he should focus on pursuing the visual arts that he found satisfying or opt for theatre, to which he was undoubtedly well suited as well.

> My desire is to get a thorough grounding in art, its theory and its practice ... Also the Anglo–French Centre's theatrical and

musical activities would help me acquire that grounding in all the arts, which will be essential to my future work. I cannot think of my painting and sculpture as being restricted to the production of easel pictures or studio sculpture, but as adapting them to more monumental works, such as frescoes, décor, stage designs and architecture...[6]

Turning his attention to the work that lay in store for the Theatre Group to accomplish in the future, Alkazi asserted the need for it to provide an alternative to what theatre in Bombay currently offered. Feverishly and in a prophetic vein, he began to identify his and the Group's key shortcomings in making relevant, contemporary theatre.

I think there should be a very serious and well-planned programme now to reorient our people—producers and audience alike—to the new and heavy demands that the theatre is bound to make in the very near future. Most of us, for instance, are confronted with a future that will find us very badly wanting in that knowledge, which, apart from its necessity for the undertaking of any cultural or creative work, will be the very essence of our mere daily being which is: *the problem of language*. Most of us who have had an Anglo–Indian education await this oncoming with a certain sense of doom, of annihilation. We have made no attempt at all to equip ourselves to face it... You, Nissim, have to convince the members of the Theatre Group that they have to settle down to learn Hindi... We need only fifteen to twenty like-minded people to bring about a vast change. Before you leave for England... plant these ideas in their mind... you must do so... I implore you!

In hindsight, this letter amounted to a kind of *manifesto*, a mission statement for the journey Alkazi would embark on in the service of culture on behalf of the nation over the next seven decades.

It is not surprising that there is a striking similarity between Alkazi's manifesto and the one his friend Souza was about to draft for the Progressive Artists Group the following year. Whereas Souza refers to the need to forge a 'language' of artistic expression that has its roots in Indian culture and tradition, Alkazi makes a plea for a strong cultural rootedness by making Hindi the main tool of theatrical communication. Thus, both youngsters, while heading west* in order to understand and appreciate international modernism, clearly saw the need to define the parameters, the philosophy and the direction modern Indian culture needed to take in the early years after Independence. In a sense, Alkazi and Souza became prophetic voices who acted as catalysts for the propulsion of Indian art from colonial mimicry towards an independent identity in a vastly expanding global world.

Years later, Alkazi summed up their intentions:

> After all the horrors of the War ... Nagasaki and Hiroshima, the Partition ... after the hectic excitement of the Freedom Movement, now that the country was free, the whole world was there before you and there was also the spirit of UNESCO ... built on humanitarian values ... and a new civilized concept of the intermingling of cultures from all over the world. We wanted to create these utopias—new cities—in which new ideas would flourish! Now there was a new dawn and we felt we should be playing our role in that new millennium. I think that was one of the things that drew one abroad ... we wanted to be educated in that ... we wanted to take as much as we possibly could from it and always, at the back of my mind, was the idea of coming back ... to share it with the people of India.[7]

Nissim and Roshen were the two people who understood the ramifications of Alkazi's ideas, which was why he suggested that they jointly go abroad to study, making it a *collaborative* mission to use the knowledge as a foundation on which to develop new ideas for the growth of theatre in India.

Sharing his thoughts with Rosh as well, Elk said in a letter to her from the ship:[8]

---

* F.N. Souza was to follow Alkazi to London the following year. In fact, on the eve of Alkazi's departure, he had urged both Souza and his wife Maria to come to London to imbibe modernity in the arts firsthand.—E. Alkazi in an interview with Amal Allana, NYC, 1999.

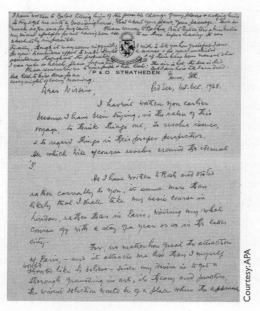

Alkazi's letter to Nissim Ezekiel, 1948

And I shall have more to say to you regarding the final arrangement of my plans and, as is the way with me, I am consumed by a burning impatience for their settling. Yes, I am always burning with impatience... I think a great deal of the future and of what I shall do when I get back and my thoughts run in many directions, but I realize that, though I may have hopes and dreams, I cannot permit my thoughts to scatter in a dozen different directions but must concentrate them on the kind of craft I am going to Europe to learn. So for the next two years, it will be painting and sculpture for me. Yet I can't kill my interest in the theatre and in the activities of TG and in my letter to Nissim, I have written at length about what I feel some of our more serious members need to undertake.

*　*　*

The initial excitement and energy Elk had displayed about going to a new country began to wear off as the long, hot days on board the ship stretched endlessly. Gradually, the thought of the lonely months ahead without a companion began to dawn on him. Hoping to bridge the distance between them, Elk wrote Rosh long, poetic letters:

My Beloved Rosh,

It is almost a week now since that day and I cannot tell whether the days have gone swift or slow. It is such a peculiar state of not feeling, not knowing, almost like a coma; though every act is a conscious act, conceived and committed, the memory of it fades, indistinguishable, among the whole host of other acts . . . But I know the day and remember the hour and the memory of those last moments is a joy for me which I must savour lingeringly and long, to last me the passage of the months to come.[9]

And once again:

. . . this is another day and it is the day and—by my watch—the hour at which we parted. But let it remain, a sad and perfumed hour within the memory.

Many hours were whiled away daydreaming about his beloved and finding it difficult to distract himself, Alkazi often found himself sinking into a state of melancholy:

And for hours too while I lie back on my deck chair drinking in the sun, I say to myself: It is eight in the morning by my watch, which means it is 10.30 a.m. in Bombay and Rosh is ironing her clothes and getting ready to go to the office and Uma is on the 'po' or in her bed, chirping away and Rosh asks her: 'Uma where's Daddy gone? Far away . . .' and the ayah begins to smile and murmurs something in her moustache in her fashion. And so I let my thoughts roam . . . until a passing ship intrudes upon the thought and sweeps it aside for another resurrection.

A week elapsed before the SS *Stratheden* docked at Aden.* The heavy torpor did not lift. In fact, the silence and solitude, along with the scorching heat, seemed fertile ground for dormant anxieties to surface. Perhaps for

---

*   Aden, now in Yemen, was part of the Bombay Presidency until 1937. The British Government considered Aden to be an important settlement due to its location, as the Royal Navy could easily access the port for resupply and repairs.

the very first time, Alkazi articulated a certain unease regarding his identity as an Arab. Rarely, if ever, had he referred to this 'identity' before. Here he alludes to it indirectly: 'On the night of the 29th at 11, we were at Aden. It was too dark to see a thing as the ship crawled wearily into the port, but you could feel the craggy rock, earthbound, sitting in somnolent silence, sphinx-like and sullen.'

Alkazi's choice of words creates a sense of foreboding—the image of a closed world. He continues: 'And then in mid-morning, the next day, I glimpsed the land of my fathers, or the islands that are part of this land. It seemed a remote land, standing austere and aloof, folding within itself its secrets, baring its barren back to the sea and sun.'[10]

It is now obvious that Alkazi was referring to Saudi Arabia, the land from where his father hailed, that stretched beyond Yemen, which is now turned away, with its 'barren back' to him. He continues by describing the Red Sea through which they are sailing adjoining Saudi Arabia:

> This sea, the Red Sea is a sluggish sea. The waves wearily licking the ship's side and, in the afternoon, an enraged sun, hissing angrily and relentlessly upon it. But much of the heat is tempered by the breeze, which grows towards evening and will not be quelled. But in the night, the sea, an ugly mass, crawls torturously with the heat it has known in the day and in one's cabin one is almost driven to death by the terrible, suffocating closeness.

In one sense, the experience of even sailing by 'the land of his fathers' evoked in Alkazi a sense of dread, fear and suffocation.

It is true that Alkazi never really defined what constituted his identity as an Arab for himself. It was only many years later that he once asked, 'Who am I, actually?' and rhetorically replied, 'A Maharashtrian Arab. Of bastard stock!'[11]

I recall that at some point he said to me, 'You know, the central theme that all great drama is concerned with is the question, "Who am I?"' This was with reference to the theme of *Oedipus*, which he said was only concerned with 'Who am I?'

It's possible that Alkazi felt a certain resentment towards the 'land of his father' at this particular juncture, in 1948, when there had been considerable communal violence in India. His family practically had to flee but had not opted to return to the 'land of their birth', as it had really nothing to offer just then.

Ebrahim was fully aware that his mother and siblings were living in highly unsettled circumstances in Karachi. Mariam was alone with the children, while Ubba was continuously shuttling between Bombay, Karachi and Kuwait. Pakistan had always been a stop-gap arrangement to give Ubba time to seek out a suitable alternative. This kind of migrant–refugee existence would unfortunately continue to be their predicament for some years.[12] It was understandable that the young Alkazi did not find the land of his forefathers welcoming.

For himself, Alkazi had made an actual physical break with his family by opting to marry an Indian and stay back in India. These were among his first independent decisions regarding where he chose to live and the kind of life he wanted for himself. Having opted for India, he needed to therefore *construct a viable identity for himself* in relation to the country, its culture and its people.

Alkazi approached the question of his identity in a unique way. Rather than seeing himself as either an 'insider' or 'outsider', he built an identity based on the widest and most liberal ideas of the day. He thought of himself as a *modern* man, open to new ideas and an inheritor of world legacies. This idea would gradually morph into his creating an identity for himself as a *world citizen*.[*] Not wishing to define himself through religion, geographic boundaries or political ideology of any kind, Ebrahim wanted to embrace pure, humanistic values.

He was very much a part of the post-World War II generation, a devastated generation that had lived through decades of power-hungry nations attempting to devour one another. In order to counteract such divisiveness, Alkazi believed that a society with ideas of democracy, egalitarian values, universalism, belief in the 'Family of Man' and the need to look beyond narrow linguistic or religious differences, must be striven for.

---

[*] My father often mentioned that although we had no cultural rootedness in any specific region of the country, our wide knowledge of international cultures gave us a broad, global perspective.

Gradually, it is these humanistic values that became the central pillars on which Alkazi built his entire approach. He believed he was the new human being born from the ashes of the old world, a phoenix arising from the dead.[*]

* * *

On 8 October, they sailed through the Strait of Gibraltar.

Putting down *New Theatres for Old,* Alkazi's mind cleared regarding what course of study he might pursue in England. This book, above all, described theatre as *performance* and not text. It was his first real introduction to contemporary French theatre and the Russian avant-garde, to the work of directors like Alexander Tairov, Yevgeny Vakhtangov, Vsevolod Meyerhold, Max Reinhardt and Bertolt Brecht. The fact that many of the stage designers, such as Marc Chagall, were famous artists was inspirational, as it reiterated for him how his own twin talents of painting and theatre could be effectively combined.

> . . . as I went out to England by ship, there was a book that had been gifted to me by a friend, which was called *New Theatres for Old* by Mordecai Gorelik and what was remarkable about this book was that it didn't deal with the commercial theatre; it dealt with the experimental theatre. It dealt with the new spirit in the theatre, whether it was in France with Vieux Colombier, Bertolt Brecht's Berliner Ensemble or Stanislavsky and later on, Meyerhold and Okhlopkov in Russia or the Group Theatre in the United States of America. There was also Jean–Louis Barrault and the Old Vic Theatre School, which had been formed. So one was excited by the ideas that one found in their writings, in their productions, in their vision of what a theatre away from the boulevard, a theatre other than the West End sort of box-office hits and successes or those of Broadway and so on. What was the new type of theatre that one should get oneself involved in?

---

[*] Alkazi made a drawing of a phoenix and adopted it as his symbol or logo for many years. It was made into a rubber stamp that was printed on the title page of each new book that he acquired for his personal library.

CHAPTER 12
38, LANSDOWNE CRESCENT
1948

'And so I found myself in London. Getting down at Tilbury Port and getting onto a train, which, in the depressing drizzle of an autumn evening and getting to Victoria Station, was one of the most unwelcome experiences that I have ever had!'[1]

Alkazi had written to his friend Baloo (B.N. Patel), who was studying in London, well in advance that he was arriving in London on 10 October at approximately 5 p.m. After inquiring with a station attendant at Victoria Station, where he alighted, he eventually found his way on foot to Baloo's lodgings at 86 Porchester Terrace. It was already past 9 p.m. when the portly landlady opened the door a crack and sceptically looked at the man in front of her. She barked at him, saying that Baloo was out and that this was hardly a decent time to come a calling. Apologizing profusely, Alkazi receded into the shadows, his cumbersome luggage now appearing to weigh more than a ton. He halted momentarily under a street lamp and fumbled in his jacket pockets for his map. Ah! He was not far from the famous Hyde Park! It might be best to sit on a bench there and contemplate what to do next. As he was about to cross the street, he heard the sound of running feet and, turning, saw Baloo waving out to him. The bags slipped out of Elk's sore hands as relief washed over him like a soothing balm. Baloo welcomed Elk with a tight embrace.

'Why, Elk, you're shivering! You're not dressed warmly enough!'

'Baloo, I'm so sorry! I did not mean to intrude so late. But tell me, have you booked me at some kind of lodging for tonight as I had requested?'

'Rubbish! You're going to share my digs until we find you something suitable to rent. I'm so thrilled to see you, Elk. Tonight's your first night in London! Let's celebrate!'

As Baloo helped Elk with his luggage, the friends chatted and caught up with the latest news from India. Baloo opened the heavy door, cautioning Elk to tread softly over the wooden floorboards so as not to wake his landlady.

The next morning, Alkazi found himself alone. Yes, Baloo had mentioned that he had an early start. A hastily scribbled note lay on the well-worn dresser, explaining what Elk should busy himself with. Lodgings had to be obtained as soon as possible, as Baloo's landlady had already objected to him having a guest. A few addresses in the vicinity where Alkazi could possibly start making inquiries topped the list of 'must-dos'. Secondly, Elk should immediately enrol in a college so that his food ration coupons are assured, without which it would be difficult to survive!

It was Monday. By this evening, he ought to get himself a place and within the week, he would surely enrol in the course. Dressing quickly, he left the house to begin what turned out to be a long and disappointing sojourn to secure a roof over his head. Initially, he was not entirely sure why he was repeatedly being turned away. It was only later that it finally dawned on him that it was because of the colour of his skin!

'Then trudging through the streets to find an accommodation, as sort of a black man, as it were, in a country that found it very strange to have Indians and so on around, was extremely difficult, extremely trying.'[2]

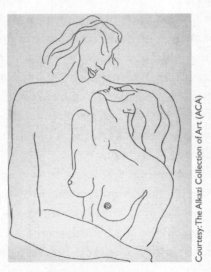

Hamlet and Ophelia, a drawing by Alkazi, 1948

The colour bar was only one of the many problems plaguing the country at this point. Britain had emerged from World War II financially drained, physically exhausted and facing a massive housing crisis. Britain had to adopt strong austerity measures in order to rebuild the country. Basic commodities such as bread, butter, meat, tea and coal were strictly rationed, as were sweets and chocolates. Electricity, too.

The indigenous white population numbered approximately 50 million, but with over half a million immigrants from Ireland and refugees fleeing from the Nazis, including over 1,60,000 Poles and Jews from Central Europe, Britain saw, in 1948, the first post-war coloured immigrants arrive on board the *Empire Windrush* from Caribbean countries such as Jamaica, Trinidad and Tobago and Barbados. These immigrants had come at the invitation of the British government, which was facing an acute labour shortage. However, there was a growing fear and suspicion among the whites that coloured people would undercut them and take their jobs. Discrimination and open racism were common, especially in public places.

All this was very shocking to Alkazi, who had never encountered racism. Writing from his new lodgings in Basil Court, where he had spent the last two days, Elk complained, 'There is a colour bar here and were it not for that, I would have gotten a place quite easily.'[3] He went on to mention that it was possible to get a more pleasant place with breakfast if he was willing to pay more, but the catch was that he would have to surrender all his food ration coupons to the landlady, which would mean he would need to have dinner and lunch out—at greater expense, no doubt.

* * *

For nearly a year now, Elk had been dreaming of enrolling at the Anglo–French Art Centre. At 8 a.m. the next day, all spruced up, he stood in front of 29 Elm Tree Road, the site of the former St John's Wood Art School where the Anglo–French Art Centre was now located. He had carefully arranged his portfolio the night before, signed and dated all his works meticulously and now, with it tucked carefully under his arm, he entered the hallowed precincts, where the promise of studying under the guidance of the most brilliant and eminent artists in the world awaited him. Looking down the corridors, a thought crossed his mind. He might actually bump into the likes of Henry Moore, Francis Bacon, Jacob Epstein,

Ronald Searle, Victor Pasmore or even Graham Sutherland! Or famous French sculptors and painters such as Fernand Léger, Henri Matisse and Germaine Richier, who, as the advertisement had indicated, would be part of the visiting faculty!

The receptionist he approached showed some amount of disbelief and surprise. 'You've come all the way from India then, have you, lad? On the strength of our advertisement alone? My, my, isn't that something? In all my years, I haven't heard the likes of that before.'

She leaned closer over the counter and said to him in a hoarse whisper, 'There's no money to be had here, lad; all the scholarships are already bespoke! You're late. The term began in September!'

'No, no, I entirely understand . . . please don't misunderstand . . . I'm perfectly willing to pay the fees.'

'Well, I never! Then you must be mighty flush! Lord of the Exchequer!'

She jumped up and disappeared into an office behind him. Returning a moment later, she said, 'Go on then, darling, no loitering! The principal will do an audition right away!'

Alkazi was taken aback that he had been granted an audition almost immediately.

'So, you're the young man who's come to us from India, then?' The principal was quite affable.

Alkazi courteously bowed low and deferentially presented his portfolio to the principal. The principal briefly hemmed and hawed through it. He finally looked up and asked a few perfunctory questions regarding the proposed length of Alkazi's stay, his financial ability to support himself in the UK and what his future intentions were as an artist. Interview done, Alkazi was asked to wait outside near the information desk.

Nearly an hour elapsed before a young woman thundered down the elaborate wooden staircase designed in the Gothic Revival style, her enormous bosom bobbing up and down as she did so and practically stripping her tight-fitting cardigan of its buttons. Lowering his eyes, Alkazi noticed that her thick English ankles were similarly bulging out of her rather tight-fitting wedge-heeled shoes. Finally, she caught her breath and called out in a sweet, syrupy, thin voice, 'Ib-ra-heeem Alkazi?'

He sprang up and hurried towards her.

'You're in!' she chimed and then, responding to his boyish good looks, she fluttered her eyelashes, toyed with her cardigan buttons and cooed, 'Sir, you may go and pay your fees . . . please.'

In total disbelief, but elated nonetheless, Alkazi bolted up to the cash counter and paid up his twelve guineas for the first three-month semester. All the officialese completed at unbelievable speed, Alkazi was handed a receipt and a book of ration coupons and told to 'run along to the Life Class!'

The Life Class! The word echoed through the corridors of his mind. A Life Class was something he had only read about—a hushed space where one created art, akin to the altar space in a church; a most sacred, hallowed space, like a rehearsal space for an actor or a gymnasium for an athlete. It was . . . he walked in . . .

Located on the first floor of the building, the Life Class studio was enormous, with an extremely high roof. A shaft of weak light filtered in through the skylight, hitting row upon row of enormous paintings that clung to the walls—portraits of men, women, kings and generals. A number of pedestals stood at one end of the room with alabaster busts of Greek or Roman senators staring out of unseeing eyes. The corners of the studio were cluttered with old, broken frames, some elaborate, some more contemporary, in the art deco style. Art books were lying open, carelessly strewn across tables. Art magazines were piled up high, along with old newspapers that were bound in stacks. Easels with incomplete works, palettes, paint brushes and palette knives congealed with multifarious hues caught his eye. Empty tea cups with cigarette butts emitted a fetid odour that combined with the acrid stench of stale alcohol and oil paint that hung in the air, as there seemed to be no visible signs of ventilation.

A few students at easels appeared intent on their paintings. One or two looked up when Alkazi entered, while another group of six to eight young men noisily chatted on the side. A bawdy joke was shared, followed by loud guffaws. Since there did not appear to be an instructor to report to, Elk sat himself down in front of an empty easel, wondering whether he should begin sketching the young teenage girl dressed in a Little Bo Peep pinafore who looked strangely out of place. She was perched on a raised platform in the centre of the room, clasping a crook in one hand and a basket of flowers in the other. Behind her, a gigantic painted backdrop of a pastoral landscape had been suspended from the rafters.

Elk was both bemused and somewhat offended by this syrupy Victorian image of a lost little girl. Were they really expected to render her? Surely, now that they had lived through the horrors of the war, he was expecting an institution such as this to be more up-to-date, challenging its students to create something deeper, more stirring of the emotions. Instead, what was this? Pure bilge. Flaccid and irrelevant. It was exactly this kind of British art that Clive Bell and Duncan Grant of the Bloomsbury group had objected to and had responded by hosting two controversial shows, in 1910 and 1920, of French modernism in London—works whose style they called Post Impressionist. Is *this* what he had come all the way here for? Academic Realism was being taught at the JJ School of Art. He could easily have done this there!

These first impressions were crowding his mind when, as if on cue, the unruly group of men began to leave the studio, while Little Bo Peep silently disappeared behind the canvas backdrop. Was the class over? Where should he go next? Gathering up his materials, he thought it best to go back downstairs to the lady at the information desk and inquire when a short, dapper black man, in a suit and bow tie, walked up to him, extending his hand.

'Charles Tucker! You new here? You look lost!'

Alkazi nodded.

'I'm a student here, too. Classes are over. Let's buzz off!'

'But it's barely 3 p.m.?'

'That's it! Want to join me for a cup o' tea? The canteen's in the basement. Get your coupons out.'

For the next hour, over a cup of tea, Tucker, eight years Alkazi's senior, regaled him with the story of his life. A man of tremendous empathy and good humour, Tucker went on to become one of Alkazi's closest friends. Even when he went home to Bermuda and rose to become one of the most renowned West Indian artists, Tucker kept in touch with Elk. But on this day, over a cup of weak English tea, the West Indian spoke about his dreams, his interest in art and why he was in England.

'I'm from Bermuda, maan, I come last year on the famous ship ... you heard of it? *Empire Windrush*? I come with 500 other West Indians.

'I was not interested in painting, maan, I was a musician. My mother taught me to play the pump organ. She used to play the organ and guitar and she teach me to play the pump organ! She sent me to learn piano when I was seven, maan.

'Before the War, I come here, to England, to study music at Guildhall School of Music and Dramatic Art! Yes! You surprised? But the War broke out in 1939 and I had to quit. I go back home.'

There was a long silence. The cafeteria was shutting down. They were the last to leave. They continued chatting on the way to the tube.

'When the war finally ended, I feel I am too old to resume my music studies! By then, I begun dabbling in painting. A few people, some Americans, they like my work and encourage me to keep at it. So last year, when the Brits invite us, I think I must not miss this opportunity to come back to England.'

'Yes, of course!'

It was already pitch-dark. They walked some more distance in silence. Tucker's story deeply affected Alkazi. What an uncertain life and what an uncertain future for an artist like him! Changing one's field, living in a distant country where you were not necessarily welcome, depending on a government scholarship—reality had to be confronted on so many levels!

'I would love to hear you play music sometime, Charles! Goodnight! Until tomorrow, then.'

* * *

On 18 October, Elk wrote to Rosh: 'This new place (Basil Court) is not very pleasant, somewhat drab and gloomy and I don't intend staying here very long. I pay 2 pounds 10.5 sh per week (2 guineas) without any meals.'

Despite not really having settled down, Elk was eager to find out what was happening in the art world that existed beyond the confines of the Anglo–French Art Centre. An advertisement in a newspaper he had browsed through while waiting for his audition results had drawn his attention to an exhibition of the 'Drawings of the Set Designs for *Hamlet* and *Macbeth*' along with 'Wood Engravings' by Edward Gordon Craig, showing at the Leicester Galleries.

Making his way to the gallery the next day, Elk found no less than twenty black-and-white drawings by Craig. A cyclostyled note mentioned that the designer had been invited in 1907 by well-known actor–director Konstantin Stanislavski to direct *Hamlet* at the Moscow Art Theatre (MAT), a project that took three long years to visualize.

Alkazi slowly absorbed Craig's images—small black-and-white sketches symmetrically arranged along the walls. It appeared that Craig had been able to convey an entire world through the simplest of means. Stripped of any kind of descriptive elements, Craig's design was a basic integration of pure form, space and light. The stage design comprised a series of tall, elegant screens that were placed in different spatial arrangements for each of the twenty scenes in the play. Their positions radically altered the shape and size of the acting area in each instance, changing now from a flat wall across the very rear of the stage for the court scene, to creating a claustrophobic enclosure for Polonius's study, as contrast. Craig had intended each area to spatially represent a character's state of mind. Craig undoubtedly considered this kind of abstraction of space an appropriate approach for creating *Hamlet* as a poetic drama.

Having absorbed the show in detail, Alkazi leafed through Max Beerbohm's catalogue note on Craig. He was very keen to pick it up at a couple of shillings, but restrained himself, thinking that he would rather save the money and spend it on things Rosh and he could enjoy together when she eventually joined him.

Strolling home, Alkazi reflected that Craig's stage designs confirmed that painting and the art of the theatre were intertwined, a realization that convinced him to never separate his twin talents. Besides, what struck him as novel was that here was an art gallery showcasing stage designs for *theatre*! It was probably this thought that prompted Alkazi to approach this same gallery a few years later for his own first one-man show.

In a letter to Rosh the next day, he described the Craig show and regarding the other works on view, he said: 'Some Moderns' drawings—Picasso, Sickert, Degas, Matisse, Signac—were also hung in the galleries for sale. The other painters also exhibiting in the same galleries—Elinor Bellingham–Smith (semi-Impressionistic characterless bilge) and William

Scott—some excellent fish and figure composition, approach: modern, direct and simplified.'

Though Alkazi was relatively young, he was familiar with the work of a large number of modern western artists and therefore he possibly felt entitled to critique their work. Roshen was perhaps the only person he shared all his ideas and thoughts with. Therefore, Alkazi desperately wished that Rosh was with him to share these experiences, and his requests that she join him earlier became more insistent.

> I think it would be wisest to leave Uma behind. If she were here going to the pictures or things like that would be entirely out of the question... I do want to say one thing though: I really believe I can't carry on without you for long. I need you very badly and I honestly believe that I must have you with me if I am to do any serious work. This does not mean that I want you to come right away—I imagine I can wait till the first of March or so. But I don't think that I'd let you go back after six months, as we had previously planned. I'd want you to remain with me and I'd like us to work together. I could go on with my painting and sculpture and you could take a course in dress designing or something like that... Further, I imagine I will be able to finish my course sooner than I'd planned—in about two years or so. So it would be alright and we wouldn't be away from Uma for too long.[4]

Drawings of the set designs for *Hamlet* by Edward Gordon Craig, 1910

The next day, he continues in the same letter:

> I haven't written this in a sudden fit of homesickness, but after having considered the matter seriously for some time. You see, there is so much I have denied you in the past in my consideration for others—time and effort and affection, which both of us could have used more profitably. Besides it's not merely remorse of conscience, but an earnest longing to make our lives together fuller, more intimate, more 'one' . . . So prepare yourself for a stay of about two years here . . .

From Elk's next letter, it is apparent that Rosh is missing him too and is very lonely, but she needs to be more convinced to update her travel plans!

> My beloved Rosh,
> I love your letters, my darling, and I love to read them again and again and again and your last letter was so beautiful although the strain of loneliness and barrenness haunted every line. I feel the same too my love; very lonely and very dejected and I want to have you close to me to feel you and your warmth and your love.
> Your letter makes me more unhappy. If the 1st of March is so far away, why not come now? What is there to prevent your coming? And since it's been decided that you are to be with me throughout my stay in Europe, then why wait? Think it over carefully, darling, and if you feel you should come now, let me know immediately so that I can make arrangements here for your accommodation.

Further letters tell us about his dissatisfaction with the Anglo–French Art Centre.

> I have been extremely depressed and unhappy at the Anglo–French every day of the ten days I have been there. I have been terribly disappointed with it—no serious study is possible; no instruction is given . . . a great many riff-raff who want to be modern and bohemian hang around the place. There was a recent exhibition of student work, which, to me, was very revealing. Most

of the work was superficial, shallow and without purpose, trying to be modern ... without having understood any of the problems of painting. Victor Pasmore was there to criticize the work—he didn't seem to think much of it. Epstein and Kokoschka will be coming there in the near future to criticize work—I hope to see them. There are about four to six students in all and they are all very unhappy here.

Several years later, Alkazi, in an interview with Samik Bandopadhyay, looked at this situation with greater insight—that this was probably not just a question of the ineptness of the teaching staff but the result of the Labour government's rebuilding policy where youngsters back from the war were enroled in colleges in subjects that were of little interest to them in order to keep them off the streets.[5]

Meanwhile, Alkazi had grown quite fond of Tucker, who suggested that they watch *Anna Lucasta,* originally a Broadway production now playing at His Majesty's Theatre at the Haymarket. Receiving rave reviews, it was the first American play that was designed for an all-coloured cast and treated coloured life without condescension.

They bought last-minute tickets 'up in the gods' (the top balcony), from where the view was so steep that you only saw 'the tops of the actor's heads'. Nonetheless, it was the first play Alkazi would be seeing in London and the friends were full of eager anticipation. Suffice to say that the production was far better than their wildest expectations.

Anna Lucasta with the all-Negro cast was terrific. The settings were naturalistic. The difficult scene changes were extremely swift. The play as played by these people bears you down with it, and it is with some despair that one realizes the long way we have to go to put on anything to touch it.

The father was terrific; his hoarse, grating voice strangled to a wheezing rasp in his throat was sustained, raised, lowered and flung with an uncanny potency and well-calculated deliberation. The old prostitute was a prostitute to her toenails; you could see, smell, hear and feel the prostitute in her ...

Direction: deft and direct.[6]

After the performance, Elk began to open up to Tucker, sharing his plans to quit the Anglo–French Art Centre and enrol at another institution—The Byam Shaw School of Art, which had been highly recommended to him. Tucker was of the same view and the next day, the two friends sought out the principal of Byam Shaw, Mr Phillips, and convinced him that they were serious students who wished to enrol immediately.

By Monday, 1 November, Alkazi began classes at Byam as well as moved out of Basil Court and into 38, Lansdowne Crescent, an accommodation he took a fancy to. With its quaint antique shops, Lansdowne Crescent was in the vicinity of Portobello Road, a hilly area with crooked little lanes, curio and junk shops, that is today considered upmarket. Alkazi would remain here till the end of his stay in England.

His lodgings was a basement bed-sitter—a tiny bedroom and a living room where Elk could paint. Though slightly more expensive than what he had planned to lay out, Alkazi thought that in the current situation, it was a wise decision, considering that it was also walking distance from Baloo's. This was convenient, as in the early weeks, Baloo was generous enough to invite him over for meals.

To celebrate, Tucker and Alkazi went to watch Laurence Olivier's film, *Hamlet*. It appeared that London was teeming with stage versions of *Hamlet* as well, and Alkazi, who had already performed the title role in Bombay himself, tore it to shreds!

> *Hamlet* was very disappointing. Even as an essay on 'Hamlet' it was lacking in power, in breadth of vision, in delineation of characters. It seemed to me an episodic version of the play, badly mauled and badly patched together and badly made to be accommodating. I can't forgive Olivier for substituting weaker and easier terms for some of Shakespeare's choicest and most heavily meaning-laden terms and phrases. I didn't care for Olivier's' interpretation—his Hamlet didn't live; there was no nerve-wracking struggle; it didn't quiver, seethe and prickle harshly... The photography was excellent and Olivier seemed to have concentrated on that, but even the best of photography and Walton's suitable music couldn't cover the defects of the whole construction and conception of the film.

This criticism may seem harsh, but it is not because I cannot see the mole in my own eye. Rather, the faults and failures of my own production have made me more sensitive to the perspectives of others. Finally, I feel Shakespeare should be left to the stage.

Alkazi himself had not yet exhausted exploring *Hamlet*. He had begun a series of sketches and drawings based on the play that reveal his remarkable talent for visualization.* For him, the word translates into visual form seamlessly. We begin to see that Alkazi is teaching himself to create drama in his paintings and paintings in his dramas!

A close identification with the central character is apparent in the fact that in most drawings, Hamlet resembles Alkazi closely, making them practically self-portraits! His muse for Ophelia is undoubtedly Roshen, who he feels has all the innocence of an Ophelia.

> The new snap of yourself that you sent me is lovely because it is so natural and unaffected. And I always want you like that darling, just as you are in all your charm and innocence and naiveté and I haven't come across a woman worth the sole of your shoe and, believe me, that's the truth. I love you and respect you . . .[7]
>
> Don't worry about relapsing with superficialities and don't be ashamed of yourself. Be yourself, be naïve and be simple—that is yourself, even if the others sometimes laugh at and make fun of your naiveté. That innocence is nothing to be ashamed of; it is something to be cherished and zealously preserved and something that I love in you more than all your other qualities. Because in your naiveté is a freshness, a virginity, a childhood innocence that I would not have you lose for all the 'smart' and 'knowing' appearances and airs in the world. Don't feel self-conscious about it. Say and feel what you feel and don't care about how it may seem to others.

---

* This suite of drawings on *Hamlet* was shown a couple of years later, in 1950, at the Leicester Galleries in London along with other works. In 2019, 'The Other Line', an exhibition on Alkazi's artworks, was curated by Ranjit Hoskote at Art Heritage Gallery, Delhi. Some of the *Hamlet* sketches are reproduced in the catalogue of the exhibition.

... It is significant that the greatest artists, writers and thinkers have always striven for and yearned for the simplicity of childhood, the freshness of vision and the vacant wonder of a child.

This you must cherish and zealously guard, especially in a world shorn of values and any living faith. And it is that alone, which abides in you, that has kept me and will keep me from suicide.[8]

The last sentence is a trifle theatrical. One feels Alkazi himself was too young at this point to have experienced 'a world shorn of values and living faith' enough to drive him to suicide! It is important to recognize that, as an artist, he allowed himself to experience life through art, art being a heightened experience of life. A lot of Alkazi's experiences and his knowledge of life and of people, accrued through studying, understanding and closely identifying with the trials and tribulations of characters in plays and/or the renditions of traumatic events in works of art. Having led quite a sheltered existence, art for Alkazi became *the* means to *access life* in full measure. It was a vital source of nourishment for his growth, development and enrichment as a person with deep and profound insight into human suffering.*

---

*   Alkazi's handwritten essay 'Imitation' was found by me among his papers. It is a brilliant analysis of the relationship between art and life.

CHAPTER 13
40,000 YEARS OF MODERN ART
1949

Wednesday, 25 January 1949. Elk and Rosh were seated upstairs, right at the front of the double-decker bus speeding towards Academy Hall at 163 Oxford Street. Rosh had been waiting for Elk at the bus stop near the Royal Academy of Dramatic Art (RADA) on Gower Street at noon, as planned. It was freezing and her hip-length woollen coat was barely keeping out the biting cold. She rearranged the woollen scarf over her head and ears before shoving her gloved hands back into her pockets. There! Finally, a bus was snaking its way towards the bus stop, but no sign of Elk yet. Just as she was about to resign herself to another long wait, she heard him call out, 'Rosh, jump on!'

There he was running towards the bus, frantically waving to the driver to hang on just a moment longer. Rosh was still undecided whether to get on when, all of a sudden, she found that he had clutched her arm and swept her onto the bus. The bus lurched to a start and both clung to one another, laughing with excitement.

'Are you alright, then?'

'I never expected that we'd make it!'

She was panting as they stumbled upstairs hand-in-hand. Finding the front seats vacant, they collapsed into them.

'So sorry I was delayed, but the improv just went on and on!'

'Not a problem. I brought you this . . . I thought you might be a bit peckish.'

Rosh dug into one of her pockets and got out a sandwich made with the previous night's leftovers of keema.

'Darling, how thoughtful of you, but I can't eat it here, Rosh! Put it away now, please. The onions will stink up the whole bus!'

'Sorry! Didn't think of that!'

Exhibition catalogue, *40,000 years of Modern Art*, ICA, London, 1948–49

'No, I'm sorry for saying "no" to your sweet thoughtfulness.'

He took her hand in his and kissed it ever so gently, holding on to it for the rest of the ride. As was his habit, he began pointing out the main shops and streets they were moving through, trying to familiarize her with the geography of the city of London and the bus routes she would need to know. Rosh nodded absently, not really paying attention—she was happy just to be with Elk, anticipating a lovely day together. They were on their way to the International Centre for the Arts (ICA), to see '40,000 Years of Modern Art'. They had planned this visit ever since Rosh arrived about two weeks earlier, soon after New Year's. The show had been the talk of the art world. In fact, it had taken all of Elk's willpower to restrain himself from rushing to see it the moment it opened, so keen was he that they should experience it together.

By now Alkazi had shifted schools once again, this time to RADA. His audition and interview for admission into RADA had created quite a buzz!* The teachers had been duly impressed by his performance of the major soliloquies from *Richard III* and *Hamlet*. When asked if anyone had instructed him in the preparation of these roles, he confessed that he had directed these plays himself! The principal, Sir Kenneth Barnes, nodded to himself; he had rarely, if ever, met such a young student who seemed to have already charted out his career with so much forethought. Undoubtedly someone to look out for!

That Elk had enrolled at RADA came as a complete surprise to Rosh. She had barely alighted from the ship when Elk whispered in her ear as he embraced her, 'Lovoo, I've got into RADA! Can you believe it? They took me in just like that! . . . It was a breeze!'[1]

'But what about your painting, Elk? What about Byams? I thought you had paid the fees and all.'

'Rosh darling! I was miserable there. They couldn't teach me a darn thing. But don't worry, I'm continuing with my painting at home. I'm really working very, very hard, I've got so much work to show you.'

---

* 'I really wanted to join the Old Vic Theatre School and I had applied to them. They said, "We are terribly sorry; we are already in September. We have our auditions and forms filled earlier, so you have to wait for the next year." I said, "I can't be waiting for the next year." So, I went to the Royal Academy and they put me through an audition and an interview; they took me right away.'—E. Alkazi in an interview with Samik Bandyopadhyay, Natya Shodh Sansthan, Kolkata, 15 March 1988.

Having decided against continuing at the Byam Shaw School of Art for much the same reason he had left the Anglo–French Art Centre, Alkazi was reluctant to try out yet another art school. It had always been his desire to study directly under a *practitioner* in order to comprehend modernism in its widest sense. It was not a particular technique that interested him; he wanted to be exposed to an approach that was flexible enough to explore a visual language and vocabulary for himself. Not willing to waste any more time, Elk concluded that he would now rather pursue an art education on his own, at home, in whatever time he could grab and turn his attention to a training in theatre.

By now, the bus was crawling towards Oxford Street and Elk, ever alert, squeezed Rosh's hand, signalling that they should begin wending their way downstairs.

Alighting from the bus, they raced towards Academy Hall. Roland Penrose and Herbert Read had established the ICA the year before in 1948 with the sole intention of educating the British public and initiating them into a playful and exciting understanding of modern art. They wanted to remedy the museums' lack of initiative in informing the British public about contemporary art movements. Their innovative approach to appreciating modern art intended to make art less sanctified, more approachable for the layman.

Herbert Read, in the ICA catalogue, outlined its objective:

> Such is our ideal—not another museum, another bleak exhibition gallery, another classical building in which insulated and classified specimens of culture are displayed for instruction, but an adult play-centre, a workshop where work is joy, a source of vitality and daring experiment. We may be mocked for our naïve idealism, but at least it will not be possible to say that an expiring civilization perished without a creative protest.

Now barely eight months later, the ICA had come up with this grand new show. It promised to be even more unique as modernist works would be placed alongside mainly African primitive art. This intrigued Alkazi greatly—that the roots of *modern* art lay in *primitive* sources. As Read mentioned in the catalogue:

The art of primitive people is no longer to us merely a manifestation of the disgusting idol worship of savages and cannibals. We have discovered in it powers of invention and expression which fills us with amazement and seems to point the way to new forms of art which can combine primitive vitality and vision with modern technique and sensibility... and one of the strange facts that emerges is that some of the earliest exhibits particularly the mammoth ivory Venus from the caves of the Dordogne (which it seems is a good 40,000 years old) appears to be the most modern in conception.

The stellar work in the exhibition, Picasso's 'Les Demoiselles d'Avignon', on loan from MoMA in New York, was being shown in London for the first time. Several African masks were to be seen, which resonated with the 126 works from prehistoric Europe, Melanesia, Australia and Africa. In the catalogue, this section was referred to as 'The Art of the Primitive People' and was contrasted with sixty-four modern artworks referred to as 'The Art of Our Time'.

It was evident right from the manner in which the entrance had been laid out that the ICA strongly believed in high design values. As they entered, Alkazi and Roshen were immediately struck by the fact that each object had not been displayed as an independent artwork but in *relation* to one another. Art from the past was juxtaposed with art from the present. Paintings were interspersed with sculptures, so that one's experience of the two-dimensionality of paintings and the three-dimensionality of sculpture was palpably physical.

For Alkazi, this was extremely instructional. An exhibition then was no longer a collection of great individual works of art. Multiple sensibilities had been brought into play, making placement, composition, audience movement, narrative, interpretation and lighting key elements that had to be orchestrated by the unseen hand of the curators and designers to create a unity of intention and expose the overall theme of the show.

Alkazi, who practised and understood the theatrical medium only too well, immediately recognized this as a kind of 'staging', a 'performance' with inanimate objects. This exhibition had a distinct bearing and influence on Alkazi's own curatorial practice and exhibition design in the future.*

The entire experience was quite overwhelming for both Elk and Rosh, who proceeded directly thereafter to the discussion on primitive art between anthropologist Dr E.R. Leach, artist Leon Underwood, psychologist Dr John Rickman and critic Fredrick Laws, which was chaired by Philip James. The discussion was riveting because it demonstrated that art could be discussed from the viewpoint of multiple disciplines. What struck both Rosh and Elk most acutely was the underlying premise, as proposed by Read and Penrose, that the source for modernistic expression indeed lay in the primeval, in rituals that were embedded in needs and desires.

Speechless with a thousand ideas and questions still buzzing in their heads, they decided to treat themselves to fish 'n' chips at a nearby ABC before they caught the bus back home, where they found Nissim asleep on the couch.

***

Yes, Nissim had arrived in London ahead of Roshen, despite Alkazi's suggestion that he plan for spring when the weather improved. But Nissim was eager to embark on what he called his 'true education' in England as soon as possible. With no more than ten pounds in his pocket, he departed from Bombay, travelling aboard the *Jal Azad* on a tourist-class ticket for which Elk's father had paid a good Rs 620.[2] After a fairly uneventful journey, Nissim, donning the secondhand woollen overcoat that Elk had picked up for him from Bhendi Bazaar in Bombay, disembarked at Tilbury Docks and, as instructed by Elk in his letters, asked the cabbie to take him to Alkazi's place. To his dismay, there was no response to his repeated knocks on the door, though a faint glow of light did filter through the tiny window of the basement flat. As they later discovered,

---

* The review in *The Studio* described it thus: 'The objects and paintings were floodlit, but deep pools of shadow fell across the avenue between them and one had a sense of descending into a kind of initiation *chambers*. The restraint of the modern work contrasted sharply with the barbaric violence of the primitive carvings but shared their power to convey invisible forces. Many people gathered from this exhibition their first, perhaps uneasy suspicion that the modern artist is traversing a field that in the past was reserved for the religious adept.'—Robert Melville, 'The Studio', 1951.

Elk had been so lost in creating his *Hamlet* drawings that night that he failed to attend to Nissim's polite knocks. Nissim then, like Elk before him on his arrival in London, had made his way through the darkness to Baloo's place. Baloo was out too, but by then his ancient Polish landlady had gotten accustomed to Baloo's stranded Indian friends arriving at odd times of the day or night for help!

Without bothering to inquire as to who he was, Mrs Kowalski turned on her heels, leaving the door open behind her.

'I suppose you are another one of them from India, eh? Get in, then, out of the cold, if you must. And shut the door behind you! First door on the right. Mr Balooooo should be back sometime tonight, I suppose. You can wait!'

In a couple of weeks, Nissim had found a job. He had heard that Krishna Menon, the Indian High Commissioner, was employing young Indians. As luck would have it, Nissim instantly cleared the interview and was offered a clerical post in the Internal Affairs Department of the Indian High Commission at India House. One of his duties was to publish a weekly newsletter. Impressed with his writing skills, Krishna Menon soon installed Nissim as the editor of the newsletter.

One of Nissim's main reasons for coming to England was to study further and before long, he duly enrolled himself in evening classes at the City Literary Institute, where the fees were low. In order to avail of this opportunity, he had given up his lectureship at Wilson College in Bombay and was already accruing a debt to his brother Joe, who sent him ten pounds a month. Despite his heavy schedule of a job and classes, Nissim nonetheless found time to devote to his poetry. 'The greater part of the day was spent in reading poetry or writing it, or listening to it, or listening to lectures on it, or visiting libraries.'[3] The varied literary culture that London offered inspired him and he often remarked that his 'real education had begun in London and that all the degrees he had accumulated so far in Bombay were by and large redundant'.

Rosh came to London barely two months after Nissim, in early January 1949, while Souza arrived six months later, on a warm day in early August 1949, adding to the sizeable group of artistic young Bombayites now in London. Besides Elk, Rosh, Nissim and Souza, there were Baloo and Homi Sethna, a Xavierite who was part of the Theatre Group.

Alkazi and Roshen in England, 1950

Another newcomer was Krishna Paigankar, a writer friend of Nissim's from Bombay.

Unexpectedly for the Alkazis, Souza parked himself at 38 Lansdowne Crescent. In his usual carefree fashion, he had not planned where he would stay in London and his efforts at finding affordable lodgings were taking longer than expected. So he was grateful for Elk and Rosh's invitation to just bung in with them in their tiny bedsitter. As luck would have it, a room on the ground floor of the same building suddenly became available and Nissim suggested that he shift there along with Paigankar, as the young Alkazis needed their privacy after all. Souza, however, was a rather thick-skinned chap and made himself impervious to Alkazi's often dark, glowering looks. Souza had genuinely come to love and admire the young Alkazi couple, finding them unusual in many ways. Opening up to Rosh over a cup of tea when Elk had gone off to RADA one morning, Souza said, 'Rosh, Elk is one of the very, very few fellows I admire! I assure you I am reticent about stating another man's merits because it usually follows that he or she has none. Flattering and cajolery are beyond me. I usually speak very frankly. That is why I have so many enemies and friends who don't like me!'[4]

'Don't be so self-deprecating, Francis! We like you. We really do!'

'You do? Then I have a confession to make! I've invited a few friends over this evening for dinner! I hope you don't mind!'

'Francis! That's not fair! You could have mentioned it earlier. What are we going to offer them to eat? We have nothing at home.'

Souza offered a sheepish grin in response!

By late evening, Rosh had sorted herself out with a menu and was busy cooking as Souza and Nissim hung around her, trying to help. The radio was on and a hushed silence enveloped the room as all of them listened with reverence to *The Waste Land* being read out by T.S. Eliot himself.

> April is the cruellest month
> Breeding lilacs out of the dead land ...

Elk sat some distance apart at his small desk, in his by now characteristic pose of Rodin's *Thinker*. Cutlery tinkled as Rosh set the table. Elk looked up with a scowl, and bringing his finger to his lips, he signalled her to keep silent. She sat down, careful not to allow the chair to scrape against the stone floor. Nissim and Souza felt reprimanded too and guiltily stopped doing whatever they were doing. 'Bloody hell!' thought Souza, 'Elk is behaving as if this is a *live* performance and that the narrator, in this case the great Eliot himself, is being disturbed!'

38, Lansdowne Crescent was barely recognizable from what it had looked like a few months ago. From a bachelor's digs with a couple of sticks of furniture, Roshen, in her inimitable fashion, had transformed it into a cosy, comfortable home. Improvising with odds and ends, she used one of her Kashmiri shawls—a cream-and-brown one with tiny paisleys embroidered on it—as a tablecloth. In the centre, she placed a jam jar with a few flowers she had picked up on her way home. The table was set with an assortment of crockery and cutlery, a few bits that Rosh had brought with her from Bombay and some plates Elk had picked up from a Salvation Army shop. These comprised their elegant dinner service! An African mask stood above the fireplace, one of Alkazi's prize possessions that he discovered buried under some old newspapers in the local Sunday flea market. Harold Clurman's *The Fervent Years* (bought off the pavement outside Foyles bookshop, with Alkazi making at least four hurried lunch-hour trips in the needling London drizzle to the place before finally deciding to buy a soaked copy of it for six pence[5]) now sat atop a pile of neatly arranged copies of Gordon Craig's journal, *The Mask*. Elk's paint brushes, pencils, etc., were in an old pewter beer mug, while his portfolio of the *Hamlet* drawings was set to one side of his desk. To the right, above the small twin bed, hung one of Bobby's paintings—a portrait of Elk. The bedside tables had photographs of Uma at different ages.[*] The warm glow enveloping the entire room came from a small art deco table lamp, making the space look cosy and lived in.

The Eliot reading was finally over.

'Chaps, this was amazing!' said Souza, breaking the spell. 'I think I'll give up reading entirely! Why shouldn't I? When I have the chance to hear T.S. Eliot himself read *The Waste Land* to me!'[6]

'This is undoubtedly Eliot's greatest work,' said Nissim, shaking his head in disbelief. What they had just experienced was indeed a historic moment.

'What say you, Elk?'

Elk looked up. 'Yes, you're right! Not that one wants to compare, but certainly *The Waste Land* is in league with Joyce's *Ulysses*. I would rank it as *the* greatest work of all modernist poetry!'[†]

'I thought it was so original to divide the poem up into several voices—male and female. It gave the rendering such a dramatic quality; it felt like a performance!' Rosh offered.

There was a knock.

'Ah! Here come our guests.'

Baloo, Homi, Krishna Paigankar and three other young artist friends of Souza walked in. The conversation seemed to fly from topic to topic as they settled down to eat. Souza was bent on regaling them with the unprecedented success of the Progressives' show in Bombay in 1949 and updating them on the imminent arrival of Raza and Husain to London. The fate of Indian modernism was hotly debated, with Souza acknowledging that though there was a great impact of the 'Medieval and Ancient Art'

---

[*] My uncles, Alyque and Chotu, would dress me up in bizarre outfits and take photos of me to send them to my parents. I was about one-and-a-half years old by this time. They would inscribe amusing lines behind each photo! In one, I am shown baring my midriff with the inscription on the reverse reading, 'No Mama, no Papa, no food for three days!' Suffice it to say, I was a plump child!

[†] These were two of Alkazi's favourite works. He also made an audiovisual of *The Waste Land* that he read out himself.

show in Delhi on all of them, influences and sources in today's art world came from everywhere.*

'It's all very well to talk in metaphors about having one's roots in one's own country. But roots need water from clouds forming over distant seas and from rivers having sources in different lands.'[7]

Roshen had cooked up a storm. Her mother's recipes of dal—hot and sweet—along with gosht ka salan (lamb curry). They wolfed it down, complimenting Rosh on her culinary skills.

Meal over, a lull descended as they sat back, satiated and drowsy. The meal had been a real treat in these rationed times. Everyone perked up again as Rosh produced a surprise dessert—stewed peaches with condensed milk,† which she had brought with her all the way from Bombay and saved for an occasion like this! The sight of a tin of condensed milk was met with jubilant applause.

'Now, Souza, do tell us what all of us have been waiting to hear from you. How is the PAG planning to continue? Can international artists join the group?' asked Homi Sethna.

Elk quietly picked up his stewed peaches and condensed milk and moved back to his corner. Nissim followed.

'What are you doing, Elk?'

'Nothing really. I wanted to show you some of my responses to the ICA show.' He then laid out his new series of work, 'Lovers 1', on his desk.

Nissim was mesmerized. 'Twenty-five works! My God, Elk, when did you do all this?'

In the background, Souza's voice was rising to fever pitch: 'And I told them to piss off! They just could not understand my intentions . . . It's a bloody racket . . . '

Rosh was chatting along with them while washing the dishes. 'Gosh, Francis, how I wish we had been there to see the show!'

---

* 'This was a grand exhibition of classical and medieval art organized at the Viceregal Lodge in Delhi in the winter of 1948. It had assembled masterpieces from museums and private collectors in India as well as from British collections. The exhibition ranged from finds of the Indus Valley civilization, the sculptures and bronzes of the medieval period and the Mughal, Rajasthani, and Pahari miniatures of later years. This exhibition had a major impact on the Progressive artists and others.'—Yashodhara Dalmia, *The Making of Modern Indian Art: The Progressives*, Oxford University Press, 2001, p. 48.

† Sweets of all kinds were rationed in England during the post-war years.

Nissim sat down to examine Elk's new work more carefully—he could swear he heard African drumbeats in his head... and a chill went down his spine! He began to read out the names of the works that Elk had pencilled in, in his neat hand, below the works: 'The Elopement', 'The Cock', etc.

The others had left. Elk had quietly slipped off to the bedroom and fallen asleep on the bed. Souza and Rosh joined Nissim around Elk's desk. Souza picked up one artwork after another and carefully put them down.

'Rosh, Elk has a wonderful potential for creating in line and colour. His drawings are deliberate and powerful, and the linear quality is the best I have seen. I promise you he will make a substantial contribution to contemporary Indian art.'[8]

Rosh looked down, carefully arranging the works back in the portfolio. Souza continued, 'He has also sincerity, not only in his work but in you. You Rosh, I think rightly, are the driving FORCE in him. You must support Elk for the furtherance of art. I am not a feminist, but I am conscious of the great influence women have on men.'[9]

CHAPTER 14
THE ANATOMY OF DRAMA
1949

The gruelling acting class had been underway for the past two hours. Alkazi had chosen to work on the character of Molière's Tartuffe. The RADA student actors had only recently been introduced to the Rudolf Laban methodology, which taught them how to construct a character from the 'outside in' and not generate the character through identifying with the character's given circumstances or emotions. Today's exercise required that there be no spoken text; the character had to be demonstrated physically by the students, relying only on body and expression.

Rudolf Laban was a Czech dancer–choreographer who had evolved a methodology for interpreting, describing, visualizing and notating all human movement into four basic categories: body, effort, shape and space. From these findings, he developed an entire system of movement exercises for dancers that was later modified for the use of actors as well. The Laban methodology aided actors in developing characters through movement.

When Alkazi joined RADA, the Stanislavski methodology was still in use and regarded as efficacious in rendering *realistic* representations of characters in the plays of writers such as Ibsen, Chekov and Shaw. However, as theatre moved away from naturalism before World War I, a significant number of small, experimental studios and laboratories sprang up across Europe to explore more innovative methods of training the modern actor to perform in a variety of styles demanded by a new kind of writing and performance. This was the time when the theatre director came into his own as the central conceptualizer of a performance. Highly individualistic Russian directors such as Meyerhold, Vakhtangov, Tairov and Okhlopkov broke away from Stanislavski (1863–1938) and created stylized and elaborately choreographed productions with huge ensemble casts conceived on an operatic scale. On the other hand, in France, the

Alkazi with his friends at the Royal Academy of Dramatic Art, London, 1949

actor–director Jacques Copeau (1879–1949) retired to the countryside to cultivate and train a handpicked group of only fifteen actors, calling themselves 'Compagnie de Quinze' (Company of Fifteen), in a methodology inspired by performing traditions as varied as the ritualistic Greek theatre, the Italian Commedia dell'arte and the Noh theatre of Japan. With no single genre or style emerging as representative of the era, it became a challenge for actor-training institutions to equip the would-be professional repertory actor with the appropriate skills required to accommodate a dazzling variety of approaches and styles demanded by highly individualistic directors.

Alongside the exciting advances in theatre was the world of modern dance, with the Russian impresario Sergei Diaghilev leading the way, followed by a host of American innovators, such as Isadora Duncan, Ruth St Denis and Ted Shawn, while from Germany there was Mary Wigman, all of whom revolted against classical western ballet, rewriting its entire vocabulary and creating a new, free form that, in many instances, was inspired by the dance traditions of the East. In fact, modern dance along with cinema, came to be regarded as *the* two new artistic mediums of the late nineteenth and early twentieth centuries, whose developments Rosh and Alkazi followed with interest, especially the work of Martha Graham that combined dance with theatre.

Overlaps between acting and dance training began taking place as it was recognized that the training of the actor's body had been neglected so far. Especially in Britain, the actor had become 'a talking head', adept at manipulating his vocal chords to the neglect of his other expressive physical skills. In order for his body to become a truly sensitive instrument capable of greater expressive power, RADA put together a rigorous acting programme, in response to which Alkazi later remarked, 'There were as many as five classes at RADA that were devoted entirely to movement—fencing, dancing, the Laban methodology, mime and mask work.'[1]

'To begin with, Mr Alkazi, how will your character *move*? Can you describe the kind of movement he may have?' the instructor, Mr Turner, queried.

'Maybe furtive and darting movements?' Alkazi tentatively responded. 'Tartuffe is always trying to conceal something, spring a surprise on people or take them unawares!'

'Good, now you're getting somewhere. What else? What about the *speed* of the movements? For instance, would they be quick or sustained?'

There was a pause.

'Well, they would be quick if Tartuffe wanted to suddenly hide himself and sustained if he did not want anyone to think he was being furtive. But if one were to choose, then I'd say sustained.'

'What would his *effort* or action be? Wring, press, flick, dab, glide, float, punch or slash?' With each word, Mr Turner demonstrated the action.

'Flick!'

Roshen with Nissim Ezekiel and Baloo in London, 1949

'So now proceed, Mr Alkazi, please demonstrate a *flicking* action at a *sustained* pace!'

Alkazi turned his back to the class and closed his eyes in an effort to concentrate. At this exact moment, the classroom door opened and the dance instructor, Ernestine Stodelle, let herself in. Realizing that she might be distracting the actor at work, she tiptoed to the back of the class and stood there, watching. There was silence and anticipation in the air.

Making use of the hush that had descended, Alkazi suddenly turned around to face the class, darting sharp looks to the left and right. Then, once again, in a sudden move, he adroitly plucked his kerchief from his top pocket and flicked it open with a flick of the wrist. Continuing to flick the kerchief hither and thither in front of his face as if driving away flies, he began to walk around the performance space at a sustained pace. By way of contrast, he shot quick furtive glances around the room from time to time, establishing a rhythm for these movements.

There were a few titters around the class. Egged on by this show of appreciation, Alkazi continued to strut around with added zeal, his wrist still flicking the kerchief. Upon spying Eva, a classmate, sitting in the front row, he stopped in his tracks and smiled at her coyly from behind the kerchief. Then, furtively looking around to check whether anyone was in sight, he approached her on tiptoe, stole a look at her bosom appreciatively and then abruptly looked away, covering his eyes with his handkerchief, as if scandalized. Looking up again from behind the kerchief, he moved even closer to Eva and then offered her the kerchief, signalling to her to cover her cleavage! Eva, enjoying being brought into the act so unexpectedly, responded spontaneously. Shaking her head, she declined his offer. Alkazi then inched even closer to her and, with a playful flick, covered the offending cleavage with the handkerchief himself and then hurriedly made the sign of the cross, followed by a deep sigh!

The entire class now burst into loud guffaws, applauding the improvisation with glee! The professor joined in.

'Not bad, Mr Alkazi, not bad! Ladies and gentlemen! We are out of time, but here are a few points. One, I hope you saw how Mr Alkazi used a considerable amount of mimetic expression to convey the intent of the scene, which contributed to the comedy. Mime and movement are what you should take away from this exercise. Not a word was uttered. Two, please note that the actor retained the flicking gesture throughout the piece, providing the character with rhythmic support for his movements. Three, the business with the handkerchief, that is, a prop, can aid the actor in characterization and add . . .'

The class had begun to disperse and some of them thumped Alkazi on the back, congratulating him. Mr Turner intervened, taking him aside. 'Now, Alkazi, in your next class with me, you will need to improvise a *costume* for yourself in order to develop the character in greater detail . . .'

'Yes, sir, of course! Thanks, sir . . . thanks! I really enjoyed the improv. This Laban method seems to throw up new possibilities for approaching a role . . .'

Alkazi was flushed with excitement. Stodelle now came towards him with the hint of a smile. Though in her early forties, she didn't look much older than Alkazi himself. She put down her leather satchel and proceeded to slip out of her skirt, revealing a taut, petite figure encased in black leotards and a black skin-fitting top. Alkazi averted his eyes immediately, not used to seeing a woman's body so casually exposed in public. Stealing a look at her reflection in the large mirrors that lined the classroom walls, he watched Stodelle sink gracefully to the floor, as dancers do, to casually slip her tiny feet into her ballet slippers and lace up the ribbons over her calves. He noticed that her blond, wavy hair was bobbed and held back in a broad headband. Aware of his gaze, she looked up slowly and when their eyes momentarily met, he noticed that they were an unusual shade of grey–blue.

Ever since he had joined RADA a few months ago, Alkazi had been struck by the precision and effortless ease with which Stodelle conducted her dance classes. Discussing her approach with his two American friends, David and Hugh, who had enrolled at RADA to specifically study how Shakespeare was to be performed, Alkazi learned from them that she was, in fact, an American and had met the great Russian director Theodore Komisarjevsky in New York a few years ago. Gossip had it that she had caught his fancy when he was still engaged to be married to none other than the great actress Peggy Ashcroft! So smitten was Komisarjevsky with the youthful dancer that he eventually divorced Ashcroft and married the graceful Ernestine, who became his third wife.

Alkazi had no idea that his teacher was the wife of a director he admired. Not only was he a refined director of operas and ballets in Moscow, he had taught the great Konstantin Stanislavski himself and worked with the brilliant Meyerhold during his experimental phase at the Moscow Art Theatre Studio. The kind of revolutionary experimentation in theatre that was happening in Russia before the Revolution was among the most daring in the world. British theatre paled into insignificance by comparison, appearing staid and uninspiring. It was only a handful of actors like John Gielgud and Alec Guinness who were well aware of this lacuna in British theatre and were consistently supportive of the idea that talent and originality from Europe be imported and nurtured to sustain the birth of a new theatre movement in Britain.

Komisarjevsky eventually left Moscow for Paris in 1919, fearing arrest by the Soviet secret police. On the advice of his friend, Sergei Diaghilev, he moved to London, where he was invited to direct the opera *Prince Igor* at Covent Garden.

As an émigré in London between 1925 and 1926, Komisarjevsky directed a succession of Russian plays that included Gielgud and Charles Laughton in their casts. People spoke in hallowed terms about how Komisarjevsky's productions of Chekhov had changed the manner in which British actors, audiences and critics understood the dramatist's works. Komisarjevsky soon became a legend in London.

For Alkazi, Komisarjevsky represented one stream of the European avant-garde that he was extremely keen to understand. Stodelle could perhaps provide him with an entry. He made up his mind to ask her if he might chat with her some time about her husband's work.

Stodelle was finally done lacing her ballet slippers. 'Mr Alkazi,' she said, 'that was fun—amusing!'

'Thank you, Ma'am!'

'By the way, you're Indian, aren't you?'

'Yes!'

'Then let me show you something! This is how a Bengali gentleman walks in his dhoti.'

Stodelle sprang up and very deftly and skilfully began to mime how a Bengali gentleman would pick up one end of his dhoti and walk like a dandy, then suddenly trip on it, regain his balance and continue. By now, the class had gathered around mesmerized at her mimetic skills. Alkazi was keenly observing how she took small, mincing steps and how she held one end of the dhoti elegantly in one hand and in the other, a swagger stick. But all this was in fact mimed; there were no props at all.

Shifting the class's attention to her hands, Stodelle said, 'Why use a handkerchief for Tartuffe? Instead, why not make him into a Bengali gentleman and see what you can do with the end of his dhoti!'

Alkazi was transfixed. What a fabulous suggestion! But how did she know about a dhoti? He was certainly going to try this out in his next Laban class. A dhoti would be his costume! Yes! Rosh could certainly help him find a dhoti and he would master wearing it!

'But, Ma'am, can you please tell me how you know so much about a dhoti? Have you ever been to India? I'm intrigued!'

'India?' she laughed, 'No, never! I met Mr Uday Shankar after his performance last week at the Haymarket. He was wearing a beautiful Bengali dhoti. I observed how he moved in it. Most elegant.'

When Alkazi looked back in interviews on his student years in England, he always made it clear that it was not *British* theatre as practised or taught at that time that influenced him but *Russian* and *French* avant-garde theatre.[2] Up until this point, I have wondered how this was possible when he was, in fact, studying in *London*? As mentioned, it was Gorelik's book, *New Theatres for Old*, which introduced him to a wealth of European theatre practitioners who had been breaking new ground for fifty years. Alkazi used the information he gleaned from the book to search for material on these theatre avant-gardists.

It became clear to Elk that modernism in both theatre and painting was basically a *European* phenomenon and therefore had to be 'imported' to Britain. In order to fill this lacuna, he actively sought out European practitioners who had relocated to London. One important person was Michel Saint-Denis. So though Alkazi was enjoying the course at RADA, the theatre school that he had really set his heart on was the Old Vic Theatre School, run by Saint–Denis who was a French director and the nephew of Jacques Copeau.

Up until the 1930s, European innovations had been largely ignored in England, as London's West End still leaned towards drawing room comedies, melodrama and musical revues; the predominant mode of acting was a kind of affected naturalism; scene design was generally outmoded and the director was not yet a force as in Europe. Many innovative British actors wanted change. Saint–Denis's work had come to the attention of well-respected theatre luminaries like Laurence Olivier and Gielgud when they saw his productions with the Compagnie des Quinze in London in 1931. It was they who suggested bringing Saint–Denis across to revitalize theatre in Britain.

Ultimately, Saint–Denis was persuaded by Tyrone Guthrie to establish a school in London. The London Theatre Studio (LTS) was founded in 1935 as a 'non-conforming' school open to experimentation with course offerings exceeding those of conventional drama programmes. Here, students took instruction in movement, dance, acrobatics, wrestling, speech, singing and mask work with an emphasis on improvisation. Among Saint–Denis's pupils were Michael Redgrave, Peggy Ashcroft, Alec Guinness and Peter Ustinov. Saint–Denis came to be known as the western world's leading authority on training for the theatre. Along with George Devine, in particular, he was credited with developing a new style and method of acting that gave the British theatre fresh vitality in those years. Critics characterized it as a new kind of realism that, in avoiding the extremes of both naturalism and romanticism, reflected the mood of contemporary society.

After World War II, Saint–Denis continued to develop his training methods at the Old Vic Theatre School. By 1949 (when Alkazi was in London), Saint–Denis had integrated a director's course with the actor's course. This expanded curriculum would become England's first programme geared to train aspiring directors and included a playwright to work with the students on collective creations. The students were taught voice, speech, music, movement, silent and spoken improvisation, comic and tragic masks, text, theatre history and performance. By all standards, this was considered radical and modern at the time and so it is understandable that Alkazi was extremely disappointed to find he was too late in his application to join the Old Vic Theatre School.

***

'Hold on to the *substance*, Mr Alkazi, don't throw away those lines!'

This was the class at RADA that Alkazi found the most difficult. His instructor was the outstanding Marjorie Boulton, a short, slightly stout, round-faced and bespectacled woman who found Alkazi's keenness to know more quite remarkable. Encouraged, Boulton became more demanding of him. She would often walk into the classroom and get down to rehearsing with Alkazi first.[3]

Boulton's subject was the 'Anatomy of Drama', which Alkazi was to fully appreciate only in later years as the *nuts and bolts* of theatre. Besides a lucid and lively study of the techniques of plot, dialogue and characterization, Bouton explained the need to understand the foundations on which drama is built, without which neither the actor nor the director would be able to *construct* a strong edifice for the performance. For Boulton, a play 'is not really a piece of literature for reading. A true play is three-dimensional; it is literature that walks and talks before our eyes.' The crucial point that she repeatedly stressed was that theatre is *performance*. Her work was to teach them how to *structure a performance*.

Mainly using texts from Shakespeare as exercise pieces, Boulton taught students to break up each section of the text into distinct sequences, units and sub-units. Each unit and sub-unit could then be worked on independently in detail and finally, when all the units were performed in sequence, the subtle changes from unit to unit would become apparent, giving the actor's performance a variety of textures built up of shifting nuances. Alkazi found Boulton's scientific and *practical* approach to transforming a text into a performance to be invaluable. He regarded Boulton as a truly professional trainer, whom 'major actresses would come to with their problems, which she would help them resolve'.[4]

'What's that book you have under your arm, Alkazi?' asked Sir Kenneth Barnes, director of RADA, as he accosted Alkazi on the steps.

'It's called *New Theatres for Old*, Sir. By Modecai Gorelik,' Alkazi said, offering the well-thumbed book.

'So, what is it about the book that appeals to you?' queried Barnes, gently.

'Sir, it's really about experimental theatre productions in Europe and the United States! There is some really exciting work they're doing . . . some brilliant directors!'

Barnes stopped in his tracks. 'Yes, I remember now; you mentioned that you used to direct in India. Do you intend to do so when you return?'

'Yes, of course, Sir, I will have to act *and* direct. When I go back, Sir, I will have to teach members of my group.'

Alkazi (left), Roshen (right), with their friends, England, 1950

Over the next hour, Alkazi was deep in conversation with Barnes in his room. It was a medium-sized room with wainscoting. Books lined the shelves from floor to ceiling. Some heavy curtains let in the pale sunlight of late afternoon. A bust of Shakespeare sat on a rather unstable-looking marble column to the right of the desk, behind which Barnes, hands behind his back, was peering over his specs at the young lad. It was already late August, so a little electric heater was on in one corner.

Alkazi was seated on an old, well-worn leather chair. Head bowed, he was solemnly outlining what he had come to England to learn, what he felt he had achieved so far and what he needed to do further. He was satisfied with the RADA course in acting, he said, but actually wished to move on to becoming a good theatre director as well. He mentioned his disappointment over not having gotten into the Old Vic Theatre School, especially since they offered an integrated course that he could have benefited from by learning a great deal about the different aspects of staging.

Barnes stood up, whipped his specs off and turned away, looking pensively out of the window.

There was a pause.

'Sir, not wanting to sound helpless or hopeless, I should confess that my wife is here, too. She wants to be a costume designer, but we can't really afford to pay fees for both of us. You see, Sir, we are running low on funds and we are not really sure whether I can even continue to afford the RADA fees, Sir.'

'Married already! Hmmm... Why so early?'

Alkazi shyly looked down. 'I don't know, Sir, we fell in love. It just happened. We also have a baby daughter!'

Another pause...

Then Barnes turned around with a faint smile.

'Well, I think we may have something for you.'

He returned to his desk and explained to Alkazi that the British Drama League (BDL), a new body, had only very recently begun a producer's course. He recommended that Alkazi join it for the last six months of his diploma. Alkazi looked up. Overjoyed. Then he was downcast once more.

'Sir, I won't be able to afford it.'

'You don't need to pay a farthing! We had planned to offer you a scholarship for the rest of your course here at RADA anyway. You're a brilliant student, Alkazi; you do know that, surely! Now those funds can be redirected towards the producer's course.'

Alkazi was overwhelmed by the gesture. 'Thank you, Sir! Thank you so much!'

Barnes stood up, signalling that the meeting was over and came around the table to shake Alkazi's hand.

'Congratulations, young man!'

With his eyes welling up, all Elk could manage was a nod. He turned to leave. Opening the door, he suddenly stopped. 'But, Sir, I don't understand. How will I be able to complete my attendance here, at RADA?'

'Alkazi, I believe you have acted in several classroom productions so far, often in the title role! That gives us a fair amount to assess your abilities as an actor. So, we shall consider your work at BDL as part of your RADA diploma; it will be taken into account.'

'Thank you, Sir, thank you very much! I promise not to let you down, Sir!

The graciousness and helpfulness of Sir Kenneth Barnes and others were never forgotten by Alkazi. To render immediate help to someone when required was a trait he emulated, helping young students in their formative years to continue their education.

*　*　*

Joining the BDL opened up a prospect of theatre that Alkazi could never have imagined. A ten-week producer's course run by Frances Mackenzie, the BDL offered lectures by Alkazi's greatest heroes, such as Michel Saint-Denis and E. Martin Browne, a specialist director of religious plays who had become an overnight sensation with his productions of T.S. Eliot's verse plays such as *The Family Reunion* and *Murder in the Cathedral*. In addition, Elk and Rosh were allowed access to the fabulous theatre archives in the Victoria and Albert Museum and the London University Library.

This was an unbelievable opportunity and Elk immediately devised a course of study for himself and Rosh for the weekends! Here were vast collections of original theatre drawings, models of stage designs, costume sketches, books on theatre, scripts, theatre backdrops and photographs of legendary theatre productions and actors through which the glorious history of world theatre was revealed.

> I made a systematic study of the theories, training methods and production procedures of the great Russian directors, Stanislavski, Meyerhold, Vakhtangov, Tairov and Komisarjevsky; of Gordon Craig and Adolphe Appia; the French theatre pioneers, Andre Antoine, Jacques Copeau, Charles Dullin, Gaston Baty, Georges Pitoeff, followed by Louis Jouvet, Jean-Louis Barrault and Michel Saint-Denis.[5]

Rosh, in turn, recounted the generosity of the officials in government institutions and museums who assisted her:

> I thought I would do a specialized course there but I had no resources. I was lucky to work with James Laver, who was the biggest authority on costume in the costume department at the Victoria and Albert Museum. And he set up a course of study for me and under his supervision, for a whole year at the Victoria and

Albert Museum, I studied the history of clothing from the earliest stages in European history. As you know, there are so many books available, but he charted out a course of studies and I did drawings, and to study what style was in the theatre, what historical accuracy was when doing plays. This gave me a very solid grounding so when I came back to India, to the Theatre Group and continued working on my husband's productions, I had at least this kind of training behind me.[6]

It was to these immense dark vaults that Alkazi and Roshen returned with the regularity of devotees each weekend. Gradually, the secrets of the great productions that Gorelik had spoken about in his book became palpable and real through vast collections of archival material that were available on them. Alkazi recollected: 'The V&A had not only one of the finest theatre libraries in the world, but also displayed original models and drawings of settings and costumes by Craig, Appia, Bakst, Goncharova, Berard, Bel Geddes and other distinguished European and American stage designers.'

Often working till the wee hours of the night, these two penniless waifs lurched home, satiated and re-energized. Dropping into bed, they made love of a very different kind—passionate, frenzied, yet gentle, born of an excitement for art and theatre coupled with an excitement for one another.

CHAPTER 15
POETRY IN PICTORIAL FORM
1950

This kind of passionate immersion into the physical realm opened the floodgates to a completely unknown world for Alkazi. It was a world that was compelling in its sensuousness and one that had been forbidden to him by his strict Arab upbringing. Overwhelmed by the experience, Elk sought to translate physical sensations into artistic expression—into the lines, forms and colours of his paintings and drawings.

The fact that Alkazi was turning out some highly remarkable and unusual works was not lost on his astute and perceptive friend Souza, who immediately recognized that Elk was moving into new and uncharted territory. Writing from London to Rosh, who was back in Bombay with me—baby Uma—Souza was unable to conceal his excitement at the sight of Elk's new series.

> 5 May 1950
> My Dear Rosh,
> For the past few weeks, Elk has been working on a series of paintings (?). Spring is so lovely in England. This is my first Spring here. But I didn't notice the loveliness of it until I was surprised by Elk's observation of it in his paintings (?). These works are small as all of his works are, painted in a few strokes of Mandarin Indian ink. This is the first impression: just a few black strokes. Suddenly one realizes that the strokes are twigs of trees . . . twigs sprouting with tender leaves and blossoming buds. Then the shock comes; a very agreeable electric shock. The twigs are 'male' and 'female' twigs twining round each other. The budding buds blossom breasts . . . the tender leaves are not modest fig leaves, but the tender splitting sprouting leaves of young women. The 'male' twig has little fruity testicles and a thorny pricky penis. The two Spring twig man and

wife entwine to procreate the Summer! Tremendously poetical the works are. Sheer poetry. I don't understand nor have the patience to read poetry in the written form. This is poetry in the pictorial form. I am not sure if these sets of works can be classified as painting, therefore, I use the (?) mark in describing them as such. But you know that Elk hates such classifications and pigeon-holing. True he works regardless of what actually painting is, or for that matter what poetry is. To him, 'life' is painting. To me, 'Painting is life'. But it will yet have to be decided what these works are. But the extremely intimate character of the work, so intimate to be shared only by his beloved wife and a few lucky friends ... this intimate aspect of the work makes such a decision a problem. The collages of the cubists are somewhat in the indecisive sphere of art. But Elk has realized a tremendously stimulating current with far reaching repercussions. However 'intimate' the works may be they must be exhibited & reproduced in book form. Most intimate letters of people have been published.

Last night, I had another surprise. He invited Nissim and me to see three more of his works. I was stupefied. I couldn't speak for long. When he asked me what I felt all I could say was I was shocked in my nervous sympathicus. The twigs had grown into men and women with their organs yielding plentiful delicious fruits and flowers. The woman's thighs open into a large crimson flower full of pollen and dewdrops. Large red beetroots hang from the man's loins, and both are engaged in a fellatio and cunnilingus position in flower patterns ... The composition is dexterous, the colour beautiful, the line delicate and the detail meticulous.

You won't get the least idea from all this ... but I am writing this to you because I am still suffering from the nervous sympathicus. You must see them for yourself and to you they will mean something else. To me, they mean that Elk has proved himself a great Poet–Artist. These paintings are not good. They are great.

Souza's praise was as genuine as it was generous. He recognized that although Roshen may have provided the impetus to awaken such passion in Elk, as an artist, he had transformed these private experiences into something beyond himself—they had become articulations that Souza described as 'visual poetry'.

Describing Alkazi's works as 'small and extremely intimate', Souza immediately caught onto their 'in-between-ness', that they could not be typically classified as 'paintings' per se. Instead, he perceptively compared them to the collages of the cubists that belonged to the 'indecisive sphere of art'. Whatever genre of art Alkazi was creating was a matter of semantics, Souza declared; the point was that they were 'great' art and should definitely appear in 'book form'. Here, Souza was possibly referring to the new genre of 'Artist's Book' that had been made popular at the turn of the century in France by publishers such as Albert Skira and E. Teriade. These books were deluxe, limited editions meant to be read as well as collected and admired as works of art.

An artist like Henri Matisse had, throughout his long and productive career, periodically refreshed his creative energies by turning from painting to drawing, sculpture and other forms of artistic expression to include the production of over a dozen illustrated books. His first book, *Poésies* (1932), included mythologically inspired images based on texts by the poet Stéphane Mallarmé, while his book *Jazz* (1947), known for its brightly coloured red *pochoirs* (stencils), is widely considered one of the most important illustrated books of the modern period.[1] It is certain that Alkazi would have come across these publications in London.

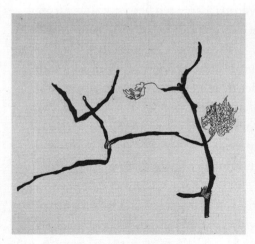 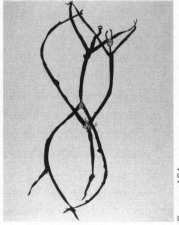

Lovers II, drawings by Alkazi, 1950

Although Alkazi had given up formal training in painting within the first few weeks of his arrival in London, he worked every day on his art with unflinching seriousness. Over the next few months, he was like a man possessed, stealing every spare moment he could grab between the demanding schedules of the producer's course at the BDL and his final acting assignment at RADA, where he was cast as the old family retainer, Firs, in Anton Chekhov's play, *The Cherry Orchard*.[2] Now that the time for his departure was drawing near, he felt the need for his works to be publicly exhibited, assessed and critiqued so as to gain some kind of response as to where he stood as an artist. With this in mind, he braced himself to approach the Leicester Galleries for a show. The gallery graciously agreed to review his portfolio. Elk was beside himself with joy that he had not been rejected outright. To celebrate, he offered to treat Alyque, his young brother-in-law, who had recently come to London, enrolled at RADA and was staying with him, to a music hall show the following weekend!*

'Have you ever watched music hall?'

Alyque could not believe his ears. He and Elk had barely exchanged a few words in the last three months since his arrival. Alyque would return home in the evening and Elk would be there painting.

'I thought I knew Elk, but then I found out that I was living with a hermit! Elk was quite a good painter. He did some fantastic paintings, very meticulous . . . I don't know why he gave it up; he wanted to be a painter as well . . . He was very keen on exactitude . . . Then I'd say, "Elk, dinner is ready." He used to come to the table with a book and read, like Bobby . . . He seemed to be in a world that was locked in; when you knocked on the door, nobody answered it.'

This was the first time in months that Alkazi had lifted his eyes from his work and acknowledged Alyque's presence.

'I have seen music hall in the movies, but I have never actually been to a live one.'

'Let's go this Saturday. It's called *Eves Without Leaves*,' Elk said.

Alyque was tickled pink! *Eves Without Leaves*! A rather graphic title! Those were the days when the Lord Chamberlain wielded his authority

---

* Alyque had by now come to London to study law but gave it up in order to devote himself to theatre. For a while, Alyque too stayed at Lansdowne Crescent and recounted his experiences of living with Elk to Amal Allana.

over matters of censorship in the theatre and nudity was forbidden on stage. However, performances in the nude could take place if the nude characters did not move![3] Moving was considered sexual! Taking their seats in a tiny, rather seedy-looking theatre, *Eves Without Leaves* had a compère who was cracking one joke after another, ad-libbing away, while the curtain opened on one tableau after another of nude women frozen in different provocative stances—without a fig leaf to cover them!

> ... that was the first time I saw a nude woman, you know ... so to me it was fantastic. What was I? I was about eighteen at the time and had never seen a nude woman! So, that was the only time I remember Elk getting out of his monk's habit, his closed-in, cloistered self, and actually crossing the road to do something that a young man like me enjoyed![4]

The awakening to sex was as liberating as was the awakening to racial equality and political rights. After the war and the relinquishing of some of their colonies, Britain had become a strong advocate of free speech, allowing citizens to publicly air their views on soapboxes at designated areas like Hyde Park Corner. Anyone could turn up unannounced and talk on any subject, making this a lively event. Elk, a seasoned debater and actor, often took to the soap box, attracting people to come listen to Nissim's poems!

'On Saturday evenings, I recited Nissim's poetry on a borrowed platform at Speakers Corner (Hyde Park), and held the podium of the Coloured Workers Association, while the Negro demagogue with bloodshot eyes, Robeson voice and mutilated, glove-covered hands, fortified himself with a snappy drink.'[5]

Roshen kept Elk and his friends abreast of news from Bombay; writing to them jointly, she jokingly addresses them as 'The Seven Dwarfs' who now have no 'Snow White' to attend to their needs! It is true that by this time, Elk, Nissim, Souza, Krishna Paigankar, Baloo, Homi Sethna and Alyque had practically run out of money, but the adrenaline still ran high when it came to heated discussions on art and theatre that related to their dreams of the future. Reminiscing, Alkazi said:

> Every Saturday, around noon, we would drift into the market at Portobello Road (a working-class district in those days and not

the tourist attraction it has since become), and buy the leftovers for our weekly rations—strings of meat, broken biscuits, a loaf of stale bread, discarded vegetables—all at reduced rates. We couldn't afford more. We would shove the whole lot together into a vessel, put it on the fire, add enough water to drown it, stir it into an unholy mess, and cackle over it, like the bearded witches in *Macbeth*. Being a poet, Nissim would distil out of this malodorous mixture a culinary concoction, which he could delicately serve out to us in meagre portions, rather like a starveling haiku. Then, true to the Bard, and in pursuit of the impossible, we would 'on our imaginary forces work' 'to make imaginary puissance', magnifying our minuscule tit-bits to epic proportions.[6]

This experience of a new way of life, in a country that had been brutally brought to its knees during the War, of the meaning and value of liberty, of the meaning and need for new expressions in art, of managing frugally—these fed into the sculpting of Alkazi's character, his attitude to life and the perspective from which he could begin to visualize a path for himself. The experiences humbled him, making him conscious that there was indeed a vast landscape he had to plough and complex interrelationships he would need to discover if he was to formulate a vision for himself to realize in the future.

* * *

As he waited for a response from the Leicester Galleries, Elk continued to work with renewed energy. The intensity and power of the sexual experience engulfed him, becoming the focal theme of a large number of the new works he was creating, many of them as series. Titling the series 'Lovers 1–4', Alkazi explored the theme of sexuality through a range of content. In 'Lovers 1', sexuality is consecrated as a primitive and sacrificial rite,[*] while in 'Lovers 2', he likens awakening to love to the awakening of nature in springtime. In these twelve elegantly delineated drawings, Alkazi depicts the man and the woman as carefree and abandoned, they are

---

[*] This series can be read alongside the draft of a storyline for a film that Alkazi had jotted down. The storyline appears biographical in more senses than one—a young man is lured to a primitive island across the seas, where he is drawn to a dark native woman. Dancing with her, he is unable to remain with her, returning reluctantly to the mainland, back to his

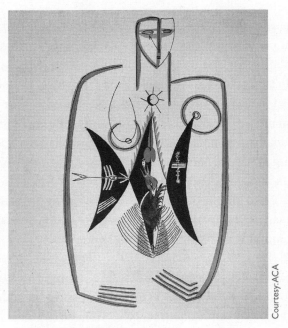

The Song of the Bride, drawing by Alkazi, 1949

visualized as twigs dancing a duet, set to a twelve-line poem by Nissim Ezekiel; 'Lovers 3' boldly depicts the man and woman in a variety of positions of coitus. The graphic nature of the subject matter is tamed by its highly stylized rendering of form, line and colour. In his *Hamlet* series ('Lovers 4'), Alkazi couples Hamlet with Gertrude and Hamlet with Ophelia in turn, highlighting the strong sexual frisson between mother and son, no doubt inspired by current interpretations of *Hamlet* as suffering from an Oedipus complex. Here, Alkazi shows remarkable control as a draughtsman, capturing the expressions and gestures of the characters through an exquisite purity of line.

Alkazi's sources are all the arts. From theatre, he explores sexuality in Shakespeare's *Hamlet*; from contemporary literature, he explores sexuality

---

wife and child. The sea, sky, wind, drums, the beautiful woman and a ritual sacrifice, are elements in common with the visuals of the series 'Lovers 1'.
Stylistically, one can relate Alkazi's choice of this theme—physical love that is set within a primitive background of people belonging to the soil—to the inspiration that European modernism found in African and Oceanic art in an attempt to return to sources and nature. This return to the primitive had played itself out in the form of the spectacular *40,000 Years of Modern Art* at the ICA, which undoubtedly affected Alkazi deeply.

in James Joyce's *Ulysses*; homosexual love is explored through the poetry of Baudelaire and Mallarme; an awakening to innocent love is found in Nissim Ezekiel's poem and in the music of Stravinsky's *The Rites of Spring*; sex as ritual is inspired by African art, particularly African and Oceanic sculpture.*

For the pictorial rendering of each of these series, it seems that Alkazi was searching for independent *stylistic* equivalents. Some series are influenced by Aubrey Beardsley's art deco style in his use of line and decoration; others echo the simplicity of Matisse's line, while the *Ulysses* works are rendered in a quasi-cubist style.

It is possible that what Alkazi was imbibing at this time from Michel Saint–Denis, whose productions he had been watching at the Old Vic and whose classes he was attending at the BDL, was suggesting an approach to him. Saint–Denis staunchly advocated that one of the key jobs of a theatre director was to discover a unique 'style' for each production. Such a 'style', Saint–Denis said, could be derived from an awareness of the popular styles in fashion design, art, architecture and furniture design of the era in question. However, in addition, the director and visualizers could incorporate these into the visual sensibility of their own era so as to give the piece a contemporary 'look' and 'feel'. Saint–Denis, as a director, had himself developed a close collaboration with extremely talented and innovative set and costume designers (like the Motley group), whom he insisted on working with repeatedly in his productions.

This was one of Saint-Denis' signature ideas,[7] and it was towards the creation of this 'style' that Roshen and Alkazi worked as collaborators, as a director–designer team, in all their subsequent theatre work. The word 'style' was more often than not accompanied by the term 'interpretation' that both Alkazi and Roshen used when discussing the approach to a new production, especially referring to its visual aspects, which included sets, costumes, colour scheme and lighting.†

Such seeping of *process* and *practice* from one medium into another would occur repeatedly in all of Alkazi's artistic endeavours. This was

---

* Being inspired by 'art' and not always by 'life directly' as an artist was the subject of Alkazi's essay 'Imitation'.

† 'Style and Interpretation' was a talk given by Roshen Alkazi to students of costume design at the Dramatic Art and Design Academy (DADA) in the early 2000s. Often, it was Roshen's costumes that helped give a second layer to Alkazi's productions. As she stated for Alkazi's productions, such as *Andha Yug* and *Suryamukh*, she found inspiration in Indian primitive

bound to be, and it is exactly this ability to move seamlessly from one medium to the other that enriched both his practices, allowing him to create complex works of art that demanded a new way of being viewed. To borrow the phrase used by Brecht, the new work demanded 'complex seeing', 'complex viewing'. Alkazi, perhaps unaware of it himself, was asking the spectator to view or read his work through multiple lenses. So, for example, in the *Ulysses* series of paper works, the viewer is required to 'read' Alkazi's take on it, in addition to using his understanding of Cubism as well as his familiarity with the original Greek myth, and finally also incorporate James Joyce's rendering and treatment of the ancient myth in contemporary terms. Thus, in order to appreciate Alkazi's artworks, the spectator was required to practically excavate them, layer by layer, in order for their multiple dimensions and meanings to be revealed. The works called for an *active* engagement from the spectator, on both the intellectual and visceral levels.

Elk laid out his fifty odd works across the floor of the tiny flat. Looking at them critically, he realized that something was missing. What was it? Yes! Conflict! He needed a second theme to act as a counterpoint to the sexuality theme. It appeared that he was constructing his first solo exhibition in much the same manner as he would structure and direct a play.

Over the next couple of weeks, several ideas were attempted and abandoned, but nothing of significance emerged as a strong counterpoint to the theme of sexuality. And then, quite by chance, the terms 'religious theatre' and 'ritual theatre' began to be mentioned quite often in the lectures given by E. Martin Browne at the BDL.[8]

---

costumes. In *Lear*, she based her style on influences from early medieval European and Celtic sources, using fur and leather. None of these productions were designed to be period pieces. Roshen basically derived their style by cleverly using a few suggestive motifs from the period but then deviating to create a style that was also modern in its feel. On the whole, Alkazi's directorial style was physical and muscular—very male, assertive and aggressive. To achieve this in the costumes, Roshen created a black body suit of just black tights and a fitted t-shirt worn as a basic garment over which she draped a cape or a tunic. This allowed the lines of the actors' bodies to be revealed in their taut muscularity. The footwear consisted of black socks, akin to ballet shoes or black boots, giving a firmness of stance and step.

* Undoubtedly, Alkazi was creatively drawn to this layered approach of seeing things. The rewriting of myth in a contemporary context was interesting to Alkazi, so *Antigone* and *Eurydice* are myths retold. Also, *Andha Yug* was a contemporary take on the Mahabharata.

Alkazi was unaware at the time that this slim, gaunt, evangelical-looking man was, in fact, considered an important theatre director in certain circles, assuming prominence prior to the War with his pageant-like productions of the verse plays of Eliot—*The Rock*, *The Family Reunion* and *Murder in the Cathedral*, productions that had, strangely enough, been supported by the Church.

> I strongly believe that the way forward from naturalism in theatre, is a return to the roots, to the wellsprings of drama, that are to be found in Greek drama and in the medieval mystery plays. Like me, several artists and writers of my generation believe that the industrialization of the modern world has bred a pursuit of the material, to the neglect of the spiritual aspects of life by modern man, whose ties with nature have consequently been snapped. Naturalism is a form that is only able to express surface truths, and is incapable of conveying the *inner* life of the spirit. What I propose is that we develop a new symbolic language, a visual and aural language of poetry, for contemporary theatre. The sources for this new approach can be sought, I believe, from the ritual theatre of the Greeks, as well as the religious theatre performances of the middle ages, performances that can take place among the people, in streets, in courtyards and in churches.[*]

Alkazi, who was sitting at the back of the class, strained forward to catch each word of E. Martin Browne. Taking out his pencil and notebook, he began scribbling notes. *This* is what he had wanted to know about—how *ancient* theatrical forms could be used to create *modern* theatre, just as 'primitive' African art was being seen as the source of modernism!

Browne shared with the students that before the War, George Bell, the bishop of Chichester, called upon representatives from Sadler's Wells, the Old Vic and the BDL to discuss the possibility of commissioning new scripts for enactments in churches. Martin Browne was invited to direct.

---

[*] These ideas of Martin Browne were to influence Alkazi. He developed them over the years and began using sites for performances. The direct influence could be seen in the pageant *The Prince of Peace*, which Alkazi staged for a church in Bandra, Bombay. This has been described by Gerson da Cunha in his chapter on Alkazi in Anil Dharker, ed., *Icons: Men & Women Who Shaped Today's India*, Lotus, 2008.

I was excited as this gave me an opportunity to try out my ideas of using the lyric form and the poetic form. So, it was inevitable that I approach that poet of great stature, T.S. Eliot, to collaborate on these exciting new experiments. In both *The Rock* as well as *Murder in the Cathedral* our discussions led to the idea of creating a Chorus which was a major device that we derived from Greek theatre, while for the visual impact we used the idea of large numbers of actors choreographed in tableaux-type formations, an idea that has it's antecedents in Medieval Mystery plays.[9]

In fact, *Murder in the Cathedral* was written by Eliot with the intention of having it staged in the Canterbury Cathedral. Many, many ideas were raging through Alkazi's mind as he walked home that evening. It was exciting to hear Browne describe the use of the actual site of the Canterbury Cathedral with its tall Gothic spires for the performance of Eliot's *Murder in the Cathedral*. Entering such a space must have awed and enveloped the audience in a mystical atmosphere, demanding their attention and devotion. The quality of light filtering through the jewelled, stained-glass windows with their figures of saints and angels would have fallen over the actors to create the aura of a Georges Rouault painting. Eliot's modern verse incanted in those medieval surroundings, charged with its own history, would have lent the contemporary performance universality and timelessness. Yes! Drama performed at a *site* felt so *organic*, so much part of the *soil*, allowing theatre to be a *ritual* where the characters and audience could be spiritually cleansed. The closed indoor proscenium stage, by contrast, appeared shallow and tawdry. An elitist, bourgeois middle-class theatre that catered to only a select few, a theatre space where one could create but a shabby illusion of the real! Alkazi wanted representational illusionism stripped away; he preferred the nakedness of the bare, damp earth. A small patch of earth with a circle drawn around it was enough to create a sanctified, consecrated space for performance. Greek theatre was just that, he thought—nothing more!*

---

* 'Gods of the Byways' was an exhibition that was part of a series titled 'India: Myth and Reality', which Alkazi curated in 1982 for Oxford/MOMA as part of the Festival of India. A photographic show of roadside shrines found in India, 'Gods of the Byways' showed how sacred spaces in India were created through the simplest of means—anointing a rock with turmeric powder and red kumkum or wrapping it with cotton thread was enough to transform the mundane into the sacred.

These ideas regarding the essential nature of theatre had begun occurring to Alkazi. They were in a germinal stage, but he would hang onto them and develop, nurture and realize them in concrete form several times through his life, creating performance spaces that were in tune and in touch with nature. What was more important to Alkazi on this late spring day in 1950, as he made his way back home in the dark, was that he had finally discovered the theme he had been searching for, around which he would create the second body of work for his art show. He did not know how he would approach it yet, but it would be around the Christ theme! The Christ theme with the sexuality theme! The Sacred and the Profane! Physical and Spiritual! These were the twin themes he would juxtapose in his forthcoming show at the Leicester Galleries. To him, this felt like an absolute revelation!

Crucifixion, drawing by Alkazi, 1950

CHAPTER 16
A MEETING OF WORLD CULTURES AND AU REVOIR
1950

Summer, 1950. Alkazi was experiencing his first day of what promised to be a utopian four weeks at Dartington Hall*—the kind of institution he could never have dreamed existed. For the past few hours, he had been roaming through the extensive 1200-acre estate with his camera, trying to capture its pastoral, sylvan charm. The eye was saturated with the rich green of the low, rolling hills of Devon, sprinkled here and there with a few barn-like structures housing the various departments of theatre, dance, music, pottery, etc. The barns appeared to be temporary structures and had a rough, handmade feel about them. A simple, flexible, open-air performance space with rudimentary levels created by tamped earth caught his attention as he strolled past. These temporary spaces were located at a considerable distance from what appeared to be the only permanent structure on the estate—a massive, majestic fourteenth-century stone castle. Here, he was told, all the students, teachers, artists and dancers gathered regularly for meals. Breaking bread together was considered an essential expression of the true spirit of community life that Dartington Hall had fostered for over a decade. In fact, the wholesome meals everyone partook of were made with the crops cultivated and cooked by the staff and students themselves, as were the rough-hewn wooden trestle tables and benches at which they sat. All the activities were aimed at making the residents of Dartington self-sufficient and encouraging them to live holistic lives close to nature, an integral aspect of Dartington's overall philosophy.

Alkazi was listening attentively to his guide as they moved towards the Great Dining Hall, not forgetting to mention all the great artists who had visited and taught at Dartington . . . As the young guide spoke,

---

* Alkazi's principal at RADA, Sir Kenneth Barnes, was once again responsible for sending him for the summer course at Dartington and getting the fees underwritten.

Alkazi was suddenly visited by an incredible vision; an entire animated scene unfolded in front of him like a teeming Pieter Bruegel painting. A vast array of humanity was dining together. Alkazi saw himself following his companion through the vast hall, humbled and awed to be in the presence of such great luminaries. He spotted the great Michael Chekhov, actor trainer and nephew of Anton Chekhov, and Michel Saint–Denis, his favourite director, sitting on either side of Beatrice Straight, an actress and daughter of the Elmhirsts's, all chatting with a group of young actors. Bernard Leach, the potter, listened with his eyes shut to a Japanese gentleman who was speaking to him in low, inaudible tones. To the far side of the table, was none other than Rudolf Laban, the innovator of the Eurythmics methodology that Alkazi had gained so much from at RADA, sitting beside Kurt Jooss, the brilliant dancer–choreographer, while Beryl de Zoete, the expert on Balinese dance, was in conversation with Uday Shankar. Dorothy Elmhirst, owner of the Dartington Hall estate, turned to take a second look at the young Alkazi, nodding and smiling at him as he passed by. Alkazi's companion now halted near Leonard Elmhirst, who was currently regaling a bevy of beautiful young dancers with a joke, sending them into peals of laughter. The laughter suddenly jerked Alkazi out of his reverie and back into the present.* Disoriented, Alkazi found himself, in fact, standing in front of his host. Rising from his seat, Leonard Elmhirst extended his hand in greeting, but then immediately withdrew it, converting it into a namaste!

'Ah! My Indian friend! Namaste! I hope your journey from London was comfortable.'

He tapped his glass and there was silence!

'Friends, let me introduce you to a charming and extremely gifted young Indian student, Ebrahim Alkazi, an actor and would-be director, I hear?'

Alkazi, taken aback at suddenly being the centre of attention, nodded shyly.

---

*　All the persons described here had at one time or another taught semesters at Dartington Hall. These were the most avant-garde artists of that generation who had contributed to Dartington's unique educational programme, enriching it. Many of them were exploring the traditions of the East, including India. In this way, students were exposed to all the arts simultaneously by a cross-section of internationally acclaimed practitioners.

Dartington Hall, 1950

'Alkazi has just completed his acting course at RADA and the new drama and producer's course at the British Drama League and, I am told, has walked away with all the top awards from both institutions!'

Polite applause.

'He is joining us at Dartington for the summer course on American experimental theatre to be conducted by our dear friends from the USA, Arch Lauterer, Hallie Flanagan and Rosamond Gilder, the editor of the *Theatre Arts Journal*.'

Alkazi recognized Hallie over a sea of heads. A somewhat severe but strong-looking woman wearing workaday overalls, Hallie waved in his direction. Elmhirst continued: 'As you know, young man, our respect for India is enormous. Dartington owes everything—its philosophy and its world view—to your great country and your esteemed national poet, dramatist and artist Rabindranath Tagore! Tagore is my guru and our inspiration.* He is responsible for all this. So please consider this place your home. Welcome!'

Alkazi was overwhelmed by this affectionate introduction. After all, he was a nobody, a mere student! As if reading his mind, his companion–guide commented as he prodded Alkazi along, 'Don't worry! You're not

---

* Elmhirst had served as secretary to Rabindranath Tagore in India between 1921 and 1925.

being singled out. Mr Elmhirst introduces every newcomer this way. He's democratic, despite his wealth and status. He wants everyone to feel relaxed and comfortable.'

Looking around, Alkazi was relieved to note that people had gone back to eating and chatting and ceased looking at him. Somewhat dazed, he was now ushered to the table across the room, where the Americans was smoking and chatting affably.

'Hi Alkazi! Come, join us.'

* * *

Alkazi felt he could not have opted for a better course as the culmination of his studies in England. Surprised that he made it through the gruelling auditions, he found he was one of the youngest in the group of forty-five selected candidates. Along with a handful of students from Old Vic Theatre School, RADA, the Royal Academy of Music and American colleges such as Carnegie, Smith and Vassar, there were major forces in professional theatre, including producers, directors, actors, dancers, writers and teachers. Together, they made up a vibrant assortment of different nationalities, ages, skills and experiences, bringing a certain multicultural dimension and vitality to their interactions.

The aim of the four-week course was to impart the teaching methodologies of American college and university drama departments, their contribution to the field of general education and the foundation for subsequent professional training. Interspersing theory with practice, the course culminated in the performance of scenes from Aeschylus' *Prometheus Bound* and Ibsen's *The Lady from the Sea* together with a modern dance–theatre piece.

The day began with Laban's movement class, followed by a seminar by the course director, Arch Lauterer, a brilliant director, teacher and designer and an expert in lighting and theatre architecture. He was well known for staging productions for Martha Graham and headed Mills College at the time. Lauterer discussed fundamentals—the conception of the drama, its relation to the stage and its deep connection with the life of man—gradually leading the students to discover links between the Greek world and Ibsen.

Imogen Holst, composer and conductor, concentrated on speech, music and choral work, while evenings were devoted to improvisations and rehearsals of both plays with Lauterer. Sessions on the use of props, modelling space through light, the value of scale and theatre architecture, were held. Afternoons were free for swimming in the River Dart and exploring the Devon countryside, with visits to Exeter Cathedral and other important sites.

Alkazi was absorbing all this like a sponge. Flanagan, now over sixty years old, spoke to the students of her visit to Europe in 1926, where she met the foremost theatre luminaries—John Galsworthy, Konstantin Stanislavski, Edward Gordon Craig, Lady Gregory, and others. Comparing the prevailing theatre conditions in America with those of Europe, she realized that not only was European theatre far more developed in its professionalism, reach, artistic merit, experimentation and appreciation of modernist trends, but more importantly, European theatre had recognized that theatre was a significant tool that helped awaken the masses to their social and political reality.

The Great Depression of 1929 found thousands unemployed in the US, leading President Franklin Roosevelt to establish the Works Progress Administration (WPA), an agency meant to create jobs. Heading the Federal Theatre Project (a wing of the WPA), Hallie Flanagan aimed at employing jobless entertainers across the US. Creating theatre for children as well as Living Newspaper plays, based on German director Erwin Piscator's concepts, Flanagan helped 12,500 actors find jobs. In New York City alone, The Federal Theatre Project played to weekly audiences of 350,000, many of whom had never experienced live theatre before.

Unfortunately, the WPA was criticized for having a political agenda, forcing Flanagan to testify before the House of Un-American Activities Committee under suspicion of supporting a Communist agenda and subverting American values. After barely four years, the WPA was abandoned.

Rosamond Gilder, the other grande dame of American theatre,[*] spoke of The Group Theatre of New York (1931–1941), which, under the guidance

---

[*] In later years, Rosamond Gilder and Harold Clurman both came to know of Alkazi's work on their visits to India. Rosamond knew him from Bombay in 1956, when she was president of the First World Theatre Conference held in Bombay in 1956, which she wrote about. Harold Clurman came to Delhi while Alkazi was director of the NSD and gave a guest lecture there in the early 1970s. E. Alkazi in an interview with Samik Bandyopadhyay, Natya Shodh Sansthan, Kolkata, 15 March 1988.

of Lee Strasberg, Harold Clurman and Cheryl Crawford, had brought the Stanislavski method to the US, modifying it for the training of cinema actors. The Group Theatre became known for its staging of contemporary work in the naturalistic mode, with an emphasis on ensemble acting.

As Gilder spoke, Alkazi recollected that this was the same group Bobby had so admired and had, in fact, named their Bombay group* after.

Alkazi was astounded to learn from these first-hand accounts how Flanagan had picked herself up and carried on working despite the US government questioning her motives. Theatre seemed to require a great deal of grit and determination, and, compared to the creative satisfaction one derives from practising it, there were no tangible financial gains.

One of the things Alkazi noted during these years of living abroad was that theatre people created theatre wherever they could, even if it meant leaving their countries. Look at Michel Saint–Denis. At Komisarjevsky. Look at Chekhov, moving from Russia to England, with talk of him setting up an actor's studio in America next! Laban from the Czech Republic was here, while Kurt Jooss had just returned to Germany—migrants, refugees, people who had tried to avoid persecution through two crippling world wars. Home, it seemed, was not necessarily one's birthplace; it was where you chose to make it.

'And me? What about me?' Alkazi thought. 'I, too, don't belong to India, yet I have decided that India is my home. So what does that make me? Am I, like all these artists, an internationalist? Perhaps artists like me work best in this "no man's land" of multiple cultures. We are from nowhere and everywhere!'

It was evident that these artists were drawing from one another, from international sources and traditions, to create a new aesthetic that went beyond their own national boundaries. Alkazi was invigorated by the idea of creating a new kind of internationalism, drawing from multiple sources.

These thoughts were passing through Alkazi's mind while he was standing in the middle of a tiny room he had unexpectedly chanced upon. The floor was filled with Indian musical instruments![1]

---

* '. . . the Theatre Group of Bombay was based, as far as I know, on The Group Theatre in America of the 1930s with Harold Clurman. And I think Bobby fell in love with the idea of creating community theatre.'—Alyque Padamsee in an interview with Amal Allana, Mumbai, 2011.

'What in heaven's name are *Indian* musical instruments doing here?' he asked one of his companions.

'These belonged to Uday Shankar's company,' he was told, 'Shankar has been teaching at Dartington Hall from time to time, and Zohra Segal too. In fact, she attended Michael Chekhov's acting classes held at Dartington.'[2]

Referring to his experience of being among international artists at Dartington as formative to his thinking many decades later, Alkazi said, 'And I wanted to create that same kind of thing in India . . . I felt, if and when I have the opportunity . . . I will try to do that . . . and to a certain extent, I tried to do that, later on, in a limited kind of way, at the National School of Drama . . .'[3]

The other half of the charm and magic of Dartington lay in its natural surroundings. What appealed to Alkazi was its expansiveness. Dartington Hall appeared to belong to a timeless era where liberty of thought and pure freedom of expression prevailed.

As Alkazi walked out into the sunlight, he saw a young girl running up the hill towards him, waving frantically.

'Mr Alkazi! A telegram for you!'

Taking it from her, Alkazi excused himself and walked rapidly towards Henry Moore's memorial sculpture for some privacy. He opened the telegram carefully, his heart racing.

* * *

The four-week course at Dartington had certainly passed in a flash and Alkazi soon found himself aboard a ship from Dover to Calais en route to Paris! He was standing on deck with his portfolio and a tiny bag tucked under his arm. This was his entire show! He had completed the last of the works on the Christ theme while at Dartington and was quite satisfied. The telegram had come from Nissim to congratulate Elk on his show being accepted by the Leicester Galleries for two weeks. It would be held under the auspices of the Asian Institute Gallery. The dates had been fixed for 18–30 September 1950. Elk was beside himself with joy. All he had to do now was mount the works, but his finances had dwindled to nothing. Where was he going to find the money? Making a quick mental calculation, Elk found that he had just about enough time to make a fleeting visit to Paris, where he was hoping to show these very works to a couple of galleries and dealers and perhaps even manage to sell a few. Then he would return to London, have his show at the Leicester Galleries and set the date for his departure to India by the end of the year. Another problem—Alkazi had no funds for his return passage either! But he would think of that later. For now, he was bound for Paris, the cultural capital of the art world.

Paris was a whirlwind. This was his second trip; the previous one in 1949 had been with Rosh. They had been thrilled to shack up with their oldest and dearest friends from Bombay, Jean and Freny Bhownagary. Jean had moved to Paris to join UNESCO in 1948 on a plum assignment as the head of mass communications, idealistically believing he could do more in Paris to further Indian art through the media there than he could have done in India!

Krishna Paigankar had joined them and together they had seen everything possible in a week—the Louvre, Notre Dame, Champs-Elysees, the Eiffel Tower, a visit to the Academie de Beaux-Arts, Quartier Latin, walks down the Seine, delightful meetings with Akbar Padamsee and S.H. Raza.

On this visit too, the Bhownagarys insisted that Elk stay with them and use the sofa in their tiny living room, as they already had a little baby girl, Jeanine. Elk thoroughly enjoyed their company. Both had a great sense of humour and Jean's interests were wide-ranging. In Bombay, he had been regarded as one of the top five comic actors of the Parsi–Gujarati stage,

(L–R) Elizabeth Clough, Arch Lauterer and Vedona Pitcher, 1950

working closely with Adi Marzban and at the *Jam-e–Jamshed* newspaper. An amateur magician—a serious hobby he shared with Hamid Sayani— Jean used 'Foo Ling U' as his stage name for performances in Bombay. What Jean had shared with Bobby Padamsee was a love of poetry. A poet himself, he also painted and produced films. Jean's excitement at seeing Elk's drawings was similar to that of Souza's. He insisted that while in Paris, Elk get a response to his work from a person like Philippe Soupault, whom he took Alkazi to meet! Soupault, a French writer, poet, novelist, critic and political activist, was a founder of the Surrealist movement in France along with André Breton.

> I didn't know who Phillipe Soupault was! I didn't realize that he was one of the great instigators of the Surrealist movement in Paris. And he said of my work . . . he read something very strange in my drawings. He read Arabic calligraphy in my drawings![4]

Elk also met up with Mulk Raj Anand, whom he knew from Bombay. Mulk was a good twenty years Elk's senior and was extremely well-acquainted with the art and literary scene in Europe, having studied in England and then spent a considerable amount of time in France and Russia. In 1936, Mulk, along with his friend Sajjad Zaheer, founded the Progressive Writers Association. One of the first Indo–Anglian writers, all three of Mulk's early novels—*Untouchable*, *Coolie* and *Across the Black Sea*—focused on the predicament of the marginalized in Indian society, earning him the respect and friendship of left-leaning artists and intellectuals like Pablo Picasso and Andre Malraux in France and E.M. Forster and T.S. Eliot in England.

Elk confided in Mulk how, as a teenager, he had come across *Untouchable* at the International Book Depot in Poona, where it was being hotly debated by Maharashtrian intellectuals! Pleased with the anecdote, Mulk guffawed with full Punjabi gusto. Turning to examine Elk's works, Mulk studied them closely. 'He found that there was a Matisse-like lyricism in my lines!'[5]

> Mulk took me around Paris and it was very, very interesting . . . he was looking for a workers' uniform! He was a very proletarian

sort of guy and he wanted to deck himself out in those kinds of clothes... those kinds of workers' clothes... as Brecht had his own sort of workers' clothes and Rodchenko... in Moscow, long before that, had also designed the right kind of outfits, like overalls, for a proletarian artist! After all, Mulk Raj Anand was a novelist of the people... and had had tremendous success in Russia... but now he was in Paris, where the Left Movement was extremely strong at this time... But more than anything else, it was Mulk Raj Anand's friendship, generosity, his taking me under his wing, as it were, a callow young man like myself... and finding time to show me not just the sights of Paris but the most stimulating, intellectual sort of centres of Paris, something I haven't forgotten.[6]

* * *

18 September 1950. Elk felt light-headed. The Leicester Galleries were a complete blur, with people swimming in and out of focus. All his close Indian friends were there, as were some from RADA, to support and cheer him on at his very first solo exhibition. He had been hugged, thumped on the back and congratulated interminably by those he knew, as well as by complete strangers. From an alarmingly empty gallery at 4 p.m., when he began to panic that no one except his friends would show up, the place suddenly exploded.

> And people like Herbert Read turn up, people like Victor Pasmore turn up, a large number of people who are very eminent in the world of art there, turn up . . . At the Leicester Galleries, because it is a distinguished gallery and they come and see my work ... and give me encouragement!*

Elk did not recognize Read and Pasmore at first, not till Souza nudged him and signalled that he go up and say hello. Both gentlemen politely shook Alkazi's hand and carried on examining the works in silence. By

---

* The Leicester Galleries was one of the few galleries that entertained showing Asian art. Asian artists were allotted a week or two at a time. This was before Victor Musgrave ran Gallery One in the 1950s, which was the first gallery to give F.N. Souza a show and launch him to recognition.

6 p.m., there was barely space to move, at which point the gallery owner called for attention and briefly introduced Alkazi and Nissim, the curator. Nissim read out a prepared note on the show. He, too, was visibly shaken at being in the midst of an illustrious art crowd. All Alkazi remembered was the reappearance of Read and Pasmore into his line of vision and them pumping his hand vigorously in approval. 'Very interesting, I shall send people to see the show,' said Pasmore with an affable grin. Their departure was a signal that the show was an unbridled success and it was now time to celebrate! In a complete daze, Elk was dragged off to the nearest pub by the six other 'dwarfs', where he was initiated into the world of spirits!

Sharing his memories of that day with me, my father said,

> And that is why, almost something like forty or fifty years later, I tried to repay the kindness of Victor Pasmore, who's now become one of the most eminent persons in the field of art in England, living in Malta in his eighties... I gave him an exhibition over here in New York... (at CICA) It was really a kind of silent tribute to him!

* * *

Sitting in the midst of chaos, with all the stuff he had collected over the last couple of years scattered around him, Elk was in the throes of packing. Not having the slightest idea how he was going to manage without money for his rent or, for that matter, his passage back to India, he had been utterly taken aback by the arrival of a letter in the morning. Reading it now for the third time just to be sure he had understood its contents correctly, Elk was transfixed. It was from H.M. Tennent, one of the largest and most well-reputed impresario agencies in London that had been around for more than a century, managing the careers of top-notch actors on the professional stage. Now, unbelievable as it sounded, H.M. Tennent were offering to put him on their roster of actors and represent him as his agents if he agreed. They mentioned that they had been impressed with his histrionic abilities in several of the final-year productions he had appeared in at RADA, including the title role in *Richard III*.[*]

---

[*] 'At that time, every student who came to the Royal Academy immediately went to Cecil Beaton, who was a great photographer of theatrical personalities. These people, when they

Speechless, he finally put down the letter! My God, this was what his fellow students dreamed about—being taken on by a reputable agent who was virtually capable of making their careers. What did this mean? He should be overjoyed! Should he stay back in England and become a professional actor? He had never thought of his future in any place apart from India, but suddenly this seemed like a distinct possibility—especially in the light of returning to a country that could not offer him a real job in the profession for which he had actually equipped himself.

The offer threw him into a complete quandary. His artist friends, Raza, Souza and Akbar, seemed to be genuinely toying with the idea of staying abroad, for the very reason that the modern art they practised had no monetary value in their own country. All of them wanted to subsist on their art, which they agreed was going to be extremely difficult in India. Maybe he should be like them, pragmatic and hard-boiled . . . and stay back.

Hoping to clear his mind, Alkazi put on his overcoat, scarf, gloves and cap and, slamming the door behind him, decided to take a walk. It was snowing lightly. In order to still his racing thoughts, he tried to paraphrase for himself what the entire experience in England had actually taught him, and secondly, to what end?

Alkazi had experienced life in a country that was rebuilding itself from scratch after being crippled by two world wars. The pride, commitment, sheer hard work and often the ploughing in of personal resources towards rebuilding their nation and civil society greatly inspired Alkazi. He had been witness to a new institution, the ICA, established on exciting ideas that sought to educate the public in the arts and set an example for larger national bodies to emulate. Likewise, in the field of theatre, stalwarts like Laurence Olivier and John Gielgud had imported fresh ideas for training

---

came to the school in the very first week, wanted themselves to be shot as actors, actresses, etc., and have various views of themselves taken . . . the left and the right profiles, etc. I couldn't afford any of that. I was never inclined that way . . . Thus, people saw you in the performances that you had done on stage. Agents would come to watch to see the new talents that are coming up. Theatrical agents were coming to these plays and I found that people were approaching me. I never ever had a theatrical agent; it had never occurred to me. They asked whether I would like to be their mustang when I left the Royal Academy! I never gave them a direct reply because I had no idea what I was going to do, except that I was very nostalgic for India and I wanted to go back to India.'—E. Alkazi in an interview with Samik Bandyopadhyay, Natya Shodh Sansthan, Kolkata, 15 March 1988.

and performance. At Dartington Hall, the Elmhirsts, in a spirit of great generosity, converted their massive family estate into a space where international artists from multiple streams could live, work and experiment together in laboratory-like situations. Interactions of this nature became the basis for an extraordinary multi-arts educational programme, where exciting aesthetic encounters between world cultures became possible, paving the way for some remarkable international fusions.

After her liberation in 1947, India too was poised for change. This was the moment that held energy, promise and potential. It was this possibility that propelled Alkazi to return. There was a land waiting to be rebuilt and there was a country that believed in high ideals—a Nehruvian India that was already talking about an 'Indian modernity'. It was the challenge of creating an 'Indian modernity' that beckoned Alkazi—his chance to make a difference, his chance to be modern, his chance to be on par with other citizens of the world...

Returning to his basement flat, he penned a short letter to Lord Elmhirst.[7]

> 6 October 1950
> Dear Mr Elmhirst,
>
> After having enjoyed your hospitality during the summer, it may seem ungracious of me to approach you again for assistance. But I am afraid I have no one else to turn to.
> I hoped through the sale of a few pictures at my exhibition to be able to pay my passage back to India. Unfortunately, I didn't manage to sell even one. I have half my fare by boat; I need the other half that amounts to 24 pounds.
> Could you please assist me?
>
> With best wishes to Mrs Elmhirst,
> I remain,
> Yours sincerely,
> E. Alkazi

A few days later, Leonard Elmhirst responded:

9 October 1950
Dear Mr Alkazi,

I am sorry you were unable to sell your pictures. I was very interested to see them.
I enclose the sum you need towards your return journey.
Both my wife and I wish you the best of luck on your return to Bombay.

Yours sincerely,
Leonard K. Elmhirst

20 October 1950
Dear Mr and Mrs Elmhirst,
I wish to thank you for your kind assistance.
I hope I prove worthy of it.
With best wishes,
Yours sincerely,
E. Alkazi[8]

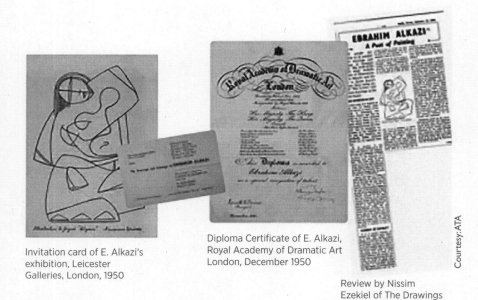

Invitation card of E. Alkazi's exhibition, Leicester Galleries, London, 1950

Diploma Certificate of E. Alkazi, Royal Academy of Dramatic Art London, December 1950

Review by Nissim Ezekiel of The Drawings & Paintings of E. Alkazi, Leicester Galleries, London, 1950

Courtesy: ATA

Alkazi and Roshen with friends, England, 1948

PART THREE

Theatre Group Bombay, 1951–1954

Miss Julie by August Strindberg, dir. E. Alkazi, Nargis Cowasji as Miss Julie, Theatre Group, Bombay, 1951

CHAPTER 17
'SOCIETY NEEDS BUILDERS—NOT ONLY OF BRIDGES AND BUILDINGS, BUT OF IDEAS AND INSTITUTIONS'
1951

'And now to real theatre. As a matter of fact, the first real theatre we have had the pleasure to watch in Bombay: The Theatre Group's performance of *Lady Julie* by Strindberg and Chekhov's *The Proposal*. Mr E. Alkazi has matured his own natural talent for the theatre in his studies and experiences abroad. In spite of his young age, he is an actor of deep power and a director whose creative hand is felt in every detail of the production and in every nuance in the acting of his cast. He has my fullest admiration for getting so much fine acting out of an amateur cast, especially for his direction of Nargis Cowasjee as Lady Julie, which is by all standards a difficult part to play because it is not typified and leads the actress from the frivolous and irresponsible mood of a spoiled and possessive maiden to the sudden awareness of a cold and cruelly revolting tragedy, which has broken in on her out of the blue of a romantic and confusing night.

'Does the stark realism of Strindberg need the dream-like atmosphere that Alkazi tried to evoke with his near-abstract decorations, which in themselves were admirable. I could imagine that the effect of Euripedean tragedy would even be stronger if developed in front of the banalest and most ludicrous of middle-class furnishings with all the details of realistic extremism. His decor was perfect for the farcical production of Chekhov's *The Proposal*, which was extremely happy in its conception, its costume and make-up and in the slap-dash speed of its performance. I, for one, am waiting with impatience for the Theatre Group's next production.'[1]

Such praise! Coming from Rudolf von Leyden,[*] a seasoned art critic and well-regarded connoisseur of the arts, was a tremendous boost to Alkazi's reputation. Leyden, though not a drama critic per se, was sufficiently familiar with European theatre to immediately recognize the significance of Alkazi's achievements for the theatre scene in Bombay.

Produced barely a few months after his return, it was no coincidence that Alkazi had selected two sharply contrasting scripts in order to showcase his range of abilities as a director. *The Proposal* was an entertaining comedy that Alkazi conceived on a flamboyant scale, with stylized sets painted by Alkazi himself along with exaggerated, carnivalesque costumes and makeup designed by Roshen.

Another reason for selecting *The Proposal* was its large cast, which helped rekindle a sense of purpose and team spirit in the Theatre Group, whose young members had felt somewhat neglected by Elk's absence for close to three years. One of the few surviving photographs of the production shows Alyque Padamsee, Bee Jefferies, Cedric Santos, Deryck Jefferies, Bomi Kapadia, Chotu Padamsee, Bapsy Sabawalla, and Minoo Chhoi among the cast, most of whom were later to become leading lights in the Theatre Group.

Alkazi's choice of *Lady Julie*, on the other hand, was chiefly for its bold, sexual theme, giving it a contemporaneous edginess that admittedly shocked audiences. With a tight cast of three, Alkazi allowed himself time to chisel stellar performances.[†]

Rather pleased with Leyden's response, Elk switched off the radio and returned to his typewriter to hammer out his talk to Theatre Group members at their first annual general body meeting since his return. He was struggling to find the right words to formulate an actor training programme for TG members, one that went beyond what he had learned at RADA. Besides the regular voice, speech, and movement classes, he

---

[*] Rudolf von Leyden, of Jewish descent, had fled the Nazis and moved to Bombay from Germany in 1933. A man of leftist views, he was hired by *The Illustrated Weekly* as a cartoonist and later engaged as the art critic of the *Times of India*. Contributing and collecting Indian artworks from various periods, organizing exhibitions, and actively promoting young contemporary artists, Leyden was a contributing editor to the leading art review magazine *MARG* from 1946 and served as an adviser for the acquisitions and art commissions of the Tata Institute of Fundamental Research, which owned one of the most important collections of post-independence Indian art.

[†] Nargis Cowasji as Miss Julie, Pheroza Cooper as Kristin and Elk as Jean.

wanted actors to gain a certain *theoretical background* as well. Not quite sure how this could be done, Alkazi got up and began pacing the room, organizing his thoughts.

Today, he was alone at his father's office at the Gobhai Karanjia Building. He had assured his father that on his return from England, he would dutifully attend 'office' for two hours every day, from 11 a.m. to 1 p.m. In return for this, he was assured a small monthly stipend, which, though insufficient for Roshen and his growing needs, was not to be scoffed at. Alkazi was assisted by his cousin, Ahmed Alkazi, who had been brought to Bombay from Saudi Arabia when the family shifted to Karachi. Ahmed managed the affairs of the firm along with Mr Alarakha, the manager, and Mehtaji, the accountant. As neither Ahmed, Mr Alarakha nor Mehtaji were well-versed in English, Ebrahim would translate notices, orders, licensing rules, etc., for them or draft responses to official letters in English. Often, there was not much to do, like today, which allowed Alkazi time to catch up with the backlog of his own theatre work. Sitting down

Miss Julie by August Strindberg, dir. E. Alkazi; Alkazi as Jean, Nargis Cowasji as Miss Julie, Theatre Group, Bombay, 1951

again, Alkazi closed his eyes and began to mentally formulate the salient points of his address.

It was quite uncanny how Ebrahim kept these two aspects of his life distinct. At the office and among Arab businessmen, he communicated only in Arabic, maintaining the etiquette and decorum expected of a young Arab. Here, he was careful never to mention his theatrical exploits, nor did he invite these Arab merchants to his art exhibitions or theatre performances. This was his secret, 'other' life.* Since he was unable to create a situation for himself in which both these identities could co-exist in an integrated manner, he learned to accept never being entirely at ease—neither in the Padamsee English-speaking theatre world he had entered nor in the isolated Arab world he had ostensibly left behind. However, what helped him in some strange way was that, as an actor, he had learned to live simultaneously in his own skin as well as the bodies of the fictional characters he was called on to impersonate—an ability that helped him cope, I believe, with the deep cultural schisms that lay latent within himself.

Alkazi removed the typed sheet from his ancient Olivetti typewriter, crumpled it into a ball and flung it into the dustbin. He had finally found the words to articulate his ideas for the first six-month acting course.

'Even though an actor may have natural talent, he still requires proper training. This means he should have complete technical control and mastery over his physical apparatus, voice, speech, body . . .'

Alkazi proceeded to spell out that the course would include a daily regimen of classes in Kathakali, mime, yoga and speech before rehearsals began. Productions to be undertaken during the course were to be drawn from the history of world drama and would include genres such as comedy, tragedy, farce, satire, etc. He went on to add how the practical aspect would be supplemented by lectures on the history of theatre as well as on literature and art of the period in order to understand the relationship between the arts and life.

Finally, a holistic programme seemed to be taking shape! But there were many issues about which Alkazi remained apprehensive. First, whether he would be successful in transforming the TG members into trained professionals. He realized that this would require him to refashion the very

---

* However, his sisters Fatima and Noorie, and their husbands and children, were familiar with Alkazi's activities in the art world.

mindset of TG members from thinking of themselves as members of a 'dramatics club' into submitting to the rigours of being trained professionally.

It was true that during rehearsals, Alkazi had already taken the opportunity to introduce them to the idea of *training* not only in acting but in all the theatre arts. But these words were uttered in a space where Elk, as director, was in control of the situation. However, the TG actors were also *members* of the Theatre Group, a group that had been set up on democratic lines, and as members of a collective, they all had a say in policy matters. Decisions were voted on through a show of hands and executive posts were held by members who were elected. Alkazi, as the artistic director of the TG, made plans and proposals for the year's activities that required the sanction of the executive committee.

Aware that his ideas differed from the basic premise on which TG had been founded, Alkazi was nonetheless determined to alter Bobby's ideas, if necessary, and give the theatre a mission he strongly believed in—as a meaningful, socially engaged activity.

> The Theatre Group has no illusions about the difficulty of the work that lies ahead of it. Since its policy is a long-term policy, it realizes that the advantages of the kind of training it is giving its members will not be fully understood or appreciated until several years have passed.[2]

As anticipated, there was resistance by the members to being trained. Another contentious issue was Alkazi's choice of plays. Some members objected to *Miss Julie* being too 'serious',[3] bordering on 'controversial' and 'scandalous'. Alkazi vehemently defended his choice, saying, 'such plays force the audience to reexamine their own moribund ideas, especially regarding sexuality and the modern woman'.

In fact, *Miss Julie* anticipated a theme that Alkazi was to explore repeatedly in the years to come in productions of Ibsen's *Ghosts*, Sophocles' *Oedipus Rex*, Strindberg's *The Father*, Lorca's *The House of Bernada Alba* and *Yerma*, Anouilh's *Eurydice* and Euripides' *Medea*. Through such texts, Alkazi laid bare the complex male–female relationship in modern society and its ambivalences and contradictions. The female protagonists were defined by their rebelliousness and unreserved sexual desires. Refusing to abide by constraining patriarchal values, the women in Alkazi's productions released raw, combustible sexual energy and were shown to be overtaken by what were referred to as bestial, irrational primitive urges, uncontrollable and overwhelming. As a result, the relationship between the sexes was strained and often agonizingly aggressive. As can be imagined, Alkazi's productions often disturbed the genteel propriety and decorum that prevailed in Bombay's middle-class, drawing room culture, which TG members were quick to point out. 'Why not do comedies? Something light and frothy!' they opined. To which Alkazi shot back, '... The problem cannot be solved by producing more comedies ... fundamentally it is a question of whether the Group can be creative, original, experimental and relevant ... For to be these things is to be truly serious ...'[4]

It was clear that many in the Theatre Group did not agree with Alkazi's approach, which he referred to many years later:

> I felt we were being pulled in different directions. On the one hand, I was interested in providing plays that gave you the experience ... the opening up of your sensibilities and of your mind through the great classics ... and through the modern experimental work that was being done in the theatre. Because I felt that was really the authentic tradition of theatre, from Greeks right down to people like Samuel Beckett. We were not going to do *Dial M for Murder* or *Witness for the Prosecution* and so on.[5]

Finding that not much had changed in the English boxwallah theatre scene of Bombay since he had left in 1948, Alkazi began to keep abreast of changes on the Marathi and Gujarati stages and was happy to see original writing in Marathi in a new format—the one-act play. Youngsters were eagerly responding to the annual inter-collegiate one-act theatre competitions sponsored by the Bharatiya Vidya Bhavan and the Mumbai Marathi Sahitya Sangh. These were fledgling attempts that, in time, would be regarded as the beginnings of a 'fringe', 'parallel' or 'experimental theatre movement in Bombay. Soon, it was youngsters working in the vernaculars, rather than those from English-language theatre groups, who showed a keen interest in receiving the kind of modern theatre training that Alkazi was beginning to impart.

Prithvi Theatre, meanwhile, seemed to have served its main mission by 1950 with *Kalakar* (artist), which spoke about the tenuous existence of the artist in today's materialistic world. Clearly autobiographical, the play reflected Prithviraj Kapoor's strained financial conditions, as he had ploughed most of his earnings from cinema into his theatre work.

In his 1948 letter to Nissim from the ship, a barely twenty-two-year-old Alkazi had foreseen that though Hindi/Hindustani groups had managed to attract a fair amount of following:

> ... their influence cannot last very long, a few years perhaps, but not much longer, because their very approach to the theatre is false. And they are working in certain shallow and transient forms, and they hardly have any people with any vision or intellectual depth... With all our deficiencies, we should be capable of setting very high standards of theatre even for the vernacular stage, for that is what we must aim at and very seriously...
>
> Who among us has even thought of making a study of Hindi? It is not merely Nissim, that we have done no such thing, but there is the majority of us, to our Mary Sethnas or our Nargis Cowasjis or our Jefferies or our Freida Arnold, there is hardly an awareness of its eventuality...

Alkazi went on to plead with Nissim to hold a meeting with TG members and convince them of the absolutely crucial need to move into Hindi, as no theatre could grow without being rooted in the language of the country.

Recollecting his 1948 thoughts, Alkazi felt it was important to raise this language issue in his address to TG members. Continuing to type, he wrote:

> The Group regards the next five years as a period of slow and carefully regulated transition from English to the vernacular. For it realizes that if the theatre movement in India is to be of any significance it must be in the language of the people. This can be accomplished by the setting up of a Hindi wing of the Theatre Group. Till then the Theatre Group will continue to produce the best European plays for the next five years or so, and hopefully

bring to the Indian theatre, all the riches of thought and experience of the West.[6]

By selecting plays from the western canon for some time, Alkazi believed that theatre practitioners as well as audiences could learn much from the thousands of years-long Western theatre tradition and be inspired to arrive at a modern, contemporary theatrical idiom for India. One of the roles he saw himself playing was as a bridge-builder between two worlds—the English and Hindi language theatres, as well as between Indian and world theatre.

Alkazi's ideas had certainly matured since he and Bobby had discussed Indian aesthetics during the rehearsals of Tagore's *Chitra*, which was to have been the next TG venture before Bobby's untimely demise. *Chitra* was the first Indian text that Bobby had engaged with. It was a dance drama and Bobby had brought in a Kathakali guru to train the cast. For him, this production was undoubtedly an experiment in narrowing the chasm that divided Indian and western aesthetics moving towards a new form of theatrical expression that relied on physical body language (dance) and mimetic skills, allowing the poetry to affect the audience at a level of sound, rhythm and word imagery. It was clear that Bobby was moving towards discovering a new grammar and vocabulary that was Indian in its sensibility.

People in the Theatre Group might have forgotten about Bobby's ideas but not Alkazi. He was acutely aware that the Theatre Group was a misfit. It was neither an amateur group providing light entertainment to an English-speaking audience or a vernacular experimental group, nor was it a leftist activist unit. It was clear to Alkazi that TG needed to forge an identity and purpose for itself.

No Exit, postcard information, Theatre Group, 1953

> Society needs artists and artists need an audience. Society needs builders of all kinds, not only of bridges and buildings but of ideas and institutions. A city like Bombay desperately needs cultural organizations which will serve it faithfully without ulterior motives of personal gain. It needs, for instance, not only a few people to produce plays occasionally, but a properly organized theatre institution, which will create a tradition of work...[7]

Alkazi firmly believed that as TG members were well-off, well educated in English and comfortably employed, they were in the right position to make sacrifices and bring about change. Perhaps Alkazi believed that the spirit with which many wealthy, educated Indians had served the freedom movement and supported Gandhi would prevail among the privileged, post-Independence middle classes towards building up a new culture for India.

What he may not have taken into account was that 'the times were a-changing' and that kind of selfless support was not always possible. Alkazi was, in fact, surrounded by a new breed of young 'Brown Sahibs' in post-Independence India, a class of people who had replaced the British by becoming an English-speaking elite themselves. Alkazi's suggestions to convert TG into a *Hindi*-language group must have set the alarm bells ringing! Was Alkazi trying to fight for Hindi from *within* the bastion of the Padamsee stronghold? The Padamsees from Dongri, whom Kulsumbai had perforce relocated to Colaba Causeway! The Padamsee children who were sent to Miss Murphy's private boarding school and whose mother, Kulsumbai, took all her children to study in England so that Bobby could go to Oxford! Would this Anglicized family now allow themselves to be turned into 'vernacs'? Alkazi was totally unaware that this move would divest them of their one trump card, the one thing that made them feel *equal* to the British—their knowledge and proficiency in speaking the Queen's English without an Indian accent!

For the next few years, Alkazi's battle to bring Hindi theatre into the Theatre Group met with all kinds of resistance, sometimes taking the shape of a class war and, at others, a war of egos.

CHAPTER 18
'LIFE QUICKENS INTO ART AND IN TURN ENRICHES LIFE'[1]
1953

So far, Alkazi had played understudy, but with growing confidence, he began to cast himself as the chief protagonist in the drama of his own life. The Prologue, during which he had accumulated *content*, *substance* and *knowledge*, was done. His return from England heralded Act 1, where he made an entry from the wings onto the world's stage, which at the moment comprised the city of Bombay. With an uncanny ability to envisage and fashion his future, he put his overall plan into action, which was to showcase his work appropriately as well as project a distinct *persona* and *version* of himself that would define him in the eyes of the world—who he was, what he was capable of and the new theatre movement he was about to launch. Alkazi spent as much time on work as he did on developing a nuanced, socially powerful and dynamic public personality—an ability he would refine through years of study and practice in impersonating characters on stage. When presenting himself in public, one often had the impression that he was playing a part, with tone, volume, clarity, emphasis in his speech and gesture, and in the stance of his body, as if put together with rehearsed accuracy for the desired response.

'Halt!'

A voice rang out from the darkness, and in a moment, Alkazi appeared from within its velvety folds with both arms raised. Making his way to the magic circle of light, he took his place centre stage, the actors scattering to make space for him.

'There's only a week until the performance, my dear friends! But even at this late stage, I want to reiterate and I will repeat to you, what this play is *about*! What it is *essentially* about! Beeeeeecause what we have seen here today is un-ac-cep-table! UNACCEPTABLE!' he roared. Bringing both his arms down sharply with a thwack to his sides, Alkazi took a step forward and kicked one of the crates lying around to emphasize his point. It fell just short of Pheroza Cooper's feet. The young actress winced and stepped back to avoid becoming its target. Silence. Alkazi immediately sprung to her side and put his arm around her shoulders, 'I hope you're not hurt, lovoo.'

She demurred.

M.F. Husain, Elk's artist friend who had been sitting next to him during the rehearsal, noiselessly crossed his long legs, glancing towards Roshen, who sat behind him. Feeling uncomfortable, Husain was not quite sure whether or not to make himself scarce. Barefoot, his long toes curled in and out.

'What we have just witnessed is a performance of tired, exhausted, worn-out OLD WOMEN! Uninspired! Lacking in thrust and energy!'

Walking to the back of the hall through a series of pillars, Alkazi turned back with a dramatic flourish to face the actors.

Now in full throttle, his performance was approaching its crescendo.

> *Murder in the Cathedral* is about M A R T Y R D O M! The play is a demonstration of the act of MARTYRDOM, and the author has to take it for granted that the audience, in order to understand the full significance of the play, is *aware* of the pattern of religious belief within which it is *possible* to contemplate such an act. *Murder in The Cathedral* presents Thomas Becket as a MARTYR... in will and in deed, with mind and heart purified, in order to be made an *instrument* of the divine will.[2]

The actors had never heard a person talk with such intensity. Eyes gleaming, Alkazi's passion energized them and made them feel like they could achieve what he was asking of them. Now his sharp eyes panned in an unblinking stare from one face to the next: Mehlli Gobhai, Manohar Pitale, George John and finally, coming to rest on Minoo Chhoi, who was playing Thomas Becket.

> Thomas is a passionate and fiery character who cannot be played apologetically. His part *sizzles* with the passion and poetry

of his life. A saint of the type of Thomas is one who *burns* with fervour and is *consumed* by an idea. Becket must be shown to be vividly *alive*. He does not walk through the play in a religious trance, pontificating! His eyes, hands and his entire body are not dead in a stupor; they are all magnificently alive! Thomas therefore has to be played on a huge scale—a titan, a giant among giants, not an awkward and diffident country priest!

On his return from England, Elk had rapidly produced four plays* for the first six-month theatre course, but it was with *Murder in the Cathedral* that he felt he had found the right vehicle to come to terms with unresolved issues, as well as come into his own as a director.

If one were to ask why he had chosen to direct such a difficult play—a verse play at that, at this early juncture in his career—or why he had chosen a Christian theme,† one would perhaps be led back to Bobby Padamsee.

For Alkazi, Bobby's suicide remained an enigma that he was still coming to terms with. He could not accept that Bobby was weak and that he had given up on life as he was unable to cope with society's adverse response to his sexual preferences.

Alkazi had been brought up in the Muslim faith, where taking one's life was considered sin—only God could take a life. But Bobby, though Muslim by birth, had not been brought up to understand the tenets of Islam the way Ebrahim had. Kulsumbai, in wanting her children to be well-educated, had neglected their schooling in the Muslim faith. Why? Did she feel it was inferior to Christianity—the faith of educated Britishers? Whatever her reasons, Bobby and his siblings had been raised in a religious vacuum that was filled by a vague, indefinable belief in Christianity, the faith of their teachers, Miss Murphy and Miss Delaney. The Irish spinsters found no resistance from Kulsumbai in bringing up the Padamsee children

---

* Besides *The Proposal* and *Miss Julie*, he produced Jean-Paul Sartre's *Crime Passionnel* and Christopher Fry's *A Phoenix Too Frequent*.

† This was the second time Alkazi worked on a Christian theme, the first instance being the suite of artworks exhibited in London. Before leaving Bombay for Delhi, he did a pageant play for a church in Bandra, *The Prince of Peace* (see *Icons* with an essay on Alkazi by Gerson da Cuhna). The theme of Christ as a crucified martyr was explored by Alkazi again in the 1960s in his charcoal and ink works of that period, exhibited at the Shridharani Gallery in New Delhi.

with Bible stories and Christian hymns. So, when a brilliant young lad like Bobby searched for some kind of mooring, it was Christianity, a faith he was somewhat familiar with, that he reached back to, perhaps by default.

Bobby's leanings towards a Christian cultural and philosophical ethos may have also arisen from the fact that the West had for centuries been inspired by Christianity to produce great religious art, literature and drama. Many of Bobby's poems were soaked in Christian thought, evoking Christian imagery. His longest and most dense and dark poem was, in fact, called *Golgotha*.*

Perhaps then, in selecting *Murder in the Cathedral*, Alkazi felt he could discover some kind of meaning in Bobby's suicide, for the play dealt with Thomas Becket's willingness to give up his life and become a martyr. As Alkazi had mentioned to his actors, 'martyrdom had to be understood within the tenets of the Christian faith, where martyrdom is considered an exalted state of being.' Was it this kind of exaltation that Bobby had aspired for?

Given Bobby's flamboyant personality and the fact that he was a young man given to heroic gestures, it was a distinct possibility that Bobby had *willingly* given up his life. He had often spoken of 'embracing Death' as one would 'a lover'! So it could be that it was not because of guilt or remorse (about being homosexual), but as a step towards attaining a heightened state of being, by overcoming the final barrier of the fear of death, that Bobby felt he would be resurrected, making his last gesture a glorified act.

It was not just while he was living but even more so in his death that Bobby assumed an elevated, larger-than-life stature, one that Alkazi felt he could not possibly compare with. 'I was terrified when Bobby's mantle fell on my shoulders.'[3] This was probably exacerbated when every TG member, without exception, compared him to Bobby.

Even Rosh compared him to her brother.[4] Elk loved Rosh dearly, but her brother had loved her more. Bobby had valued Roshen's opinions; he had put her on a pedestal. As a result, Alkazi was competing against a chimera, a memory of Sultan Padamsee, and trying desperately to prove—to his wife and to his friends—that he was equal to, if not better, than the great Sultan Padamsee. Bobby's invisible presence, like Hamlet's father's ghost, initially paralysed Alkazi. Finally, in grappling with this play, Alkazi

---

* The place where Christ was crucified. Also referred to as the Mound of the Skull.

was, in some senses, rationalizing the meaning of Bobby's life and death for himself.

* * *

Members of the Theatre Group who participated in the first course[*] were somewhat taken aback at being back 'in class' and studying the 'theory of drama'. At the same time, they found the experience novel and 'fun'. At the time their production of *Crime Passionnel* was invited by Sir Hirjee Jehangir[†] (the owner of the Jehangir Art Gallery) to be staged in Poona. Alyque Padamsee, who played one of the gunmen in the play, reminisced about how the entire group[‡] were Sir Hirjee's personal guests at his beautiful home and were delighted to be transported into a world of aristocratic luxury:

> ... it was a beautiful place—like a castle with a tower—very British Raj. And we stayed there ... it was wonderful because Sir Hirjee had this long table, just like you see in the movies, about fifty feet long, with chairs and butlers in livery, serving you! And that was the first time when I heard, 'Sir, what would you like to drink?' So I said, 'What have you got?' He said, 'Sir, we have lemonade, we have raspberry, we have Vimto ...' and so on—soft drinks. At every meal, we were served soft drinks first, which was unheard of! Anyway there we were at sit-down meals ... course after course being served! It was all very strange for me. We were used to our Indian style, sitting at the horseshoe table at home—with all the food dumped on the table ... but this was a new experience.

As the course came to a close, Alkazi said it had been a mere 'introduction' and suggested that the same actors continue their training

---

[*] Pheroza Cooper, Alyque Padamsee, Sylvester da Cuhna, Bomi Kapadia and Minoo Chhoi.

[†] Sir Cowasji Jehangir's younger son, Sir Hirjee Jehangir, served as chairman of the Jehangir Art Gallery for forty years. Of a scholarly bent of mind, Sir Hirjee devoted his time to studying history, literature and art and doing social work. He was a dedicated patron of modern art and encouraged several artists, from K.H. Ara to Jehangir Sabavala. Collecting the paintings of promising young Indian artists became his passion.

[‡] Alyque Padamsee, Hamid Sayani, Pheroza Cooper, Roshan Kalapesi and her sister, Cedric Santos, Sylvester da Cuhna and, of course, Elk and Rosh.

into a second course that would be for the duration of a full year! The TG members felt Elk was carrying things too far. Since his return, they had been moving from one production to the next at breakneck speed, with poetry readings every Thursday and play readings or talks every Saturday evening, leaving little time for much else.

For most TG members, this kind of work, commitment and time, which Alkazi felt was required of them, was not what they had signed up for. Joining TG during their college days, with Bobby at the helm, had been quite a different story. Now they were older and had jobs and families. They had certainly not anticipated that they would be called upon to dedicate themselves to a nation-building project. As Alyque Padamsee recalled:

> Bobby was full of fun and what he loved was that after rehearsals, there was always a party. Always. We would be drinking tea and having chips, laughing and joking and talking. No one wanted to leave after the rehearsals. There was this wonderful spirit that made me feel that I not only work in the theatre, but I play in the theatre! It's a lovely feeling, it's an all-encompassing feeling that 'this is my life'.
>
> But Elk was very strict at rehearsals—you could not laugh! Sylvie and I used to treat rehearsals as fun. For us you did your part and then you cracked jokes... like that... but Elk was very serious.[5]

Elk's 'seriousness' was nonetheless making an impact on audiences. Poetry readings and talks were not limited to members but were open to the general public as well, so that they too could sensitize themselves to modernity in contemporary art forms in a holistic manner. Attendance at these activities was gratis. These kinds of supplementary activities gave the TG a certain prestige among the affluent and influential elite of the city, who became both patrons and audience for Alkazi's multifaceted events.

Such activities required venues, and soon Alkazi co-opted the use of the terraces at Kulsum Terrace and Chotu Terrace, as well as the large, spacious drawing room of Deryck and Bee Jefferies at Meher Mansion opposite the Cooperage Maidan, for play readings, while the terrace of Rehmat Manzil at Churchgate, where TG member Ashraf Jairazbhoy lived, was often used for Theatre Group meetings.* In a way, using homes added a certain personalized touch that allowed Alkazi and the Group to get to know their audience and build a community.† However, even at this early stage, Alkazi realized that in order to be taken seriously, the Theatre Group must have its own premises, so he was constantly on the lookout for viable options, even before he returned from England.‡

Although Bobby's rehearsals had always taken place in the large Kulsum Terrace drawing room, Kulsumbai did not readily extend the same generosity to her son-in-law! Because of her reservations, both Alkazi's productions of *Hamlet* and *Richard III* had been rehearsed in our tiny third-floor flat before my parents' departure for England, with our furniture parked in the public passage outside our front door. Now rehearsals of the acting courses too were threatening to explode into our flat, sending my father out on a desperate search for a rehearsal space.

A sudden stroke of luck! Alkazi discovered a large hall in the Fort–Kala Ghoda area, which was occupied by the Institute of Foreign Languages (IFL). It had been established by Charles Petras,[6] an artist who, like the better-known trio of émigrés, Rudolf von Leyden, Walter Langhammer and Oskar Schlesinger, had escaped from Nazi Germany, settling in Bombay. At the outbreak of World War II, Petras had been interned as an enemy alien at a camp in Dehradun.§ On his release, he became the manager for Hilde Holger, an émigré dancer,¶ while simultaneously establishing the

---

* Working on these open-air terraces appealed to Alkazi because he felt they were spaces that could be used for a major part of the year, leading him to build an actual theatre, Meghdoot Theatre, on his own terrace at Vithal Court in 1960. This was followed by another open-air Meghdoot Theatre on the lawns of Rabindra Bhavan, New Delhi, when he became the director of NSD.

† In fact, Alkazi remembered how Roland Penrose and Herbert Read had thrown open their own homes for salons and discussions in the early years of the ICA when they suffered a lack of funds.

‡ 'Elk is in want of accommodation for the Theatre Group ... I spoke to him about your house in Kalyan ... Please go and meet Mrs Alkazi regarding this matter.'— Souza in one of his letters from England to Raza, 17 February 1950, in Ashok Vajpeyi, ed., *Geysers: Letters between Sayed Haider Raza and His Artist-Friends*, Vadehra Art Gallery, 2013.

§ Petras was interned along with other Germans, Austrians and Italians who were thought to be Nazi sympathizers by the British Government. This was the same camp where the cinematographer Josef Wirsching and his family, of Bombay Talkies fame, were interned as well.

¶ Hilde Hoger was a Jewish expressionist dancer from Vienna who fled Germany in 1939. Charles Petras helped her flee to Bombay. In 1940, she married Parsi homeopath Dr Boman Behram. In 1941, Holger founded a new school of dance in Bombay. Among her collaborators were Indian dancers Rukmini Devi Arundale, Ram Gopal and Uday Shankar.

IFL, which became well-known as a meeting place and mediation centre. Known to the Progressive artists, Petras supported Syed Haidar Raza with his first solo show at the IFL in 1950. In many ways, Petras was one of those 'war émigrés' who participated in and supported the development of modernity in Indian art.

Alkazi approached the IFL for use of the space. Petras graciously agreed to let the TG have it on weekends. A space in the centre of Bombay's art district, located practically opposite Jehangir Art Gallery, next to Chetna and the Bombay Art Society—there could not have been a more appropriate venue for the kind of work Alkazi was doing as the IFL was frequented by an international crowd as well as students, all of whom gradually became a committed audience for Theatre Group productions.

What excited Alkazi about the IFL space was that it did not have a regular proscenium stage but was simply a large empty room that could be used in a flexible manner. He could creatively rearrange performance and audience areas for each production.

In Ibsen's *Ghosts*, for example, the action took place in the centre of the space, arena style, with the audience encircling the actors. It required the director to conceive of the production 'in the round' from multiple viewpoints, like a cubistic sculpture.

Murder in the Cathedral, the production currently in rehearsal, was conceived frontally, with the audience facing the action unidirectionally. Alkazi arranged the seating so that a wide central aisle divided the audience into equal segments, resembling the seating arrangement of the congregation in a church. By allowing entries and exits of characters to take place through the aisle and by placing a large painted crucifix directly in line with it in the depth of the stage, Alkazi created a sense of the audience being seated in church.

* * *

The day's rehearsal for *Murder in the Cathedral* has concluded, and Elk and Husain are deep in conversation. Elk leans back in his chair, legs extended, his hands behind his head, holding forth. Husain nods from time to time; his eyes survey the height and width of the hall, absorbing the space.

'Husain Saab, this production is on a vast scale; it is truly a directorial challenge for me. This is a fairly abstract verse play, something I have never attempted before. As a director, my interest has now shifted to *form*. It is the *form* rather than the *content* that I'm struggling with.

'This challenges the actors as well, because now I'm not asking them to delineate individual characters; there are no *star* roles in this kind of play for anyone. But I'm asking the actors to work as groups, jointly, as a chorus. This is entirely a choral play, with characters conceived of as different choral groups—there is a chorus of women, a group of priests and a group of knights, all of which call for conceiving of them as *ensembles*, as representatives of ideas.

'Visually, I have treated them as blocks or groups. As you saw in the rehearsal, their movements have been choreographed, as one would for a group dance, but they do not always replicate one another's movements. Their voices, too, have been composed with tonality in mind, more like a musical score. In keeping with the modernist abstract style I am trying to achieve, music is not melody or mood, but a series of abstract sounds that accompany the articulation of the chanted text.

Murder in the Cathedral by T.S Eliot, dir. E. Alkazi, Minoo Chhoi as Thomas Becket, Theatre Group, Bombay, 1953

'My attempt is also to integrate many mediums together—painting, live music, choreography and a new sense of lighting that sculpts the actor in space. I believe all these art forms come together in the art of the theatre!

'This way of conceptualizing is unprecedented for me and therefore an artistic challenge! It is a risk to have no narrative storyline. The play is just the exposition and expansion of an idea. This is a play of only one action, a murder—the rest of it is ruminations around death.'

Husain stood up and walked into the depths of the stage area. Elk stopped talking.

'No need to stop. Please continue; I'm listening.'

Alkazi carried on: 'You see, Husain Saab, the basic structure of this modern verse play corresponds to the *ritual* structure of ancient Greek tragedy! What I want to do in this production is to foreground this *ritual* aspect, mainly visually, in the sets, props, costumes and, of course, choreography.'

Husain suddenly got down on all fours, placed his sketchbook on the floor, and began sketching.

'An idea I had was, Husain Saab, to introduce a half mask for the chorus of women.'

Husain looked up, interested.

'Not like a conventional Greek mask. No, no, something that looks much more modern and yet is extremely basic and primitive. It would be wonderful if you could design it!'

'Hmm... *Dekhte hain*!' (We'll see!)

Husain returned to his sketching.

Roshen, though at some distance, was listening in. Holding up a generic tunic-like black gown, she said, 'I've taken the idea for the chorus women's costume from the Greek *chiton* and I'm planning to combine the gown with a headscarf that will completely cover the hair—that's a bit of a medieval touch, like a caul! This way, the uneven hairline will be hidden and the face will be framed more formally. The whole idea is to achieve a more stylized look, which will become more prominent, especially now if you're planning to add masks, Elk.

'For me, the play has an allegorical dramatic style and I want this to be rendered as one would an abstract painting. Use only the bare essentials of the appropriate line. Let's not forget the play is also like a stark, medieval morality play.'

'I don't know about all that, Elk, but come, take a look!'

Alkazi stood up and motioned to the actors and Rosh, who was helping them try on their costumes, to gather around Husain. Mrs Hodgson, Antoinette Dinez, Katy Umrigar, Usha Amin, Pheroza Cooper, Hilla Divecha and Minoo Chhoi eagerly came forward, peering down at Husain's sketches.

On one side of the page, Husain had adroitly sketched a tall, elongated figure of Christ, crucified, using very stark, basic outlines.

'I feel this crucified Christ figure should be approximately twelve to fifteen feet tall, the maximum we can fit in this hall. I will be painting it on a black canvas sheet, which we can suspend from the ceiling. It will serve as a backdrop, and these two pillars,' he pointed to them, 'we can cover them with similar canvas sheets painted with these figures of the Virgin Mary!'

Husain passed the sketchbook to Elk, who eagerly pored over Husain's handiwork. He noted how Husain had tried to get the height and scale of a church with the enormous figures of Christ and the two figures of Virgin Mary. Also that he had followed a pictorial style for the Christ and the Virgin Mary figures, inspired by the elongated figures found in medieval Gothic church windows. The manner in which he had delineated the drapery of the robes of the figures, using thick, dark outlines was reminiscent of the thick, black iron bands that firmly held the pieces of stained glass in the windows of churches in place. Other sketches included an idea for a half mask for the chorus women, which Elk could swear had the feel of African masks! Husain's blending of influences from medieval western art along with African primitive art, both arising from rituals, appealed tremendously to Elk. He found it totally unbelievable that Husain had understood his suggestions so effortlessly and had responded with such immediacy! Alkazi felt an instant rapport with his artist friend.

'Amazing! Just amazing,' Alkazi looked gratefully at Husain, who was putting away his sketching implements.

Walking out with Husain, Elk called out to Rosh to meet them across the street at Chetna, where Nissim would be waiting.

'I'm dead tired, darling! I'll see you at home later,' Roshen replied, adding that Pheroza would drop her home.

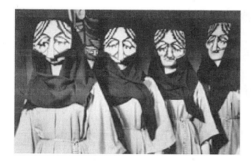

Murder in the Cathedral by T. S. Eliot, dir. E. Alkazi, set design by M.F Husain, Theatre Group, Bombay, 1953

'Rosh, I don't know how you do it,' moaned Pheroza, 'All I can say is that I'm totally pooped! I hope your dear husband is going to finally give us a break after these twelve shows of *Murder* are over! My parents complain every single day that they never see me any more!'

'I doubt it very much, love! Jai Hind College has been booked for the shows of *Antigone* already! There's no letting up in sight!'

The room was filled with universal moans as the actors folded their costumes and returned them to Rosh.

* * *

There was barely any traffic around Kala Ghoda as Husain and Alkazi crossed over to Chetna. Husain was barefoot. The streetlamps shed pools of light around them. Rhythm House was closed for the day. A couple of stray beggars were preparing to sleep, laying out their ragged sheets on the bare pavement. Both men absorbed these sights but did not refer to them.

'Alkazi, I'm really enjoying this theatre work with you. It reminds me of my days when I was painting hoardings. An opportunity to paint on such a massive scale . . . *bahut maza aa raha hai* (I'm really enjoying it)!'

'No, no, it's an honour for us that you agreed. By the way, are you planning to go abroad, Husain Saab? I heard you might join Akbar and Raza in Paris.'

'*Nahin, nahin,* (no, no) that was just a passing thought! There is so much to do here in our country; we have so much life here; this has to be depicted. Things are moving so fast! How does one capture this excitement and this speed of change that's happening here? Time runs, gallops—like a wild horse!'

'So you're going to paint horses, then? Wild, untamed horses?' Elk asked in jest.

Husain stopped dead in his tracks. 'You've just articulated my thoughts, Elk! I can't believe it!'

They walked some distance in silence.

'Yes! Horses! I will paint horses! Horses are a good metaphor for *time*—time that never stands still. My horses, like lightning, will cut across many horizons."*

'Husain Saab, what can I say? You're a poet *and* a painter! Speaking of which, I see another poet sitting in that corner!'

They had entered Chetna and were looking around.

Elk pointed to the secluded table where Nissim sat, absorbed in a book. They joined him.

'Hello, Nissim! So sorry for being late! What can I say? Husain Saab kept us busy, showing us his sketches for the set of *Murder*! It's going to look spectacular, Nissim! This man is a poet and a genius! I'm so happy today. I realize that my two dearest friends are poets! What more can one ask for?' They all chuckled.

'*Accha, Khuda Hafiz . . . Milta hoon . . . Ek do kaam hain . . . Aap log baithiye . . .*' (Goodbye . . . I'll see you later . . . I have some things to take care of . . . Carry on.)

Before they could invite him to join them, Husain had vanished.

* * *

---

* 'In 1952, Husain travelled to China where he studied the pottery horses of the Song dynasty. These horses from myth and legend became the building blocks for one of the artist's most enduring themes. In China, Husain also met the painter Qi Baishi, an artist known for his monochromatic paintings of animals with a minimalist use of line to achieve form and movement. This condensing of mediums and minimal application greatly inspired Husain.'—Sotheby's, Maqbool Fida Husain, Catalogue Note.

'A small something for you, Elk,' Nissim said, shyly pushing a packet covered in brown paper, tied with a string across the table.

'What's this? Another gift? Really, Nissim, you shouldn't have! We haven't even given you a wedding present yet!'

'Go on, open it!'

Elk slid the book out of the wrapper. A fairly thick paperback presented itself: *A Time to Change* by Nissim Ezekiel!

'I wanted you to be the first to see it.'

Slowly and very carefully, Elk turned to the title page and there stood the dedication: *For Elk and Rosh, who were part of my life changing.* Elk looked up slowly at Nissim as his eyes welled up. He stood and came across to Nissim, who stood up too, awkwardly. Elk caught him in a bear hug. Nissim's wire-rimmed oval specs nearly slid off the edge of his very thin nose. He was not used to such a physical display of affection.

'You don't know what this means to Rosh and me. I'm deeply touched, Nissim. Truly, deeply touched. We have done nothing to deserve this.'

'Honestly, Elk, were it not for you and Rosh, I would never have been able to go abroad. As you know, the experience has completely altered my life and my thinking. I just wanted to acknowledge that in some way.'

Nissim had recently returned after three years in England. He was keen to spend more time on his creative writing and not return to teaching at the university if he could help it. As luck would have it, he landed a job on the very day of his return! The *Illustrated Weekly* offered him an associate editorship at a princely salary of Rs 440 a month![7] This reassured Nissim's parents, who immediately suggested that the twenty-eight-year-old Nissim settle down. Accordingly, a suitable wife was found—Daisy, a Baghdadi Jew. The couple were married in November of the same year and lived with his parents and siblings at The Retreat on Bellasis Road in Byculla.

Elk had been awaiting Nissim's return, eager to install the artworks he had shown at Leicester Galleries, which Nissim had curated and written the catalogue note for. For this major event, Elk had rented the newly opened Jehangir Art Gallery. He was also keen to use Nissim's editorial expertise to fashion the small, new publishing venture he had recently initiated, *The Theatre Group Bulletin* (TGB). Handing Nissim a copy of the very first issue, Elk proudly explained that though the *TGB* was a 'little magazine',[8] what the bulletin had to say was of no 'little' consequence! To date, there was no other theatre group in Bombay that believed in the importance of creating a platform for the discussion of ideas between the arts.

'No one imagines drama to be a concrete reflection of society's aspirations, an expression of its tragic conflicts. Drama gives voice to human beings at their most authentic, intense, and fruitful moments.'

'True Elk, but the point is, will there be enough people who will subscribe to the Bulletin? It has to be financially viable; otherwise, it will soon close down.'

'Don't say that, Nissim! We shall find a way; we *must* find a way to sustain it! When people see the kind of serious work we are doing, they will step forward to support us. Of that, I am sure! But right now, it's imperative that we get our ideas out there, *and* the surest way of doing that is through the printed word. Only the printed word carries weight. Also, the Bulletin's reach will be not only across India but across the world too! Mark my words!'

'Ok, so even if we *do* manage to raise some funds, what kind of content are we looking for?'

'New ideas! The Bulletin's first task is to propagate new ideas! Stimulate discussion on theatre through essays on European and Indian modernism and reviews of current productions and exhibitions. All the arts should feature—dance, literature, film, theatre and the visual arts—should be discussed side by side, so we can recognize and understand the deep-seated relationship between them.'

Theatre Group Bulletin covers: January 1954 and October 1954

'Elk, I would love to get my hands dirty brewing such a cocktail! But the point is, who will we get to write? On theatre? On art? We don't have good art critics!'

'Exactly! That's why we need to encourage young people like Freny Bhownagary, who has a sensitivity towards all the arts, to write. Also, because she lives between Bombay and Paris, she's up-to-date with the latest trends. You too, Nissim, must write regularly on painting; you have a gift for it! And let's get your young friend Krishna Paigankar to write about current trends in literature. Philoo Contractor could be mentored. We need to write about the work of Husain, Souza, Gaitonde, Akbar and Tyeb! I want us to promote Indian modernity in the visual arts in the Bulletin as well! One way of doing that is to use their paintings as the cover image of *TGB* issues from time to time.'

'Great idea!'

'The Bulletin is also a *critical* journal. It *criticizes* others; it criticizes *itself*. It believes that an *uncritical* life is not worth living, for to be uncritical is to be blind, driven by urges and appetites, but without conscious purpose and direction. Since we will have little space at our disposal, we will rely on our *point of view*, on what is suggested by a few hundred words, rather than any exhaustive survey of a subject.'[9]

'Hmm, have you introduced this scheme to the TG Committee?'

'I will, I will! I'm going to show them this first issue at our next meeting.'

'Do you think they'll buy the idea? Agree to all this hard work and this expense?'

'Shall I be frank with you, Nissim? Between us, I'm not really waiting for their approval. If you and I are convinced, that's enough for me! Actually, barely anyone understands my ideas—they can't see the larger picture. They think I'm *too serious* and the plays I select to produce are *too serious*. Well, my answer is, let's try and take our audiences along with us, make them see how and why we select to do certain types of plays and *prepare* our audience for what they might never have experienced before.

'For example, I've written about how we are going to stage *Murder* at the IFL[10]—that it will not be a regular proscenium theatre experience, but one that is conceived for an empty space. I've indicated how they will be seated and how the audience will be limited to fifty people so that it becomes an intimate experience. You see, I don't want the audience to simply dismiss the production as incomprehensible, strange and unfamiliar. Instead, I want to help them understand and appreciate the reasons why a particular approach has been adopted by the director: that it is no longer just the histrionic ability of the actor alone to ensure the success of a production, but the entire vision, concept and treatment of the material in the hands of a director that make a powerful statement. In a way, I'm coaxing and inviting the audience to come on board with us on an exciting journey to experience new ideas of modernity without apprehensions or misgivings."

'True, true, I can well understand…'

'Then again, many of our members are wondering why they need to be *trained* in acting! They don't seem to realize that *no theatre movement is possible without good actors*; they have no serious concern with FUNDAMENTALS! Most of our members just want to get on the stage and show off! Unfortunately for them, theatre is just a hobby. Well, to hell with them! I really don't have time for the fripperies of amateurs!'

Pause.

Elk had worked himself up. Visibly distressed, he stood up and signalled to the waiter to bring the bill. They paid in silence. Walking towards the exit, Elk changed the topic.

'How's Daisy? Sarah? Joe?'[†]

'Everyone's fine! Except, Elk, I find it so difficult to get some privacy to write. There are so many of us living at The Retreat! The only way I survive is by fleeing as early as I can every morning to escape the tyranny of domestic life!'[11]

'Well, if it's any consolation, it's a bit of a squeeze for us too. Now that we have Uma, and then there's the ayah and the boy.[‡] It's become impossible to rehearse at home. Actually, Nissim, that's one of the reasons why we need to talk to Madhuri Behn. I hope you don't mind, but I've fixed up

---

[*] In the years to come, essays and articles on world-famous directors would appear in the *TGB*, illustrating how in modern theatre, the director played an authoritative role in crafting a performance to become an artistic, integrated piece that emanated from a singular vision. These were new ideas at this point. Let us remember that before this, there had been only stage managers who organized productions and it was only people like Alkazi, Sombhu Mitra, Utpal Dutt and Habib Tanvir, who constituted the very first generation of theatre directors in India.

[†] Sarah was Nissim's sister and Joe was his brother, who married Khorshed Wadia.

[‡] 'The boy' is a generic term we used in those days to indicate a young male servant helping around the house.

to meet her and Soli Batliwalla tomorrow morning. I need you to come, Nissim. Let's find out what they're planning to do with the Bhulabhai Desai Institute. I've heard they want to make it into an arts centre of sorts. I wonder if they would be willing to give Theatre Group some space there. We need some permanence, Nissim, a rehearsal space, a library.'

* * *

Elk was surprised to find the lights on in the bedroom. Rosh and the ayah, Yowjaan, were attending to Uma, who was howling in pain as she was suffering from an ear ache.

'She's been crying non-stop ever since I came home. I don't know how to soothe her. I've used ear drops, but they don't seem to help! Elk, do you think we can call a doctor now?'

Yowjaan hurried to the kitchen, returning with a poultice of roasted ajwain (carom seeds) and a hot *tawa* (griddle). Sitting next to Uma, she began dabbing the warm poultice around the child's ear. In a few minutes, it seemed to have a magical effect and Uma gradually stopped screaming and began to drop off to sleep.

'*Bai, fan band karo, Baby abhi soyenga. Aap log khana khao.*' (Madam, turn off the fan. The baby will sleep now. You and Sir should have dinner.)

'Haven't you eaten yet, Rosh?'

'No, I was waiting for you.'

They moved to the tiny living room and sat at the fluted dining table with legs made in the design of trees with stylized branches. The stools were part of the dining table set, carrying out an art deco tree design as well.[*] Alkazi's paintings hung on the walls. Nudes and a five-foot-high Christ, all of which he had prepared for his exhibition held at the JAG. On the far side was one of Bobby's paintings—the one of two seated nude men.

'Elk, I wanted to tell you—Mummy called me this morning and mentioned that Alyque said that he does not want to only act in plays. He wants to direct plays too, for TG. He feels he has the confidence.'

---

[*] This set of furniture was used on the set of *Miss Julie* by Alkazi as the kitchen table. We would use all our personal furniture, clothes and props often in productions, as we never had enough resources to get sets, costumes and props, especially for productions. Therefore, we would often be without a dining table, chairs, lamps, etc., for extended periods!

Nissim Ezekiel giving a talk at Alkazi's exhibition at Jehangir Art Gallery, Bombay, 1952

Elk looked up with a scowl.

'What? What did you say, Rosh? Direct! Alyque wants to direct? Hah! He's just not serious! He and Sylvie are just not serious! They laugh and joke their way through classes... like the Kathakali class, I'm told! Besides, Alyque did not even complete his course at RADA. He should wait and gain more experience. Really, Rosh, you should know better!'

Pause. They served themselves in silence.

'Well, what do you think? What shall I tell Mummy?"

'Nothing. Don't tell Mummy anything! If Alyque wants to direct, then why hasn't he spoken to me? Why has he asked Mummy to talk to you?' Alkazi's voice had started rising. 'How am I to have *any* authority in the Theatre Group if family members begin to *meddle*?'

'I mean, I don't think Mummy was trying to interfere. She was just trying to help!'

Pushing his plate aside, Elk stood up.

'I'm just so *fed up* with the lot of you! *Totally* fed up! How can one work with any sort of clarity of thought? It's just impossible! Not possible!'

With that, Alkazi stormed to the front door.

'I don't think it's fair for you to ask me to deal with your whole family! It's too much! I'm claustrophobic . . . AND . . . There's not an inch of space to move in this bloody house.'

He walked out, slamming the door behind him. The baby started crying.

'Elkins, please, where are you going? Aren't we going to eat?' Roshen's voice fades after him.

Elk passes 'the boy' smoking a beedi in the dimly lit corridor. The poor fellow jumps up as soon as the 'Saab' passes him by without acknowledging his presence and Saab disappears down the staircase, three at a time. The entire stairwell is filled with the stench of urine. Paan stains glisten in the corners of every landing. At the building's entrance, an oldish-looking Russian prostitute is an undefined mass of sagging breasts and heavy hips. Alerted by the possibility of a customer, she strikes a pose by lifting her straggly red hair with one hand and hitching her skirt up to the crotch with the other.

'Darrrling, want to come with me tonight?' she hisses through bloodied lips.

Elk breathlessly rushes past her, fleeing into the fetid street. He tries to lose himself in the folds of the darkness as the tuneless song of the prostitute hag follows him.

I went to see my darrrrling, last Saturday night,
I went to see my darrrrling, the moon was shining bright
I went to see my darrrrling, and what do you think she said?
She said she would not marry me, if the rest of the world were dead.

He reaches the Gateway of India, still breathing heavily. Gradually, his equilibrium is restored as a cool breeze from the Arabian Sea whispers across his brow.

CHAPTER 19
HEADING FOR A SPLIT
1953

Elk was in an ebullient mood! The day had begun on a note of excitement. He had received a letter from the board of the Bhulabhai Desai Institute (BDI), mentioning that they had agreed to grant premises to the Theatre Group from August 1953. It was now April. Elk's thoughts flashed forward into the future as he rapidly formulated a scenario that he would put into action over the next couple of months. Finally, *finally*, they would have their own premises! Finally, the TG could plan its activities in advance and not be dependent on the availability of auditoriums or homes of members for their productions, readings, talks, etc. Finally, they could start giving shape to an *institution*! The BDI was *ideal* for his work. To be among other artists—painters, musicians, dancers—would be tremendously prestigious. He had overheard Madhuri Behn saying that Ravi Shankar and the Vajifdaar sisters would be holding classes there too, and that the painters Akbar and Husain had already requested studios. The best part was that Madhuri Behn, Soli Batliwala and the rest of the BDI Board had created a trust to support and patronize all the arts and would charge the TG a token rent of Rs 1 a day! What more could he have asked for?

Passing Roshen the formal approval letter, he finished the remains of his breakfast of a fried egg and two toasts. Rosh was still not ready but sat there looking exhausted, trying to down a cup of tea. Not noticing her condition, Elk went on, 'Darling! Rosh! Can you believe it? This is a major turning point for us . . . huge! We must set up a school of drama as the focus of TG's activities—the cornerstone must be a drama *school* on totally professional lines. Rosh, it will be the first of its kind in India! There will be no turning back after that!'

Rosh smiled weakly, putting down her cup of tea. She looked rather pale. She was three months pregnant and morning sickness seemed to be the norm these days.

'I've decided, Rosh, we must get everything in order. To begin with, it's absolutely essential that we have a first-rate *library* of theatre books and, of course, books on art, poetry, etc. We should now branch out into doing art exhibitions. As I said, the visual and performing arts must go hand in hand! My idea is to do a series of exhibitions on modern art . . . and so, I feel, it's imperative for me to go to London and Paris immediately. I can't be ordering books from here. It will be much simpler to go and pick them up myself. I've thought about asking my father for some help. I think he will agree. After all, it's for an important cause, darling! To educate people! What do you think?'

Looking up, he saw that Rosh was moving towards the bathroom, her hand covering her mouth.

'Oh darling, I'm so sorry, you're not feeling well . . . how thoughtless of me to just carry on like that,' he said, helping her to the bathroom, where she promptly threw up.

'Yowjaan, *thoda paani lao, please, bai ke liye.*' (Please bring some water for Madam.)

Rosh took a few sips and then walked to the bedroom to see if Uma was ready.

'You carry on upstairs, Elk; it will take me a few minutes to get dressed. They must all be waiting.'

'Come along, Uma darling! Put your sandals on.'

'Ok, Daddy! How do I look?'

'Oh my God! You look so, so beautiful, darling! Who got you this lovely dress?'

'Mummy made it for me!'

'Oh my God! Beautiful! You look like a princess!'

Elk lifted Uma up in his arms, took a look at himself in the full-length mirror, adjusted his cravat, arranged his front lock, and off they went, up to the fourth floor.

The KT drawing room was bustling with the whole family. Deryck was supervising a sofa being shifted to the terrace by the two house boys. A photographer and his assistant were following them with their equipment, suggesting where the sofa should be placed to get some good light for the photographs. Bee was in a pale blue chiffon sari. She was about six months pregnant and was following three-year-old Renan around with a bowl of porridge. Running away from her, he collided with Elk and Uma, who were just entering.

'So sorry, Elk! Renan! Stop right here and say sorry to Uncle Elk!'

'It's okay, Bee! Hello darling, Renan! Look who's here?' and he put Uma down. The cousins ran off to the terrace to play hide-and-seek.

'Candy, please help me feed this child! He's becoming naughtier by the day!' pleaded Bee.

'Don't worry!' said a very adult thirteen-year-old Candy. 'I'll keep them busy with the doll's house Elk Uncle made for me!'*

Elk strolled across to greet Hamid Sayani, who was sitting apart from the rest as he usually did, eager not to fraternize too closely with the Padamsee clan. Dressed in his customary white bush shirt and trousers, he was smoking, with a box of Capstan cigarettes and a lighter in his hand. Jerry, his wife, sat next to Kulsumbai across the room. Draped in a beautiful white chiffon sari with a three-quarter-length sleeved blouse and a pair of pearl earrings, she looked calm and composed, her naturally volatile emotions soothed for the moment by an anti-depressant. Her equally beautiful little daughter, the delicate Pooh, aged two, was sitting on her lap in a muslin dress. Alyque, in his thick, horn-rimmed spectacles, sat to Kulsumbai's right. Kulsumbai, in her long, floral Khoja farak, her teeth stained red by years of chewing paan, was cracking supari (betel nuts) with her cutter, collecting them in a small aluminium tray on her lap.

'Good morning, Mummy!' Elk greeted her.

She pretended not to hear him, turned to Jerry and said, 'Ask who wants tea.'

Rebuffed, Elk turned to move on when Kulsumbai turned back. 'Did you say something, Alk?'

Elk turned back, 'I was just saying . . .'

Before he could answer, she cut in, 'Where's my daughter?'

---

* This doll house was made by Alkazi for Candy's eighth birthday. It had two floors and was very realistic, with tiny furniture and paintings on the wall as well as lights that could be turned off and on. Shades of his interest in stage design.

'She'll be up presently . . . a little morning sickness.'

Again, Kulsumbai ignored Elk's answer and turned to say something to Alyque. Elk felt slighted but was determined to stay cheerful. He had much to celebrate and was not going to allow his spirits to be dampened. Making himself scarce, he walked into his father-in-law Jafferbhai's room, where the latter was enthroned on his sofa-cum-*jhoola* (swing). The wall behind him was adorned with colour-tinted photographic portraits of his numerous brothers and one sister, forming an apt Padamsee family backdrop to his rather commodious frame.

'Salam Alaikum,' Ebrahim said politely in greeting.

Jafferbhai nodded and indicated the sofa opposite him. Ebrahim sat down while his father-in-law continued to slowly rock back and forth on his jhoola.

'Hamed Saab *theek thak hain? Business kaise chal raha hai?*' (Is your father alright? How's business?)

'*Alhamdulillaah*' (Praise be to God), replied Ebrahim, touching his chest with his right hand and formally bowing his head slightly.

Jafferbhai's living space could be considered the equivalent of an Arab diwaniya, the men's drawing room, where the head of the family would receive male guests. In most Muslim households, this room would have been the first one outsiders would enter, with women and children's quarters located more towards the interior. However, in this household, Kulsumbai with her anglicized ideas had opted for a formal, western-style parlour, designed as the very first room guests, both male and female, would enter.

The décor was certainly meant to awe. Everyone who entered was duly dazzled by the drawing room's splendour and scale. Its cut-glass chandelier descending from a twenty-five-foot-high ceiling reflected the golden hues of the lush Persian carpets. Overlooking this sumptuous display of middle-class wealth were multiple life-sized, hand-tinted photographs of the Padamsees gazing down on their guests from their gilt frames. It was from this centralized drawing room that Kulsumbai reigned over her kingdom. She was the Queen Mother as it were, and this was where her children and their spouses, friends and grandchildren paid obeisance to her with ritualistic punctuality. Kulsumbai's Wednesday dinners for the adult members of the family and Sunday lunches with the entire family were legion. Her mouth-watering Khoja cuisine was served at her majestic horseshoe-shaped dining table, where, besides the family, it was an open house for TG members and their friends.

Through such means, then, did Kulsumbai, my grandmother, become a virtual legend in theatre circles in Bombay, playing the role of grand hostess to her family's theatrical activities. It was here in her drawing room and at her dining table that the Padamsee theatre dynasty merged with the larger theatre family and community of middle-class Bombay, allowing her children to continue the legacy of English theatre in Bombay that Sultan Padamsee, her golden-eyed, brilliant son, had initiated.

It was from this pivotal position that Kulsumbai closely guarded Bobby's *gaddi* (position of power). 'Whom would the Theatre Group gaddi go to?' was a loaded question. Who it would be was still, according to her, an open question. She would judge for herself whether this 'Arab' was fit to replace her son! And so she waited for the right moment to make the right move.

'Ok everyone, come along! Line up, please! Family wise . . . First the three daughters with their husbands, then with their kiddos and then the whole family together.' Deryck was ushering people from the drawing room onto the mosaic-floored terrace, where the sofa had been placed in front of the white slatted trellis screen.

Kulsumbai joined the others, ensconcing herself on the terrace swing and continuing with her supari cutting. From here, she had a clear view of the entire clan. The family photograph was an annual event she insisted on. The photographs were proof of her ever-expanding family. She was proud that one of her sons-in-law, Deryck Jefferies, was British, so dependable and always willing to help. Of the other two, Hamid Sayani and Elk, she had reservations about whether they made good husbands and fathers.

'Ok, the Alkazi trio, Rosh, Elk, Uma, you're next,' Deryck called out, stage-managing the entire event.

'But Rosh is missing!' said Bubbles.

'No, no, here I am! Hello Mummy . . .' Rosh came in draped in a green sari with a boldly embroidered border. She looked petite and pretty. With tiny kiss curls arranged on her forehead, the rest of her hair, which was cut

(Top row, L–R): Deryck Jeffries, E. Alkazi, Hamid Sayani, Alyque Padamsee, Chotu Padamsee and Aziz Padamsee; (bottom row, L–R): Candy, Uma (Amal), Roshen, Renan, Bapsy, Zarine and baby Ayesha (Pooh), Bombay, 1953

in steps, flowed down to her shoulders in large waves. With a delicate black mole painted above her lips, there was no doubt that she looked like an Indian version of Hollywood star Rita Hayworth.

'Are you feeling ok, Roshen? You're looking a bit pale,' inquired Kulsumbai.

'I'm fine, Mummy!' Roshen called out as she took her place next to Elk.

Kulsumbai shifted her gaze to Elk. So there he stood, that wily Arab! Kulsumbai thought, sizing him up. Today, he seemed to be in a very good mood, cracking jokes with everyone. Why was he so talkative today? She had always been unsure of this man with camel eyes! Shifty! She was well aware of his theatrical endeavours having a positive impact on Bombay audiences, who had never imagined receiving such cultural bounty at their doorstep. She overheard the aspiring youngsters who partook of her weekly dinners talk about the growing respect and admiration Elk elicited, while others whispered that those who occupied the highest echelons of society were making overtures of support for the Arab in his ventures.

This kind of information had begun to rankle with Kulsumbai. How could Elk have the *audacity* to come into her drawing room and lord it around here, in Bobby's place, cracking jokes? It was true that he had worked quite hard, but who did he think he was, shunting Alyque off to do some inconsequential play readings at Chotu Terrace? This Arab was getting too big for his boots! Bossing everyone around! He could get out, as far as she was concerned.

Alkazi, of course, was completely oblivious to Kulsumbai's meandering thoughts that were being fanned on a low flame, so full was he of memorizing the announcements he was going to make at the TG meeting this evening.

* * *

Seated in a circle on the terrace of Rehmat Manzil, above the popular restaurant Gourdon & Co. in Churchgate, members of the TG were chatting amiably. Ashraf Jairazbhoy, one of the members who occupied a flat in the building, had sought the landlord's permission for the use of the terrace from time to time. Lectures on the modern novel had been held there earlier in March of the same year. Today, a cool sea breeze relaxed them, with many coming to the meeting directly after a hectic day at the office.[2]

A small table had been placed at one end of the circle at which Alkazi sat. At exactly 7 p.m., he began his address, as president, to the twenty-odd members who had assembled. Amjad Ali, his old school friend and now a member of the Group, was taking down the minutes, while Abdul Shakoor, ever obliging, bustled about making arrangements for the tea and biscuits that would follow.

Elk began by breaking the thrilling news of the TG having been granted premises at the BDI.

'By arrangement with the trustees and through the generosity of Mrs Desai, the Group will have its Reading Room, Office and Rehearsal Room on the first floor of the BDI. The large terrace, a beautifully proportioned room and the other amenities of the place make it an ideal centre for a group such as ours. Henceforth, all TG activities will be centered at the Institute.'[3]

There was a round of applause.

'Hear! Hear! That's wonderful, Elk!'

'Yes, and therefore, in response to BDI's generosity, I feel it is only right that we invite Madhuri Behn Desai herself to be on the Theatre Group executive committee. Daughter of the illustrious Bhulabhai Desai, she will bring tremendous prestige to the Group!'

Ashraf Jairazbhoy called out, 'I second that!'

Other voices chimed in, 'Hear! Hear!'

'Also, I would like to add that it is now time that the presidency of TG pass on to someone else. As outgoing president, I propose Mr Nissim Ezekiel. His deep knowledge of all the arts, especially literature, poetry, painting and theatre, along with the fact that he is on the editorial boards of two highly respected magazines, *Quest* and the *Illustrated Weekly*, makes him an ideal candidate. I propose Nissim Ezekiel.'

'I second that,' said Khorshed Wadia, Nissim's sister-in-law-to-be, and a few others assented.[4]

'And now to our forthcoming activities.'

Alkazi read out the details of the third acting course they were to embark on, which would be for ten months and cover seven productions.

'The plays will be in this particular order:

1. *Huis Clos* (No Exit) by Jean-Paul Sartre
2. *The Physician in Spite of Himself* by Molière
3. *The Love of Don Perlimplín* by Lorca
4. *Oedipus Rex* by Sophocles
5. *Volpone* by Ben Jonson
6. *The Three Sisters* by Chekhov
7. Shakespeare's *The Tempest*

Let me add here that though we hope to trim our subsidiary activities like lectures and so on and to concentrate chiefly on the production of the plays...'

Alkazi, Roshen and Uma (Amal), Bombay, 1953

There was an audible sigh of relief in response to the theory classes being reduced. Alkazi raised his hand to indicate that he wished to continue.

'We shall nonetheless be organizing a series of *exhibitions* covering the history and development of modern art.'

'Exhibitions! Why exhibitions?'

'I am keen on this because I had promised the students of the last course a series of lectures on the subject of art. These exhibitions will be in fulfillment of that promise.[5] These exhibitions (which will consist of prints) will be held at a suitable venue, probably the newly opened Jehangir Art Gallery, and they will be in this order:

1. A large exhibition tracing the Growth of Modern Art
2. The Beginnings: Delacroix, Courbet and the Impressionists
3. Degas
4. Toulouse-Lautrec
5. Renoir

6. Cézanne
7. Cubism: Gris, Braque, Picasso, Minors
8. Surrealism: Breton, Dali, Max Ernst, Tanguy, Miró
9. Matisse
10. Paul Klee
11. Pablo Picasso

There was genuine surprise coupled with considerable shock among the members at Alkazi's announcement of eleven exhibitions! Who was going to find the money for these and who was going to do all the work? Changing the subject, Alkazi directed the attention of the members to the need for a library for the benefit of the students in their training programme.

'I am personally willing to fund and support this library initiative, which is central to a training institution. I am willing to travel abroad, to London and Paris, as soon as possible to make a selection of books. My going there would be a quicker and less expensive way of acquiring the books rather than ordering them by post.'

Side by side, Alkazi mentioned that he would be purchasing prints of modern art, which would be used in the exhibitions he had spoken about. In his absence, Nissim would oversee the activities that had been planned for the next few months.

'And now to the last item on today's agenda. As I have mentioned before, after every production, we will hold a post-mortem of our latest production, subjecting it to severe critical scrutiny. This will be with regard to all aspects of the production, from the acting, direction, costumes, props and impact on the audience, as well as an analysis as to how we have fared with the management of the production as a whole. Today, our first post-mortem will be of our production of *Ghosts*.'

So far, the evening had been a mix of alarms, surprises and good news. A few members not involved in the production excused themselves. Others took a cigarette break and sipped on the by-now-lukewarm tea. Alkazi then invited P.D. Shenoy, who had been asked to keep a production diary of *Ghosts*, to begin the post-mortem. What followed would be deeply etched in the memories of those involved for years to come. As Alyque Padamsee recollected more than half a century later:

'I remember there were just twelve of us in the course and were double cast in *Ghosts* ... We were also being taught Kathakali ... Sylvie and I were hysterical because Kathakali was like a foreign land to us, so we used to joke and laugh during Kathakali practice. We were also taught yoga.

'And Elk had a guy who was like his "chamcha" (actually the assistant director) called P.D. Shenoy. And PD used to sit and rehearse the play with us sometimes (Alkazi was training Shenoy to be a director) ... and we thought PD was making notes about how one directs a play ...

'We did the play and it was totally fine. I really enjoyed it. Elk made us do a lot of homework, very good background research on the characters, etc., and the production ran quite well! It was a very small hall, so we did quite a few shows and then he called for this post-mortem!

'And as I remember it, he sat there (at the meeting). Elk had a little table and desk and PD sat next to him at another desk and there was this post-mortem of *Ghosts*. Elk said, "Now not many of you know that P.D. Shenoy has kept an entire record of this production ... the first of its kind ... and it is one of the Group's most valuable possessions ... I ask you, PD, to please read out." So, PD began, "The rehearsals of 16th May ... We started rehearsals ... I have to note that Alyque and Sylvie came late and so on. Next ... 30th May ... We did rehearsals again, though they were on time, both these same gentlemen were laughing throughout."

'Suddenly, one found that one was in the dock! It was like Kafka's *Trial*, you know! Suddenly things are being held against you ... for laughing! We called it having good fun! And there in the Kathakali class, you know, PD pointed out, "Alyque refused to wear ballet shoes and he was not wearing any shoes ..." and things like that! And he went on and on like that, for half an hour!

'We were getting hot under the collar, Sylvie and I, and then Elk said in a semi-democratic way, "So, any questions?"

'So I asked, "What is this? I mean why has everything been written down? I mean, yes, certainly we had fun ... and I really was not exactly very serious ... but we performed, and I thought the whole thing went off well. I thought the whole thing is about are you any good as an actor?" After all, we wanted to be assessed as actors!'

Suddenly, Elk sprang out of his chair. Bellowing at full volume, he articulated each word separately as he spat them out.

'No, no! The theatre is LIFE . . . everything that happens at rehearsals must be according to a certain pattern of LIFE that I have laid down for the Theatre Group!'[6]

Stunned silence. No one present forgot that evening.

Later that week, Rosh suffered a miscarriage.

CHAPTER 20
LULL BEFORE THE STORM
1953

Alkazi stormed out of the meeting and blindly strode towards Marine Drive in a rage. Walking the better part of the night, he castigated himself for not being able to control his temper. He *had* to control himself. But, for *God's sake*, it was sheer agony to try to persuade these people that the theatre required sacrifice and hard work!

This evening, the tensions that lay under the surface had erupted and would henceforth begin to manifest themselves in strained relations between members of the Group. Alyque and Sylvie had been singled out and referred to as the disruptive, non-serious members who were unwilling to submit to Alkazi's very disciplined way of functioning. The embarrassment was even greater because Alyque was Elk's brother-in-law! Three sons-in-law of Kulsumbai Padamsee were involved in the TG, but only one son—Alyque. Being Bobby's kid brother, Alyque had never been considered a contender for TG's leadership. Deryck was the more practical one, while Hamid, though a very talented actor, was shy and retiring. So Alkazi had been the unanimous choice to take over the reins of the TG, most closely mirroring as he did Bobby's artistic pursuits and talents.

Clearly, it was not Alkazi's competence that was in question here; it was his *legitimacy*! As time passed, it was his growing reputation that rankled most with Kulsumbai, especially since Alyque had opted for theatre rather than law, for which Kulsumbai had sent him to study in England.* Alyque had flatly refused. 'Within a few weeks, I gave up the idea of law when I learned that I would have to spend my evenings studying briefs and would

---

* Kulsumbai had hoped that Alyque would take up the legal profession and follow in the footsteps of Mohmmad Ali Jinnah, whom she greatly admired.—Candy Bhatia in an interview with Amal Allana, USA, 2018.

not have time for rehearsals!' said Alyque, 'and I opted instead for RADA, where Elk was!'[1]

Finding RADA too rigorous, Alyque dropped out and returned to Bombay to join St Xavier's College. Alongside, he began to participate in TG productions under Alkazi's direction. Alkazi had frankly been disappointed that Alyque had not found it necessary to be professionally trained, which signalled to the other TG members that theatre required only talent and no hard work! To somehow compensate for this, Elk had begun casting Alyque in serious roles, such as Engstrand in *Ghosts*, while also giving him play readings of the classics to direct. This was meant to help Alyque gain directorial experience.

Both Kulsumbai and Alyque had definitely misread Elk's responses. Kulsumbai felt Alyque was being deliberately sidelined by Elk by not allowing him to direct a full-fledged production of his own. To add insult to injury, Alyque had been publicly reprimanded! This would have infuriated her!

As rapidly as Elk had lost his shirt that evening, the pressing exigencies of his forthcoming trip abroad soon took precedence. His remorse receded. Equilibrium restored, he soon forgot about how the blow-up might have affected Roshen. Avoiding any reference to the matter, he brushed it under the carpet. This was my father's usual way of dealing with most emotional matters—he would simply sidestep them and behave as if they hadn't occurred while my mother Roshen was too timid to bring up contentious issues, lest they lead to yet another outburst. And so I assume matters festered in the deep, dark corners of her soul without resolution. Elk's silence on the Alyque matter eventually became quite unbearable, because within a week of the incident, my mother suffered a miscarriage. This immediately won her some sympathy from her mother, who was extremely solicitous of her daughter's condition. Elk's departure for Paris and London came as a relief to all concerned, allowing the tension to dissipate and disperse.

* * *

Keen to learn more about the French theatre and the art scene, Alkazi spent more time in Paris than London on this trip.[*] Away from the noise

---

[*] Alkazi had met John Mitchell in London as a student. The latter was looking after the library of the BDL. Now, in 1953, Alkazi met him again in London. Mitchell, who came to know

Catalogue and display, *This Is Modern Art*, Jehangir Art Gallery, Bombay, 1950s

and stress of pressing deadlines, this was a period of recuperation for him too. Prone to being depressed without company, shopping of any kind—for art works, books, home furnishings, clothes, anything at all—gave my father an adrenaline rush, relaxed him and gave him immense satisfaction. The book-hunting excursions were no doubt a repeat of his delightful childhood escapades to the International Book Depot in Poona.

Spending an entire day wandering through warrens of decrepit, out-of-the-way bookshops on ancient Parisian streets was exciting. Within no time, Alkazi would befriend the bookshop owner, pumping him for more information on other books while also eagerly inquiring about the release of forthcoming publications. So it was quite common for me, in later years, to be informed at bookshops I frequented that, 'Your father, Mr Alkazi, is one of our most esteemed customers. Such a knowledgeable gentleman, with such refined manners and a taste for well-brought-out books!'

This time around, Alkazi had an agenda. He combed Parisian bookshops with books in English from dawn to dusk—jotting down titles,

---

Kamaladevi Chattopadhyaya later, attended the First World Theatre Conference organized by ITI and the Bharatiya Natya Sangh in Bombay in 1956 along with Rosamond Gilder. Mitchell was one of the persons who highly recommended Alkazi to Kamaladevi, saying that Alkazi was, in fact, the most qualified to take on the directorship of the NSD.

names of publishers and prices—and spent the evenings compiling them, subject-wise, into comprehensive lists of plays, dramatic criticism, acting, movement, speech, stage design, lighting, stage management, costuming, make-up, etc., as well as allied fields that included the visual arts, music, dance, mime and masks.

He was thrilled to discover rare and out-of-print books, such as the copiously illustrated publication of the productions of Stanislavski's *Moscow Art Theatre* in Russian, Adolphe Appia's *La Mise En Scene Du Drama Wagnerian* (1895) and *Die Musik und de Inszenierung* (1899) in German. The photographs alone in the MAT book were a treasure, while Appia's writings on stage design were like sacred texts that Alkazi had been waiting to devour. He was determined to get them translated by a TG member immediately on his return.

Today, Alkazi is known as much as an art collector as a theatre educator, so it is interesting to note that this 'theatre library' was his very first and fledgling attempt at making a serious *collection*. Theatre people and visitors to BDI were highly impressed with Alkazi's collection of books on all the arts. Soon, painters like Akbar and Husain were asking to borrow books, but Alkazi was not at all keen on lending them. This was a collection that was *handpicked*, he said, and he did not want his books filched. Which *did* happen, much to his unspeakable annoyance, by none other than people like Satyadev Dubey!

The supporter of this library enterprise was none other than Ubba, my grandfather, who had encouraged Ebrahim at a young age to collect books. In later years, in answer to why he became a collector, Alkazi would say, 'I was, in fact, following in my father's footsteps . . . he had built a meticulous collection of great Arab literature and poetry for us as children in our home in Poona . . . and I had been put in charge of its maintenance'.[2] Elsewhere, Alkazi talks about his early fascination for books arising out of being asked by the Jesuit priests at St Vincent's School to help maintain the school's library. For Alkazi, a library was one of the cornerstones of any institution of learning, and now that he had acquired some space, he built a library at its core.

Besides books, Paris had exciting theatre to offer, theatre with a mission to reach the common man. Furthering this idea was Jean Vilar, actor, writer, director and founder of the Festival d'Avignon, as well as artistic director of the Theatre National Populaire (TNP).

Throughout his career, Vilar not only championed the concept of popular theatre, he was committed to placing the public at the centre of artistic creation and maintained that the theatre should be a public service. At TNP and the Festival d'Avignon, Vilar altered the timings of the performances to accommodate the needs of the working-class man—light meals were available before the performances, free leaflets provided a background to the play and the actors, tickets and complete texts of plays could be bought at modest rates while public discussions on plays were initiated.

Repertoire-wise Vilar focused mainly on the classics but also proposed modern texts by foreign writers like Bertolt Brecht, Georg Büchner, Paul Claudel, etc. Prominent actors and visual artists, such as Alexander Calder, and musicians were invited to collaborate.

Vilar's approach inspired Alkazi, especially his views regarding *popularizing* and *democratizing* theatre. Alkazi's idea in later years of doing festivals at historic sites such as the Purana Qila or Feroz Shah Kotla, so that large audiences could attend, the mixed repertoire of plays, both classic and contemporary, the modest pricing of tickets and the leaflets for the audience enabling them to receive a background on the play could have been inspired by the Avignon experience.

The *TGB*'s September 1954 issue included an article by Jean Vilar titled 'Avignon, Where All is New'. Introducing the article, Alkazi wrote: 'This article is to introduce our readers to the approach and attitude of a significant worker in the theatre movement—an approach which in many ways serves as an eye opener and an inspiration to those theatre workers in this country who have dedicated themselves to a similar task.'

Likewise, in the October 1954 issue of *TUB*,* Alkazi included 'What Is the Friend's Association of the Theatre Populaire?' by Henri Laborde. Alkazi introduced it thus:

> We publish here a statement issued by the President of the Friends Association of the Theatre Populaire, which explains the relationship of this organization to the ideas and practice of the

---

*   In October 1954, the Theatre Group had split up and Alkazi founded a new group called the Theatre Unit. He took over the Bulletin, which was rechristened the *Theatre Unit Bulletin* from this issue onwards.

parent body. For the category of membership called FRIENDS in our own society, the THEATRE UNIT, we have drawn our inspiration chiefly from the ideas expressed here. In working out the structure of the THEATRE UNIT therefore, we have not hesitated to draw upon the experiences of similar organizations serving the same ideals in other parts of the world.

By stating that he shared similar ideals and goals regarding the future of theatre with international theatre organizations like the TNP, Alkazi reiterated his belief that the Indian theatre movement should be aligned with and be part of a larger *world* theatre movement that was democratically conceived, with its core concerns being public education and engagement.

* * *

Alkazi had also gone abroad to purchase a large number of prints or reproductions of art works for his forthcoming series 'This is Modern Art'. This idea, to showcase reproductions, not original artworks, would have far-reaching repercussions. What Alkazi did with the shows in 1954 was to realize in practice what the great French art historian André Malraux propounded as a unique theory in his *A Museum Without Walls* or *Le Musée Imaginaire*.

Malraux proposed that since no museum in the world could assemble large numbers of artworks at any given venue, the only way this was possible was through reproductions and photographs. This kind of assemblage would lead to significant new curatorial practices where objects from totally disparate and different cultures could be juxtaposed and contextualized in new ways. Malraux wrote:

'Imaginary Museums could shake the authority of old institutions and pave the way for us to think about cultural democracy in a different way, and allow for all heritage to be seen as the common heritage of mankind.'[3]

Malraux's philosophy appealed strongly to Alkazi, as it suggested that all art belonged not only to the country of its origin but to mankind as a whole, making all traditions and cultures part of a *common heritage*. This thought was becoming fundamental to what Alkazi believed in— *that world cultures were our common heritage to be drawn from and to sustain us.*

This was Alkazi's approach in 1953, far ahead of its time. He had already begun drawing on multiple traditions to create a new performance language for the stage and a pictorial language for his artwork. In search of the basic and fundamental sources of performance in creating a modern idiom, Alkazi had already looked towards primitive African and ancient Greek sources. On this visit to Paris, what he saw at the Marigny Theatre, for example, was Jean-Louis Barrault's return to the Commedia dell'arte tradition as inspiration for a new approach to acting. Barrault, a student of Jacques Copeau and Charles Dullin, was using his body as the prime instrument of an actor's tool kit, combining it with the use of masks as well as mime. Alkazi, who was already interested in dance as well as choreography, was excited by Barrault's stronger focus on visual expression rather than on the theatre's customary reliance on the dramatic word as the primary means of communication. Such exposure to the modern usage of the Commedia tradition would have a considerable bearing on Alkazi's future work in India both as an actor himself and a trainer. Going back to earlier *performance* traditions, such as African rituals, Greek theatre and the Commedia dell'arte for use in a modern idiom, could make Alkazi the first Indian *intercultural* practitioner to consciously draw on and embrace world performing traditions.

Inasmuch as Alkazi saw himself as drawing on world cultures, he saw himself as a *world citizen* and therefore made it his business to comprehend the histories of other cultures. As he looked around, met people and saw the art of France, he began to sense more clearly that he was at the very birthplace of the French Revolution, among people who had fought for and defined the very meaning of liberty, equality and fraternity. France was a country whose thinkers, writers, painters, poets and theatre practitioners had resisted totalitarian regimes and responded by creating radically new, modern works of art that were informed by that spirit of resistance and its aftermath—deep despair.

Existentialism was France's philosophic response to the annihilation and devastation caused by World Wars I and II. On this particular visit, it resonated with Alkazi to the extent that he would, for the next couple of years, produce some of the most important French Existentialist plays by writers such as Jean Anouilh, Jean-Paul Satre and Albert Camus. Anouilh's *Antigone* and *Eurydice* were especially close to Alkazi as they revisited Greek myth in contemporary terms. The culmination of this cycle of Alkazi's productions was possibly Samuel Beckett's *Waiting for Godot*, which he directed in 1961. Hailed as one of Alkazi's landmark productions of the Bombay years, it rivalled several international productions of the play.

On the whole, this trip to Paris stood apart from the ones he had made during his student days back in 1949 and 1950. Now he was a professional theatre practitioner who was knee-deep in propelling an entire group to enter the mainstream of theatre. The high quality of productions and serious social engagement that he witnessed in French theatre made Alkazi realize that the Group would have to aspire for far greater professionalism.

* * *

Returning with renewed vigour, Alkazi's enthusiasm was greatly dampened when he learned that during his absence, the production of Jean Giraudoux's *Amphitryon 38* had been postponed and some public lectures had been cancelled. For Alkazi, such cancellations reflected a gross neglect of the TG's social obligations.

In Paris, he had the time to reflect on why the TG lacked cohesiveness. He felt that although he had struggled hard to pull the Group up by their bootstraps to a level that satisfied some minimum standards, he had not really succeeded in changing fundamental attitudes. Members still felt that they could dabble in theatre. Since bringing up these matters at annual general body meetings had not really effected a change, Alkazi, on his return, took recourse to airing these shortcomings through his editorials in the *TGB*. Taking such issues into the public arena, and that too in writing, upset several TG members who felt these were internal matters. But Alkazi held his ground, saying that since the Group was a *public* institution, matters should be frankly and openly discussed.

In the editorials 'The Need to Build' (*TGB*, May 1953), 'Are We Too Serious?' (*TGB*, June 1953) and 'Some Observations' (*TGB*, July 1953), Alkazi directly addressed TG members on the need to look within, on the social responsibility of theatre, as well as the urgent need to connect their work with their counterparts working in Marathi, Gujarati and Hindi. Differences continued to simmer over the next few months, but Alkazi was too busy to attend to them just then.

Two matters of importance occurred at this time. One was the launch of a Hindi section for the TG at BDI, which had been Alkazi's long-cherished dream. Alkazi put P.D. Shenoy in charge of overseeing it. It was launched with the production of three one-act plays: *Man and Superman*, directed by Darshan Chabada; *Footpath*, a dramatization of the refugee problem written and produced by Deepak Naidu; and *Jutha Khab*, a farce by Shaukat Thanavi, directed by Amin Sayani.

The other matter that Alkazi was pleased about was that the TG had been invited to be affiliated with the Theatre Centre, Bombay, which was a branch of the National Theatre Centre founded by Kamaladevi Chattopadhyaya. This national federation of theatre groups was formed at the instance of the International Theatre Institute (ITI), set up by UNESCO, for the pooling of resources and exchange of ideas on theatre on an international basis. For Alkazi, working as part of an international forum was very important, so when TG was offered an honorary secretaryship of the Theatre Centre in Bombay, Alkazi was quick to depute Mr Lelin, a TG member, to take charge.

Kamaladevi was a key player in the theatre movement during these years. She had the ear of Prime Minister Jawaharlal Nehru, especially in matters of cultural policy, and had accordingly kept the PM abreast of Alkazi's initiatives in the area of imparting theatre education in a modern, scientific way. It was not long before Alkazi was invited by the Ministry of Education, New Delhi, to give a series of talks on 'Play Production and the Organization of Youth Groups for Dramatics'. These were part of the youth leadership training courses for universities in Bombay State. The purpose of the camp was to train the staff of colleges for leadership work. Alkazi's eagerness regarding such nation-building projects was evident.

At the same time, Alkazi was working hard towards mounting the ambitious series of exhibitions, 'This is Modern Art'. Conceiving them on a large scale,[4] he hired the prestigious Jehangir Art Gallery for a week a month. Bombay's influential elite, such as Homi Bhabha, came forward enthusiastically to support Alkazi, loaning him several originals from their private collections, while the French and Italian consulates collaborated by providing Alkazi with high-quality prints or reproductions along with wonderfully produced art books for display at the exhibitions. Films on art would also be screened, so that 'This is Modern Art' became a keenly anticipated public event.

It was during this time that Alkazi came into contact with key international figures in the art world. In early January 1954, W.G. Archer, Keeper of the Indian Section at the Victoria and Albert Museum, London, attended two talks in Bombay: 'Poetry and Romance in Indian Art' at the Bombay Art Society and 'British Art' at Jehangir Art Gallery and Bombay University. It was on these occasions that Alkazi introduced himself to Archer.

8 February 1954 was the opening of the first part of 'This is Modern Art—A Survey'. Munroe Wheeler, one of the trustees of the Museum of Modern Art (MoMA), New York, happened to be in Bombay and much to Elk's delight, he agreed to deliver a lantern lecture on modern art at the opening. Two films were also shown during the course of the exhibition: Luciano Emmer's *The World of Hieronymus Bosch* and Norman McLaren's *Fiddle-dee-dee*.

* * *

The relocation of the TG to the aesthetically pleasing premises of the BDI situated on the seafront at Warden Road, away from the confines of an increasingly claustrophobic Kulsum Terrace, was vastly liberating. The BDI was a neutral space dedicated to professional work. Here, Alkazi felt his intellectual horizons widen, as did his audience. The proximity to his artist friends who had studios at BDI—Husain, Akbar, Gaitonde and Tyeb—allowed him to closely keep abreast of their work. One notes that, though friends, Alkazi was able to maintain a critical distance from them, allowing him to assess their work objectively. In Alkazi's review of the Progressive Artists Group's second exhibition (February 1954), he observes that 'the Progressives are unable to sustain their integrity as a group any longer, as there is no common ideology or stylistic approach that binds them together, each artist having already developed a highly individualistic trajectory of his own.'[5]*

Other artists at BDI included the three Vajifdar sisters—Shirin, Roshan and Khurshid—who conducted dance classes there, and Pandit

---

* Alkazi is proved right. By the end of 1954, the PAG disbands as a group.

(L) Nissim Ezekiel, Isamu Noguchi, Nargis Cowasji and Alkazi, *This Is Modern Art*, Jehangir Art Gallery, Bombay, 1955; (R) Alkazi, and Mr and Mrs Rudy von Leyden at the Picasso exhibition, *This Is Modern Art*, Jehangir Art Gallery, Bombay, 1957

Ravi Shankar in music. Thus, BDI began to be regarded as *the* centre of intense interdisciplinary artistic activity and today, we look back and regard it as *the* significant space in Bombay of the 1950s and early 1960s, where experimental activity of a high order was taking shape. Such fertile ground served to inspire a new generation of youngsters apart from Alkazi's theatre students, such as Nalini Malani (painter), Shyam Benegal (filmmaker) and Girish Karnad (playwright), who later remarked that the explosion of artistic activity at BDI in those years had a seminal bearing on expanding their horizons.

Alkazi now began searching for accommodation for us. My parents fell in love with a small two-bedroom flat at Cumballa Hill in a five-storey building named Vithal Court, which was still under construction. It was on the top floor, with a fabulous view of the sea. Walking distance from BDI, Roshen, by now pregnant once again, was overjoyed at the prospect of being closer to Nuruddin and Akbar Padamsee, her two favourite first cousins who lived across the road at Taher Mansion on Nepean Sea Road. Both were young intellectuals whose company Rosh sought for deep and stimulating discussions on art, theatre and literature.

These new arrangements did not go down well with the Padamsee camp. Feeling somewhat neglected, with Elk's attention focused on organizing programmes at the new BDI premises, Alyque retreated into a sullen and morose mood. He had been nursing dreams of directing a large production of *The Taming of the Shrew* for some time, but his suggestion had been turned down by the managing committee of TG, saying they did not have the resources just then. Kulsumbai, who was closely monitoring the events as they unfolded, found this an opportune moment to challenge Elk's growing authority over the TG's affairs. 'After all, TG was something Bobby had started, so her son, Alyque, had a right to continue it, she felt.'[6] One must not forget that these are matters of the blood, matters that defy rationality. And so, in a sense, Alkazi's life, unknown to him, began to take on the mythic contours of a Greek tragedy, where the young hero is pitted against the Furies, who hurl him towards his destined end.

Kulsumbai now came forward with an offer to underwrite all the expenses of Alyque's production herself. Elated, Alyque immediately informed the managing committee of his intention to begin rehearsals. The committee could not object as funds had been made available. As Alyque recollects:

> Pearl, my sisters, Jerry and Bee . . . you won't believe it, but these three young ladies went out of their way . . . walking up and down Colaba Causeway . . . asking every shopkeeper to give us an advertisement for Rs 500 for the brochure! Finally, they collected Rs 5000! I remember the figure! . . . And we were able to put on *The Taming of the Shrew*. I must say that we were very ambitious, considering that it was my first production! Chotu, my brother, designed the sets and Pearl played the Shrew . . . she played Petrushka . . .[7]

As expected, Alkazi was enraged over his authority being undermined in this way. He was already facing considerable flak from TG members for mounting *art* exhibitions, which, they reminded him, were not strictly within the purview of a *theatre* company. Alkazi, aware that the schism in the Group was widening, decided to lie low for the moment and not to take up the *Taming* issue right away.

Before *Taming* opened, the end of February 1954 saw seven shows of a Molière comedy directed by Alkazi, *The Physician in Spite of Himself*,[*] staged at the terrace theatre of the BDI. Visually innovative and comic in

---

[*] Akbar Padamsee and V. Gaitonde collaborated on painting the cutout sets and designing the masks, while Roshen suggested they also paint the trimmings on the costumes, highlighting the folds, etc., all of which gave the production an illustrated look. The use of mime and movement reinforced this kind of treatment.

its overall treatment, *Physician* was a runaway success, an important factor considering the criticism by TG members that Alkazi only did tragedies and was unable to draw enough of an audience.

Alyque's *Taming*, slated to open the following month, was also a comedy, and in a sense was competing with *Physician* for box office appeal. Alyque and Alkazi seemed to be locked in a popularity contest!

The Taming of the Shrew was staged at Jai Hind College on 29 March 1954. The cast consisted of Gerson da Cunha, Pearl Waiz, Zarine Wadia, Abbas Abbas, Danny Singh, Zarine Sayani, etc. Although the performances by Pearl and Gerson were commendable, the rest of the cast, according to a review by John Smithard that was published in the May 1954 issue of *TGB*, were 'out of their depth, covering their shortcomings by resorting to loud and hammy performances'. Alkazi seems to have used this rather negative review of *Taming* as a peg to hang his next few editorials on: 'The Necessity of Criticism' (March 1954), 'Amateur or Professional' (May 1954) and 'Criticising the Critic' (June 1954).

These editorials by Alkazi were particularly provocative and harsh because they insistently questioned the complacency of the amateur who lethargically practised theatre as an evening 'hobby'! In them, Alkazi categorically stated that in order to maintain the 'highest standards' of professionalism, half-baked productions should not be produced under the banner of the TG; that there was an urgent need to be *self*-critical; and that the Group's intentions needed to be absolutely transparent vis-à-vis the public. In a sense, Alkazi's editorials were becoming open letters to the Group, where he was giving members an ultimatum of sorts, insisting that there be no fence-sitters; he was asking them to choose between his way—that was the hard professional way—or the other softer, easier and amateur way.

In April–May of the same year, an incident occurred that rose to national prominence and rocked the art world. Akbar Padamsee was asked by the Bombay Police to remove two paintings called 'Lovers 1' and 'Lovers 2', from his exhibition being held at Jehangir Art Gallery. The so-called offensive paintings showed a nude couple, with the man gently caressing the woman's breast. The works were described as 'obscene' by the police as they overstepped the bounds of decency and morality. Akbar refused to remove the works, opting instead for imprisonment if it came to that.

Roused by this, the artist community held a meeting at the Artists Aid Centre to discuss the issue. Most of them advised Akbar to remove the paintings, as he was sure to lose the case. Akbar was appalled at the weak-kneed response of his fellow artists. The only people who supported Akbar were Husain, Alkazi, Nissim and Rudy von Leyden. Eventually, Akbar won the case. Alkazi's decision to stand by Akbar in a way demonstrated his views that an artist must stand firm in the defence of 'artistic freedom and integrity'. It foreshadowed the stand Alkazi would take in the months to come as the chasm widened between those in the TG who were willing to make sacrifices for the theatre movement as professionals and those who were happy to engage with theatre in a more laissez-faire manner.

Being a consummate director, Alkazi had so far successfully staged Act II of this 'break-up drama' during which time he lay low. Then, in a sudden move, in June 1954, he decided to leave Bombay for a few months. The chief protagonist having disappeared, the other camp was left bemused and uncomfortable about what lay in store. But this was a part of Alkazi's strategy—to create a lull before the storm, a suspenseful pause that helped to set the stage for Act III, where, as per the rules of dramatic construction, the conflict would explode in a climax.

As I look back and study the chronology of events as they unfolded, I am beginning to see that Alkazi had been closely watching Kulsumbai's moves and countering them indirectly, blow for blow. He had understood that Kulsumbai's larger game plan was to somehow oust him from TG and make way for her son, Alyque. She must have been seething with rage at Elk's successes. But Elk held strong beliefs in the efficacy of art, and all the work he had done so far was built on those ideals. For him, there was a tremendous amount at stake, and he was damned if he would come out of this 'petty family feud' business as the mauled victim. As a result, over the past year, he had systematically secured the continuation of his work and his family's welfare in a shrewd, practical manner.

Things did not just happen to Alkazi by coincidence or by lucky chance. Opportunities did not 'magically' arise. More often than not, there was an element of stage-managing events in the direction Alkazi wanted them to take. Briefly stated, what he had done over the past year was to

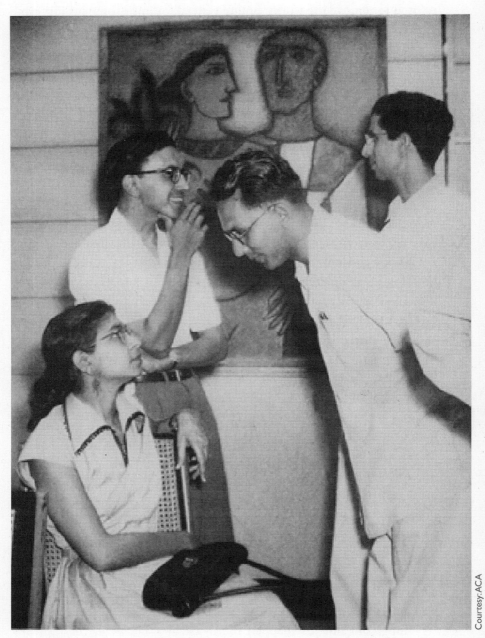

Alkazi and Roshen with Nissim Ezekiel (right) and H.A. Gade at the opening of Akbar Padamsee's solo exhibition, Jehangir Art Gallery, Bombay, 1954

actually set the stage for the break between him and the Theatre Group. He desperately wanted his independence, which would allow him to try out his own ideas without hindrance or opposition.

Alkazi realized that his efforts were being seen, appreciated and acknowledged. This came home to him even more clearly when, in 1954, he was formally invited to design the syllabus for the National School of Drama that was soon to be set up in Delhi and would function under the umbrella of UNESCO's Asian Theatre Institute.

The importance of developing a theatre syllabus for a *national* educational institution was not lost on Alkazi. Its ramifications on the future development of Indian theatre as a whole and his career, in particular, seemed immense. The years spent studying, understanding, transforming and shaping ideas of modern theatre had helped him gain a clearer perspective of what needed to be done. With this invitation, his vision began to assume the proportions of a gigantic national theatre project! Yes, he began to feel that a new India was finally on its way and he was eager to participate in the shaping of new educational art institutions that he believed were fundamental to providing solid foundations for the future development of a modern society. Though so young, Alkazi had been given this incredible opportunity. With an unknown, tantalizing future beckoning him, Alkazi was in a hurry to move on.

CHAPTER 21
THE BREAK-UP
1954

It had been decided that my parents would first travel to London and I would follow later, meeting them in Beirut in June 1954. This would allow the three of us almost two months to get to know my paternal grandparents, uncles and aunts and, for the first time, feel part of the Alkazi family.

By then, my mother was in the third month of her pregnancy. She had never really had the opportunity to get to know the rest of the Alkazi family, except for Noorie and Fatty. Understandably apprehensive about how her in-laws might receive their *Indian* daughter-in-law, Roshen's fears were soon allayed by the warm welcome she received from Munira, Lulu and Faiza, Elk's three other sisters, and his two brothers, Sulaiman and Basil. Wildly excited to meet Ebrahim, who was obviously an elder brother they all doted on, all the siblings and their parents were in high spirits. Ebrahim's zany humour, his way with words and the passionate manner in which he described the work he was doing in Bombay excited and inspired everyone! London was Ebrahim's beat, and over the next few weeks he waltzed the family through all the favourite haunts of his student days, introducing them to Souza and his wife, Maria, and the writer Krishna Paigankar. With a bevy of Arab beauties on his arm, Ebrahim was in his element, taking them to art galleries, museums and performances.

Rosh was relieved to see Elk relaxed and in high spirits with his family—the tension of the previous weeks evaporating with every passing day. Retiring and discreet by nature, Rosh spent most of her time befriending her mother-in-law at home. Ummi had been born and brought up in Bombay and was keen that Roshen fill her in with the latest news and converse with her in Hindi. Roshen's interest and talents as a cook endeared her to Ummi, their conversations often centring on unusual recipes. It was on this trip that Ummi taught Roshen how to prepare jareesh, margoog and tashreeb, Arab dishes that Ummi said Ebrahim was especially fond of. My mother soon mastered them, much to my father's delight, popularizing them at her dinner parties in Delhi in the years to come. They were dishes that I too, in turn, was taught, and those that we cook regularly at our parties even today.

After Ummi and Ubba retired for the night, Rosh would settle down to share her thoughts on art, literature and theatre with Munira and Lulu, who were intellectually bright and full of questions and insights. When they insisted, Roshen would read out her own poems to them. Faiza, my father's youngest sister, and my mother, a brilliant costume designer, shared sartorial tastes, as Faiza had a unique talent for designing clothes and jewellery that fused Arab and western traditions.

After leaving India, Ubba had more or less retired but kept his business contacts going in Kuwait, Bahrain, Dubai, Muscat, Aden and Basra, cities he had actively traded with from Bombay.* Wanting their children to further educate themselves, Ummi and Ubba had decided to temporarily set up house in London after Karachi. Basil was only twelve years old and boarding school in England was an option they were considering. Sulaiman had begun to study economics at the University of Westminster, while Ebrahim encouraged his sister Munira, already a gifted painter, to look for opportunities to study in London. Although London did not feel like home to Ubba, he was somewhat familiar with British culture and the English language because of his many years in India. In the long term, Ubba's preference was to live in an Arab-speaking country. Beirut seemed the answer with its invigorating Mediterranean climate and cosmopolitan outlook, which also appealed to Ebrahim's sisters, who had enjoyed a great deal of freedom, having grown up in India, and were unwilling to adjust to the conservatism of an Islamic state.

After a couple of weeks in London, the large Alkazi family proceeded to Lebanon to spend the rest of the summer in a beautiful chalet in the mountains. From Beirut, my father found time to fulfil a longtime promise

---

* He began to invest in a number of start-up companies, like the Oil Tanker Company, the Kuwait Airways Corporation, the National Bank of Kuwait and the Arab Jordan Bank. *History of Kuwaiti–Indian relations: The Complete and Illustrated Encyclopedia 1896–1965*, preparation, collection and documentation by Hessa Awad Al-Harbi, first edition, 2017, copyright 1999–2021, Dar Al-Masila.

to his mother, that was, to accompany her on Haj, which made him a 'Haji' as well.

This was my first trip abroad, ever! I was all of seven years old and would travel by plane alone! My excitement knew no bounds.* I was rather a compact, self-confident child, and, as I remember, I had no anxiety at all about travelling alone by plane. I was handed over to the air hostess, who promised to take special care of me on the trip. I sat there very properly in my seat, wearing one of my new dresses, looking out of the window and virtually daydreaming about the gifts I had been promised by my parents from Hamleys, the most famous toy shop in England! I had asked for a pair of dolls, a male and a female, which I was promised would be handed to me the minute I landed. As my parents gathered me in their arms to cover me with kisses at the Beirut airport, I noticed they were not carrying any gifts. I immediately asked where the dolls were, only to be told that they had only been able to get the girl doll, which was waiting for me at home, but had not been able to get her counterpart. I wept inconsolably that whole night, lying between my parents. Was it that even then, at the age of seven, I had sensed an unspoken rift between them? I have never been sure whether the other woman had already come into our lives. Maybe she had.

However, the holiday in Beirut was wonderful. We went to Baalbek, watched a performance at the ruins, ate at small cafés dotting the mountain sides and went for long drives. Lulu smothered me with gifts that taught me to sew and weave. Being the only kid around, I was always the centre of attention. And if I remember right, it was from this point on that I began to be called 'Amal', not 'Uma'. Amal was my Arab name, so these uncles and aunts only ever knew me as 'Amal'.

Back in Bombay, the monsoon had appeared in all its glorious force and drama. As we drove home from the airport to Kulsum Terrace, waves lashed the Breach Candy rocks. My mother looked a bit exhausted and the strained look returned. Elk had told her during the trip that they were

---

* My two Arab aunts in Bombay, Noorie and Fatima, were given the task of acquiring a brand-new wardrobe for me, especially for this international trip! They took me shopping and bought me the most beautiful outfits. I had to have a small purse for my passport! And a new suitcase. My Arab aunts were always impeccably and fashionably dressed in the latest trends, as were their children, so I felt very, very special being taken out shopping by them. Until then, all my clothes had been designed by my mother and tailored by the local darzi!

The Physician in Spite of Himself by Moliere, dir. E. Alkazi, Theatre Unit, Bombay, 1954

about to enter a glorious *new* phase of their lives. That the times ahead were, in a sense, a *new* beginning, that the Bhulabhai Desai Institute was such a splendid venue for their *new* work, that the *new* flat at Vithal Court was to be completed within a month and how wonderful it was that a *new* baby was on the way. He confided that Ubba had promised to increase their monthly allowance as they would have far greater responsibilities from now on. 'Rosh darling, there is no need for you to worry—no need at all!' But Mum just looked out of the taxi window into the far distance; she did not hear what Elk was saying; she did not feel his hand in hers squeezing it in a gesture of solidarity. All she knew was that there was a dull ache of tension in the pit of her stomach. That her life was changing and things would never be the same again.

* * *

As the August issue of *TGB* came hot off the press, the TG members called one another, suggesting that Elk's article, 'To Further the Cause of the Theatre: A Plan for the Reorganization of the Theatre Group', be read immediately. They did not entirely comprehend what it was that Elk was trying to say through it. Did he mean to change the *constitution* of the Group? How was that possible? Within a few days of its publication, however, Elk invited all the TG members to a meeting on the terrace of the BDI.

The rain had abated, the terrace was still wet and the air tangy with a taste of salt. Several stood watching the sunset, which today appeared to have set Bombay aflame. At 7 p.m. sharp, Elk briskly walked up the steps to the terrace, followed by Nissim and Roshen, who took their places with the rest. Elk nodded greetings to a couple of members and seated himself in front to face them. All naturally fell silent.

Looking stern and preoccupied, Elk deliberately left a pause, as if gathering his thoughts. Of course, this was not so, as he knew exactly what he was going to say. In a few moments, his voice rang out in clear, sharp tones:[1]

'By now, most of you might have read my article in the August issue of *TGB*. In that, I have asked the Group to reshape its entire policy and organization, I am asking the Group to take what I consider to be the next logical step in its development, in light of present-day conditions.

'The reason being that I feel it is important that from time to time we should reshape and reorganize our ideas because that way the Group becomes a live, growing, developing organism and not a fossilized institution. Today, our experience and understanding of the theatre are deeper than what they were several years ago. Those same old ideas have served their purpose; we have outlived them. What I am suggesting is ways in which the Group can be fully mobilized, as it were, to play its rightful part in the Indian theatre movement.

'The Theatre Group cannot be content today with the role of a small amateur organization serving college students or a narrow circle of theatre enthusiasts in the city of Bombay. Our work must have repercussions on the Indian theatre movement as a whole if it is to truly fulfil its aim of "furthering the cause of the theatre in all its various aspects...", which our constitution states.

'How, then, can the Group play a more direct and dynamic part in shaping ideas concerning drama and theatre in the country? *By setting a standard. By creating and establishing a tradition.* A long string of artistic successes does not constitute a tradition. We can establish a tradition only by formulating a way of doing theatre: by systematizing methods of training the actor, the producer and the scene designer. Such a tradition can be consolidated only through a school, a regular academic institution.

'Obviously, we must then begin to conceive of the Theatre Group as a much more weighty and responsible institution than it is at present. As its functions expand, its responsibilities increase, and the full burden of these responsibilities must be shouldered by a managing committee that fully realizes what the Group is committed to.

'The founding of a drama school—that in itself is a grave decision. It means we need a building to house the school, a director and staff to run it, and students to keep it going. That would mean revising the entire constitution and organization of the Group, as it now stands.

'This is how I think the Group should be reorganized:

Theatre Group
(The General Organization)

School | Two Repertory Companies | Wardrobe | Workshop |
Bulletin | Library | Other Activities

'The School should form the core of the Theatre Group, its heart and soul. It should set the standards and create the tradition of the Theatre Group. Therefore, the demands of the School should be severe and uncompromising. The School should be an exemplary institution in its discipline and its training; it should prove an inspiration and set a precedent for similar prospective institutions in the country. To be a graduate of a Theatre Group School should be a real distinction.

'There comes a time in the life of every purposeful institution when members are faced with the responsibility of making graver decisions than they may have bargained for. We can remain where we have remained for the past ten years: struggling valiantly and enthusiastically to serve a cause, the full measure of which we never really understood. Having understood it now, we can still decide to remain where we have so far comfortably been—aspiring but never *fully* committed.

'But if we are to be honest with ourselves and sincere when we say that our purpose is "to serve the cause of the theatre in all its various aspects", then there is no other way for us but to be *fully committed*. If that is truly our aim and not a mere catchphrase uttered in a moment of idealism, then we must accept the difficulties, make the decisions and undertake the projects that lead to the fulfilment of that aim.

'We must decide now. Today, there is tremendous enthusiasm in theatre all over the country. Every educational institution, every municipal corporation and every national body speaks of building theatre. There are drama festivals and competitions galore. Naturally, the air is full of half-baked ideas regarding drama, theatre, architecture, scenic design, play-production, and so on at all levels, from the primary school teacher to the member of parliament. There are many illusions under which most drama enthusiasts are suffering—well-intentioned, but nonetheless harmful. We must help clear the air. We must nip some of these illusions in the bud. By our own example, we must show the real way in which theatre can be served and be made a vital force in the lives of people.

'This is our responsibility. We cannot shirk it. Through the years we have watched, not without misgivings, our shadow outstripping us. Today, the prestige and status of the Group is greater than the Group itself. The Group must begin to live up to itself...'

A deathly silence engulfed the gathering. A few people coughed uncomfortably.

Then Elk asked rather democratically, 'Any questions?'

A lone voice of a woman piped up, 'It's all very well, Elk, to say we will take up the responsibility of running a school, but we need teachers. Besides you, where are the teachers?'

'A good question, Pheroza. So that's exactly what we want to do: train some of you to become teachers,' Elk responded with a gentle smile, Pheroza being one of the most dedicated and talented of the Group—in fact, she was the Secretary.

'But then, what will happen to the fact that we are a group that mainly stages plays. Most of us want to act, to direct...'

'As you can see, we are doing plays, but through them we are training you to act, to direct, to design—all aspects of theatre. Once a number of you are trained, you will become members of a repertory company, but until such time, I will be very clear with you: there is only one way for us to do theatre and that is to be trained as *professionals!* I am *trained* to do theatre and I have set down a pattern and developed a course. And frankly, I think there should be only one director in the Theatre Group.'

Sylvie,[*] who could no longer restrain himself, stood up and blurted out,

'Well, I don't agree with that! Bobby started the Theatre Group and I think the idea was that we should fan out so that everyone would be involved. Some will direct, some will do set design, someone will act, and so on...'

Elk retorted categorically, 'No, I am sorry; the kind of stuff being done is not the kind of theatre I believe in.'

Elk's answer seemed to have unleashed everyone's tongues and everyone began speaking at once. Mehlli Gobhai, sitting at the rear of the group, sprang up and shouted above the rest, 'Excuse me, Elk, you talk about your beliefs in the theatre and all that, and all the time we listen! All these things are so high-sounding . . . that's fine! But theatre is also a human kind of a thing . . . and all this other stuff you talk about is just a facade.'

Elk, unable to tolerate this insolence, was beside himself with rage! He boomed: 'Facade! FACAAAAAADE! . . . What do you mean, Gobhai? It is not a *facade*! It's reality! It's my life! I put my life into this. I have put my *entire life into theatre,* and you call it a FACADE?'

Alyque and Sylvie, who were too young to grasp the enormity of the proceedings, began to giggle, as if this were a schoolboy altercation. Rosh buried her face in her handkerchief while Nissim advanced to Elk, whispering in an undertone, 'It's alright, Elk. Let's just calm down.'

'I am absolutely calm, Nissim! But let it be said in no uncertain terms that in one institution, you cannot have *two* approaches. So, you all should make up your minds! Decide! Anybody who wants to work with me,

---

[*] Sylvester da Cuhna, who passed away on 20 June 2023, was an actor–director and had his own advertising agency. Brother of Gerson da Cuhna and married to poet Nisha da Cuhna, his son is Rahul da Cuhna, the theatre director who has taken over his father's ad agency.

either you come in your entirety or you go in your entirety. I know people will want to have a foot in both camps, like "We will act with you from time to time". I say, "No". Make up your minds, because it's not a question of just acting with me; it's a question of being part of a *movement*, part of a concept of what the role of theatre is in society . . .

'I am resigning from the Theatre Group. I am starting the Theatre Unit. Those who want to join me can join me; those who don't want to, need not.'

With that, Alkazi walked out.

Years later, my father told me: 'And what was extraordinary was that the moment I formed the Theatre Unit, people ran off and locked up all our stuff, removed our locks on the godowns—three huge godowns of properties that we had been accumulating over the years—and all the lighting equipment—the finest collection of lighting equipment that we had—and I said, "I don't want a thing! What is this? How ridiculous it is to reduce our relationship to that level! Here are the keys; all that stuff is yours. I do not want a single pin from the Theatre Group, and I do not even want the name 'The Theatre Group'!" So, we founded the Theatre Unit overnight! And there was Nissim who was with me and later on, Usha Amin, Kersy Katrak, Bomi Kapadia, Minoo Chhoi, Nargis Cowasji, Pheroza Cooper, Kusum Behl, etc. So these were the people who continued to work with me . . .'

Years later, Alyque said to me: 'And so that was the schism, not just in the Theatre Group, but a schism in the family as well. And then Rosh and Elk became, you know, as if they were in a foreign land, in the Theatre Unit . . . and Deryck, me, Hamid and Jerry were together in the Theatre Group. And in all this, my mother, Kulsumbai, said, "Theatre Group was born in Kulsum Terrace and it stays in Kulsum Terrace!" And I said, "Fine! I will not use Bhulabhai Desai Institute . . ." and that was that at that time.'

Poster of *Miss Julie* by August Strindberg, dir. E. Alkazi, Alaknanda Samarth as Miss Julie, Theatre Unit, Bombay, 1960

PART FOUR

Theatre Unit Bombay, 1954–1962

Poster of *Antigone* by Jean Anouilh, dir. E. Alkazi, Kusum Behl as Antigone, Theatre Unit, Bombay, 1955

CHAPTER 22
THEATRE AS A WAY OF LIFE
1954

'*Ahiste, Ahiste! Koi jaldi nahi hain.*' (Slowly! Slowly! There is no hurry!) My father was directing the four labourers hoisting a massive two-ton piece of freshly quarried stone up the five flights of Vithal Court to Flat Number 13!

'*Dum lagake!*' chanted two of the labourers.

'*Hoshiyar!*' responded the other two.

'*Dum lagake!*'

'*Hoshiyar!*'

The chanting created a rhythmic beat that the labourers followed with their footsteps, heaving the stone up step by step. It also brought the neighbours to their doors, curious to find out what all the hullabaloo was about.

'What is happening? Why is this stone going upstairs? Alkazi Saab, what is the meaning of this?'

Mr Sarraiya, a tenant of the second floor, pushed his way forward to the front of the crowd.

'Such heavy, heavy stones will affect the foundations of this building! *Yeh pagalpan hai*, this is sheer madness. Have you taken permission?'

Children kept squeezing forward ahead of their parents to gleefully watch the feat, screaming out '*Hoshiyar!*' along with the labourers, adding energy and zest to the joint effort.

'You will see soon enough, Mr Sarraiya! Please come over to our flat for a cup of tea to see where I'm placing this beautiful stone!' my father replied politely with a friendly smile.

Mr Sarraiya harrumphed off, 'I shall complain to the landlord!'

The Poonawalas, the Manjis, the Basrais, the Maniars and the Bhikajis—all residents of the various flats at Vithal Court—were getting used to the strange objects going in and out of Flat 13 on the fifth floor. And... My God! The number of people who seemed to visit these Alkazis on a daily basis! Unbelievable! However, this Ebrahim Alkazi fellow seemed to be courteous and pleasant enough—always politely greeting everyone when passing them by on the staircase or amusing the children with a joke or prank. They also noticed how he never insisted on having a designated space in the compound to park his car, something that most of the other residents endlessly squabbled over. He just quietly parked his Humber Hawk outside the compound, along the opposite pavement.

With a final heave, the stone was brought in through our front door and, under strict instructions from my father, cautiously lowered next to the only load-bearing pillar of the entire 800-square-foot studio apartment.

'*Saab! Hamne yeh kaam aapeech ke liye kiya! Bhagwaan ki moorti samajkar, isko dhyan se uthakar is pahad pe chadhaya hai aapke liye! Lao!*'

Roshen Alkazi, 1955

Haldi-kumkum do! Iska sthapana honaach padega.'
(Sir, we have done this job only for you! Considering it to be the sacred idol of a god, we have carefully brought it up this mountain just for you! Give us the turmeric and kumkum. We need to install it with due rituals and reverence!)

My father was somewhat taken aback by the labourer's conclusion. But our old maid, Yowjaan, though a Goan Catholic, immediately understood what he meant. She ran off to the kitchen to get some turmeric, while my mother, who was lying down, pointed to her tiny kumkum box lying on the makeshift dressing table. The older labourer dabbed the stone with yellow and red powder, while Yowjaan lit an incense stick and sprinkled some grains of rice on the stone. All joined their palms together in reverence and shut their eyes, the labourer intoning a small prayer. Yowjaan handed out some jaggery as *prasad* (devotional offering). Anointed and blessed, from this point on, the stone seat became the sacred centre of our new home, our new life and our new way of looking at ourselves in relation to the world around us. It was a universe that was capable of being magically transformed and animated through a few simple, ritualistic acts. The mundane became sacred, requiring only belief in the existence of its magical potency, in much the same way, I suppose, as we were able to conjure up a make-believe world in our theatre work.

Bringing in an unspoiled, natural element into a man-made environment was to become one of the signature features of my father's design aesthetic. In different corners of the flat, he introduced a few walls clad with roughly hewn grey flagstones, which stood in juxtaposition to the smooth, white plastered walls. This design feature was carried out unobtrusively. For example, a narrow wall in one corner was made of grey flagstones, while diagonally across from it, at the other end of the studio flat stood another, narrow, three-and-a-half-foot-high stone wall of the same material, with an elegant slim, long black glass placed on it, serving as a modernistic dressing table-cum-mantlepiece for my mother's cosmetics.

In a similar manner, the large west-facing French windows along two sides of the flat served the purpose of allowing nature in, with plenty of natural light and air flooding into the studio apartment throughout the day. Since we were on the topmost floor of the building, these large windows afforded a spectacular view of the sea and sky, allowing us to witness and experience the phenomenal changes in Bombay's skies from cloudy to clear to dark and brooding, marked by torrential rain and flaming sunsets. The consciousness of the vastness of the universe, in all its diversity, was something my father wanted us to love, cherish and experience, with him often calling us to stand with him on the tiny balcony to witness it.

We were also sensitized to the passing of time as artworks of different periods, epochs and cultures dotted the landscape of our domestic environment. A centuries-old stone sculpture of a couple, or *dampatti*, standing with palms together in the namaste position, was installed outside our front door to welcome guests in. The house was also home to modern and contemporary artworks, from Husain's *Three Nudes* (1954) and Tyeb Mehta's arresting lithograph *Man* (1957) to Adi Davierwalla's sculpture of a buxom *Nude* (1958), Bauhaus and Jane Drew-inspired furniture, as well as traditional masks from Japan (Kabuki), Bali, Sri Lanka and Africa. Each object was placed with careful consideration so that a cross-cultural dialogue was set up between them, leading the eye from one to the other. To see parallels, contrasts and similarities between objects and styles of different cultures and periods had seeped into Alkazi's presentation of art as a whole, informing a new curatorial approach that he was developing, the seeds of which were evident right here in our home, shaping how we lived and responded to art as part of our day-to-day experience.

Our flat was perhaps one of the first of its kind in Bombay to celebrate such new ideas of an international modernist style in art and architecture, no doubt inspired by the presence of the great Swiss–French architect Le Corbusier, who had been commissioned by Prime Minister Nehru to design an entire new modern city for India, Chandigarh. On his multiple trips to the country, Corbusier and his team had befriended several influential, wealthy Indian families, such as the Sarabhais of Ahmedabad, who offered 'Corbu' private commissions to design their homes along with the interiors. Corbusier's was an unfussy 'international style' that reflected an industrial, modern feel in his architecture of the major public buildings of Chandigarh, where he used massive unpainted concrete slabs, dictated by clean lines, simplicity and functionality. In other instances, as in the Sarabhai homes, his approach differed. Here, he made use of indigenous material, adopting traditional masonry in construction and using ethnic decorative features like roughly carved wooden balconies and door frames, thus combining the local and the global into a new, fused international aesthetic.

The Sarabhais, basically mill owners from Gujarat who had supported Gandhiji during the freedom movement, had always shown a keen interest in all art forms. Now, their interest in modern design extended to establishing an advertising agency called Shilpi in Bombay. Before long, Nissim was on their payroll, and my father took up assignments at Shilpi to work on several exhibition projects with the industrial and advertising photographer, Mitter Bedi, who not only shot all of Alkazi's theatre productions from this time onwards but was to become my father's lifelong friend.

Cosmopolitan Bombay had been developing into a centre of Indian architectural thought for some time—many British and Indian architectural practices were based in the city, and the Sir J.J. School, under Claude Batley's direction, was regarded as the country's foremost architecture school. Walter Langhammer, Rudy von Leyden and Emmanuel Schlesinger were equally interested in design. Von Leyden contributed articles to *Marg*, while Langhammer's dinner parties and salons, much like Mulk Raj Anand's 'at-home-soirees', were social hubs where aspiring young artists and architects rubbed shoulders and exchanged ideas.

Mulk Raj Anand had returned from studies abroad and, along with Anil de Silva, had established *Marg*, chiefly devoted to art and architecture. Although all-Indian in its scope, it was international in terms of its contributors, with essays by distinguished art historians such as W.G. Archer, Ananda Coomaraswamy, Hermann Goetz, and Stella Kramrisch, introducing the Indian public to the latest international scholarship on Indian traditions. Coverage of modern architecture and its implications for India was also central to the mission of the journal in its early years. As a result, 'no publication did more than *Marg* to make the Indian upper middle classes, whose considerable education did not usually encompass art and architecture, more aware of these aspects of their heritage.'

Our home also reflected a certain openness and a new understanding of sexuality. Sex was no longer taboo; it was natural, beautiful, liberating, compelling and true. Banishing Victorian prudery, my father had placed in our home an exquisite bronze Shiva–Parvati, each poised on a single foot, the other leg entwined around each other's waists, copulating in energized stillness. They were engaged in the ultimate act, the dance of creation, while an angelic Bodhisattva Padmapani sat composed in lotus position, her half-closed eyes looking inward, reflective, with a beatific Mona Lisa smile hovering across her lips. Images such as these, of sheer beauty, grace and intensity, illuminated our lives as we were growing up.

There was no doubt that we had to 'learn' to inhabit a new kind of domestic environment in a simple, uncluttered manner. Such a visually rich space reflected the new progressive views of its owners as people invigorated by world cultures. At this moment, my mother, Roshen, is recumbent on the bed, delicate and rather fatigued, in her seventh month. Alkazi cannot help but marvel at her infinite grace and beauty—a mother with her unborn child, dozing under the painting of Husain's three white nudes.

The Vithal Court flat had been designed as a single comprehensive space where my parents' beds were placed near the two tiny balconies to one side. A couple of chairs and a centre coffee table took up the central area, denoting the drawing room, while a low dining table with four stools and a bench designated the dining area. Not far off were my brother Feisal and my beds (his was on casters beneath mine and was pulled out at night). Each space flowed seamlessly into the next, and my mother was often asked how she managed with no privacy—for dressing, for private conversations, for sex—away from the prying eyes of the servants and children.

'When will the phone be connected, Elk?' my mother asks tentatively.

'Darling, didn't I mention that we are not installing a phone? No need; it will be a terrible nuisance,' says Elk soothingly.

'But . . . how will we manage without a phone?'

'We'll manage just fine! But tell me, how do you like the flat? Isn't it stunning? I want to make this the most beautiful home in the world . . . just for you!'

'Thank you, darling.'

'And it's so convenient . . . just a stone's throw from the BDI.'

'Hmm . . . true.'

He lies down next to Rosh for an afternoon siesta. He puts one arm across his face. I look on, happy that my parents seem calm. Away from KT with its Khoja Victorianism, its clutter, its noise, its lack of sophistication—

here, for the first time, Alkazi has an opportunity to build a new life from scratch, a life where he envisions a new and free relationship with his wife, an opportunity to develop a group of people to work with who believe in his passion for being more inclusive, experimental, less conservative and conforming.

My mother opens her eyes, staring at the ceiling. She has no idea how Elk has the ability to cut himself off from everyone with surgical precision. How he can sever close ties and make a swift, clean and merciless break with the past—a rupture with her family, their college friends, and not even mention the split. She has begun to understand that his way of coping is keeping himself busy with insurmountable challenges that fill his days with work, work and more work. At the moment, he is engrossed in rehearsals for the new production of *Oedipus Rex*, in which he has taken on the lead role, and is preparing for the new school. Elk seems to stride forth undaunted, with energy, enthusiasm and sheer discipline, which leaves Rosh gasping as she struggles to keep up.

Elk had taken over the *Theatre Group Bulletin* and renamed it the *Theatre Unit Bulletin*. The first issue (October 1954) carried the resignation letters of Nissim, Rosh and himself under the bold heading 'Why We Have Resigned'. Alkazi felt strongly that since the group was a public institution, it was morally incumbent on the three of them to be totally forthright about the reasons for their resignations, leaving no space for rumour-mongering or ambiguity.

How did all this affect my mother? I asked Alyque several decades later.

He responded, 'I think above all, Rosh must have felt helpless . . . this was an artificial cutting off of the umbilical cord. For us, it felt like Elk and Rosh had become part of another world. But what could Rosh do? After all, she was his wife!'

***

It was an open house at 41 Pali Hill, a kind of salon hosted once a week by Chetan and Uma Anand, to which Shenoy was taking Alkazi this evening. Shenoy had spoken extremely highly of Chetan Anand, a theatre director turned film director of *Neecha Nagar*, a film that had won the Palme d'Or at Cannes in 1946, gaining him instant international recognition as well as the respect of his peers in the film industry. No less talented was his young wife, Uma Anand, a stage actress who had played the female lead in *Neecha Nagar*. Besides her considerable abilities as a screenplay writer, she was a professional radio artist, not to mention that her father, G.C. Chatterjee, had been the principal of Government Law College, Lahore, pre-Partition, where she and Chetan had met. Performing together in collegiate plays, they fell in love and were married soon after.

Passionate about theatre, Chetan found employment as a drama instructor at Doon School, leading the couple to relocate there during Partition. Within a year, they moved to Bombay and formed their own theatre group, Hindi Manch, while seeking more lucrative opportunities to utilize their creative abilities.

Their residence at 41 Pali Hill was a two-storey bungalow in which the Anands, their little son Ketan, and Chetan's two brothers, Vijay and Dev Anand, occupied the first floor, while Zohra Segal, along with her dancer husband Kameshwar, son Pawan and daughter Kiran, were ensconced on the ground floor. This evening, the young intelligentsia of the film industry flowed seamlessly across both floors, spilling out towards the beach and disappearing under a thick canopy of stars towards the sea. Groups of people were scattered around, lounging on chairs, seated on the floor or perched on ledges, while others sat on the sand or stood around with whisky glasses, but mostly cups of tea. Guru Dutt, Mohan Sehgal, Raj Khosla, Balraj Sahni, Safdar Mir, Ali Sardar Jafri, Shanti Bardhan and Sahir Ludhianvi, along with aspiring youngsters who worked in either IPTA or Hindi Manch productions, and there sat Damayanti Sahni, Zohra Segal and Uzra Butt, all currently making their mark in the last of Prithvi Theatres' productions.

This was Bombay's leftist intellectual crowd, from whom Alkazi had so far distanced himself, assessing their work with a certain degree of scepticism. Had he been too harsh in judging them? Was he correct in assuming that although they appeared articulate and energetic, they were already vaguely aware that the sheer pressure of the film industry on their creativity would eventually defeat them? He already noticed signs of their art being diluted to a popular level to meet the demands of commerce.

Alkazi could not understand how these very writers and directors who had migrated to Bombay, investing the industry with powerful leftist ideas, who had been inspired in theme and form by the great Russian writers and avant-gardists of the Russian cinema, as well as by German Expressionism—how could they so easily sell themselves?

As he made his way through the tightly packed bodies, Alkazi recognized a few people in the dim light. Kaifi and Shaukat Azmi graciously greeted him with an *adaab*, while K.A. Abbas, whose one-act play the Theatre Unit had recently produced as part of their first steps towards working in Hindi, greeted Alkazi effusively and immediately embroiled him in a lengthy conversation.

'I hope you are aware, Alkazi Saab, that I am no longer in IPTA!'

'How so? I thought you were one of the founders of IPTA, here in Bombay!'

'I was . . . but in 1948–49, CPI stalwarts filed a case against me for writing a preface to Ramanand Sagar's novel, *Aur Insaan Mar Gaya*. It was about the inhumanity that the riots engendered. A literary inquisition took place, and I was denounced by my ex-comrades and expelled from the PWA and IPTA! My rejoinder was not allowed to be published in *Naya Adab*, the PWA journal, despite my being one of its three editors! Can you believe it?'[1]

Shenoy seemed to have disappeared. In a sense he had become Alkazi's right-hand man, helping him realize his long-cherished dream of working in Hindi. Joining the Theatre Group soon after Alkazi had returned to India, PD's interest was to become a director himself. Shifting with Alkazi to the Theatre Unit, PD was gradually being handed over the charge of overseeing the Hindi section of the brand-new School of Dramatic Arts that Alkazi was about to launch. It was in this connection, to locate and test the viability of getting more students in search of professional training, that Shenoy suggested to Alkazi that he get to know an influential section of intellectuals and would-be actor aspirants who normally flocked to such gatherings.

As Abbas picked up a conversation with another guest, Alkazi took the opportunity to slip away and settled down in a discreet corner from where he could observe the crowd. From his perch, Alkazi noticed that there were a number of beautiful women dotted around. Dressed in casual cotton salwar kameez, they did not appear film-starry at all. In fact, they spoke easily with intelligence and confidence, an attitude that Alkazi appreciated. These were the new breed of India's *modern* women—

educated, professionally oriented, and definitely material for today's theatre, he thought!

As his eyes roved over the crowd, they settled on two rather attractive women in saris, chatting and smoking quietly. One was tall and stately, with her hair severely drawn back in a rather manly fashion. The other had her back to him. Slim with slightly stooped shoulders, she turned and saw Alkazi looking in her direction. She said something to her companion and they moved forward towards him with wide smiles. Alkazi stood up rather awkwardly and shyly emerged from the shadows.

'Welcome, Mr Alkazi! How wonderful that you could make it! Shenoy did mention that you might come along today. Come, let me first introduce you to one of my dearest friends, Hima Kesarkodi, a very fine actress, I may add. By the way, Alkazi, Hima and I saw your production at the Bhulabhai Institute the other day, the Molière one. You were simply brilliant! Your sense of timing and movement in comedy—one was simply dumbstruck!'

Flattered by the compliment, Alkazi smiled.

'And you are?'

'Gosh! I'm terribly sorry! How foolish of me not to introduce myself! I'm Uma Anand, the host!'

Uma Anand's voice was warm, friendly, melodious and cultivated, no doubt.

'Chetan! Look who's here! Alkazi!' Uma called out, as Chetan and an older, tall, striking-looking man emerged from behind a bush. Dressed casually, with wavy hair and a kind, handsome face, Chetan extended his hand in a warm greeting. The two men sized each other up in the blink of an eye. Shaking hands, Alkazi congratulated Chetan on *Neecha Nagar*.

'That's old hat now. You must watch my new film *Taxi Driver* with my brother, Dev Anand, in the lead. Let me have your candid opinion!'

'Chetan! Don't forget! We're going to see Alkazi's forthcoming production, *Oedipus Rex*, at that new venue at the BDI that you've not seen yet. Also, Alkazi is about to open a new acting school there.'

'Really? That's wonderful news! God knows, the industry is in dire need of trained blokes,' Chetan pointed generally around, 'all severely in need of training!'

'I'm glad you think so.'

'Tell me, Alkazi, have you managed to find some talent yet?'

Alkazi had begun to relax in the presence of someone like Chetan Anand, who appeared to be on the same wavelength as him.

'If I may be frank with you, Mr Anand, the student actor is already half ruined before he assumes training, most of which necessarily consists of undoing the harm already done to him in the preceding years. He comes with certain preconceived notions of the art of acting, which he has picked up through watching amateur or professional theatre or films. To him, acting means the imitation on the stage of his favourite screen idol!'[2]

They all burst out laughing.

'I hope you won't mind my adding that the Indian actor, even when he is talented and hardworking is often both ignorant and indifferent to the *arts* . . . to painting, sculpture, music, literature and architecture! The result is that he never notices the *mediocrity* or frequently, the sheer *vulgarity* of the setting in which he functions. He is prepared to wear *outrageously* designed costumes in *fantastic* colours or suffer the indignity of moving among bric-a-brac bought for the occasion from Chor Bazaar! This tradition of *unaesthetic* nonsense that is today acceptable to *thousands* in the Indian theatre must be smashed up relentlessly! One should have absolutely no patience with it!'[3]

Dev Anand, Uma and Chetan Anand, 1954

There was a brief, stunned silence as Alkazi's little audience of four were somewhat taken aback at the intensity of his tirade!

'Well, well, Alkazi! You certainly are a man of uncompromising views!'

'By the way,' said Chetan, 'this is Rafi Peer, my star in *Neecha Nagar* ... *trained*, not *untrained*, by none other than Max Reinhardt in Germany!'

'You were at RADA, I believe?' said Rafi to Alkazi. 'Would love to join Uma and Chetan to see your *Oedipus*!'

'Yes, certainly, welcome! You all must come. I look forward to that.'

While Chetan and Peer carried on perambulating through the guests, for the next couple of hours, Alkazi had the two women, Uma and Hima, in thrall, regaling them with his elaborate plans for the school of drama and for working towards theatre as a serious profession. Both of them were mesmerized by the scale of his vision and the depth of his ideas. His eyes sparkled, his words were precise and his voice trembled with excitement. Alkazi seemed to have great clarity as to where he wanted to go. It was only as Uma listened to Alkazi that she realized how much she actually missed theatre. It was after a long time that she had come across a person as passionately involved in theatre as she had always been. Cinema was fine, and maybe Chetan did not miss theatre, but for her, theatre was *the* medium of her choice. It was live and vibrant, and this man, Alkazi, spoke so eloquently of his own passion for it. It shook her from inside; it was quite unnerving.

As they bid goodnight, Uma added, 'By the way, Alkazi, it just struck me, would you consider doing your production of *Physician* as a radio play? Radio is a good source of extra income for actors! I'm a producer of the *Women's World* programme on AIR. I could talk to my colleagues in the drama section. Let me know!'

CHAPTER 23
HOSTING SPENDER
1954-55

'In November of Catherine Wheels and Rockets
This luring ranter, man and boy,
Proved Guy Fox true, and burned on a real fire.
His rhymes that stuffed his body with a straw,
His poems he shed out of his pockets with squibs and string
and ... and wire.
The crackling Ghost Thorn crowned him with spiked joy.
Where he sang, burning, round his neck a cupped bag
"Pennies! Pennies for the Guy!"'[1]

Stephen Spender's American-accented voice floats on the afternoon breeze wafting in through the windows of the terrace summer house of the Bhulabhai Desai Institute, enveloping the small group sitting in rapt attention.[2] It is Spender's poem about the death of his close friend, Dylan Thomas. The handsome young poet in shirtsleeves had removed his jacket earlier in the day in a symbolic gesture, making it easier to exchange views more freely. Approximately ten Theatre Unit members make up his attentive audience, among them Alkazi, Roshen, Nissim, Mary Sethna, Khorshed Wadia, Pheroza Cooper, Bomi Kapadia, Manohar Pitale and Minoo Chhoi. Roshen, in sun goggles, seven and a half months pregnant and positively glowing, sits alongside Elk and Spender. With such an eminent poet in their midst, Rosh has sprung to life, the interaction possibly reminding her of the poetry sessions she had so enjoyed with Bobby and his friends on the KT terrace.

On Spender's arrival earlier that morning, Alkazi had introduced him to the work of the Theatre Unit, showing him photographs of their productions, copies of the *TUB*, and exhibition catalogues of 'This is

Stephen Spender addressing members of the Theatre Unit, 1954

Modern Art', not forgetting to mention with some pride that they had held a public poetry reading with recordings of Spender's poems along with those of Edith Sitwell and C. Day Lewis the previous year.[3] After a light lunch, the group settles down to listen to Spender read a selection of his poems. He reads sensitively and clearly, his choice of poems veering in favour of those with social commitment, along with some personal ones, such as one on his daughter.

He rounds off the session with the one on Dylan Thomas, mentioning that it had not yet been published. A member of the group points out that today, 9 November 1954, is Thomas's first death anniversary. Visibly moved, Spender pauses after the poem and then mentions that he has never read it aloud before. The day has indeed been a memorable one for all and Alkazi is especially pleased that Spender has acceded to their request for an audio recording of his reading to be played later to a larger audience.

Over the last month, Alkazi has run into Uma Anand on a couple of occasions, where she offers to be of assistance to him in his theatre work. Alkazi suggests that since Spender is in town, it would be significant if she could arrange an interview with him on All India Radio (AIR).[*] Uma

---

[*] In her unpublished autobiographical note, Uma Anand mentions that she interviewed not only Spender, but many visitors that Alkazi hosted at the TU.

readily agrees to take it on herself, on the condition that Alkazi will fill her in on Spender's background and help formulate some suitable questions.

Alkazi shares with Uma that he has been an ardent admirer of Spender since his student days in England. He is well-acquainted with Spender's passion for all the arts, borne out by his close kinship with W.H. Auden, Christopher Isherwood, T.S. Eliot, Lucian Freud and Henry Moore—writers, poets and painters whom Alkazi too admires greatly. Having lived through the wars, Spender believes that art and literature are able to transcend political and ideological divides and help find a common humanity. His acceptance of the editorship of literary magazines such as *Horizon* and *Encounter* is in pursuance of the same goals.

Encounter is a magazine aimed at promoting an 'East–West Encounter'. The publication is responsible for Spender's visit to India, providing him an opportunity to interact with Indian authors and intellectuals whom the magazine will ultimately cultivate and promote in their journey towards supporting new modernisms in Asia.

While researching my father's era for this book, I noticed that, from approximately the mid-1950s onwards, Bombay had begun to see an influx of artists from the United States. Preceding Spender by a few days was the editor of *Theatre Arts Journal*, Rosamond Gilder, who attended the First World Theatre Conference in Bombay organized by the Bharatiya Natya Sangh and sponsored by the International Theatre Institute (29 October to 5 November 1954). This was followed by Monroe Wheeler, director of the Exhibitions and Publications Outreach Program of MoMA, New York, who met my father and was impressed with his efforts at disseminating modernism through 'This is Modern Art'. This led Wheeler to regularly gift Alkazi prints for forthcoming shows. The year 1956 saw the huge MoMA photographic exhibition 'The Family of Man', curated and designed by Edward Steichen, open at Jehangir Art Gallery, before circulating to several cities in India. Isamu Noguchi, an American architect and sculptor of Japanese origin, began visiting India as his interest lay in the architecture of the ancient Nalanda University. Noguchi's visit to Alkazi's exhibition 'The Cubists' in 1958 was documented in a photograph in my father's collection. Another visitor was Joseph Campbell, the American scholar of comparative mythology and religion, with his wife, the dancer Jean Erdman. Both were invited to speak on the growth and development

Stephen Spender looking through photo albums of Theatre Unit productions

of modern American dance at the Theatre Unit by Alkazi, while Alexander Calder, the American artist of kinetic sculpture, conducted a workshop for Alkazi's students at The School of Dramatic Arts. Alkazi displayed Calder's mobiles at his 'Matisse Memorial' show, as well as included one of them in his stage design for Strindberg's *The Father* in 1958.

Those were years when the Cold War was at its peak. Nehru's socialist leanings towards the USSR were sought to be balanced by the USA. The latter attempted to influence 'leaders' of Indian society, including artists and intellectuals, in their quest for 'freedom of speech' and 'peace', core 'democratic' values that were upheld by the USA in their resistance and fight against the Iron Curtain policy of the Communists. It was only many years later, in the 1960s and 1970s, that it became evident that the CIA had indeed been funding a significant number of cultural activities, including the visits of people connected with the arts to India. Through agencies such as the Indian Council for Cultural Freedom and the United States Information Service (USIS), the CIA had funded books, journals, translations, readers' digests, festivals, conferences, seminars, exhibitions, radio, film and book programmes, including the funding of *Quest*, the magazine that Nissim Ezekiel had been invited to edit right from its inception in 1954.[4] Unaware of the CIA's involvement, Hindi writers such as Mohan Rakesh and Agyeya, along with Indian writers in English such as Adil Jussawalla, Gauri Deshpande, Gieve Patel, etc., vehemently protested when they found out that they were being used as pawns on the chessboard of USA–USSR politics.[*]

Even if funded by the CIA, such intense cultural activity had a positive side as well. It contributed significantly during those formative years towards nurturing a cosmopolitanism and internationalism in Indian poetry and fiction in English and the vernaculars, as well as establishing a transnational dialogue between Indian and American writers, thinkers and artists.

We should not forget that among those who visited India were some of the most eminent American scholars, artists and writers, widely recognized as *the* cutting-edge modernists of their time. Their visits became opportunities for a person like my father to personally get to know them. He often invited them to our tiny home in Vithal Court to share a simple meal and it was over these homely, informal lunches or dinners that we learned of an evolving post-war American culture that had begun to make a dramatic shift away from European Modernism. American art was reacting against traditional artistic conventions and asserting, for example, that art did not belong in institutions like academies, theatres, museums or concert halls but had to be accessible to all. Furthermore, new mediums such as photography and cinema had to be recognized as belonging to the spectrum of not merely popular but high forms of modern art. These ideas certainly fed into Alkazi's knowledge of the new directions contemporary art was taking.

Even as a student in Britain, Alkazi had gleaned that America supported new thinking on the art of the future. Many years later, in the 1980s, these experiences led my father to eventually opt for the US over Britain or France as the country that could potentially work as a home for an institution with an international perspective.

*　*　*

---

[*]　In a posthumously published interview, the modernist Hindi writer Mohan Rakesh acknowledged India had been 'a chess board . . . between the United States' ideologists and the USSR's ideologists', and many intellectuals 'were being made pawns in the game'.—*Journal of South Asia Literature*, Mohan Rakesh, K.P. Singh, Azhgar Wajahat, 1973, Vol. 9.

On 26 December 1954, Alkazi was in New Delhi, opening his new production of Sophocles' *Oedipus Rex*.[5] The Theatre Unit had been invited to participate in the Union Government's first National Drama Festival at Sapru House, New Delhi. Playing on the national stage for the first time to a packed hall of discerning theatre lovers, critics, officials of the Ministry of Education and the Sangeet Natak Akademi, Alkazi's production was hailed by the festival as outstanding and received an 'Honourable Mention'.

In Delhi, Alkazi was introduced to Ashfaque Husain, joint secretary, Ministry of Education, and Prof. G.D. Sondhi,[*] sports adviser to the Government of India, who informed him of the government's plan to hold a month-long theatre training course at Subato, near Shimla, inviting Alkazi and his team to conduct it.

On the same visit, Alkazi befriended Dr Charles Fabri, a Hungarian historian and archeologist, who had recently shifted to Delhi from Lahore after marrying Uma's close friend, Ratna, a textile designer. Fabri was also the art and theatre critic for the *Statesman*. Alkazi met Romesh Chander as well, a graduate of Government College, Lahore, and an erstwhile Trade Union leader, now a journalist at the *Patriot*.[†] These were among Delhi's theatre buffs, a small coterie whom Alkazi met for the first time, inviting both Chander and Fabri to contribute articles to *TUB*, where Chander henceforth functioned as the Delhi correspondent!

* * *

The new year saw eleven shows of *Oedipus Rex*, beginning on 8 January 1955. My brother Feisal was born the very next day, 9 January. My father was absolutely thrilled to have a son, making Feisal the first Alkazi grandson in the family! For my mother, too, it was a wondrous occasion, as 9 January was Bobby's death anniversary, leading friends and family to speculate whether Feisal was a 'reincarnation' of Bobby!

---

[*] G.D. Sondhi was known to the educationist from Lahore and Uma Anand's father, Prof. G.C. Chatterji. Sondhi's achievements included building an open-air theatre at Lawrence Gardens along the lines of a Greek theatre with a skene building and an orchestra.

[†] Romesh Chander was a colourful character who had organized a workers' theatre in Lahore (during World War II), performing street plays at factory gates.

Oedipus was a major success with housefuls, unheard of for a tragedy.* It had a strong cast of Nargis Cowasji as Jocasta, Alkazi himself as Oedipus, Bomi Kapadia as Tiresias, the soothsayer, Shenoy as the shepherd, and Pheroza Cooper, Hilla Divecha and Vijaya Jaywant as the chorus women. I was seven at the time and played Antigone, the younger daughter of Oedipus, while Antoinette Diniz, who later married Gieve Patel, played Ismene, my elder sister. We made our entry at the very end of the play when Oedipus, with his eyes gouged out, bids farewell to us, his children, and we cling to him, begging him not to abandon us! The image of my father howling and weeping in despair with blood coursing down his cheeks can never be erased from my memory.

The originality of the *Oedipus* staging also probably accounted for its success. Performed on the rear lawns of the BDI, directly on the grass, with no elevated stage, the audience sat facing the stage and on the same level as the actors. Another group of audience members were seated at a height of about twenty feet above the acting area, along the parapet of the BDI terrace. Bombay audiences had never before experienced this steep bird's-eye view of the stage from a height. Maybe Alkazi sought to simulate the view a fourth-century member of the audience would have had from the top row of a Greek amphitheater! Adding to the visual experience was Alkazi's stark and bold set design. As Vijaya Mehta (née Jaywant) recollected:

> The lawns looked like a satiny green carpet, surrounded by big and small bushes. At the rear of the performing area were two huge bamboos that had been erected about fifteen feet high. Across them was another twelve foot bamboo tied horizontally. Over this abstract entrance structure was thrown a large blood-coloured sack cloth. That is all. The verdant green surroundings were serene and beautiful, and marring all this was the blood red sack cloth! How else could a subject like *Oedipus* be portrayed? This was Mr Alkazi! He looked for drama in all art forms.[6]

Alkazi's productions had now begun to attract an entirely new audience. Uma Anand brought along the Anand clan—Chetan, Goldie

---

* Akbar Padamsee was back from Paris and designed the brochure cover with the drawing of an elongated Greek mask!

Roshen and Alkazi at the Theatre Unit Ball, 1955

and Dev—along with her friends from the film industry, youngsters like Wasi Khan, Satyadev Dubey and Amrish Puri. An increasing number arrived from Marathi, Gujarati and Hindi–Urdu theatres. From Marathi theatre, there were experimental playwrights Mama Warerkar and P.L. Deshpande, Durgabai Khote—an actress who had heard about Alkazi from D.G. Nadkarni—while Damu Jhaveri and Dina Pathak from Gujarati theatre came out of curiosity and excitement to watch Alkazi's modernist stagings.

Alkazi made the effort to perform *Oedipus* and other TU plays at the Elphinstone and Ismail Yusuf colleges. Thus, further excitement and interest in Alkazi's activities were generated, helping to effectively spread the word about Theatre Unit's School of Dramatic Arts, which was to be launched in July of the same year.

* * *

Over the following months, all the members of the Theatre Unit were entirely caught up in preparations for a theatre ball to raise funds for the proposed School of Dramatic Arts.[7] Alkazi had requested the Bhulabhai and Dhirajlal Desai Memorial Trusts to collaborate with TU to create a high-profile Theatre Ball Committee comprising prominent citizens of Bombay, such as A.J. Wadia, Madhuri Behn Desai, Roshan Sabavala, Soli Batliwala, Sophie Natrajan, Pheroza Cooper and Bapsy Sabawalla. Bapsy wholeheartedly supported Alkazi in his theatrical efforts, her only caveat being that Alkazi cast her in small roles from time to time! On this occasion, Bapsy got a large number of corporate houses of Bombay to advertise in the Theatre Ball brochure!

The Theatre Ball became the talk of the town! Held at the Taj Mahal Hotel, the ballroom was candlelit and especially decorated to create a theatre-like ambience. Tickets for dinner were offered at Rs 15 per head and served at buffet booths designed to remind one of Alkazi's past productions: 'The Archbishop's Larder' for *Murder in the Cathedral*; 'Bernada's Kitchen' for *The House of Bernada Alba*; and 'The Grecian Urn' for *Oedipus Rex*. Hostesses were attired in period costumes, making this the talking point of the entire event. There was also a 'Mughal Window' where *paan* was offered with attendants suitably costumed in Mughal outfits! Freny Talyarkhan compered the show with wit and skill, while Mickey Correa's band provided live music. The Governor of Bombay, Harekrushna Mehtab, graced the occasion. He arrived at 11 p.m. but

Members of the Subato workshop with Alkazi, 1955

made up for it by keeping the audience entertained with his speech and then staying on till well past midnight! Roshen, an avid ballroom dancer, could not stop snapping her fingers to the lively rhythms of the band and, after much persuasion, convinced Elk to join her on the dance floor. Elk, though a brilliant actor, was a terribly shy dancer! Unable to keep up with Roshen, he soon began clowning around, much to the merriment of the onlookers! At the end of the evening, a cheque for the handsome sum of Rs 30,000 was handed over to the Theatre Unit by the Bhulabhai Dhirajlal Trust. There was much applause and Alkazi was in his element! This was the beginning of fulfilling his long-cherished dream of establishing a proper training school for theatre practitioners.

***

Their youthful energy and excitement allowed Alkazi, Rosh, Nissim and Pheroza Cooper to board a train the very next morning and depart for the month-long Subato Summer Camp, near Shimla. Under the auspices of the government's Youth Welfare Committee, Sondhi had enrolled a group of university teachers from Bombay, Delhi, Punjab, Kashmir, Nagpur and Saugor (Madhya Pradesh) to be trained in theatre. Alkazi was to teach acting and production, while Roshen taught costume design, Pheroza taught speech and Nissim gave lectures on dramatic literature and criticism.

It is from the sylvan surroundings of Subato that we find the first three personal letters from Alkazi to Uma Anand. These were written on the last few days of the course and it becomes evident that they have grown quite close since they first met approximately six months ago.

The letters reveal that Uma is in Kashmir and has not yet written to Alkazi. They suggest that he is developing deep and abiding feelings for Uma, which he refrains from articulating directly. Written in a poetic vein, he describes his distracted state of mind: how he wanders through the garden like a stricken lover, communing with nature while desperately awaiting a missive from her. On 20 April 1955, he writes:

> All day long, the cries of birds, ecstatic—sparrow and bulbul and myna and koyel and rook and wood pigeon. Murdering, stabbing cries: somehow, they go deep down within me.

Silence yet. No word from Kashmir. Is one's joy so great as to know no words? One cannot help feeling more than a little anxious.

While he wanders around, forlorn, all God's creatures seem oblivious of his predicament, enjoying themselves in gay abandon. In this little garden, just below the house is a tiny lotus pool, neither round nor square but the shape of a squiggle and there, some four or five generations of frogs stir up such a cacophony so as to put the creatures of Aristophanes to shame. I would never have believed that frogs could make such strange sounds, for they were not just croaks but an infinite number of musical variations. High-pitched and low, staccato and long-drawn-out, rising and falling and leaping and swooning and bubbling and groaning.

One impertinent and shameless hussy reclined naked on a lotus leaf, in the manner of Madame Recamier and blurted in my face the most filthy obscenities. She must have been to a harlot with her lack of modesty and her unbecoming airs, and around her a flirting of young beaux and silly... wandered suggestively. I flung a stone among the pack of them and they wiggled their bottoms at me and fled to deeper haunts.

The whole place is a modest Garden of Eden...

In another instance, Alkazi philosophizes on the dignity and beauty of nature that humans thoughtlessly despoil.

28 April 1955

When three days ago, we lowered it (a flower) into this bowl we could not escape a feeling of faith. To sever a flower, to abduct it from its relations and friends, to bear it away from the touch of wind and sun and travelling beetle, and to enthrone it with solemn human dignity in a bowl—there's something unbearably absurd and unbecoming in the act.

What shamed one into silence was its dignity. Over this small watery kingdom it asserted its rights; it assumed a power over everything around it—and over us too—which astounded us. It assailed us with its own beauty, which it kept to itself. What pulsing volcanic energy, used with what still restraint, summoned from what deep, dark, mysterious source, made this flower unfurl itself petal by petal in the early morning and close itself to sleep at night.

It rests here in tranquil self-assurance, knowing that when the time comes for it to close, the strength will come too, in its proper measure. It humiliates us by the manner in which it has assumed its destiny. From moment to moment, it fulfils itself, not fevered or desperate or anguished. It has gathered the world around itself only to discard it, to claim to be nothing more and nothing—not even by a breath—less than itself.

I believe that part of Alkazi's wonder and love of nature comes from his Islamic background, wherein the Quran extols the beauties of 'Nature' as manifestations of God's creations. The 'Artist' in Islam is held in the highest esteem precisely because he or she is a person who seeks to follow God's example by creating beauty. Therefore, a love of nature is by extension, an expression of one's appreciation and love for God. It is precisely because of this that neither Hamed Alkazi nor his wife Mariam ever objected to their children becoming artists; in fact, they greatly encouraged and supported the idea.

CHAPTER 24

THE SCHOOL OF DRAMATIC ARTS: MODERNITY AND PROFESSIONALISM ON STAGE
1955

Kusum and her sister Pratima hurried up the slope leading from Warden Road to the entrance of the Bhulabhai Desai Institute. Wide, curved steps followed the shape of the spacious bungalow, giving the single-storey structure an elegant, palatial look. The young girls were a year apart—Pratima, the older one, was seventeen and attending music classes there. It was already 3.15 p.m., and she was late. The walk from Navroji Gamadia Road had taken longer than usual today, as the strap on Kusum's sandal had suddenly snapped.

Pratima sprinted ahead, shouting, 'Try and fix that, Kusum! I'm rushing off!'

Practically in tears, Kusum kicked off her sandal and sat on the broad ledge of one of the French windows encircling the capacious veranda. The salty sea breeze dried up the tiny droplets of perspiration that had collected on her dome-shaped brow. Fair, with classically beautiful features and large, chestnut brown eyes, people were always drawn to young Kusum, with her petiteness, soft-spoken manner and melodious voice. She was bored and lonely these days, as she had finished her Senior Cambridge exams at sixteen and had a whole year to kill before she joined college. So, she took to accompanying her sister to the BDI thrice a week.

'Good afternoon, Mr Alkazi!' a student's voice rang out.

'Hello, Sir!'

Mr Alkazi was seated at a desk partitioned off from the corridor. Looking up, he smiled and returned to his work! Then, looking up again, his attention was drawn to the young girl, who looked quite distraught.

He walked up and asked with affectionate concern, 'I see you sitting here sometimes. Are you attending any of the classes, young lady?'

Flustered, Kusum stood up and said, 'No, I'm waiting for my sister to finish her music class.'

'Would you like to watch an acting class while you wait?'

Kusum was taken aback. Mr Alkazi seemed so polite and kind.

'I don't mind, actually!' she said shyly.

This was Kusum's first introduction to Alkazi and the School of Dramatic Arts (SDA)! Her eyes shone as she watched student actors impersonate different roles. Later that evening, she prevailed upon her parents to permit her to join the SDA. Little did they realize that she would be pursuing her lifelong calling. Under Alkazi's tutelage, Kusum Haidar (née Behl) was to rise to histrionic heights, becoming one of India's illustrious actresses who played some of the most complex characters ever written for the stage—Antigone, Eurydice, Blanche du Bois and Yerma.*

Pheroza Cooper teaches acting at the School of Dramatic Arts, Theatre Unit, 1955

Opening in July 1955, Alkazi had established a comprehensive, two-year programme for the SDA. Shenoy and Alkazi were the senior course instructors for acting, improvisation and student productions; Nissim taught dramatic literature and Pheroza Cooper, who had undergone formal training at RADA and again under Alkazi, taught speech and mime. Professionals like Zoe Bebbington, an elocution teacher in a Bombay

---

* These were directed by Alkazi. However, Kusum also acted with other directors, including Habib Tanvir, Joy Michael, Amal Allana and Zuleikha Chaudhari. She also taught voice and speech at St Columbus School.

school, taught diction; Guru Pannikar took Kathakali classes; B.K.M. Iyengar taught yoga; and Joglekar, a professional make-up artist from the Marathi stage, taught make-up. Swept along by subjects she had never heard of, Kusum reminisced:

> We had a variety of sessions on voice production, speech, movement and improvisation. Mr Alkazi often took individual classes. We learnt Hindi and Kathakali, and had music and art appreciation classes. The improvisation classes were conducted by Mr P.D. Shenoy—a fabulous teacher . . . one of the most well-read persons I knew. He introduced us to the works of Kierkegaard, Camus and Satre . . . Then people started doing their plays . . . and then I was shocked when Mr Alkazi cast me as Antigone! I didn't even know what a play was![1]

In fact, it was to a rehearsal of *Antigone* that Shenoy brought another young aspirant, Vijaya Mehta (nee Jaywant),[*] to observe the session. Vijaya recollects:

> P.D. Shenoy took Viju to a rehearsal that was at Mr Alkazi's residence. Viju was sitting in a smallish hall and just seven to eight feet away the scene between Haemon and Antigone was being rehearsed. During the course of the rehearsal, Mr Alkazi instructed the actor playing Haemon to embrace Antigone in fervour and kiss her. Both the actors were perturbed at first. But rehearsing repeatedly made them comfortable . . . There was one person in the audience who was completely stunned—Viju. She had never witnessed a kiss between a man and a woman in her entire life . . . In those early years, Viju's middle-class Maharashtrian sensibilities received many jolts . . . Theatre Unit took her through a lot of 'non-Maharashtrian' experiences.[2]

---

[*] Vijaya Jaywant belonged to an eminent Maharashtrian theatre family and was the cousin of film actors Nutan and Tanuja. In her autobiography, *Zimma*, she refers to herself in the third person as Viju.

It was evident that Alkazi's reputation as a serious teacher of theatre was spreading in the vernacular theatre community. Endorsements came from eminent Maharashtrian playwrights such as Mama Warerkar and critics such as D.G. Nadkarni. Meena Chitnis, son of Leela Chitnis, and Vijay Anand, brother of Chetan and Dev Anand, enrolled as well. Vijay Anand encouraged Satyadev Dubey, who had come to Bombay from Bilaspur, to join SDA too.

Apart from the SDA, Alkazi expanded his activities to include directing plays with students at colleges such as Elphinstone College. It was here that the young Alaknanda Samarth, along with her colleagues Farida Sonawala, Shiamak Shahvakshah, Yasmin Mody, etc., participated in Alkazi's productions of Molière's *Sganarelle* and Christopher Fry's *A Phoenix Too Frequent*. Alaknanda, who played Dynamene in *Phoenix,* showed remarkable spark and potential, which Alkazi was quick to recognize.

> My darling Rosh,
>
> The Elphinstone plays got over last night. There were three shows in all—Sat, Sun, Mon—with full houses on the first two nights. All in all, they went over excellently with the audiences...
>
> *Phoenix* was a much more mature and polished piece of work—comparatively... In Alaknanda, who comes from a cultured family of actresses (Shobhana Samarth is her aunt, Nutan her cousin), we have someone who speaks English beautifully and has a natural flair for acting. She is good in comedy as well as serious plays; Hindi too. So let's groom her...[3]

With a growing number of students, members of the Theatre Unit, such as Cedric Santos, Amjad Ali and Abdul Shakoor, gave unstintingly of their time after office hours to assist with the management and administration of a now formal institution that ran a regular, six-day-a-week theatre training programme.

* * *

It is important to understand the rationale behind Alkazi's need to build a 'national' language for theatre. At the historical juncture of

Independence, the move towards cultivating an 'authentic' Indian identity had taken precedence, and Hindi had been adopted as the country's official language. However, ten years had already elapsed since Independence and people began questioning whether there was such a thing as 'an authentic Indian language' in a subcontinent of multiple languages, races, religions and lifestyles. Multiple regional voices began to protest the imposition of Hindi across the country. They demanded that their languages and cultural differences be acknowledged.

Language was also a matter of concern for urban writers who wrote in English. Questions were raised as to whether they could legitimately be regarded as 'Indian' writers as they did not use a mother tongue. Bombay poets, spearheaded by none other than Nissim Ezekiel, demanded that not just English, but a colloquial version of English laced with Hindi and Marathi words, become acceptable.[4]

In the midst of these strong views being expressed, Alkazi felt he had to approach the language issue in a rational manner. He had neither political issues with Hindi nor an emotional attachment to it. As a theatre educationist, he had to decide whether students of acting should be taught to speak fluent Hindi or English. Where was it likely that his students would end up practising their craft? The answer was probably in the film industry, which basically functioned through Hindi–Hindustani, or alternately in vernacular languages such as Marathi or Gujarati that commanded sizeable audiences.

Deciding that the language of instruction at the SDA would be both English and Hindi, Alkazi insisted that all students from English-speaking backgrounds, as well as those whose mother tongue was other than Hindi, would need to learn Hindi as they would be doing plays in both Hindi and English. Accordingly, a Hindi teacher was engaged by Alkazi and SDA students were required to appear for government-approved examinations in the Hindi language.

The dearth of plays in Hindi prompted Alkazi to encourage students to write and stage plays. Translations of Western classics, such as *The Heiress* by Ruth Goetz and Augustus Goetz, based on the novel *Washington Square* by Henry James, was translated and directed by Moneeka Misra[*] in 1956.

---

[*] Misra was then a teacher at the SDA. She later married Habib Tanvir.

This was followed by Shakespeare's *Julius Caesar* in Hindi, a classroom production performed in the arena style. Jean Anouilh's *Antigone* was performed first in English and then in Hindi, with Kusum Behl in both* and Meena Chitnis and Satyadev Dubey playing the lead roles.

* * *

At a staff meeting held at the conclusion of the SDA's first year, it was decided that the SDA would increasingly dedicate itself to working in Hindi. Staff members suggested that in order to attract larger numbers, the school prospectus should be printed in Hindi and advertisements inserted in vernacular newspapers. This, coupled with SDA's affordable fees, would encourage students from diverse classes and backgrounds to enrol.

Perhaps unknowingly, Alkazi had brought together two mutually exclusive, insular camps that did not normally socialize or fraternize with one another. The erosion of social class and linguistic differences undoubtedly led to a greater understanding of one another, but at the same time, created a certain amount of unease, especially among upper and middle-class families, whose daughters began to enrol. Vijaya Jaywant tellingly recounts:

> Once Viju decided to pursue Theatre Unit and turned her back on the Hindi cinema, Bhai's attitude towards her changed drastically. Bhai (Vijaya's brother) had realized that the people connected to the Theater Unit were from the corporate world, travelled abroad and in spite of being non-Maharashtrians they were well-read. He had also made a note of Babasaheb's opinion. Babasaheb trusted his friends, Nissim Ezekiel and Soli Batlivala. Poor old Baiji was left to her own devices and was busy worrying. Her problem was not a simple question like 'Who will marry Baby?', but would she now catch hold of a Parsi or a Muslim or even a much elderly married person? She was plagued by this horrible worry![5]

---

* The Hindi production of *Antigone* had Meena Chitnis as Creon and Satyadev Dubey as Haemon. Both were SDA students at the time. This production was later taken to Delhi along with *A Phoenix Too Frequent* by Alkazi. These were the first productions to introduce both Alaknanda Samarth and Kusum Behl to the Delhi audience in 1955–56.

As social transitions of this nature were evolving, it is interesting to try and grasp how Alkazi was being perceived, especially by the 'vernacular' group. My guess is that they held an ambivalent opinion of him. While on the one hand he was venerated as a learned guru of the arts who was helping them gain an international and modern outlook that contributed to their upward mobility as the new 'vernacular' elite, Alkazi was also viewed with a certain amount of suspicion and scepticism that became more pronounced once he arrived on the national scene.

* * *

Having put a strong core team of teachers and administrators in place for the SDA, Alkazi went on to envisage how a professional theatre movement could grow out of the school. His idea was that, subsequent to receiving all-round basic training, the actors would be absorbed as interns into what he called the Theatre Unit's Repertory Company. Here they would have an opportunity to act with more experienced actors and engage in professionally mounted productions. Thus, by creating two entities, a school and a repertory, Alkazi sought to establish a direct link between the actor training programme and professional practice.

This kind of synergy of one institution feeding into another had been developed in Russia by Konstantin Stanislavski between his professional company, The Moscow Art Theatre, and his acting school-cum-laboratory, The First Studio, in 1912. Similarly, in 1935, a module was devised by the great director–pedagogue Michel Saint–Denis, who established a theatre school, London Theatre Studio, which continuously fed a repertory company, The Old Vic, with fresh talent. On completion of their course, youngsters would act in smaller roles alongside stalwarts such as Laurence Olivier, John Gielgud, Peggy Ashcroft and Vivien Leigh in West End productions before finally launching into their professional careers. This kind of direct link between training and practice also, importantly, provided for a continuity of approach to an acting methodology that could be built upon and developed from one generation to the next as an ongoing, cohesive tradition.

* * *

The fare Alkazi planned for the Repertory Company was 'World Classics'. As can be imagined, the actors back then in the 1950s had no idea as to how these plays from the western canon were to be performed, having neither read nor watched productions of them (except the occasional Shakespeare play that came to India). It meant walking into completely uncharted territory for the performers, the director, as well as the audience.

As a director, Alkazi devised original ways to help actors enter the text. Much of his rehearsal time was spent familiarizing the cast not just with the text but also stimulating their imaginations with images of the art, architecture and costumes of the period through slides, books, films, etc. He also sensitized them to the original language by making them listen to recorded music and poetry of that era. The rehearsal process, therefore, was an immersive experience into the lifestyle and history, the arts and the philosophy of a bygone era.

Regarding the 'acting style' required for a particular play, Alkazi believed there were no standard ways of enacting a Shakespeare, a Shaw, an Ibsen or an Anouilh character. Therefore, weeks were spent in 'laboratory mode', trying to *discover* an appropriate approach. For Alkazi, the body is a dynamic instrument that is the most expressive tool in the actor's arsenal. Freny Bhownagary references a performance she saw of Alkazi in and as *Richard III* at RADA, where physicality appears to be one of the hallmarks of Alkazi's own instinctive approach to acting:

> In 1949, I saw Alkazi as Richard III, in an end-of-term performance at the Royal Academy of Dramatic Art, London, where he had just completed his first year. He seemed to me then to possess more of the mannerisms, vitality and liveliness of a French actor, in particular, Jean–Louis Barrault, than any English actor I could think of. He had a natural talent for using mime and bodily movements in his acting, which is understandable considering that this is the Indian way of expression. Like the French, we speak with our hands and facial expressions just as much as with our voices. Alkazi had not seen the French stage at that time so there was no question of his imitating it; there was just a certain natural, uncultivated similarity.[6]

* * *

Acutely conscious of his role as an instructor, Alkazi chose scripts that could be used as vehicles for actor training rather than fulfilling his creative needs as a director. For example, he selected *Murder in the Cathedral* to work on speech, while *The Physician In Spite of Himself* became an exercise in exploring body and movement.

'In no other production could the urgent need for movement have made itself more manifest than in this one.'[7] In an insightful article published in the *TUB*, Alkazi outlines the rehearsal process for this movement-driven production.

After a few failed attempts at finding their way into *Physician* through readings and discussions, he and the cast

> ... felt that the words provided a skeletal framework for the more elaborate clowning and comic business we would have to develop, in much the same way as a script for a COMMEDIA DELL'ARTE performance...

Recognizing that the greatest weakness of their productions lay in the poor, inconsequential movement of the actors, and the inexpressiveness of their bodies, Alkazi said:

> We now started with IMPROVISATION—that is, the enactment of scenes or episodes on the stage without the use of speech... Confronted with the difficulty of trying to communicate through a medium they had never used [the actors] began to discover that, though mute, the body can become the most telling of instruments... They began to realize the need for observing things afresh, for experiencing emotions anew.

After weeks of improvising, the whole first act was played in mime. To their surprise, the play sprang immediately to life. It became obvious to them how the script was nothing but a framework for the vigorous slapstick of the Commedia Dell'Arte.

Alkazi followed up this process with a lantern lecture on the history of mime through the ages, with particular emphasis on the remarkable influence of the Commedia dell'arte on Molière. But Alkazi still found it difficult to dispel the self-consciousness that was the bane of the amateur actor. How can the actor novice be persuaded to act without being thwarted by his own inhibitions? One of the ways is by providing him with a mask.

Wearing a mask gives the actor a strange but reassuring sense of anonymity. Since his face is covered, he loses his identity, becomes suddenly a being other than himself, and permits himself to indulge in all sorts of capers, contortions and uninhibited movements which he would be too self-conscious to do in his own guise. Concealed behind his mask, he feels he can observe without being observed, and this gives him the courage to perform with the greatest freedom before an audience.[8]

The Physician in Spite of Himself by Moliere, dir. E. Alkazi, Theatre Unit, Bombay, 1954

But what the mask does not do is grant the actor unlimited freedom. It offers the actor a persona, ready-made with all his distinguishing features, quite different from those of the actor's own. Out of this painted face of papier mâché or cardboard, an entire individual has to be created.

The whole body must be built round the face, the arms, the fingers, the legs, the shoulders, the haunches, the tilt of the head, the gait and finally the speech. In every single detail, the actor's body must learn to conform with the mask it wears. The transformation must be complete—as it can never be in the case of a performance without a mask.

To create such a character, then, the actor must come to know his mask in its infinitesimal detail. He must live with it, regard it as his alter ego, recreate himself in terms of it. As our production has shown, this is more difficult than it sounds . . . It will indeed be a sad moment when, on the last night, each actor bids farewell to the face which he has for so many months come to accept as his own.

**

By 1960, Alaknanda Duriaud (née Samarth) had completed the two-year course, been inducted into the Theatre Unit and cast in two powerful productions for the Theatre Unit Repertory:[*] August Strindberg's *Miss Julie*, where she played the title role opposite Alkazi as Jean; and Jean Anouilh's *Eurydice*, where she acted opposite Zul Vellani, an experienced actor and radio voice.

Fifty-five years later, Alaknanda, at the age of seventy-five, shared her experience with me, outlining with great clarity what she had imbibed.

> I have no visceral memory of the very first read-through, rehearsal or even the very first performance. So it must've happened naturally without fear, anxiety or conscious pedagogy.
>
> *Miss Julie*, in which both Mr Alkazi and I played the leads, is an overwrought play about overwrought characters. It is a psychosocial drama which is today constantly reworked and replayed, such is its staying power.
>
> But Mr Alkazi, in that play, and in all the others I did with him, bypassed, completely jettisoned working through psychological realism. There was no talk of 'motivation', 'characterization', 'backstory', at least to me.

---

[*] The word 'Repertory' was soon dropped.

(L) M.F. Husain's drawing of Alkazi's production of Euripides' *Medea*, Theatre Unit, Bombay, 1961; (R) *Antigone* by Jean Anouilh, dir. E. Alkazi, Kusum Behl as Antigone, Meena Chitnis as Creon, Theatre Unit, Bombay, 1955

There was no exploitation above all . . . no emotional exploitation of the actor's frailties, no voyeurism or psycho-dramatic confessionals. In today's often self-indulgent, commercially power-driven workshop culture, this seems quite unbelievable.

What Mr Alkazi did, as I recall, was distance the text in a workman-like way, fairly quickly like a craftsman chipping away at his material.

He did this by giving shape not to 'moves' or 'actions' or 'blocking' (though that word was current then) so much as freeing entire visual images—energy fields—in the text.

If the actor absorbed them, filled them in, flowed wholeheartedly with them and believed in them, the rest followed. The actor was part of an entire image.[9]

I believe that this brief assessment by Alaknanda carries the essence of Alkazi's methodology of working with actors, that is, of freeing the visual images evoked by the text and offering them as inspiration and guidelines for the actor to physicalize the role.

* * *

Alkazi was not only impacting his actors but his audiences as well. By all accounts, *Miss Julie* was a startling production conceived of as a modern ritual. It spoke to the blood, awakening in the audience the need to take cognizance of the deep sexual desires of its young female protagonist. Watching Alkazi's productions, based on modern aesthetics, was a decisive moment for the young Girish Karnad.

> . . . seeing Alkazi's plays triggered an impulse that took me back into my own background. It did not take me out. One great thing I learnt from *Eurydice* and *Antigone* was this was what you could do with your myths . . . Suddenly it was clear to me what was wrong with our pauranik plays . . . So, the modelling of *Yayati* was very much an influence of Alkazi, of Anouilh . . . it came from actually seeing them played out on stage. My first play, *Yayati*, really the whole confrontation between Chitralekha and Yayati, is straight out of *Antigone* . . . I must acknowledge that it was Alkazi's production of *Antigone* that impacted it.[10]

More importantly, Karnad understood the kind of modernity that Alkazi was leading Indian theatre towards.

> I think Alkazi's contribution to our work was not where it took us, but what it took us away from. The dominating figure those days was George Bernard Shaw. So a modern play meant a living room . . . that was modern to us. And Alkazi took it away. He said, 'No, that's not it!' The great advantage to us was that he looked to Europe, leaving England aside. He did *Hedda Gabler* . . . he was interested in European playwrights and their plays, particularly with female protagonists. That was a complete education for us in theatre.

*　*　*

The experimental nature of Alkazi's work attracted newer and larger audiences. There were, of course, the Bhulabhai artists—Husain, Gaitonde, Tyeb, Prafulla Dahanukar and Jatin Das, as well as Akbar Padamsee and Bal Chhabda, while the older theatre regulars included Mulk Raj Anand,

Rudy von Leyden, Sham Lal and Nuruddin Padamsee. Nissim was instrumental in interesting a growing tribe of young Indian poets and writers such as Dilip Chitre, Arun Kolatkar, Keki Daruwalla and Adil Jussawalla. They constituted an informed and critical audience for Alkazi's plays. An entire new generation of filmmakers such as Shyam Benegal and Mani Kaul and playwrights such as Mohan Rakesh and Girish Karnad not only watched Alkazi's productions but also attended his exhibitions, film shows, workshops and talks by eminent international and national personalities such as American dancer–choreographer Martha Graham, American artist and landscape architect Isamu Noguchi, American sculptor Alexander Calder, the British-born Indian anthropologist and ethnologist Verrier Elwin, Indian–American writer Santha Rama Rau and Bharatnatyam dancer T. Balasaraswati.

* * *

While he was aware of his fecund role in the Indian theatre movement by now, Alkazi's innate modesty did not allow him to boast of the important news he had formally received. Tucking the item away discreetly in the December 1955 issue of the *TUB*, Alkazi announced:

'The Unit has the honour of having one of its members being called upon to draft the syllabus of the National School of Drama, an institution which the SNA proposes to start soon.'[11]

This was followed by a letter inviting Alkazi to read a paper on the training of the actor at the first National Drama Seminar to be organized in post-Independence India by the Sangeet Natak Akademi in New Delhi in March–April 1956. Alkazi went immediately to his desk to pen the editorial for the March 1956 issue of the *TUB*:

> On the 25th of this month, Vice President Radhakrishnan will inaugurate India's first National Drama Seminar . . . One aspect strikes the discerning observer as substantially neglected. A viable form of modernity must be achieved as an instrument for the progress of Indian theatre. We may speak nostalgically of our ancient stage arts, functioning in an integrated rural pattern of life on hilly slopes with lamplight and moonlight sufficient for their high office. But the modern need is for permanent stages, well

planned auditoriums, lighting equipment, greenrooms and club rooms, parking space for automobiles and garden areas or lounges for refreshment etc. Theatre today is a complicated organizational venture as much as it is a creative art. In a society that is being rapidly and systematically industrialized, through successive five year plans, the theatre cannot sustain itself on the meager essentials of village troupes and itinerant travelling companies. It must face the challenge of cinema and other modern forms of entertainment with its own external attractions of space, time and architecture... Theatre is an art of infinite variety. If the first Drama Seminar puts our specific problems in some such perspective, it will have served a useful purpose.

These were and continue to be the terrifying conditions under which we in the theatre exist and struggle. Alkazi's words from sixty-five years ago serve to remind us that not much has changed in the government's support of theatre in our country.

CHAPTER 25
THE THEATRIC UNIVERSE OF POST-INDEPENDENCE INDIA
1956

Alkazi was extremely annoyed that he had been slated to deliver his paper on the third and last day of the seminar. People would be bored and exhausted by then, he thought, and his paper would not receive the attention it deserved. He had worked long and hard on putting together his ideas on training, added to which was the pressure of Uma's remark before he departed, 'I've heard there are some people who are banking on you to make an impression with your paper, Alkazi!' That rankled him throughout the journey. What exactly did she mean by that? Which people were banking on him?

As the train pulled into the New Delhi railway station, Alkazi saw Romesh Chander, a short fellow in sola topi, frantically waving his handkerchief in all directions. Before they could even exchange 'hellos', Romesh was insisting that Alkazi stay with him.

'No, no, Elk, I insist you stay with us! There is absolutely no formality at all. After all, it's only a question of a few days, old chap! I know that SNA guest house only too well! Infested with mosquitoes! And the food—it's inedible! At home, you will be comfortable with us. We are Lahoreans after all! *Mehman nawazi* (hospitality) is the one thing we pride ourselves on!'

'Romesh, it's really sweet of you, but honestly, I can't put you out like this!'

'Alkazi! Not another word! Uma wrote and told us that you enjoy a good meal! So Padma has cooked teetar (quail) for dinner tonight in your honour! I promise you won't regret it!' With that, Romesh bundled Alkazi's tiny suitcase into the dicky and they bumped along the wide streets in his jalopy. Paying little attention to the traffic, Romesh talked non-stop and braked suddenly every so often, despite the fact that there was hardly any traffic to speak of! Alkazi finally surrendered to Romesh's

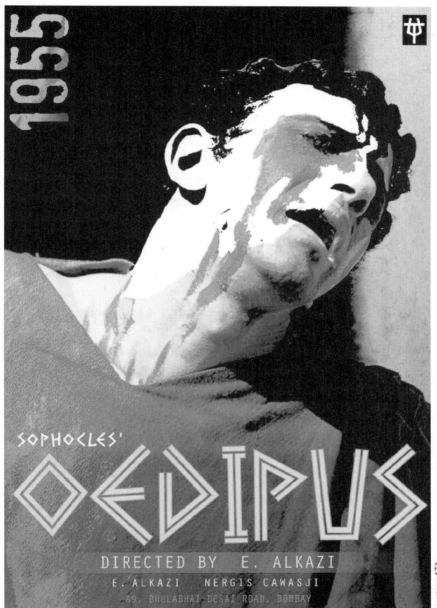

Poster of *Oedipus Rex* by Sophocles, dir. E. Alkazi, Alkazi as Oedipus, Theatre Unit, Bombay, 1955

persuasions, and, zoning out his chatter, he withdrew into himself to soak in the unfamiliar sights of a new city.

On his earlier visit, there had been no time to enjoy its sprawling layout. The weather was hot and dry—a thin, hazy veil of dust hung in the air through which one could see Delhi's tree-lined avenues ablaze with their bright yellow laburnum trees in full bloom—so different from Bombay's clear blue skies and swishing palm trees! The full glory of Lutyens's architecture hit him as they circled around the famed India Gate, catching a glimpse of the Rashtrapati Bhavan at the far end of the Raj Path as they did so.

That evening, Padma's brother Hali Vats and his wife Sheila Bhatia joined them for dinner. The couple were originally from Sialkot, Pakistan, and had shifted to Delhi post-Partition and immediately established an independent group, Delhi Art Theatre. Sheila, an erstwhile IPTA worker, carried strong socialist views and appeared to be an energetic woman who had directed a few Punjabi operas, including *Call of the Valley*, which Alkazi had seen at the National Drama Festival. It had been followed by Balwant Gargi's *Kesro* and *Dukhe Khet*. As Sheila explained to Alkazi, her main preoccupation in creating operas in Punjabi was to use Punjab's rich folk musical heritage in innovative ways. She was currently collaborating with a young, talented singer, Shanno Khurana, on a libretto for her new production of Waris Shah's *Heer*.

Romesh seemed pleased with how the evening was progressing, regaling his guests with anecdotes of his incarceration as a Trade Union leader, until they finally shifted to lighter topics, such as who would be attending the seminar the next day (as well as those who had been left out!), allowing Alkazi to get a whiff of some Delhi theatre gossip.

As the evening wore on, Alkazi began to fade while Hali came into his own. Obviously enjoying his Scotch, Hali grew more and more loquacious and spirited, and Alkazi observed how Hali would begin most of his sentences in English and then deftly switch over to Punjabi, punctuating every few sentences with loud guffaws, slapping Alkazi on the back as he did so! After dinner, the hosts looked around and noticed Alkazi missing. Looking for him all over the flat, they located him fast asleep on the floor of one of the verandas! Horrified and amused, this incident would become one of those oft-repeated anecdotes about the 'strange and unfathomable

Alkazi!' In later years, whenever I happened to meet either Romesh or Hali, they never ceased to repeat to me, 'Beta, I don't think you know, but the first time I met your father, he slept on the floor of our veranda, just like that! He refused to sleep on the bed!' My father's version of the incident was that he found the weather extremely hot and opted for the floor, which was much cooler!

* * *

Alkazi adjusted the knot of his tie, centring it, and held himself erect, as he and Romesh Chander entered the portals of the grand Sapru House on Barakhamba Road. Home to the Indian Council of World Affairs (ICWA) and named after its first president, Tej Bahadur Sapru, the building had only just been completed the year before, in 1955. Alkazi's keen eye was quick to take in the syncretic synthesis of its architectural styles. While the gateway bore an Islamic influence, its pillared façade showed the influence of Hindu architecture, with the entire edifice capped by a Sanchi-style stupa dome. What held the diverse styles together was the overall colour scheme—white walls with red sandstone highlights, which were tempered down against the lush green lawns surrounding the building.

As they mounted the steps, one of the first people Alkazi recognized was Dr Charles Fabri, who greeted them both effusively. Falling in step with them, Fabri tapped the large, brown Manila envelope tucked under his arm and whispered to Alkazi with a twinkle in his eye, 'Alkazi! I've brought you the article I promised on ancient Indian theatre. My assumptions are based on absolutely newly discovered evidence! Very exciting!'

Alkazi nodded, thanking Fabri effusively and saying he would definitely include it in the forthcoming May issue of the *TUB*. Meanwhile, a few young women in tightly draped khadi sarees were greeting the guests with namastes and ushering them towards the first-floor auditorium. The hall was already packed to capacity and Alkazi noticed Dina Gandhi and Adi Marzban gravitating towards him.

'*Arre baba!* Where were you last night, Elk? *Khare khar*, (I swear!) we searched high and low for you all over the guest house!' exclaimed Adi.

Before Alkazi could apologize, someone from the dais called for order, asking everyone to take their seats as Vice President Dr Radhakrishnan had arrived.

The procession of dignitaries entered the auditorium and slowly made their way down the aisle to the stage, festooned with large loops of marigolds. Dr Radhakrishnan looked extremely distinguished in his impeccable white achkan, dhoti and turban. Alongside him were Dr P.V. Rajamannar, chief justice of the Madras High Court and chairperson of the Sangeet Natak Akademi (SNA) and, of course, the chief crusader of the entire event, the gentle, self-effacing, but determined Kamaladevi Chattopadhyaya. Wearing an elegant dark silk saree with a broad, dull gold border and a tiny flower tucked into the little bun at the nape of her neck, Kamaladevi was the undisputed Czarina of the theatre world—not only was she the vice chairman of the SNA but also president of UNESCO's International Theatre Institute (ITI), which was established in 1948.

A sense of national pride swelled in Alkazi's heart as the national anthem struck up, providing an aura of solemnity to the occasion.

'The important place the theatre occupies in the cultural life of the nation cannot be denied . . . Rabindranath Tagore once said that a nation's culture is judged by the standard of its theatre . . .'[1]

As Chief Justice Rajamannar went on, Alkazi found a moment to take a look across the room. An event could not get more 'national' than this! Theatre practitioners and scholars from across the country were meeting for the first time in one place to share their thoughts on contemporary theatre and how it should be developed. It began to dawn on Alkazi how fortunate he was to be part of this select group of forty people who were being given the opportunity to contribute to what would become the cultural policy of an entire nation—a new nation! This was indeed a historic event!

'. . . Drama creates the conscience of the age. We cannot make people good by Acts of Parliament. Nor is it possible by constitutional provisions to remove deep-seated social prejudices. We influence social behaviour by creating public opinion. I have known many playwrights and actors who have worked hard at the task of raising standards of behaviour in our country.'

The vice president was speaking slowly and sagely. Alkazi was impressed that, though his experience of theatre seemed limited to the ancient classics, from which he quoted extensively in Sanskrit, Dr Radhakrishnan seemed aware that one of the fundamental tasks of theatre was to assume its social responsibility.

Declaring the seminar open, the vice president concluded: 'I hope your deliberations will arouse public interest in the theatre movement and the art of the drama, and thereby result in the improvement of our standards.'

Alkazi felt as if the vice president was talking to him directly, telling him that very high standards were expected of him. There and then, Alkazi resolved to rework his paper—there was no question of returning to Romesh's tonight! Mosquitoes be damned, he needed peace and quiet to reflect on what he was going to say. It was certainly proving providential that he had been slotted to make his presentation on the very last day. This would give him the opportunity to listen to others, comprehend their thoughts and then plan his responses accordingly.

I have often wondered how the people in Delhi's government circles even got to hear of my father's efforts. I would hazard a guess that it was not only the high quality of his productions that had become the talk of the town in Bombay but also the speed and variety of his programmes. Within a few years, Alkazi had become a recognizable public figure, enhanced no doubt by his skills at public speaking as well as his acting abilities. Kamaladevi Chattopadhyaya was among a growing number who kept abreast of Alkazi's activities.

What Kamaladevi perhaps also appreciated was Alkazi's comprehensive awareness of the international theatre scene and his keenness to be part of it. Simultaneously, Alkazi was knowledgeable about the visual arts, architecture and design, all of which added substantially to his dynamic personality. Alkazi was seen as a proactive citizen who served public interest in nation-building through the arts.[2]

By 1954, the three national akademis of visual arts (Lalit Kala Akademi), literature (Sahitya Akademi) and performing arts (Sangeet Natak Akademi) had been established under guidelines suggested by Maulana Abul Kalam Azad, the then minister for education and scientific research. Clarifying their functioning to Kamaladevi over lunch one day, Azad had said, 'The akademis will be autonomous in their internal working and will include in their composition not only state representatives, but equally representatives of important organizations and distinguished individual artists. The akademi of dance, drama and music, the Sangeet Natak Akademi will be the first to be set up.'[3]

(L–R) Dina Pathak, Sombhu Mitra, Dr Rajendra Prasad and E. Alkazi at Rashtrapati Bhavan celebrating the SNA's First National Seminar, 1956

Knowing of her deep and abiding interest in the arts, Maulana Azad nominated Kamaladevi as vice chairman of the SNA, assuring her of his full support while reminding her that the running of the SNA would rest mainly with her since the chairman Dr Rajamannar's duties as chief justice in Madras could keep him busy. Meanwhile, Panditji had made it clear that he was very keen that a National Theatre be established and for that to happen, it was inevitable that an institution for training in the dramatic arts be instituted as the first logical step. This being Nehru's second decade in power, he had prioritized the creation of major national institutions, believing that they gave public life a structural density that helped to sustain an open society. Keeping in step with the PM's wishes, within a year of its establishment, the executive board of the SNA recommended the setting up of a national school of drama.

Kamaladevi drew the attention of Ashfaque Husain, the joint secretary of education and scientific research, to Alkazi as a suitable candidate in the area of theatre training. A keen supporter of the theatre himself, Husain made a special visit to meet Alkazi at BDI.[4] Suitably impressed with the SDA, he reiterated the invitation for Alkazi to draw up the blueprint for a syllabus for the proposed new school.

The government's keenness to announce a National Theatre among other institutions as part of India's Second Five-Year Plan* led Kamaladevi to realize the need to hold the National Theatre Seminar in March–April 1956. To this end, the country's distinguished scholars of classical and folk theatre, educationists and theatre practitioners from professional and amateur groups of various regions representing all the major Indian languages were invited to voice their views towards evolving a national theatre, one that could have a distinct identity of its own and yet be modern. It was this body of experts at this seminar who would, in principle, support and ratify the idea of establishing a theatre training school. Kamaladevi was hoping that this would be one of the key outcomes of the seminar.

Several decades later, theatre scholar and author at University of Wisconsin-Madison, US, Aparna Bhargava Dharwadker, noted the significance of the seminar unequivocally,

> With a meticulously detailed agenda, it was going to be the first sustained exercise in historical self-positioning—an early post-colonial reflection on the singular problematic of a multilingual theatrical tradition that had classical and pre-modern as well as colonial antecedents . . . The object of the commentaries and exchanges among the delegates was to relate this complex legacy in theatre to the aesthetic, social and political needs of a new nation and to develop a program for 'the future Indian drama'.[5]

This seminar was going to be an attempt at cultural policymaking in the cause of nation-building. The akademis saw themselves as an integral part of this modernizing project, one of their main jobs being to 'relocate' the 'traditional arts' into 'modern institutions'.

---

* The Second Five-Year Plan (1956–1961) refers more substantively to culture. It is here that we see the earliest references to the provisions made for the institution of SNA, the other akademis for the arts and letters, a national theatre, children's museum, the National Library (Calcutta) and the Gallery of Modern Art, plans supporting the development of Hindi and the regional languages and programmes for the support of the national archives, and the colonially constituted disciplines of archaeology, anthropology and Indology. Notwithstanding the Second Plan's identification of these programmes, culture yet again plays a subsidiary role in education, particularly with regard to its administration and access to financial support.

But who were these theatre practitioners with divergent views who had been invited to participate in a seminar that was to decide the future cultural policies of the nation?

This was a new, enthusiastic breed hailing from the educated middle class who, since the 1940s, had virtually taken over from where the commercial Natak companies had left off and moved to the film industry. Distinguishing themselves by being 'amateurs' who did not stoop to crass commercialism, they were passionately committed to modern theatre and styled themselves as the new messiahs of 'meaningful' theatre. In them, Kamaladevi saw the possibilities of a modern movement emerging. It is interesting to note that people from this very group would shape the contours of contemporary Indian theatre over the next few decades.

Looking back, it is likely that Kamaladevi too, like many others, believed that professional Parsi Natak company practitioners (along with the other commercial companies that functioned in different languages) were neither sophisticated nor competent enough to do justice to either India's glorious theatrical legacy or to modernity. She was also clear that a 'national' theatre could not commit itself to an ideological orientation.

Kamaladevi prepared the ground for new ideas by bringing these relatively recently established amateur theatre groups together under the single umbrella of the Bharatiya Natya Sangh (BNS) in 1954. A non-governmental body, the BNS was conceived as a national federation of theatre organizations with units all over India. Kamaladevi strongly supported the Nehruvian idea that there should be a constant striving towards unity—in politics as well as cultural life. The BNS was therefore envisaged as an agency to build kinship between the rich variety of India's cultural forms through talks, discussions and seminars. Its nation-building role was to act as a facilitator to coordinate and promote activities, not to be a creative body itself. In a massive effort, Kamaladevi had been able to mobilize more than 300 amateur and professional groups and institutions to affiliate themselves with the BNS through its twenty-six regional centres, or natya sanghs, across the country. Most delegates at this seminar were drawn from among BNS affiliates and were therefore well-known to Kamaladevi. Her relationship to them, built over the years, would now allow her to navigate and steer the shrill and divergent voices she was sure would surface during the seminar and help towards building consensus and fielding feasible, practical recommendations.

In keeping with Nehru's idea that foreign expertise would be required in building up national institutions on modern, international lines, Kamaladevi further proposed a prestigious tie-up of the BNS with an international body, the ITI.

It was Rosamond Gilder who initiated the idea of the ITI, as she was committed to the cause of internationalism and theatre. Persuading UNESCO to include theatre, she claimed, 'theater is one of the most effective vehicles for the dissemination of the principles of international understanding, international cooperation and world peace' and that 'the stage speaks an international language', and 'by exchanging productions of other nations with ours, we will create an international understanding and appreciation of the talents and customs of all countries'.[6]

Internationalism recognized that the world had shrunk and that all nations were reliant on one another, thereby acknowledging that the cultures of different countries could influence one another. The idea that 'authentic', 'national' traditions alone could be the source for future modernisms was fiercely argued over the next three days at the seminar. In all, fifty-two papers were presented and the question was raised: Should India's classical traditions be authentically 'revived' to give post-colonial theatre its 'Indian' identity?

Giving deference to Sanskrit drama, Dr V. Raghavan was the first to be invited to read his paper. He proposed that since Sanskrit drama was *the* 'authentic' classical tradition of Indian drama, it should be revived and made the source from which modern Indian theatre would germinate. This idea was generally refuted with playwright Adya Rangacharya asserting that Sanskrit drama had ceased to exist when it stopped talking to the common man. Mulk Raj Anand agreed that although it no longer corresponded to contemporary experience, it was 'a tradition of the imagination', from which contemporary playwrights and producers could be inspired.

Other respondents, such as Kapila Vatsyayan, felt that Tagore's plays came closest to Sanskrit drama, while the always outspoken Fabri interjected with, 'Sanskrit drama was a courtly drama patronized by the courts and supported by people who had nothing to do but flirt with court ladies!' He added, 'I do believe you should bring Sanskrit drama down from the dusty shelves of Sanskrit scholars and present it in a slightly modernized form!' As can be imagined, there was a storm of protest over this remark led by J.C. Mathur, who exclaimed, 'What is there in court intrigues that is so shockingly unacceptable to the present generation? After all, such scandals have always interested the populace... Why should Sanskrit *prahasans* (farce) alone stink in the nose of Dr Fabri?'

Alkazi raised his hand to speak. Bringing the discussion back on track, he suggested: 'Historical and literary research alone will not help us much in the profitable use of our ancient heritage, unless we test the ancient plays by playing them exactly in the way they used to be played in the past. In one western university, in order to produce Greek drama, they have an entire department to develop it and to perform it in the ancient style for limited audiences. A similar thing can be done with Sanskrit drama in our country.'

Agreeing with Alkazi's suggestion, Kamaladevi summed up by suggesting that research and experimentation with classical drama should be encouraged through government support and that exclusive playhouses be established for traditional and classical drama. These would work as laboratories where students could research classical drama.

The next topic on the agenda concerned whether and how the living folk performing traditions could influence the development of modern Indian theatre.

Alkazi listened carefully, making mental notes and absorbing the points of view of delegates such as Dina Gandhi, Balraj Sahni and especially Dr Suresh Awasthi, all of whom vehemently espoused the cause of folk theatre being absorbed by the contemporary, while at the same time lamenting the fact that folk theatre needed to be 'saved', as it was being irredeemably damaged by the influence of tawdry Hindi films. At this point, Alkazi stood up, making the point that although he too was in favour of using folk forms as they were 'living' traditions, he was at the same time conscious that practitioners like themselves may not be the right people to decide the fate of these traditions.

'We want to educate the Bhavai artists. We want to teach them how to read and write and how to behave like educated persons like us. But we do not for a moment consider that the nearer they reach us, the quicker would they discard the arts of their forefathers...'

Delegates of SNA's First National Theatre Seminar, 1956: (L–R) E. Alkazi, Sisir Bhaduri, Balraj Sahni, Dina Pathak, Sombhu Mitra and Balwant Gargi

Some delegates objected to the crude language and obscenities that were used in Bhavai. Again, Alkazi countered with the view that what we may consider crude and vulgar constituted part of the intrinsic vitality of the Bhavai form: 'Should we be so proud and puritanical as to evaluate every art in the light of our own moral code? When the police say that the Dramatic Performances Act had to be promulgated to stop vulgar stage shows, we demand to know who gave them the right to do so? May we not ask ourselves who gives us the right to purify the Bhavai forms?'

His remarks undoubtedly touched a raw nerve. To some, it probably appeared that Alkazi was throwing in the gauntlet and challenging the credibility of the august assembly. Was this the youngster who had been asked to frame the syllabus for the proposed theatre training institute? There was a certain arrogance about him, despite his polite, unassuming attitude!

The seminarists reassembled for the final question that remained to be debated: the place and position of western theatre in relation to contemporary Indian theatre. Though Mulk Raj Anand had been assigned the topic, it was evident that he was neither able to concretely defend nor criticize the influence of the western tradition on contemporary theatre, as he himself, as a writer, was very much a part of that historical process.

In many ways, it was Alkazi's paper titled 'The Training of the Actor' that tackled this thorny issue with simplicity and directness. 'Theatre is a prrrrractical art', my father would always say, deliberately rolling his 'r's' by way of emphasis, 'Solutions to theatre's problems should always be tackled in a down-to-earth, prrrrractical manner!'

The final moment had arrived. Alkazi drew a deep breath and composed himself. Launching into the substance of his paper extempore, Alkazi began by describing the overall goal of actor training, painting the larger picture in sweeping poetic and dramatic terms:

> Acting, one affirms, is an **art**; the actor is an **artist** in the theatre. He is both **creator and interpreter** of another's creation. The actor's instrument is his **body**; in this he is at once the creator and the thing created. These assumptions partially determine the type and quality of the actor's training. But in this connection another factor cannot be ignored—namely, a society's conception of the **nature and function** of the theatre.[7]

Then, immediately taking the bull by the horns, he went on to discuss the challenges of incorporating Indian traditions of Sanskrit drama and folk theatre into contemporary Indian idioms and forms of expression.

> What **determines** the training of the actor is the **present** state of theatre in India . . . Should the Indian actor be able to interpret **all** the varieties of forms and styles that he finds before him? . . . Sanskrit drama demands **formal** treatment of conversation, posture, diction and movement . . . then there is the modern **realistic** treatment, and finally . . . **folk** drama . . . Therefore, **what should be the style of acting that the present generation of Indian actor adopts** as the medium of his interpretation?

A past master at holding the attention of his audience, Alkazi took his time, proceeding at a measured pace. Punctuating his words with carefully selected gestures and pauses, he continued in a step-by-step manner, gathering momentum.

> What **I** believe is this; a **style** of acting must find its place as the **contemporary expression of a tradition** which has come down through history . . . But in India there is a **schism** . . . We have no **continuous** logical and historical development as they have it in the West . . . Apart from brief, enigmatic written references, we have **nothing** to go by which would give us a **graphic** idea of theatre architecture. Were there any **buildings** for dramatic performances, or were plays performed in a **temple** or **palace courtyard**, or simply in the **open air**? Is there any development in the manner of play presentation? What kind of **make-up** was used? What type of **costumes** did the actors wear, and was there any development in costume design on the stage? These are **crucial** questions to which **precise** answers must be found based on **irrefutable evidence**, if we are properly to understand our theatre heritage.
>
> In Europe . . . theatre went through a score of styles in writing, acting and production, which present a line of logical, historical and artistic continuity. This constitutes the **European** theatre tradition . . . **By a strange conspiracy of circumstances, there is such little material on the Indian theatre.**

The audience was listening in pin-drop silence, as if at a performance!

> Our modern productions of Sanskrit plays make me uneasy and raise great doubts in my mind. I witness a play written in the classical style, according to obviously rigid and highly formalized conventions, performed by actors who resort to a **pseudo-realistic style** of acting, in settings achieving a certain **shabby naturalism**. However appreciative the Sanskrit student may be of the play as spoken by the performers, the **incongruity of the entire production is aesthetically excruciating!**

Alkazi could sense members of the audience tensing up. The traditionalists and folklorists pursed their lips, not appreciating that Alkazi was voicing such strong opinions publicly.

> . . . but there are **new** ways of looking at the situation . . . of which we should not be afraid. It is reasonable to suppose that with the breaking down of **physical, political and cultural barriers** between countries, the achievement of **any** nation **anywhere** in the world, in **any** field of art, becomes a contribution to **world art**, and the **common heritage of all mankind.** Under **such** conditions, we cannot help foreseeing an **overwhelming** impact of **every type, style and form of the foreign theatre on the Indian and vice versa.**

Now every word was chewed and spat out with a pause between each: 'Thus, there is not only a **cross-fertilization of the West and the East,** but also of the **Eastern past and the Western present.**'

Referencing the impact of eastern theatre on a genius like Bertolt Brecht, Alkazi led to his climactic point using a deep base tone: 'Clearly, out of all this, an **international style** is bound to emerge, just as it has in **architecture, painting, music, sculpture, and particularly the applied arts,** with superficial national deviations and idiosyncrasies.'

Now, Alkazi held a dramatic, pregnant pause before delivering the next sentence, which was a loaded one—one that he had calculated would give weight and substance to his argument as it was an endorsement of a grand Nehruvian vision.

> It is no **accident** of history that **Le Corbusier**, one of the most **progressive and revolutionary** European architects of today, should be entrusted with the task of **raising out of Indian soil a new Indian city**. It is only **a vivid sign** of the times. And what is happening in the field of **architecture** is happening in **the theatre** and indeed all the arts, though in a subtler and less spectacular manner.

He saw Kamaladevi nodding sagely. Alkazi knew that he had, in projecting the yet-to-be-realized contemporary Indian theatre as taking its place among the spectrum of revolutionary and progressive art forms in the world, as well as obliquely comparing his own vision and beliefs to those of a great architect like Le Corbusier, succeeded in projecting an image of himself as a man with an expansive and inclusive futuristic vision. Finally, he climaxed with a fearless, energetic articulation of a future that would be connected with the past, yet be free from constraining shackles.

'This stupendous ferment of ideas and cross-influences presents no dangers, and holds no terror for all that is vital and authentic in the arts. **It destroys decadent forms, shibboleths, fake traditions...**'

Thus, Alkazi through his speech had pushed for a strong internationalist approach that suggested that a new 'national' tradition be born out of a cross fertilization of different cultures towards the creation of an 'international' expression. Indeed, this was the last thing conservative traditionalists wanted to hear! It shattered the idea of creating a new 'Indian' form using 'authentic' Indian sources alone!

Romesh, Fabri and Ahindra Choudhury raised their hands to applaud but were soon hushed by others...

Undaunted, Alkazi now carried on with practical suggestions as to the kind of inclusive approach he was proposing for a new 'national' school:

> ... the school may avail itself of one of several methods...
> It may be felt, for example, that Kathakali embodies a system of physical training—in terms of movement, gesture, rhythm and mime—ideally suited to the Indian actor. On the other hand, another teacher may arrive at the same results through another system, as that of Dalcroze's eurhythmics, or the methods of Rudolf Laban. In these cases, the ends certainly justify the means.

As a trainer of contemporary actors, Alkazi knew that his job was to prepare actors to be able to play a large variety of roles drawn from a wide spectrum of world classics, each requiring a different approach. Therefore, to train an actor in one particular technique or style would be limiting.

Next, he went on to the very real problem that a teacher of acting would encounter:

Acting [to the new entrant] will mean the imitation on the stage of his favourite screen idol . . . The difficulty of the teacher's task will also lie in his fight against the litter of sterile conventions and defunct traditions, which suffocates the contemporary Indian theatre and which the student will have in all innocence assiduously encumbered himself with . . .

His body has to be rejuvenated, to come alive again, shorn of all false modesties, inhibitions and complexes. The actor has slowly to make the discovery of his body for himself, in all its intricate mechanism, and its evocative beauty, an instrument which has to be sensitive, flexible, perfectly tuned, so as to respond effectively to the actor's imagination and reflect accurately his ideas.

In conclusion, Alkazi said:

The most a school of acting can therefore do is to create the bracing intellectual and artistic climate conducive to the development of the actor's gifts. In such a school, therefore, a student will undergo formation as an artist which is much more than training. This first principle will demand the direction of the school by a person of sufficient artistic strength and achievement to promote a certain point of view. I use the word 'promote' and not 'impose' . . . The actor has to aspire to the state of mind of a **Poet**, a **Lover** or a **Fool**!

An uncomfortable silence.
The audience was somewhat taken aback by Alkazi's last remark; there was a hesitant titter of laughter, followed by scattered applause. How seriously should this man be taken? Was he joking or was he serious?
Alkazi was quick to sense hostility underlying the few questions that followed. Although no one really challenged or discussed Alkazi's proposition, neither was it universally endorsed. This was understandable coming from diehard scholars such as Dr Raghavan, who were trying desperately to make space in the Akademi for the support of classical theatre. But it was in a person like Suresh Awasthi, basically a scholar of Hindi and a vociferous promoter and upholder of reviving and supporting

folk theatre, that Alkazi sensed a couched and vigorous opponent to his modernist ideas. Awasthi, on this occasion, did not lock horns with Alkazi but smoothly deflected from Alkazi's main point by asking rather superfluous and general questions regarding what constituted good acting and good producing (directing). Alkazi immediately recognized this as a tactic to shift attention away from and negate the importance of his proposal. The other person who sensed the sharp polarity of opinions being expressed was Kamaladevi. But being a wise and circumspect woman, she found it in the best interests of the Akademi to wait and watch.

So this was the national arena where the rubber met the road. This space, the Akademi, was where Alkazi's brand of *internationalism* would be challenged repeatedly. This is where Alkazi met his current and future adversaries and opponents. He sensed their discomfort at the possibility of his arrival on the national stage. Their thoughts, though unspoken, were easily comprehensible to the acutely sharp and sensitive Alkazi. Undoubtedly, they felt he was an outsider on many counts. He worked in English theatre but was making claims on Hindi-language territory. Besides, he hailed from nowhere! Who was he, actually? Was he a Parsi? He had relatively quickly made a reputation for himself in Bombay. Was he seriously considering shifting to Delhi? There was Nemi Chandra Jain in the corner, bearing a quizzical look. He seemed to know Awasthi well. Both Awasthi and Jain were staunch 'Hindiwallahs'. At the same time, they supported contemporizing folk traditions.

Alkazi had listened carefully to the discussions over the last few days. He was sure that in the years to come, it would be these very issues that would become even more contentious. In fact, it would be these very issues that would define the course that the contemporary theatre movement would take.

What constituted the 'national' was a fraught question, and, over the next few decades, Alkazi would slowly begin to decipher what the term meant to him.

As Girish Karnad mentioned in an article in *India Today* in December 2005, 'There was a great clamour to describe what was national and Alkazi was one of the few to define that term for us.'

CHAPTER 26
MADRAS MOTHER: THE NEED FOR ROOTS
1958

As the train sliced through the landscape like a knife, Rosh could feel the relentless onward movement of her life towards unknown destinations. The last few years had been eventful and now as she sat there in the second-class compartment with only one lady co-passenger asleep in front of her, Rosh, for the first time ever, was about to bring in the New Year, 31 December 1958, entirely on her own. Sitting on the cusp of the new year and waiting for the minute hands on her wristwatch to align themselves perfectly one above the other, a sudden gust of wind swept into the compartment, unleashing Roshen's hair from its hairpin and allowing her to experience a rare sense of release and physical abandon.

Roshen could not believe that it was only the previous year, in July, that she had made the same journey from Bombay to Madras with the children. Today, as I pen these lines, I ask myself where my mother found the courage to make such a momentous decision to simply take us out of school and put us on a train with her to a city she had never visited before and where she knew no one. And why had she, this time around, opted to leave us children with my father and make the journey on her own? Feisal was barely three and a half and I was just about eleven. Were these multiple journeys of leaving Bombay for long and short spells of time experiments my mother was carrying out to discover ways in which she could somehow release herself from my father? Or were these her journeys into self-discovery? As a young woman who was barely thirty-three years old, I doubt that my mother had clearly articulated the reasons for her flights. All she knew was that she was experiencing a dull pain that had curdled into a tight knot, embedded itself into the pit of her stomach and lain there for years. The weight of the pain had grown unbearable and Roshen knew she had to somehow get rid of it. For this, Roshen had longed, prayed and waited. Yes, Roshen, my mother, waited long and hard for a miracle to happen, to be released from her pain.

The first ten years of her marriage had been overtaken by relentless and ceaseless activity generated by Elk—of making and sustaining a theatre group and of building a presence for himself in a highly competitive city. There had been no real time for personal issues. Elk seemed satisfied to have such an able and devoted work colleague in Rosh. In fact, he could not do without her even for an instant, as she mentioned to me in later years:

> Elk grew very dependent on me . . . he didn't like to have a rehearsal if I was not in the room! He would send someone to find out where I was, that I should come to the rehearsal and sit. And I suppose I did everything for the play, from ticket-selling to costumes to any other donkey work that is needed for a production. So I was indispensable and I suppose that was the strongest thing—that I was indispensable to him in his work.[1]

But that was not the only role Rosh wished to play in life. She was a person of far deeper probing, a person who was in search of herself—actively, relentlessly and intimately. Roshen reflected on herself, her life, the inner needs of her soul and her needs as a woman. Only knowledge of all this would give 'meaning to life', she would say.

Roshen was an avid and eclectic reader, of not just fiction and poetry but also works that opened up new ways of understanding the human mind and human behaviour. Psychoanalysis, especially the unconscious and the inner world of dreams, fascinated her. Freud, Jung, Adler and, of late, the new books by Simone de Beauvoir that voiced a radical new philosophy—Existentialism, where ideas of free will, desire, rights and responsibilities and the value of personal experience were explored through the lens of gender. In *The Second Sex*, Beauvoir opened up a Pandora's box on subjects like marriage, partnership and fidelity, provoking Roshen to look beyond the conventional understanding of marriage. She sought to involve her husband, Elk, in the exploration of these exciting new topics. They had intense discussions regarding the new kinds of relationship between men and women that bore little resemblance to the prudish, Victorian marriage standards of the day. Rosh cited that de Beauvoir and Jean-Paul

Sartre had entered into a lifelong 'soul partnership' that was sexual but not exclusive, nor one that involved living together. What about members of the Bloomsbury Group? Virginia Woolf, Vanessa Bell and Duncan Grant outraged people with their unconventional lifestyles. Expressing a spirit of rebellion against what they felt were unnecessary constraints and double standards! Politically liberal, they also held liberal ideas about sex, leading to multiple relationships outside of marriage!

'What do you think, Elk, is it actually possible to agree to your spouse having other relationships? Maybe de Beauvoir is right! After all, who has made all these rules about marriage?'

'Rosh, do please stop! This is too embarrassing; besides, it is theoretical! Let's get on with the job in front of us. Don't we have to go to the rehearsal now?'

Elk was always evasive. Roshen's discussions on marital fidelity clearly unnerved him. He wondered if Rosh had come to know of his growing closeness to Uma. If so, should he bring it up and make a clean breast of it? He did not really like to be secretive; it made him feel somehow unfair, impure and dishonest, and the last thing he wanted was to be dishonest with Rosh.

At night, however, as they lay in bed, Rosh would, in all innocence, return to the thoughts that had begun to preoccupy her.

'You know, darling, I read another bit in *The Second Sex* today, which mentioned that women are as capable of choices as men and thus can choose to elevate themselves, move beyond the "immanence" to which they have previously resigned, and reach "transcendence", a position in which one takes responsibility for oneself and the world and thereby one chooses one's own freedom.'

That's true, thought Elk. Uma, as a married woman, was independently deciding the steps she was taking with regard to her relationship with him. If he did not feel Uma was wrong for loving him, then could Rosh not do the same too? Surely, she too should be able to choose her life and her partners? After weeks of internal debate and torment, Elk finally confessed to Rosh that he cared for Uma, but that in no way did it diminish his love for her, his wife and the mother of his children!*

---

* My guess is that this news broke after my brother, Feisal, was born, sometime after the Subato Camp trip in March–April 1956.

T. Balasaraswati, Roshen's guru

What was my mother's response? From what I remember, there were long periods of erratic behaviour on both their parts for years.

Bouts of so-called 'normalcy' in my parents' behaviour shifted unannounced to bouts of depression, especially on my mother's part. Dark, brooding moments when the two of them kept silent for hours—nay days—still haunt me. At our Vithal Court flat, without walls behind which my mother could hide, or cry or scream, in a cavernous hollow where arguments could not be engaged in at decibels matching the searing intensity of their emotions, where the air would be thick with unspoken accusations, a sense of betrayal and unexpressed pain. Often, towards evening, the lights would *not* be turned on, which was frightening for my brother and myself, who, while sensing the tension, would silently continue to play cards or Snakes and Ladders in the dark. In general, my mother wore the look of a rejected, abandoned, frightened animal. Unkempt with red, swollen eyes, she roamed around in her dressing gown or slept interminably under the influence of sleeping pills. At times, she disappeared on to the terrace for hours or, even scarier, disappeared from the house altogether, only to have my distraught father anxiously search for her all over Bombay. More often than not, my mother would be discovered at her mother Kulsumbai's home, as she knew Elk would think twice before following her there as he remained an unwelcome son-in-law. We kids would then be sent across to KT to be with our mother, accompanied by our ayah Yowjaan. After a few weeks, we would all return once again to Vithal Court and life would go on.

It was strange that Kulsum Terrace provided Roshen with a natal home but not at all with an understanding parent. Kulsumbai never volunteered to ask Roshen what the matter was. Her affection and sympathy towards Roshen's predicament stretched only as far as saying, 'This is your home; come anytime; the doors are always open.' Kulsumbai could never say, 'Leave your husband. He is causing you trauma.'

Of course, through all this, my parents' theatre work somehow never suffered. Living by the adage that 'the show must go on', every deadline of every performance was scrupulously met, every talk, every exhibition was mounted on time. This kind of schizophrenic life, all smiles and so-called normalcy with outsiders and dark welts of silence and stumbling over chasms of guilt with insiders, became the norm. Our cover-up performances were highly convincing. But then, as I look back and around me, I guess families don't really wear their hearts on their sleeves! It's a strategy for survival.

The knowledge of the presence of another woman in her husband's life who was the object of his affections seemed to prompt my mother to nurture and cultivate a separate circle of friends. Not that they were not known to my father, but he would now mostly avoid their 'dos', excusing himself by saying that he was either 'too busy' or 'Rosh, you carry on with your armchair critic friends—you know I can't stand so much intellectualizing about art. I'm sorry, but these people just have no idea what it takes to be an artist!'

The group met regularly on the top floor of Taher Mansion, where her first cousin Nuruddin Padamsee's drawing room was transformed into an *adda* for intellectuals long before his brother, Akbar Padamsee, envisaged the Vision Exchange Workshop on the second floor of the same building in the 1970s. Nikki, as he was called, would appear in his white bush shirt, trousers and open sandals to take his place among the guests at his evening soirees, where the conversation flowed seamlessly from one week to the next as if the guests had never left! Here, Bombay's latest theatre productions, films, exhibitions and new literature were hotly debated, critiqued and often torn to shreds! The inner circle included Akbar and his beautiful French wife Solange, the documentary filmmaker Jean Bhownagary along with his highly excitable, sharply witty and intelligent wife, Freny, while the dour Sham Lal, assistant editor of the *Times of India* and his Madonna-faced wife Vimla brought their political views to bear on most topics. A very young Dilip Padgaonkar also dropped in occasionally. I remember that it was the French New Wave Cinema of the 1950s that was most animatedly discussed and it was through a person like Bhownagary that the group learned of filmmakers like Jean–Luc Godard, Claude Chabrol and Alain Resnais. Moving between France and India, Jean, Freny, Akbar and Solange updated their friends in Bombay about experiments in New Wave cinema in editing and visual style to create narrative ambiguity. Jean explained how the new ways of filmmaking made use of portable equipment that required little or no set-up time, resulting in a new documentary style of approaching fiction.

My mother glowed with excitement as the conversations moved effortlessly from one art form to the next, allowing them to discover the relationships between them. I would often tag along as Kabir and Munira, Nikki and Shahbibi's children, were around my age (and my second cousins), and together with the two beautiful daughters of Sham Lal, friendships were forged between us youngsters too. By merely hanging around, we were exposed to and imbibed a lot about the modern movement in art. Needless to say, what we children looked forward to most was the sumptuous dinner of Khoja cuisine that Shahbibi would lay out, buffet style, on the tiny sliver of a veranda, after which the much-awaited home-made custard apple ice cream would appear!

Jean, a gifted painter, sculptor, poet, engraver, potter and filmmaker, had been working at UNESCO in Paris since the 1940s and like so many of their contemporaries, he and his wife yearned to return to India not only to discover their roots but to aid in the nation-building process. Finally, Jean managed an appointment for himself at the Films Division in Bombay to be 'on loan' from UNESCO from 1954–57 to transform the organization. As deputy chief producer, he invited Indian artists from different fields—musicians, painters, sculptors and dancers—to collaborate and create a cross-fertilization of ideas through the process of filmmaking. As a creative documentary filmmaker himself, he realized his vision of nation-building through a cinematic exploration of Indian art. 'We started by trying to make films that would help build the nation so that we, as a subcontinent, may be enriched by our very differences,' Jean told his friends. Producing several highly acclaimed documentaries on Indian art and culture, Jean's landmark documentary, *Khajuraho*, on the temples in the 'city of gods', went on to win several international awards.

Fresh from Paris, Freny had been exposed to the work of theatre directors such as Jean Vilar, who were finding their roots in traditions like the Commedia dell'arte, leading Freny to discover in Bombay a similar indigenous form of 'popular theatre' in the Bhangwadi tradition (the popular urban Gujarati tradition), where music and drama were integrated. Rosh and Freny would rush off to shows at Girgaum, returning to regale their friends of its vivacity and hybrid kitschy-ness. Meanwhile, Akbar was trying to grapple with the theory of *rasa* as it pertained to painting through a study of Sanskrit.

Down the road, at the Bhulabhai Desai Institute, Elk was similarly engaged in getting himself tutored in Hindi and Gujarati and producing western plays in translation (*Antigone, Bicchu, Julius Caesar, The Heiress*). Concluding his series 'This is Modern Art' on western modernism, Alkazi now focused on Indian modernism, chiefly promoting the Progressives through exhibitions, talks and essays. Likewise, for the *TUB*, he began commissioning articles on Sanskrit drama (V. Raghavan, Charles Fabri), the contemporary Indian theatre movement in Marathi and Bengali (Mama Warerkar, D.G. Nadkarni, Sombhu Mitra, Kiranmoy Raha) and Indian tribal dance (Verrier Elwin). Alkazi himself reviewed contemporary plays such as *Paisa* and *Dekh Teri Mumbai*, while the latest offerings from cinema such as *Khajuraho* and *Pather Panchali* were written about along with M.F. Husain's drawings and paintings of Satyajit Ray's film that Alkazi immediately exhibited.

From the mid-1950s on, a growing number of educated, middle-class intellectuals and artists like my mother questioned whether their westernized education had not estranged them from their own culture.

> Mummy sent us to an exclusive school called Miss Murphy's School on Altamount Road, run by two Irish ladies, where only princes and princesses of royal families came ... Mummy felt that we would get some idea of other things if we mixed with the 'right' kind of people. As a result, we were totally out of place with our own family, like our cousins, aunts and uncles in Dongri. It was as if we were a different breed. We were the Brown Sahebs. We could not relate to them.[2]

For my mother, it was not just a 'politically correct' move to discover one's indigenous identity; her search served a deeper, more *personal* need. It was clear that Simone Weil's *The Need for Roots* affected her deeply.[*] Roshen would confess to the Taher Mansion group that discovering

---

[*] In the book, Weil diagnoses the causes of the social, cultural and spiritual malaise afflicting twentieth-century civilization, particularly Europe but also the rest of the world. 'Uprootedness' is defined as a near-universal condition resulting from the destruction of ties with the past and the dissolution of community. Weil specifies the requirements that must be met so that people can once again feel rooted, in a cultural and spiritual sense, to their environment and to both the past and expectations for the future.

herself as an Indian was a spiritual need and that even as a youngster, she questioned her identity as a Muslim as she found this aspect of her upbringing had been totally neglected.

> For instance, religion in our house... There was no emphasis on studying the Quran or saying our prayers or keeping the Ramazan fast; I don't remember either of my parents saying this was ever necessary! I showed an interest in the Quran when I was about fifteen when I came from England and insisted that Mummy keep a maulvi for me to read the Quran to understand what it was... but I don't think anyone else among the children took it up at all. I also studied how to say the prayers, but it was more an intellectual search for something. I was looking for answers to things. If I was a Muslim, why did I not know anything about Islam? And this slowly led to a search for myself, and my roots as to who I was.[3]

What further confused Roshen was the fact that, despite not being practising Ismaili Khojas, her parents performed elaborate, quasi-religious rituals. I clearly recall participating in a ritual as a pre-pubescent girl in connection with a vow Kulsumbai had made after receiving a boon from a *pir* (holy man)—that no harm would come to her next child (as she had miscarried several times). My grandmother would invite seven virgins to take part in the ritual where she would have to bathe them, wash their hair, and finally wash their big toe in water and then drink that water herself! This would be followed by a grand feast in which the poor of the Khoja community were fed. I remember distinctly that as the young girls of the family, we cousins had to participate and thereby, as a family, we offered thanks for the continued health and happiness of our loved ones.

'Surely these were not Islamic rituals?' my mother questioned. Islam did not have rituals. These were perhaps Sufi and Bhakti traditions that had gradually crept into and embedded themselves into Islamic practice in a region like Gujarat where there had been a significant number of conversions and intermarriages among faiths. My mother found that the entire Khoja marriage ritual, for example, was akin to Hindu marriage practices, and that images of the Hindu god Krishna appeared as one of the prophets in an

Islamic calendar of that area; that the Khoja *dua* (prayers) were in Gujarati, not in Arabic; they were not recited, but sung like Hindu *bhajans*.

Trying to make sense of these contradictions around this time, two members of our family, Akbar and Roshen, took it upon themselves to seriously inquire into the Padamsee family's ancestry. Perhaps this would help to clarify who they were, which tribe they belonged to, the original name of their ancestors, the location of their ancestral village, why the Padamsees had migrated to Bombay, etc. In short, they were searching for the 'facts' of their own *personal lineage*—their *roots*.

With no written history available of our antecedents, my grandfather, Jafferbhai Padamsee, presented himself as the sole custodian of the Padamsee genealogy. Accordingly, a date and time were set with Akbar and Roshen, as Jafferbhai sat ensconced on his throne-like sofa jhoola, one foot tucked under him and the other on the floor, regulating his back and forth swinging movements. Thus, the archival session began!

For the very first time, the story of our ancestry began to unravel from my grandfather's beetle-stained red mouth, to be captured on the plastic coils of the Grundig tape recorder that Akbar had especially hired for the historic occasion. As the spools hypnotically rotated, my grandfather, in a trance-like reverie, divested himself of a tale that no one in the family had heard before.

> You see, this is what happened . . . our family was very poor. They had barely enough to feed themselves from day to day. Then, one day, a stranger arrived with his cow. He said he was on a journey and needed somewhere to rest for the night. Our ancestors immediately welcomed him and the old woman rustled up a decent meal with whatever scraps she had and treated the stranger with graciousness and warmth . . .

Speaking in a mixture of Hindi, Gujarati and English, my grandfather held forth for what appeared to be many long hours, with Rosh and Akbar spellbound and me flitting in and out of the room, but only to pee. Servants brought in cups of tea by way of refreshment from time to time, while Jafferbhai, dervish-like, rocking back and forth with eyes half closed, insisted that he not be interrupted for his meals or his afternoon siesta—nothing! He wanted to concentrate and get it right.

The next morning, they woke up to find that the stranger had vanished! They were surprised to see that he had left his cow behind. Believing that he would return soon, the old couple fed and tended to the cow . . . only to realize that she needed to be milked. They milked her and then, knowing that the milk would curdle, they sold it in the market and collected the money they got in a tin for safekeeping until the stranger returned to collect his cow . . .

The grandfather clock chimed distantly, but we were so engrossed in the telling that we lost count of time and place. My grandmother made a few perfunctory visits from her room to see how far we had gotten, only to be shooed away by the wave of a hand by my grandfather, who had possibly never restrained his wife from interrupting him ever before! But this was *his* moment, *his* family's story, a *Padamsee* story that was being recorded for posterity. And NO Kulsum Devji, no daughter of any Justice-Pashtish of Peace-Bees, NOBODY could now interrupt his flow of thoughts.

Months passed and they continued in this way, selling the milk, making it into cottage cheese and selling it and always collecting the money for the stranger, whom they awaited . . . Years elapsed. But the point is that the stranger never reappeared . . . The old couple died and their children carried on being caretakers of that money . . . never believing it was theirs . . . but they were custodians of it . . . And that is how it has been going on . . . that is how we did well for ourselves . . . by not being greedy . . . knowing there is nothing in this world except the blessings of the Almighty . . . nothing really belongs to us . . . we are only temporary caretakers.

By midnight, it was finally done.
What kind of history was this, thought Rosh? The story moved effortlessly between the real to the surreal. From history, it had become unfettered, losing all sense of time and place, and had entered the timeless

zone of myth to join the ranks of folklore. The history of the Padamsee family had metamorphosed into a series of images that were ephemeral. There were no facts here that could be manifestly held on to. The actual story had been lost in translation and had become a parable. Roshen and Akbar were amazed that no reasonable answer was available as to the family's current wealth and good fortune. It was not due to an ancestor's sound business acumen but his 'good deeds' that we owed our comfortable existence!

This investigation into the Padamsee family roots came at a time of turmoil and uncertainty in my mother's life. The anchor of her life, my father, seemed to be drifting away, reducing her status to a nobody (if she wasn't someone's wife, who was she?). And now it seemed her sense of self as a Padamsee too was becoming insubstantial. Though she had scant belief in miracles, she felt a desperate need to *believe* in something, in someone, to be shown the path.

One day, quite by chance, Roshen decided to attend a dance recital on her own. From Colaba, where she was staying with her mother at the time, Roshen travelled all the way to Shanmukhananda Hall in Sion by bus. And that was the day something 'magical' happened! Roshen had her moment of revelation. She watched T. Balasaraswati dance! A sublime presence, with inner grace, detached. That day, Roshen instantly knew that she had found her guru—a guru who would lead her to discover herself and her roots!

* * *

Following her instincts, Roshen wasted no time, packed her bags and ours as well (Feisal's and mine), and we boarded a train to Madras to live there for close to a year. Balasaraswati had obviously found my mother's plea to be her student compelling. Roshen clarified that she did not wish to be a professional dancer; she simply wanted to learn and understand the ancient art in greater depth.

My father appeared to support the idea, probably thinking a change of scene would ease matters between them. Money, though extremely tight, was provided so that my mother could get herself a comfortable home.

Sending you Rs 1000 . . . Paid Encyclopedia Britannica Rs 150 plus 2/4 for M.O. Paid Mehtaji Rs 50 a week ago towards rent.

Daily budget Rs 4 maximum... Kiss the children a thousand times and yourself. Miss you all a great deal. Trying to work hard. Wrote something on Akbar which I'm expanding for the Bulletin...[4]

After the first week at Woodlands Hotel, my mother rented us a bungalow in Nungambakkam, not far from my new school, Good Shepherd Convent. We led a quiet, routine-filled life and my mother managed a bit of socializing with a few friends who happened to be in Madras—Dr Narayana Menon, who was at AIR, and his wife Rekha, and artist Krishen Khanna, the then general manager of Grindlays Bank in Madras, who occupied a sprawling bungalow along with his wife Renu, their two girls, Malati and Rasika, and son Karan.

For Roshen, the year in Madras was intense. Bala and she seemed to hit it off immediately. As a special privilege, my mother was given private tuitions by Bala at her home in the mornings. Practice was interspersed with discussing the *Natyashastra* and the history and traditions of Bharatanatyam. My mother also came to understand the fraught existence of the Devadasi community, to which Bala belonged. Bala, as a dancer, occupied a distinct historic space as she was both the custodian of an ancient art and therefore occupied a position of respectability as a national treasure, while her (outcaste) Devadasi status still lingered, becoming an impediment to her sense of security.

It was wonderful to watch an intimate relationship blossom between Bala and my mother, a sisterhood between an extremely brilliant traditional artist and a young, modern woman in search of herself. Bala increasingly sought Roshen's advice on matters pertaining to developing her career both in India and abroad, topics that can be glimpsed from the warm correspondence they continued to share until the end of Bala's days. Bala's mother Jayammal, Bala's brothers, the great flautist Viswanathan and Ranganathan, the mridangam player, as well as Bala's daughter, Lakshmi, all warmly welcomed my mother and us children into the charmed inner sanctum of their family. Roshen developed a taste for Kanjeevaram saris, grew her hair, which she coiled into an elegant bun with a *gajra* encircling it, sported a bindi and attended concerts and recitals with Bala. Visiting the Music Academy, she met and discussed Sanskrit drama with Dr V. Raghavan, while evenings were spent being tutored in Carnatic music

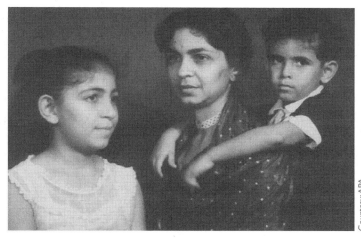

Roshen with Amal and Feisal, 1958

at home. Effortlessly slipping into a world grounded and steeped in tradition, which she had known only as a distant observer, Roshen began to feel she belonged, as her quest to understand the roots of our very ancient civilization started being fulfilled through this deeply immersive experience of Bharatanatyam at the feet of India's greatest exponent, T. Balasaraswati.

* * *

Meanwhile, my father was busy directing Molière's *The Miser* in Bombay, while additionally, due to financial constraints, he took up an actor training course for a group in Bandra called Nalanda.

> The Nalanda people have advertised quite widely re: my classes (including, I believe, in the Bombay Man's Diary) So I'll probably do it, even if there is a little talent, twice a week. The Rs 180 would be welcome. We're very short of money and every day brings a new bombshell.[5]

Elk went on:

> The financial situation is pretty desperate. We owe the following large amounts: Amal's fees: Rs 180; Standard Lit: Rs 150; Yusuf,

the furniture man: Rs 330; Veena's: about Rs 250. (Rs 100 which I borrowed from Karson & the rest for repairs on our car which is at present in a pretty bad condition.) Another headache. Veena's now ask to pay cash on the spot before they give you delivery of the car! I really don't know what to do because apart from the above there are still a few others: Schema Rs 150; Chetana: Rs 60; the Artists Aid Fund Centre: over Rs 200.

This month, I have had to borrow small sums of Rs 10 & Rs 20 from people like Hilla & Cedric & Amjad, which is most embarrassing. I am sorry to catalogue these financial woes to you but I really don't know what to do.[6]

By now, there was talk of the Asian Theatre Institute merging with the National School of Drama (NSD). The Ministry continued dialogue with Alkazi, trying to assess whether he would be willing to get on board as director of the NSD in addition to developing the syllabus. From his letter to Roshen, it appears that he was uncertain.

> Ashfaque (Husain) will be here for a couple of days & wants to see me. Mama Warerkar asked to see me and wants me to head this School (NSD) which he says should be located at Bombay and not in Delhi. I said No. If you are so anxious to get me it's because you have respect for my work & faith in it. I've only been able to do it because I've been independent. If you really wish to help me, give me financial assistance and land and allow me to work in complete freedom. He seems anxious to help.[7]

At this point, it seems that Alkazi preferred to remain in Bombay, reluctant to lose his independence and the freedom to pursue his own vision.

Despite the mounting anxieties, my father always made it a point to write cheerful letters to us children in Madras, cracking jokes and making light of matters. One of his delightful letters to me:

16th November 1957

My darling Amal,

I opened your letter where you had closed it. But you had closed it so soon.

I hope you are not still feeling week (sorry, mistake, weak weak weak) and that you are eating plenty of liver and onions and ayah's toes. By the way, ask Mummy about that medicine for my friend in Bermuda.

Three days ago, the weather was very bad with mist and dampness like every day in England. It made me miserable.

Hence, I live on tea and stale bread and thoughts of you. I hope I shall see you all soon. Love to Feisal, Mummy & Fatty Bumpkins, the Ayah.

Your sad Dad,
Elk

Please tell mummy her letters are always under stamped and that every time I have to pay 4 n.p. but that I wouldn't mind paying 4000000000000000000000000000000000000000000 for one of her letters!

Missing us terribly, my father took two weeks off to come down to Madras, from where the four of us took off on a fabulous trip to the famous temples of South India. Renting a car, we went to Kanchipuram, the city of a thousand temples. The silk-weavers district was a special delight for Mummy, who bought herself a few saris. Next, we visited Mahabalipuram, the ancient port of the Pallavas, from where we proceeded to Thanjavur, associated with the spread of Carnatic music and home of traditional Tanjore paintings. We then visited the Meenakshi Temple at Madurai and finally ended our trip by spending a glorious evening watching the sunset and sipping coconut water while lolling on the beach at the southernmost tip of India—Kanyakumari!

The trip seemed to realign my parents and they appeared to be quite happy and at ease, all of which helped to reinforce our ties as a family.

* * *

Throughout our stay in Madras, my father had been extremely supportive of my mother's desire to seriously pursue her study of Bharatanatyam. However, on our return, Roshen sensed a certain aloofness in Elk's attitude. She had hoped that her absence would have brought him and Uma to their senses, that they might have realized that theirs was a short-lived infatuation and that what was at stake here was the break-up of an entire family. Instead, in the ten months of our absence, it appeared that Uma had actually shifted out of her husband's home in Pali Hill and had settled down with her children in a flat at Nepean Sea Road, not far from where we lived.[8] She supported herself through jobs at the *Illustrated Weekly* and AIR, and her friend from Delhi, Shona Ray, a textile and interior designer and cousin to Satyajit Ray, visited from time to time.[*]

What distressed Roshen further was that Alkazi had cast Hima Kesarkodi in the title role of *Hedda Gabler*. What was Elk thinking by bringing in a close friend and confidant of Uma's into their midst? Hima had never worked with them before—she was neither a TU member nor one of Alkazi's students! Worse still, Elk cast Roshen opposite Hima as Mrs Elvsted, making the undeniable parallel between the triangular relationship between the characters in the play and their own personal lives painfully evident. Roshen regarded this as a public humiliation in front of their family, friends and associates and it intensified her sense of rejection. Ironically, as it so often happens, the emotional tensions in an actor or director's personal life somehow translate into electrifying theatre onstage. Alkazi's casting of Hima as Hedda, a complex and unsympathetic woman, and Rosh as the seemingly weak Mrs Elvsted, along with the rest of the cast and the spectacular staging, made this one of Alkazi's most nuanced, polished and powerful productions.

The first night over, the sense of relief was short-lived as a scathing review of the play appeared in the *Times of India* (TOI) the next morning.

---

[*] In a letter from Uma Anand to Alkazi in 1977, after the news of Shona Ray's death, she wrote, 'She has been a vital part of me ever since in '57 she came to share our sweet flat in Job Palace.' I had no idea that Uma and my father shared a flat in Job Palace in Bombay.

Alkazi, worn out and emotionally drained, could not contain himself. He shot off a sharp rejoinder to the editor of *TOI*, which appeared in the 'Letters to the Editor' column the following week.

There was a counter reply from the *TOI* critic, followed by letters from Laeeq Futehally, Soli Batliwala, Chunilal K. Madia, V.S. Gaitonde and Shona Ray and others, broadly supporting Alkazi's stand. Another letter was from a Mr K. Kittu, who claimed that the Theatre Unit's production was in no way even 'worthy of notice', while one Mr V. Grenfell was distressed to find the *Times of India* 'turned into a battleground over a current production.'[9]

The Theatre Unit announced a public discussion at the Bhulabhai Desai Institute, turning the event into a public forum where the artist and critic would lock horns. Inviting Bombay's top intellectuals to participate in a public discussion on the production, Alkazi had Rudy von Leyden preside with Sham Lal, assistant editor of the *TOI*, D.G. Nadkarni and himself as the producer, express their views. The place was packed to capacity, making the evening a landmark event in the annals of theatre history where Alkazi refused to accept 'the sanctimonious and self-righteous tone of the critic', which aimed at stifling artistic experimentation and the right to artistic freedom. Alkazi lambasted:

> I practice an ephemeral art that is rendered still more ephemeral by crippling economic conditions. I cannot leave it to posterity, as the writer or artist can, to pass its verdict on my work. Nothing remains of my creations except the memories retained by those who have seen them. That is why it is important, from my point of view, for people to see my work while it is in existence for a mere six days and pass their judgement on it.[10]

'. . . and not be influenced not to attend by some third-rate hack' . . . is what he might have added! Referring to Mr Grenfell's letter, which sought to admonish him as the producer for carrying on 'these kinds of sinister skirmishes publicly in newspaper columns', as it diminished public decency and decorum, Alkazi, clearly beside himself, spat out:

> The fact of the matter is that these 'sinister skirmishes' are symptomatic of a general dissatisfaction with the present state of

criticism—literary, film, art and drama. It is only natural that this dissatisfaction should find healthy expression in the columns of a newspaper...

Mr Grenfell invokes propriety, and the drama critic of the *Times of India* talks of table manners. This same 'shocked' strain is evident in the writings of those who called Ibsen's works 'an open sewer', dubbed Joyce obscene, Lawrence a guttersnipe and Sean O'Casey a third-rate pen-pusher wallowing in filth. These 'enemies of the people' carried on their individual fights not only in the columns of newspapers but also in courts of law. Today, they stand vindicated in the eyes of the world.

Unquestionably, this event became something of a cause célèbre, catapulting Alkazi into the position of being regarded as a spokesman of the theatre fraternity as a whole, who was putting himself on the line in order to defend the cause of freedom of expression, the ethics of theatre practice and the dignity that should be afforded to the theatre as a profession, as a medium of artistic expression.

* * *

With *Hedda* behind them, Roshen was determined to keep her commitment to returning to Madras to complete her studies, but at the same time she was hesitant to leave Bombay for any extended length of time, as it might adversely impact her teetering marriage. Weighing her options, Roshen decided to return to Madras on her own, *without* the children, leaving us in the care of our father instead. However, she would reduce her stints in Madras to two months at a time. Handing over the keys of the cupboards along with Rs 120 to me, an amount that was to take care of food and sundry expenses for a month (on an average of Rs 4 per day!), my mother psyched me into being a 'good little girl' who should write down the daily *hisaab* (accounts), take charge of handling the servants and play substitute 'Mummy' to my little brother, Feisal, in her absence—all of which I, at the tender age of eleven years, accomplished with due diligence, as my daily letters to my mother in Madras testify. I remember seeing my mother off at the station on 30

December 1958 (which is where I began this chapter), tears of sorrow and abandonment coursing down my cheeks. The next day, I penned the following letter:[11]

> My Darling Mummy,
>
> How are you? I am not feeling so bad that you have gone. Please write and tell me when you are coming. Today, Daddy brought Feisal his watering can. This morning I and Feisal had a wonderful time painting the tanks and Daddy has painted a tank, we brought down some plants and put them on the verandah, we also went to B's house this morning and had fun, we are going on Friday too. Feisal is now playing Natak-Natak and Daddy is talking to his friend.
> Happy New Year! Must close now.
>
> Love
> Amal

My letter of the very next day testifies that besides giving my mother news of our routine, I had taken it upon myself to inform her of any of my dad's 'unusual' activities. It is clear that I was quick to recognize signs of the cracks in their relationship.

'Yesterday night, Daddy marched out of the house with a suit on, and Feisal asked him where he was going and Daddy answered he was going out for New Year, and we asked him where, and he did not answer.'

In other letters, written on 5 January and 7 January, I comment on the fact that Dad is out of sorts:

> I have so much work to do and the ayahs do not do as they are told, and Daddy gives me long lectures (today he is giving one).
> I take my medicines regularly. I cry when I think of you, but Feisal does remember you but does not cry. We are now preparing for Feisal's birthday. Daddy does not let me send letters without his permission.

In yet another letter, I mention that my father seems depressed:
'Daddy was looking sad.'
My mother responds:[12]

'You write that Daddy seems sad because I haven't written him. But I have written 5 letters to him, so he must be worried about the play, I think. Let me know how he is?'

It is from this time that the tone and tenor of my mother's letters begin to tell a completely different story as to her state of mind. My mother seems to have begun to emerge as a butterfly from its chrysalis; she no longer needs to be complimented by Elk that she is his 'Botticelli's Venus', nor does she want him to profess that he misses her desperately. For the very first time in her life, my mother has had the courage to travel alone by train, stay by herself at a hotel and even shift to a modest shared room at the YMCA. Despite the initial awkwardness of being stared at as a woman by herself without a male escort in a restaurant, she has begun to enjoy the smell of freedom and the excitement of anonymity that Madras offers her. Her letters are bright and energetic and describe her days as being full of meaningful activity. In one of her letters, she reflects on the thrilling prospect of being engaged in a creative endeavour that is entirely her own.

> Today has been a very exciting day for me. I was discussing Bharatanatyam with Bala—one of the reasons why I felt why it did not take on meaning for people today was the rigidity of the formal patterns created by the dancer on the stage and how the stage was never used fully. Also, how, interesting formal patterns could be created with two or more dancers together. She, of her own accord, suggested I try some such experiments with her students at the class! I was staggered to know that she approved of experimenting with traditional forms. This support and opportunity to try out some of my ideas is very exciting, for here I have the musicians, Bala to guide and trained students. I hope I will be able to do something worthwhile.[13]

Roshen is also thrilled to find that the costumes, which she was invited to design for British director Peter Coe's production of *Twelfth Night* with the Madras Players, are being greatly appreciated.

The Madras experience allowed my mother to begin believing in herself. Observing how a person like Bala had to suffer several setbacks, both financial and reputation-wise, in the process of building her career, was a lesson for Roshen to understand how women especially had to struggle in order to make something of themselves. For Roshen, Bala exemplified a woman artist who had been able to transcend the mundane and take her art to another level of experience. It began to dawn on Roshen even more clearly that it was only in creating *art* that a human being could find harmony and fulfilment.

By now, she had grown more confident of getting Elk and herself through this troubled patch of their marriage. In a letter to him, shortly before her return to Bombay, she offered him her unstinted support, stating that she unwaveringly believed in his vision and capacity.

> Darling,
>
> I will really help you solidly. Together, darling, we can achieve anything, believe me nothing is stronger than the belief we have in each other and the will we have to help each other.
>
> In all the activities you take up, always lay the greatest emphasis, and spend most time and thought, on the real creative work of producing plays or acting. The outer shell, like the place we work in or the richness of sets, etc., are not so important. They may impress people, but finally our work is the productions you give out, your interpretations of great dramatists. Also your ability to teach acting. I am not saying this in disapproval of anything you do, or have done, I have far and as much faith in you and I know that you are always going in the right direction. But this feeling you have, that unless something solid is established now, otherwise the future is bleak, is quite wrong. If you mean your own theatre, it is your own ability to create, that is your source of solidity and no one can take that from you. So long as you go on creating, the future can never be bleak.[14]

CHAPTER 27
ALKAZI'S WOMEN: AGENTS OF CHANGE 1958–61

If there was an exhibition that embodied my father's 'internationalist' philosophy, it was 'The Family of Man', which had been shown in Bombay's Jehangir Art Gallery in 1956 as part of its travels across the world.* This phenomenal photographic exhibition was curated and designed by Edward Steichen, the head of the photographic section of MoMA, New York. I remember being totally mesmerized as my father held my hand and led me through a maze of huge blowups of faces. Conceived as a response to the horrors perpetrated by the war, Steichen refused to highlight the devastation and grimness of the war; instead, he focused on the people's will to *live*, to *survive*! Today, Steichen's approach reminds me of Brecht's advice to his actors to 'play the opposite' in order to make your point!

A row of narrow, nine-foot-tall cupboards stretched from floor to ceiling across the length of an entire wall of our Vithal Court flat. Very 1950s in its design, behind its Burma teak elongated doors lay a world I would feast on every evening as soon as I returned from school. Throwing down my satchel, I would fling open the refrigerator door, grab the large bowl of freshly cut fruit, smother it with malai (fresh cream), pluck a book or magazine from one of the cupboards and settle down cross-legged on a very Jane Drew-looking chair to spend the next half hour in a state of total bliss!

I was inevitably drawn to illustrated books and magazines like *Plays and Players*, which my father regularly subscribed to, revealing the latest Old Vic productions or books on modern dancers, and, of course, my

---

* In 1956–57, it travelled to seven cities, the highest number within any country: Trivandrum, Ahmedabad, Agra, Madras, Bombay, Delhi and Calcutta.—From *Pictorialism to Realism: On Marg's 1960 Issue*, Sukanya Bhaskar, ASAP Art, May 2021 issue, https://asapconnect.in/post/163/singlestories/nation-building-and-photography

old favourite, 'The Family of Man' catalogue with its images of peasants, factory workers and artisans—people close to the land who worked with their hands. These were the first socialist-inspired images I had ever set eyes on and they left an indelible impression, shaping my own aesthetic in later years.

My father would often reference 'The Family of Man' exhibition in his talks on art or in rehearsals. I believe it awakened in him a deep and abiding interest in photography as a creative medium as well as a historical document. In later years, this developed into a passion, leading him to create an expansive collection of rare nineteenth-century photographs. The design aesthetic of the exhibition also left its traces—the huge blow-ups of faces suspended at different heights, many above eye level, was an idea that Alkazi developed to compelling effect in the layout of his own exhibitions. Also of great interest to him was the juxtaposition of images with poetic texts that played off one another to create an exciting new audio-visual experience that induced alternative ways of 'seeing' and 'reading' artworks.*

On a more humane level, the exhibition featured images of ordinary people whom Alkazi had always been sympathetic to in daily life. 'There was sunlight and beauty to be found everywhere,' he said. My father would always end his productions, even deep, dark tragedies, on a note of hope, never despair. This constituted his belief in mankind, 'the essential oneness of humanity throughout the world' that Steichen had so remarkably achieved in his landmark exhibition.

From where I sat, I could see my mother at the far end of the flat furling and unfurling her lightly starched, gauzy cotton sari around her, looking over her dainty shoulders at herself in the full-length mirror. Her movements had become lighter and more graceful under Balasaraswati's rigorous training, while her figure had filled out slightly—a slim waist resting on curvaceous hips. This was the time after her afternoon nap and cup of tea when my mother would be getting ready to attend rehearsals. My father was currently rehearsing *Miss Julie*.

---

* A decade later, Alkazi was to devise two innovative 'slide programmes' based on *The Waste Land* and *Brecht: The Years of Revolt*, where he experimented by combining music and spoken text (including poetry) with slides of paintings and archival photographs.

On her return from Madras, my mother had taken her cousin Nicky Padamsee's advice to consult a psychoanalyst, as he felt it might help her come to terms with her anxieties. In those days, going to a psychoanalyst was frowned on, but my mother persevered, confiding in me in later years that she had found the analyst's suggestion to write down her recurring dreams[*] and feelings an invaluable exercise in understanding her deep-seated fears and looking at her life more objectively. It was around this time that my mother began penning her thoughts, filling up notebooks, until she gradually taught herself to abbreviate and contain her responses and emotions into exquisite haiku-like poems. This was my mother's strongest quality; she always found ways to channelize her pain and anguish into something more constructive and creative. First, it was dance and now poetry. Here, in her poem 'The Search',[1] my mother reiterates the need to understand:

> To know beyond the fact,
> To grasp the core of meaning
> This is the futile search,
> But barren husk
> Is all the mind can reach
>
> Beyond the mind there is a truth
> A truth which must be found
> This force within moves blindly forth
> Impelled against the will
> It batters down each feeble wall
> With elemental power
> This seeking, searching soundless thing
> This pounding from afar
> Denying all that has been known
> Demanding evermore
> Pursuing with relentless grip
> The all-consuming flame

---

[*] He helped her recognize a dream she constantly had, that of a tall blank wall that she was trying to get through. He explained that she confronted two walls in her life: one was her mother, who had never shown affection and the other was her husband, who was headstrong.

Whose touch destroys yet reaffirms
The life force within.

*   *   *

Making good on her word, my mother, on her return from Madras, wholeheartedly supported my father in the hope that this might strengthen the bonds of not just their marriage but, more importantly, prevent the dissipation of the work they had collectively built. Now, as they lived through this dark, unsettling period of their lives, both my parents made herculean efforts to avoid their work becoming collateral damage caused by their strained relationship. Somehow, my father created some of the most intense, masterful productions of his entire career during this turmoil-filled period.

Alkazi's relationship with the two women he was so closely involved with must have preoccupied him. As with all artists, life becomes the raw material to shape into art and one sees Alkazi using his own understanding of the conflicts that Roshen and Uma were experiencing reflected in his choice of texts. Uma, willing to forego the security of her marriage and live independently on her own terms, was even so facing the repercussions, whereas Roshen felt betrayed, ignored and unacknowledged. In his own family, Alkazi had observed how his mother and five sisters had yearned for the freedom to explore a world beyond the four walls of their home. So did the young actresses he now worked with, struggling daily against parental and societal prejudices to pursue a public profession like theatre.

Undoubtedly, these were times when women were the agents of change, the new protagonists. Therefore, it was the woman in her multiple guises—with all her uncertainties, assertions of selfhood, suppressed anger and hysterical breakdowns—that became the major theme that preoccupied Alkazi in his productions between 1956 and 1961.

It was the classics that he would invest with contemporary significance: Strindberg's *The Father*, Ibsen's *Hedda Gabler*, Anouilh's *Antigone* and *Eurydice*, Strindberg's *Miss Julie*, Lorca's *The House of Bernada Alba* and *Yerma* and Euripides's *Medea*—each a powerful, woman-centric play that allowed Alkazi to explore the psyche of the modern woman.[*]

---

[*] In assessing Alkazi's contribution to Indian theatre, Girish Karnad rightly observes that we in Indian theatre were lucky that Alkazi steered us away from Britain's drawing room comedies and turned our attention towards Europe with his choice of women-centric plays

Miss Julie by August Strindberg, dir. E. Alkazi, Alaknanda Samarth as Miss Julie, Alkazi as Jean, Theatre Unit, Bombay, 1960

'If a work of art embodies within itself some seed of universal and perennial significance, it grows with the passage of time ... and allows for several interpretations.'

In search of plays of 'timeless' relevance, Alkazi discovers that *The Father* has the dimensions of a Greek tragedy, challenging him to open it up to a 'universalist' treatment.

> This tragedy cannot be enacted on a domestic level. It cannot be confined to the four gloomy walls of a Scandinavian home, nor can Laura and the Captain be regarded as characters representative of a particular small town at a particular period in history. That view would make the play mean, sordid and parochial. *The Father* is a work of larger dimensions; its theme is of universal significance, and the problem it poses is an eternal problem. It is a tragedy in that there is no way out; no rational sensible solution can alter the implacable course of events.[2]

---

from there. In a sense, all our major playwrights, such as Mohan Rakesh, Vijay Tendulkar and Girish Karnad himself, soon followed with powerful new women-centric plays.

Hedda Gabler by Henrik Ibsen, dir. E. Alkazi, Hima Devi as Hedda Gabler, Theatre Unit, Bombay, 1958

In his treatment of the text, Alkazi relocates the story in a timeless zone of myth and ritual re-enactments, envisioning the characters as 'archetypal' entities representing 'elemental forces'. Such a reading of the text was surely inspired by the modernist approaches of Carl Jung and Joseph Campbell, where human behaviour was being seen as the product of the 'collective unconscious'. In describing how he envisages the play, Alkazi wrote:

> The scene is not a living-room; it is a battlefield on which two elemental forces confront each other. These forces are so stupendous as mental configurations, and also in their destructive physical power . . . In this fight to the finish, the antagonists use every resource of mind and body to outdo each other. There is something 'animal' in the struggle . . . It is a matter of the survival of the fittest. And this 'animal' feeling can only be communicated

if the actors assume the characters of animals. Laura in the second act is a serpent, cold, hypnotic, diabolically cruel, coiled round a brave, forthright, leonine Captain.

Taking his analogy further, Alkazi designs a set where he removes all semblance of naturalistic detail, where nothing descriptively suggests a Scandinavian parlour; instead, he visualizes the location as 'an arena of combat':

> Our setting is an isolated arena (the scene of combat) raised above the actual stage, with only the most essential requirements. Every property or item of furniture is a poised, tense witness to this deadly struggle. Rearing above the arena, and facing each other diagonally across the stage are two forms, a tall ominous horned figure on the one side; on the other the male form, shooting upwards, bursting into flower. Above the male, is a curved female shape, overhanging the acting-area, like a cloud.

Following the director's interpretation, Roshen eliminates all extraneous details and decoration that suggest a specific historical period and creates stark, dark costumes of rough texture. The snug fit allows the animal-like movements to become more apparent.

Here we see Alkazi moving towards a more modern, abstract, essentialist approach that is reductive and suggestive rather than historically accurate and descriptive. As a painter–director, Alkazi prefers to build strong tableau-like images that are static and iconic, placing them at crucial points in the development of the narrative—images that he believes will linger in the spectator's memory long after the performance evaporates.

> The eyes and the ears remember. In recollecting a performance, only a few moments will remain vivid in the memories of the spectators . . . These are moments when the dramatic event has been compressed into an Image of compelling truth and power . . . They are not accidental. It requires all the skill and cunning of actors and producer to sum up each scene in a significant image.

Each of these images has to be so composed and so timed as to build up to the requisite dramatic intensity.[3]

The creation of images was part of the total performance language that Alkazi was exploring as a director. He sought to speak to the 'dark regions of the blood' so that the audience 'experienced' the play at a deep, subliminal level. This was illustrated in his next venture, a stunning new production *Miss Julie* in 1960.

> A great work of art affects us on several levels of consciousness. Drama at its purest is apprehended not only by the intellect but also by the intuition . . . The meaning of a speech as spoken by an actor may be mentally registered by the audience; but by its cadence, its rhythm, the quality of the voice, the stance of the actor as he speaks the lines, it will affect the pulse of the audience, however imperceptibly. A shriek, a moan, a sigh, a laugh, silence, the sight of blood, the lighting effects, will affect an audience at a much deeper level than merely the level of the mind.[4]

Alkazi recognized that *Miss Julie* dealt with primal instincts and its impact depended on the director's ability to make palpable the indescribable physical attraction between the antagonists.

> The perennial, primeval conflict is the essence of this play. Its impact is penetrative; it infiltrates into levels of consciousness in the human psyche and explodes there with shattering force. I am referring now to the elements in it of myth and ritual.[5]

The midsummer night, the bacchanalian dance, the blood and the sacrifice of the greenfinch are the visual and aural elements that Strindberg uses to highlight the ritual quality in the play. Alkazi describes how by sensitively integrating the texture of the set with the music, the costumes, the lack of make-up, the texture of light moving from twilight through the dark cave of the night and ending with the morning sun, he hopes to achieve the requisite texture of a sexual ritual.

Looking back, from 1989 to his experience of witnessing a performance of Alkazi's *Miss Julie* in Bombay in 1960, Karnad, who himself went back to Indian myth and folklore as material for contemporary themes, shares how deeply the production impacted him:

> One of the first things I did in Bombay was to go and see a play, which happened to be Strindberg's *Miss Julie* directed by the brilliant young Ebrahim Alkazi. I have been told since then that it was one of Alkazi's less successful productions. The papers tore it to shreds the next day. But when I walked out of the theatre that evening, I felt as though I had been put through an emotionally or even a physically painful rite of passage. I had read some western playwrights in college, but nothing had prepared me for the power and violence I experienced that day. By the norms I had been brought up on, the very notion of laying bare the inner recesses of the human psyche like this for public consumption seemed obscene . . . What impressed me as much as the psychological cannibalism of the play was the way lights faded in and out on stage . . . We stepped out of mythological plays lit by torches or petromax lamps straight into Strindberg and dimmers. The new technology could not be divorced from the new psychology. The two together defined a stage that was like nothing we had known or suspected. I have often wondered whether it wasn't that evening that, without being actually aware of it, I decided I wanted to be a playwright.[6]

* * *

It had now been a full ten years since my parents' return from England in 1951 that they had spent pursuing theatre without it providing them any financial stability. In fact, their personal resources had dwindled substantially. To support and run an institution was an uphill task and I remember this being an incessant topic of conversation between my parents. It was often a cause of tension as my father's plans and activities only grew, and my mother, who sympathized with her artist husband, was equally heartbroken when there were insufficient resources to fund his ideas. From the meagre monthly stipend that my father received from his partnership in his family's spice company, she scrimped and saved from monies that were earmarked to cover our household expenses. However, there were occasions when my mother was unwilling to forgo her household monies in favour of TU projects. Such resistance immediately sent my father into a fit of rage. Finally, he would bellow out, 'That's fine, Rosh! Close down the blasted Theatre Unit for all I care!' And with that, he would make a theatrical exit, banging the front door behind him as punctuation! My poor mother, invariably shaken, would try to stop him saying, 'Elkins! Please don't worry! I'm sure something can be worked out! Elkins, please don't go!'

At the moment, Elk's urgent need was to secure a dedicated space of his own for his work. He had outgrown the BDI. Not knowing how long the TU would be welcome there caused him great anxiety. Having been given the use of the space gratis, Soli Batliwala had gradually begun charging substantial amounts towards maintenance and sundry expenses and was impatient with delayed payments. One of the rooms allotted to the TU was abruptly withdrawn, leaving them with only one large studio to conduct SDA classes and repertory rehearsals. Besides, the BDI had lost its exclusive charm and solitude, becoming too noisy with art, dance and music classes, artists' studios, Bal Chabra's Gallery 59, a bookshop, etc., making performances in the open air impossible. This forced the TU to once again rent auditoriums across the city at exorbitant rates, severely curtailing the number of performances to just the three or four that they could afford. What Alkazi needed was a smaller auditorium where his student–actors could grow over a larger number of shows. Then, as if the gods had heard his lamentations, a solution presented itself from out of the blue!

'I went up to the terrace of our building one day and suddenly things fell into place! I looked around, studied the space and found that with some amount of re-arranging of the water tanks etc., I could accommodate a small eighty-seater auditorium on the terrace . . . totally self-sufficient in all respects! Excitedly, I inquired of our Gujarati landlord whether he would grant me permission to build one. Being a shrewd businessman, he did some quick calculations, and within a few moments readily agreed to rent us the terrace for a sum of Rs 150 per month. It was unbelievable!'

In the blink of an eye, my parents decided to monetize our family's life insurance certificates, gave up the idea of buying a new car and took an advance on our monthly installments from the spice company. My father had enough to design and build an exquisite, perfectly proportioned, open-air auditorium on the terrace of our building, naming it 'Meghdoot' (cloud messenger) after Kalidasa's famous poem!

Though this project was undertaken to serve his own need for space, the Meghdoot exercise was also geared to set an example to architects, theatre practitioners and government bodies that simple theatres could be erected almost anywhere, at low cost, and if the space was designed intelligently, could lend itself to the performance of even the world's greatest classics!

And that is exactly what Alkazi took upon himself to do. He created two magnificent productions, *Medea* and *Waiting for Godot,* the first an epic Greek tragedy by Euripides set in the fifth century and the other, one of the greatest post-war plays set in a barren wasteland.

Waiting for Godot by Samuel Beckett, dir. E. Alkazi, (L–R) Kersy Katrak as Vladimir, Gerson da Cunha as Pozzo, Manohar Pitale as Estragon, Theatre Unit, Bombay, 1961

The audience would arrive at Vithal Court, and begin their sojourn up the six flights of steps to the terrace as there was no elevator! Once they arrived, to their right was a tiny 'foyer' area to which they could retire during the interval for coffee. The toilets were tucked away behind the water tanks on the opposite side. The orientation of the stage was such that a wide expanse of sky and a sliver of the stormy Arabian Sea would form a natural backdrop to the action. The majority of the audience (approximately eighty people) were accommodated on nineteen white rising wooden bleachers facing the performance space. Another fifteen to twenty people were seated along its right on two raised bleachers. Before each performance, we would roll out long, green, narrow mattresses along the bleachers for extra comfort. There was no raised platform to denote the stage, with the performance taking place directly on the floor. The performance area was approximately 45 feet across and 40 feet deep. Actors made entries and exits from both sides of the stage from behind white Japanese-looking slatted screens. Simple light poles had been erected on the two sides, while the sound and light consoles were accommodated behind the slatted screens from where the operators got a clear view of the stage.

My father had innovatively designed two dressing rooms under the high rising bleachers. These were equipped with a long wooden rail each, on which the costumes were hung after the *dhobi* had pressed them. Each dressing room had a makeup table, with light bulbs framing the mirrors. There was no wastage of space whatsoever.

The Meghdoot project somehow became the glue that held our family together—the excitement of my father building upstairs, the fact that rehearsals were on again just above our heads, costumes were being fabricated and ironed in our flat! With shows every weekend, the whole place came alive with laughter and activity. My father barely ever left the building, which meant that we had him around all the time! What was even more binding was the fact that all four of us were in the production of *Medea*. My father played the Messenger, my mother and I were chorus women and Feisal was Medea's son. We were really and truly a tightly knit theatre family!

Now my mother always seemed to be in high spirits! This was also perhaps due to the fact that there seemed to be a thaw in the Theatre Group/Theatre Unit relations. Alkazi, with his mercurial temperament, had abruptly changed his stance, turning loquacious and generous, inviting TG actors to participate in TU plays! Suddenly, Gerson da Cuhna, Usha Amin and Kersy Katrak crossed the floor as it were and were cast in major roles in *Tartuffe, Yerma, Medea, Waiting for Godot, Suddenly Last Summer*, etc. Rosh was overjoyed; it felt like old times—a veritable family reunion!

Audiences were absolutely enthralled with the majestic production of *Medea*, in which Usha Amin possibly gave the greatest performance of her life. Playing the jealous tribal queen Medea with suppressed fury, Usha conjured up a tremendous primeval presence. Alkazi's set was stark, consisting of a single wooden door set in a highly textured, ruined wall, whitewashed and pierced with thick metallic arrow-shaped protuberances. Gieve Patel, a young medical student at the time, attached himself to my father, playing the role of the Tutor. Vividly recollecting how Alkazi worked on plastering the Medea wall himself, he said,

> I got to see the inner workings of theatre . . . I saw Elk actually working physically—creating a screen wall using plaster of Paris and splashing it down with a cloth to give the effect of a ruined house front. These were beautiful actual encounters with theatre that will be with me always.[7]

The 'door' had become one of the most prominent of Alkazi's visual leitmotifs, assuming various shapes, sizes and designs in various productions such as *The Proposal* (1951), *Miss Julie* (1951), *Oedipus* (1955), *The Father, Miss Julie* (1959-60) and *Medea* (1960). For him, the door symbolically marked the threshold that separated the inner from the outer world.

'The place is the final place, the last, lone, ultimate place—Death's door. As in Greek tragedy, the door is never used casually. It is the threshold from life to death.'[8]

All of fourteen years, and cast as one of the chorus women, so caught up was I in Medea's rage that I can still recollect how my hair stood on end when Usha strode through the door. Holding the door open, her gesture was one of contained fury, like a leopardess ready to pounce; the sky and the sea behind her were a perfect background to visualize elemental forces unleashing themselves.

Looking back, I feel that in the process of erecting Meghdoot, Alkazi had ultimately discovered in nature the appropriate backdrop for his tragedies. This was his first step towards moving fully outdoors. Even at the BDI terrace theatre, the stage area had been covered while the audience sat in the open. Suddenly, here at Meghdoot, Alkazi's productions gained an epic grandeur by virtue of being performed under a vast canopy of the stars. For Alkazi, building this theatre was a truly liberating and rewarding experience where he had arrived at an understanding of the essential nature of the theatrical experience as being part of a collective ritual.

The terrace theatre seemed to evoke new responses from the actors as well. Gieve Patel mentioned,

> The elements of the open air . . . I mean one of my most beautiful memories is that Usha used to come after work, both for the rehearsals and for the final performances. She had a shower before coming so that when she came her hair was still wet and plastered down, but because of the breeze on the terrace of Vithal Court, as the play progressed, her hair dried and began flapping around her. It beautifully expressed Medea's growing passion . . . It was visually stunning to see that.[9]

Meghdoot elevated Alkazi's stature considerably. Artists, intellectuals, students and visitors to Bombay all made it a point to attend performances there. The fact that it was a strenuous climb up the six flights made it even more offbeat, giving it an air of being an avant-garde, experimental space. Catering to a limited audience of just eighty to ninety people in all also gave it an air of exclusivity. It was always 'house full'!

One evening, Husain arrived to watch a show of *Medea*. Little did we know that he had brought his drawing sheets with him and was sketching away in the dark. Mysteriously disappearing after the performance, he returned early the next morning with a rather bulky portfolio tucked under his arm. He strode in barefoot in his inimitable style, sat opposite my father at the dining table and, after a pause, placed the portfolio in front of him.

We were intrigued. My mother, Feisal and I crowded behind Dad to take a look as my father carefully undid the ties. The very first image startled us—a snarling Usha Amin as Medea, teeth bared, hissing and rabid! One by one, my father slowly absorbed each of the thirty odd drawings, laying each sheet down carefully over the other. Images of Jason, rows of spears, the doorway, steps, old men, soldiers were delineated by Husain in all their stark simplicity. It was amazing how Husain had been able to capture the horror of those times as well as the essential quality of Alkazi's production through a few adroit strokes of black ink.

Alkazi was overwhelmed. Silently and meticulously, Alkazi reassembled the drawings, returned them to the portfolio, which he handed back to Husain.

'I'm speechless, Husain Saab. These are superb. I'm so honoured.'

'No, no! These are for you, Elk!' said the gentle Husain, pushing the portfolio back towards his friend. 'It's not my creation, it's yours!'

I could see that there were tears in my father's eyes.

***

There is another memory that somehow provides an apt conclusion to this period in our lives. Out of the blue, Husain asked if he might paint a portrait of us as a family. Did this idea come to him as a result of seeing all four of us together in my father's production of *Medea*? Was this to be a kind of 'Portrait of an Artist's Family'? Whatever Husain's reason, we were all elated. I remember how each of us 'sat' for him for a few moments, not more, as he rapidly sketched.

Several weeks later, Husain arrived with the completed painting. We stood around as he unfurled his canvas and laid it out on the floor. There we were, back-to-back, arranged in a circle, each looking in a different direction. There was a pregnant pause while my father walked around absorbing the canvas from various angles, probably taking time to arrange his thoughts into an adequate response. But before he could do so, it just came out, just like that: 'Husain, I don't really know what to say, but I just don't respond to it. It somehow does not seem to capture . . .'

Before he could complete his sentence, there and then, on the spot, Husain tore up the canvas in front of Elk and Rosh and us two children, the long-drawn-out ripping sound echoing through the flat.

Husain smiled and said, 'I will make another one. No problem.'

Leaving the shredded canvas on the floor, Husain quietly exited.

Why was my father's reaction so negative? Was it the idea of us being depicted as a 'family unit' that was going to be preserved for posterity on canvas that disturbed him? Did he feel it did not represent the full truth of his life, of our lives? Was he uncomfortable with the idea of leaving behind 'a lie'? Was it out of guilt? Fear? Shame? Or a sensitivity towards what Uma's response might be?

My parents looked at the long strips of torn canvas. My mother began silently weeping and went and lay on the bed, while my father collected the mutilated strips and pieced them together on the floor once again. But they did not align. He looked carefully at the canvas once again, knelt down and then silently rolled the pieces up and put them away neatly in a narrow cupboard. There they lay for years, untouched, until I came back to live in Vithal Court when I got married in 1971, looking at the pieces now and then as I cleaned the shelves.

My Dad walked out of the house, shutting the door behind him. I took Feisal's hand, moved across the desolate landscape of the polished floor towards the fridge, opened it to look for something to eat and was calmed into the domesticity of the present by the sound of the sharp whistle of the pressure cooker as it let off steam.

CHAPTER 28
DIFFICULT DECISIONS
1961-62

Elk walked down the steps swiftly, his heart hammering in his chest. The world around him seemed to blur into insubstantial nothingness. He crossed the compound, looking around for his car. Where the hell was the bloody car? He was about to question one of the usual alcoholic louts who hung around downstairs when he remembered that he had *sold* the car! To build the *theatre*!

Crossing the road towards Allabeli Irani Restaurant, he passed Venus Chemists, from where Miss Kutty, daughter of the owner, emerged wreathed in smiles and said, 'Sir, I was just about to come. I'm just taking my lunch, Sir.' He had hired Miss Kutty as an assistant to help sort his personal library in the afternoons after her college. He absentmindedly waved to her and strode on, passing Dayanand Stores, Habib Hajam's Precious Haircutting Saloon, Dr Kagalwala's Clinic, the lane to Omer Park, the bus stand, onwards towards Yeh Woh, the antique shop, My Own Studio, the photography shop, the comic shop, the paan shop and the nariyal paani (tender coconut water) shop. Darting past the gate of the Bhulabhai Desai Institute, he spotted the artists Gaitonde and Prafulla Dahanukar walking down the driveway in his direction. They waved to draw his attention; he nodded, making a dash for it across the road towards the seafront, only to be nearly knocked down by a speeding taxi! Screeching to a halt, the taxiwallah yelled out, '*Arre! Jara dekh ke chalo bhai! Bewde ke mafik idhar se udhar ladakta hain, sala!*' (Hey! Watch where you're going! You're stumbling around like a drunk!) Without responding, Alkazi broke into a run. All he knew was that he did not want to meet anyone! NO ONE! Scandal Point, the American Embassy, Breach Candy Hospital, Mafatlal Park . . . Elk was totally out of breath. Finally, he reached the junction of Bhulabhai Desai Road and Peddar Road—Mahalaxmi! He made a sharp left turn after passing the temple, where the bells were persistently ringing and eventually, there it was, the open sea and Haji Ali Dargah! Unable to continue any further, Elk just staggered a few more steps and then buckled and collapsed heavily onto the seafront ledge.

Perspiration streamed down his face, the back of his neck—his clothes were drenched. He felt an overwhelming need to lie down and did so on the narrow parapet, one arm crooked beneath his head like a pillow, the other covering his eyes. It was not sleep that he needed, but some clarity of thought. He was not in a good place, filled as he was with a sense of self-loathing, guilt, nausea.

He was deeply ashamed of himself—the manner in which he had responded to Husain's work was unacceptable! Why had he been so abrupt and insensitive? Was Husain, through 'The Alkazi Family Portrait', trying to allude to something? He hated the thought of his private life being under any kind of scrutiny.

Anyway, it was true that his life was completely messed up! He and Rosh had been going through this 'Uma dilemma' for so many years now, yet no resolution seemed to be in sight.

What was he to do? Everyone in Bombay knew them—the famous Alkazis! Rosh's family, the Padamsees, and Uma's family, the Anands, were no less public figures either. They had overlapping social circles of friends, acquaintances and colleagues, and then there was the Arab community in Bombay. All of this made it impossible for his private life to remain private. It was only possible to meet Uma behind the closed doors of her flat. Suffocating! Under such circumstances, what position could he possibly offer Uma in his life?

Then there was the larger question. Was he going to allow his personal matters to impact his work? His future? The missives from the ministry had become urgent and persuasive. He had received long letters from John Mitchell and Charles Elson mentioning that they had strongly recommended his name to Kamaladevi as the only suitable contender for director of the NSD.[1] For the past few years, Alkazi had been fending off the ministry, saying he was 'too young' for the post and that it was 'unethical' for him to serve as director since he had designed the syllabus himself. By delaying a decision, he was well aware that the job might be offered to someone else. But he was willing to take the chance, as he needed time to equip himself for such a major responsibility. This was why he had spent the last few years testing out the efficacy of a similar syllabus at the Theatre Unit's SDA.

But now he could no longer stall the ministry. Ever since its inception in 1959, everything had seemed to go wrong at NSD.[2] UNESCO observers had recently visited the school and been dissatisfied with the manner in which work was progressing, recommending, in fact, that UNESCO discontinue its grant to the school. Satu Sen, the director, had left, leaving N.C. Jain, an administrative officer at the Sangeet Natak Akademi, temporarily in charge. Sombhu Mitra had been approached, but he declined the post, while Utpal Dutt was possibly not considered because of his political affiliations. It was then that Mr Mazumdar, vice chairman of the SNA, came to meet Alkazi in Bombay and said, 'I've been told that you are the best person for this job. Do you want to take over? Or we are going to close it down.'[3]

Now, Alkazi sat up, smoothed his hair and looked out. The sun was low, about to sink into its watery grave. How majestic this vision was—the sky, the sea, the ancient mosque out there surrounded by the turbulence of the waves—an oasis of solitude in the midst of turmoil!

While looking for his handkerchief, a letter presented itself from one of his pockets! Opening it, he found it was from Lulu, his sister in Beirut. Among other news, she mentioned that she and their youngest sister, Faiza, would be taking Ubba to London for his cataract surgery. Ah! His beloved parents and family! In all the clamour of events over the past few years, he had barely found the time to stay in touch.

From a distance, the muezzin's call to prayer distracted him from the letter and awakened him to the present. It was dark now. The streetlights had been turned on. Elk got up and began to walk towards the *dargah*. He needed more time to think.

Maybe this was the right time for him to consider a change. True, he had achieved a lot in these years in Bombay. He had trained people at the SDA like the young Vijaya Jaywant and Satyadev Dubey, who showed leadership potential and great promise in introducing new ideas to the Marathi and Hindi theatre scenes. He would be more than happy for Dubey to continue working in the Theatre Unit and develop Hindi theatre in Bombay! He had created a space for women's issues to be acknowledged on stage, a space for women in the theatre to be respected. He had finally convinced theatre people of the need to be trained, leading to the sprouting up of short- and long-term courses in Bombay conducted by groups like the INT and the Natya Sangh.[4] Many of his students, such as Alaknanda Samarth, Kusum Behl, Yasmin Mody and Zarine Engineer, showed great talent and were on their way abroad to pursue further studies in theatre. Moreover, he had built and grown a substantial audience for good theatre in Bombay and had set high standards through his productions. Perhaps it was time for him to move on and build the foundation for a strong national theatre movement on modern lines! This, of course, was the great lure of Delhi—he would have an opportunity to work on a *national* level and scale. Whereas these thoughts filled him with excitement, energy and hope, the very next moment he would become despondent, overcome by feelings of guilt. The thought of letting down all those people who had so dedicatedly worked with him and been part and parcel of his journey thus far, what about them? Should he just dishonourably walk away from them and think only of himself?[5] And what about Rosh and the children? What about Uma?

By now, Elk was on one of the terraces of the dargah. He stood there looking out into the night, the faint strains of a *qawwali* (devotional singing) filling the silence.

Later that night, he spoke to Roshen. 'Rosh, I need to go away for some time to be on my own. There are a lot of issues I need to seriously consider. I feel we have reached a watershed moment in our lives. It's time to consider new options, both personal and professional. I'm planning to spend time with my parents. It will help me sort things out.'

Prior to his departure, my father was silent and introspective. There were no rehearsals. Taking out his drawing board and implements after several long years, he settled down to try and capture in charcoal drawings the wondrous beauty he had experienced at Haji Ali.[*]

*　*　*

My father's extended trip abroad, from April to August of 1961, lifted his spirits. The instability of his life in Bombay, the constant anxiety about

---

[*] These charcoal works of landscapes, still lifes and nudes were featured in the exhibition 'The Other Line', Art Heritage, New Delhi 2019, curated by Ranjit Hoskote.

money and the striving to be successful in a field that was not organized had made him short-tempered and, at times, aggressive. Being within the loving embrace of his family was comforting and healing. His upbeat mood was apparent in the tone of the many letters and postcards he sent us from the different cities he visited.

Alighting at Bahrain, Ebrahim begins to rediscover the Arab world. He is impressed at how rapidly the city is modernizing. He is overwhelmed by the graciousness and generosity of cousins he barely knows. He enjoys sitting at their shops, having a cup of qahwah; relishes the sumptuous Arab meals he is invited to in their homes and attends the daily prayers at the mosque. He no longer appears to be in denial of his Arab identity. On the contrary, he appears at ease and comforted by a sense of belonging. His next stop is Kuwait, where his brother Sulaiman continues to source business opportunities, as do other Arab merchants who are returning from India.

On to Beirut, where he meets his parents, along with his sisters Lulu, Faiza and Noorie with her husband Abdulla Al-Bassam and their children, who have left Bombay and are now settled here. Munira is in London studying art at the Central School of Art and Design. Ubba proudly mentions to Ebrahim that Crown Prince Faisal of Saudi Arabia visited their home. Noticing one of Munira's paintings (of a mother nursing her child), he asked, 'Whose work is this?'

'My daughter Munira's,' Ubba shyly replied.

'Send her to London or Paris,' Prince Faisal urged, adding, 'It is there that she will flourish as an artist!'

Ubba was amazed at the open-mindedness of Prince Faisal. 'He is ushering in a new era!' Ubba confides.[6]

By now, oil had been discovered in Saudi Arabia, so with new-found confidence, Prince Faisal was encouraging Arab businessman, who had lived abroad and cultivated modern ideas to return to the homeland and assist in the process of building a new nation. He extended a personal invitation to Ubba and his family. Ubba thanked him profusely and said he would seriously consider it.

Ebrahim falls in love with Beirut, too. Located on the Mediterranean coast, it is regarded as the 'Paris of the East', a veritable European city with balmy weather, an azure blue sea, charming winding streets and outdoor cafes reminiscent of those in France, Italy and Greece. Charmed by the ambience, Alkazi saunters through its undulating narrow streets and even orders a couple of tailored suits for himself. Dipping into bookshops, he invariably ends up enjoying a glass of wine along with a Lebanese meal at a roadside cafe. His sisters all being regular theatregoers, Ebrahim is taken to theatre performances, art exhibitions and the annual festival of opera, theatre and music at the ruins of Baalbek.

The Alkazis and Al-Bassams have never felt more at home. Beirut offers them a culture that is a mix of Lebanese, Arab and European, where women enjoy complete freedom to move around. My father mentions all this to us in his letters so as to expose us to another hybrid, international lifestyle that he feels we might find enriching and that we might fit into. He has a growing awareness that I will soon need to go to university. So, for example, he writes to me about Kuwait's new university as well as the American University of Beirut (AUB) as possibilities to consider.

* * *

Prince Faisal visits the Alkazi home in Beirut, in early 1960s; Munira Alkazi's painting *Mother and Child* behind them

It is only now, sixty-five years later, while researching for this book, that I discover a set of letters from Uma to her sons written from Europe during this time. Slipping away from Beirut and his family for a couple of weeks, Alkazi visits Venice, Athens and Paris, where Uma joins him. Relieved to be together away from prying eyes, Uma and Alkazi discuss future plans, including the NSD job.

What could have made Uma anxious over the past one year was not knowing where she stood with Alkazi, as he did not appear to be severing his ties with Roshen. In fact, she noted that he was now spending most of his time at his new Meghdoot Theatre. People began to attribute Meghdoot's success to the efforts of 'Elk and Rosh', a couple who, in people's eyes, were reuniting as a team with renewed vigour. Uma, now more than ever, sensed that she had been cast in the role of the 'other woman', and had begun feeling neglected and isolated. Even now, after so many years of their relationship, she could only meet Alkazi clandestinely.

'Alkazi! The NSD should be the next logical step to you realizing your dreams.'

Voicing his reluctance, Alkazi argued back: 'Uma, wiping out the past as it were is something I really cannot do so easily. Whatever I have achieved has been in Bombay. And the thought of starting anew in a city, which I know very, very little about and which is literally a minefield, is frightening!'[7]

But Uma persisted. Alkazi's move to Delhi would perhaps provide her an opportunity to somehow seal their bond. She went so far as to suggest leaving Bombay herself and following him to Delhi, if necessary, if that could give him greater confidence to make his decision.[*]

'And Alkazi, don't worry, I will be there by your side and introduce you to a wide circle of gifted and supportive friends who already know of your work here. Many are in important, influential positions. You will need all the support you can get in a new place.'

Many years later, my Father told me:

> And so it was Uma who encouraged me and she said, 'Look! You have been struggling around over the years in Bombay and

---

[*] This did, in fact, happen.

you have come to the top of your profession there, but now there is the tremendous challenge on a national scale! Do you want to take it or do you not want to take it? And I felt the time had come for me to take on those challenges.[8]

Meanwhile, my mother in Bombay was anxiously awaiting news of my father's decision regarding the NSD job in Delhi. Writing from London, where he met up with the family once again for his father's cataract operation, he said: 'Yes, I have accepted. But for you, the safest is always to say you don't know—even now.'[9]

My father kept his plans close to his chest. In the nine months that he was in Bombay before departing for Delhi, he directed a pageant play with a cast of over 100 amateurs for a church parish in Chembur. Gerson da Cuhna, who was to direct the event, felt it was beyond him and, with only three more weeks to go, he approached Elk to take it over.

The Prince of Peace, based on the first few chapters of the New Testament, was staged at the end of December 1961. The actors did not utter a word as Alkazi worked out a pattern of mime and movement for them, creating tableaux, which they executed while Gerson and Alkazi read the matching verses from the Bible. The music was drawn from Vivaldi's 'Beatus Vir', among other choral selections. *The Prince of Peace* was Alkazi's first large production, a spectacle, where he faced an entirely new set of challenges as a director. It was a novel experience for my mother too, as it forced her to conceptualize the costumes for massive groups rather than individual characters. Much to everyone's surprise, she banished satin and fake velvet to use hessian instead. As Gerson wrote in his assessment of Alkazi:

> The production was a spectacular success. We had experienced the touch, the invention and the management typical of Ebrahim Alkazi. He had seen at once that his parish cast was so concerned about the lines and diction that everything else was lost. As soon as they were released from speech, they were suddenly transfigured. They donned a natural nobility and grace, as he had sensed they would. He had elected to use some of the best writing in the English language, the words of the Bible. He had also worked lke lighting. He had recognized a challenge in the theatre and an opportunity

Alkazi and Uma Anand in Venice, 1962

to help. Cues were never to be missed. These qualities, merely glimpsed in *The Prince of Peace*, would soon move centre stage, in the drama of his deeds to nurture a straying national theatre in India.[10]

My father's final production in Bombay at the Meghdoot Theatre was Tennessee William's *Suddenly Last Summer*, with shows stretching practically till the day of his departure. At the time, Feisal and I were spending our summer holidays in Mahabaleshwar with our grandmother, Kulsumbai, and Padamsee cousins. Our mother had just joined us when Feisal and I received this letter:

23rd May, 1962

My darling Amal,

Now that Mummy is with you, it must be such a relief. Your last letters showed how starved you were for her. I hope you will at least really enjoy the last few days of your holiday in Mahableshwar.

Your letters have been so neat and handwriting so lovely and the spelling mistakes so few that I am really proud of you. You must keep this up—it will prove useful to you all through your life.

As you know our play (*Suddenly Last Summer*) was washed out by rain last Saturday and there is renewed likelihood of it being washed out today. If that happens, we shall refund people's money at the gate straightaway and call the whole thing off. It will be great pity if this production of ours does end like that.

I am leaving for Delhi on 30th and shall be away for about a week. It must be terribly hot over there. So Mummy will tell you, I am taking this job of Director of the National School of Drama. It will be a great challenge and I fear the conditions will be quite tough but one cannot sit back like a lord all one's life and do just what one wants to do. There's very little feeling of achievement in that. It is much more creditable to achieve one's goal under the most difficult conditions. Besides, here is an opportunity to do work on a country-wide scale.

I shall probably leave for the Delhi job in the middle of July, or it may even be little earlier than that because of student interviews, organizing the year's work, etc. Of course, I shall miss you all terribly, but I hope to come down to Bombay frequently and during the holidays you could come up to Delhi and we could go to places in the north for a change, I am sure you will love that.

And now a few words for Feisal.

My darling Feisal,

How are you getting along with your walks to distant points and getting lost and torchlights and stretchers?

Here, all your girl friends are pining away for you! They ask about you all the time, and are dying for you to produce them in a play. So come back soon for their sakes as well as mine.

Give Mamma, Amal and all the others my fondest love,

Daddy

My father left for Delhi two days before our return from Mahabaleshwar. With true Arab–Nejdi stoicism, he did not feel the need, nor indulged in emotional farewells ever. For the same reason, he did not allow his friends and colleagues to congratulate him on his new job! Instead, in typical Alkazi fashion, he just silently vanished from Bombay on 30 May 1962.

As Cedric Santos, secretary of the Theatre Unit, told me in 2019 when I interviewed him:

> Elk never told us anything. He just went. One Sunday morning, we had a meeting at Soli Divecha's house. We sat around and very solemnly Roshen tells us, 'You know Elk has gone and he is not coming back and we've to run the Theatre Unit.' So there were Soli, me and your mother running the Theatre Unit, wondering what we should do.[11]

CHAPTER 29
IN LIMBO
1962-63

The next year and a half, from mid-1962 to the end of 1963, was a period of tremendous flux and instability in our lives. It was decided that my mother and us kids would not shift to Delhi immediately as it would affect my studies, seeing that I had only two years left to complete school. The NSD job had not been regularized yet, nor was my father keen on burning his boats in Bombay until he was completely sure that the new position was suitable for him. Living apart for close to two years taught all four of us as a family to cope as best we could and discover new ways of relating to one another. Since there were no mobile phones and trunk calls were expensive, our only option was communicating through letters. The innumerable letters exchanged between us during these years testify to the fact that our separation only served to intensify the bonds between us.

My father's absence made me feel deeply insecure. While I was a rather confident young fifteen-year-old, I felt a desperate need for his strong and sheltering presence. Now, the house felt empty and abandoned without any rehearsals or comings and goings.

> 15 June 1962
> Dear Dad,
> How are you? I must not forget to add how your School is, how is it? You must be busy doing it up.
> Well, here in Bombay, we are not particularly cheerful without you. The house is so quiet and hardly anyone has come over except, of course, Dubey. He is present for lunch, dinner, tea and sometimes breakfast. He wants to know if we can keep him as a

non-paying guest, with boarding and lodging. Rather forward of him (as usual) but Mum refused!*

4 July 1962
My beloved Feisal, Amal & Rosh,

Well, here's the Director of the National School of Drama installed now in his office and his home. The office, as well as the School is pretty messy; the painters shabbily, half-heartedly slap whitewash and paint all over the place—whitewash where there should be paint and vice versa, and I carry on a running battle with them. The carpenters are busy on my little arena stage which should be ready in ten days. Tomorrow are the interviews and we expect between 50 & 75 applicants to turn up. Perhaps it will take us more than one day...

I trust you are all well and cheerful. Amal is now the Home Minister and Feisal in charge of Foreign Affairs. Rosh is of course the Queen Mother. You must always bow or curtsy to her, kiss her hand and ask her 'Your Majesty'—for example, when you knock on the bathroom door, you must say, 'Your Majesty, how long will you be on the po?' Her Majesty will probably reply with a salute of 21 guns which will land her in it!...

Give Yowjaan my best wishes—also Rita[†] and accept all my love.

Daddy

---

[*] Satyadev Dubey was hoping to make use of the Theatre Unit and the Meghdoot Theatre for his own work. He would ask to borrow a book from my father's vast library, which had not yet been shifted to Delhi. Very few books were ever returned, much to my father's annoyance.

[†] Rita Montero was the daughter of the car cleaner—Pedro, an alcoholic. With no mother to care for her, she lived in a chawl full of sex workers. Roshen informally adopted Rita and brought her to live with us at Vithal Court, seeing her through her education.

23 July 1962
My beloved Amal, Feisal & Rosh,

This is a letter for all three of you but especially for Amal because for the last few days you, Amal, have been constantly in my thoughts. I miss you a very great deal and wish you were here with me. But Inshallah you will all be here soon—just till October—let me know which date so that I can have everything in readiness . . .

29 July 1962
Dear Dad,

. . . While I am writing this letter to you the whole house is quiet for it is 6 a.m. I feel lonely without you, for remember how we used to sit and have breakfast together?

Mummy and Feisal are fast asleep and Yowjaan is pottering around preparing breakfast.

I am really looking forward to coming to Delhi. I want to see all those lovely monuments and other things like the School, and of course I want to see you most of all . . .

11 August 1962
My Dearest Rosh, Amal, Feisal,

I am sorry for the long break. Somehow the days slip by and one does not realize it has been so long since one wrote . . . Well, our labours are not over yet, though we managed to get the School to look presentable and even impressive on the first day. Rudy Leyden was there for the opening and most of the Advisory Committee and they all seemed most impressed, particularly those who had known it in its previous state.

We have provided quite a lot of amenities for the students— liquid soap and towels in all bathrooms, lots of stone seats in shady places in the garden, a games court. On the opening day, we showed some films including *Leonardo Da Vinci* and yesterday

A Dancer's World, The Open Window & *Country Cathedral*. There are very frequent power breaks—that is, your electricity is suddenly switched off for 3–4 hrs—and these, of course, are a great nuisance.

Yesterday I had Jean & the Thapars over at the School and after that we had a very pleasant evening together, when the Halis joined us and ended up with dinner at Moti Mahal. But though enjoyable, I find it very tiring, particularly after a hard day at the school. You must remember that I not only run the School, supervise as many classes as possible and take my own lectures but I have to

Nissar Allana, Matheran, 1964

attend and prepare for endless Committee meetings—all sorts of Committees: to select people to be sent abroad, or delegations or as performing artists; to pass judgment on design for the Indian Pavilion at the next New York World Fair; to give one's views on theatres here and so on. I realize how much power one wields in Delhi—it is quite amazing.

27 August 1962
Dear Dad,

How are you? Why have you not written for such a long time? But it doesn't matter whether you write or not so long as you are well and happy...

We went to a film yesterday, *Bridge to the Sun*. It was a good film. The man in the film reminded me of you.

We went to see Dubey's *The Caretaker* on Wednesday. I did not like it very much. The three characters did not act in connection with one another, but separately...

31 August 1962
My Beloved Feisal, Amal, Rosh,

I thought I had better write to you at once since Mummy has given me such a terrible firing in her letter. I started crying when I read it, then said to myself 'What's the use; they can't hear you so far away—so I stopped. Then it started raining outside.

Well, let me first tell you about the award.[*] We that is, all the award winners, about 10 or so, had to sit on the stage in a straight line facing the audience with the President of India in the centre. Then, one by one, we were garlanded. Then, one after the other, we went and stood in front of the President while the citation was read out by the Vice Chairman of the Sangeet Natak Akademi (I am sending you a copy of the citation). Then I did a 'Namaste' to the President and accepted the award. This consisted of a gold-washed

---

[*] Alkazi received the SNA award for stage design in 1962.

Roshen, Bombay, 1962

plaque with a lotus motif, an embroidered shawl, a Kashmiri plate and a cylindrical sandalwood box with the award certificate in it. You will be proud to know that I got the longest applause of all the winners. I think it was because I appeared to be the youngest of those present and people want to see young people (about 40!) coming up now. Anyway, it was a most moving and thrilling experience and my only regret was that you were not there to share it with me.

After the function, most of the audience came on the stage and mobbed us wanting our autographs. Of course, all my students were there and most excited about it all.

Well, it's over now, and since the work of the School had been interrupted by this function, I had to work doubly hard to make up for the lost time. I am producing 2 plays simultaneously in the School, and the Hindi of one of them is extremely difficult. I have a tutor who comes early in the morning. Then at 8 a.m., I rush off to the School and return by the evening and immediately I have to work out the moves for both plays for rehearsals next day, apart from preparing my lectures. I direct the School and lecture 2–3 hours every day—which no Principal ever does. Also I have to supervise the teaching in the other classes as well as the work of the carpenters in the workshop.

4 September 1962
My Darling Dad,

I am so proud of you. Mummy, Feisal and myself dashed off early on Sunday to the pictures so as not to miss the news, but unfortunately, they showed a documentary instead. We were really most disappointed. We decided to go to another film so as to see you and therefore we went to another film yesterday and we saw you! You looked so young compared to the other award winners and you were undoubtedly the handsomest! You really looked smashing. I nearly mistook you for Elvis Presley!!!

You were looking rather plump in the film. (By that, I mean that you have put on more weight) You look fit and fine. All my friends have seen you in the film and they all ask me why you were on the screen and so now I have decided to wear a placard on my back and write 'I am the daughter of the one and only Mr E. Alkazi, who has won the award and has come on the screen'. All the girls come and tell me 'Oh how cute your Dad looks!'

Your loving daughter
Amal

Compared to my father's hectic and exciting life in Delhi, ours was domestic and low-key. Trying to make up for his absence, my mother made every attempt to keep us busy, entertained and cheerful, filling our days with picnics, trips, Sunday lunches and movies at my grandmother's house with the rest of the Padamsees, Jefferies and Sayanis. My mother's close friends remained the Bhownagarys, the Husain family, the Akbar Padamsee and Nuruddin Padamsee families, the Sham Lals and the Ezekiel family. We continued to visit art exhibitions and the theatre and, with my mother becoming the dance critic for the *Times of India*, I often accompanied her to recitals. But I also remember that when we had nowhere to go, a cloud of depression descended, especially as evening fell, and a kind of claustrophobic silence enveloped all three of us in the flat. My mother, attuned to my teenage moodiness, began taking me out for long walks during these twilight hours. At times, she would take me to Bombelli's with its garden café, where both of us would order a cup of coffee each and nurse it for over an hour, making small talk or observing the comings and goings of the other patrons. It was during these quiet moments together that my mother began confiding in me about a few details of her life with my father, my role imperceptibly shifting from daughter to confidante.

Without a demanding husband to occupy her thoughts or dominate her activities, Roshen, for the first time, was able to pattern her life in a manner that suited her own temperament and rhythm.

The education and upbringing of children, including the differently abled, were of great interest to my mother. In this, she had been influenced by the ideas of Maria Montessori, who articulated that it was during early childhood that attitudes and neurosis took root. My mother devised a job for herself at the Sir JJ Hospital, where she spent a couple of mornings a week with physically and mentally challenged children, using play and recreational activities of different kinds to help them.

Using the Montessori Method for the all-round development of my brother Feisal, my mother surrounded him with educational Montessori toys and encouraged him to write stories, act and produce plays from the age of five or six! Feisal made beautiful paintings and stage designs, developed a sense of independence and humour and had clear leadership skills! My mother also began theatre classes for children and did a couple of children's plays in Hindi, *Patte Nagri* and a puppet play based on the *Panchatantra*, in the Meghdoot Theatre. In both, she cast children living in our building along with my cousins and the children of Husain, Nuruddin and Sham Lal.

These educational activities that my mother took up left an indelible impression on Feisal, who would opt for social work and children's theatre, along with working with physically and mentally challenged children, as his lifelong engagements.

I believe it was during this time that my love and admiration for my father grew and deepened. I began to understand that the path he had chosen, though admirable, was an uphill one for which sacrifices had to be made. I was at an impressionable age, and, in many respects, he became my role model. I aspired to emulate his discipline, stoicism, hard work, passion and attention to detail.

This had begun ever since I was twelve, when I began observing the Ramadan fasts with him. He was very proud that I had the stamina and discipline for them. Even though he was away, I somehow wanted him to know that I had not slacked off and continued keeping them. I also began to take my schoolwork seriously and, for the first time, began to do well in class. My father was extremely pleased and encouraging, all of which gave me a great sense of confidence and pride in my achievements.

Amal, I was so thrilled to learn you had come 7th out of 40 girls in your class. Congratulations! It's really wonderful. But I knew you had it in you to do really well and I am convinced you can do even better. Please keep up the excellent work. You have only 2 more years in school and if you do excellently and work solidly (not just for the exams) in these 2 years, you will be laying firm foundations for the rest of your life. Not only for further studies or to get a job, but for the shape of your own personal life. These 2 years will form your taste in all things, clothes, books, music, people etc. So you must see that these years are not wasted or just allowed to drift by. I am sure you will make something very beautiful of your life.

I now began to receive independent letters from my dad.

14 July 1963
My darling and most precious Dad,

Hi! We haven't received a letter from you for over a week, do write soon. How are you? I miss you very, very much and think of you a lot. You write such beautiful letters to me. I am not worthy of even a line of them. My precious Dad, I feel that you all treat me too well. I don't give you anything in return. I am trying to kind of repay you back by working on my studies. The tests are nearly over and I can now settle down to some solid reading.

Since you left, I have read *To Kill a Mockingbird* by Harper Lee. I finished *Portrait of an Artist as a Young Man*. I read *Jane Eyre* for the second time and am now reading Thomas Hardy's *The Mayor of Casterbridge*. It is truly a great book. The restraint with which Hardy uses his words and yet he is not stingy with them. Have you read it? If not do try. I am going to read *Oliver Twist* next as I haven't read it yet ...

16 July 1963
My darling Dad,

I am so worried about your School and your work. Don't give it up for anything in the world. You must promise me that you will not. Please look after your health as it is as important as your work. As I have mentioned before, let there be nothing to stop you from calling me to Delhi ... God bless and keep you from any harm and I send you all the love in my heart.

With millions of tons of love and kisses,
Amal

P. S. I love you very, very much
Love,
Amal

It was exactly around this time that a big event occurred in my life. I met a boy—Nissar! It was by chance that I was introduced to him by my cousin Kabir Padamsee. Classmates and good friends, Kabir and Nissar had opted for biology and had planned to practice their skills of dissecting on frogs. One evening in June 1963, Kabir invited me over to watch. Nissar's attention was completely diverted from the poor drugged frogs, his eyes seeking to connect to mine. Years later, he would describe our romantic first meeting jokingly as 'love at first frog'! Within the short span of a week, one rendezvous followed another, with Nissar persistently arriving at my school bus stop every day with a single red rose in one hand and a little love missive in the other! I wrote to Dad, full of excitement:

18 July 1963
My darling Dad,

... As I told you in my last letter that I have made friends with a boy named Nissar. He has come over to see me twice this last week. I hope you do not mind this for it is as healthy to make good friends with boys as with girls. I know that you will not object for you have a balanced mind and I hope you will understand me ...

Lots and pots of love,
Amal

25 July 1963
Darling Amal,

Forgive me for writing on this awful paper. But I am in my office and trying to write this letter in between classes.

Will you also forgive me for not having replied earlier to your lovely letters. But the truth is that I move around in a sort of daze. I have so much to do, that I do not know where to begin. However, these excuses of mine are endless, you know. Perhaps I am not as young as I used to be.

But I am thrilled that you are. I am as excited about Nissar as I would be if he were my friend. I am terribly happy for you. Certainly, you can have him over. I am sure he's as intelligent, serious and sincere as you are, and if he has your marvellous looks, I shall be very, very happy. But looks, of course, are not the most important thing.

How old is he? Where does he study? What are his hobbies? What does his Daddy do? Please let me know all about him.

I am sending him as a gift, a little box for cufflinks and pins and old teeth and glass-eyes and that sort of thing. I hope he'll like it. It's only a little token from me—and tell him if he's good, I'll put on an entire production for him!

Darling, in the midst of your new happiness you must not forget your school work. Sweetheart, I know I don't really need to remind you about it. But I want you to do really well in your studies this last year. In previous classes, it did not matter so much how well you did so long as you passed. But in this final year, your whole future depends upon the standard you achieve. So please do work extremely hard.

I have sent the little gift with ANTHONY TOYNE who was here a couple of days ago. I have told him you'll pick it up from his place—so please do so.

I have also bought Feisal a gift, which I shall be posting today. Please give Feisal and Mummy my fondest love and tell them they'll be getting special letters from me.

Love,
Daddy

29 July 1963
My most, most, most precious Dad,
I was really happy and sincerely enjoyed receiving your beautiful letter. I am so, so glad that you understand me and don't disapprove about my friendship with Nissar. I cannot tell you how happy I am to think that you love me so much and care for my friends. I read Nissar your letter and he was very touched that you had thought of him and had sent him a present. We shall be going over to Anthony Toyne's house this evening to pick it up. Thank you very, very much for liking him . . .

Your loving daughter
Amal

This non-conservative and welcoming approach to a topic like a boyfriend was quite amazing. I was permitted to meet Nissar at home with my mother hovering around in the background!

Meanwhile, since my father's move to Delhi, my mother, Feisal and I had made two enjoyable trips there. Throughout this period, my mother continued to insist that we shift to Delhi, but my father still seemed reluctant. It was only on the eve of our third visit, during the October 1963 holidays, that my father suggested that only Feisal and I come to visit him, not Roshen. On arriving in Delhi, the reason soon became apparent—Uma Anand had already moved in to live with my father, along with her parents!

I had just turned sixteen and had absolutely no idea about how I should react. My father said nothing and behaved normally, so with a great deal of guilt and shame, I mentioned nothing of Uma's presence to my mother in the letters I wrote to her practically every day. When the time came for Feisal and me to return to Bombay, my father kept postponing the date, saying, 'Stay a few days longer; I will miss you.'

* * *

It was 9 p.m. My father, Uma, her parents, Mr and Mrs Chatterjee, Feisal and myself were silently having dinner seated at the round wooden dining table at 16 D Nizamuddin West. The radio was belting out the day's news when we were startled by the sharp ring of the doorbell. Diwan Singh, the servant, pattered down to open the door and came back up to announce that there was a woman at the door asking for my father. My father looked a bit confused and hurriedly went down to see who it was, only to return within a few minutes with my pale, exhausted-looking mother—a battered suitcase in hand.

Dead silence. We all just stood up, caught in the act as it were!

The old Chatterjees disappeared into their room, as did Uma.

The rest of the turmoil-filled night was spent with my parents talking in hushed, aggrieved tones and asking us children to go to sleep, which was impossible given the circumstances. I remember weeping inconsolably the entire night, my face bloating into a red balloon as feelings of fear, insecurity and shame overtook me in turn. I just wanted to disappear.

My mother told me years later that she sensed that things were amiss as my father had not sent us back after the holidays. She had also heard from her cousin Nuruddin that Uma had shifted to Delhi. Without giving matters a second thought, she immediately boarded the train to find out for herself.

Surprisingly, my parents spent the entire night making decisions at lightning speed regarding our futures. We would shift to Delhi immediately; Kusum Behl, now married to Salman Haidar and living in Delhi, was contacted to help us find a decent flat. I would complete my last year of schooling in Delhi. Barely six months had elapsed since I met Nissar and I wept bitter tears that I would be separated from him so soon. I was, however, assured by my mother that we could meet during the holidays.

Trying to squeeze sixteen years of a full married life into a dozen or so tin trunks, ten suitcases and other ungainly-looking packages and bundles, my mother and I completed the job of packing for Delhi in less than two weeks. Bidding farewell to a way of life at Vithal Court that we were never to experience again as our magical home, we hoisted our worldly goods into the brake van of the Rajdhani Express and along with a reluctant Yowjaan and Rita, the girl my mother had informally adopted, we clambered aboard the second-class vestibule. Twenty-four hours later, exhausted and full of soot, we alighted at New Delhi Railway Station. It was 25 November 1963, a bitter, cold, foggy, damp day.

I distinctly remember that my father was nowhere to be seen on the horizon. Instead, Hassan, his peon from the NSD, had been deputed as the one-man reception committee since 'Director Saab' was 'very busy'. My mother, visibly shaken by my father's absence at the station, took a deep breath and proceeded to herd us and the mountains of luggage towards the exit to find a taxi. After what felt like an age, two taxi cabs with luggage carriers were hired at a price fixed by my mother after much haggling to accommodate all our goods and chattel, and so began the arduous journey to C-442 Defence Colony, our newly rented flat. The ungainly vehicles lumbered out of the gates of the New Delhi Railway Station and merged into the teeming urine-stenched streets, with everything becoming a blur. The babel of a very different type of Hindi being spoken was disorienting, making us feel like strangers, insecure and helpless as we entered a completely new and rather brash world—one that we were totally unprepared for.

An Actor's Family by M.F. Husain, 1959

PART FIVE

National School of Drama
New Delhi, 1962–1977

Aashad Ka Ek Din by Mohan Rakesh, dir. E. Alkazi, Sudha Sharma as Mallika, Om Shivpuri as Kalidasa, National School of Drama, New Delhi, 1962

CHAPTER 30
AASHAD: PUTTING HINDI THEATRE ON THE MAP 1962-63

It is tempting to read of Alkazi's early encounters and reception by the Hindi theatrewallas of Delhi in the early 1960s as the story of a western-educated Bombayite who was presumptuous and conceited enough to think he could teach Delhi theatre buffs a thing or two. Alkazi was poised to confront an already atrophying institution that had been unable to sustain itself through imaginative progression in imparting theatre studies to youngsters. The NSD staff had been appointed by the Nehruvian government even before Alkazi's arrival, leaving the new director with little scope to select his own team. Sheila Bhatia, Shanta Gandhi, N.C. Jain, Govardhan Panchal, Dev Mohapatra, Panchanan Pathak and Indu Ghosh—all highly talented former IPTA members from different wards—had once bonded closely in the anti-imperialist days; now, given the constraints of working in a government institution, they did not always work as a cohesive team. To Alkazi, they often appeared parochial and regional-minded and, with a few exceptions, were limited in pedagogical skills. The NSD had been around a good three to four years (1959–62) before Alkazi's arrival, but its impact was negligible on the Delhi theatre scene, far less across the country. Moving swiftly with a number of simultaneous activities, there was nothing slow about Alkazi. He was an intellectual powerhouse, exacting, demanding and intolerant of excuses.

As a second-year NSD student in 1962, Sai Paranjpye recalls:

> And then suddenly, a miracle occurred! A storm called Ebrahim Alkazi was appointed director of the National School of Drama in 1962, and a metamorphosis took place almost overnight. He was a positive force and exuded vitality. With his arrival on the scene, a

languorous institution was jolted out of a deep slumber, shaken up and plunged headlong into action.[1]

The manner in which Alkazi implemented drastic changes over the following sixteen years is best illustrated by the near-indelible memories that NSD students carried of him into the future. One was of their new director, *jhadoo* in hand, cleaning the filthy latrines of the Greater Kailash bungalow where NSD was then housed. Another anecdote that entered theatre lore was the spectacle of Alkazi, along with his students,

> ... standing in the middle of the courtyard, my pants rolled up to my knees, dipping my hands into cow dung and plastering the walls of the hut, the floor and the door frame of the set I had designed for *Aashad Ka Ek Din* . . . The students were with me, explaining and demonstrating how it had to be done.[2]

'They must have been shocked to see you, the Director, doing menial work!' said Rosh, passing Dad the jareesh, an Arab dish that was fast becoming a Sunday lunch special at our Defence Colony home. It was one of my dad's favourite dishes, especially during the winter months in Delhi. My mother, Feisal and I, a rapt audience of three, hung onto his every word as he relived his initial experiences at NSD.

'Shocked? Rosh! They were positively stunned into disbelief!' Dad replied with a wicked glint in his eye.

What Alkazi probably wished to convey through such public enactments in the rehearsal room was that producing theatre was a strenuous enterprise! That theatre was a job where you would literally dirty your hands with shit and that there was no place for any kind of puritanical caste system or hierarchy in theatre! It was as simple as that!

Anecdotes such as these would be repeated by students from one generation to the next, accompanied by whispers about Alkazi's regular outbursts of rage, which shook the very beams of an already crumbling building. Directed mainly towards mental and physical apathy and sloppiness, they were part of Alkazi's ammunition against Delhi's 'civilized babudom' whose attitude he felt was generally detrimental to the growth of a liberal theatre arts school whose aim was to fashion highly skilled professional theatre artists. Often, staff members too were at the

Alkazi, Roshen, Amal and Feisal having tea on the terrace of C-442 Defence Colony, New Delhi, 1964

receiving end of Alkazi's wrath. He could never comprehend why they did not challenge themselves to improve further[3] and instead quickly fell into the trap of complacency of having secured a 'government job for life'! As can be imagined, such frontal attacks against members of the administration and academic fraternity would ultimately lead to resentment that would fester over the years and, when the time was ripe, lead to retaliation and rebellion. But for the moment, the thirty-six-year-old Alkazi was quite happy to be considered the new enfant terrible of the Delhi theatre world.

My father then went on to regale us with the near-derelict condition of the institution when he arrived.

'The place, rented from a tent wallah, was filthy, Rosh! The corners of rooms were spat upon with paan! Students unashamedly went around with their beedis! Local shopkeepers, paan wallahs, beedi wallahs and washermen, came to me and said that money was owed to them! Why? Because the students' stipends were still pending!'[4]

'Really? How shameful!'

'Next, I asked to see the theatre and was promptly informed that there was none! Can you believe it? A drama school without a theatre! So, within no time at all, I got my students to clean up the place and immediately got down to building a small mini theatre right there in the backyard!'

In a letter to us, soon after his arrival in Delhi, my father wrote of this in great detail.

23 July 1962

Darling Amal, Feisal and Rosh,

The building, painting, repairing and scraping work at the School has been relentless...

The work in the courtyard is practically complete. I have a lovely shaded patio area with two stone seats. On either side of the fountain have been planted two lovely trees with pink blossoms. On one side, there is a large egg shaped rock in a cluster of small pebbles. The roof of the patio area will be tiled tomorrow. Inshallah.

The wooden stone shed in the inner courtyard has been painted white and altogether, this whole area looks much more spacious...

The auditorium is practically ready. All the innumerable wires for the lights have been very neatly fixed on wooden strips fixed to the wall near the ceiling. The arena stage platforms, as well as the platforms for the auditorium have been neatly polished, and the curtains, which are being dyed light and dark brown will be ready Inshallah, by the 25th.

One of the first things my father would do when initiating a new project was to completely overhaul and remodel the look and feel of his work environment along clean, simple and aesthetic lines. Keen to make use of the elements available to him, the landscape with its undulations, stones, shrubbery, existing trees and water bodies ignited his imagination, and he would soon be busy making neat sketches of the general layout. As with all new projects, there was always a sense of eager excitement and anticipation to complete them in the shortest amount of time.

Alkazi's spatial aesthetics took into account the movement of the user. From the point of entry through the garden, Alkazi designed the path an audience member would take en route to the auditorium, providing him with a variety of visual and sensory experiences, anticipating that an audience member might enjoy sitting in the shade of a roofed structure, refreshed and soothed by the sound of the bubbling water of the fountain.

* * *

Next, Alkazi turned his attention to developing theatre in Hindi. Ever since 1948, he had held onto the idea that working in a *national* language was the basis on which the growth of a *national theatre movement* depended. Aware that he had only limited success in promoting Hindi theatre in Bombay, he wished to rectify that in Delhi.

However, in assessing the situation, he found that Hindi had never really been considered a language for theatrical or poetic expression, resulting in a paucity of dramatic literature available in the language. This was despite the valiant efforts of Bharatendu Harishchandra (1850–1885), Munshi Premchand (1880–1938), Jaishankar Prasad (1890–1937) and Upendranath Ashk (1910–1996), who had championed the cause of Hindi theatre but achieved little success in staging their works. This was unlike Bengal and Maharashtra, regions that had experienced a virtual renaissance in playwriting and staging by the turn of the century. Throughout this period, it was Parsi Natak companies, performing in Urdu, that had serviced northern India. Though Parsi theatre could be considered an antecedent to Hindi theatre, a majority of Hindi playwrights refrained from being associated with a genre that had by this time fallen into disrepute, what with its blatant commercialism and pandering to popular taste.

Changes, however, began to take place in the mid-1940s with the establishment of IPTA on an all-India basis with its Delhi chapter performing in Hindi. This, along with Prithvi Theatre visiting from

Bombay with their Hindustani plays,[*] helped build a small audience for more serious fare in Hindi and Hindustani in the capital. Independence saw the resettlement of thousands of refugees in Delhi from Lahore. Among them were top professionals—doctors, lawyers, intellectuals, artists and academics. With cultivated tastes in Urdu poetry, literature, theatre, dance and painting, they became the nucleus of New Delhi's intellectual and art-literate, middle-class audience.

Ardent theatre lovers among them included Inder Lal Dass, who established his repertory company, Little Theatre Group, in Delhi in 1948, while Sheila and Hali Vats established Delhi Art Theatre, through which they revived Punjab's folk music tradition in operatic form. English-language groups such as Unity Theatre gave way to Yatrik, an amateur theatre group that emerged out of the drama society at St Stephen's College. Other groups, such as Five Actors Club, performed in multiple languages—Hindi, English and Punjabi—at Sapru House.

Commenting on the state of Delhi theatre, Alkazi said:

> Merely doing plays of one kind or another is not a sign of dramatic awakening . . . But more than dramatic activity . . . one seeks a certain social, political or philosophic awareness or sensitivity. This does not seem to exist, and where it professes to, it is in clichéd and hackneyed terms. You cannot make a contribution to twentieth-century theatre with nineteenth-century attitudes and tastes . . . A group has to have an intellectual and philosophic base, a point of view, an attitude to life that one strives to shape, develop, mature . . . And the first and last word that defines that attitude is honesty—intellectual honesty.[5]

The exception, Alkazi pointed out, were the efforts of Begum Qudsia Zaidi and Habib Tanvir, whose work held integrity and promise. Tanvir had shifted his base from IPTA to Qudsia Zaidi's private amateur group called Hindustani Theatre, established in 1955.

As the name suggests, this group's language served as much as its distinguishing feature as was the kind of fare they were promoting. Zaidi,

---

[*] These were performed at Regal Theatre in Connaught Place, which was later to become a cinema hall.

though, of course, well-versed in Urdu, was rooting for a more 'Indian national' language that drew from both Persian and Sanskrit sources, one that was more colloquial and simpler to understand. Her idea was to construct a more intelligible democratic language. Returning to the roots of Indian playwriting, i.e., Sanskrit dramas, Zaidi began to experiment by translating Sanskrit classics into this new *boli*. Thus it was that the Sanskrit classic *Mrcchakatika* was translated into Hindustani by Qudsia Zaidi herself and directed and staged in Delhi in 1958–59 by Tanvir. The following year, Tanvir split from Hindustani Theatre and set up Naya Theatre along with his wife, Moneeka Misra.

Scattered theatrical activity of this nature led Alkazi, in the early days, to describe Delhi as a 'cultural desert' without focus or goal. It was no wonder that Hindi writers such as Mohan Rakesh and Dharamvir Bharati had to remain content with their plays being simply read or staged as radio plays in this rather bleak Hindi theatre landscape. Alkazi realized that there was an immense amount of work required to establish some kind of Hindi theatre movement in Delhi. He decided to make it the business of the NSD to nurture and encourage new playwrights in Hindi through the performance of their plays. He believed this would allow Hindi theatre to gain an audience and evolve an identity of its own.

* * *

My father had not yet directed a play in Hindi (plays in Hindi had been directed by Shenoy at the Theatre Unit's SDA in Bombay), so this was going to be a great challenge for him. Given his lack of familiarity with the language[*] and culture, many of his peers had been apprehensive about his appointment as director of the NSD. Opposition also came in the form of 'the prevailing drama groups in Delhi opposing the idea of such a school as it would have superseded their own groups,'[6] mentions Ashfaque Husain. Therefore, Alkazi's first public production in Hindi in Delhi was a kind of 'presenting of his credentials'. He was well aware that much depended on a favourable response from Delhi's audience to these first few productions

---

[*] Alkazi hired a Hindi tutor and would diligently read entire plays with him. He had also hired Gulab Das Broker in Bombay to teach him Gujarati, and, the following year, a Sanskrit teacher.

and that their success would go a long way towards his being accepted as the unquestionable choice to head the country's first national drama school.

> I had to take up that challenge because they (Delhi theatre people) thought . . . who is this bastard coming to teach us about Indian theatre . . . this firangi . . . this Bombay guy! Because here I was, a man coming from Bombay and people merely assumed that because this chap comes from Bombay, he has no understanding really of the Hindi language. I had to prove myself and therefore I took on these challenges, I deliberately took on a play like *Aashad Ka Ek Din* to show people, to demonstrate to people—I want to show you what I can do and what my understanding of theatre is, not merely of the Hindi language, but also of theatre![7]

Alkazi planned his strategy with military precision and political acumen. His first move was to enter the tight bastion of the 'inner circle'. Walking straight into the 'den' of the so-called 'Hindi wallah writers' camp', Alkazi caught them unawares by selecting the works of the most experimental and celebrated of the Hindi New Wave, or *Nai Kahani*, movement. Mohan Rakesh was basically a short-story and fiction writer, while Dharamvir Bharati was a poet, a writer and the editor of *Dharmyug*, a prestigious Hindi literary magazine. Alkazi had been warned by members of his staff not to touch these two plays (*Aashad Ka Ek Din* and *Andha Yug*) as their Hindi was too Sanskritized, they were tedious and they were *radio* plays, so not stage worthy at all! Ignoring their apprehensions, Alkazi found that their themes held tremendous contemporary relevance. He was sure he could win over Rakesh and Bharati—two writers of the Hindi literary firmament who held modernist ideas not dissimilar to his own—with his directorial skills.

Aashad, a play with a rural background, was the story of the Indian villager, whose lifestyle, pace and values were succumbing to the inevitable onslaught of urbanization. Interestingly, Rakesh had set the play in the Gupta period, with Kalidasa, the Sanskrit poet of that era, as its protagonist—a writer from the village who receives accolades from the court, prompting him to migrate to the capital, Ujjain.

I felt it was a very important work. I took it up because it was a great challenge to me personally; I felt that the basic theme was very interesting and was autobiographical to Mohan Rakesh himself—where he identified himself with a classical playwright like Kalidasa, and where the problems, the issues and the conflicts are similar to his own struggles today.[8]

This mix of history and the present, entwined into a single entity, was a modernist strategy that Alkazi too had attempted while contemporizing myth in productions of Anouilh's *Antigone* and *Eurydice*. The fact that both he and Rakesh were grappling with similar concepts was reassuring. In hindsight, I feel that both Rakesh and Alkazi had certainly been influenced by Eliot's path-breaking essay, 'Tradition and the Individual Talent', where Eliot expounds on the modern writer's attempt to simultaneously encapsulate both 'timeliness' as well as 'timelessness' in his writing. I believe that this essay profoundly influenced Alkazi's understanding of the relationship between tradition and modernity in relation to contemporary art as a whole.

However, it was not just Rakesh's conceptual treatment that attracted Alkazi to *Aashad*. The plot, in many ways, echoed Alkazi's own personal journey. We see an idealistic artist drawn away from his village, his roots and his muse, leaving for the capital, where he begins to enjoy the prestige and fame showered on him. Falling in love with another woman who helps him build his career, he fails to return to his first love. Referring to this aspect of the theme, Alkazi said,

> ... It was a play that did not deal with merely the life of Kalidas, but by analogy, it was concerned with the plight of the creative individual and with his ties to his genius, and his ties to the human beings around him, and how human relationships are sacrificed for art ... As a creative artiste, 'Can you use other human beings? ... can they be used merely as fodder for your creative mill?[9]

Aashad is perhaps Alkazi's only production in which we get an oblique glimpse into his private life. It could be counted among the few where, as a director, he was able to completely internalize the experience, resulting in an exquisitely crafted mise en scène that sparkled with delicate, nuanced performances from even young and inexperienced student actors such as Suddha Sharma as Mallika, Om Shivpuri as Kalidasa, Meena Williams as Ambika and Sai Paranjpye as Priyangumanjari, among others.

Presenting rural India on the stage, Alkazi was adamant that it should not be an exotic, folksy or valourized version of Indian village life, but shown in all its simplicity and rawness. He opted for Zolaesque authenticity in the scenic design.

Rakesh located the action in the courtyard of Mallika and Ambika's home. Alkazi used part of the actual tiny courtyard of the NSD building as his stage. With no platform to indicate a raised level for the performance, the audience felt as though they were seated in Ambika's courtyard. A door leading inside was visible on stage right, piercing the hut's exterior wall. Opposite, on stage left, was a door that led from their courtyard to the outer world. Framed between the wall of the hut and the outer door was the *angan*, making it a transitional space between the inner and outer worlds where the private and public exchanges between the characters occur. A single tree with a seat around it was placed on one side of the courtyard,

Aashad Ka Ek Din by Mohan Rakesh, dir. E. Alkazi, Sudha Sharma as Mallika, NSD, New Delhi, 1962

becoming a focal point. In the process of designing his first 'Indian' set, Alkazi was discovering a whole new world of spatial aesthetics beyond the westernized or Arab ones he was familiar with. The floor now became important as characters sat, worked and conversed while seated there. Alkazi found his students to be the best guides in matters of authenticity.

> You see, a greater part of them (students) came from villages and this was precisely how they built their own homes... using cow dung to plaster the floor, the walls... thatching the roof... all this was germane to most of the students. For the urban students, using brooms, sinking their hands into cow dung, scrubbing floors—the whole experience seeped into them so that they identified, willy-nilly, whether they liked it or not! These common chores seeped into them and made them act naturally and behave naturally within such surroundings. And that is partially the vitality of this play ... its reality, its genuineness, its directness, its simplicity ... that's what makes it authentic.[10]

It was now close to 4 p.m., and the sun was coming through the large, glazed window panes of the dining room, casting deep, lengthy shadows across our makeshift slatted dining table, which was actually a Japanese-looking bench that my father had designed for an exhibition! We had been sitting around it for a good two hours after lunch with the food having congealed on our fingers—so completely mesmerized were we with Dad's account of this new Indian play he had staged! We had missed such sessions for far too long in Bombay, and this made us feel like a family once again, despite him not living with us.

'Elk, I never thought you were ever that interested in naturalism of this kind. You're talking about the smell and touch of real mud, of cow dung. Why? I thought your aesthetics leaned more in the direction of stylized realism?' my mother asked with genuine surprise.

'Hmmm, that's true. I have always been against naturalism. But more than that, I have been against the *pathetic* rendering of realism on stage. And therefore, one has to get rid of all the notions of this kind of tawdry proscenium theatre aesthetics and concepts. So, we brought the reality of everyday life to the audience through the very smell of the stage, which was plastered with cow dung before every performance, to give an authentic experience to the audience, even as they came into the space. And therefore, I think that you need to use your common sense, but that common sense has to be part of a *poetic* imagination. And so the prosaic elements have to be *lifted* to the level of *poetry* through theatre.'[11]

'Well, that's a unique way of looking at realism, I suppose,' mused Rosh.

Mum stood up to clear the dishes. Dad followed, collecting more dishes and moving towards the kitchen, where Mum was piling them up to be washed later. Feisal and I followed with the water glasses.

'Rosh! What are you doing? The dishes can't be left dirty until tomorrow morning, when Chameli (our maid) comes! Please, all of you, get out of the kitchen! I will do the dishwashing in a jiffy.'

'But Dad, you can't! Let me do it. Really!'

'Out of here, young lady! I'm the best dishwasher in the world!'

Refusing to budge, my father just stood there, waiting for the three of us to troop out. Often, we discovered that Dad just disappeared without saying goodbye, returning to 16 D Nizamuddin West, where he lived with Uma. It was clear that he did not really like saying goodbye, so he made his exit as invisible and unobtrusive as possible. Wandering into the kitchen in search of him half an hour later, I saw that he had left the kitchen spic and span. The washed dishes were arranged in neat rows, and the spoons and forks were laid out to dry in descending order of height—tall to short!

* * *

Alkazi directed *Aashad* as a low-key, mellow chamber piece. Paced at a slow tempo, time, manifested in Mallika's patient wait for Kalidasa, seemed to eke out. Filled with silences and pregnant with unspoken thoughts, much was conveyed by creating the appropriate mood, and not relying on words alone.

> I tried to use extremely quiet and subdued lighting. I used unmade up actors playing these village characters, to show the internal workings of their minds, of their hearts, of their longings . . . This subdued lighting not only suggested the night-

time, it suggested a pitiful sense of togetherness, and also of loneliness, of being able to communicate, but at the same time, of the distance between the two characters ... One must remember that this was around the time of Satyajit Ray's *Pather Panchali*, etc., so there were many things in common, that kind of simplicity, that kind of rawness, that kind of realistic approach and so on.[12]

Without perhaps being aware of it, my father had instinctively discovered a style and treatment for *Aashad*. His mastery and sensitive handling of stage elements allowed him to discover a visual and theatrical language equivalent to the Nai Kahani style of writing that Hindi writers such as Rakesh, Kamleshwar and Rajendra Yadav had begun to cultivate in their handling of the short story genre from the mid-1950s onwards, where the environment speaks and all is not communicated merely through the words.

Right from the start, Alkazi insisted on NSD productions with students being open to the public so that the work of the school could be tested, vetted and assessed by a live audience. This was considered revolutionary, as earlier, students performed only in classroom productions. Now, full-fledged productions for the public kept everyone on their toes! Lights, costumes, sets, music—every aspect was gone into, practically making it a detailed, hands-on learning experience.

The impact of Alkazi's first production of *Aashad* surpassed all expectations. Audiences in Delhi had never experienced this kind of staging before. Abandoning the proscenium theatre and moving towards what was then termed 'open staging', where a dynamic, close interaction between audience and actor was possible, the production gained in both intimacy and power, with actors having to eschew loud theatricality. Described as the first open-air production to have ever taken place in the city, Alkazi's production of *Aashad* suddenly attracted new audiences—academics from Delhi University, such as Frank Thakurdas, Rati and Richard Bartholomew; playwrights such as Balwant Gargi and Nora Richards from Punjab; and university students. Ranjit Sabikhi, a well-known architect in Delhi, told me recently that the first time he saw my father was in 1962, when he, Shona Ray, Biren De and Mini Boga, all youngsters then, had gone to see Alkazi's *Aashad Ka Ek Din* at Kailash

Colony. Sabikhi remembers how he was struck by the design and layout of the little garden, which Alkazi had transformed into a mini paradise with its pond, flowers, gazebo and stone seats, besides, of course, the originality of the intimate staging. With a carefully crafted production like *Aashad*, Alkazi was undoubtedly creating a quiet revolution on a small scale.

Throughout his tenure, Alkazi was keen on the public being privy to the magical transformations he was affecting at the NSD, not only in terms of carving out new spaces for performance but also in inviting them to attend guest lectures that were basically meant for the students. As a result, he cultivated a vivacious atmosphere, enlivened by his own warm, welcoming graciousness. Hindi writers such as Agyeya, inheritors of the Jaishankar Prasad and Premchand legacies, along with young writers such as Dharamvir Bharati, Kamleshwar, Rajendra Yadav and Rakesh, were invited by Alkazi to share their thoughts and ideas through lectures and poetry readings at NSD. For them, it appeared that the young, dynamic Alkazi had suddenly seized this vacant space and filled it with meaningful activity, placing Hindi-language theatre at the centre of his concerns at a national institute like the NSD. Overnight, Hindi writers began to gain prestige and prominence and felt encouraged to write more plays. Not wishing to lose momentum, Alkazi immediately announced his next production, *Andha Yug*, Dharamvir Bharati's verse play for the radio based on the Mahabharata.

CHAPTER 31
ANDHA YUG
1963

It was 1963 and India had just lost a war. A man from Bombay turned the ruins of Feroz Shah Kotla into a stage for an epic play about the cost of violence. This was my guru, Ebrahim Alkazi, a director with an eye for the theatrical, who created his production of *Andha Yug*, a production that changed the course of Hindi theatre forever!

Mohan Maharishi,[*] a student of Alkazi at NSD, was vividly recalling the historical significance of Alkazi's production of *Andha Yug*. Maharishi had participated in the production himself fifty years earlier, Maharishi had played Sanjay, the messenger who carries the dreadful news of the rout of the Kauravas to their parents, Dhritarashtra and Gandhari.

What was the right way to tell a mother that her sons are dead? I did not have the emotional resources for this task. I was not able to get what Mr Alkazi was asking of me. He was tense.

And then one day, miraculously, '*it* happened'.

The rehearsal floor was rough and I was asking to be murdered. I came down the ramp. Ashwatthama rushed at me with a naked sword, but instead of defending myself, I slid on the floor and

---

[*] Maharishi, an NSD graduate, would also go on to become director of the school. He was speaking to the *Indian Express* in 2015 on the occasion of a massive exhibition, 'The Theatre of E. Alkazi', which Nissar and I had collaborated on as a tribute to my father in his ninetieth year.

Andha Yug by Dharamvir Bharati, dir. E. Alkazi, Meena Pethe as Gandhari, NSD, New Delhi, 1963

Courtesy: ATA

held his feet. 'Kill me, kill, kill, kill . . . and spare me the anguish of meeting Dhritirashtra and Gandhari,' wailed Maharishi as Sanjay.

Alkazi was watching; he had suddenly become quiet.

'When I slid to the floor, I bruised both my knees and was bleeding . . . I did not want to live. Ashwatthama did not kill me and I reached the palace of the Kauravas with the gruesome tale of death and devastation.'

'Coming out nicely,' said Alkazi.

1963. India had just lost a war with China. The Cold War was raging and the atom bomb was the new shape of fear. Alkazi had chosen *Andha Yug*, set during the last days of the Kurukshetra war, when Ashwatthama strode in rage, prepared to use the ultimate weapon to annihilate mankind.

It was not just the play's topicality, its anti-war thrust, that drew Alkazi to it. The shift to Delhi had somewhat destabilized my father, bringing him face to face with the fact that the cosmopolitan temperament he had cultivated in Bombay and abroad were clearly insufficient to understand the vast transformations taking place across the subcontinent. Restless and uneasy, he instinctively reached back to source material, searching for scripts that would help him understand the origins of Indic culture. What drives the country? What makes its people tick? What were their thoughts and value systems based on? Alkazi tried to shrug off the baggage of European modernism he was carrying, embarking now on a foundational journey towards a deeper 'discovery of India'.

Besides a formal study of Hindi, Alkazi simultaneously began to tackle the root language, Sanskrit, a fact that added considerable weight to his already legendary reputation of being unrelenting in his pursuit of knowledge. As a journalist mentioned, 'Rising at 4 a.m., Ebrahim Alkazi sits on his terrace swaying back and forth and chanting lines from the Mahabharata . . . he is being taught by a Guru so that he can do justice to his play *Andha Yug* . . .'[1]

His personal library held key works on India such as *Epics, Myths and Legends of India* by Paul Thomas, James Tod's *Annals and Antiquities of Rajasthan*, Verrier Elwin's *The Tribal World of Verrier Elwin*, Stella Kramrisch's *The Art of India Through the Ages*, etc. Alkazi now realized that though these were truly great Indologists, their observations were at times coloured by an Orientalist perspective. He sought the views of younger

Indian scholars by attending lectures and reading books and articles by historians such as Romila Thapar, Irfan Habib and Bipin Chandra. Dr Moti Chandra's comprehensive account of the costumes of India, Mohan Khokar's scholarship on Indian dance, Dr Pramod Kale's contemporary understanding of the *Natyashastra* and the research into Sanskrit drama by Dr V. Raghavan brought forth a fresh understanding of India's complex culture through its manifestations in the various art forms.

By 1962, at the age of thirty-seven, Alkazi had not only seen the great architectural monuments of India, he had also travelled extensively across Europe. He now began to look at the origins, sources, iconography, history and sociology of India in an informed and meaningful manner, making the next five decades his most intense period of study. From prehistoric times to the twentieth century, each project Alkazi undertook (in theatre and/or the visual arts) became an opportunity for him to study and uncover one more layer in the culture of this subcontinent. Here was a lifelong student who never stopped absorbing knowledge and was systematically piecing together the vast mosaic of thought and ideas upon which he gradually began to graft his understanding of Indian modernity. What is interesting is that at each stage he expressed his newly acquired knowledge not theoretically but in the palpable, creative terms of a theatre production or later, in his curation of exhibitions. These creative endeavours give us a glimpse into the long journey of self-discovery he had undertaken to 'be' an Indian and also towards 'becoming' an Indian.

Alkazi, therefore, regarded both *Andha Yug* and *Aashad Ka Ek Din* as *source* plays. Through them, he sought to uncover many fundamental aspects of India's *core identity*. Through *Andha Yug,* Alkazi came closer to learning about India's value system and philosophy as explored in the Mahabharata epic, while *Aashad* gave him an appreciation of the artistic sensibility of the great Sanskrit poet–dramatist Kalidasa, India's veritable Shakespeare. Interestingly, *Aashad* also lent itself to examining India's rural reality (as did Premchand's *Godan*, which Alkazi would adapt for the stage the following year in 1964 as *Hori*). From now on, Alkazi would engage with the idea of India between these two polarities: India as a myth and India as a kind of documentary reality. Many years later, both these aspects of India were articulated by Alkazi in his curation and shaping of a mammoth exhibition at the Museum of Modern Art (MOMA) in Oxford, UK, for the Festival of India in 1982, which, in fact, he named 'India: Myth and Reality'.

Explaining that his choice of *Andha Yug* was because it belonged to a seminal period when a crystallization of Indic civilization occurred, Alkazi said:

> The Mahabharata suggests to me a 'new' people in a 'new' land. The first terrible onslaughts had already been accomplished (the Ramayana in which the 'new' people established their supremacy over the local tribes), and the first attempts at achieving settled kingdoms in which the principles, concepts and ideas contained in the early Shastras could find concrete expression. Then, very early, evil corrupted and eroded these new people—within 500 years, fratricidal wars almost destroyed them totally. No wonder that the aftermath of that crisis on the brink were the stultifying centuries of Brahmanical tyranny. But up to and including the age of the Mahabharata, the questions were not of small differences, as between levels and classes of society; they were the enormous fundamentals of human thought. Man was not engaged in arguing with man; he was confronted by the challenge of the elements (Nature and Divinity). He was slowly evolving or divining in flashes of intuition and insight into vast fundamental concepts. The date of the Gita is unimportant. What is important is its inclusion in the Mahabharata. Why? Because Krishna preached his doctrine of duty and non-attachment to a fellow human. Can you imagine him preaching right and wrong to a fellow divinity? What mockery Indra or Agni would make of ETHICS. It is man's terrible destiny to be conscious of moral values in an amoral cosmos. Nature obeys inexorable laws relentlessly; gods obey no laws—they flout them. Gods being, I suppose, man's envious embodiments of total irresponsible idea-and-action. The whole poem, posing the questions of evil, corruption and destruction, formulates questions that were the first cornerstones of a culture that would then, through the ages, be petrified into a civilization.[2]

Staging a production like *Andha Yug* challenged Alkazi tremendously, both as a director and as a stage designer. He realized that most Indians had grown up with stereotypical visual impressions of characters from the Mahabharata and Ramayana. These impressions were by and large imitations of how the nineteenth-century artist Ravi Varma had repeatedly represented them in his calendars and paintings, and which the Natak companies further endorsed and popularized in their depictions of mythological characters in dramas. One of Alkazi's challenges lay in attempting to exorcize such entrenched iconography from public memory. As he argued,

> His (Ravi Verma's) vapid, sentimental, melodramatic visualizations of scenes from the Ramayana and the Mahabharata in a tasteless Victorian manner have surely nothing to do with the great periods of Indian art. One has only to compare the Mahabharata frieze at the Kailasa Temple, Ellora, with Ravi Varma's anaemic, pseudo-academic interpretations to see what one means.[3]

'. . . How to restore the masculinity, the dignity, the direct quality, the physical energy and the monumental stature of characters such

Blind King, drawing by Alkazi, 1960s

as Dhritarashtra, Ashwatthama, Duryodhana, Sanjay, Yuyutsu and Gandhari?' he asked himself.

The only way to do so was to go directly to the characters themselves, firmly rejecting the tinsel interpretation they have suffered in art and theatre and summoning them up anew out of our knowledge of human emotions and out of our own experience of life. Only then could we begin to see these characters as archetypes and not merely models of clay venerated in empty platitudes.

In order for the actors to visualize the dignity and loneliness of such archetypes, Alkazi referred them to classical Indian sculpture and to Biblical characters and incidents.

These two sources of inspiration worked in separate ways: from the sculpted grace and serenity of classical Indian and Buddhist sculpture, they could glean a sense of style and repose beyond the frailty of human action. From the more realistic western art—such as Rembrandt for Gandhari and Dhritarashtra, the violence in Goya's war etchings and Delacroix's battle scenes for Ashwatthama—they could learn to appreciate the sweep and power of monumental movement.

Another directorial challenge was to discover a theatrical form that could project the epic sweep and power without turning into a Hollywood-style extravaganza. 'It is not grand lavish sets or elaborate, expensive costumes that can give the full weight and substance of ideas of universal significance, depicted through the actions of almost super-human characters. This can be realized only through the creation of a specific style.'

In his 1965 essay 'Style in Theatre', the word 'style' was publicly used by Alkazi for the first time. It perhaps meant little or nothing to most other contemporary directors, but to Alkazi and Roshen, a unity of 'style' was the ultimate criterion on which a well-realized production could be judged.

Ever since Alkazi had been introduced to the idea of 'style' by his mentor Michel Saint–Denis, both in lectures at the British Drama League as well as through his book *The Rediscovery of Style*, Alkazi had come to understand that the true job of the director was to first deconstruct the text and then gradually discover for it a unique and specific visual and performative style.

The director was to convey his ideas to his team of collaborators—the stage designer, costume designer, lighting designer, makeup designer, music composer, choreographer, etc.—all of whom would then need to fuse their aesthetic treatment towards creating a single, unified stylistic approach. In time, such carefully conceived and structured performances came to be regarded as independent artworks in themselves, elevating the position and status of the director to one that was on par with the author.

Clearly, Alkazi was introducing the idea that theatre was a *performance art*, not *literature* performed on stage! He was creating a *language* of *performance* that was distinct from the *language* of *words*. It was this *art* of *performance* that Alkazi was teaching his students. In doing such large and challenging productions, Alkazi's students had the opportunity to observe him at rehearsals as this new type of director, a conductor of multiple mediums.

What they also observed was that he was not teaching them to stand centre stage and declaim lines or become 'real' characters; he was teaching the actor to be restrained, to hold back and to regard himself as only *one* of the mediums through which meaning and emotion were being imparted. Lighting a scene in a particular way, for example, could create mood and emotion; the physical composition of characters with one another was capable of creating telling relationships; an actor's relationship to the scale of the performance space could evoke qualities like power or loneliness. The modern actor needed to understand that he was not the sole or central means of communicating meaning on stage, he was only 'one' of the elements in the grand design of the production.

Likewise, modern plays were no longer about the trials and tribulations of great individual characters but increasingly about entire societies, races, different classes or genders, and it was in the complex relationships between such groups that the meaning lay. Therefore, actors now had to earn to play as 'an ensemble', rather than as 'stars'.

With this kind of training in mind, it is not difficult to understand why Alkazi insisted on teaching through an 'integrated' syllabus through which students were trained in *all* aspects of theatre, from sets, costumes, masks, makeup, lighting, etc. Within a few years of his arrival, he extended the NSD diploma course from two to three years—the first two years with general, integrated courses, and the third devoted to one of three specializations—acting, direction or stage management.

The idea of an integrated course was completely novel in 1963. Most drama schools in the West continued to train actors to play stellar roles or prepare them for character parts—whether it was the Royal Academy of Dramatic Art (RADA), London Academy of Music and Dramatic Art (LAMDA) or the Actor's Studio under Lee Strasberg, as Alkazi was to see for himself the following year when he visited the US. The sole exception was Saint–Denis, who had designed integrated syllabi both for the London Studio and the Old Vic School, insisting that theatre language be understood as a collaboration of artistic inputs. In Europe, scenic and costume design were part of the training in art schools, as set design for centuries had basically consisted of painted backdrops.

Apart from the subjects offered, an exciting learning experience was to observe Alkazi direct and design productions. Many from the *Andha Yug* cast alone, such as Mohan Maharishi, Om Shivpuri, B.V. Karanth, Ram Gopal Bajaj and K.M. Sontakke, who were basically actors, later developed into extremely competent directors, inspired by this experience.[*]

Alkazi was one of those highly gifted and creative individuals who took care of most of the aesthetic considerations of his productions himself. He had trained himself to be accomplished in all these disciplines and therefore needed no collaborators with the exception of a costume designer, a role that Roshen filled. She remained his one constant and key collaborator throughout his career, with him relying on and trusting her judgement completely.

It was in designing costumes for the stage, more than anything else, that my mother's own creative abilities found their fullest expression. The process began with her sitting patiently at my father's rehearsals, trying to gauge the particular style that he was attempting to fashion. What were the thoughts and imperatives that guided a director's approach to a specific

---

[*] This could also be said of the actors Alkazi trained in Bombay, a few of whom went on to become leading directors in their respective languages—Vijaya Mehta, Satyadev Dubey, P.D. Shenoy and Antoinette Diniz.

play? Was it the socio–political reality that he wished to foreground? Was his handling of the crowd scenes going to be in bold, sweeping strokes, with masses of extras moving in blocks? Or was he attempting to express the inner, tentative, febrile lives of individual characters? Or was it a dark, womb-like, clammy earthiness that the costumes would require to evoke to help create a context for the sexually loaded theme of Lorca's *Yerma*, for example?

> . . . of the approximately 150 to 200 plays that I designed costumes for, the majority were for my husband . . . we were working as a team . . . I knew what he was thinking before he even expressed it to me because I watched every rehearsal and heard everything he said, and so it was from that where my ideas would grow . . .[4]

Wondering what kind of historical period she should set *Andha Yug* in, Roshen picked up a clue when Elk casually mentioned that he was going to discard classical music because 'the aalap was too refined and sophisticated; instead, I have chosen primitive-sounding folk and tribal chants for their feel of "hordes", of the raucous, hard-pressed cries of human beings at the end of their tether.'[5]

Referencing back to the costumes of one of the early periods in Indian history, the Mauryan, she decided to create a style that was a blend of the quality found in the sculpture at Sanchi and Bharhut, along with primitive and tribal accessories found in the jewellery of North-eastern hill tribes, where bones and beads rather than gemstones were used decoratively.

For the basic male attire, she opted for dhotis made of rough, thick, hand-spun fabric. Bare chests were partially covered by full-length cloaks held together with leather and metal fastenings. Leather sandals for the warriors were used to accentuate stride, while leather wristlets gave a certain masculine accent to hand gestures.

Gandhari was the only female character. Though majestic in her bearing, Roshen gave her no jewellery or accessories to denote her status. Her costume consisted of a simple *lehenga*, a long-sleeved tunic, and a black shawl—all made of undecorated, thick handspun cloth. She wore her hair loose, giving a certain unkempt wildness to her look. Gone were the *mukuts* (crowns), elaborate jewellery and *gota*-trimmed satin costumes used in Natak company productions! Here we saw a fierce breed of men and women—bleeding, dishevelled, war-torn, with ravaged faces and shattered hopes, 'at the end of their tether'.

However, the costumes were not literally torn, bloodied, burned or in rags, which would have reduced the stature of these characters to a realistic scale. Alkazi needed to maintain the epic, universal quality of the poem, to not let us forget that this was a huge war on a cosmic scale—a war that had robbed human beings of their morals, ideals and values.

Roshen realized her costumes had to hold their own when seen against the dominating environment that Alkazi had chosen for this production, the site he had discovered during his morning walks to various historical monuments.

> I was very careful in choosing a site such as Feroz Shah Kotla. Its towering massive rough-hewn walls—pitted, scarred and broken—exuded a brooding, somewhat oppressive atmosphere, which was just right for the play. There was a quality which the elements, the sun, the wind, the rain, added to trees and stones over a long period of time giving them a living character which can never be artificially achieved within a theatre. The very authenticity of such a background forces the actor to confront himself and to act with honesty and sincerity, with a total lack of artificiality in performance as well as in costume and make-up.[6]

Alkazi felt the site itself would allow him to explore 'space and scale' in performance.

> In the performance itself everything becomes a matter of scale: the scale of the human figures; the scale of the 10 ft. wheel in relation to the great flight of steps, to that of the rearing walls behind; the scale of the actor's gesture in relation to all these; the scale of the human voice (undistorted by microphones) in relation to the characters they are depicting and the open space in which the words must be spoken and yet remain expressive.

Andha Yug by Dharamvir Bharati, dir. E. Alkazi, NSD, New Delhi, 1963

The young K.M. Sontakke, who was assistant to Alkazi on the production, remembers the strong visual impact of the production.

> In *Andha Yug* Alkazi Saab reached his creative peak. The vast field of the Mahabharata battle scene was recreated with great theatricality among the old remains of Feroz Shah Kotla. By using this as his performance space he disentangled himself from using clichéd idioms. Selecting a 70-foot long and a 35-foot high wall made of pakhali stones as a backdrop, Alkazi Saab added two arches at one end of the wall. The central playing area in front of the wall was covered with a platform that was 30 feet wide and 60 feet long, rising to a height of 3 feet. From here, 17 steps lead to a higher level.
>
> Brooding over these undecorated levels was a tattered flag that fluttered atop the high wall where a flock of vultures was perched and a few human bones lay scattered. These mortal remains lit by flame-torches used in the production were glimpsed from time to time creating an atmosphere that crossed the limits of time

and space and carried the spectators into a trance. The echoes of Ashwatthama's anguish, Gandhari's curse on Krishna, Sanjay's outcry to stop Vyadh from destroying Krishna, elevated one from one's normal consciousness.[7]

Alkazi himself summarized his production thus:

> Finally to see events portrayed in this manner in the open air against the vast sky with its moving clouds, gives a sense of the remorseless and inevitable passage of time, of human action as an infinitesimal part of the limitless sky and the inexorable cycle of nature. The cries of birds in the night, the distant barking of dogs, the rustling of trees, the gentle caress of the night-breeze imbue the experience with authenticity . . . I see Gandhari small, lost, lonely, a mere speck under a huge suffocating bowl of the sky, a frenzied, protesting speck, a cursing atom in the act of explosion, detonating a chain reaction of vengeance against the whole Yadav clan . . . minute, helpless, unable to stop what has been started. But being human, open to suffering, to realizing her part in the terrible game.

For Alkazi, fratricidal war between brothers in the Mahabharata rekindled memories of the divide between Hindus and Muslims, between India and Pakistan. Feroz Shah Kotla was drenched in this history. It was one of the sites where thousands of refugees from Pakistan had languished for many months. Much like the characters in *Andha Yug*, the refugees saw themselves as either victims or witnesses to hatred.

The impact of the eight performances in October 1963 was huge. This was the story of the aftermath of the Partition, which had played itself out within the living memory of the spectators. Each performance brought in a larger audience. Such were the crowds that Pandit Nehru himself asked to attend the performance that was making waves. Alkazi's stature soared overnight!

The third bell rang and there was still no sight of the PM. He was held up in a meeting! Alkazi was being himself when he insisted on beginning on time, PM or no PM! Minutes later, Panditji and a few others had to be led to their seats in the dark. Flurrying security men did not know where to station themselves. The play continued for some time without a break, and then suddenly cries of *'Maaro! Kaato!'* rent the air. The audience froze. Security men who had been absorbed in the play sprang up to surround the PM, as they thought there was an attempt on his life! Actors who were shouting these slogans were barred from entering the stage! Alkazi swiftly and quietly reassured the security that this was part of a scene in the play. With so much drama both on stage and off, there was no question that Alkazi's *Andha Yug* would be long remembered![8]

The one thing that no one in the audience missed was that the play was both a prophecy and a warning: another war was raging, one that could turn more vast and destructive—the Vietnam War, which was then entering its ninth year.

CHAPTER 32
THE METAMORPHOSIS OF DELHI: THE INDIA TRILOGY 1964-65

One day, my father overheard a low-ranking secretary in the ministry casually mention that the top floor of Rabindra Bhawan was vacant. In a heartbeat, Alkazi convinced the ministry that he wished to relocate the NSD there. Apart from its central location, NSD would also be housed in the same building as other key cultural institutions—the Sangeet Natak Akademi, the Lalit Kala Akademi and the Sahitya Akademi. Exposure to the other arts would certainly sensitize NSD students as to their interconnectedness.

In those early Nehruvian years, the akademis were instrumental in galvanizing cultural activity, providing substantial state support to the arts through their five-year plans. Acquiring art for national collections, commissioning works, holding national-level seminars on cultural policy for contemporary Indian art and acknowledging excellence through the conferring of annual awards—all this patronage encouraged painters such as M.F. Husain, Akbar Padamsee, Gaitonde, Krishen Khanna and Tyeb Mehta (interestingly, those who had studios at the Bhulabhai Desai Institute) to gravitate to Delhi. As key representatives of modernism, these artists, like Alkazi, were on the brink of establishing themselves at a national level. They began to receive important commissions for murals and sculptures for newly designed public buildings; their advice and presence on committees for key national projects were sought by the government. New galleries began to spring up—Kumar Art Gallery (1955), followed by Chemould of Bombay setting up a sister concern in Delhi, Kunika Chemould Art Gallery (1965). Influential people like Raj and Romesh Thapar shifted to Delhi, publishing their magazine *Seminar* from the capital, as did Patwant Singh, editor of *Design* magazine.

The government simultaneously allotted land to big industrialists such as the Bharat Ram and Charat Ram families, who established the Shri Ram

Centre for Performing Arts (early 1960s), Kamani Auditorium (1971) and the Shriram Bharatiya Kala Kendra, a school of dance. I.L. Dass was granted land to build the Little Theatre Group Auditorium, which housed a permanent theatre repertory that he ran. All these sprang up in the vicinity of the akademis at Mandi House. Across the road, Sundari Shridharani, a dancer who had been a pupil of Uday Shankar in Almora, Uttarakhand, established the Triveni Kala Sangam (1963). Designed by Joseph Allen Stein, an American architect who had shifted base to India, Triveni was established for the promotion of the arts. Triveni continues to be an iconic arts complex with multiple art galleries, dance, music and photography studios, and a delightful open-air theatre and café.

Almost immediately on his arrival at Rabindra Bhawan, Alkazi, finding the premises inadequate, consulted with the building's architect Habib Rahman, for permission to remove a wall between two rooms on the third floor in order to carve a space for an eighty-seater mini auditorium! By February 1964, seventy-two people, including Prithviraj Kapoor, witnessed a performance at the new Studio 1, of Sophocles' *Oedipus Rex* in Hindi, directed by Alkazi, with Om Shivpuri and Sudha Sharma in the lead roles. Designed by Alkazi himself, Studio 1 was fully equipped with a lighting grid, a lighting booth, a beautifully sprung wooden floor and adjoining green rooms. Built entirely in-house (including its elegant leather chairs for the auditorium) by the carpentry section of NSD under the guidance of master carpenters Tarseem Lal and Daleep Chand, weekend shows of NSD productions from the 1960s onwards popularized Studio 1.

When one thinks of *King Lear*, one is apt to visualize a vast expanse of moor and heath, where, in his terrible journey towards self-realization through the tortuous labyrinth of madness, the King, reduced to 'a bare forked animal', finally finds redemption and release in the simple love of his daughter, Cordelia. Alkazi decided to stage possibly one of Shakespeare's most gigantic epics in the compact Studio 1!

What prompted this daring decision? The answer is 'necessity'. Alkazi was a firm believer in utilizing whatever was available. The small stage, with a cunning use of a very few stark and primitive bas-relief murals and innovative lighting and sound, gave the impression of a limitless moor, while the costumes designed by Roshen gave the characters a

Alkazi with Dr Zakir Husain at the exhibition Etchings by Munira Alkazi and Drawings by E. Alkazi, Shridharani Gallery, New Delhi, 1965

primitive grandeur. However, it was Alkazi's ability to extract intelligent performances from his student actors that made productions like *Lear* significant.

* * *

Alkazi's next project was a 300-seater open-air theatre on the lawns of Rabindra Bhawan. Naming it Meghdoot after the theatre he had built on his terrace in Bombay, Alkazi mischievously describes how he circumvented all official permissions in securing this space for the NSD.

> So while the three akademis held their leap-year meetings over coffee and cashew nuts (government servants seem to be an ineradicable species of nibbling rodents), we had the space cleared with the help of our students, engaged two masons on daily wages, and built the exquisite open-air theatre you see there today called Meghdoot at a cost of something like Rs 12,000, an amount that must have been covered at least ten times over through box-office receipts. The akademis must spend the same amount on every rickety annual function of theirs, I imagine. (Do check, just for the fun of it.) A little later, the chief architect of the NDMC stumbled across the unauthorized structure. I thought he would institute legal proceedings against me. All he did was ask from where I got the masons who did such superb brickwork![1]

The inauguration of Meghdoot was scheduled to coincide with Alkazi's production of *Hori* (1967), a dramatization of Premchand's novel *Godan*, which I have identified as the third play of his 'India Trilogy' (*Aashad Ka Ek Din, Andha Yug, Hori*) (though Alkazi himself may not have viewed them as such). The rationale behind his choice was possibly that all three were original works in Hindi that would go a long way in laying the foundations for Hindi drama.

As with his treatment of *Aashad* and *Andha Yug*, in *Hori* too, Alkazi did not wish to represent India sentimentally or with frills. The image of an emaciated old man squatting and drinking a thimbleful of water from a chipped earthenware pot that Alkazi used on the cover of the brochure (photograph by Richard Bartholomew),* pointed to a grainy, documentary-style quality he was aiming for.

The unique performance spaces Alkazi had selected for both *Aashad* and *Andha Yug* had gone a long way in contributing to their success. In the instance of *Hori* too, Alkazi once again lit upon an apt site.

> I was keen to do plays in the open air. There was a plot of land behind the three akademis and so I quietly went into that space and looked around and I found this tree—and I felt it was an incredible character... and I felt I could use this tree and make it the focal point of the set.[2]

Elaborating on the dry and parched peepal tree as the centre piece of his setting, Alkazi said, 'Looming above a few ramshackle huts, the tree assumed poetic dimensions, symbolizing the strength and forbearance of the protagonist peasant, as he weathered not only the exigencies of nature, but also suffered the ruthless exploitation of the local zamindars.'[3]

Alkazi knew only too well that expensive auditoriums drained most of the resources of small theatre groups, so the *Hori* project also became an opportunity for him to demonstrate to his students (and the amateur theatre groups of Delhi) that theatre could be done anywhere.

'Our effort has been to put up a small theatre that can be an example of simplicity, economy, functionalism and also, we hope, of a certain beauty. Elegance and dignity can be achieved without any undue extravagance or ostentation.'[4]

* * *

Not content to be known as a brilliant director, a superb actor trainer and a stage, lighting and theatre designer, Alkazi also introduced himself to Delhi audiences as an accomplished artist, installing a large exhibition of his own recent artworks along with those of his sister, Munira Alkazi, at

---

* 'This is a photograph that was taken by Richard Bartholomew, who was the secretary of the Lalit Kala Akademi and one of the most brilliant photographers. And it was this picture of an Indian peasant that inspired me to create a kind of texture, the kind of loneliness, the kind of hungry spiritedness of this individual on to the characters in the play.'—From Alkazi's Lifetime Achievement Award speech in 2009.

the Shridharani Gallery in 1965. Charles Fabri describes Alkazi's multiple talents in 'The Two Alkazis':

> It has been frequently said that the theatre and the ballet combine, if not all, at least most arts, painting, music and poetry. It is, hence, not surprising to find a theatrical expert such as Mr E. Alkazi interested in painting and drawing. Mr Alkazi is a great actor and producer, a designer who makes his own sets, costumes and stage property, and who firmly holds the opinion that all his students ought to be well acquainted with the history and the tendencies of art.[5]

All of sixteen, I helped my father install the show. I distinctly remember as one entered the Shridharani Gallery (it was our first show ever there), one noticed the narrow black screens placed along the white walls at intervals as backdrops to the works, making the space appear mysteriously dark and sombre. My father's drawings comprised portraits, landscapes,

(L–R) Tyeb Mehta, Sakina Mehta and M.F. Husain, Etchings by Munira Alkazi and Drawings by E. Alkazi, Shridharani Gallery, New Delhi, 1965

still life and nude torsos, which were arranged in groups of three or four. Not all were hung at eye level. Some were stacked in double rows, while other independent works were displayed on 30-inch-high white pedestals sloped towards the viewer. These resembled music sheet stands and were dotted around the central area. Other works were displayed on similar, 1-foot-high pedestals running along the gallery walls. Whereas most drawings were Imperial size, Alkazi had created three life-size works—'Baptism', 'Crucifixion' and 'Embalmed Christ'—that were dramatically mounted on the central wall at the far end of the deep gallery, becoming the focal point of the show. Alkazi's design of the show was unusual because it allowed for a more active, spontaneous engagement with the works, as a pre-designated route had not been charted out for the viewer.

'It is difficult to consider Alkazi only a Sunday painter, an amateur who dabbles occasionally in art,' wrote Fabri. 'Most of his drawings are of considerable size, such as his life-size Christs and enormous heads of men and kings. The word "dramatic" instantly springs into one's mind, and not without reason. For his drawings have a strong dramatic quality, not based on theatrical elements, but rather on the emotional impact that they tend to create . . . Most of his works are essentially experiments with lighting effects—the sort of work one expects an experienced stage director to try out with a production of a Greek tragedy or Shakespearean drama—and out of this sombre ground his tragic human figures loom slightly into the light.'

This exhibition, coming a decade after his first one in England, showed a considerable departure from his earlier pictorial language. Gone was the calligraphic linearity and decorative primitivism of his earlier work. The genre of landscape particularly seemed to have captured Alkazi's imagination during his last years in Bombay, where he had made a series of seascapes, each identified with a barely recognizable architectural structure. Though these drawings were small in scale, Alkazi was able to capture a sense of the vastness of the sea and sky. Incidentally, these works coincided with the period of his directing productions like *Medea* and *Waiting for Godot* on his open-air terrace theatre, thus marking the period when he shifted from the indoor proscenium stage to the open air.

Wandering through Delhi's monuments during his early morning walks, he began to notice how history and the natural elements left their

Landscape, drawing by Alkazi, 1960s

traces on the pitted, ruined walls. In a similar manner, they bear down on the pitted and scared physiognomies of the protagonists he now begins to draw. Texturizing the surface of his paper, both man and environment receive a similar treatment, reflecting both an inner and outer spiritual breakdown. It is these ruined inner and outer landscapes that Alkazi expresses in stark black-and-white portraits of characters like Dhritarashtra and Gandhari, old prophets and headless nudes. The lack of distinction between Man and Nature is most powerfully realized in 'Reclining Figure of Christ', a long, narrow horizontal work where Christ's reclining body can be mistaken for an undulating landscape. In Alkazi's unique visualization of his resurrection, Christ is shown to have become one with the earth.

* * *

With the Sangeet Natak Akademi Award for stage design in 1962 and several productions under his belt, within a span of a few years, Alkazi came across as a young, multi-talented dynamo. Theatre personalities from across the country and the world made it a point to include NSD in their itinerary when in Delhi. Prominent among international visitors were the brilliant film director Elia Kazan and the influential John Houseman. Houseman was one of the key figures of the Federal Theatre Project who had worked alongside Hallie Flanagan and Orson Welles to bring modern concepts of theatre to the US. Alkazi recounts:

> Houseman was completely astounded by the kind of approach that we had! By the kind of syllabus we offered... by the intensity... by the wide nature and the depth of the training that was being provided ... and he felt that this was something that was totally lacking in the American theatre training institutes![6]

Houseman recommended that Alkazi be invited to visit the US 'to observe first-hand the activities of the drama departments of American Universities and to study the organization of theatre, collections and museums.' This was to be Alkazi's first trip to the US.

The post-war world had looked towards the US as a country that had embraced change. Through the war years, American scholars had imbibed European modernity, which inspired them to foster and build institutions with an open and liberal attitude towards artistic experimentation, transforming a city like New York into the new cultural capital of the world. The Actor's Studio, established in New York City in 1947 by Elia Kazan, Cheryl Crawford, and Bobby Lewis (members of the erstwhile Group Theatre, 1931–41) had become well-known as 'the home of Method Acting', which Lee Strasberg had derived from the ideas of Stanislavski. During his month's stay in NYC, Alkazi visited The Actor's Studio thrice a week, meeting and exchanging notes with Strasberg. Alongside, he visited several universities that offered drama as a subject at the undergraduate level.[7]

New York also had an exceptionally vibrant art scene. Alkazi's mornings were devoted to actor studio visits, afternoons to impeccable exhibitions at the Met, MoMA and the Guggenheim and evenings packed with watching theatre—Alec Guinness in *Dylan*, *The Blacks*, *The Trojan Women* with Mildred Dunnock as Hecuba, *The Deputy*, *After the Fall*, *Marco Millions* and *Six Characters in Search of an Author*. Alkazi managed to catch up with Joseph Campbell, the anthropologist, and his wife, Jean Erdman, the modern dancer, who had been invited by Alkazi to give a talk at the Bhulabhai Desai Institute in Bombay. Alkazi notes that his visit to Martha Graham's studio was one of the highlights of his trip. Another was his personal interaction with Saint–Denis at a theatre conference.

> Well, for me to be side-by-side with these people ... and to be given the honor of working on the syllabus for the Lincoln Centre

of Performing Arts, for the Juilliard School of Drama*... was a great opportunity.[8]

Alkazi visited Cleveland, Seattle, San Francisco and Los Angeles, but it was New York that made the strongest impression on him. He fell in love with the pulsating city and especially with Greenwich Village—'Will probably go to one of those Beatnik joints. I love the Village—it is the most delightful and lovable section in NYC.' An entire generation of young Beatniks was challenging the more conservative elements of American society and were instrumental in bringing about a new non-conformist approach to fashion, film and literature.

Alkazi found this refreshing and felt that, on the whole, modern American society was more willing to experiment and was in a fluid, transitional state, creating a culture that was alive and responsive to the moment. Alkazi had always had the spirit and energy of a pioneer, whose interest lay in discovering new places where he could lay down roots and build small yet meaningful institutions for the kind of work he wished to promote. I mention these initial positive responses on my father's part to America here as they mark the moment when perhaps Alkazi was discovering that a new global culture was in the making, one that might be receptive to his own Indian culture. Several visits later, and when circumstances in his life changed considerably, it was to the US, and New York in particular, that Alkazi turned his gaze as a possible city where he might live, rather than London or any other European city whose culture he was certainly more familiar with.

*　*　*

While new, innovative and exciting projects were continuously envisioned and realized, on a personal level, my parents were trying to arrive at a feasible solution as to how they might function as a family. My father's insistence on a separate home with Uma reaffirmed that he was not willing to live dishonestly. He refused to continue hiding from either

---

* This was the time when the renowned Juilliard School in New York City, funded by the Rockefeller Foundation, had decided to integrate a Drama Division into its Music and Dance School. Alkazi was one of the key international experts to contribute to the syllabus being drawn up.

my mother, us or the rest of the world the fact that he was living with a married woman. It is only recently that I have discovered (by reading some of his old letters) that he had actually prepared my mother, before her decision to move to Delhi, to face this eventuality. (This was even before she quite unexpectedly appeared on that fateful night in October 1962 to discover that Uma and her parents had already moved in with my father!)

Dear Rosh,

... Both of us are old enough and experienced enough to know that we are not the young teenage lovers we were. A great deal has happened to both of us and we have both changed ... But whatever our individual shortcomings I do not think it is right to ourselves, our children, our relationship with each other, to continue a façade of pretence and show, merely to 'save face' as it were. By doing that, we are distorting our personalities and indulging in a grotesque game ... Children are wise and brave and they have tremendous inner resources. If we use them as counters in any emotional blackmail between us, then of course we inflict our unhappiness on them, and make them suffer for our sakes.[9]

The live-in arrangement with Uma, besides causing immense pain to my mother and us, must have created something of a scandal in Delhi society. Alkazi and Uma were seen together in public; they attended plays and receptions; they gathered a close circle of friends around them and they regularly hosted intimate dinner parties. This was not difficult for Uma to organize as many of her friends and family were already in Delhi. But the picture was far from rosy, as my father had to simultaneously withstand a storm of disapproval. He was intensely uncomfortable with being scrutinized. People were watching him, his students were watching him, his staff was watching him. Rumours soon began to circulate as to whether Alkazi was 'morally fit' to occupy such a high public office. 'I do not know how much longer I can continue here,' he confided to my mother soon after he shifted to Delhi.

17 June 1962

My dear Rosh

I find myself in a rather unpleasant situation here, one which may even turn ugly. The failed students* with a representation, then threats, then the most brazen and shameless sort of vilification make one uneasy. I have never come across anything so foul in my life. The matter was taken to the Advisory Committee, which rejected the student's representation; they then went to the Vice Chairman who did the same. The matter has now been raised with the Ministry—God knows what the Ministry will do with it.

At every stage, there have been even more new and fantastic charges levelled against me. It is obvious that a few staff members are also involved...

Naturally, this unpleasant situation was abhorrent to my father and he was all set to resign. However, it's possible that our arrival on the scene, as the NSD director's legitimate family, may have helped quell the dissent and assuage the ruffled feathers of Delhi's sanctimonious babus.

As children, we never questioned their arrangement, as my mother, though worn-out and depressed from time to time, appeared to have accepted the inevitable at some level. I often wondered why she agreed to relinquish her position as his wife in public rather than the other way around. Why had she not insisted on living with him in his official residence and turning a blind eye to him continuing his relationship with Uma as the 'other woman' in another flat? Though I often asked my mother, I never received a satisfactory answer. Of course, I did not have the gumption to question my father. He would have thought I was being highly invasive and disrespectful. The only plausible reason I can think of is that they both believed in living truthfully.

In his letter, my father outlined a dignified manner in which we, as a family, could jointly face the social stigma that we would probably have to

---

* Alkazi had not allowed some students to be promoted because of poor performance in their examinations.

confront. Putting up a united front would reduce the amount of hurt and pain for all concerned, he felt.

> If on the other hand, the situation is rationally and sensibly unfolded to them (the children), and if in our own relationship we maintain our sincerity and dignity and continue to preserve and show our abiding respect for each other, then we will not, and our children will not have to hide our heads in shame.
> ... I want you please, please, to understand. I do not wish to desert you or not look after you, or sever communications with you. Nothing of the kind. But I would like us both to accept an adjustment in our relationship, to agree to live apart and to come together with the children wherever we or they feel the need...
> Forgive me if I have hurt you. I have not done so intentionally.
>
> Love
> Elk

In hindsight, I would say that my father's suggestions provided both my parents and us with sensible and sensitive parameters within which we could continue to respect one another as family members and, at the same time, accept my father's independence. How this could be realized in practice was, of course, left to my mother to sort out!*

Roshen was good at making a little go a long way! Working within limitations was something she excelled at, whether it was a tight budget within which she had to manage household expenses or the budget of a play or, as in this case, make something of the limited interactions we would have with my father. They were, I suppose, her 'survival kit'. Though she somehow managed to live by 'the truth', it was terribly painful for her. She asked, 'You say you wish to live "in truth", but is your life with us now a lie?' Pouring her feelings out in letters, poems and diary jottings, she

---

* As youngsters, we were often confused, finding it difficult to choose between the parameters set by society and the ones our parents presented. I suppose being brought up in the arts, where freedom of choice is highly prized, helped. What this experience did teach us was to accept many different kinds of relationships and that it was important to build partnerships based on truth and trust.

repeatedly asserted, 'one does not choose to love this or that person; it is a truth that cannot be denied'.

Despite the searing pain, my mother accepted my father's terms that we move to Delhi but live apart from him, rather than us staying back in Bombay. *Accepting* this disadvantageous position was very painful and it took years—perhaps a full decade—before we got used to the unfair circumstances that we had been placed in.

The one thing that kept my mother going during these early years in Delhi is that she continued to partner with my father in his theatre work. He reluctantly agreed that she design costumes for his NSD productions, strictly on condition that she would not be paid for her services (my father would never tolerate being accused of nepotism), nor would she be credited directly as 'Costume Designer' in the brochure. My mother's love and passion for the theatre far outstripped any kudos or money she might receive. Designing costumes and watching a creative being at work was its own reward.

> Watching rehearsals was a kind of learning. I watched him all his life, directing all his plays . . . every rehearsal that he had ever done in the theatre at the National School of Drama, Theatre Unit, Theatre Group. For me that was more real, that world, than the outside world, because it was so exciting. Because he was visualizing dramatic moments. Life is not full of dramatic moments . . . but here in the theatre you have intense moments being played out before you, so sometimes I used to wonder whether it was the outside world that was real or whether it was this world that was real.[10]

It soon became awkward for my mother to go to the NSD, because within a few months Uma had found herself a job at the Sangeet Natak Akademi as editor of the *SNA Journal* on the Arts. Her office was on the third floor of Rabindra Bhawan, while NSD was located on the fourth. Though Alkazi and Uma did not commute together to work, it often happened that my mother and Uma collided with each other in the lift or on the staircase, much to my mother's acute embarrassment.

There were other uncomfortable occasions too, for example, when my father attended public functions with Uma; if by chance my mother and I were at the same function, there was an embarrassing moment when we would avoid eye contact and not greet one another. Then again, at most performances, both my father and Uma would be guided towards the front rows, while my mother and I would sit some distance away from them towards the back. Often, after the show, my father would slip off with Uma in his own car, leaving my mother and me to fend for ourselves. More often than not, we could only afford an autorickshaw home and not a taxi, making us feel rejected and pathetic. The embarrassment and humiliation my mother and I felt were so intense that it would take us days to recover.

Incidents like this, especially those played out in full public view, made my mother feel undermined, vulnerable and unworthy of her husband's affections. Despite fleeing to Bombay every summer and winter, life in Delhi, without the backing and support of her own family or close friends, led to a great sense of isolation, loneliness and despair that my mother was unable to shake off for many, many years. She wrote:

> The weight of loneliness is like a stone
> Which slowly sinks into the dark tarns of the soul
> There trembling eddies form
> Rippling vainly towards a distant shore
> Where no one waits
>
> Its form is round and smooth
> Its sinking slow and sure
> And as it sinks the grey becomes
> A black oppressive thing
> Against whose deepening power
> There's no escape.

It is clear that traces of Bobby's suicide continued to haunt my mother as a possible, final solution.

CHAPTER 33
THE WAR CYCLE
1965

The showdown between my father and me was totally unexpected and took place against an immensely theatrical backdrop—one of the oldest theatres built by man, at Epidaurus in Greece. This was regarding my future!

My father had promised that if I excelled with a first division in my Senior Cambridge examinations, a holiday in Greece and Italy would be the reward. This meant a lot to us as a family, as it would be the first time that we would enjoy a holiday abroad together. Initially stopping over in Beirut, we were engulfed by the warmth of the Alkazi clan. My aunts immediately fell in love with Feisal with his witticisms and jokes, his talent as a little artist and his love of acting! As for me, a sixteen-year-old teenager, I was taken in hand forthwith to undergo a total Pygmalion-like metamorphosis! The bouffant hairstyle that I had cultivated, a la Brigitte Bardot, was now considered archaic and chopped off, and voila, there stood a young beauty with short hair and a fringe. I was taken on shopping sprees and fitted out with new outfits to look fashionable while on the holiday—polo necks with pleated skirts, accessorized with the latest pointed-toe, low-heeled shoes! A touch of the early Beatles look took the form of rather large, round sun goggles that I wore for the first time.

Barely had we touched down in Athens before my father whisked us off to the Acropolis, so keen was he that we should visit the impressive site without delay. In fact, he selected a cosy hotel at the foot of the great monument so that we might enjoy a view of it, especially at night when it was effectively lit up.

Then there was the Acropolis Museum, which housed enormous repositories of ancient Greek statuary and art. My mother, who had already begun some research into ancient Indian costumes, was excited to see how

Alkazi and Roshen on holiday in Greece, 1965

the drapery of the Indian sari could be traced back to its Greek antecedents found in Gandhara art. Such immersive experiences were followed by lazy lunches in quaint, whitewashed cafes where we partook of fresh salads, souvlakis and dolmades, accompanied by my parents sharing a carafe of red wine. After a quick afternoon siesta, the day was topped off with a performance of a Greek tragedy at the Theatre of Dionysius.

Epidaurus, the highlight of our trip, was saved for the last. We sat among 5000 spectators at a grand performance of *Medea*. Enacted in the ancient Greek style, with the actors wearing masks and tall, heavy *kothornos* boots, it was an unforgettable experience. When we returned the next morning to study the theatre in greater detail, Mummy and Feisal wandered off while Dad held my hand as we ascended to the topmost level of the auditorium. The fragrance of olives and grapes filled our nostrils while we sat in silence, taking in the panoramic view of the fourth-century BCE auditorium with the mountains and the sea beyond providing a salubrious background.

My father had always held the Greek theatre in the highest esteem. Speaking in low, confiding tones, he began to unwind:

Amal and Feisal on holiday in Greece, 1965

'See, darling, you should understand how this performance space, dug into a hillside, into the very belly of the earth, has been created by one of the greatest civilizations in the world—the Greek civilization, which is the birthplace of not only theatre but also of philosophic concepts, of democracy, of citizenship.'

'But how does it relate to us in India?'

'Not just to India, darling! It relates to the entire world. The concept of theatre being performed within nature, against a cosmic, timeless landscape is something that inspires me.'

'Really?'

'Yes, for instance, our little open-air theatre on our terrace in Bombay was an experiment in this direction.'

'Dad! All this sounds so exciting. I want to be part of it. I want to know more about all these things. I think I'll join the NSD.'

In a trice, my father sprang up, his mood completely altered.

'Blasted rot!' he thundered across the landscape! The excitement of a second ago had vanished and there were ominous black clouds darkening his brow.

'You will do *nothing* of the sort, Amal! It's been *decided* . . . you are going to do your BA at a college in Bombay! You said yourself, that's what you wanted to do!'

'But Dad, I only said that because I didn't really know *what* I wanted. I know now that I don't want to do a BA. I don't want to go to Bombay. I'm realizing more and more that it's theatre that I love doing.'

'This is *ridiculous*, Amal! You need to graduate. It's very, very important for your future career. You can always do theatre side-by-side.'

'No! I refuse!' I shouted back. 'I'm *not* going anywhere. You can't *force* me.'

With that, I burst into tears and ran off, blindly searching for my mother through a veil of tears. My father just sat down in a dark, glowering mood, having no clue how to deal with an adamant teenager.

It was true that, until then, it had been assumed that I would go to Bombay to do my BA. This would finally allow me to spend more time with Nissar, who was at Elphinstone College for a year, after which he would be joining the Sir JJ Hospital for his MBBS. Although my heart pulled me towards Nissar, it somehow dawned on me that this was not the right time for me to leave my parents and my home. Everything was still so fragile between my parents and, young as I was, I realized that I, for some reason, was a kind of glue that held them together, preventing the edifice of their marriage from completely collapsing. In a way, I felt duty-bound to be there to console my mother and cheer her up whenever she felt low. Joining the NSD appeared to be the best solution—to do what I loved best, as well as not leave my parents and home just yet.

It was the first time in my life that I was making an independent decision. In fact, I refused to speak to my father for more than a week! Finally, a point was reached when my father actually *forbade* me from joining the NSD. Rebelliously, I went off and filled out the application form on the last day. I had certainly graduated from the coy, giggling girl I had once been, into an obstinate and insistent young lady.

***

The next three years were the most formative in my life. All my understanding and experience of living and breathing theatre had been imbibed through osmosis. Now at NSD, I was made to approach each area of theatre as a separate 'subject'.

Over three years, I learned that theatre had a history, an evolution and was practised differently in different parts of the world. We had to write papers on a variety of subjects and prepare elaborate project books on set design, costumes and lighting, complete with scale drawings. Later, in the final year, a full prompt book based on our final-year student productions had to be produced.

My notebooks came back with red markings scrawled across my neatly written pages as Alkazi, especially ruthless with me, cancelled out irrelevant paragraphs and made scathing remarks in the columns, often shaming me into realizing my inadequate knowledge, analytical powers or poor imagination. I gave up lunch and was glued to the library, making notes in whatever free time I managed to squeeze out of our hectic schedule.

I'd always felt like an inadequate actor. Now, I was even more terrified and self-conscious, as I did not feel at home speaking Hindi. This was glaringly apparent in Euripides's *The Trojan Women*, where I was double cast with Uttara Baokar as Andromache. In a climactic scene, I had to deliver a huge lamentation speech on learning that my husband has been killed in the war and my little son is to be thrown from the ramparts to his death. Disbelief, pain, anguish, horror, loss—I had no idea how to generate these emotions. I was all of eighteen years old in 1966 and had no life experience to speak of. I was stilted and, at best, made crying sounds with my voice.

My father was probably at his wit's end with my piteous efforts. One day, he must have decided that enough was enough. We were rehearsing in the small studio theatre. At one point, he stood up frustrated and delivered my monologue in the way he felt it should be articulated, interspersed with enormous groans and animal-like howls. Everyone on stage and those observing from the auditorium looked from him to me as I weakly tried to imitate him. This continued for a while, with little improvement. Then, all of a sudden, he sprang down the steps of the auditorium, strode towards me and before I could grasp what he was about to do, he gave me a resounding slap across the face! I was so stunned, I just broke down. I could not stop the sobs. He stood there, goading me on, insisting, 'Now go on, say your lines, say them!' which I did, through my sobs and runny nose. Mercifully, he did not interrupt me again and the rehearsal continued.

It dawned on me much later that the slap not only helped release my pent-up emotions, it was also a lesson in understanding how shaken, helpless and yet vengeful Andromache needed to be in this scene. Subsequently, I begged Om Shivpuri, several years my senior, who was also acting in the play as Menalaus, to slap me hard before I went on stage. Of course, the poor fellow refused to do so, leaving me to discover resources of my own.

* * *

I would regard *The Trojan Women* (1966) as one of the pivotal productions of Alkazi's career, a powerful anti-war play that belongs to a series of *political* works that I will refer to as Alkazi's 'War Cycle'.

Alkazi's War Cycle was spread across the same decade that saw the efflorescence of contemporary Indian theatre when writers like Mohan Rakesh, Adya Rangacharya, Girish Karnad and Vijay Tendulkar discovered their own authentic voices in their own languages. They became the first generation of Indian playwrights to express contemporary urban reality with all its uncertainties. Concerned with the breakdown of society, their themes ranged from the passing of the feudal order to unemployment, urban ennui, the breakup of the family unit and the modern woman's attempt to break out of the stereotypical roles assigned to her. In foregrounding these issues, they revealed the troubled psyche of a society in transition.

Alkazi's antenna, however, was attuned to larger *political* issues that concerned his generation. He began to move away from the domestic drama of Ibsen and Strindberg to a larger international arena where the growing threat that the Cold War could erupt into a Third World War was becoming a disturbing reality. It was around this time that Alkazi began to study the plays and theories of Bertolt Brecht. Deeply affected by them, Alkazi's fundamental ideas on art began to alter. In an early essay on Brecht, he wrote:

> The generally prevalent attitude at the beginning of century was and is, that art was 'above the battle,' that it need not concern itself with political or economic matters, that these were too mundane and of transient interest . . . Art, it was maintained, should be concerned with timeless and universal human values . . . But man is born in a specific time and at a specific place. The very concept of man changes from epoch to epoch as society is in a constant state of transformation. Therefore the idea of 'universal' man attached to abstract ideals moved by abstract emotions, and externally valid abstract ideas, is nothing more than a fallacy. The individual is shaped by social, political and economic circumstances which in turn have been shaped by other human beings, and not by gods, or by blind fate, or by mere chance.[1]

Such a shift naturally began to affect Alkazi's choice of plays. 'Unless we can begin to identify those characters from a piece of dramatic literature with characters whom we see in our newspapers every day, I don't think that we will be able to establish the relationship between theatre and life.'[2]

Feeling an urgent need to express contemporary reality, Alkazi toyed with the idea of directing *Mother Courage*, but abandoned it in favour of *Waiting for Godot* in 1961, whose context, though left undefined, exuded a distinctly contemporary sensibility. In *Godot*, Beckett depicted the wasteland left behind by World War II. The protagonists, Estragon and Vladimir, were fragments of complete beings eking out their bleak existence in a sterile landscape. Unable to differentiate between the past and the future, they existed in a continuous 'present', which I believe is a state of helplessness that people experience living as they do under the continuous threat of a nuclear holocaust.

Andha Yug (1963) was Alkazi's next anti-war play. Carrying an urgent message of the horrific outcome of a fratricidal war between cousins, Alkazi contextualized the play against the memory and trauma of the Partition and the Indo–Pak tension along with the 1961 war with China. With *King Lear* in 1964, Alkazi continued to explore the theme of the 'blindness' of the monarch, whose hubris led the country to civil war. For Alkazi, the play reflected the current condition of India, where regional forces had begun to tug at the integrity of the country, especially after Nehru's death.

By 1966, the world's attention was focused on the explosive Vietnam War, then in its eleventh year. By selecting *The Trojan Women,* Alkazi sought to radically expose the apocalyptic devastation caused by the war. As a director, his challenge lay in attempting to discover a new, relevant *form* for its staging, one that would foreground the contemporary relevance of the ancient text.

***

Before Alkazi launches into rehearsals of *The Trojan Women,* in May 1966, he is invited on an eighteen-day visit to West Germany to attend a theatre conference. This is his first visit to the country, where besides absorbing West German theatre, he crosses over to East Berlin to witness great productions at Brecht's theatre, the Berliner Ensemble.[3]

> In marked contrast to the glittering splendor and elegance of the new theatres in West Germany stands Brecht's Berliner Ensemble. It presents a cold, grey forbidding exterior, solemn and lugubrious. The banners and posters on the façade have a clear cut, practical simplicity and a proletarian earnestness and simplicity of purpose. The modest foyer, the carpeted corridors and staircases have a quiet working-class dignity and lead one without any seduction of gloss or form, to the auditorium . . . An immaculate white half curtain is stretched taut across the proscenium. Beyond it is the

stage which in Brecht's conception is something like an operation theatre where skilled deft hands controlled by cool scientifically detached minds dissect social institutions in the manner of the surgeon with his scalpel.[4]

Noting how the approach to acting differed significantly on both sides of the Berlin Wall, Alkazi says of theatre in the West:

> Sequences are worked up to climactic moments in an almost predictable manner, one broad stroke of emotion after another building up in pitch and volume. With such massive rhinocerean effects hurled at the audience one has a sense of being bludgeoned and battered . . . One can only begin to understand Hitler's exploitation of this predilection among the German people and see how he had succeeded in capturing their imagination in such an amazingly short span of time. Likewise one can understand Brecht's mistrust of and antagonism towards this style and his arduous patient struggle to evolve an entirely new vocabulary of the stage.

Analysing the approach to acting at Brecht's theatre Alkazi continues: 'The acting of the Berliner Ensemble . . . is completely relaxed, light, casual and effortless in manner... The entire action is distilled into a poetic gesture which goes beyond the restricted meaning of the realistic event.'

Writing to Roshen before his return, Alkazi, obviously inspired, says, 'In our production, the soldiers must appear massive and heavy with impressive and brutal-looking helmets (I have a design), long cloaks and solid round shields, heavy textures and clanking chains. I shall have at least 12 soldiers and want to use them effectively.'[5]

Like a painter of 'war' or 'history paintings' that depict massive scenes of carnage, victory marches, coronations, etc., Alkazi begins to fill the stage with larger numbers to convey a sense of power, domination and suppression. His directorial notebook of *The Trojan Women* has sketches visualizing such 'crowd scenes'. He conceives of groups along with their accompanying properties, such as flags and spears, which he integrates into his visual compositions. He also indicates how these images are to be lit. It is clear that he wishes to create emotion through the movement, choreography and composition. 'This is the manner in which I tried to communicate ideas through visuals, which were far more eloquent than mere words could be,' he said in later years.

* * *

The Trojan Women evolved into a heavy, brooding, 'masculine' performance. It was conceived in bold, choreographed sequences of Hecuba and a female chorus where the two were fused into an indivisible unit that was further visually enhanced by them all wearing black costumes.

Since the entire cast was made up of women, with the sole exception of Menelaus, the play became the *woman's version of how she sees and responds to war*. No longer pitiable victims or bystanders, the women are witnesses to crimes, shown to have political agency and a voice. This is a chorus of *women* and not old, wise men who become the conscience of the people, as in other Greek tragedies.

In *The Trojan Women*, Alkazi eschews descriptive scenography and opts instead for an empty white cube as the performance space. He sets up three white walls, flat and untextured, along the sides and back of the stage. The screens (for lack of a better word) are used to project larger-than-life shadows of the actors in silhouette. In this way a three-dimensional scenography is substituted with constantly changing choreographies of the massed bodies of the soldiers and/or the chorus of women.

Denuding the stage had begun prior to *The Trojan Women*. It began with *Waiting for Godot*, where Alkazi used an empty stage with a single tree. Much like a landscape painter, Alkazi began to highlight the 'texture', 'look' and 'ambience' of his basically empty environments to evoke and communicate the essential quality of the play rather than use actual descriptive set pieces. In *Aashad Ka Ek Din*, it was the *texture* and *smell* of the *cow dung walls* that Alkazi used to convey the earthy beauty of Kalidas's village, while in *Hori*, it was the Peepul tree that was used as the poetic focal point of the action. In *Andha Yug*, 'the pitted walls of the ruins of Feroz Shah Kotla blasted by the elements or by earlier wars' were what Alkazi chose as living, speaking environments for these productions.

In *The Trojan Women*, Alkazi went a step further. He relinquished colour and restricted all the costumes to black.[6] By removing colour and texture and leaving the stage completely bare, he denied himself all extraneous emotive and descriptive elements that could tug at the audience's emotions. Instead, he attempted a Brechtian objectivity and presentational approach. The bare, wooden stage was also used for its ability to produce sound, so that the periodical thudding and stomping of soldiers' boots or the clanking of heavy metal chains dragged along by the prisoners of war resounded in the empty space.

Wishing to represent contemporary reality in a stark documentary fashion, Alkazi made a bold directorial intervention by introducing lantern slides into a live performance. Through them, he was able to provide statistical and visual data of a documentary nature.

> Instead of the Prologue, which is the discussion between Athena and Poseidon, which I thought would be rather difficult for our people to take in, I used a set of ten slides. They came from Greek sculpture depicting the horrors of war. Superimposed on them were subtitles explaining that this was a play which Euripides wrote against his own country when it was engaged in imperialist

Trojan Women by Euripides, dir. E. Alkazi, NSD, New Delhi, 1966

wars. My idea was to provoke our own people into realizing the need to have a certain social consciousness in working in the theatre.

As an Epilogue, I used ten slides on the horror of war of the last 150 years, I tried to demonstrate this through the etchings of Goya from his Horror of War series, continuing onto pictures of World War I, World War II, the Indo–Pakistan War, etc. I tried to indicate that the Hecubas, the Astyanaxes and the Andromaches are people whose faces we see every day in the newspapers, either in the shapes of corpses littering the streets, or in the harrowed faces of the women in Vietnam or of the villagers who are surrounded by troops no matter to which side they belong.[7]

Delhi audiences responded appreciatively to these newer ways of communicating, making the production something of a landmark. However, there were others like young theatre director Rajinder Nath, who had taken to writing theatre reviews, who strongly criticized the production.

A great tragedy which could have become a very vital experience, became one long, hounding drone, signifying nothing. Even with the imposition of three irrelevant slides at the beginning and after the play, as if to give it contemporary significance, it failed as a propaganda play, if by any chance that was the intention of the producer. May one ask the need for this? Was the producer thinking that Euripides' play in itself is not enough to evoke anti-war feelings and therefore he resorted to this technique or was he only interested in demonstrating his skill in handling a mechanical device? . . . If at all the play is anti, it is anti-audience . . .

The producer has so far failed to convince that his is a sensitive ear for the language of the play. Consequently what happens in this play is that the visual elements predominate so much so they become ends in themselves. Instead of helping the play . . . they distract from it entirely . . .[8]

I have quoted this review at length as it summarizes some of the points that Alkazi's critics were to use against him in the coming years. We have to remember that it was a time when language played a major role in

Tyeb Mehta drawing of Euripides's *Trojan Women*, dir. by E. Alkazi, NSD, New Delhi, 1966

national and regional politics. To add to this, the artists and intellectuals working in Hindi in Delhi were provoked by a relative stranger's entry and success into 'their territory' as it were! Rajinder Nath, quoted above, was considered one of the 'authentic' representatives of Hindi theatre in the city, which clearly Alkazi was not. Therefore, Alkazi's suitability to head a 'national' institution in the 'national' language was regularly brought up and viewed as an alarming tendency. But these were still early days and my father was energetic and battle-ready to weather all manner of criticism!'

By criticizing Alkazi's work as being too 'visual' what becomes apparent is that Nath was unaware that Alkazi was, in fact, affecting a shift from the older 'word-based', literary approach to a theatre that would free the actor from being a 'talking head' and allow him to use his entire being as a total, expressive tool. The term 'Total Theatre' began to be increasingly bandied about and, in fact, that same year in 1966, an important event—the 'East–West Theatre Seminar' was organized to discuss the multiple theatrical means that could be employed to make a new form of theatre.

---

* Assessing his own production of *The Trojan Women* a decade later, he asserted with confidence: 'I think *The Trojan Women* was one of the most serious plays I have done. Here I was confronting an artistic as well as a social solution on the stage.'—E. Alkazi in an interview, *Journal of South Asian Literature*, Vol. 10, No. 2/4, 1975.

CHAPTER 34
THE EAST–WEST THEATRE SEMINAR 1965–68

Alongside *The Trojan Women*, Alkazi was knee deep in creating two exciting audio-visual presentations—*The Waste Land* (1965) and *Bertolt Brecht: The Years of Revolt* (1966).

Brecht: The Years of Revolt was Alkazi's attempt to introduce Brecht's ideas to an Indian public. Presenting Brecht in the context of his times, Alkazi's canvas was the cultural landscape of Germany during World War I and II. He combined visually powerful works produced by painters, writers, designers and directors of this period with sketches of their sets, along with documentary photographs of both wars. Alkazi's soundtrack was likewise a pastiche of Brecht's songs, poems, music from his plays and popular music of the era, along with a brief commentary by Alkazi himself. Through such a treatment, Alkazi sought to connect and relate Brecht's socio-political and cultural background to the new kind of theatre language he was forging. By highlighting Brecht's personal background, the wars, the kind of society it bred, and the response of artists to their socio-political scenario, Alkazi was able to evoke the complex reality that Brecht experienced while 'changing his country more often than his shoes,' fleeing and living in exile, in a bid to avoid the Fascist hordes that had gained control over 'the Fatherland'.

Using lantern slides and a recorded soundtrack, Alkazi spliced sound, image and text together in a tangential manner so that the visuals did not literally serve to illustrate the text but played off of them to create associated meanings.

The new theories of montage in cinema that had been proposed by the Russian film director Sergei Eisenstein, where he explained that by intercutting unrelated images together, newer meanings could emerge, had clearly inspired Brecht. This led him to arrive at a new fragmented structural form for his 'Epic' theatre, where he juxtaposed written texts in the form of titles that described the action of scenes alongside projected statistics, while the performance on stage consisted of prose sequences interrupted by songs and often narration.

In *The Waste Land* too, Alkazi drew visuals from the war drawings of Henry Moore along with a reading of Eliot's text in such a way that he was able to maintain the autonomy of two monumental works by Britain's greatest artists. The drama critic of the *Times of India* summed up the experience as follows:

> What the programme sought was a total experience of the mood of the poem as well as its movement of thought and imagery. The visual images that the slides offered were not merely illustrative; they ran from the literal to the tangential and the antithetical. The experience of the poem was thus sought to be cumulatively enriched, with the imagination teased but not confined.
>
> Mr Alkazi's reading was sensitive, well-flighted in a dramatic range of voice. We received the emptiness as much as the counterpoint irony, the panic of loneliness, and the incantatory rhythms that shadowed Eliot's later work. The musical accompaniment, mostly from Kodaly's Sonata for Unaccompanied Cello, took up the inner resonance of poetry during pauses in the reading. Altogether, a worthy programme and a good experiment, orchestrated as a piece of music, and one that should be widely seen and heard.[1]

Totally self-reliant, Alkazi required no creative team to mount these programmes. They were 'solos' that Alkazi conceived, directed and 'acted' in, along with handling all aspects of the presentation himself. To the audio track, he added music, songs, and sound effects while meticulously selecting images of drawings, paintings and photographs of the period that he shot himself from books.*

---

* My father rose early each morning and, after his first cup of tea, awaited the sun to shift to a particular position that would be appropriate for shooting stills. Always in the throes of preparing for an illustrated talk or supplementary material he wanted to show the students, he would spend hours selecting, shooting, labelling and numbering slides and photographs from theatre and painting, especially. Over the years, he built up vast libraries of these

Each soundtrack was approximately forty-five minutes in length and accompanied by about 200 slides.

For each presentation, Alkazi arrived hours ahead of time to check and recheck the order of the slides. Seated in the centre of the auditorium, Alkazi, with full concentration, changed 200 slides as noiselessly as possible himself. Both of these programmes were highly appreciated both in India and abroad, where they were frequently shown at seminars, conferences and to lay audiences.

* * *

Alkazi and Joan Littlewood at East-West Theatre Seminar, New Delhi, 1966

slides, which were titled and put into albums in alphabetical order. In this sense, he was a builder of archives and libraries right from his youth. This occupation of shooting in the early mornings continued on terraces or balconies wherever he was in the world. As can be imagined, he became fond of buying cameras and lenses for this purpose. These reels were given for printing to Mahatta & Co. and he eagerly awaited the positives. This, of course, was a prelude to his interest in photography.

The year 1966 was also when the East–West Theatre Seminar was held in Delhi on the theme of 'Total Theatre'. I was in my second year at the NSD and distinctly remember sitting on the floor of the conference room at Vigyan Bhawan from 24–27 October, along with fifty other NSD students and repertory members, listening with rapt attention to playwrights, producers, actors, directors and technicians from twenty-seven countries. This was the first large international theatre seminar to be held in post-Independence India, where views on a new form of theatre were exchanged.

The young Samik Bandopadhyay was present along with the most important practitioners of theatre and dance: Sombhu Mitra, who led the Indian delegation, Dr V. Raghavan, Rukmini Devi Arundale, Mrinalini Sarabhai, Shiv Kapoor, Ajitesh Bandyopadhyay and Nemichandra Jain, along with international delegates who included Joan Littlewood, John Houseman and Käthe Rülicke-Weiler. Bandopadhyay recollects that before his speech, Alkazi presented *Brecht: The Years of Revolt*, after which he 'spelt out his vision of the post-colonial Indian theatre and the role of the NSD in helping to realize it'.[2]

Alkazi mentioned that today's playwrights and directors were desperately searching for a means to express contemporary reality in a viable form. While some were returning to their roots in a post-colonial bid to assert their 'Indian' identity, others continued to draw sustenance from the West. A genius like Brecht had unabashedly drawn from both eastern and western theatrical traditions and had 'evolved a theatre of dialectics, a theatre that concerned itself with significant movements in contemporary history'.

> His plays show the important historical role of the common people, not in the unsubtle manner of Socialist Realism propaganda, but with great perception, imagination and sensitivity. Brecht created a form of theatre which makes the audience aware of the dynamic role they have to play in the transformation of their own society from one of greed and exploitation, to one of equality, freedom and justice. And the theatrical means Brecht used were those employed in the epochs of great theatre in the East. It was particularly from India, China and Japan that he learnt the use of

conventions and devices which lifted the theatre experience to a high level of artistic achievement and of theatrical poetry. By studying Brecht therefore we could be poised to rediscover our own dramatic heritage.[3]

Alkazi's words drew the ire of Joan Littlewood, who abruptly stood up, protesting that 'India should first solve its problems of those hungry buggers and bastards, those who sleep on the pavements of Delhi, before thinking from where it can devise modern theatre!'[4] All eyes turned in her direction. In the midst of our self-righteous theatre community, here stood a hot-headed woman sporting a crop of short, unruly hair and wearing factory worker-type dungarees. Using a working-class lingo that was deliberately cultivated to shock and upturn middle-class propriety, Littlewood, in no uncertain terms, was asserting her proletariat leanings.

On another occasion during the seminar, Littlewood, without warning, performed extempore one of the smutty songs from her 1963 production of *Oh! What a Lovely War!* where she had made use of several Brechtian devices and brought about a revolution of sorts on to the staid British stage. Her pithy, aggressively rendered song suddenly made it clear to me how a 'critical attitude' revealed itself in performance. This seminar, on the whole, opened my eyes as a wannabe young theatre director to an entirely new approach to performance. It encouraged me to scrutinize the robust folk theatre performances that had been organized for the seminar delegates in the evenings more carefully. Somehow, Brecht and our folk traditions had begun to speak to one another in a new yet unfamiliar way.

My father, in his inimitable, intelligent way, was able to sum up the basic ideas that had been discussed over the four days:

'If the purpose of Total Theatre is not merely to use a variety of means but to make an impact on many levels at once—the sensory, the imaginative, the instinctive, the intellectual and the spiritual—then it is striving to do what all great art does. Although 'form' is something we are searching for, I am not for any kind of revivalism. In fact, I offer a warning: when faith or myth are no longer alive, the forms in which they are enshrined fall into decay. The aesthetics of that form are inseparable from the religious impulse contained within them. Today we no longer have faith, but are excited by the forms.'

Rosamond Gilder, the president of the International Theatre Institute (ITI), concluded, 'These meetings are as theatrical as you can make them! You have the choruses and you have the explosions. These are valuable and, from my experience, seminars may be a lot of hot air, but during that period of warmth, you have a living contact, say between a Miss Joan Littlewood and a Mr Alkazi!'

* * *

Although directors such as Sombhu Mitra, Habib Tanvir and Utpal Dutt had been inspired to combine folk traditions along with some Brechtian narrative devices in presenting plays like *Nabanna* (Sombhu Mitra and Bijon Bhattacharya, 1944), an ancient Sanskrit text like *Mrrchakatika / Mitti ki Gaadi* (Habib Tanvir, 1958) or a political one like *Kallol* (Utpal Dutt, 1965), Brecht's impact on the whole had been limited to a few creative individuals. Now Alkazi, at the NSD in Delhi, was looking to disseminate the ideas of Brecht officially, as he was convinced that after Shakespeare and Ibsen, it was Bertolt Brecht from the European tradition who would possibly be a significant catalyst to usher in change.

In 1968, Alkazi was invited to represent India at the *Brecht Dialog*, organized by the ITI and the Brecht–Zentrum at the Berliner Ensemble.[*]

On the sidelines of this visit, Alkazi finalized that the study of Brecht would be incorporated into the official curriculum of the NSD. What followed over the next few years, was the study of Brecht under the guidance of international Brecht experts, whom Alkazi insisted on having as NSD's first instructors in Brechtian theatre.

---

[*] The symposium marked Brecht's seventieth birth anniversary. Alkazi carried with him a photographic exhibition on the Folk Theatre in India that was installed in the lobby of the Berliner Ensemble. He also presented *Bertolt Brecht: The Years of Revolt*.

CHAPTER 35
NEW NARRATIVE STRATEGIES: BRECHT AND FOLK THEATRE 1967-69

In May 1967, in a letter to her younger sister Candy, who was studying in the US, my mother wrote, 'Elk has become quite an international theatre personality and has been invited every year to other countries . . . I think you are going to see him soon! He might be there for your wedding!'

In June, my father undertook his second trip to the US, where he met Carl Weber, a professor and theatre director at Stanford University. Weber had been a first-generation student of Brecht's and one of his assistant directors at the Berliner Ensemble, accompanying the troupe on their European tours. Believing that a student could learn more through actual practice than through volumes of theory, Alkazi was convinced that Weber was the right person to direct NSD's first production of a Brecht play, *The Caucasian Chalk Circle*. Weber was also the first international director to be invited to work with NSD students.

As promised, my father took a couple of days to attend Candy's wedding. Since he was the lone family member present for the occasion, he was keen to do something special for the young couple.

'Elk invited Andy, my husband-to-be, and me to the Russian Tea Room in New York for high tea! A very posh place! Trying to put us youngsters at ease, he began jesting around. He decided to name the red-haired waitress who was serving us "Natasha" and every now and then he called out to her theatrically, "Natasha! Come dance with me!" Shy and reticent by nature, Andy was bemused and alarmed by Elk's display of theatrics in public.'

It was 2018, when Nissar and I were sitting around Candy's dining table in her Connecticut home, that she narrated the following: 'We had requested your father to be Andy's best man at the wedding, to which he readily agreed, but on condition that he play the role of the mehendi walli as well. The night before the wedding, Elk settled down to paint my hands with mehendi that he had brought all the way from India. Holding my palm, he began to decorate it with exquisite peacocks and floral designs. The only problem was that he kept falling asleep, as he was still jet-lagged. I kept saying, "It's alright, Elk, there is no need for mehendi," but he kept insisting and then dozing off again, prolonging the process, which continued for half the night!'

* * *

Alkazi had clearly outlined during the East–West Theatre Seminar that Brecht and Indian folk performing traditions should be studied alongside one another to open up new, hybrid forms of theatrical expression. He now proceeded to put his ideas to the test.

It was 1968 and I was in my final year, when the school was introduced to the Bhavai performing tradition of Gujarat. We were to take part in a Bhavai *vesha* (skit), *Jasma Odan*, under the direction of Shanta Gandhi, an acknowledged scholar of the form. Over several months, we were taught to sing and dance in the Bhavai style, with Shantaji modifying the traditional vesha to become more compact and suitable for city audiences. To add to the authenticity of our experience, traditional *bhoongal* players (trumpeteers) were brought to Delhi, as were voluminous embroidered Gujarati ghagras and seductive backless cholis that we saw and wore for the first time! Cast in a tiny role as Subz Pari, I was exhilarated to be part of a vivacious and energetic production. The vesha's free-flowing narrative form and its stock characters—the two jesters Rangla and Naik, who acted as comic narrators—set the tone and provided a racy pace, their witty political asides to the audience bringing the house down, with the songs and folk dances adding to the production's instant appeal.

Jasma Odan was hailed as a landmark production that marked the beginning of 'authentic Indian' contemporary theatre. Playwrights were liberated to discover an alternative to the rigid three-act structure of western naturalistic drama, as well as the fact that the use of prose, verse and song gave a multilayered texture to the script. For Delhi's audiences, *Jasma* was their first exposure to this traditional rural theatre. They responded with spirited enthusiasm, which necessitated that the shows be extended.

Jasma Odan, dir. Shanta Gandhi, Meena Walwalkar as Jasma, NSD, New Delhi, 1968

Jasma Odan also opened the floodgates to a massive *new* audience—an underprivileged one that extended beyond the urban middle class that modern theatre normally catered to. Quite by chance, the dhobis, malis, shopkeepers, etc., along with their wives and children who lived and worked in the vicinity of Mandi House, began to be drawn to our daily rehearsals held in the open-air Meghdoot Theatre. Their enthusiasm prompted us to do shows for them as well.

So excited was my mother (who did the costumes) with the fact that a traditional form had found mass appeal that she insisted on accompanying the production on tour to the sugar factory of Mawana, where we performed for an audience of up to 4000 factory workers, as well as to a tiny village in Hastinapur. Penning her observations, Roshen said the post-performance interactions with these audiences made it clear that this play had different meanings for levels of society other than the usual Delhi audiences. Such audiences held differing views on the subject matter of the play. Some understood it as a story of the support of a dutiful wife for her handicapped husband; for other villagers, it came across as the fulfilment of karma. The exposure of corruption, the dealings between labourers and officials, the curse of the dowry system, or Jasma's love for life as seen in her refusal to remain in heaven, preferring to remain on earth, were some pertinent observations Roshen made on the theme and message of the play that came across to factory workers. The fact that Jasma, as a woman, had agency and could choose her partner was also seen as an important theme.[1]

However, *Jasma's* success was later analysed and even criticized at the Roundtable Seminar on Folk Theatre organized in 1971 by the SNA. Many felt it was not 'authentic' folk theatre; it was 'a cultural appropriation of a people's genre by urban educated artists for their entertainment'. As Erin Mee stated, 'With *Jasma Odan*, Shanta Gandhi was clearly trying to do too many things at once—to modernize Bhavai, to train NSD students

Threepenny Opera/Teen Take Ka Swang by Bertolt Brecht, dir. Fritz Bennewitz, Manohar Singh (Macheath) Uttara Baokar (Polly) and Suhas Joshi (Lucy), NSD, New Delhi, 1970

in Bhavai, and to present an urban public with an entertaining version of Bhavai.'[2] This begged the question: Who was this exercise for? Was it for the rural folk? To revive and preserve their older forms? If it was, the project of revitalizing and preserving folk theatre for its practitioners at the rural level, a major aim of the SNA that had been recommended at the 1956 seminar, was clearly not being addressed.

For Alkazi, however, the study of folk traditions was simply a training tool that he believed his students needed to imbibe through practice. Such skills would allow them to discover for themselves the usefulness of traditions to their own approaches to the 'modernist' theatre enterprise. Accordingly, NSD began to host eminent gurus to work with the students. In 1970, Fritz Bennewitz from the GDR had been invited to do Brecht's *The Three Penny Opera/Teen Take Ka Swang* with the NSD. I had accompanied Bennewitz as his assistant director. This was followed by invitations to Shozo Sato, a Japanese director, to do *Ibaragi*, a Kabuki play in the traditional style, followed by Shivram Karanth to impart the Yakshagana style to the students. Between 1968 and 1972, NSD was a veritable theatre laboratory where tradition and modernity interfaced, leading to some pathbreaking experiments.

Such a liberal approach with far-reaching implications for developing a modern theatre movement won accolades not only for Alkazi but also for NSD, which came to be known as an avant-garde institution that produced graduates who were not only technically accomplished as actors, directors and technicians but young, thinking artists who were engaged in experimentally pushing the boundaries of theatre.

* * *

With NSD behind me by mid-1968, the question of my future loomed large. One possibility was that I would go to Yale and join the excellent scenic design course under the famous stage designer, Wilfried Minks. The other option was to study in Germany. On 12 April 1968, my mother wrote to Candy that they were thrilled that I had secured a two-year scholarship to continue my study of Brecht's theatre in his very homeland, the German Democratic Republic. In preparation for my departure, I decided to enrol in a three-month intensive course studying the German language at the Goethe Institute in Pune.

The Caucasian Chalk Circle by Bertolt Brecht, dir. Carl Weber; Uttara Baokar (Grusha) and Nadira Zaheer (Village Woman), NSD, New Delhi, 1968

Back in Delhi after the language course, I found Weber and his extremely attractive wife, Marianne, chatting with my mother as they sat around our dining table in Defence Colony. For the next six weeks of rehearsals of *The Caucasian Chalk Circle* the couple were our personal guests, comfortably housed in the living space on our spacious *barsati*.

Before departing for East Berlin, I took the opportunity to observe Weber at work on *The Caucasian Chalk Circle*. Other than the fact that the play had been translated into Hindustani and had an entirely new musical score composed by the Bombay-based, highly eccentric composer Vanraj Bhatia, Weber's production minutely followed Brecht's own visualization of the play that he had directed for the Berliner Ensemble. What Weber was re-creating then was known as a *modelbuch* production, a veritable copy of the original one directed by Brecht. This was significant for NSD students, as it allowed them to gain insight into the direction of one of the greatest directors of the twentieth century. Alkazi was always keen on learning from the source.

Viewed historically, Weber's modelbuch production could be considered the first 'authentic' Brecht production to be produced in the country. It is also significant that over 100 people, including students, faculty, stagehands, carpenters, musicians, designers, etc., were exposed, first-hand, to a modelbuch production. These were the people who were later responsible for spreading Brecht's ideas and legacy in India.

* * *

With each passing day, my mother became increasingly nervous about my being away for two long years. She was not confident about her and Feisal managing on their own. I, too, was uneasy about leaving them, although my father reassured me repeatedly that he would be in closer touch with them in my absence. And then, as if in answer to our concerns, Kekoo Gandhy, the well-known Bombay gallerist, out of the blue, offered my mother the position of director of the Kunika Chemould Art Centre, which he had established in Delhi.

My mother, though flattered, was hesitant to take on a major responsibility at this juncture. However, with some adjustments regarding timing, and with Kekoo and Alkazi's assurances to assist her in every way possible, my mother finally agreed to join on 1 August 1968. Everyone was of the opinion that being involved in interesting, creative work would take her mind off depressing thoughts.

With Kunika Chemould, a new chapter unfolded in my mother's life. A whole new profession revealed itself to her, one that she began to value. Over the next few years, she built an independent career and identity for herself that was apart from being the 'wife' of Alkazi, or the lifelong supporter of *his* creative work. The fact that she was earning also helped build her self-esteem.

With Kunika Chemould, my mother's social circle expanded. Painters, writers, architects and filmmakers who frequented the gallery were invited home to share meals with us. Close artist friends from Bombay, such as M.F. Husain and his family, Tyeb and Sakina Mehta and their family, Akbar Padamsee, Gaitonde, etc., had relocated to Delhi by this time, giving my mother a chance to rekindle old friendships. They were very fond of Roshen, trusted her opinion on art and were delighted to have her handle their work professionally. In Delhi, she had learned to live a quiet, reclusive life, totally unlike the hectic one she had known in Bombay. But now the city began to grow on Roshen, her 'Bombayite' identity gradually disappearing along with her 'Bambaiya' Hindi. 'Delhi is so much more a part of the *real* India than Bombay... Bombay is culturally still so *Anglo-Indian*,' my mother would often point out to her siblings Alyque, Bee and Jerry, as well as to old friends like Nuruddin, Nissim and Gieve, whom she kept in touch with on her annual visits to Bombay.

***

A few months prior to my departure for the GDR, Cyrus Jhabvala, the feisty Parsi principal of the School of Planning and Architecture (SPA) and husband of well-known author and screenwriter Ruth Prawer Jhabvala, offered me my very first professional assignment: to direct a play with his architecture students. I selected Ernst Toller's *Masse–Mensch/ Man and the Masses*. By any standards, it was a huge undertaking, not only because it had a large, unwieldy cast, but as a novice director with wild ambitions and no sense of reality, I decided against staging the play at a regular auditorium, opting instead for an actual factory site.

With beginner's luck, I located a small hot mix plant within walking distance of the SPA. It had just the constructivist look I wanted—pipes, railings and metal rungs to climb up and down, and its machine was installed in a metal-roofed, corrugated shed.

Written as an early Expressionist drama, Toller, unlike some of his contemporaries, saw the machine as an instrument that would bring about a socialist utopia. *Masse–Mensch*, written in 1920, showed the tragic attempt of a woman factory worker to bring about a mass revolution among her co-workers in order to lead them to eschew violence and embrace the idea of peaceful coexistence.

Unable to find a suitable actress to play the central female role from amongst the students in the architecture college, I invited Amba Sanyal, the vibrant daughter of the actor Sneh Sanyal and the legendary artist B.C. Sanyal.

I remember my father being one of the earliest audience members to arrive on that fateful day of the first performance of the first play of my professional career. In tow was a very special guest of his, Badal

Sircar. My knees were knocking as I glimpsed them from the makeshift backstage tent, wending their way around the exhibition of blow-ups of Expressionist artist Käthe Kollwitz's powerful series on factory workers that I had installed behind the bleachers. Professor Jhabvala arrived soon after and sent for me.

'What are you doing backstage? Please mingle with the audience.'

I cringed.

'Go meet Badal Da! He has especially come to see the show. Go on, there is no backing down now!'

I went up to Badal Da, who congratulated me on the originality and aptness of my choice of a public site for the play, the Kollwitz installation and for selecting such a difficult text as my maiden venture. How could I have been such a fool to select this? (I thought to myself!)

By now, audience members were arriving in large numbers. Word-of-mouth had spread among the student community of Delhi University that an unusual performance was taking place at a factory. A large number of NSD students arrived en masse. Then, Romesh Chander, the theatre critic (who reviewed it the following day), Sneh and B.C. Sanyal, Frank Thakurdas, Sheila Bhatia, Joy Michael and finally Mummy and Feisal, who joined Dad in the front row. I was thankful not to spot Uma Anand, as my mother sat next to Dad, preening and accepting all the congratulations on my behalf, even before the show had begun.

During the performance, I did what I have always done subsequently—huddle backstage, mouthing all the lines along with the actors or busying myself with helping them with costume changes. The rest of that particular evening remains a blur. But there were no two ways about it: the performance was declared an unmitigated success. On the way back home in our Standard Herald, Badal Da sat in the front seat with my dad driving, while Mum, Feisal and I were in the back. Badal Da spoke animatedly about his shift from architecture to playwriting and how he was now anxious to experiment further.

'I want to cultivate an alternative performance strategy that I will call "Third Theatre"!'

'What are the first two theatres, if I may ask?' queried Alkazi.

'The first is folk theatre; the second is urban theatre of the middle classes, that is done on the proscenium stage that mimics naturalism, one that cannot express the increasing complexity of urban life. So, through the Third Theatre, we want to break this legacy inherited from the West. While I am not in a position to do anything for rural theatre, I want to borrow from folk forms to serve my purpose. I want it to be a kind of theatre that can be performed anywhere, in an open courtyard, a room or in the streets, where there is no division between the audience and the actor—a democratic theatre, a participatory theatre!'[3]

My father nodded.

'By the way, Alkazi, have you taken a look at my new play, *Teesvi Shatabdi*?' said Badal Da, changing the subject.

'Indeed, I have! And if you allow, I want your permission to produce it, Badal Da.'

'Alkazi, please don't be so formal! It will be an honour! I will be delighted!'

'But I need to seriously talk to you at some length about certain interventions I would like to make in the script,' Alkazi slipped in, adding, 'Could we meet tomorrow at the Triveni Kala Sangam café and discuss matters over lunch?'[*]

'Done!' quipped Badal Da, evidently pleased. We had arrived at Banga Bhawan, where he was staying. 'Goodnight, then!'

Mum slipped out and got into the front seat next to Dad.

A comforting, reassuring silence descended over the four of us. We felt like a normal family, driving home in the silence and darkness of the night.

* * *

As Alkazi dozed off in his favourite chair after dinner that evening, it was one of those rare occasions when he allowed a sense of fulfilment to overtake him. Normally, his thoughts were plagued by lists of work he had yet to accomplish, always feeling that there were not enough hours in the day to complete them. But somehow, today was different. For some reason, he sensed a closure of some kind; he felt the first phase of settling down in Delhi was behind him. He stood up and went to the tiny veranda. Looking

---

[*] Alkazi had lunch punctually at 1 p.m. every day for years at the Triveni cafeteria, which was virtually across the road from NSD. Always occupying the same table that was informally reserved for him, it became the place where Alkazi regularly met people—an informal adda of sorts. A host of other artists and writers also patronized Mrs Acharya's café and it was the equivalent of Chetna in Bombay in the 1950s and 1960s.

across the blue landscape bathed in moonlight, he took a deep breath. The faint aroma of *raat ki rani* flowers wafted across the stillness and silence. 'More important than all the achievements of my career is the fact that in my personal life, Rosh and I have come to terms with one another and are growing closer as a family. She looked so vibrant and radiant this evening,' he reflected, 'so serene and beautiful watching Amal's play.' He had secretly taken her hand in his own in the darkness of the auditorium and squeezed it. Without turning away from the stage, Rosh had reciprocated with the trace of a smile flitting across her lips.

Elk sighed and moved inside. He kissed the framed photographs of his parents and sister Faiza that were placed on his dressing table, then walked to his bed. As he was about to lie down, his chest swelled and tears welled up in his eyes. He was ever so proud that Amal had been accepted as a student in the GDR and would have the opportunity to see the work of some of the greatest directors in the world. As these thoughts overtook him, his body relaxed and he lay down, falling into a deep slumber.

Amal and Nissar's wedding, Bombay, 1971; (L–R) Chotu Allana, Roshen, Nissar, Amal, Alkazi, Nurunisa Allana, (seated) Feisal

CHAPTER 36
REACHING OUT
1972

The Kunika Chemould Art Gallery is filled to capacity with Delhi's most prominent intellectuals and artists. It is the opening of Gulam Mohammed Sheikh's *Recent Paintings and Prints* being presented by Roshen, who has come into her own as a prominent gallerist in Delhi. Roshen's success can be attributed not only to the kind of art she presents but also to the intelligent positioning of her shows, such that viewers have begun to grasp the contemporary artist's search for an indigenous identity. Chatting with visitors this evening, Roshen refers to Gulam's exploration of a contemporary idiom through his engagement with the older Mughal miniature tradition.

Besides Roshen's strenuous efforts to build a vibrant art scene, a part of Kunika's success also lies in its prime location at the Central Cottage Industries Emporium on Janpath. 'The Cottage', as it is commonly referred to, is an offshoot of the All India Handicrafts Board (AIHB), the brainchild of Pupul Jayakar, Kamaladevi Chattopadhyay, Lakshmi Chand Jain and Fori Nehru, established in 1952. On its advice, the CCI was set up to support craftspeople and has rapidly become the largest and most stylishly designed outlet for handmade items from across India. Kekoo Gandhy's suggestion to take over the Kunika Arts Centre at Cottage, an initiative begun by the Rockefeller Foundation, and convert it into a contemporary art gallery, Kunika Chemould, was welcomed as an excellent idea, as shoppers would be exposed to both the finest selection of traditional as well as contemporary Indian art under one roof.

Replacing Richard Bartholomew, the art critic who had been the previous director of Kunika, Roshen directed her energy towards showcasing not only the senior generation of artists of the Progressive Group but a host of youngsters, graduates of either the Baroda or

Shantiniketan art schools. Jeram Patel, Nasreen Mohamedi, Bhupen Khakhar, K.G. Subramanyan, Gulam Mohammed Sheikh and Jagdish Swaminathan were actively promoted by Roshen, making them household names among Delhi's top intellectuals and opinion makers.

Kekoo Gandhy was well aware that Roshen's close association, particularly with the Progressive artists, substantially contributed to the amicable relationship they developed with the Kunika gallery, while her being Alkazi's wife opened doors into Delhi's select government and intellectual circles. Besides this, Alkazi's fulsome support of Roshen could be gauged by his considerable skill in spotting new artistic talent, while his regular presence at Kunika openings gave the gallery a certain celebrity status.

Alkazi had deliberately stationed himself at the entrance of the gallery, an excellent vantage point from where he was able to greet people. With his arms folded across his chest, Alkazi was assessing the phenomenal growth of the art scene in Delhi and the potential it held for further expansion. Alkazi ruminated that Roshen had done a remarkable job, too, with underplayed grace and ease. Today she looked particularly radiant playing the hostess in her 'salon', with many young, not to mention 'older' artists, vying for her attention. He must remind her not to get overly friendly with these bounders! 'They're scoundrels . . . most of the artists!' he muttered under his breath.

Alkazi was wearing a dark blue, well-tailored, mid-thigh-length collarless kurta over white Aligarhi pyjamas. This had become his standard outfit after his shift to Delhi, providing him with a certain 'urban Indian ethnic look', which added a casual, debonair flair to his charismatic personality. From where Alkazi stood, he observed Tom Keene immersed in a conversation with the former US ambassador, Chester Bowles, both on a visit to India. Keene had been involved in the handicrafts movement along with Kamaladevi from the 1950s onwards, spending many years in India with his family. A lover of contemporary Indian art, he had melded seamlessly into the Indian art scene, developing deep and abiding personal friendships with artists and critics. It is interesting to note that the US continued its soft cultural diplomacy by way of grants, seminars and literary magazines, etc. In fact, the Rockefeller Foundation requested that Keene select and invite key Indian artists and art critics for extended

(L–R) Geeta Kapur, Renu Khanna, Tyeb Mehta, Sakina Mehta, Himani Mehta, Nasreen Mohamedi, Roshen Alkazi and Khorshed Gandhi, Kunika-Chemould Art Centre, New Delhi, 1970

residencies in the US, where they could interact with their counterparts. Krishan Khanna, M.F. Husain, Tyeb Mehta, K.G. Subramanyan, Gaitonde, Jyoti Bhatt and Richard Bartholomew were among the recipients.

A sudden flurry of activity near the staircase and there, out of the blue, Indira Gandhi appears with Mulk Raj Anand. Accompanying them is Som Benegal, one of the key officials of the Cottage Emporium, while the rest of the entourage includes Usha Bhagat, Amie Crishna and Raj and Romesh Thapar. Part of the 'inner coterie', Satish Gujral is bringing up the rear. Grabbing Husain's arm, he communicates through hand gestures and sounds: 'I just kidnapped her and told her she must come to the opening, even if for five minutes! It will boost the artists' morale, *yaar*. Roshen! Where is Roshen? Husain Saab! *You* talk to her; I'll find Roshen.'

Husain just stands there, totally bemused.

'Take Madam around, *yaar! Tu baat kar*! (Talk to her).'

Meanwhile, Mrs Gandhi has started walking around the gallery. Turning to Mulk Raj, she whispers something and then, with practiced ease, looks blankly into the middle distance. Despite being in close proximity to the general crowd, Mrs Gandhi is able to maintain her distance and composure. Looking around, she spots Alkazi and gives a brief nod in his direction, a small, tight smile cracking across her lips. Alkazi is unclear as to how to respond. Should he nod back? Should he move forward to greet her? What comes to him instinctively is to offer a kind of formal half-bow. By the time he looks up, Mrs Gandhi's gaze has shifted and the momentary smile has disappeared. Roshen, who is watching this silent mimetic exchange, was to capture the quality of Mrs Gandhi's estrangement from her surroundings in a poem that she penned several years later, in 1977, titled 'On Indira Gandhi'.

> She sits alone
> and looks across to where she
> > once had been
> the bridge now crossed
> the time has come to count
> > the gain
> or loss—of years spent
> racing through this land
> in search of truth—yet
> some would call it power
>
> The line she drew—was straight
> as if she saw the end was light
> but blinding light can force the
> > night
> She sits aloof
> and looks across—
> > alone

* * *

Alkazi could not boast of personally 'knowing' Mrs Gandhi. However, he had attended several meetings chaired by her. In fact, it was just a few months earlier, in December 1971, that Alkazi had unexpectedly been summoned to a meeting where the forthcoming Republic Day Parade was to be discussed. Normally, officials from the defence forces, the President

Indira Gandhi and Mulk Raj Anand at an exhibition opening at Kunika-Chemould Art Centre, New Delhi

and the PM's security and the PWD officials attended. This year, Mrs Gandhi insisted on being present herself. A representative of the Defence Forces was the first to address her.

Asking for her permission to speak, he apprised the PM of how the Indian Army had vindicated itself in the 1971 war. Since Indian units were still in forward locations at the Bangladesh–India border, Army Headquarters had recommended that the Republic Day parade in 1972 be called off.

A frown creased Mrs Gandhi's brow and she dismissed the idea forthwith, her words conveying her steely determination to move forward with the parade. At the Beating Retreat parade, she later articulated her reasons for this:

'There is a victory to celebrate and there are tributes to be paid. The victory of the 1971 war has earned a euphoric response from the country. After the glorious rout of Pakistan from East Pakistan with our assistance, a new nation, Bangladesh, has been born. We have assisted in the release of Sheikh Mujibur Rahman from behind bars. It therefore becomes our bounden duty to celebrate these events with even greater fervour and fanfare! Our victory should become vividly apparent to our people, that India stands for Democracy and Freedom. The loss of Indian martyrs who fell in the cause of the nation's fight should never be forgotten!'

It was for this reason, Mrs Gandhi said at the meeting, that Alkazi was being invited to devise a rousing, ten-minute visual enactment to present with dramatic clarity the historic emergence of a new nation, as a fitting tribute to the martyrdom of our jawans!

Alkazi's mind was agog with what he regarded as a huge commission. My God! Stage the birth of a nation? His imagination immediately sped forward to visualize a huge battle-scene sequence!

It was decided that the event should take place at Vijay Chowk on 27 January as part of the Beating Retreat ceremony.

Over the next few weeks, Alkazi was seen pre-dawn at Vijay Chowk, rehearsing! It was the dead of winter and with the fog and freezing temperatures, the cast consisting of 200 jawans along with fifty actors was kept on the go by Alkazi. He realized soon enough that the space at Vijay Chowk was larger than what he had envisaged. He requested an extra contingent of 200 jawans. Untrained as actors but good at taking orders, this 400-strong unit was made to enact battle sequences. Dressed in appropriate uniforms denoting the three outfits involved in the 1971 war (Pakistani, Mukti Bahini and Indian), the jawans were given dummy rifles to use as props. The 'real' actors were selected for key dramatic moments like engaging in hand-to-hand combat that required emoting, while the jawans were part of mass formations composed at the periphery of the space.

Alkazi was well aware that his job as a director in this instance was to create a spectacle that required drama and scale. As a young director myself, I was keen on observing my father dealing with this kind of theatrical event, especially how the untrained jawans were being incorporated. Attending a few rehearsals, I noticed that Alkazi's approach was to give the jawans clipped orders through a megaphone, like an army commander. To halt a sequence mid-action, for example, Alkazi would blow on a loud whistle! The whole affair appeared more like he was conducting a military campaign! Interestingly, Alkazi's assistant was an army captain on horseback! His main job was to gallop off to relay Alkazi's instructions to different groups of jawans spread across the vast space. At times, Alkazi himself would literally run, hurling himself from one end of Vijay Chowk to the other, yelling out instructions. Wearing a balaclava, woollen gloves and a huge coat and muffler, Alkazi looked like he was dressed for the North Pole. The entire experience was undoubtedly a unique one for my father and he would often recount anecdotes related to it to his friends and students with great enthusiasm.

Years later, Romi Chopra would vividly describe to me the final performance of the 1972 staging at Vijay Chowk.

'Thinking about it even now, my hair stands on end, Amal. Your father was a master of the dramatic and poetic. The battle sequences—the fall of Indian jawans, a woman wrenching the national flag of Bangladesh and planting it into the soil as she fell dead, paying the price for freedom— was the kind of mise en scène that made for stirring drama. Your father visualized this event on a massive scale, using music too—Bengali patriotic songs mostly—very effectively. There was not a person in the audience that cold, wintery evening at Vijay Chowk including Mrs Gandhi and Sheikh Mujibur Rahman, who was not moved. To me, this remains one of the finest sequences of drama I have ever witnessed. It evoked in the audience a powerful sense of national pride!'

Though haggard, shrunk and exhausted, Alkazi remained in a heightened state of euphoria for days together after the event. The thought that he had been given the opportunity to create a dramatic sequence in the name of the country and its pledge to democracy thrilled him in a new way, suddenly connecting him to a larger public and a far wider constituency. This is what he had always wanted: for theatre to be mobilized for a larger 'national' purpose beyond its artistic and creative intent and become a means to bind people together and bring about a change in consciousness. Such projects made Alkazi intensely aware that it was his 'business to try to discover what form of theatrical experience could reach those millions of people who live in the villages and who spend their lives on the pavements of the cities.'[1] He became less and less interested in performing plays for select, upper middle-class audiences, the so-called intellectuals, and began to envisage schemes of touring with his plays to smaller towns and villages.

S.K. Mishra, 'Chappie' to his friends, was a bureaucrat and art lover who was, at the time, the dynamic chief secretary to the chief minister of Haryana, Bansi Lal. Highly impressed by Alkazi's skill at realizing his ideas, Chappie began involving Alkazi in interesting public projects.

In 1972, he invited Alkazi to conceptualize a pavilion for Asia's first International Trade Fair at Pragati Maidan, an event that was envisaged by Indira Gandhi to project India as an emerging economic giant in Asia. Determined to make an impact, Mrs Gandhi invited India's top architects, such as Raj Rewal and Charles Correa, to design world-class modern pavilions, such as the Hall of Nations and the Hindustan Lever Pavilion, for the fair. Alongside, each state was required to create their own pavilions, showcasing the strides they had made since Independence. Chappie took this opportunity to invite India's top creative artists—M.F. Husain, Mulk Raj Anand, Shyam Benegal and documentary filmmaker Sukhdev—to make films highlighting Haryana's development, while Alkazi was asked to design the Haryana Pavilion. The films were screened on a spectacular 360-degree diorama with surround sound, while popular movies were screened in a Haryana Roadways bus that had been installed on the first floor of the pavilion, drawing teeming crowds. Alkazi's successful design won them the best pavilion jury award.

Another successful public project in 1968 was the reading of Mahatma Gandhi's autobiographical work, *My Experiments with Truth*, in serialized form over a span of fifty-two weeks on All India Radio. Alkazi regarded this as one of the highest privileges of his career, where, as an actor, he lent his voice to convey Gandhiji's inspirational thoughts and ideas to an audience of millions. Empowering moments such as these made the trials and tribulations of pursuing an altogether uphill career in theatre worthwhile. At such moments, Alkazi seemed to identify completely and seamlessly as a 'son of the soil'. It was uncanny how he had emerged as a true Indian from the chrysalis of a true-blue Arab!

'Alkazi, where are your parents from?' someone once queried.

'How inquisitive people were! Stupid woman . . . as if it mattered!' he thought to himself.

'My mother was a circus acrobat! A bareback horse rider!' he shot in her direction.

Clearly bemused, but then noticing the twinkle in his eyes, the lady pouted.

'No, please, Alkazi, don't make jokes! Really, I want to know where you are from?'

Alkazi gave her one of his disarming smiles and disappeared into the crowd.

***

Mrs Gandhi left Kunika Chemould with her entourage, and immediately everyone in the gallery seemed to breathe freely once again. Alkazi took this as a cue to depart too. As he made his way towards Mandi House, he was taken by surprise to find himself being dragged along by more than a hundred demonstrators, shouting slogans against the government, its corruption and the prime minister's overbearing attitude. Not wishing to be caught up in what could easily turn into a nasty melee, Alkazi battled his way in the opposite direction.

This brief episode momentarily took him back to that fateful day in August 1942, when he was unwittingly caught up in the Quit India March in Bombay. Except back then, the mood had been upbeat and his countrymen were energized in their fight for freedom. Whereas, thirty years later, one could sense an underlying frustration. It was widely acknowledged that

> the Congress Party remained captive to powerful land owning and business interests and that upper castes still dominated (its) leadership . . . Politics was consumed by rank ambition, opportunism and intrigues . . . the thick underbrush of a hierarchical and corrupt political culture flourished and spread on the thin topsoil of democracy. It was against this elite-dominated and corrupt political culture that the streets exploded in anger . . . (with) gheroes, dharnas, rural and urban insurrections . . .[2]

Alkazi had acutely begun to sense that injustice and corruption at every level were pulling people down into a deeper quagmire of moral degradation and despair. Living in Delhi and moving through the corridors of power, he was appalled to find people ingratiating themselves with their senior officers, feeling the need to be favoured by an 'inner circle'.[3] Rumours spread that he was one of the 'favoured ones'! He baulked at the very thought! He was merely doing his job, for God's sake! Just because he insisted that the government allow him to develop the NSD into an institution of national importance and allow it to forge links with other major institutions such as the Film and Television Institute, Jawaharlal Nehru University and Doordarshan—links that would become employment avenues for NSD's graduates—such aspirations were interpreted as him 'expanding his own network and pushing himself forward, using the NSD to acquire national and international stature for himself!'

'Why can't people see that you are working for the greater good, Elk?' Rosh slipped in tentatively, knowing this was an extremely sensitive topic for my father.

As expected, Elk snapped back, 'Don't be so gullible, Rosh! Malicious lies regarding my intentions are no longer just tidbits of idle gossip being whispered by the hoi polloi at dinner parties; they are views intentionally planted in the national press with the sole purpose of hurting and ruining my reputation and my career! There is a growing lobby that is attempting to dislodge me! As you well know, my success is irksome to many! It just shows them up, with their incompetence and their mediocrity!'

'That's true! But . . .'

'There are no 'buts', Rosh! Please remember, I'm always viewed as an outsider! I'm not a Hindi wallah! Nor a Delhi wallah! I have no lobby! I'm a bastardized, westernized box wallah in their eyes! They're upset that I have made it to the national level by sheer dint of my hard work and merit. Bombay has an altogether different work ethic and culture. In a commercial city like that, one's success is rated on one's performance, not on which caste or community you belong to, nor, for that matter, what your blasted mother tongue is.'

'He is beginning to lose some of his idealism, becoming cynical and bitter, something quite alien to his intrinsic nature. This is not good,' my mother would confide in me.

'Does he feel defeated, Mum?'

'Nooo,' said Mum, 'He's resilient, your dad! I strongly believe that his talent, vision and perseverance are more than enough for him to tide over these difficulties! You'll see!'

This was a difficult period for my father. He frequently complained of feeling let down and listless, his previously buoyant spirits and optimism flagging. He also often complained of being unable to sleep well at night and experiencing terrifying nightmares. It was true that he had become more suspicious, not knowing whom to trust any longer and having the distinct feeling that people were conspiring against him. A kind of paranoia had set in, and it began to be said that he carried his resignation letter in his pocket at all times, threatening to leave the institution at a moment's notice.

Pushing such thoughts aside, Alkazi had reached Rabindra Bhawan, crossing the lawns towards Meghdoot Theatre. Collecting his thoughts before meeting the actors, he remembered what Girish Karnad had said to him about *Tughlaq*:

> What struck me absolutely about Tughlaq's history was that it was contemporary. The fact that here was the most idealistic, the most intelligent king ever to come on the throne of Delhi, and one of the greatest failures also. And within a span of twenty years, this tremendously capable man had gone to pieces. This seemed to be both due to his idealism as well as the shortcomings within him, such as his impatience, his cruelty, his feeling that he had the only correct answer. I felt that in the early sixties India had also come very far in the same direction—the twenty-year period seemed to me very much a striking parallel.[4]

Not wanting to talk about the contemporary situation directly, Alkazi felt that this play effectively reflected the trials and opposition a visionary leader faced while trying to function within a corrupt political scenario, not unlike the one that Alkazi currently felt himself trapped in.

'You must understand that Tughlaq is the most misunderstood emperor in Indian history. He was a man of tremendous vision and so advanced for his time that his ministers and subjects could neither comprehend his ideas nor keep pace with him. The gap between Mohammed and his people, therefore, widened with his frustration and their bewilderment gradually transformed into hostility and bitterness . . .'

Alkazi was addressing the cast of *Tughlaq*. It was an unusually late after-dinner rehearsal, as they were barely a week away from opening night. Alkazi took this opportunity to remind the cast, especially Manohar Singh, who was playing Tughlaq, about aspects of the character that needed to be highlighted.

'The kind of impact the play should make on today's audience largely depends on the manner in which the central character is portrayed . . . Manohar, there is a thin line that separates lunacy from genius. Play Tughlaq rationally, not emotionally; otherwise, Tughlaq will come across as a madman, a self-serving lunatic. Our job is to show that he was a genius—far ahead of his time! He only loses control when people refuse to understand his logic.'

Clarifying Tughlaq's genius, Alkazi went on: 'Imagine! Tughlaq was the *first* emperor to visualize India as one political administrative and cultural unit. He was the *first* Muslim emperor who wished to sweep away all barriers between Hindus and Muslims, between the ruling classes and the common man. He was a man who visualized India as one *nation* . . .'[5]

Manohar nodded, a pensive look on his face as he tried to absorb what his director was suggesting. The entire cast was listening with rapt attention. At such moments, Alkazi was confident that he had succeeded in forging a bond with his students. These were mostly youngsters from smaller towns and villages who had decided to dedicate themselves to the art of theatre! He felt morally bound to nourish and nurture them and bring about a change in their lives, their circumstances and their intellectual growth. He was convinced that these were the people that mattered, they were the future, and therefore they were the ones who understood what he wanted to do. They would stand by him and stand up to those carping, petty-minded critics so keen on bringing him down.

This particular cast of *Tughlaq* had some of NSD's most brilliant actors, each painstakingly trained by Alkazi himself. There was Manohar Singh playing Tughlaq, Surekha Sikri and Uttara Baokar were doubled up as Sauteli Ma, Naseeruddin Shah as the Machiavellian Aziz, Rajesh Vivek Upadhyay as Najeeb and Anang Desai as Barani. Younger repertory members included Pankaj Kapoor, K.K. Raina, Vijay Kashyap, Raghubir Yadav, Vasant Josalkar, Prem Matiyani, Vasudev Namdeo, Dolly Ahluwalia and Nutan Surya.

These ex-graduates were employed on an ad hoc basis by an ad hoc NSD Repertory Company. Regularizing the company into a permanent one, with jobs secured for three years, had been one of Alkazi's earliest proposals to the government. For one reason or another, the approval had been delayed, resulting in a sense of insecurity among the repertory members, who were considering offers coming their way from the Bombay film industry. Many had stuck on with the Repertory out of sheer loyalty to Alkazi, believing he would continue to fight on their behalf with the Ministry.

'Ok! Let's start in ten minutes! No wasting any time! From the top!'

Actors begin to scramble and take their positions backstage. Meanwhile, Alkazi strides up the steps of the Meghdoot Theatre and sits on the topmost level of the auditorium.

By now, Rosh has arrived at Meghdoot. She has designed the costumes based on her meticulous research of this medieval period and has decided that all her research must go into a second book on Indian costumes. She sits quietly at some distance from Elk, taking out her notepad and pencil to make notes.

The third bell rings. The lights dim in the auditorium and come up on stage. The opening crowd scene—Alkazi feels the crowd needs to spread out further compositionally, but restrains himself from interrupting the run-through! Tughlaq enters with his entourage to address the populace. There seems to be a lot of fumbling regarding positions. A few actors trip on the stairs in their long robes. Unable to restrain himself any longer, Alkazi stands up.

'Continue while I rearrange you; don't stop.'

Alkazi rushes down to the stage and moves actors around, placing them across the multiple levels to create arresting stage pictures of singles and groups. This is his forte, which comes directly from his study of compositions, especially large history paintings.

He returns to his seat and makes a few notes, never allowing his focus to move away from the stage. He signals for Rosh to join him.

'Something has to be done about the turbans, Rosh! They keep falling off! Also the length of the costumes, the actors are tripping.'

'They need more time to get used to the costumes! Can we start having full dress rehearsals from tomorrow, please?'

He nods, not wanting to take his eyes off the stage. It's become a messy rehearsal.

The prayer scene is going on, where the attempt is made to assassinate Tughlaq. Alkazi's mind quivers as he recognizes the same kind of conspiratorial lack of loyalty among Tughluq's courtiers to their king as the school's staff have to him ... a spineless, ineffective lot!' The scene seems to be dragging on—uninspired and weak! Alkazi's ideas begin to escalate and it suddenly dawns on him how the scene should develop from this point until its conclusion. He rushes on to the stage, virtually pushes Manohar Singh aside, and without a pause, takes over the role of Tughlaq, enacting the entire scene himself. At the same time, he maintains his own identity as the director, instructing the other actors in their moves, gestures and

Tughlaq by Girish Karnad, dir. E. Alkazi; Manohar Singh as Tughlaq, NSD, New Delhi, 1972

postures. Never allowing his energy to flag, it is remarkable how his leaping onto the stage has electrified the action. Manohar stands apart, drinking in every action, while he feeds Alkazi his dialogues, one by one, which Alkazi repeats in his own explosive manner. And then suddenly, Alkazi grabs the dagger from one of the courtiers' cummerbunds and swivels to face Sheikh Imamuddin, grabs him by the collar with his left hand and throws him down on the floor. Before the rest can register his actions, he straddles the Sheikh going down on his knees and drives the dagger into his chest, once, twice, thrice—repeatedly over a dozen times, not stopping, till one of the courtiers finally says, '*Janab! Woh mar chuke hain!*' ('Sire! He is already dead!') Alkazi continues the thrusts, simultaneously shouting out, 'BLACKOUT! FAST FADEOUT!'

Roshen and the rest of the onlookers are shattered. There is a deathly silence as Alkazi quietly returns to his place in the auditorium.

'Next scene . . . Continue!'

Roshen, alone among those present, understands the depth of her husband's seething anger and humiliation. The dark clouds are gathering over them. Things may no longer be the same.

* * *

It is past midnight. Alkazi walks into his flat and finds Diwan Singh, his servant, still awake.

'*Saab, telegram aya hai, shyam ko.*' (Sir, a telegram arrived earlier this evening.)

DAD IN HOSPITAL. COME AS SOON AS POSSIBLE!

* * *

In 1971, soon after I returned from the GDR, Nissar and I were married and were living at Vithal Court in Bombay, where he was pursuing his MS as a resident doctor at G.T. Hospital. Now, in May 1973, I was about to deliver my first child, Zuleikha. There was much excitement and my mother came to Bombay well in advance to be present at the birth of her first grandchild. Dad was supposed to follow as well, but this was not to be as several telegrams pursued him until he found himself on a flight to Beirut to visit his father, who had lain in a hospital for close to a year, suffering from cancer. However, this was not all; the family's problems had multiplied. My father's sister, Munira, the artist, had decided to settle down in Ibiza, in

Spain, the island well-known for attracting hippies. My father, as the eldest brother, was given the responsibility of going to Ibiza and prevailing upon Munira to give up this rash scheme and return to the family fold.

After attending to his father in Beirut, my father spent a couple of weeks with Munira. It was clear that Ebrahim was unable to cope with Munira's volatile temperament or her hippie friends, who were all squatting in a large barn-like peasant's home. She refused to budge, and my father was about to return to India when he was called back to Beirut, where his father had taken a turn for the worse. By the end of the summer of 1973, my grandfather was gone.

This was the second loss to the Alkazi family, the first being the death of my father's eldest sister, Fatima, who had also succumbed to cancer in 1969. Perhaps for the first time, my father became aware of his responsibilities as the eldest son towards his mother and especially his unmarried sisters, who would now have to be cared for. It had been a fatiguing few months coping with one family crisis after another, and along with the growing tensions at NSD, Alkazi was completely worn out.

(L–R) Anupam Kher, Nissar, Amal and Zuleikha, Chandigarh, 1974

He wrote to Uma, saying, 'Every moment is a longing to be back with you, every aching step a thought of you. Darling, please, please let us go away to Shimla or somewhere... anywhere... in the hills... I need to reassess and realign.'[6]

Around the same time, Kunika Chemould closed down. This came as a shock to my mother, who noted in her diary:

> It's funny how five and a half years of work can be wiped out in a moment. I cannot understand the logic of it, this is what hurts. At one moment, one has a 'place in the sun', an office that was an extension of my home, work that involved me and propelled me forward by its own impetus. And now the emptiness again, the struggle to find a meaning and a sense of security, to redefine oneself, to find avenues to utilize one's possibilities and energies, channelize them into work that is worthwhile.
>
> But what is the use of writing and complaining, I must find the right work and start again—there seems no other way out! But the main thing about the work was that it shut out the pain and loneliness almost throughout the day—there was no time to think.

CHAPTER 37
PURANA QILA: SCALING NEW HEIGHTS 1974-76

Ebrahim was unable to sleep. He tossed and turned anxiously, his mind straying towards insurmountable hurdles and inevitable failures. His main differences were with the Akademi, particularly with people such as Suresh Awasthi.

Nehru's dream of reconstructing the nation needed a powerful and unitary concept of 'nationalism' to reorganize all the productive forces in the country. Culture was very much a part of the reconstructive process that needed to be systemized and brought under one umbrella and for this purpose, the three national academies had been set up: the Sangeet Natak Akademi, the Lalit Kala Akademi and the Sahitya Akademi. The desire to modernize Indian theatre by introducing professional training at a national school was part of the same reconstructive cultural policy designed and initiated by the Nehru government.

However, after Nehru's death, without a strong leadership, taking India's pluralistic culture towards modernity through democratic consensus became a complex matter. A new breed of rather shrill intellectuals made their way into key cultural institutions, assuming prominent positions. In 1965, Suresh Awasthi, a gaunt, intelligent, highly strung academic, became secretary of the SNA and, in a sense, Alkazi's boss. Alkazi and Awasthi did not see eye to eye on a number of key issues concerning the nurturing of a new Indian modernity.

Awasthi had reiterated at both the SNA's Round Table Seminar of 1971 and the Emergence of the National Theatre Seminar of 1972 that 'experiments were being made to use and revitalize folk forms and traditional theatre' by modern theatre directors, leading him to believe that these were 'definite signs of the emergence of a "national" theatre'. As a consequence, SNA began to support artists who made use of

Alkazi rehearsing Dharamvir Bharati's *Andha Yug*, Purana Qila, New Delhi, 1974

indigenous performance traditions, upholding their claim of being the makers of modern 'Indian' theatre. A hue and cry was raised by several playwrights and directors, objecting to such a narrow view being taken of contemporary theatre. They argued that it was not for the Akademi to dictate which influence was legitimate or authentic. Furthermore, government resources should not support only one type of 'Indian theatre' and define it as 'authentic'. For several years, this would remain a contentious issue. Marathi playwright G.P. Deshpande stated:

> ... is it at all necessary to define national theatre? My response would be—no. Because most of the people who are trying to 'create' a national theatre or advocate national theatre begin with definitions. They seem to say, this, my dear chap, is what Indian theatre is. Do it. Or if you don't do it, we aren't interested in you.[1]

Remarking on revivalist and reactionary tendencies overtaking the Akademi, Aparna Dharwadker mentions that individuals such as Suresh Awasthi, Nemichandra Jain, Kapila Vatsyayan and Adya Rangacharya veered towards valourizing indigenous performance and demonizing 'western influenced' theatre.

> ... a move that subjects the complex body of a new socialist–realist, existentialist, absurdist, Brechtian and broadly leftwing political drama in India to a process of ideological erasure. In the same measure that the traditional and the folk are invested with originality, creativity, authenticity and Indianness, the forms of contemporary urban theatre that do not participate in the revivalist movement are reduced to inconsequence.[2]

Polarization within the SNA was clear, with two broad camps emerging—Alkazi and his 'internationalism' (wrongly termed 'westernization') and Awasthi with his 'theatre of roots'.

At the heart of the matter lay the vexed question of what was meant by 'national culture'? Would the Indian government exclusively support 'modernity' with strong links to tradition or a 'modernity' that absorbed influences organically from across cultures?

Right from his earliest days, Alkazi had singularly asserted:

> Our present predicament has nothing to do with what we consider to be 'Indian' and what 'western', though we seem to be obsessed with problems of cultural identity. We should essentially be concerned with what is feudalistic, backward looking, reactionary on the one hand, and that which is rational, egalitarian, reaching out to the future, on the other. We should be much more exercised over our basic humanity than over the question of Indianness. When we are in the midst of this horrible caste, communal and regional wars, should we accept the prejudices out of which these arise as being an essential part of our Indianness, or should we reject them outright as outmoded, regressive and inhuman? Do we not see signs of the sickening 'Aryan' myth being raised? In a whipped-up frenzy of this kind, do we not see the danger of a cultural fascism?[3]

It is amazing that, as far back as fifty years ago, Alkazi was able to see the writing on the wall! His brand of nationalism was already losing ground.

* * *

Showing vision and capacity, Alkazi's performance as director of the NSD for over thirteen years was regarded as nothing short of impressive. However, he had never felt that establishing a training institution was his only and ultimate goal. He recognized only too well that training was only the first step towards the next phase, which was to create an infrastructure for the practice of the profession. Right from his early days in Bombay and then later at NSD, he was quietly evolving a comprehensive blueprint for the development of professional theatre across the country. Crystalizing his blueprint further, Alkazi prepared an impressive formal document that he submitted to the government for implementation in the Fifth Five-Year Plan.[4]

He divided his 'national scheme' for 'Developing Theatre Arts in the Country During the Coming 15 Years and Priorities for the 5th Five-Year Plan' into four simple sections, where 'a piecemeal ad hoc approach to planning will not do. We must have constantly before us the overall total picture and action must be taken sequentially in time, maintaining the perspective of the total picture.'

Detailing a plan for the proposed National Theatre as his topmost priority, Alkazi stated that no practical step had been taken in that direction for the past 16 years. Its significance lay in it being an integral part of the training and purpose of the NSD. Describing its benefits, Alkazi continued:

> A National Theatre will help establish and give status to the theatrical profession thus drawing the best talent from the country . . . It will give the profession a dignity and place in the social order, which it now lacks. The basic groundwork has been done; we have gifted actors, directors, playwrights and technicians able to come up to high international standards.
>
> The talent coming out of the National School of Drama has never been given the chance to develop its full potential. [This has] created a sense of frustration and deep resentment. Despite the apathy of officialdom . . . the past graduates of the School have rendered significant service to the theatre movement. This needs to be recognized, and opportunities to work on a national scale need to be provided immediately.
>
> A scheme for the building of the National Theatre should be undertaken immediately. The site is already available at Nos. 3 and 5 Rajendra Prasad Road.

Alkazi also suggested the following changes be made in the structure and status of the NSD:

- NSD be made autonomous, i.e., its severance from its parent body, the SNA.
- NSD's Repertory Company become autonomous, i.e., it should be separated from the NSD.
- Larger premises be given to NSD.

Alkazi's proposal was handed over for appraisal to the Khosla Committee, which was preparing a report on the progress of the SNA.

Within a year, the Khosla Committee responded that Alkazi's scheme was feasible and practical and recommended that four aspects of the scheme be implemented: the establishment of the National Theatre, autonomy for the NSD, autonomy for the Repertory Company and the allotment of more space for the NSD.

* * *

Months elapsed and there was still no news on the implementation of his approved schemes. As expected, the SNA was not at all happy with the Khosla Committee's endorsement of Alkazi's request for severance from them. Alkazi began to realize that those officiating felt no urgency to push his proposals through. According to him, he was surrounded by a society whose citizens deliberately pulled each other down.[5] Unable to function in such an uninspired, claustrophobic, foetid atmosphere, Alkazi began to lose patience and grew short-tempered. His peace of mind was shattered and he was convinced that those around him would never allow his national scheme to fructify. 'I'm fighting a losing battle! Maybe it's time to leave!' he often repeated. At the same time, he felt he could not betray his students. He had asked for their commitment to work hard for a future. Where would they go without jobs?

* * *

Having spent the entire night tossing and turning, he finally gasped awake, emerging from what seemed like a nightmare. What time was it? Not yet dawn. He lay down once again, rising at 5.30 a.m. Following the routine he rarely deviated from, he made himself a pot of tea, warmed the milk, put tea cosies on both the kettle and the milk jug and settled down with his first cup. At 6 a.m., he heard the thud of the newspaper hitting the downstairs door. The headlines attested to the fact that even decades after Independence, the country was mired in issues pulling it even further apart. The only way the present dispensation seemed to cope with unrest was to come down heavily on dissenters. On the whole, the Akademi appeared to be a microcosm of what was happening in the rest of the country.

Taking out some contact sheets from his briefcase, he settled down to mark photos of the Purana Qila he wanted enlarged. A particular photograph caught his attention. The archway known as the Humayun

Darwaza, with its domes and walls, seemed to create a natural backdrop for a performance. Instantly, he was able to visualize a stage with seven acting areas that could be created against the imposing backdrop. A thrill of excitement coursed through his body! He had wanted to perform at the Purana Qila ten years ago. When he had proposed the scheme to M.C. Chagla, then in the Ministry, he had immediately earmarked it to be sanctioned.

'Well, the significance of which Chagla, with his understanding and foresight, had immediately sensed and sanctioned in one day was stalled for ten years by Ministry officials, through what seems to have been sheer meanness and pusillanimity.'[6]

This morning, with renewed vigour and determination, he resolved to approach the Ministry and the Archaeological Survey once again. He was so palpably excited that he could barely contain himself at breakfast.

'Darling! I have this brilliant idea', he said, sitting down to his toast and eggs. 'I am determined to get the Ministry to sanction the theatre at Purana Qila! I'm planning a month-long theatre festival there. *Andha Yug*, *Tughlaq* and *Sultan Razia* . . . they will be magnificent at the Purana Qila. These three productions are going to be my swan song.'

'Your swan song? Alkazi, whatever do you mean?'

'I think I've done enough for the NSD, Uma! I refuse to continue if they refuse to let me grow! Why are they still sitting on my proposals approved by the Khosla Committee? My idea is to do these three productions splendidly. I'll show them what I'm capable of. And at the end of it, if they still refuse to give the NSD its autonomy and get on with a National Theatre, I will have every reason to walk out!'

Alkazi swung into action, and after tremendous persuasion, the Ministry agreed to the temporary structure of Alkazi's design of a theatre at Purana Qila. That was enough for my father. He began construction immediately, supervising it himself.

While this work was underway, a trip to Japan had been planned for February 1974. Alkazi had always admired Japanese aesthetics. Its sparseness and economy of expression resonated with his own aesthetic preferences, which combined the linearity of Arabic calligraphy with the eschewed formal geometry of Bauhaus modernism. The design of Alkazi's NSD office underwent a change on his return and reflected such eclectic

Tughlaq by Girish Karnad, dir. E. Alkazi, Manohar Singh as Tughlaq, NSD, New Delhi, 1974

taste! A slatted wooden nine-inch-high platform covered half the floor space. His desk sat on the raised platform, backed by a traditional, wooden Noh theatre backdrop painted with a pine tree. Installed on one side of the desk was a real tree trunk stretching from floor to ceiling. A seating area for guests was furnished with slatted wooden benches.

The director of NSD unmistakably conveyed that his brand of modernity drew from international, especially Asian cultural sources.

His Japan visit became an occasion to see a range of Kabuki, Noh and Bunraku performances for the first time. Excited by Japanese theatre, art and architecture, he wrote to Uma:

> Very exciting here, everything—both the traditional and the modern are of such an extraordinarily high standard, it makes me feel very stale and uncreative in comparison. Nonetheless will spur me on to much harder work.
>
> You must get Vanraj to Delhi by the 7th or 8th. Have Kabuki (Kathakali ideas for *ANDHA YUG* with orchestra and Chorus on stage) and a new approach to the Son-et-Lumiere.[7]

Alkazi was in his element. Creatively, he felt he was taking a step in an entirely new direction. *Andha Yug* was going to be his first intercultural production in which his experience of Greek tragedy, traditional Indian forms and Japanese theatre would come together.

The entire NSD and Repertory Company were involved in the project. This was going to be a triumph! Rosh, who had worked under Shozo Sato on the Japanese costumes for *Ibaragi*, was challenged to come up with new ideas for this production.

> Set against the old monument of the Purana Qila in Delhi and imaginatively styled by the director in a very formal Japanese manner with a great deal of tableaux formations and much use of the entrances exits of the gateways of the Old Fort and its steps for royal processions. Against such a powerful setting we realized that masks would be needed to enlarge and formalize the facial expressions so as to project the actors more forcefully. Costumes

Andha Yug by Dharamvir Bharati, dir. E. Alkazi, NSD, New Delhi, 1974

too were designed so that they could enlarge and extend the human body and its gestures. I realized that there were two cultures I could draw inspiration from—India and the Japanese theatre . . . I finally arrived at a 'style' created from a mixture of elements from the Yakshagana dance drama and Japanese Kabuki . . .[8]

***

On 15 April 1974, the Summer Festival at the Purana Qila Theatre and the Studio Theatre kicked off. The Purana Qila festival, with *Tughluq, Sultan Razia* and *Andha Yug*, became the most talked-about cultural event of the decade. The originality of its venue made it a much-sought-after event. Tickets were sold out! Most interestingly, ordinary people from Old Delhi were seen in the audience for the first time. Here was a public space right next to the Delhi Zoo where the common man felt he could enter without intimidation. These were plays about Indian history and Indian politics being performed in Hindustani. Alkazi, standing at the gate to receive his audience each day, felt enormously gratified watching burqa-clad women attend performances. All these years, it was this audience he had been seeking to address. He wanted to offer them high-quality theatre that did not condescend to 'popular' taste, theatre that had a social conscience, that instructed *and* entertained. This was Alkazi's prototype, his ideal of what constituted 'national' theatre.

* * *

Finally, the bomb was dropped! On the last day of the Purana Qila Festival, 15 May 1974, it was officially announced that Alkazi had resigned! A general wail went up as screeching headlines announced Alkazi's departure—EXIT THE KING . . . GOODBYE, MR ALKAZI! DRAMA AT THE NATIONAL SCHOOL! Everyone was shocked. They wanted him back—the Ministry, the Akademi, the students, the theatre community, the public! Alkazi was feverishly pursued. For the Ministry, he was their showpiece, a grand Nehruvian with dreams and plans. As for the general public, they had just witnessed what he was capable of with his memorable Purana Qila festival. Alkazi knew he had played his cards right. Now all he had to do was sit tight and wait for the Ministry to come around. This was his strategy to get what he wanted.

Suspenseful months followed, with the national press providing daily updates on the status of his resignation. It was 'imminently possible', they said, 'that the reputable Mr Ebrahim Alkazi may no longer continue as Director of the National School of Drama.'

When Alkazi sent in his resignation to the SNA, he did not assign any reasons. In a TV interview a few days later, he put forth artistic reasons. He said he could do ten times more work than he had been doing at the School. He wanted to do things on a bigger, all India scale . . . For thirteen years, he had been teaching only fundamentals to the neophytes and he now felt he could put his talent and energies to better use if he resigned.[9]

Soon, Alkazi was invited to a SNA board meeting.

When he appeared before the SNA Board to explain why he couldn't take back his resignation, he gave a long list of impediments that were in his way: he felt constrained and strait-jacketed working in the SNA–controlled set-up. The whole thing took a different turn. It became a tussle between the SNA and Mr Alkazi. The SNA felt that a child whom it had mothered and brought up was being snatched away. It felt the host of vague charges of inefficiency; red tapeism and eventual interference were being hauled up to give it a bad name. Why had such specific charges not been brought to its notice and consequently to the governments' all these years? After all the PM has always been connected with its (SNA's) working and if the School was looking for some more money and facilities, they could be routed through the Akademi ... It was not the SNA but the Government which had ... constrained the more ambitious programs and schemes of Mr. Alkazi.[10]

The SNA Executive Board sent its recommendations to the Department of Culture, suggesting that they confer on them and that Alkazi's resignation be kept pending until then. Meanwhile, the Ministry independently held meetings with Alkazi, where they assured him that his demands as per the decisions of the Khosla Committee were being seriously considered. This meeting was followed by a Ministry delegation. Frank Thakurdas noted:

'Oddly enough, 10 days later (after his resignation) ... the Government deputed three persons to invite Mr Alkazi to examine whether the Bhawalpur House, formally occupied by the USIS, could be considered as its new home. We spent several hours with the experts and gave our demands ...'[11]

June, by all accounts, was a stressful time for the Government, what with J.P. Narayan deciding to hold a mammoth rally in Patna seeking to destabilize the Indira Gandhi government. Alkazi least expected the Department of Culture to find time to resolve his proposals on that very day, 24 June 1974. A letter was received by the SNA stating that the Government had agreed to grant full autonomy to both the NSD and the Repertory Company.

The letter caused a furor in the SNA. Shanta Serbjeet Singh, one of the senior-most theatre and art critics of the day, described in detail the response of SNA members to the government directive:

SNA members were furious that a decision concerning its school had been taken by the Government without consulting the

SNA and disregarding their decision that a full discussion on the matter be held with the DoC before any of Alkazi's demands were met. Members of the SNA Executive Board felt the Ministry had undermined its decision and position and that these were arm-twisting tactics on the part of Mr Alkazi. They felt it was wrong for a high powered body like the SNA to yield to this kind of (government) pressure.

Serbjeet Singh continued that several points of view on the subject were hotly aired in the same meeting:

> ... Important and influential SNA Board Members supported Alkazi—Speaking on his behalf, P.L. Deshpande, the vice chairman, SNA said, 'Alkazi is a Theatre guru'. Dr Narayana Menon added, 'There is only one Alkazi in the whole of India', while Balwant Gargi strongly endorsed Alkazi being retained, 'No one person in India knows all aspects of theatre as Alkazi does, no person has put them to such supreme creative use as he has.' Though these persons supported Alkazi, the consensus was against him. 'Who does Akazi think he is anyway, a God?'[12]

Meanwhile, Alkazi was officially on 'leave pending retirement' until 15 September. He left for London in August to be with his ailing mother, as well as to make a short trip to meet technical experts at Phillip's headquarters in Holland in connection with the forthcoming son et lumière on the life of Jawaharlal Nehru planned at Teen Murti Bhavan.

In Alkazi's absence, N.C. Jain, the senior-most teacher, officiated as director. There was turmoil at NSD as anti- and pro-Alkazi supporters began voicing their opinions and demanding that 'the Khosla Commission report be implemented pronto, at least as far as delinking was concerned.'

While in London, Alkazi received a detailed letter from Uma, who was still working as editor of the *SNA Journal*, informing him of the situation.

> At office, in the afternoon, some students came to inform me that the 2 o'clock news on AIR had announced that NSD was to be set up as an independent body. It turned out to be not quite

as simple as that. The Minister had made a statement in reply to a question re the Khosla Comm. Recommendations, that at present the Ministry was not empowered to issue directives to the akademis, but that a Bill was to be issued shortly to thus empower it. He did also state that NSD should then be made independent of the SNA. So it still waits.

In a way, I am glad you have been absent. Every two or three days there have been big write-ups in the paper regarding autonomy. Theatre workers meetings mainly organized by March Group (Kohli; Suhail etc.) but joined by others and a 'confrontation' by a large delegation of these chaps at SNA with V.C., Secretary etc. I think P.L. has begun to see the light and is now wavering. Now that the Minister has openly said a Bill is to be introduced, I think they are feeling shaky—though Tanvir is still trying to do his little bit in the Rajya Sabha about 'the Ministry's unwanted interference' in the working of the akademis. In any case it will come about and you will have an uphill task. Jain and Co. have been doing their best (or worst?) and the result is an eroding of effort and work in the school. Vaishnavi and Co. took their petition to the Ministry and were unable to see Nurul, but handed it personally to Mukerjee who assured them that the Khosla Comm. would go through and you would come back. Jain got to know this. Created a ruckus. Threatened to rusticate Vaishnavi and removed him from being Student Rep. Also threatened all those who went to the Ministry and said he'd write to their parents etc. The students maintained that they had not represented against the interests of the School but merely given a petition requesting that the Khosla Comm. Recos be implemented—which they had read of in the papers. But Jain is being quite vicious about it. Meetings with Staff &/or students frequently. It came out quite bluntly that the Staff (most of them) are anti the move . . .[13]

The air was thick with rumours as to whether Alkazi's resignation would be accepted and, if so, who would be his likely successor. Opinions from Bombay's Satyadev Dubey came with, 'Rajinder Nath is tipped off as the future successor to the present director of the NSD', but Dubey added that Rajinder Nath was perhaps unsuitable as he 'has always irritated people by his aloofness, which his enemies have called arrogance.'[14]

'In the first week of September, Mr N.C. Jain permitted Mr Rajinder Nath to do a play in the Open Air Theatre, with the help of the students of the School. The play was *Suraj Ka Satwan Ghoda*. It only sharpened the wagging tongues.'[15]

Finally, 15 September arrived. No one at NSD had received any directive from the SNA or the Ministry regarding Alkazi's resignation. Both as a theatre director and as an actor, Alkazi understood only too well the impact of well-timed entries and exits. Describing the incident to us later, he said, 'On 15th September, to everyone's complete surprise and shock, without any announcement, I simply strode into my office at NSD! There was Mr N.C. Jain occupying my chair! The expression on his face was one of complete shock! Tremendously flustered, he stood up and,

Sultan Razia by Balwant Gargi, dir. E. Alkazi, Rohini Oka as Razia, Naseeruddin Shah as Jamaluddin Yakut, NSD, New Delhi, 1974

not knowing what to do or say, stammered, excusing himself from the room. I said nothing and sat down to resume my duties as if nothing had happened! Within minutes, the office staff started buzzing around me and we were back to business as usual!'

No one was aware of the assurances from the government on which Alkazi had returned!

* * *

When one reflects back on this episode, one realizes that Alkazi had deliberately made his resignation a public matter. In a TV interview, he said that he felt it was time for NSD to move out of the constricted little space it was occupying as a sub-department of an ageing akademi, and that he wanted it to join the league of exciting universities. He wanted to make cross-cultural and international collaborations for the NSD; he wanted to make theatre a household entertainment by entering into tie-ups with the national television network like Doordarshan. But he could only do this from a position of leverage, of autonomy.

Speaking frankly to the media served one purpose: it focused attention on the significance of culture in our lives. Alkazi's attempt was to make all the stakeholders in theatre, including the public, focus on the need for the growth of cultural institutions for the future of the country. He made the survival of theatre a public issue. In a sense, this was the stand Alkazi had taken with regard to his resignation from the Theatre Group in 1954, when he had openly published his resignation letter in the TG Bulletin, and then again in challenging the *Times of India* theatre critic to take part in a public debate! Now, once again, by appearing on TV, Alkazi had underlined the fact that he saw his position as head of a cultural institution as a public office, which brought with it responsibility and accountability to the public.

Alkazi's ideas made keen sense to Serbjeet Singh, who summarized the situation in no uncertain terms:

> What now? Most serious theatre people in India would agree that the NSD has reached a plateau from where it must take off into a National theatre embracing all parts of the country or else it must stagnate or die. We asked Balwant Gargi what he had to

say about an Arab setting up India's National Theatre. He said: 'Theatre is a language. Any theatre anywhere in the world is always centred on the director. He leaves his imprint, his dynamism and his style on everything connected with the group and it is often seen that actors, designers and others move away with the director, very much in the way the clientele of a Chinese restaurant shifts along with the cook. As for Alkazi being an outsider—though I can't think of someone more of an insider as far as theatre is concerned—Tyronne Guthrie (a Britisher) went to Minneapolis to set up a National Theatre and a Frenchman (Michel Saint-Denis) was invited to set up England's first National Theatre (Old Vic and Royal Shakespeare companies). I think everywhere it is a tradition to ask an outsider to organize such a dynamic and far-reaching thing like a National Theatre movement.

It would seem then that now is a psychic time, a time in history to set up the National Theatre under Alkazi's baton. Money for the purpose should be contributed by the Education and Culture Ministry and the I and B Ministry. As for the Akademi, if the government must placate the ego of pompous elders it could leave the NSD under its tutelage where it would soon become another happy little Kala Kendra. But the National Theatre must be set up outside the pale of all this and since there is only one Alkazi, the choice of who should lead it should be relatively simple.'[16]

As forthcoming events made clear, the choice was not as 'simple' as Serbjeet Singh had suggested. A lobby of Alkazi detractors was aligning forces and had begun to minutely examine and protest against these proposals.

CHAPTER 38
ALKAZI OUSTED!
1977

Being part artist, part clown, part military general, or even a monk by temperament, my father's protests against the establishment took many interesting forms, ranging from the aggressive to the absurd and even hilarious! It was during these years, when my father's reputation had become larger than life that he was invited by Dr Pran Talwar and his lovely wife Raksha to a Sunday luncheon. The Talwars were hosting several internationally acclaimed immunologists at the All India Institute of Medical Sciences (AIIMS) and invited their artist friends to join them. Wishing to make it a casual occasion, Dr Talwar's invitation stated, 'Dress Code: Bush Shirt Only!'

It was a clear and bright Sunday morning as Alkazi and Uma rang the doorbell to the Talwar's home and were ushered into a drawing room adorned with some splendid works of the Progressives.

Dr Talwar wrapped Alkazi in a capacious Punjabi bear hug, accompanied by much backslapping and guttural laughter. Introductions followed, Dr Talwar making it a point to boast of Alkazi's many accomplishments to his foreign guests. What the good doctor did not notice were the expressions of surprise and embarrassment that seemed to spread across the faces of his guests. It finally dawned on him that most of his guests greeted Alkazi effusively, after which their eyes furtively travelled down to Alkazi's nether regions. Following their gaze, Dr Talwar was shocked to see that Alkazi was not wearing any trousers!

Hurriedly cornering Alkazi to one side, Dr Talwar asked with alarmed concern, 'Alkazi what's all this! Do you need to use the bathroom?'

'Not at all, Pran,' Alkazi quipped, and moving blithely to the centre of the room, he addressed all those assembled, 'I came dressed as you advised! Your invitation card clearly mentioned "Bush Shirt Only"!'

After a momentary pause, the entire gathering burst into laughter.

Playing pranks and indulging in rather crazy, outlandish behaviour was my father's way of releasing tension! Clowning was a way of cutting himself down to size in order to erase the image people had of him being solemn, too reserved or downright arrogant! Being a consummate actor, his jokes and pranks were superbly timed, feeding into his undoubted charisma and mystique.

* * *

When Alkazi returned to NSD after his resignation, he did not wait for the Ministry's formal approval of the School's and the Repertory's autonomy. Moving ahead with new plans of taking theatre to the people, he organized a tour with *Mrrchakatika* and *Tughlaq* in which both the School and Repertory Company participated. In this, he received tremendous support from his, by now, old friend S.K. Mishra, who continued as chief secretary to the Haryana government.

> Can you imagine the colossal exercise we embarked on? It was like a military campaign . . . in one spell of 24 hours, the School gave 4 different performances at 3 different sites: the first at the Municipal Club, Ambala, on an 80-foot stage, to an audience of 3000, the performance continuing almost till midnight; next day, two performances at Jamuna Nagar, 40 miles away, at 10 am and 3 pm on a small 24 foot platform; at 7.30 the same evening back at Ambala to perform at the Sirhind Club . . .
>
> From there we went on to give 24 performances in 10 towns in 21 days, before audiences totaling well over 50,000 spectators: factory workers, village folk, university students, audiences in mofussil towns. At the Pinjore Gardens beyond Chandigarh, we set our plays against the charming late-Mughal buildings and waterways. In a sense, we revived the traditional practice of entertainments in water-pavilions, which hark back to pre-Mughal times, not for the secluded pleasure for the court, but for the general masses.
>
> By confronting the students each day with a totally new situation, we were trying to toughen them up in preparation for

their professional careers. They were forced to adjust in a matter of hours to the unique problems of each local situation, and to come up with practical and ingenious solutions on the spur of the moment.

Besides, we intended to bring the students face to face with the brutal social and economic realities of life in India. They watched the government machinery at work—in an agricultural university; a sheep farm; a village hospital; a district court; family planning centres; housing schemes; social welfare projects; irrigation schemes.

Exposed to all this, how could the social conscience of the student not be stirred? Aware of the enormity of our national problems, how could he not acquire humility and realism? How could he fail to ask himself what the relevance of theatre is to the life of the common people?

Such an exercise, on a national scale, would, over a period of ten years, generate all the discipline we need in our country.[1]

Biren Das Sharma in his article 'How Apolitical Is Cultural Policy—the NSD Example' makes an important observation on how Alkazi's theatre work epitomized both the idea of nation-building in the Nehruvian sense as well as his view of the 'conspicuous transformation of the world' in the post-World War decades.

Alkazi's very desire to challenge and eventually change the existing notions of theatre practice in India, to intervene in a planned and systematic way, was part of the same Nehruvian dream of social change. The so-called Alkazi model was designed to give young theatre workers a strong social base in their theatre work. Alkazi took the school out of the classroom to initiate a process of learning through experiencing theatre as a living process—he wanted to emphasize the sociology of theatre practice.

* * *

In early 1975, to Alkazi's relief, the Ministry kept its word and allotted Bhawalpur House to NSD for its new headquarters. With an additional 20,000 square feet at his disposal, Alkazi immediately got down to renovating the campus, involving the students in the exercise. The older Rabindra Bhawan premises, along with the seventy-two-seater Studio Theatre and Meghdoot Theatre, were retained as homes for the Repertory Company. With this move on the part of the Ministry, Alkazi was somewhat reassured that his proposals would finally be implemented.

June 1975 was a dark and unpredictable month that witnessed the declaration of the Emergency, which immensely disturbed my father. Several creative individuals he knew were being picked up. Civilian rights were being mercilessly curbed. As an artist, he valued freedom of expression above all else! Would this government job deny him this basic freedom? Was he willing to be gagged in order to retain this position? Artists had begun couching their criticism of the regime in dimly disguised metaphors, as M.F. Husain had done in his 'The Triptych in the Life of the Nation', 1975. The first canvas was titled 'Twelfth June', 1975. It showed Janaki, daughter of the Earth, set high up in the sky

> beyond the reach of the accusing fingers from a headless body named Janta. The second titled 'Twenty-fourth June, 1975', depicted Mother Earth, shaped like India, in turmoil, with her gaze fixed on the scales of justice. The third and most controversial called 'Twenty-sixth June', 1975, was an image of Goddess Durga riding a roaring tiger, determined to eliminate evil.[2]

'Surely Husain was playing a dangerous game that could seriously backfire,' Alkazi reflected with some concern.

Sensing that the tense political situation could possibly delay the decision on NSD's autonomy, Alkazi decided to lie low. This provided him with the mental space to look beyond the walls of NSD to another field. Roshen was on the verge of establishing a new art gallery, an idea that she had casually suggested to S.K. Mishra, who had instantly responded by offering a space for what became The Black Partridge Art Gallery. Elk decided to support Rosh in her new endeavour. Located in Haryana Bhawan at Baba Kharak Singh Marg, the gallery's first exhibition, 'Six Painters: Premiere Exhibition', in 1975, brought together the works of Eruch Hakim, Gulam Mohammed Sheikh, K.G. Subramanyan, Laxma Goud and Tyeb Mehta. Encouraged by the response from artists and a growing art public, a further plan to set up a folk art museum in Haryana took shape. Inviting the eminent craft historian Haku Shah to join her, they travelled the length and breadth of Haryana, selecting folk artefacts for the collection.* These were fledgling initiatives on the part of the Alkazis to support the idea that craft should be considered on par with fine art. Discussions, talks and films along with exhibitions, enlivened the Black Partridge space, illustrating that an art gallery need not be considered a commercial space exclusively but could also become a venue for the circulation of new ideas on culture.

* * *

Finally, by December 1975, the long-awaited 'autonomy' status was officially granted to NSD, delinking it from the Sangeet Natak Akademi as well as its earlier affiliation with the Asian Theatre Institute.

For Alkazi's critics, alarm bells began to ring. The ongoing Emergency made them feel that autonomy for NSD would centralize power with Alkazi. Now, with additional funds allotted to NSD along with its new status, they feared that Alkazi might not include amateur groups and actors from other states in his national schemes and instead favour NSD graduates exclusively. The major grudge of the theatre groups was that no other theatre institution received anything close to the largesse that the government showered on the NSD, forcing them to subsist on next to nothing. 'Theatre is like a perennial patient in India lying on a sick bed— the government just giving it enough oxygen to keep it breathing—but never the injections to get it up and kicking. Why not mercy killing if the patient is not worth it?' opined Rajinder Paul.[3]

The simmering discontent against Alkazi began to gather momentum, finding expression in reviews of NSD productions. These became opportunities for Alkazi's detractors among the press to focus on the 'stifling' atmosphere in NSD because of the director's 'authoritarian' approach. Alkazi's actor training methodology also came in for flak; they said it was geared to develop not individual talent but half-baked clones of Alkazi himself. Then again, the oft-repeated accusation of Alkazi's preference for scripts from the western canon to the neglect of contemporary Indian playwriting was continuously referred to. Additional

---

* Unfortunately, this was wrapped up as Roshen resigned from Black Partridge in 1977 to begin her own art gallery with Alkazi.

allegations against Alkazi included nepotism—of favouring his family! This was because my mother designed costumes for his plays, while I, like other former NSD graduates, had begun to be offered work at NSD from time to time. Finally, eight years after graduating, with several major productions behind me,* I was asked to direct a play for the Repertory Company, *Aadhe Adhure*, my father making it absolutely clear to me that I would not be paid a penny for the assignment. Of course, no press report found it necessary to mention this. As it so happened, *Aadhe Adhure* (1976) turned out to be an important production. Receiving kudos, it managed twenty-nine house-full performances in its first run, a feat few NSD productions had achieved. Perhaps, a non-Hindi wallah person like myself making a success of a Hindi contemporary classic may have ruffled more than a few feathers. Also, the fact that Nissar and I were making our presence felt on the Delhi theatre scene must have been perceived as yet another generation of Alkazis waiting in the wings to take over. Oblivious to the politics of the situation, Nissar and I simply saw ourselves as strugglers, like the rest of the theatre community.

* * *

It was December 1976. Repeat shows of *Aadhe Adure* were going on. I happened to be at the Repertory Company the day the news of its autonomy arrived. Manohar Singh was overjoyed! Clasping a few files, we crossed the street to Bhawalpur House to relay the news to my father.

My father was elated at the news, but apparently not too many others were. People in the theatre world felt that the next step would surely be the announcement of the National Theatre under Alkazi's stewardship. Determined to finally oust Alkazi from the directorship of NSD, a major smear campaign was launched against him by multiple factions. Among them were members of NSD's staff, mainly retired, who were nursing old grouses and wounds, as were members of the SNA; another coterie consisted of so-called Hindi theatre wallahs from Delhi, Bombay and

---

* Between 1971 and 1975, Nissar and I established The Workshop, a small theatre group in Bombay where we did several fairly complex productions in quick succession—*A Man's a Man, Three One-Act Plays, The Good Woman of Setzuan, Hayavadana, Exception and the Rule, Three Penny Opera, Miss Julie* and *Spring Awakening*. This was followed by *The Designer in the Theatre*, a huge exhibition pertaining to the art of stage design in India and abroad. Mounted at JAG, we also showed it at the LKA Gallery in Delhi.

Kolkata. Other factions included former students who had been waiting in the wings to claim important posts in the NSD. This became an opportunity for them to band loosely together. Alkazi loyalists consisted of the current lot of NSD students and the members of the Repertory Company.

Alkazi's detractors strategized that the only way to really attack him was from the inside, i.e., to dismantle his lobby. This was easily accomplished. A student from Delhi University, M, who had been enrolled in the NSD turned out to be a kind of 'professional' student agitator who needed a playing field for his politics. At NSD, he had begun demanding that a student union be instituted, with him angling for the position of student union leader himself, but his demands had remained unaddressed. The Alkazi detractors approached M to help them oust Alkazi. M readily agreed.

M swung into action. He was a past master at organizing huge protests at Delhi University. Swaying the minds of seventy-five NSD students and a few members of the Repertory Company was child's play for him. Along with another NSD student, he orchestrated that the campus be converted into a kind of rally maidan. For days together, the students were encouraged to not attend classes and instead sit in dharnas on the lawns in makeshift tents. Banners and placards with anti-Alkazi slogans were pasted on the walls of Bhawalpur House facing the road. The entry gate was likewise covered with angry slogans to draw public attention. Press personnel were allowed free entry to the NSD campus on the pretext of needing to report on the situation. They penned down the long tirades against Alkazi's rule by one student agitator after the other that blared out on microphones all day, interspersed with rhythmic slogan mongering. Students demanded better living conditions and higher scholarships, blaming Alkazi for turning a deaf ear to their demands, while the substance of the rhetoric focused exclusively on Alkazi's alleged undemocratic manner of functioning, his dictatorial ways, his nepotism, his self-aggrandizement, his habit of playing favourites, etc.

Let us not forget that these protests were being staged at a time when national elections were being held and it was becoming evident that Mrs Gandhi was going to lose her support. Alkazi's detractors saw this as the ideal opportunity to bring him down, as he would soon lose the Ministry's support. On 21 March 1977, as predicted, Mrs Gandhi was defeated, losing her Raebareli seat to J.P. Narayan.

On 30 March 1977 was the opening of the Hindi adaptations of *Sotoba Komachi*, a Noh play, and *Bhagwad Ajjukiam*, a classic Sanskrit prahasan, which I was directing with the second-year students of NSD. I was rehearsing during this entire period, so both Nissar and I were on campus. We were privy to the manner in which events were unfolding and the unspeakable behaviour of many NSD students who overnight switched affiliations, busy heaping humiliation and disrespect on my father in full measure. Those were unimaginable weeks that one lived through. To see my father walk past all the slogan mongering and lying diatribes being screamed out against him was painful, and yet it was elevating to watch him walk calmly across the compound from the School gate without a trace of emotion crossing his face and disappear into his office.

All through those horrific days, Alkazi refused to lower himself to the level of the street. He was well aware of what he had done for NSD; he was confident that he had made the right choices. So throughout this unseemly episode, he kept his self-respect intact, refusing to utter a word or retaliate with animosity or bitterness. On a few occasions, Alkazi was asked to address the students, which he did, but the cacophony of shrill outcries drowned him out. It was terrifying to see a man who once wielded so much power, in front of whom people actually stammered and quaked, be rendered totally powerless.

Those agonizing days have been described by Reeta Sondhi as 'the years 1976–77 were generally bad for the School—one may say they were in bad taste apart from being positively harmful. There were some fanatics and deliberate trouble-makers who created controversies and general indiscipline among the students.'[4]

One of Alkazi's most virulent attackers, Kavita Nagpal, a theatre critic, took it upon herself to write pieces against Alkazi week after week, maligning his intent, capacity and overall vision. Determined to make the NSD protest appear as a student's uprising against the dictatorial rule of Alkazi, she wrote:

> The fearful silence of the long stifling months has burst in a vociferous airing of real and imagined grievances in almost every area of public life. A section of the students of the centrally-controlled National School of Drama—the only one of its kind

in the country—issued an open letter demanding an immediate public inquiry into the functioning of the School, whose history they asserted 'is a story of growing concentration of power and increasing alienation of its members.'

They deplored the 'cultural insularity, erosion of educational standards, despotic administration, lack of democratic participation, absence of an organized body of creative opinion and a system of patronage . . . and demanded a democratization of the administration with adequate student representation in all policy and decision making bodies.[5]

Cultural columnist Uma Vasudev, who had been around in Delhi during this period, set the record straight when years later she spoke to ex-NSD graduates who still hankered and prayed for Alkazi's return.

'What happened in 1977 was a planned conspiracy of bureaucratic decisions and vested interests to make Alkazi's position untenable. It went beyond any student dissidence, with the result that the institution he created has never been the same again.'[6]

Disillusioned and in sheer disgust, but with a heavy heart, Alkazi resigned from the National School of Drama on 11 May 1977. It was not the virulent critics, not theatre people, nor his own beloved students who prompted him to take the final step. It was his realization that the pettiness of those in power could not find it in themselves to support his brand of futuristic schemes. Tremendously pained that this, in fact, was the new harsh reality, he said of a moribund bureaucracy:

> There is a lot that our commissars of culture in the last twenty years have to answer for, and history is not going to let them off lightly. They have vitiated the national cultural scene with their pettiness and paranoia; their own embittered frustration; their sickening hysteria. They have crammed the akademis and other cultural bodies of the government with incompetent, servile functionaries; they have reduced them to dismal, arid, fetid charnel houses of culture. The occasional, spasmodic flicker of activity in them resembles nothing so much as the last twitches of an animal in its death throes . . .[7]

Practically uttering a curse, my father walked away not just from the turgid darkness that engulfed the National School of Drama but from theatre altogether. Like Ram going into *vanvas*, the next fourteen years would be spent in exile from his beloved theatre.

PART SIX

Art Heritage, CICA, Sepia
Alkazi Foundation for the Arts
New Delhi, New York, 1977 . . .

Untitled, etching by Munira Alkazi, 1960

Courtesy: ACA

CHAPTER 39
OPTIONS
1977

As the civil war in Lebanon raged between Christians and Muslims (1975–1990), leading to the loss of thousands of lives and an unprecedented exodus of one million people, the uprooted Alkazi family once again packed their bags, left Beirut and continued their nomadic search for yet another homeland. Hamed Alkazi, still well-respected as one of the grand old Arab merchants of Bombay, had been offered Kuwaiti citizenship for himself and his family by the ruling Al–Sabah family. Now Sulaiman, my father's middle brother, got down to the gruelling job of laying the foundations for a business in Kuwait. My grandfather was no more, and I'm told the young man set up a shed on a street corner and began a car repair workshop, gradually building himself up to securing an exclusive dealership of Honda cars in Kuwait by 1977.

Thus, Kuwait became our paternal homeland. It was here that my parents found refuge after the NSD storm. A deafening silence enveloped every aspect of my father's life. In many ways, the city reflected his state of numbness. Kuwait was a city of few buildings, sand and a sizeable population of uneducated *bedus* (Bedouin) who remained tribal in their ways. For many hours of the day, Ebrahim stood in the scorching heat on the balcony of his brother's home, looking out over the parched compound with its arid, withered shrubs. Sulaiman and his wife, Laila Mussalam, were always loving and respectful of Ebrahim. They generously shifted their children out of a tiny room, which was somewhat isolated from the rest of the house, so that my parents could have some privacy. Mealtimes were when my father conversed perfunctorily with the family and no one, not even my mother, disturbed his preoccupations. She had immediately taken leave from her job at Black Partridge Gallery, sensing his need for her presence. For days, she just kept watch from a distance, aware that this was a turning point in her husband's life, a time for reckoning when he was considering multiple options regarding his future.

Ebrahim visited his mother and his sister Lulu every day at their small flat on the seafront. Massaging Ummi's feet, feeding her soup and cracking jokes, he never once divulged to her or the family the extent of humiliation he had suffered at NSD. The Alkazis had the uncanny ability to sense one another's pain without it being articulated. Unlike the Padamsee siblings, who freely shared intimate details of their lives with one another, the Alkazis were reserved yet cheerful, their anxieties never disturbing the daily routine of work, prayers, sleeping, eating and fasting. I often questioned my mother about these two radically different ways of coping with problems. In her opinion, not talking about the issues led them to fester and grow. However, I saw some value in the Alkazi stoicism that allowed one to introspect and discover solutions that perhaps came from the teachings of the Quran—a sura from here or there possibly providing one with a philosophy and world view from which to seek answers. In the case of the Alkazi siblings, I observed that most of them learned to channelize their pent-up anxieties into creative pursuits—Munira and Basil being artists—while my great-great-grandfather was a poet. My father ascribed these artistic leanings to both his mother, Mariam, as well as his grandparents. On one occasion, he was delighted to find a book of my great-grandfather's poetry at the Kuwait airport bookshop!

There was no doubt that my father was deeply wounded by the NSD debacle, so much so that he was now actually considering giving up theatre altogether! In a series of letters to Uma, which he writes in the still afternoons when my mother is resting, he stresses that he cannot return to 'amateur' theatre and talks about embarking on 'a new phase of life', 'a new career'. At the same time, he continues to daydream of a comeback to theatre

> . . . to do occasional productions with the Repertory Company or with the Rep. & the School combined . . . I (should) be offered a visiting Professorship . . . a CARTE BLANCHE offer: to do whatever plays I liked, with actors of my choice, and with no budgetary restrictions—of course up to a point. This would enable me to maintain my hold on the theatre and groom talent

which can be useful... Also, without the burden of administration and the daily routine of teaching, I could do good creative work. I could do three productions a year over a period of just three months... I could also stake a claim on Radio and TV rights of those productions. But it would have to be worked out in such a way that it did not interfere with my new career. We could restore Purana Qila to its glory and do the type of theatre I have always wanted to do...

I am thinking of CYCLES of plays: a cycle of Chekov plays—*The Seagull, Uncle Vanya, The Three Sisters, The Cherry Orchard* on consecutive nights... What a fantastic opportunity for the actors—doing a new Chekov character each night. Shows four nights a week for three months! The same televised!

Then we could have a cycle of Shakespearean plays, of Greek plays, of Strindberg, Ibsen, Molière—and then be kicked out for doing Western plays![1]

In her letters to him, Uma suggested that Alkazi shift from theatre to film—feature films or documentaries. She retained her contacts and interest in the film industry despite her separation from Chetan Anand and, with her sons moving in that direction as well, she probably thought moving back to Bombay would be beneficial. However, the film industry, with all its uncertainties, did not appeal to my father. Though a risk-taker, he was not the kind of person to be dependent on the diktats of a fickle, market-driven industry. Instead, he proposed setting up a gallery of Islamic art and antiquities.

> This would not be a junk shop but would specialize in good works of art. The clientele would be collectors, museums and people with discriminating taste... The advantage of this scheme over the previous one (of T.V. films and documentaries) is this: we do not require a large set-up (studios, laboratories etc.); not so much investment on equipment (cameras, lights, consoles etc.)... Also, we would be entirely on our own, we would be dependent on no one else. Besides, this is quieter, less strenuous work and as we get older, this is an important factor to bear in mind.[2]

Was my father's interest in Islamic art a possible attempt to try to understand his own roots? Perhaps. What he got down to immediately was to brush up on Arabic.

> From today I start my Arabic classes—they sting you for 5 dinars an hour, a minimum of 12 hours a month, which means Rs. 1800!!! for 12 hours of tuition. Just think of that. And I have yet to find out what the quality of the teaching is. I shall take it for a month at the most and then work on my own. Of course, one improves rapidly with the constant conversation practice, but I do want to come to grips with the literature and the poetry...[3]

Within a month of his stay in Kuwait, my father had come to terms with his departure from the NSD.
'NSD. I have washed it out of my system now and have no feelings towards it, and would not like to hark back to it sentimentally.'
In order to sever ties completely and unequivocally with the institutions he had been involved with, he wrote in the same letter:
'Please see that there are no hold-ups at the SNA in releasing my Provident Fund!'[4]

* * *

What my father did not write to Uma about, but what my mother wrote to Feisal, me and Nissar was that he was discussing possibilities of doing something in Kuwait with Najat and Ghazi Sultan. Ghazi had studied architecture at Carnegie Mellon and Harvard's Graduate School of Design, and on his return to Kuwait, he began to design both private and public buildings. His innate love of art drove him and his sister Najat to establish the Sultan Gallery in 1969. Sharing their dreams with my parents, Ghazi and Najat spoke of their gallery's mission to promote 'young Arab artists'. The sudden influx of oil money allowed Kuwait, even

> before Doha, Dubai or Abu Dhabi, to be regarded as the city with the boldest ambitions in the Gulf. In the 1970s, everyone from I.M. Pei to Andy Warhol travelled to Kuwait to build, show, experience and experiment in an atmosphere that was flourishing

under the care of the sudden oil boom. There were poetry readings, public performances, avant-garde fashion statements . . . Official and independent arts infrastructures were taking shape, thanks to the influx of cash and waves of influence rolling in from Beirut, Bombay and Baghdad.[5]

On 21 March 1969, Sultan Gallery was inaugurated with the work of Kuwaiti artist Munira Al Kazi (my father's sister) and Iraqi artist Essam Al Saidin.

I would say that Munira Al Kazi was the most important Kuwaiti artist of those times. Her show with the Iraqi artist and architect named Essam Al Saidin in 1969 at Sultan Gallery was . . . the first major art show held in the Kuwaiti private sector. A

Munira Alkazi in her studio in London, 1963

printmaker and graphic artist, Munira was a member of the Arab Art Group and actively exhibited in Europe and the Middle East during the sixties and seventies. Her works are in major collections abroad.[6]

There was an instantaneous meeting of minds between Ghazi, Najat and my parents. They not only shared ideas about supporting new art in their respective countries but were bound by a common past. The Sultan family were originally Kuwaiti merchants and, like the Alkazis, had settled in Bombay for years before returning to Kuwait after the discovery of oil in 1959.

The other point of contact was that Ghazi was married to Aruna Kohli, a Delhi girl known to close friends of my parents, Kusum and Salman Haidar. Aruna and Ghazi travelled frequently to Delhi and in time they built a distinguished collection of contemporary Indian art.

Ghazi was keen that my father join them on their mission of supporting Arab art. The Sultans suggested that Alkazi prepare a blueprint to establish a National Arts Centre in Kuwait with him at the helm. Alkazi had all the necessary qualifications, they said—the vision, the experience, the leadership skills. His family was well-known, he was of Saudi Arabian–Kuwaiti descent (my grandmother was Kuwaiti), he spoke Arabic and, of course, his sterling work in India had been universally acknowledged. Resources for such a project would be more than sufficient, as Kuwait was modernizing rapidly.

My father seriously considered the idea. Here was a chance for him to return to his roots and make a fresh start by establishing a modern art scene in an Arab country.

Soon, my father was formally invited to present his proposal to a select gathering of ministry officials along with the leading artists and intellectuals of Kuwait. The entire Alkazi clan was in attendance, excited that Ebrahim may be spending more time with them in the coming years.

Although he had made an official proposal, doubts still assailed him on whether to leave the country of his birth or not. The matter resolved itself because, despite Najat's heroic efforts to take the project forward with the Kuwaiti Ministry, bureaucratic holdups delayed decisions. By then, my father had lost interest and his mind sped forward to what he could accomplish *now, immediately*.

'Life is too short! I have no time to waste on people who cannot make up their minds', he declared, springing up from his chair. 'Don't you understand, Rosh, we need to build on our past knowledge and experience and weave that tremendous experience into our future work!'

'Then it's clear we should continue with theatre, isn't it? Before NSD, we were making massive strides with the Theatre Unit. Can't we revive it?' my mother suggested.

'Ridiculous Rosh! I refuse to go back to amateur theatre! It's simply unsustainable for us to plough our own resources into a field where there are no returns whatsoever! No, no, no! We must look beyond theatre to art and culture as a whole!'

Pondering, my mother got up to pour herself another cup of tea.

'Rosh! Sit down... Yes! I have it! Listen carefully, we will establish our *own* art gallery. I haven't forgotten my promise to our Bombay audiences, that we would follow up on our "This is Modern Art" series with a whole slew of exhibitions on modern *Indian* art!'

'It's a good idea, but...'

'No ifs and buts, Rosh. An art gallery is perfect! Can't you see, I will now be more mobile? I am no longer tied to a job. Our gallery will serve two cities, Delhi and Bombay, if not more. We can also start some activities here, in the Middle East, which will give me a chance to learn more about Islamic art. And Ummi will be so pleased to have us coming and going frequently. Rosh, darling. There is no doubt. We make a perfect team. We will definitely make this work!'

My father walked towards her and spontaneously lifted her up into his arms. 'Aren't you thrilled, darling?' he whispered into her ear.

'Um... yes,' Roshen responded, melting into his embrace.

They remained still and silent for an unbelievably long moment. It had been aeons since he had shown Roshen physical affection, something she had always yearned for.

Taking her face in his hands, he said, 'So it's settled then, my love! We're back together as a team.'

Rosh nodded and then nuzzled her head closer into his chest. She knew then that a new chapter of her life with Elk had begun. She had been waiting twenty-three years for this moment.

CHAPTER 40
ART HERITAGE: UNFINISHED BUSINESS 1977

To the often-asked question of why he left theatre, my father's answers were always varied. One of them went so:

> I had decided that at the age of 50, I'd stop whatever I was doing and do something else. I'd seen the sadness of people who are retiring. They cling to their jobs and plead for extensions. And what do they do when they retire? . . . Embroidery; bazaaring for the wife, walking the dog. I mean, how often can you walk the dog? I didn't want to shuffle out of a job, I decided I'd move on to something new.[1]

At barely fifty-two years old, Alkazi was determined not to lose the momentum he had generated over the years of building a formidable reputation and a vast audience of acolytes, whose interest he now sought to channel into a related artistic stream—the visual arts.

Discussing what shape and form Art Heritage should take with Rosh, Alkazi was convinced that the choice of venue for their new venture was critical to its success. Triveni Kala Sangam was his first choice and when he learned that the basement was up for rent, there was no stopping him. Besides its architecture, Triveni's appeal for Alkazi lay in the fact that it was bustling with writers, painters, actors and artists, an atmosphere that came closest to Bombay's Bhulabhai Desai Institute. Like the BDI, Triveni was a privately owned public arts institution that was freely accessible to all. It was run by a woman with instincts and values very much like his own—Sundari Shridharani was a Nehruvian, idealistic and pragmatic. Besides, Triveni was in close proximity to the akademis, the Shriram Centre for the Arts, Little Theatre Group, Kamani Auditorium and the

M.F. Husain: A Retrospective, by Art Heritage, Lalit Kala Akademi, New Delhi, 1978

National School of Drama, making it the centre of an exciting cultural hub at Mandi House.

Alkazi may have left the theatre world, but it was not in him to easily relinquish his responsibility towards an institution he had built and the students he had trained. Greeting former students effusively at Art Heritage, cracking jokes while listening to ideas for their latest projects, my father continued to morally support his students, never missing an opportunity to attend performances of their plays or be by their side in times of illness or stress. Several NSD graduates, such as B.V. Karanth, B.M. Shah, Ratan Thiyam and Mohan Maharishi, would each assume the mantle of NSD director over the next decade. It was heartwarming to watch them arrive at Art Heritage to seek the advice and blessings of their guru.

* * *

If anything, Alkazi was a planner and visionary. The idea of establishing an art gallery was not an end in itself but only the starting point of a larger idea. He saw Art Heritage as the 'India' base for an 'international' plan towards the promotion of Indian art. His scheme was not a business one, i.e., to find a global market for Indian art, but one of promoting an understanding of contemporary Indian art, which was developing its own brand of modernism and speaking to a post-colonial world. As the director of such a small but unique institution, Alkazi was confident that he could establish a powerful and influential presence in the international art world. However, before venturing abroad, it was key that he put down strong roots in India.

Alkazi had been carefully surveying the art scene from the wings ever since Roshen began working at Kunika Chemould. He recognized that quality art was being produced thanks to institutions such as the Baroda College of Art, Shantiniketan, the Sir J.J. School of Art, the Madras College of Art, etc. However, it was the *promotion* and *understanding* of art that was inconsistent, with barely a few family friends and art lovers attending shows at Delhi's galleries.* 'This situation can only be rectified if people understand art, or why would they buy it or even visit a show?' Alkazi remarked.[2]

Art education in most countries is imparted through *national* institutions like museums. It was depressing for Alkazi to find that in India, museums such as the National Gallery of Modern Art (NGMA) and the Lalit Kala Akademi, or quasigovernmental societies such as the All India Fine Arts and Crafts Society (AIFACS) had, thirty years after Independence, become sleepy bodies, concerned with conferring annual awards, paying scant attention to exciting new work or engaging viewers with the country's art history.

> With art melas threatening to bombard us from two contradictory sides, the Lalit Kala Akademi and the All India Fine Arts and Crafts Society... with its year-long programme of garden exhibitions of all kinds of wares from terylene saris and chappals to bedsheets and towels, with a few sculptures thrown in here and there was already one big mela![3]

* * *

---

* Sale of contemporary works of art through a professional gallery was unknown on the Delhi scene until Virendra Kumar arrived on the scene in the mid-1950s. With some expertise picked up in dealing with art objects in the course of his years as a sales assistant in Dhoomimal, the old stationer's shop in Connaught Place, Virendra set up the Kumar Gallery and pioneered a new set up for promoting art and artists, by paying monthly retainers to Husain, Ram Kumar, etc.

Stepping into such a disorganized field, it is not difficult to believe that Roshen and Ebrahim Alkazi's fresh arrival into the art world was heralded with much fanfare, eliciting headlines such as 'Art Heritage Impresses' or 'A New Gallery is Born'. The *Morning Echo* predicted:

> Where goes Roshen Alkazi, there goes the event in art. From Kunika Chemould and Black Partridge of yesteryears to Art Heritage now Roshen has been blazing a trail in this esoteric field. When she opened her new shop, Art Heritage, at Triveni Kala Sangam in October this year, everyone knew that another chapter had begun in the histories of art galleries in the capital.[4]

Art Heritage's inaugural shows (October–December 1977) demonstrated that here was a gallery where one would learn to decipher the often confusing visual language of modern artistic expression. While presenting a group show of mainly established artists—M.F. Husain, Akbar Padamsee, K.G. Subramanyan, Gulam Mohammed Sheikh and Bhupen Khakhar—Alkazi, with conscious deliberation, also included the young artists Nalini Malani and Gieve Patel, giving their work equal prominence. Again, by having Malani's work in such a male-dominated line-up, Alkazi demonstrated his confidence in her talent and gravitas, not

Roshen Alkazi at the Shamshad Husain solo exhibition, Art Heritage, New Delhi, 1989

just as a 'woman artist', but simply as an artist to reckon with. Without stating it in so many words, Alkazi communicated that it was not a question of seniority or gender that affected Art Heritage's choice of art.

The second show was equally surprising—a solo of etchings by an unheard-of young artist, Devraj Dakoji. Printmaking had been generally regarded as a lower medium than oil painting because it was reproducible. Alkazi's choice made it clear he did not believe in the superiority of one medium over another. A short note in the catalogue by seasoned critic Richard Bartholomew was also Alkazi's way of subverting hierarchical norms. It asserted that Art Heritage was primarily a gallery that discovered and supported rare, new talent. Secondly, this new talent would be contextualized against the legacy of an established, older guard. Art Heritage would therefore always be in the avant-garde, introducing new ideas, new mediums and difficult works.

Two international collaborations followed. One with the British Council, 'Contemporary Trends in British Art', and the other, an expansive exhibition of post-war Bulgarian graphics. These kept the audience abreast of *international* trends in art, situating Indian art in a wider, global context. This kind of systematic planning of each season is where we see the mind of Alkazi as an art educationist at work.

* * *

As with his theatre work, so too in the field of art, Alkazi was keen to relate *art* to *life*. His selection of art stemmed from his profound belief that art should closely connect with the present circumstances, not just as a document of the times but also as a critique.

> Some of our artists are in a dream world of their own. It always amazes me how little has come of our traumatic experiences and been reflected in our art. Where do you find the trauma of Partition in the work of Indian artists? There is nothing about the national struggle either, except the odd Tripura poster that Nandlal Bose did for the Congress session, and not one painting of the Bhopal gas disaster. It's as if these terrifying historical experiences didn't exist and that it's the business of the artist to carry on with his own personal experiences. Such a narcissistic view is debilitating,

it destroys you as a human being. An artist should primarily be a critic of society. Daumier, Goya, Hogarth—all of them were. Criticism needn't be destructive; it should rouse the people to think. One purpose of art is to make people sensitive to what's wrong in society...[5]

These were new ideas in evaluating art that went beyond the traditional ideas of art being appreciated for its serene, aesthetic beauty. 'The Cyclonic Silence', 1978, Art Heritage's very next show in Bombay and Delhi, was gritty and hard-edged where Husain and Laxma Gaud, in two divergent mediums, responded to the devastating cyclone that lashed Andhra Pradesh. Alkazi the curator, described the searing quality of these works:

> Husain transcends the obvious depiction of human suffering and achieves a veritable catharsis, a purging of the emotions of pity and terror... Husain dips his hands into the open wounds of humanity; invests the agony of mankind with a quality of visual poetry and by miraculous transformations such as these restores to art its quiescent dignity and its healing touch. This is one of the rare inspired moments in the history of art when the creative vision of a great artist confronts the onslaught of a staggering disaster with serenity and poise, and transforms the slings of death into the quickening impulse of renewed life. We are indeed privileged to be witnesses to that miracle.[6]

Alkazi's ability to communicate the meaning of artworks through his talks and essays was uniquely his own. Allowing his audience to arrive at a deep understanding of the work on an experiential rather than just a cerebral level, Alkazi spoke of the compelling, hypnotic power of Laxma Gaud's small ink drawings in the same show, thus:

> No camera eye could have probed so dispassionately into the cruelty of nature and the callousness of officialdom. The contorted forms of man and beast and battered utensil seem to emit a silent agonized cry against the blind fury of the elements and hurl an

outraged accusation against the inhumanity of fellow human beings. They are an imprecation and a curse. The small ink drawings have a compelling hypnotic power, an explosive energy, a refusal to surrender to the cold bleakness of death... These searing, haunting drawings of ravaged humanity have the same rage and power as Goya's 'The Disasters of War', and the same enduring quality. Long after these scenes of natural catastrophe have faded into oblivion, Laxma's drawings will remain, a document and an accusation.[7]

It was not long before photography began to feature within the hallowed sanctum of a fine arts gallery. It was the ability of photography to capture the quickness of life that drew Alkazi's attention to this democratic art form. The fact that an inner narrative could be excavated from beneath seemingly ordinary and mundane images appealed to Alkazi. He writes of the poetic intensity of Satish Sharma's suite of works in the 1985–86 Art Heritage catalogue:

> The horror pictures of Satish Sharma seize us by the throat... Maimed children pick their way, insect-like, on all fours, through littered streets; their eyes neither beseech nor yield; they accuse. The outraged modesty of a woman explodes into fierce rage against a couple of city thugs. Crowds are on the rampage, destroying cars, looting property, setting human beings ablaze. The city is one vast charnel house. Human life is literally, in a matter of moments, reduced to ashes. This is the ultimate horror. For the death of that one man spells the doom of all humanity. It marks the end of civilization. It makes a mockery of all our utterances, converts our dreams into hideous nightmares.
>
> Here in these pictures we are dragged to the bottom of the abyss, beyond despair, beyond redemption and hope. We can only stare with horror and stupefaction. And the feeling slowly seizes us that we ourselves cannot be absolved of the guilt.
>
> The shame and humiliation of being an Indian today.

Alkazi was not only supporting art whose subject matter emanated from the day's newspaper headlines, but he also venerated artists like

Akbar Padamsee, whose sculpted heads were able to catch the spiritual essence of life.

Padamsee's scrutiny takes him away from the outward resemblance, from the fleeting and transitory, to the essence. Accordingly, as Giacometti before him felt constrained to do, he evolves his own phenomenology of perception, based, in his case, on principles of portrayal from classical Sanskrit sources: to seize upon that quintessential state of mind and being which goes beyond physical characteristics. In this precisely lies the paradox of all art: how, through the gross and the material, to signify the spiritual.

It was through such simple yet evocative explanations that Alkazi was able to train generations of viewers over the years to appreciate and read the visual language of a vast range of art that he displayed.

'I believe that art going must become a habit, therefore, in order for that to happen we have to promote art regularly and in a sustained manner. We cannot afford to lose patience but have to doggedly continue with our mission.'[8]

* * *

Alkazi was one of the first to recognize the significance of women artists and that the subject matter and treatment of their pictorial language were distinct from that of men. From the 1970s on, he consistently promoted women in group shows, but more often in solos.[*]

Looking back, artist Navjot Altaf said,

> Alkazi Saab selected me to be in the first Women Artists' show ever held. He had come to Bombay and had asked me to bring my work for him to see at Vithal Court. It was pouring with rain, but I somehow got there. 'The thing I like about people,' he said,

---

[*] This included Nalini Malani, Arpita Singh, Zarina Hashmi, Nasreen Mohamedi, Rekha Rodwittiya, Anupam Sud, Mona Rai, Arpana Caur, Jaya Ganguly, Meera Devidayal, Kristine Michael, Kishori Kaul, Gogi Saroj Pal, Ira Roy, Bharti Kher, Ketaki Sheth, Tara Sabharwal, Kavita Jaiswal, Tina Bopiah, Sabrina, Sunanda Khajuria, Gouri Vemula, Latika Katt, Jyotsna Bhatt and Ira Chaudhari.

'is if they keep their appointments. I thought you may not come because of the rain. It seems you are serious.'

Alkazi wanted each woman artist in the show to make an impact, so it was an impressive, large show for which he had rented all three galleries at Triveni. There were about 24 works of mine on view. I had priced my work at Rs 1500, but Mrs Alkazi sold them for Rs 1000 each. She said firmly, 'You have to keep standardized and reasonable prices.'

Alkazi had a catalogue with each show and a written note. This was something very new. The Alkazis were trying to professionalize the art movement.

I remember my father insisting on graphic artists carefully numbering their print editions, as well as signing and dating their work. Ensuring that a name be ascribed to each work rather than lazily titling them as 'Untitled 1', '2' etc., Alkazi often helped artists name their works with poetic brevity. How to maintain works in good condition, frame them, restore them, if necessary, and photograph and document works for future reference were details that Alkazi introduced to the art scene. For the first time, someone in the art field was emphasizing the need to educate, professionally promote, disseminate, care for and restore art in a systematic, professional manner.

While Alkazi was generous and supportive, he was equally ruthless and exacting in demanding the highest standards of his artists. As Anupam Sud recollects:

> When I brought my works to the gallery and showed them to Mr Alkazi a few days before the opening, he just turned away. 'Not good enough! We cannot show these works. The exhibition is cancelled!' I was speechless. I could barely hold back my tears! It was only later that I understood that Alkazi was right... I would have ruined my career with a weak show.[9]

**

Alkazi was acutely aware that national art institutions had so far neglected to create substantial, representative holdings of Indian modernity that would constitute a historical canon. Without a cannon, vested interests were likely to misrepresent the history of Indian modernity. Alkazi felt it imperative to counteract this possibility by '... the scrupulous study of Indian art over the past two hundred years in order to perceive the significant strands in its development and to view the art of today against that broad perspective.'[10]

One way was through *retrospectives*. Again, this was the job of national institutions that Alkazi now chose to undertake.

> My feeling really was that on the one hand, while there is an ephemeral aspect to the theatre, in that it does not last, it only lives on in the memories of people, there is also, unfortunately, a similar kind of ephemeral quality to art in India ... in that it is not really looked after, there are no serious public collections, to promote art and in order to safeguard it. There is no real consistent policy to safeguard these artworks and to keep them on, as treasures for future, for future generations ... and also for the present generations to be able to learn a great deal from. And so I felt, that from time to time, it would be important for me to put up retrospective exhibitions of those artists who had made a significant contribution to contemporary Indian art. And so when my wife, Mrs Alkazi, asked me to be associated with her, I said to her that I was not really interested in selling paintings ... in peddling paintings ... And it was a wonderful exercise for me, because they (the retrospectives) gave me a clear idea of the development of this particular art form, in relation to the development of the theatre also, which we had studied from the nineteenth century on. And I felt that it complimented the kind of work that I did.[11]

Between 1977 and 1997, Alkazi set himself the formidable task of mounting twenty-three retrospectives of major artists from the pre- and post-Independence periods. The Progressives were undoubtedly fundamental to Alkazi's reading of contemporary Indian art and he located them squarely at the centre of Indian modernity. Therefore, the Progressives—M.F. Husain, F.N. Souza, Akbar Padamsee, Ram Kumar, Tyeb Mehta, Satish Gujral and Krishen Khanna—were among the first to be awarded canonical status through large retrospective shows. Another

Alkazi in conversation with S.K. Mishra at Art Heritage, 2008

strand was from Bengal with Ramkinkar Baij, Chittaprosad Bhattacharya, Haren Das, Gobardhan Ash and B.C. Sanyal, leading onto Somnath Hore, K.G. Subramanyan and Bijon Bhattacharya.

A roundup of the printmaking scene, '50 Years of Printmaking' (1980), was followed by a retrospective of the works of Devyani and Kanwal Krishna, Jyoti Bhatt and Anupam Sud, perhaps the youngest printmaker to receive a retrospective at Art Heritage.

Alkazi's respect for sculpture was acknowledged in his retrospectives of Adi Davierwala, Dhanraj Bhagat, Somnath Hore, Sankho Chaudhuri and Himmat Shah.

In general, these retrospectives marked the formal acknowledgement of these artists as the exponents of India's modern art movement. It is interesting to note that, to date, Alkazi's canonization of these artists remains largely unchallenged.

The retrospectives became opportunities for Alkazi to research and collect a significant amount of documentary material on each artist. Each retrospective also required the recording of interviews with the artist about his or her life and times. As professional art historians and curators were few and far between at the time, Alkazi either conducted these interviews himself or sought out young graduates of newly founded art history departments and others, including Mala Marwah, Anita Dube, Archana Hebbar, Gayatri Sinha and Roobina Karode. Alkazi was perhaps among the first persons in the field of art to carry out such scholarly investigations that were published in the retrospective catalogues. The collated material drawn from multiple sources was systematically ordered into folders, filed and labelled by Alkazi himself. This was long before the advent of computers!

Looking back at her early interactions with Art Heritage, Roobina Karode, who currently holds the prestigious position of chief curator and director of the Kiran Nadar Museum of Art in New Delhi, recollects that Alkazi's passion and respect for artworks and artists served as unforgettable lessons in her understanding of art.

> When Alkazi Saab showed me an art work, he would handle it with so much care and respect, irrespective of whether it was the work of a lesser known artist or a major one... For him it made no difference... This was one of the ways he taught me to be closer to the work... so that I could actually begin to see it.

* * *

Around this time, Alkazi had begun searching for and acquiring older publications, old art journals, newspaper articles and reviews in both English and the vernacular languages that would be required for future research. As he went along, he became convinced of the importance of this exercise. Such an archive would serve as an invaluable resource for future art historians. He was also aware that it was vital for him to have access to this kind of resource material if he was going to promote Indian art abroad. Over the next few years, at each step of this exhausting process, Alkazi felt frustrated, realizing that we in India had neither the technology nor the skilled personnel to undertake this momentous project in a scientific manner.

Yayati by A. Ramachandran, a painting in twelve panels, 1986

The turnover of exhibitions at Art Heritage was breathtaking, with as many as twenty exhibitions annually. Over a span of thirty-three years, from 1977 to 2010, Alkazi curated and designed 642 exhibitions, a Herculean task by any standards! 'If art viewing has to be inculcated among the public as a habit, it is our job as gallerists to programme consistently excellent work on a regular basis throughout the year,' he said.

* * *

The overwhelming response to Art Heritage exhibitions in Delhi emboldened my parents to travel with a couple of shows annually to Bombay, where they would rent Jehangir Art Gallery. However, my mother was keen to establish a more permanent presence for Art Heritage in the city. A perfect solution presented itself when she discovered that the young Pheroza Godrej was interested in establishing her own small gallery at Bhulabhai Desai Road. However, Pheroza confessed that she neither had the knowledge nor the experience to handle an art business. Roshen suggested a collaboration between Art Heritage and Pheroza's Cymroza Art Gallery. It was decided that Art Heritage would annually send a selection of shows they had already shown in Delhi. Commenting on Roshen's mentorship, Pheroza said:

'Your mother guided us in everything . . . packing, billing, hanging, lighting, transporting . . . We at Cymroza copied the style of Art Heritage in everything—in the catalogue size and layout, the captioning . . . even the style of the posters and invitations. Our openings were followed by dinners just like your mother would organize in Delhi. In fact, we continue that tradition even today!

'In all, Art Heritage and Cymroza collaborated on approximately seventy to eighty shows between 1984 and 1994! Saroj Pal Gogi, Manu Parekh, Devraj Dakoji, Latika Katt, Anupam Sud and many, many more were among the artists we exhibited that Art Heritage introduced us to.'[12]

Pheroza ends with an Alkazi anecdote!

'Sorry, but I can't resist telling you about this incident, Amal. You see this was before I had ever met your father. He invited me to the Taj for lunch. We planned to meet in the lobby. I said I would be wearing a pink kurta so that he would not have any trouble spotting me.

'"You will have no problem spotting me," your father replied, "I will be the ugliest man in the room and the shortest!"'

CHAPTER 41
BRITAIN: DEVELOPING A SENSE OF HISTORY 1979-82

While establishing Art Heritage, my father began to simultaneously travel to Kuwait and the UK, getting acquainted with the complex cultural networks that operated in each country. Recognizing the need to travel as and when he pleased, he decided to become a non-resident Indian (NRI), finding employment at Al Falak Fine Arts, a foundation set up in Kuwait by his brother Sulaiman Alkazi for the promotion of international arts. The only snag to becoming an NRI was that his time in India was limited to three months a year for the first few years. This meant that my mother would have to shoulder most of the day-to-day responsibilities of Art Heritage.

While trying to establish a new career and mission for himself abroad, personal family matters made demands on him from time to time. For example, Alkazi was unable to attend the retrospective he had organized for Adi Davierwalla's work at Jehangir Art Gallery in February 1979, as he was needed at his youngest sister Faiza's bedside in London. Faiza had been diagnosed with cancer and had to undergo prolonged treatment in London. This kept my grandmother and the Alkazi siblings shuttling between Kuwait and London until her eventual demise in October 1979. Concerns for his sister Munira in London, who continued to experience protracted episodes of depression, also clouded the year. My father coaxed and cajoled Munira to keep working while he personally oversaw the printing of her etchings in an attempt to draw her out of herself.

> It is an extremely difficult job working with Munira and trying to get things steadily organized regarding the printing of editions of her work... Also at some time or the other she will have to go to hospital for about 3 weeks to get her off her medication... Munira

is so distinctively an individualist and has lived and worked so totally apart in her own world and with her personal techniques, that it is almost impossible for someone else to simulate the same.[1]

He also planned to publish a book on Munira, as she was regarded as the foremost Arab woman artist of her generation. In this context, Alkazi began meeting 'superb printers' and publishers in London.

Publishing, Alkazi found, was a serious and respectable way to gain entry into the art world in Britain, a direction he now began to seriously pursue.

'I am thinking of books on Indian art, architecture, beautiful India ... truthful not exaggerated or vulgarized. There is a fantastic market for all this over here. And we can get adequate financial sponsorship. Just let's get down to writing the things ... leave all the rest to me ...' he wrote to Uma, who was in the process of researching her own book, *Mansions of the Sun*.[2]

Alkazi was not wrong in his assessment of the phenomenal India/Raj nostalgia that was sweeping the UK at this time. In 1981, Salman Rushdie's *Midnight's Children* won the Booker Prize, while Richard Attenborough's film *Gandhi* (1982) drew avid media attention and eventually a number of Oscars. On its heels came an entire spate of Raj-centric films based on E.M. Forster's *A Passage to India* (1984) and Rudyard Kipling's *Kim* (1984), while *Mountbatten: The Last Viceroy* (1986), Paul Scott's *The Raj Quartet/The Jewel in the Crown* (1984) and M.M. Kaye's *The Far Pavilions* (1984) became extremely popular television series.

There was also a growing academic interest by Indian and British scholars in understanding and reevaluating the impact British culture had on India.

The nineteenth century was now a period that Alkazi began to find significant in the history of Indian art.

> I was really interested in working out for myself the antecedents of modern Indian art ... and that meant going backwards slowly in time to the '70s and the '60s, and the '50s and so on, to the early years of the century. I mean going back, if possible, to the middle of the nineteenth century ...'[3]

Alkazi began to study late eighteenth and early nineteenth centuries—drawings, paintings, prints and water colours by British artists, such as William Hodges (1744–1797), Thomas Daniell (1749–1840) and William Daniell (1769–1837), and began to be seized by a passion for them. London was still a veritable treasure trove where the work of landscape artists was not yet considered 'high art', while aquatints and etchings were often found tucked away on the back stands at flea markets at relatively affordable rates. In most cases, it was a network of small vendors with whom such picturesque scenes of India were available, many of whom had inherited a large number of these prints from their parents or grandparents who had served in India at one time. Befriending dealers whom he found extremely knowledgeable about their wares, Alkazi gradually picked up the odd watercolour or aquatint. Before long, Alkazi began to feel the need to build up a decent visual archive of the history of Indian art, an effort that no one else had undertaken so far.

> I started acquiring works of art—drawings, etchings and paintings, as well as photographs, over a period of 30 years or so. From the 1960s and 70s, I travelled a great deal to Europe, Asia, the USA and the Latin American countries looking for interesting material at auctions and in specialized shops, which were run by extremely well-travelled, knowledgeable and scholarly people who were always on the look-out for rare material for a regular, steady client.[4]

It was only a matter of time before Alkazi discovered the work of Indian painters, often drawn from Mughal ateliers, who were commissioned by British officers to create artworks for their personal collections or for the East India Company. Employed and supervised by British artists, Indian painters were trained in the techniques of western art, while European paper replaced the traditionally prepared ground used for miniatures. The work of Indian artists of this period came to be known as the Company School.

Excited and wanting to disseminate his knowledge, Alkazi approached Mildred Archer, an expert on the Company period, who had catalogued the East India Company's collection of paintings housed at the India

Office Library along with Toby Falk, an expert on miniatures, to write and bring out books and portfolios on Company drawings for him. The subjects ranged from 'The Marquis of Wellesley Collection' of the flora and fauna of India, to 'Skinner's Album', a set of Company drawings created by Indian artists of Skinner's private army. Karl Khandalavala, reviewing 'The Tranquil Eye', 'Between Battles', 'The Marquis of Wellesley Collection' (Alfalak/Scorpion, 1985) mentions,

> A lot of interest in the Raj at this time. As Alkazi says his purpose is to explore those areas of Indian history which have hitherto received scant attention and to bring to notice work that is often anonymous or by little known artists ... All these years the stress has been on Mughal, Deccani or Pahari paintings. Alkazi has also set a standard in publishing compared to the indifferent and poor production standards of our museums.[5]

Alkazi's interest, as Khandalavala points out, had always been to 'uncover hidden talent'.

> Disparaging things have been said about the works of Indian artists who utilize these styles. The suggestion being that what was produced was a bastard style and uneasy mixture of Indian and western. Actually the finest works show the Indian artist capacity for quick and imaginative assimilation and the creation of works of originality and vigour.

The British had a long and respected history and tradition of collecting, and it was interesting to see how my father began to educate and groom himself into becoming a passionate scholar and collector, one who knew his collection inside out.

> England was the most interesting hunting ground for me— it had been a far-flung and expansive colonial power well before other continental countries and had set up educational institutions and museums of meticulous scholarship. I learned a great deal from scholars all over the British Empire who were extremely

knowledgeable, shared their knowledge, and took their vocation very seriously.[6]

He became a regular visitor at major auctions held at reputed auction houses like Bonhams, Sotheby's, Christie's, etc. His sartorial tastes were altered too. He discarded the kurta–pyjamas of his NSD days and appeared more formal in expensive suits and ties, elegant loafers, a man of means no doubt, but always fashionably understated!

***

For the moment, Alkazi's acquisitions began to be housed in his tiny rented flats in Kuwait, London and Delhi, and, as can be imagined, all his homes began to burst at the seams with piles of books, stacks of paintings and heaps of portfolios encroaching on dining tables and spilling onto sofas and floors (albeit in neat piles). Notices and messages like 'V. IMP. DO NOT TOUCH!' were appended to parcels and heaps. The growing number of artefacts was one of the reasons why my father categorically refused to allow anyone in the family to spend even a few days in any of his flats. 'Go and stay in a guest house or hotel,' he would bark, 'I have no place for anyone.'

***

From 1979 onwards, Alkazi also began to get in touch with a couple of galleries in London through introductions by Maria Souza, F.N. Souza's first wife, who now had a gallery of her own. He noted that it was 'not going to be easy to break into the gallery circuit in the UK.'[7] While interest in modern Indian art was limited to a few Indophiles, Asia lovers and antiquarian enthusiasts in the UK, he had a strong hunch that with the renewed interest in India as well as its growing Indian immigrant population, it might be the right time to promote an artist like Souza in the West in a substantial way.

Alkazi had kept abreast of Souza's career with keen interest. There was no doubt that the kind of attention Souza garnered in the West had been remarkable—Stephen Spender had endorsed him by publishing his biographical fragment, 'Nirvana of a Maggot', in *Encounter*. Furthermore, Spender introduced Souza to Peter Watson, who immediately included three of Souza's works alongside those of Francis Bacon, Henry Moore, Graham Sutherland and Ivon Hitchens in his ICA show of 1954, where all three were sold! Finally, Victor Musgrave offered Souza a one-man show at his Gallery One in 1955, an exhibition that art critic John Berger devoted an entire page to in the *New Statesman*. All this was promising to secure Souza a lasting place among the leading British artists of his generation.

The initial enthusiastic response to Souza was followed by a relative low ebb, with the exception of the artist finding a generous and admiring patron in Harold Kovner, an American businessman who was so taken by Souza's work that he acquired 200 of his paintings between 1956–1960. It was due to these earlier triumphs that Alkazi sought to build up and promote Souza, discussing this with Musgrave.

By the early 1980s, Alkazi began to be both visible and well-respected in the London art and publishing scenes. Increasingly, international collectors, scholars and museum directors made it a point to visit the Art Heritage gallery. Presenting himself as the Indian gallerist who mounted formidable exhibitions and offered museum-quality works to collectors, Alkazi was careful that Art Heritage be viewed more as an institution than an 'art shop'. Always stressing that he was building up an archive for the purposes of study and scholarship, he was taken seriously by young international collectors such as Chester and Davida Herwitz from the US, Ghazi and Aruna Sultan from Kuwait and Masanori Fukuoka from Japan. Artists such as Howard Hodgkin and Timothy Hyman, scholars like Robert Skelton and Deborah Swallow from the Victoria & Albert Museum, T. Richard Blurton from the British Museum, buyers from the Tate, the Museum of Mankind, etc., put Art Heritage on their 'must visit' list. These contacts were crucial for Alkazi to cultivate, as he was preparing to promote Indian art abroad in a substantial way. The ideal opportunity presented itself when he heard about the Festival of India in the UK, which was being planned for the following year, 1982.

Alkazi sensed this was his big opportunity. He immediately devised a formidable project consisting of a series of exhibitions on Indian art and culture. Looking for a like-minded collaborator and institution, Alkazi was introduced to David Elliott, the director of Oxford MOMA, by Musgrave.

Writing to Uma in an elated mood from Kuwait in July 1981, Alkazi said:

> Now to come to some fantastic news which is absolutely confidential, which I am discussing with you as it involves not only some of our own publications, but also our future:
>
> Victor Musgrave has been able to get for us the Museum of Modern Art, Oxford for a huge exhibition of Indian art. This is not only a stroke of luck, but also an incredible scoop because it is most certainly the most prestigious and most beautiful art gallery in England.
>
> I am trying to sell them a package deal:
>
> Exhibition of Contemporary Indian Painting
> Exhibition of works of Five Indian Photographers
> Exhibition either of Pithora Paintings (artists painting on the spot there) or Photographic exhibition: Gods of the Byways
> Film Festival: Young Directors of last 10 years
> Documentary Films complementing the above four exhibitions
>
> If I manage to pull it off, it will be an absolutely stunning achievement for us, for the present and the future. Because it will immediately put us on the world map of art . . .[8]

Alkazi was keeping his fingers crossed that his project would be accepted in its entirety by MOMA. If he succeeded, it would be the first step towards realizing his final aim, which was to promote contemporary Indian art abroad. 'This will be a superb beginning', he wrote, 'It could not be launched from a better platform . . . It will take us all over the world, and it will open doors for us. And nobody before us will have done it in as comprehensive and committed a way.'

Alkazi was also shrewdly keeping an eye on the political mileage that the festival was garnering from the two collaborating countries—India and Britain.

After the present spate of riots, the British government is going to bend backwards to appease the Blacks. I am keeping a close watch on the TV coverage from England and the changing attitudes, actions and statements of Mrs Thatcher and the conservative government as a whole, as well as the reactions of other European and American spokesmen are very revealing. This has been such a terrible but salutary shock that they will have to do something drastic about it. And that will be to the benefit of the Blacks. Because from now on no other policy is possible . . . So I think the British government will try and make as great a propaganda success of the India Festival as it possibly can. And that will be useful for us.[9]

The Indian government, too, was prioritizing the festival, as it was being seen as part of Indira Gandhi's strategy to alter the image of her governance and project a positive image of her leadership to a western audience at a time when her credibility was at a low. The festival was conceived to showcase the 'traditional' along with the 'modern' arts and sciences, symbolic of centuries of civilizational continuity. The central theme was 'continuity and change' in the context of the unity and plurality of Indian culture. It was clear that both governments were conceiving of the festival on a massive scale.

Alkazi's was, of course, a unique take on this theme. His proposed series of exhibitions was an attempt to introduce the British public to a new India—an India beyond the Raj that they knew. His curatorial thrust would be distinct from the official contemporary art exhibition that was going to be held at the Royal Academy of Arts in London. For far too long, India had been regarded as an 'ancient' civilization, carrying forward age-old traditions and customs into the present. Alkazi's entire emphasis was to project the *modern* art of a *modern* nation, not 'the modern art of an ancient civilization'. Through his selection of *contemporary* Indian painting, *contemporary* photography, *contemporary* cinema, Alkazi wished for the British public to engage with a *new* India through multiple mediums. Alkazi's India was a *raw* India that was still struggling to cope with 'the trauma of the Partition, cope with economic disparity, urban stress and yet maintain its secular,

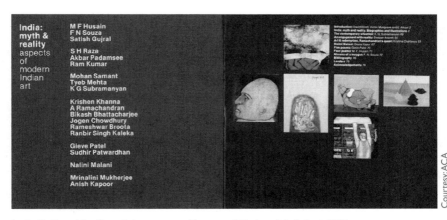

India: Myth and Reality, catalogue pages, Museum of Modern Art, Oxford, 1982

democratic values'. Through the work of *younger* voices in painting, cinema and photography, Alkazi wished to showcase how India's young artists were responding passionately to their times, creating a new Indian modernism that drew from tradition while also being well aware of international trends.

Elliott was excited by Alkazi's holistic approach and immediately embraced the proposal. As a scholar of Asian modernity himself, he was interested in, 'countries that had long artistic traditions who were now modernizing'. One must remember also that in agreeing to Alkazi's promotion of officially 'unrecognized' and 'unvalidated' artists, Museum of Modern Art, Oxford, as a museum, was running the risk of supporting unvetted work. The very fact that there was a 'modern' art movement in India at all, as Alkazi claimed, was regarded in Britain in those days with a great amount of scepticism! As Elliott mentions:

> a lot of people regarded India as a 'Third World' country and not 'modern' at all. Many thought it was a 'backward' ex-colony and on top of this, there was significant racial prejudice against Asian immigrants . . . Even Howard Hodgkin, who was on my board, a collector and connoisseur of classical Indian art, was uninterested in contemporary Indian art, apart from that of [his friend] Bhupen Khakhar . . .

By accepting Alkazi's proposal in toto, Elliott was using MOMA's autonomous status to his advantage. Elliott also leveraged his reputation as a young museum director who had a history of excelling in unusual shows. Musgrave, on the other hand, was not a museum man but an independent gallery owner of Gallery One, known for its serious promotion of 'Outsider (Asian and Black) Art'. Managing to convince his board, Elliott confirmed Alkazi's five-part series of shows under the overarching title of 'India: Myth and Reality'.

Finally, on 5 August 1981, Alkazi was able to send a jubilant telegram to Uma: 'So we have landed it after all, and the hard work begins.' The telegram to my mother read: 'Entire Oxford Project approved. Stop. Finalize with artists. Start collecting works.'

Working ceaselessly through the year, Alkazi coordinated the multi-pronged project long-distance through letters, telegrams, phone calls and a few fleeting visits to India with Elliott and Musgrave in tow for the final selections. Jyotindra Jain, Komal Kothari and Haku Shah, as craft experts, were invited to curate 'Gods of the Byways: Wayside Shrines of Rajasthan, Madhya Pradesh and Gujarat', an exposition through fifty photographs and artefacts, while young film director Pradip Krishen curated and coordinated the Cinema and Documentary section—a film festival of 'New Wave Indian Cinema; Screen Idols: Indian Film Posters from the 1950s to the Present' along with some documentaries and audio-visual programmes created by Debu Dutta. Ace photographer T.S. Nagarajan oversaw the quality of printing and enlargements of 'The Other India: Seven Contemporary Photographers' (Jyoti Bhatt, Raghav Kaneria, T.S. Nagarajan, Pablo Bartholomew, Foy Nissen, Mitter Bedi and Dashrath Patel), while Uma Anand was general editor of all three catalogues published for the occasion.

These four shows were conceived of as satellites to the centrepiece—'Aspects of Modern Indian Art', which comprised a staggering 180 artworks by nineteen artists co-curated by Alkazi, Elliott and Musgrave that were to be displayed across the museum's three galleries.

It was from the collection of Chester and Davida Herwitz in Massachusetts, USA, that Alkazi needed to borrow a large number of works for the show. Chester and Alkazi had always shared a love–hate relationship. Both had a great sense of humour and a passion for art. Chester had always trusted Alkazi's judgement on the quality of art, prompting him to acquire a large number of works from Art Heritage. Although Alkazi did sell works to Herwitz, he was never really keen that Indian artworks be acquired by private collectors abroad, as they would no longer be available for viewing by scholars and the lay public in India.

The following letter from Alkazi to Chester illustrates the tongue-in-cheek manner in which Alkazi often got his way in embarrassing, prickly situations.

7th August 1981

My Dear Chester,

I have been able to bring off what promises to be a very exciting project. The Museum of Modern Art, Oxford has accepted a scheme of mine to present a series of exhibitions from 9th May to 8th August 1982, which will include Contemporary Indian Art. Tribal and Folk Art, Contemporary Indian Photographers and Young Indian Film Makers.

The Contemporary Indian Art show will comprise 180 works of about 15 artists. Each artist will be represented by a fairly large cross-section of about 12–15 works (at least each major artist); the younger artists would perhaps be represented by about 6–8 works each. This should give viewers an idea of the significant trends over the last 10–15 years.

Some of the artists I have in mind are: Souza, Husain, Samant, Subramanyam (terracotta), Akbar, Tyeb, Ram Kumar, Krishen Khanna and Gaitonde among more established artists. Among the younger: Nalini Malani, Laxma Gaud, Sudhir Patwardhan, Gieve Patel, Jogen Choudhury and Vivan Sundaram.

Would you consider loaning works for this show from your fine collection?

I do not know whether you are talking to me or not. If you are not talking to me, please write to me immediately to say so. And if you are talking to me, please phone me collect at 617671, Kuwait, and tell me that you will be writing to me. In any case, please let me know what is what and who is where. And if that is difficult, please

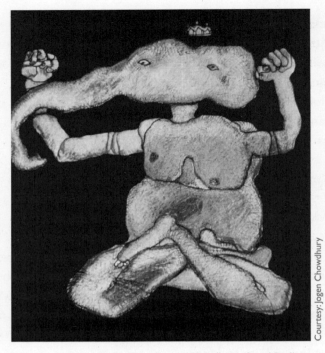

Ganesh with Crown, Jogen Chowdhury, 1979, India: Myth and Reality, Museum of Modern Art, Oxford, 1982

put an advertisement in the New York Times, Agony Column, and I will understand.

Under your influence, I learn that Husain is now jumping into bed in the Indian films. So long as it is not with an elephant, that's fine.

I'm thinking of coming to the States, but I'm told you have your SAM missiles lined up against me on the eastern coast.

In any case, write and send us all your hate.

Fondest love to Davy,
affectionately,
Elk, the Scarab.

Of course, Chester and Davida were totally disarmed by Alkazi's charm and wit and loaned him whatever he asked for.

* * *

Nissar and I made it a point to be at the opening of what promised to be a seminal art show of Indian art abroad. Wrapping up nine months of intense work as set decorators on Richard Attenborough's film *Gandhi*, we dashed off to London. Arriving at the museum well ahead of time allowed us to get a sense of the show as a whole. I still remember being taken aback by the sly quote from Rabindranath Tagore that greeted us at the door: 'I strongly urge our artists vehemently to deny their obligation to produce something that can be labelled as Indian art.'

The catalogue helped to succinctly contextualize the theme:

> The title 'India: Myth and Reality' might imply a contradiction. However, the indivisibility of myth from contemporary reality is a central facet of Indian culture and inevitably this is expressed in many artists' work... It is a paradox that in a subcontinent revered for its tradition of non-violence, conflict, cruelty, terror should be at the core of its art and myth. It is in this common ground that ancient epic and contemporary painting so often meet. There is a rawness to life in India, which while it does not preclude happiness, is striking, sometimes terrifying, to the western eye.

India: Myth and Reality, Museum of Modern Art, Oxford, 1982

The Fall by Tyeb Mehta, 1976, India: Myth and Reality, Museum of Modern Art, Oxford, 1982

Courtesy: Mehta Family Archives

The introductory segment of the show was rather overwhelming. It comprised thirty outstanding works each of Husain and Souza—both founders of the Progressive Artists Group and precursors of modernism in India.

Looking back, there appears to be a certain deliberation in Alkazi's choice of Souza and Husain. Both series of works were largely mythic and civilizational in their themes. By selecting a Muslim painter who powerfully visualizes a Hindu epic, the Mahabharata, and a Goan painter whose works are suffused with a Catholic preoccupation with the ideas of sin and redemption but whose pictorial language arises from the influence of sensual and sculptural classical Hindu art, Alkazi drew attention to the fact that both were actually drawing from a common pool—a *syncretic* confluence of multiple cultures not limited by their own personal religious orientations or political beliefs. Their genius lay in transforming those influences into a modern idiom. Exhibited alongside the work of Pablo Picasso in Sao Paulo, Husain's 'Mahabharata' series had already acquired a certain iconic status. One wonders if this kind of curation would be welcomed in our country today.

As one moved on through the exhibition, taking in the works of Tyeb Mehta, Krishen Khanna, K.G. Subramanyan, Meera Mukherjee, Sudhir Patwardhan, Nalini Malani, Gieve Patel and Anish Kapoor, what became apparent was the Indian artist's intense need to 'hammer out a pictorial language true to the rawness of the times'.

One of the important points made by critics and visitors was that 'despite superficial resemblances, contemporary Indian art was not a second-hand reworking of tendencies in the West, nor was it a withdrawal into a romantic past'.[10]

Four decades later, when an interviewer in conversation with Elliott referenced 'Aspects of Modern Indian Art', she said, 'Looking at the list of artists you included in the exhibition of modern and contemporary art, for example, many of those are names that have become much more familiar to British audiences today. I would argue that your exhibition contributed significantly to that process of canon formation.'

In response, Elliott said, 'Absolutely. It reflected the remarkable strength of work made by Indian artists from the period of Independence to the early 1980s—this has only relatively recently been widely acknowledged.'[11]

By promoting relative newcomers on an international platform, Alkazi was inviting a younger generation of Indian artists to take their place among international modernists.

CHAPTER 42
THE PASSAGE OF TIME
1983-84

For any celebrity, returning to the humdrum normalcy of daily life after a period of hectic activity and public acclaim is utterly unbearable. The year 1982 had already been an overwhelming one, what with the Oxford MOMA show, Alkazi hardly had time to process his mother's passing, which had finally caught up with him. Finding no future direction presenting itself to him in concrete terms, he felt all the more disheartened and depressed. What irked him was that he had been unable to clearly pinpoint the exact nature of the work he wished to pursue abroad. The time spent in England had taught him that although India and Britain shared a common past, there were very few private or official art institutions in Britain willing to form international partnerships.

The next few years were chiefly spent adjusting to the constraints of his NRI status. Limited to spending only eighty-nine days a year in India, he spent the rest of the nine months on his own, shuttling between Kuwait and London. Isolated, lonely and disenchanted, he often referred to himself as 'living in exile' or like a 'refugee', weighing whether living apart from the family and Uma for such long stretches was worth it. The stress of working in multiple countries meant the loss of tight control over work. 'I do find it difficult and frustrating working from a distance, not having matters under direct and immediate control. It is not satisfying for me, patching together what other people are doing . . .' This was despite the fact that my mother compensated with her sheer level-headedness and experience in running a gallery.* With a skeletal staff of two peons and Debashree Haldar, her assistant, she single-handedly installed massive projects like the major retrospectives.

---

*   The K.G. Subramanyan retrospective in 1984 was Roshen Alkazi's 200th show.

Rosh dutifully sat by the phone at 9.30 a.m., almost every day of those years, awaiting Elk's 'trunk' call. Without preliminary niceties, he would begin, 'Rosh, now let's get down to business!' Pen and pad in hand, my mother would meticulously jot down the work he listed. Art-related chats would be followed by brief exchanges on family matters; my father was always concerned when it came to health or monetary requirements. It was through these phone calls then that my parents managed their lives across time zones.

The stints in London became longer than those in Kuwait, prompting my father to get a tiny one-bedroom flat at Ovington Square in Knightsbridge which he set up with Uma. In order that we spend more time with him, my mother suggested that she, Nissar, our three children, Zuleikha, Tariq and Rahaab, and I practically spend every summer in London in a rented apartment across from his. In addition, I would visit my father on my own for two- or three-week stints. These were when I had the pleasure of having him all to myself. He would spoil me with small gifts, proudly show me the rare and beautiful acquisitions he had made and take me to movies, plays and interesting restaurants for meals. Our outings usually began with a museum show at the Victoria & Albert Museum, the Royal Academy or the Tate, which he had planned in advance. Towards the end of my stay, I would go off on my own, mostly to the bookshops Foyles and Waterstones, where I would hunt for interesting theatre books. By the end of my stay, I would have totted up a substantial bill, which my father would generously pay.

One morning at breakfast, he said, 'I'm going to take you to an American artist, Judy Chicago's most brilliant show called "The Dinner Party".' Till date, the experience of that show remains vividly etched in my mind—my first experience of installation art! It was not in a gallery but at The Warehouse, a vast, dark, barn-like shed.

A huge triangular-shaped dining table (48 feet on each side) and chairs were laid out in the centre of the space. Only the table was lit; the rest of the space was dark. Places were set for the thirty-nine most famous women from history, all imagined to be partaking of a grand feast. (Ninety-nine more names were inscribed on the table's base). Each plate was painted with a vulva and each placemat, cutlery and crockery were inscribed with their names. All the objects were hand-made, hand-embroidered, sensuously painted and crafted in ceramic by the artist! Extremely visceral!

'The Dinner Party' was my very first exposure to 'feminist' art. Making me tingle all over and rendering me speechless, the extraordinary experience of a fictitious female feast stayed with me for many years. It was only much later, when I became aware that I was indeed practising what could be termed 'feminist' theatre myself, that I realized why it had impacted me as it did. Looking back, I find it quite amazing that my father apparently noticed traces of feminist theatre practice in my directorial work long before I did.

* * *

Looking forward to his restricted days in India, my father planned his visits carefully. Parched of intellectual stimulation, especially in a place like Kuwait, my father wrote to Uma: 'I want GAY, lively parties every second day in Delhi, and I don't want the same old fogies and the same old crones. I want to be with POSITIVE, VITAL, EXCITING, DYNAMIC, OPTIMISTIC, DELIGHTFUL PEOPLE—NO CHEST BEATERS!'[1]

Parties apart, workwise, his schedule was packed! Often arriving in Delhi on the morning of the opening of a show, he would head directly to the gallery. The following days were crammed with planning the next season with my mother, supervising the printing of the next catalogue,

Alkazi and Roshen, Kuwait, 1983

giving books he had acquired to be bound, seeing to the framing and restoration of older works, meeting artists. Often, he would make a quick day trip to Baroda or Shantiniketan to see the work of some new artists.

* * *

Adjusting her work schedule to allow more time with my father, my mother decided to set up home with him in Kuwait, where they began to spend two to three months each year. This was the place, in the heart of his family, where Roshen felt she was completely his wife, where she did not have to share him with Uma. She would have instinctively known that my father would never take Uma to Kuwait.

In Kuwait, my mother developed strong and loving ties with my father's sisters and began to experience and understand an Arab way of life with its simple yet stately grace and beauty. The holy month of Ramadan, followed by Eid celebrations, was a major annual event, which my mother introduced into our lives in Delhi in a less elaborate form. In Kuwait, she began to wear abayas and was introduced to family and friends as 'Om Feisal' (Mother of Feisal). More than anything else, living with my father in Kuwait allowed my mother to discover a totally unknown side of Ebrahim—his Arab self, one that barely played out when he was in India. Roshen eagerly sought to understand this side of her husband, where a totally different set of values, parameters and behaviour patterns operated. She felt it would help her understand his complex personality better and come to terms with his often baffling decisions and responses.

She noticed that over time Elk discarded western attire altogether in Kuwait and began to dress in *jalabiyas* (long kaftans), complete with the keffiyeh, or head scarf. She noticed that he would unobtrusively slip out of a room at prayer times to offer namaz. He observed the Ramazan fasts. Speaking fluent Arabic, she saw how he conducted himself publicly in Arab society, observing all Arab protocols in his interactions with women. With Arab men, she was amazed to find how family and acquaintances deferred to his age, giving him full love and respect, the youngsters kissing his hands, the older men embracing one another three times. The fact that Ebrahim was Hamed Alkazi's eldest son always won him a respected seat at the table. On one occasion, my father happened to be in Kuwait when an elderly, distant relative passed away. Attending the funeral, my father later told me, 'I was brought by the deceased family to stand at the head of the line of the bereaved family, as hundreds of people filed past, condoling with me. Only then did it strike me that I was the eldest and therefore the head of the Alkazi clan! They all seemed to know me, but I knew none of them! I was so ashamed. I suddenly felt the weight of responsibility I carried as the eldest member of the family.'

In the Arab world, Alkazi was no lauded artist, theatre educationist or art connoisseur. Here, he was the eldest Alkazi who was expected to carry on the family legacy true to the Nejdi code of honour and, most especially carry on his father's unblemished reputation earned through great charitable deeds and honest dealings. In India, he had *grown* roots, *learned* to be an Indian, fought to be accepted. In the Arab world, he was unquestioningly welcomed and respected despite his years of absence in India. In a sense, I suppose my father, during these latter years of his life, was the prodigal son quietly trying to come to terms with his 'other' neglected self.

By now, my mother had maintained a steady correspondence with her sisters-in-law, Noorie and Lulu. Though they knew of my father living with another woman in India, they never directly referred to it but hinted that it was not uncommon for an Arab man to have more than one wife, as long as he treated them both equally. However, 'A man with two wives is like a coolie/donkey!' they chuckled, quoting an Arabic proverb, leaving Roshen to figure out what that meant.

So it was in Kuwait that my mother regained her lost ground and began to bloom once again. It was here that she quietly and purposefully made it a point to build a small, beautiful home for herself and my father where they shared a togetherness that sustained her faith in him. My father, too, began to appreciate her loyalty, devotion and perseverance in holding the family together. My mother encouraged Feisal and me, along with our respective families, to make frequent visits to Kuwait. This consolidated our sense of family.

When we first arrived in Delhi, we were just a small family of four. If the weather was fine, on Sundays, my father would whisk us off for picnic lunches at various historical monuments. If lunch was to be at home, my father would arrive around noon after having visited Chor Bazaar around the Jama Masjid. Often, Feisal and I accompanied him there. Being a regular, vendors would call out to him as they would have kept aside particular issues of art magazines or objects like lamps or old prints that he had asked them to source that could be used as 'props' for his productions. My father would rarely haggle over the price as he was so grateful for the tremendous effort these vendors had taken to procure things especially for him, making him a prized customer!

By the mid-1980s, we had grown as a family. I think with the addition of grandchildren, my parents increasingly realized their seniority and responsibility towards family. Sunday lunches became more elaborate occasions. My mother took great pains to prepare a delicious feast, designing the menu around special Arab dishes that my father enjoyed or the Khoja dishes like ek handi and aab ghosht learnt from Kulsumbai. A cool glass of beer preceded the mouth-watering lunch. The conversation was always scintillating—intelligent discussions pertaining to an art event, a new book, a film or, of course, politics. One could see my father visibly relaxing in such a convivial atmosphere. My mother made it a point to invite a visiting artist or a relative to join us and sitting around the table after the meal, we would nurse mint and cinnamon-flavoured red tea from tiny golden glasses, a la Kuwaiti style, and chat for hours. My father would gradually come into his own. With us as his attentive audience, he played the part of the paterfamilias to the hilt, holding forth with amusing

Manohar Singh, Alkazi and Indrani Rahman at Sohna Farm

anecdotes of his travels or describing brilliant exhibitions he had seen or performances he had witnessed!

* * *

One visit my father never failed to regularly make was to his farm. Leaving at 6.30 a.m. or 7 a.m., he and Uma would head out to Sohna in Haryana and breakfast there. The few acres he had acquired were opposite the farms of publishers Patwant Singh and Raj and Romesh Thapar, and to one side, his immediate neighbour was Sundari Shridharani. On the advice of his architect friend Habib Rahman, he built a small farmhouse consisting of three rooms and an inner courtyard with a garden, while stone sculptures of various deities dotted the otherwise open landscape.

Nature had always held a fascination for Alkazi. Installation of tube wells, painting and repairs, planting of hedges and the harvesting of wheat and vegetables were occupations that my father now, for the first time in his life, began to enjoy immensely. Attired in corduroy outfits, topped by a tartan cap and swirling a neat swagger stick that could be opened to form a perch-like seat that offered him a brief respite when he took a round of the estate, he was transformed into a 'gentleman farmer'.

Having a small parcel of land nestling at the base of the Aravalli Hills, a whole new world seemed to open up for my father. He found it peaceful to be out in the open, away from the hubbub of the city. His body would relax and unwind in the salubrious landscape, echoing with the sound of bird calls. Looking out over the lush green fields, he would often daydream about transforming these few acres into an idyllic abode where artists could live, work and be sustained by nature.

Having left the National School of Drama in 1977 . . . it (the land) gave me the feeling of creativity, gave me the feeling of doing something, which was really productive and worthwhile, and I think it gave me a kind of renewed energy, to get into new perspectives and that perspective was the perspective of art, contemporary Indian art. But without this kind of open space, you can't really do it, because this is what sustains your mind,

your intellect, your spirit, in an extraordinary kind of way . . .
And I think that one can understand the whole business of
Stanislavski taking his actors to the countryside . . . to be in touch
with nature. The same thing happened at Tolstoy Farm . . . where
Gandhi started this whole movement in South Africa . . . It was
associated with a farm—with productivity . . . Yes, the whole
idea of community.[2]

* * *

Surprisingly, in June 1984, Alkazi was invited to collaborate with American composer Philip Glass on his opera, *Satyagraha*. Apparently, on a visit to India in 1973, Glass had been impressed by Alkazi's production of *Danton's Death* at NSD. Based on Gandhi's philosophy, *Satyagraha* was being considered as an Indo–US collaboration to be staged at the Metropolitan Opera in New York as a special event for the festival and Alkazi was invited to direct it.

Back to theatre! And that too, for such a prestigious international production. Alkazi was surprised, shocked and apprehensive. A two-week trip to the US was planned for late July 1984.

> Philip Glass & I hit it off very well, indeed. He seemed very stimulated by my critical but constructive reactions to his opera.
>
> The whole production . . . has to portray the participation of enormous masses in political motion and the withdrawal of the individual with his still centre of meditation from which he acquires the strength of his soul-force. How can the arbitrary helpless individual face up to the overwhelming power of materialist & totalitarian societies. This production should show/demonstrate how one individual DID & therefore how man can.[3]

Alkazi knew he needed to make the most sense to a Western audience. He continued:

> . . . We need to give it an international historical background: Gandhi's methods of non-violent revolution which involved

the mobilization of the poor, illiterate masses set against the totalitarian & violent approach of Western nations: Nazism in Germany; Fascism in Italy; Franco in Spain; Stalinism in Russia. Against this background the rebellion & purposeful examples of individuals like Schweitzer, Pasternak, Mother Teresa. We have to choose such episodes and individuals with which audiences in America, Europe & India can identify, & yet they should not be stale or commonplace through over exposure already . . . against such an international background of events, the relevance of Gandhi would emerge very strongly . . . particularly because of the nuclear holocaust by which it feels threatened.

Alkazi was charged and excited. His proposed treatment contextualizing Gandhi's peaceful strategy against momentous world events enlarged the canvas to a vast civilizational scale.

He returned to Delhi in September 1984, where he apprised Mrs Gandhi of the project. She assured him of all assistance with material from the government's archives. The rushed week was spent absorbing several documentaries on Gandhiji as well as collecting visual documentation.

*　*　*

On his frequent trips to New York since 1983, Alkazi had renewed his ties with Souza. The positive response Souza's work had met with at Oxford MOMA reassured Alkazi that he had not been mistaken in his assessment of the artist's international calibre. It was unfortunate that he had not been recognized in his own country.

> It's a disgrace that Souza, who has played such an important role in projecting the meaningfulness of Indian art abroad, should not be officially recognized just because he doesn't have an Indian passport. It's so petty. If you love your country despite everything, that's a true measure of your patriotism.[4]

It was unfortunate that by living abroad, Souza had often been pigeonholed as being a 'Commonwealth' or 'diaspora' artist. In addition, his idiosyncratic temperament, his alcoholism, his behaviour towards women in particular, his uncensored criticism of institutions and governments were also major factors that impeded his success. Alkazi, however, was more forgiving of Souza's shortcomings, understanding that it was the artist's passion for art and his frustration at not being recognized that drove him to all kinds of excess. Determined to resurrect and install Souza to his rightful place on the Indian and international art scene, Alkazi began to visit Souza's home studio in NYC. He was stunned by the quality of the work. Noting the abysmal conditions in which the artist was living, Alkazi asked if he required assistance. Souza, overwhelmed, asked for a monthly stipend, which Alkazi agreed to.

Unable to stand dirt and disorder, my father, as was his habit, immediately rolled up his sleeves and began to clean and organize Souza's studio apartment himself. Photographing the works, organizing them chronologically, collecting write-ups—the task was enormous as everything was in a shambles. To assist in this massive undertaking, Alkazi also hired Souza's assistant on a separate monthly salary. When in London, Alkazi undertook the same work himself, as substantial material still remained with Souza's first wife, Maria, who resided there.

So it was from 1983 onwards that Alkazi began to invest substantially in Souza, while at the same time planning a major retrospective and a book on him. Souza vacillated between being grateful—'Dear Elk, Thanks for the lolly, (6000 pounds)'[5]—and being overconfident in his own abilities as an artist:

27 October 1984

Thanks to you I am doing some superb paintings. As I wrote to you, I feel now that it is essential to exhibit my paintings not only in India, but in the West, to show how far Modern Art has advanced! My paintings unfold a new world in form and colour. You will see that hung properly in an exhibition hall, my new paintings will dazzle the eyes and minds of people who see them ... I could do with a little more money ... Even to set up a 'studio', the cost of canvas and paint has sky rocketed, has to have an initial expense ...

F.N. Souza's *Portuguese Gentleman*, 1952

In the same letter, Souza penned a kind of prose poem describing himself as:

The Last Of The Red Hot Modernists!

I am the last of the Red Hot Modernists
I am polishing Modern Art,
Refurbishing it. What Vlaminck.
Soutine, Braque, Rouault, Picasso,
Matisse, Buffet, Dubuffet, etc.,
Didn't do, I am doing!
I am painting the conclusion of Modern Art, which
Cezanne, Gauguin and Van Gogh had started.
My conclusion is that Modern Art
Is eclectic with a personal style;
A style so personal, that the
Eclectic is not apparent.
The eclectic, together with style
Clinches aesthetics: Aesthetics is the
Science of Beauty—a very modern concept.

Simultaneous to what I am doing, forging new images, is a literature describing it that is growing in which the paint and words are equally colourful! Even off-colour when needed! You are an artist and a master (after all you have the credentials for it . . . I was present at your graduation from RADA) of the eloquent word, you will be the first to appreciate what's going on: something brand new in Art and Literature which couples aesthetics with a linguistic style, as mine does, are bound to stimulate, entertain, elevate and massage the minds of thinking people who are fortunate to behold this new culture of the mind through words and aesthetics![6]

Three days after Souza's letter to Alkazi, Mrs Gandhi was assassinated.

* * *

As Delhi was engulfed in flames and we in Greater Kailash Part II, our home, we heard about hundreds of Sikhs being butchered, we bolted our doors and sat tight. On about the fourth or fifth day after the event, we stole out under the cover of darkness, managing with great difficulty to get a few airline tickets out of Delhi to Bombay. We were numbed by the real presence of death at our doorsteps, something none of my generation of 'Midnight's Children' had ever experienced.

It had barely been five weeks since Alkazi had met Mrs Gandhi. Shocked as the whole world was, she, for all her faults, was one of the few people whom Alkazi admired. Unable to contain himself, Alkazi provided a kind of personal obituary to her:

> It's the end of an era—and the beginning of another. The end of one specific period of my life as well, because though I was not involved in the political scene & was certainly not part of her immediate circle, I could at all times sense her encouragement & sympathetic response. Of how many politicians & heads of state could it be said that they have a genuine, live interest in the arts, traditional and contemporary, to the extent of being involved with mundane trivialities of management & support? I am grateful for what she did for the arts.[7]

A few days later, Alkazi wrote to Souza:

> My dear Souza,
>
> With the death of Mrs Gandhi, the art scene is going to be pretty bleak from the sales point of view for a pretty long time. First of all, she was genuinely interested in contemporary Indian art, and with her encouragement came official patronage on a substantial scale both in India as well as through exhibitions abroad...
>
> Art follows the course of political power, however distressing that reality may be. In the passing away of Mrs Gandhi, the status of Indian art abroad has also been dealt a severe blow. I am sorry

to sound like a gloomy prognosticator. But there is no escape from reality, and some sensible strategy will have to be worked out for these devious times.

Best wishes,
Alkazi[8]

CHAPTER 43
CICA: A GLOBAL IDENTITY 1985-86

Twenty-four Indian and foreign artists[*] had been invited to share their work and ideas at an international symposium, the 'East–West Visual Arts Encounter', organized by the Goethe Institute in Bombay along with the National Centre for the Performing Arts in early 1985. The 'encounter' was threatening to collapse. Responding to a remark made by Mark Prent, a Canadian artist who observed that he did not know that there was such a thing as 'contemporary' Indian art, an infuriated Souza declared: 'It appears to me that in their ignorance, the white artists have come to Bombay to show the Indians their art, but instead have been confronted by better art than theirs and have become envious...'[1]

Nissim Ezekiel, by this time regarded as one of the most reputed art critics in Bombay, cast an embarrassed glance at Ursula Bickelmann—both were conveners of the seminar. Interrupting Souza, Nissim attempted to maintain a semblance of decorum during the proceedings![2]

'Really Souza! Let's not get personal... There is no need for this kind of...'

'But there is, Nissim! There certainly is! Look here! Let's call a spade a spade! Ernst Fuchs from Austria has been going about telling the Indian artists, "Why are you copying the West? Why are you imitating us?" That is a misinterpretation of modern Indian art. It is not copying the West at all!'

Pochkanawala, the only woman artist present, approached Souza. Using dulcet tones, she hissed between her teeth, 'Francis, *Yeh hamare guests hain!* (They are our guests!) ... *Suno ... aisa nahin bolne ko mangta*

---

[*] Ernst Fuchs, Mark Prent, Peter Nagel, Wolfgang Laib, Peter Kinley, Claude Lagoutte, Robert Marx, Dieter Jung, Henry Leo Schoebel, S.H. Raza, Bikash Bhattacharjee, F.N. Souza, Pilloo Pochkhanawala, Balan Nambiar, G.R. Santosh, Jeram Patel, Manjit Bawa, Prafulla Mohanti, Tyeb Mehta, Gulam Mohammed Sheikh, N.S. Bendre, Sunil Das, Tapan Basu and Bhupen Khakhar.

tumko (You mustn't say such things) . . .' She trailed off, her poor Hindi failing her at this important juncture.

'No Piloo, no! We're all *equal* here', barked Souza, 'There are no guests and hosts . . . We're all *artists*! . . . This kind of bloody condescending, colonial attitude will not be tolerated anymore . . . They are not the ones to pass judgement on our art . . . whether ours can be considered modern or not! . . . Let me share an amusing observation I made. When Fuchs showed us his video, he had *sitar* music on the soundtrack! Fancy that! What it amounts to is that white artists appropriate other cultures, but when others do it, they tell them, "Why are you imitating us?" Get my point?'

Souza was in his element! This event marked his re-entry into the national art scene in India and he took every opportunity to remind his audience that it was Raza and he who were the founders of India's modernist art movement.

Heated arguments erupted in other art forums as well, making it apparent that Indian artists were no longer willing to kowtow to the West. They were asserting their identity. Representing a wide range of artists at Art Heritage, Alkazi reaffirmed this, 'Taken as a whole, the works of Indian artists reflect an astonishingly wide gamut of styles, techniques and pictorial language, confident and original. Grounded in unquestionable artistic skill, Indian artists are aware of worldwide trends, but secure in their own individual identities.'

On another occasion, Alkazi predicted, 'Indian arts will acquire world status soon . . .'[3]

To an extent, this new self-assertion had come in the wake of Indira Gandhi's shy and unassuming pilot son Rajiv Gandhi romping home with a thumping majority in the general election held in December 1984, soon after her assassination. He was able to give the youth of the country hope of a bright future where the economy began to open up to multinational investments.

Economic self-confidence was reflected in the buoyancy of the art market as well, so Souza, for example, was very pleased to find a growing interest in his work during this visit. Pundole Art Gallery immediately offered him a solo, while Dhoomimal Art Gallery bought several of his works, as did the Parsi art collector Jehangir Nicholson.

On hearing reports of what was happening, Alkazi, sitting in New York, was understandably furious, hurt and felt taken advantage of. All along, Alkazi's understanding with Souza had been that he would support the artist as he prepared new works for the forthcoming retrospective that Alkazi was planning. With Souza selling his new work to other gallerists and collectors, he had not only betrayed Alkazi's trust in him but also scuppered his larger plan of making him an international celebrity.

Alkazi said nothing. He simply withheld the next installment of Souza's stipend. This incensed Souza, who, instead of apologizing, lashed out at Alkazi, accusing him of not keeping his word about doing the retrospective. Instead, retrospectives of other artists, such as Somnath Hore and K.G. Subramanyam, were being held at Art Heritage. How long could he wait? There was no end to Souza's diatribes, with him often writing more than one letter a day, each more insistent, vengeful and abusive.[*]

Although such unpleasant incidents left my father wondering whether investing so much of his time and resources and providing emotional support to artists was worth it in the long run, he was also not one to be easily deflected from his main course, which remained building some kind of a lasting legacy for the furtherance of an understanding of art.

* * *

Having spent a considerable amount of time between the UK and the US, my father's ideas were undergoing a change. He began to question the relevance of exclusively supporting and promoting Indian art. That would amount to a limited, 'nationalistic' project that had never been his intention. He recognized that the world had shrunk and that the time was ripe to support *international* art. This would become the core idea around which he decided to build an institution in the US.

Alkazi's choice of the USA arose from the fact that it was a country of immigrants that had been receptive to a changing dynamic between world cultures from the days when it had opened its doors to European refugee artists and immigrants back in the 1920s and 30s, transforming it into the Mecca of the modern art world. Then again, from the Cold War years of

---

[*] He was perhaps the only person I know who spoke to Alkazi without an iota of restraint, often saying that he took such liberties because of their relationship that went back to the 1940s.

the 1950s onwards, the study of Asia's peoples, policies and cultures had become the focus of American political strategy in its attempt to thwart a rising Communist influence. However, from this political strategy was also born a genuine interest in the contemporary arts of India, China and Japan, which led to the emergence of major institutions such as the Asia Society, the Hawaii East–West Institute, the Asian Arts Museum in San Francisco, the Asian Cultural Council, etc., all of which contributed to supporting a new intercultural art's practice. Alkazi wanted his new institution to participate in this international discourse.

An institution builder, Alkazi now began to envisage a space where artists, scholars and laymen could interact and delve deeper into new scholarship. He wanted contemporary art to be shown alongside historical archives! Art needed to be studied, not necessarily bought. Towards this end, Alkazi continued to search for a person who could help materialize the architecture for such an institution and create a module for its functioning.

* * *

It was almost by chance that Alkazi met Dr Bhupendra Karia. Alkazi had been invited to speak on photography at the International Centre for Photography in New York in October 1985 by the institution's co-founders, Cornell Capa and Karia.

Alkazi was impressed by Karia's wide range of experience as a teacher, theorist and curator, as well as a practising photographer. Karia, in turn, was excited to learn of Alkazi's ideas for establishing an institution in NYC. Alkazi detailed how his activities, besides Art Heritage, were focused on improving working conditions for artists as well as creating a market for their work in India and abroad. So far, his programmes included exhibitions, publications, grants to students and artists, the purchase of artworks and the documentation of oral and visual archives. Alkazi now wished for this work to come together within an institutional framework in the US.

Karia asked Alkazi if he would like him to prepare a feasibility report to create such a structured organization to incorporate such diverse activities.

It appeared that Alkazi was finally on his way! Karia was intelligent, practical, invigorating. The fact that he was an Indian, known in India to the arts community, and well respected in American academic circles reassured Alkazi that he was the right choice as a collaborator.

Bhupendra Karia and Alkazi at CICA, 1988

By 7 February 1986, the Centre for International Contemporary Art (CICA) was incorporated as a not-for-profit organization.

The Center for International Contemporary Arts, New York has been conceived for the promotion, development and documentation of contemporary art, providing a dynamic forum for the interaction of contemporary painting, sculpture, ceramics, photography, film, architecture and the traditional crafts. CICA will present gifted but inadequately known artists in venues, national and international, where the work can be assessed, and take its place within the framework of the world art scene.

The Centre will document and preserve materials in all disciplines in an Archives of Contemporary Arts which will be available to serious scholars, professionals and students internationally.

Through Fellowships, Scholarships and Travel Grants, CICA will aid artists, scholars and students. A Publications Program has been planned where CICA hopes to interest other institutions in collaborating on specific projects.

Alkazi and his CICA team were overwhelmed by the cascade of enthusiastic responses from scholars and art institutions. Among them was artist and writer Timothy Hyman, who noted that while nothing like this had happened so far, the project might be too ambitious. Hyman believed that an institution that proposed to look at all art from across the world side by side would inevitably have to evaluate them according to new criteria rather than in light of the well-established canons of western art history.

In his letter to Alkazi, Hyman said:

> What makes the project so valuable to me, is the truly international (i.e., intercontricentral/intercontinental) emphasis. By implication such an institute could break into, subvert and undermine the suffocating pattern established in recent Western Art, but essentially in New York: the endless succession of avant-garde styles, each of them all-powerful at any one time . . . This pattern has become in recent years even more absurd and shallow, more stripped even of any 'progressive' overtones; and their shame, many curators and museum—people throughout the West have been guilty of complicity . . .
>
> What your institute can do—simply by pushing a wider perspective—is to replace this Fashion emphasis by something more lasting. The kinds of manipulation of the art . . . (e.g. by the Saatchi's in Britain, a well-documented CIA falling of American abstraction in the '60s) that have been taking place over the last 20 years, are only possible within a closed system—where people are ignorant of what is going on in India or Africa or Eastern Europe—or else were 'born yesterday'! By finding a wider and less centralized diet, you can be of great help; nothing is more provincial than the 'mainstream'!'

Responses such as Hyman's suddenly allowed one to sense the magnitude of Alkazi's proposition, i.e., of the necessity of re-reading modern art from *multiple* cultural perspectives, not just the single western one that had dominated it to date. Alkazi, in a sense, as an Indian and an Asian, wished to challenge the status quo.

Alkazi's exhibition at the Oxford MOMA in 1982 had asserted the arrival of a modernity in Indian art. But now he was widening that premise to include art from all countries! It appeared that Alkazi was bent on putting this Western modernist genealogy to the acid test of scholarship at CICA, where new international modernities would be discovered, documented, shown and discussed!

Meanwhile, Alkazi's personal collection continued to be documented, as all this material would eventually feed into the CICA Archives, especially the contemporary Indian art documentation that Alkazi planned to eventually publish as an encyclopedia on contemporary Indian art in thirteen volumes.

A much-discussed subject at early CICA board meetings was the choice of its first art exhibition. The success of CICA depended almost exclusively on the impact its first show would make. A proposal by David Elliott and seconded by Karia was to show the avant-garde work of the young Yayoi Kusama, a highly eccentric Japanese woman artist who had left New York to return to her homeland, Japan. Rejected by the avant-garde art world of New York, Kusama remained isolated and unrecognized despite having spent many years in NYC. The young Alexandra Munroe, now heading the Asian section of the Guggenheim Museum, was taken on to research Kusama extensively and produce a well-documented catalogue for the show. The Kusama project was over two years in the making, with Alkazi insistent that it be of the highest curatorial and art historical standard to illustrate how CICA proposed to promote international artists 'whose creativity had not been recognized, nor had they received enlightened support or adequate exposure essential for their own development'.

***

It was now 1986—almost nine years since my father had resigned from NSD. It had taken him all these years to lay down some kind of international foundation for his future work. Now that CICA was finally on its way, my father felt he could breathe more easily.

Another load off his chest was the reconciliation with Souza. Their falling out had been a source of pain and disillusionment for him. Souza was one of his oldest friends—practically a brother! The patch-up was short and sweet, with Souza emotionally confessing that Alkazi was the only person who really understood his art, and he felt so privileged to be 'like one of those great Renaissance artists who were supported by Venetian Doges (Alkazi)! Elk, you inspire me to give of my best! Your money is being well spent!' The childhood friends embraced. Alkazi assured Souza that CICA was indeed preparing to mount a large show of his work in 1991 in NYC. And that showing the work of an Indian artist for its launch would deflect from CICA's international USP.

* * *

Quite unexpectedly, Alkazi received news that he had been awarded the prestigious Kalidas Samman for his contribution to theatre. My father found it rather amusing that the very people who were largely responsible for his ouster from NSD on the grounds that he was too 'western', now seemed to have no qualms in hailing him as the 'doyen of *Hindi/Indian* theatre'. Perhaps Alkazi posed less of a threat now that he was no longer head of NSD, besides which he appeared to have moved away from theatre altogether. However, Alkazi was rather shrewd. He refused to be relegated to some corner and memorialized like some ageing has-been. From now on, he made it his business to be a keen observer, critic and watchdog of the country's cultural policies. Using his independent status as well as his growing international stature, Alkazi became unrelentingly outspoken about the sorry state of cultural patronage in the country. He emphatically asserted that despite not holding any public office, he continued to serve the country, both at home and abroad, through his private initiatives as an individual, as the government appeared to have lost the drive, capacity and vision to develop cultural institutions and raise them to international standards. 'The emphasis in India is all wrong. The official approach of sending exhibitions through embassies and cultural organizations does not work. There are works of remarkable stature in India, but we lack the curatorial premise for setting up exhibitions for which presentation, selection and strategy are essential!' Clarifying his role and the role that an institution like CICA could play in the US, Alkazi said, 'I hope to be a catalyst for the art scene in India, not only for creative art but also for research.'[4]

NSD, too, appeared to be back in the news around this time. Ratan Thiyam had recently been installed as its director. It was noted that

'Students had been agitating to get a permanent director as the institution was floundering (as) NSD Directors had come and gone faster than yo-yos.'[5] Thiyam said he wished 'to restore NSD to its lost glory . . . lost somewhere due to politicking, strikes, inactivity, indifference of teachers, students and foremost of former directors.'[6] Of late, past graduates of the NSD had been complaining that they had still not received their diplomas since Alkazi's departure ten years ago. They now demanded that Thiyam arrange for them to receive their diplomas from the hands of their guru himself.

It was NSD's silver jubilee year. Thiyam approached Alkazi, inviting him to confer the diplomas. Alkazi's initial response was to refuse. Acceptance meant re-engaging with the institution. Thiyam persisted, convincing Alkazi that he was the only person who could assuage the raw feelings of anger and resentment that had built up over the years against the institution. Alkazi ultimately relented, as he could not bring himself to refuse help.

I thought it was unbelievable! Imagine going back to the very same NSD that had rejected him! I was his daughter *and* his student. I had witnessed the ugly scenes of his ouster in 1977, the terrible wrenching pain he had suffered as a result of his resignation. And now I wondered how they would receive him. Would they allow him his dignity, which they had so cruelly snatched away? He was much older now. He would not be able to bounce back as easily, I felt. I anxiously watched the whole situation unfold from the sidelines.

* * *

15 March 1987, Bhawalpur House, morning: I have been at NSD since 8 a.m. Past graduates have been arriving from the evening before, but the bulk arrives now.

> Each arrival is invested with the dramatic . . . As autorickshaws and cabs draw up at the gate of Bhawalpur House and past graduates spill out, they are greeted with great whoops of joy. Notes are exchanged as they are borne triumphantly inside the building, where the atmosphere is near festive—teachers recognize familiar faces with warmth, self-appointed representatives from the present

and past batches go around collecting 'chanda' for Holi, which is around the corner... A telegram has been sent to the magistrate in Bhopal to allow Mr B.V. Karanth, involved in a case of attempted murder, to attend the celebrations and receive the honor to be bestowed on senior faculty members. Mr Karanth is himself a student of the school and has also been its director... Mr Ratan will also be receiving his diploma which he himself will be signing! Others expected include Mr Naseeruddin Shah, Mr Om Puri, and Mr Raj Babbar. The NSD is celebrating its Silver Jubilee Year and a convocation is underway as twelve long years of delay come to a close... Alkazi has travelled all the way from London to deliver the Convocation Address...[7]

15 March 1987, Bhawalpur House, afternoon: Alkazi alights from his car. Two hundred students rush to greet him. Some press people begin to click photographs. Alkazi's face lights up and radiates intense happiness as hands reach out to touch him. 'Sir, you remember me? Sir, let me touch your feet.' Sir is dressed in a grey suit with a mauve shirt and a dark blue grey striped tie. Like a sleek and elegant Pied Piper, he is followed by a phalanx of students down the corridor, where Thiyam and Dr Awasthi

Alkazi with former NSD students, including Naseeruddin Shah and Om Puri, at a reception in his honour in Bombay

await him. Awasthi, still chairperson of the SNA, utters a few words of welcome. Alkazi lights the lamp with studied grace and proceeds to inaugurate a small exhibition of photographs of NSD's past productions. Thanking the director for inviting him, Alkazi moves on to talk about the importance of theatre photographs.

> If you were to take a play, a massive play, for example, like *The Caucasian Chalk Circle*, if you were also to take a play that deals with the overthrow of a government, a play like *Danton's Death*, which is about a revolution, if you were to take a third play like *King Lear*, which is also concerned with revolution, what are the differences in your approach that you're going to deal with in these productions that are going to distinguish one from the other? One worldview of Georg Büchner is completely different from that of Shakespeare, though he was also related to him and one worldview of Bertolt Brecht, who took from Buchner and also happened to take from Shakespeare. It is these various lessons that we have to pick out from photographs because photographs are, after all, our productions, like the drawings of a great artist.[8]

Past and present entwine as students acknowledge that they are in the presence of their guru. They begin to settle down on the floor, drinking in Alkazi's every word. Even the corridor is jam-packed. The older graduates have tears in their eyes as memories flood back of their classes with him.

Jagdamba, the old NSD peon, wipes his eyes and says, '*Pehele jaisa lagta hai. Accha hai, Saheb ghar laut aye.*' (This is just like before. It feels good. Sir has returned home.)

I nod, barely able to hold back my tears.

15 March 1987, Kamani Theatre, evening: The hall is packed. On stage are Ratan Thiyam and the chief guest, Union Resource Minister P.V. Narasimha Rao.

A beaming Rohini and Jaidev Hattangadi, both of the same batch, actor Raj Babbar resplendent in a green silk kurta, Pankaj (*Karamchand*) Kapur, Raghubir Yadav of *Massey Saheb* fame, Alok Nath and Anita Kanwar, unrecognizable as Haveli Ram and Lajoji of *Buniyaad,* all occupy the first few rows, waiting to receive their diplomas.

The moment Alkazi appears on the dais, the whole audience rises. The air is filled with rapturous, never-ending applause—a standing ovation for several minutes. There is nostalgia in abundance, but the irony of the situation is not lost on anyone.

After much requesting from Alkazi for the audience to calm down, they finally comply and he begins his address:

'Standing before you today, I feel like a man who, after a long absence, has returned to his family...'

Once again, the applause rises to a crescendo. Once again, it is quietened.

'But what a large and extended family! I am no longer a chacha, or uncle, as you affectionately call me (laughter), but indeed a grand-uncle (laughter). Some of you have grown to be chachas in your own right and have assumed the shape appropriate to that status.'

Riotous laughter and claps!

'Unlike the men, however, our women graduates have not changed; they are as beautiful and not a day older than they appeared ten years ago!'

Commotion! Whoops of joy!

'Many of you have acquired an army of worshipful fans; a great many of you, as TV stars, have become household names; and I believe that every day scores of newborn babies are being named after you!'

Uncontrolled laughter!

'My sabzi wallah tells me that Pankaj Kapur has been responsible for the steep rise in the price of carrots, and it has been reported that many TV aspirants have taken to chewing that vegetable in the belief that the practice will rub some of Pankaj's talent off on them. I asked Pankaj if this was true and he rudely said to me, "Shut up, Kitty!" So I obediently went and shut Kitty up!'

Students get up and begin to laugh and whistle. Others dance in the aisles. Ushers try to control them...

The chief guest, Narasimha Rao, looks completely baffled by the turn of the evening's events. He was possibly expecting a sedate ceremony.

Alkazi continues to lace his speech with great wit and humour and is repeatedly drowned out by prolonged applause and whistles! Undoubtedly thrilled by the response he is receiving, he repeatedly requests that the audience save their applause for the end as he still has some 'very marvellous things to say.'[9]

Then, abruptly, the tone and tenor of Alkazi's address alters. An underlying sterner, harsher ring becomes evident. He begins to turn the tables.

'The NSD owes more to you, its students, than you owe it, for you yourself have upheld the ideals that the school itself has neglected. The school is a pale shadow of your achievements.'

Turning to face the chief guest, Alkazi squarely hits out hard at the NSD, severely criticizing its declining standards.

'The theatre world has watched with pain as the school has reeled from one disaster to another. It has regressed, going back twenty years.'

Referring to the change from the 'specialization course' he himself had put in place to a so-called 'integrated course', he said an enormous mistake had been made.

'The present syllabus can be taught in three months, not three years. It is one that is not even fit for amateurs!'

Alkazi's bead-like eyes pan across the audience. They are dead silent.

'Is this all we can offer after twenty-five years of existence?' His voice rises.

Pause. He allows this to sink in.

'Can we allow the future of several generations of students to be brought to ruin? Does it not behove all of us—we the past faculty, the present staff, and you the alumni—to do something about it? Change and growth do not mean the mindless dismantling of what has taken decades to come into being.'

Describing the intensive training programme he had put in place, Alkazi moves on to talk of the contribution NSD alumni had made to society.

'Our graduates have changed the very image of the actor in his profession: from a baby-faced, hip-swinging, characterless, mindless, sentimental moron, a mockery of contemporary Indian reality, which he professes to represent, to the image of a serious, thoughtful, questioning, intelligent, sensitive being, tortured by the hypocrisy, the social injustice, the sheer living hell of our present-day situation. Here are feeling and thinking individuals who have not looked upon themselves as fodder for the idiotic commercial mill of escapist fare, but persons who have accepted the responsibility of awakening our nation into consciousness of its grim reality, into respect for the dignity of work, for thoughtful analysis, the sustaining of a conscience that will not be stilled.'

The address took no less than thirty minutes. Alkazi, in those moments, had not allowed his words to be wasted or to fall on deaf ears. The point he made was the need to be accountable to oneself, to society, to the nation. Concluding on a softer, quieter note, he held his audience spellbound till the last word he uttered with directness and simplicity.

'As always, I have been overwhelmed by your love. That little corner in your hearts has been, for me, a token of immortality. I live through every one of you, no matter in what remote region of the world I may be. You know this; you sense it. I share your sorrows. Your happiness sustains me.

'People spend their lives yearning for heaven in their afterlife. For me, your love has been my earthly paradise. Greater joy hath no man than this.

'This love that holds us all so close—can it not move mountains? Let that love unite us all in the case of our beloved NSD.'

The audience went wild as Naseeruddin Shah, Om Puri, Raj Babbar, Pankaj Kapur, Rohini and Jaidev Hattangadi, Anita Kanwar, Alok Nath et al. came on stage to receive their diplomas. Ratan Thiyam himself exited and returned again to touch his guru's feet, genuflecting in a complete *sashtang pranam*! There was practically a riot, as emotions by then had reached fever pitch!

That evening, real life and fiction merged. No one had seen so much laughter and so many tears being shed at the same time. The 1987 NSD convocation turned out to be an incredible homecoming for Alkazi, a family reunion that told him that his legacy was intact.

***

16 March 1987: My father has invited all the students to spend the day at his Sohna farm. Nissar and I go ahead to make arrangements for food, etc., to be catered from lunch through tea.

The weather is perfect, even at noon. It's springtime with beds of flowers blossoming—pansies, petunias, dog flowers and cosmos. Students arrive in buses. Lunch over, they lounge here and there. Some gather around

Alkazi, who is in high spirits and cracking jokes; others, who are meeting after a long time, take leisurely walks across the estate. Manohar Singh, Surekha Sikri, Uttara Baokar and, of course, Marathe, are the eldest, still members of the Repertory Company. They have their own set of admirers huddled around them. After a cup of strong, sweet tea, the sun begins to set behind the Aravalli Hills. Alkazi, apart from the rest, surveys his farm, strewn as it is with actors. For a moment, he imagines how Stanislavski must have felt at his dacha with his band of actors. 'If only we could all live in a place like this as a community, work together, create great productions together!' His reverie is broken by a young girl who shyly says, 'Sir, we must go now . . . it's growing dark.'

Gradually, the golden moments begin to fade. They have to return. 'Sir, we are so thrilled. Sir, we are so blessed. Sir, please direct us in a play.

Alkazi with Manohar Singh, 1996

Sir, we will leave everything and come work with you . . . Sir, when could we meet again? Sir, may I write to you?' Girls weep, 'Sir, please don't give up on us . . . don't forget us.' They climb into the buses that speed away, dissolving into the night.

Kuldeep Kumar, a reporter from the *Sunday Observer*, stays behind, as Alkazi has promised him a long interview. His last key question is:

'Alkazi Saab, yesterday you said, "Can we see our life's work being ruined?" Then why have you kept yourself away from theatre since you left the NSD?'

Alkazi sits back in his wicker chair and, in a tone of resignation, admits defeat.

> Well, to begin with, when I left the NSD, I left it because I felt that an atmosphere had come into the institution that was not at all conducive to creative work. It was an atmosphere of politics, pettiness, and an atmosphere that no longer had any faith in the basic principles or requirements of the institution. A kind of demoralization had set in. I felt that if I continued to be there, I would become involved in the politics and I did not want that to happen. I don't think any artiste would like to get involved in the shabby politics of this kind. After all, an artist is a person who has to go out in the world and prove himself by the quality of his work. That's it. His politics are the quality of his performances, not pulling strings, not the manipulating, not the trips abroad, not the contacts with the higher ups, not the participation in festivals, and so on and so forth . . .
>
> Looking back with hindsight, now I feel sorry I left NSD, I should have been there for another 15 years. I feel a sense of guilt about it . . . but there are certain temperamental qualities . . . I had to save myself . . . I could not afford to lose my sense of hope . . .[10]

My father and I walk Kuldeep to the gate. A small group of loyal acolytes are still sitting on the veranda, chatting with Uma. Manohar springs up, 'Sir, you must rest now; we will leave! It's been an emotion-filled two days . . . You must be tired!'

'Rubbish! Nonsense! Just sit down, Manohar Bhai! Meeting you all never tires me! I'm totally rejuvenated! See? Fresh as a daisy! Come along, Dhingra! Where's that bottle of Scotch I got from duty-free that you have been hiding? Let's crack it open!'

Alkazi with his students, Time and Talents Club Lifetime Achievement Award, Bombay, 1998

CHAPTER 44

THE RISE AND FALL OF CICA
1987-91

With six months at his disposal in India as an NRI now, Alkazi became increasingly visible on the art scene. He prepared a new series of illustrated talks. One was a reworking of an earlier version of *The Waste Land*, recorded in his own voice, which was shown alongside 'The War Drawings of Henry Moore'. Another talk, 'Henry Moore: Sculptor of the Apocalypse', reflected on the artist's sculptural response to the devastating impact of the two world wars, a theme Alkazi had consistently explored in stage productions throughout his career.

However, two other talks, 'Song of Mexican Earth', on the Mexican muralist Diego Rivera, and 'Man of Fire', on José Clemente Orozco, were on an entirely new subject—resistance. A few visits to Mexico had left Alkazi completely in awe of the massive murals of these artists on public buildings depicting the searing history of their country post the Mexican revolution. Developing his talk through historical time, the revolutionary social and political environment, the nationalistic fervour, the workers and peasants urge to stand up to tyranny and take their destiny into their own hands,[1] Alkazi took the audience through the Mayan phase, the Aztec phase, the Spanish conquest and colonial occupation. Visualized through a leftist perspective, these muralists had dedicated their work to the nation, celebrating and giving visibility to the dignity with which the Mexican people had offered resistance.

Not only was Alkazi impressed by the outstanding artistic merit of these public artworks, but it reinforced for him the idea that it was high time that an *alternative* reading of modern art be made, one that went beyond the single Eurocentric reading of art history.

'Till today, there is no substantial study of the works of Rivera and Orozco, even those in Mexico are not on a scale commensurate with

Alkazi with Yayoi Kusama and Bhupendra Karia at the opening of her show at CICA, 1989

the talents of these creative giants. Encyclopedias of contemporary art dismiss them almost in scoffing terms, or with such grudging praise as to be insultingly patronizing.

'The history of contemporary world art has to be *re-written*, and from perspectives other than the stereotyped and hackneyed ones of Paris, London and New York. There are views of the world, attitudes to life and measures of judgement other than those imposed and sacrificed by purveyors of taste in the West. And it is about time we took a fresh look at things, with our own eyes, and had the courage to form, and stand by our own independent judgements. We are politically free, but culturally enslaved. Surely it is time we started to struggle for our cultural emancipation.

'If I sound angry, I think you will find by the end of this session some justification for my anger.'

It was becoming abundantly clear to Alkazi that the evaluation of artworks, artists and art theories was not necessarily objective but controlled by political, social and financial interests as well.

'This is the imbalance I have set out to rectify at CICA,' my father explained to a group of journalists after one of the talks, 'and it is for this reason that I have now made it a point to travel the world and see for myself how many great traditions and artists have been *excluded* from the history and story of art! I have begun to educate myself on the state of modern art in countries as remote and far flung from one another as Bali, Australia, Japan, Holland, Ireland . . . meeting artists, historians, museum directors and curators.'

As he went along, it became more and more clear that what Alkazi was attempting at CICA was indeed unprecedented, bold and ambitious. In practical terms, Alkazi's attempt was to build global communication by bringing to light the full spectrum of information related to worldwide contemporary endeavours in art.

By the time CICA was formally inaugurated with the Kusama retrospective on 27 September 1989, it had collected material on 48,000 artists, with special focus on non-western countries such as the Soviet Union, India and Japan. Among the many reports of CICA's new, unique space, Jill Llyod said,

> The opening for the Centre for Contemporary Arts (CICA) in New York on 27th September will mark an important development in the study of art in our times. The inflationary effects of so much commercial activity around contemporary art in the eighties has left little time for reflection and scholarship. In this sense, the foundation of a non-profit organization to provide an information service on contemporary art, an exhibition program, internships, publications and a reference library in the heart of New York is a welcome and refreshing new departure. CICA will attempt to deconstruct traditional ethnocentric criteria for judging contemporary art and present a global picture.[2]

The Yayoi Kusama show consisted of her collages, reliefs, sculptures, prints, oil on canvas and mixed media works, which were tastefully displayed at the spanking new 10,000-square-foot premises at 724, Fifth Avenue, across from Trump Towers. The catalogue was impressive. No fewer than sixty interviews were conducted by Alexandra Munroe, the guest curator, and writer and researcher Reiko Tomar. Alkazi had been correct in selecting Kusama—she was a woman artist, forgotten and rejected, controversial. Fiercely independent, she was now sixty years old. In normal circumstances, these would have been grounds to reject her, but Alkazi felt that on the contrary, they would act in her favour, as all said and done, her work was brilliant but had gone by unrecognized. The exhibition was hailed as her comeback, which led to the consequent exposure and fame she now enjoys in the US, if not in the world.

Photographs of the event attest to my father's high spirits throughout the evening. Alkazi was absolutely bursting with pride and joy that the institute of his dreams had finally been born!

* * *

Alkazi with Amal at the opening of the Yayoi Kusama show at CICA, 1989

And then it happened. On 2 August 1990, Iraq invaded Kuwait. My parents happened to be there, stranded! They had stopped over in Kuwait on their way back from Europe before heading back to Delhi to start the new season at Art Heritage.

Perhaps it had been too good to be true that my father was finally enjoying the fruits of his labour at CICA. After the successful Kusama show, CICA inaugurated 'Art from Britain', a series of four one-person exhibitions exploring a wide spectrum of the British art scene, aimed at conveying a sense of both the current preoccupations of artists and their antecedents: 'David Olivant: A Goodbye to Grunewald' (February–April 1990) followed by 'Max Vaux: From Pigment to Light' (May–June 1990), 'Michael Kidner: At-tension to the Wave' (July–September 1990) and 'Victor Pasmore: Nature into Art' (November 1990–February 1991).

Sitting in Kuwait with a war raging around them, CICA was furthest from my parents' minds. Three other Alkazi families were residing in the same apartment block as my parents. Luckily, my aunt Lulu was in London, but my aunt Munira and my cousin Laila Alkazi and her children were in Kuwait. Across town, my uncle Sulaiman and his large family were all in town. Everyone's first reaction was shock and disbelief, but this was coupled with the feeling that the crisis would be over in a few days.

Our building was situated on the seafront. My father stationed himself on the veranda for hours, trying to sight enemy ships on the horizon. However, what he did spot a few days later were some young Iraqi soldiers loitering around the building. He immediately withdrew from the veranda, fearing the worst. Those young boys looked inexperienced but were toting machine guns! Fights were breaking out and they were turning aggressive, not allowing residents to leave the building even when the curfew was lifted.

My young cousin Omar, Sulaiman's son, managed to get a travel pass and visit the family in our building with food once a day if he could. He shrewdly befriended the young Iraqi soldiers, bribing them with food and cigarettes so that they would allow him upstairs.

Glued to the radio the whole day, my father found it difficult to tune into the BBC. Of course, trunk calls were out of the question! We, in Delhi, had absolutely no news! Sulaiman was keen that my parents leave Kuwait, as they could perhaps be more useful to the family from outside. Since the Iraqis had taken over the airport and commercial flights were no longer operating, people were constantly planning to escape through other avenues. The options seemed dangerous and were not always successful. Huge sums were being offered to cars, taxis and buses to somehow smuggle people across Kuwait's borders. Everything was on the black market, especially the hiring of transport. Food and petrol were being sold at a premium and everyone was running short of funds. Sulaiman's entire time was spent trying to find ways of getting liquid cash. The banks had been notified not to issue any money. However, a welcome relief to Kuwaitis outside the country was the government's directive to the National Bank of Kuwait to give them a certain amount each week for their living expenses.

In Delhi, we felt helpless. We were in touch with Kusum and Salman Haidar on a daily basis for news of my parents. Salman, a high-ranking bureaucrat in the Ministry of External Affairs, assured us that he was doing his utmost to see that my parents got safe passage. He had alerted the Indian Embassy in Kuwait, informing them that the Alkazis were stranded there.

A full month elapsed before my parents were finally contacted by the Indian Embassy. I.K. Gujral, the Foreign Minister, had gone to Kuwait and was poised to bring back a full posse of Indians stranded there by military aircraft. We were informed that my parents might be on that aircraft.

That night, as I closed my eyes, I suddenly felt as if a blinding white light was shining on me. Opening my eyes, I found that it was pitch dark. I realized then that this was a sign. The light for me represented my parents. I knew at that very instant that my parents were out of danger. The next evening, while watching television, we suddenly spotted my parents on screen. There they were, safe and sound, my father resolutely holding my mother's hand tightly in his own and marching her towards the airport exit, while the TV commentator reported the arrival of the first batch of Indians rescued from Kuwait.

* * *

November 1990, nearly three months since my parents returned from Kuwait. Uma is away in the hills with her family, my father is in Delhi restlessly awaiting news of the Gulf War's developments. He carries around his small portable transistor radio everywhere—to Art Heritage, in the car, to the farm—anxiously wanting to know the latest news. Everything remains in a state of flux, with some of his sisters and nieces in London and his brother Sulaiman now in Bahrain with his son Hamed, trying to get him into a school. Rosh is in Delhi getting ready for her cataract surgery, while Uma is not well, having been diagnosed with diabetes. On top of all this, my father remains unclear about how to handle his CICA affairs in the US.

Today, he has invited some of his closest friends, Ghazi Sultan, Salman Haidar and Kusum, to the farm. Since his return, he has had time to attend to the farm regularly. It appears well-kempt. He has built a new room and is getting the flooring done as well as the paving outside.

Alkazi with Kusum and Salman Haider at the Sohna Farm, Haryana, 1990

A car sweeps in through the gate. Switching off the radio, he ushers the three guests onto the veranda. They settle down to a cup of steaming coffee, with Diwan Singh in attendance. Ghazi has just arrived in Delhi, managing to bring his old mother out of Kuwait to safety.

'My God, Ghazi! How in heaven's name did you manage that?' my father asks incredulously.

'As God is my witness, Ebrahim, it was a harrowing experience! It literally took us five days to get from Kuwait to Amman . . . but we were indeed lucky, as we left by the very last convoy of buses.'

'Really? And how did your mother manage?' asks Kusum. 'She is so frail . . .'

'I have no idea. She seemed to have summoned strength from somewhere and was able to endure the inhuman conditions in those terrible refugee camps . . .'

There is a pause as they take it all in.

'But conditions in Kuwait are hardly better', Ghazi continues, 'The torture inflicted on people there and the miserable atmosphere . . .'

'Please give me news of my family. Any news at all. Your sister Najat and my niece Laila are part of the resistance I hear! I hope they are being careful,' my father said.

'Najat and careful?! She just shoots her mouth off and Laila is no better!'

'Najat is bringing women together to offer resistance,' says Kusum, 'I've been getting dribbles of news from here and there.'

'Yes, we're proud of them, Kusum, but Najat should not put herself out there so openly.'

'She can't help herself,' says Kusum, who was in school in Bombay with Najat, 'Najat is a firebrand.'

'Is Munira safe?'

'She seems okay!'

'Alhamdulillah! Any news about my flat?' my father inquires, adding, 'I locked it and gave the keys to Laila to keep an eye on it.'

There is a long silence. Then Ghazi looks up.

'I thought you already knew, Ebrahim. They barged into your flat, pushed Laila aside. She put up resistance . . . they tore her clothes and abused her. Suddenly, their officer arrived. She was saved, but they raided the entire flat. All paintings and books were gutted. Everything! I'm sorry to be the harbinger of this terrible news!'

My father went deathly silent.

'Thank you for telling me. I had no idea,' he added a moment later.

'It's hardly any better here, Ghazi. My accountant tells me that one can no longer rely on the Government of India extending the 150-day limit for NRIs despite these extraordinary circumstances. He feels that the present dispensation is weak and the situation will continue like this for the next few years until the elections.'

Not one to dwell ceaselessly on depressing subjects, Alkazi sprang up.

'Come! Let me show you some of our exciting acquisitions!'

Taking out a Solander box, Alkazi flipped open the lid and very carefully began to show them one old etching at a time from his growing collection.

It had been a quiet, insightful afternoon with Ghazi, Salman and Kusum. Their conversation had allowed Alkazi to clear his mind. He had gleaned quite a lot from them about present conditions in both India and Kuwait, as well as some perspective on what the immediate future held in store for him in the US. The coming months brought more news of greater financial losses. This was enough for my father to decide on his next steps. Sitting down at his desk on 7 February 1991, Alkazi penned the following lines to the trustees at CICA:

> The latest situation vis-a-vis my family is as follows: The large building on the sea front, in which two of my sisters and I had three separate apartments, has been razed to the ground by allied bombing. This means that, apart from losing our homes and all our belongings, our entire life's work has been destroyed: 200 paintings of my sister Munira, by all accounts, the most distinguished artist in the Arab world; the creative writings of my sister Lulu, a highly respected Islamic scholar; my entire library, a collection of over 100 paintings and more than 15,000 slides on art, and all my writings.
>
> My brother Sulaiman, the sole agent in Kuwait for Honda cars, has lost 900 cars and hundreds of motorcycles, apart from having his offices, showrooms and warehouses destroyed. He is now in

London with part of his family, and together we have estimated that we have 33 family members outside Kuwait to provide for, and another 24 stranded in Kuwait.

As head of the family, I have to assume the responsibility of providing for them.[3]

With that, Alkazi stepped away from CICA. The process of winding down its affairs took more than a year. Honouring his commitments to exhibitions and publications until 1992, my father made it a point to make substantive gifts of CICA's books, data and equipment to other important institutions in the US that could use them, among them the MET, the Smithsonian and the Asia Society. No doubt the closing down of CICA was very painful for my father, but as he said, 'life repays one back in inscrutable ways!'

One can only imagine the heights Alkazi could have scaled with CICA had fate—in the form of the Gulf War and the post-9/11 Islamophobia in the US that swept so mercilessly across his path—not prevented him from reaching the pinnacle of his endeavours.

CHAPTER 45
CIVILIZATIONAL CHRONICLES
1991-99

After the closure of the Centre for International Contemporary Art, Alkazi waited to assess the post-Gulf War response to Muslims in the US before establishing a new venture. Biding his time, he converted part of his homes in London and New York City into workspaces, still believing that his collection of photographs could best be cared for abroad, where the latest technology in archiving, not to mention professional scholars and restorers, were readily available.

Alkazi's next priority was to conceive of an effective way to promote and disseminate his photography collection. While CICA had been established for the study of the visual arts as a whole, Alkazi now felt it necessary to create an independent institution dedicated to the exclusive study of photography. Over the years, he had started to believe in the significance of photography as 'the independent new art form of the twentieth century':

> And I felt it was important now with *this great art form of the twentieth century,* which had become universally pervasive and uses a language that is universally understood by all mankind. Hence, the extraordinary success of that exhibition 'The Family of Man', which did more for the ideas of peace and universal brotherhood than any act by the United Nations or UNESCO.[1]

Positioning photography as *the* new visual medium of the twentieth century, Alkazi asserted that 'photography has replaced painting' in many respects. Although he admired photography's ability to precisely represent reality, Alkazi saw the photograph more in the nature of a *document* of history.

Every photograph, no matter what its quality, is a historical document. It is a fleeting moment frozen in time. But it lives on by virtue of the signs it provides, the messages it sends out regarding the person, the time, the place, the action. Each photograph is as full of clues as a police shot taken at the scene of a crime.[2]

The photographs of nineteenth-century India held special significance for him. He observed that the British had systematically and formally documented every aspect of Indian life and culture using the camera. This made their photographic coverage a vast archive of the colonial period and an invaluable resource of India's complex heritage that would be of use to all manner of professionals, be they historians, sociologists, economists, architects, anthropologists, archaeologists, art historians or cultural historians. The fact that India's national institutions did not have the foresight to preserve these priceless treasures prompted Alkazi to undertake their acquisition himself.

One of the great tragedies was the fact that about twelve or thirteen years ago (1991), the firm of Bourne & Shepherd,[*] which had been set up by Samuel Bourne in 1863, and which had then been sold to the Indians at the time of Partition, went up in flames and that meant about a *130 years of Indian history was reduced to ashes* . . . and I felt a deep, deep sense of loss there, and I came across some of these images through book fairs, through dealers and at auctions.[3]

Alkazi made it his personal mission then to acquire substantial holdings of important albums and simultaneously obtain supporting archival material in the form of books, maps, journals, diaries, letters, journals, newspapers, government records, biographies, memoirs of Indian rulers, British officials and civilians, along with travelogues and postcards. Giving his collection a generic title, 'The Alkazi Collection of Photography' (ACP), Alkazi was determined that it be rivalled by none.

* * *

---

[*] Bourne & Shepherd was not only the oldest photographic studio in India but the oldest running photographic studio with branches all over the world. It finally shut down in 2016.

By now, my father was in his seventies and suffered intense bouts of remorse. 'My actions and behaviour in many instances were reprehensible,' he would moan. 'I was so ill-tempered! So ill-mannered! Such an insufferable grouch!' What he especially regretted was the manner in which he had walked out of the Theatre Group, the Theatre Unit and finally, his resignation from the National School of Drama. Though he felt completely justified in leaving these institutions back then, as he grew older, more mellow and more circumspect, he sought ways to make amends, at times re-engaging with those he was estranged from or by acknowledging the contribution of even his most severe critics. These occasions were often played out in full public view and helped restore a sense of equilibrium to the theatre community, which, by now, had venerated him as the 'Father of Indian Theatre'.

An emotional reconciliation between Alkazi and the NSD had already taken place during the convocation in 1989. Now, we were taken aback when my father accepted the invitation to direct three plays[*] for the NSD Repertory Company as part of their silver jubilee celebrations.

Tick-tock, tick-tock, Alkazi's heels hit the floor at a brisk pace as he walks down the corridor of the NSD Repertory Company premises.[4] Ironically, it has been exactly fourteen years since Alkazi, like King Rama of the epic Ramayana, returned from vanvas. Despite the salt and pepper beard, there is a distinct spring in his step. He sports a no-nonsense expression as he enters Studio 1, a theatre that he himself designed and built twenty-five years ago. Placing his diary and pen at perfect right angles to the tabletop and without preliminaries, he barks out to those assembled in the auditorium, 'Okay, let's get down to business! *Din ke Andhere Mein.*'[†]

The actors scramble to their positions, while the haughty-looking Zohra Segal, whom Alkazi has specially invited to play the title role of Bernarda/Qudsia as a guest actress, takes her place among them.

---

[*] The three plays are Girish Karnad's *Rakta Kalyan*, Shakespeare's *Julius Caesar* and Federico García Lorca's *The House of Bernarda Alba / Din ke Andhere Mein.*

[†] By now, Repertory Chief Manohar Singh, along with Surekha Sikri, Uttara Baokar, G.S. Marathe, Pankaj Kapur, K.K. Raina and Raghubir Yadav had resigned and migrated to Mumbai in search of better prospects in films and television. This time around, Alkazi showed much enthusiasm for training newcomers like Seema Biswas, Swaroopa Ghosh and Alka.

Alkazi's return to theatre becomes an ideal opportunity for Nissar and myself to film him at work. Midway through this task, I sense that it is near impossible to document such a rich and varied life. 'What will we actually achieve?' I ask. 'There is literally no archival footage available of your father directing. This opportunity cannot be missed,' insists Nissar, who has grown close to my father over the years. They share an unspoken bond of mutual respect and affection, yet neither oversteps the bounds of the familial relationship, each maintaining a certain formality in their exchanges. My father's unwavering trust in his son-in-law has arisen from Nissar's fierce sense of loyalty, not just towards me but towards all members of the family, a trait that reassures my father that he is dependable.

The camera is on Alkazi as he instructs Seema Biswas (Martirio) in a difficult sequence, where Martirio is sexually aroused by the pounding, sensual music played by villagers as they pass under her window, while at the same time attempting to suppress an orgasm. In Alkazi's demonstration of the sequence, he never allows his performance to become literal, keeping it teetering suggestively on the edge. By now, a penetrating, voyeuristic silence has descended over the theatre. We are transfixed as a seventy-year-old male actor renders the sexual arousal of a young woman. It is unbelievable how Alkazi's histrionic abilities have not diminished despite long years of not having stepped on the boards.

These days, my mother, too, is at her buoyant best, overjoyed that my father is back at the theatre with three plays for her to costume. After the rehearsal at Rabindra Bhawan, my parents cross the Mandi House Circle and, with equal elan, they enter another sanctuary, Art Heritage. There is a sense of liberation and ease as they float between these two worlds of theatre and art.

**

In response to Alkazi's three productions, aspiring young actors urged him to return to teaching, believing in his ability to mould raw talent into successful theatre or film careers. Unable to ignore their persuasiveness, Alkazi established a small, unpretentious private school of drama, The Living Theatre, in 1991, where he offered a production-oriented course to a maximum of twenty-five students.

Of the eleven productions he mounted for Living Theatre between 1991–96, three stood out as significant: In the *Oresteia*, a Greek trilogy comprising *Agamemnon*, *The Libation Bearers* and *Eumenides*, Alkazi examined the destruction of an entire lineage, the House of Atreus, by individuals consumed by greed, lust and power. In Mahesh Elkunchwar's trilogy *Wada Chirebandi*, the chronicles of an aristocratic Maharashtrian family across three generations revealed the disintegration of an entire class who were unable to withstand the rapid onslaught of urbanization upon a countryside. *The Royal Hunt of the Sun* described the destruction of the indigenous Inca civilization by Spanish colonizers, who plundered Peru's gold and converted the people to Christianity.

Alkazi's choice of plays at this mature stage of his career shows a vastly expanded canvas on which even larger swathes of history are investigated. His interest now extends beyond the personal fate of historical individuals like Tughluq and Sultan Razia to include entire societies, nay civilizations, in the throes of momentous transformations.

Rehearsal of *The Orestia*, dir. E. Alkazi, Living Theatre, New Delhi, 1995

Alkazi's return to active theatre in these latter years brought his distinguished theatre career to a dignified, fitting close rather than the hurriedly aborted one that had occurred at the time of his resignation from NSD in 1977.

* * *

In most instances, Alkazi was the kind of man who achieved what he had set out to do. However, his attempts to mount a large show on Souza eluded him for one reason or another. In Alkazi's estimation, Souza was one of the greatest artists of the twentieth century, comparable to names such as Pablo Picasso and Francis Bacon. In the Indian context, he believed that Souza's importance lay in the fact that he had 'resolved the dilemma of style as no other modern Indian painter had done so far'.[5]

Unsuccessful in exhibiting Souza internationally, Alkazi resolved to mount a Souza show in Delhi. Startling, bold and controversial, the show Alkazi curated in November 1996 foregrounded Souza's Catholic upbringing as the essential impulse that drove his work.

> Souza's works, despite all his protestations and statements to the contrary, are soaked in his Catholicism. An obsession with the idea of 'Original Sin', a deep sense of guilt at being driven by physical desires and sexual excesses, repentance through mortification of the flesh—all these pervade his works, particularly the provocatively erotic ones. He sees EVIL as an implacable phenomenon that hangs like a dark cloud over our lives.[6]

Alkazi brought alive sixty works in an impressive, experiential installation of church-like surroundings at the Arpana Art Gallery in New Delhi. As critic Sunil Sethi described it:

> Dotting the exhibition space with wooden Goan crucifixes, carved altar pieces and images of Christ in his mother's lap, a massive red carpet ran like an aisle down the centre of the gallery space, as in a church. In this way, Alkazi set the stage for the representation of an entirely new Francis Newton Souza whose works were deeply rooted in his Goan ethos.[7]

F.N. Souza: A Retrospective, Art Heritage, Arpana Art Gallery, New Delhi, 1996

After being walked through the exhibition by Alkazi, Sethi left the venue with a strong sense that

> the lives of Souza and Alkazi, two tempestuous titans, have been intertwined since their early youth, and now in their early seventies, their conversation has not yet ended . . . The show also says something about a singular obsession, of how madly, truly, deeply a collector can feel about one artist, and over a fifty-year friendship with estrangements and rapprochements, become, if not the keeper of the painter's soul, at least his spiritual alter ego.

* * *

Despite their advancing years, the 1990s surprisingly became one of the most active phases of my parents' life in art. Their overarching aim was to focus on *consolidating, sharing* and *disseminating* their knowledge of art with wider and wider audiences.

Opening up their collections of paintings, drawings, prints and sculpture in two shows—'Masterpieces from the Alkazi Collection, Part I & II' (1995 and 2003)—served to contextualize trends in post-Independence

The Alkazi Collection

A collection is not a haphazard conglomeration of art objects accumulated over the years, with no clear purpose or larger view in mind. A collection is a revealing reflection of the taste and discrimination of the collector and of his aesthetic sensibility. In many ways, a collection implies a distinctive, idiosyncratic view of what constitutes "quality" in art, fortified, hopefully, by a sound knowledge and understanding of art history.

One acquires art works to satisfy an inner need that goes beyond acquisitiveness. Works of art should form an integral part of the collector's life. They should give him the same sustained joy, stimulation and solace that one discovers in a soul-companion. They are sentient objects to be contemplated and communed with. They should widen one's horizon, stir one's deepest emotions, and, through the values and attitudes enshrined in the work, give one a sense of upliftment and release.

We have had the privilege of being closely associated with the art movement in Bombay in the forties, and have enjoyed intimate and lasting friendship with artists of that generation in India, and abroad.

In Delhi, since the early sixties, Mrs Roshen Alkazi has run one art gallery after another with conspicuous success, patiently and steadfastly rousing the general public to an appreciation of and respect for contemporary Indian art.

In the course of more than thirty years she has discovered and fostered the talents of generations of artists, most of them then totally unknown, who are now names to reckon with in the art world.

In addition, scholarships, travel grants and stipends on a one or two-year basis have been provided to a large number of promising artists, and their works have been shown on a regular, continuing basis at Art Heritage.

Cover: F.N. Souza: *The Host*

From *Masterworks of the Alkazi Collection*, exhibition leaflet, Shridharani Gallery, New Delhi, 2004

ment. Such seeds are to be found in the works of M.F. Husain, and K.G. Subramanyan, among others. A recent exhibition served the purpose of a brief introduction to the Collection. The series of shows to follow will strive to share with viewers the quality, range and depth of works so as to be of use to the serious scholar and lover of art.

E. Alkazi

Somnath Hore: *Bird*

F.N. Souza: *Goan Peasants*

From *Masterworks of the Alkazi Collection*

Indian modernity. Defining his overall criteria for selecting works for his collection, Alkazi wrote in the modest leaflet:

> A collection is not a haphazard conglomeration of art objects accumulated over the years, with no clear purpose or larger view in mind ... One acquires artworks to satisfy an inner need that goes beyond acquisitiveness ... Artworks are sentient objects to be contemplated and communed with. They should widen one's horizon, stir one's deepest emotions and, through the values and attitudes enshrined in the work, give one a sense of upliftment and release ...
>
> One is interested not in acquiring works by 'fashionable' artists, but rather in the serious, often lonely, quest of artists who shun the limelight, reject the seductions of the marketplace and pursue their vocation with compelling passion.[8]

During these prolific years, Alkazi also reached out to larger audiences through a six-part television series titled *Indian Art and Modernism* (1995–96),[9] with two episodes providing the art historical background, while the other four episodes were devoted to Rabindranath Tagore, Amrita Sher-Gil, M.F. Husain and F.N. Souza. As anchor of the series, Alkazi introduced each artist as representative of his or her own specific political, social and cultural environment. While analysing their key works, he articulated each artist's development of a unique pictorial language that ultimately contributed to the creation of a complex 'Indian modernity'.

Alkazi's intention was for the series to serve as an introduction to contemporary arts practice. His focus was to assist the lay viewer to appreciate and learn to 'read' pictorial language. As always, he eschewed the intellectual jargon that he felt much of the new writing on art relied on in favour of a simple, direct script.

* * *

While Art Heritage continued with its regular programme of exhibitions and talks, it became apparent that my father's attention was increasingly focused on his photography collection. The year after he launched ACP in Delhi in 1998 through a major exhibition called *Shadows at Sunset*, he launched Sepia International Inc. in New York. By this time, he was somewhat reassured that the political climate in the US was more amenable to Muslims.

Acquiring an old, ramshackle 4000-square-foot property in Chelsea—the centre of the photography district of New York—Alkazi, along with young Indian designer–architect Nandini Phookan, transformed it into an elegant, state-of-the-art institution. Sepia International Inc. was envisaged as both a photography archive for students and scholars as well as a commercial gallery. 'Re Orientations: Photography from South Asia 1845–1920' was Sepia's maiden exhibition, which showcased works from Alkazi's nineteenth-century collection, the curatorial thrust being to revisit colonialism in India, with the aim of educating a western audience.

As Sepia presented exhibitions of brilliant Indian photographers such as Raghubir Singh, Ketaki Sheth, Dayanita Singh, Vivan Sundaram and Richard Bartholomew, with a no less prestigious roster of South Asian and Latin American photographers such as Kenro Izu, Tomako Sawada, Edward Grazda and Marissa Roth, among others, it made a tremendous impact in the few years of its existence, filling American audiences in with India's past and present through exhibitions films, talks and seminars. However, once again, Alkazi's success was short-lived, as barely two years later, in 2001, the World Trade Center was attacked. Though Alkazi dug

Alkazi and F.N. Souza, during the shooting of the TV series *Indian Art and Modernism*, 1995–96

Entrance to Sepia International Inc., New York

in his heels for some more time, his visits to the US became less frequent until Sepia finally shut its doors in 2009.

* * *

My mother's failing health from 2000 onwards was also one of the reasons for my father not wanting to be away in the US for long stretches. Uma, too, kept indifferent health and had become rather weak and frail.

In my mother's case, we soon realized that it was no longer possible to care for her at home. For four long years, she lived in a small, quiet nursing home with all of us in round-the-clock attendance. Sensing that her stay at the nursing home would be indefinite, my mother requested permission to bring in a few things from home.

Kishori Kaul's paintings were the first to arrive. Her glorious impressionistic renditions of flowers instantly flooded the room with soft, incandescent hues. Potted plants for the veranda were followed by a microwave oven that allowed us to make tea for my mother's visitors. Enthused by the makeover, I suggested that we also change the faded curtains and upholstery to her liking. The nurses looked on with genuine glee as Roshen transformed the drab, sterile hospital room into a cosy, comfortable little home for us. Her brother Alyque, when in Delhi, dropped in to have lunch with my mother, who ordered her maid to cook his favourite gosht ka salan and bring it to the nursing home. Her sister, Candy, came to Delhi for long stretches to spend time with her. Watching the two of them chat away relaxed the underlying tension of her illness that preoccupied all of us.

It was touching and wonderful to see my father, full of love and good humour, attend to her every need. Sitting by her bedside every evening for a couple of hours after he returned from Art Heritage, he kept Rosh abreast of all activities at the gallery, which helped distract her from her health. During these long years, he diligently helped her complete her second book, *Medieval Indian Costumes*, but most importantly (and as usual), their discussions concerned the future—of the gallery and the photography collection.

Right from the late 1990s, my father's main concern was to find a safe home for his valuable photography archive. Finally opting for Delhi, he established the Alkazi Foundation for the Arts (AFA) in 2006. AFA was primarily a research archive that would continue research on his collection as well as serve as a rich repository of related material for use by visiting scholars. The Alkazi Foundation's programme included disseminating—through exhibitions and publications, both in India and abroad—aspects of India's colonial history that coincided with the birth of modernism. As was his passion, my father continued to build a handpicked library of his dreams.

***

In a document on a 1990–91 notepad inscribed in his firm, neat hand, Alkazi expressed his thoughts regarding the relevance of his photographic collection to the personal journey of his life. He wrote:

> The two fields that I have explored as part of my professional career have been those of theatre and the fine arts. These are important areas that deal with the history and the present state of mankind. Societies do not exist in a vacuum. History, archaeology,

anthropology, philosophy and psychology are indispensable and integral parts of that scrutiny. The camera has played an important role in depicting those states and interpreting them in visual terms.

Once we have given ourselves that brief as a student of the history of mankind, our field of investigation both deepens and expands with the development of technology that science reached, beyond the verbal into the visual...

What sustained me was the depth and persistence of my passion; the wide range of my visual exploration; a ceaseless and unrequited quest for knowledge and for insight into human behavior; and an awareness of the inter-relatedness of the arts on one hand and of the arts and sciences on the other.

The work I did in the theatre was my discipline and my training ground. The depth, insight and sensitivity that I brought to my work were integral parts of my aesthetic, humanistic and spiritual discipline.

Such quests are love quests...

Who am I? An attempt by man to discover himself tracing back his physical, psychological and philosophical development begins with his effort to recognize himself in terms of his own past/by tracing his destiny backward in time. Hence his curiosity about his antecedents... In my own case, it was a matter of tracing my family antecedents: who my parents were and, step by step, generation by generation, to trace my lineage backwards to my first photographically documented Arab ancestors.

Every effort is made to complete the picture, item by item, as in a pictorial puzzle/(jig-saw) piece by piece.

I have attempted to unravel myself to myself, to begin with, through my work in the theatre as an actor and as director.

I find myself frequently as an enigma unto myself: dense, inscrutable, incomprehensible and I cannot go on, hanging up there in the intangible void...

Roshen Alkazi, 1974

Courtesy: Pablo Bartholomew

CHAPTER 46
I DO NOT KNOW, LORD, ARE YOU THERE?
2007

27 September 2007. My mother passed away in the early hours of the day. Time dissipated into a blur for all of us. Feisal and his wife Radhika, Nissar and our children, Zuleikha and Rahaab, our daughter-in-law Nandita, our devoted housekeeper Agnes, my mother's driver, Najeeb, and our office staff Debashree Haldar and Alek Nayak—all of us, with the exception of my father, furiously bustled around making the requisite arrangements.

My father receded into some dark space, away from the hubbub of organizing the bathing of the body, finding a white shawl in which to wrap her, getting Najeeb to sit up the whole night and say the namaz in the room where her body lay, the incessant conversations about who's coming, who's going, airline tickets, Alyque's stay at a hotel, etc. Nissar, Feisal and Rahaab divided duties—death certificates, cremation arrangements, organizing an ambulance, etc.—while Zuleikha's children, Zanskaar and Zaarya, wore dazed expressions as this was their first experience of a family member's funeral. I recollect existing in a kind of blurry no man's land between being ever alert to practicalities and breaking into uncontrollable sobs that overtook me, racking my body.

***

30 September 2007. Roshen's memorial service. The Triveni auditorium is packed to capacity. Silence. Followed by more silence, except for the music wafting in—a sombre, reflective piece selected by my father. The aroma of incense is overpowering. On the stage, a large photograph of my mother shows her in deep contemplation, looking inward, reflective and beautiful. A massive arrangement of white flowers surrounds her portrait.

I look around for Feisal. I am concerned about him. He was always so close to Mum.

My father and I take our places in the front row. The music fades out. My father's recorded voice is heard on the speakers. He quietly informs us that he has decided not to address the gathering in person as he is afraid of breaking down. Charged with emotion, his voice trembles slightly as he proceeds to say a few words about my mother—her loyalty and steadfastness towards him, her acute aesthetic sensibilities and her great compassion for others.

One by one, Alyque Padamsee, Geeta Kapur, Krishan Khanna and Feisal narrate their experiences with Roshen. The room is filled with images and impressions of her. I am exhausted. I shut my eyes and zone out for a while. As a finale, my father's recorded voice returns to read my mother's poems. His voice quivers. One senses his struggle to go through with it, yet each word is enunciated slowly, quietly and clearly, foregrounding the austere beauty of Roshen's thoughts.

'I will now read out four poems by Roshen,' he says.

> I have lived on the fringe of the leaf of your love
> Sensing the sap that runs through its veins
> All the green far away, as I hide on the rim
> Holding fast to this mast, as I sway in the wind
> There is rain all around and the shelter is slim
> But so light is the raft and the journey so long
> That I long for the day when I rest on the ground

Silence.

The next poem is 'I Do Not Know, Lord, Are You There?'

My father continues reading until all four poems are done. The poems are exquisite and speak of her readiness to embrace death.

It is clear that the memorial service has been cathartic for all. I glance at my father. He looks tired, his suit crumpled. He gets up. People crowd in on him to offer condolences. I watch him wander away towards the entrance alone and before we notice his absence, he has vanished. The last thing I overhear him say to someone is, 'It was the power of art that sustained Roshen and me every day of our lives.'

Alkazi at Cop Shiva's show My Life Is My Message, Art Heritage, 2013

Courtesy: Rama Veeresh Babu

CHAPTER 47
DISAPPEARANCE
2016

My father stopped speaking entirely. Before that, his exchanges were limited to 'My darling!' Every time he saw me, he called out 'My daaarling!' most lovingly, throwing his arms wide open to envelop me in his warm embrace.

Soon enough, these words eluded him too. He would sit in a chair with a book in his lap, totally absorbed and quite content. He would not be reading the book as much as examining the visuals that embedded themselves on the retina of his eye; from there, they probably lodged themselves in some corner of his consciousness. From time to time, he would pass his fingers over the pages in order to 'feel' the images as if they were palpable. Greedily absorbing them, Alkazi's gaze would then shift to real life—the ordinary life around him. Alkazi had trained his eyes over the years to shift directly from art to life and vice versa, never feeling the necessity of words to help him see the relationship of one to the other. This total absorption in the visual experience was one he probably carried over from theatre, a field that required the acute observation and study of human behaviour.

Over the years of his silence, we began to sense as well as accept his evaporation into an ether-like state of insubstantiality. Watching this process of his disappearance, one began to understand that perhaps the secret of life lay in slowly moving towards losing one's identity and becoming transparent and invisible. One was reminded of the words spoken so passionately by him about the artist's need to distance himself.

An artist belongs to no political party, an artist belongs to no religious ideology, an artist has to distance himself from each one of these in order to see each one of these objectively... and finally, he has to release himself, and distance himself from himself.[1]

* * *

Sitting in silence with him under the shade of a tree on the lawns surrounding Humayun's Tomb, while I enjoy the flowers, the refreshing air and watch the squirrels frisk around, Jomol, my father's nurse, pours him a cup of steaming sweet tea and then dunks his favourite Nice biscuits in the tea to feed him. His eyes sparkle momentarily as he nods, thanking her for her efforts. Sitting out in nature, my father appears content. It is peaceful to sit with him. A soft breeze rustles the leaves of the tree. I lean back and close my eyes as some of his thoughts play in my mind.

I like to work in the open air, under the arching sky, at historical sites, preferably ruins, pitted and scarred by time, because they convey immediately the fundamental idea of the fragility and discontinuity of human existence; because the visual 'weight' of the past provides a salutary 'mindscape'—one of the essential elements in drama—and enables us to see the pitiful human events on the stage as minute particles of a vast, relentless cosmos.

The director's text book is his own life and the lives of those around him—in his home, with his family, in the streets among fellow human beings, in his motherland and in the world as a whole. That life in the raw is, after all, the stuff of literature, drama and cinema—of the cataclysmic calamities that continue to tear our world apart, as they have done for thousands of years. Our book of reference is that cruel, crafty, pitiless world that is our inheritance today. It is our duty and moral responsibility to study that horrifying history dispassionately, but with a passion for the truth, with humility and with a profound sense of moral responsibility, and to ask ourselves seriously: What is the legacy that **we** shall leave behind?[2]

BORN ON 18 OCTOBER 1925, EBRAHIM ALKAZI PASSED AWAY ON 4 AUGUST 2020. HOWEVER, HIS LEGACY LIVES ON THROUGH THE WORK AT THE INSTITUTIONS HE FOUNDED—WORK THAT CONTINUES TO THIS DAY.

Portrait of the Alkazi and Allana families; (standing, L–R): Radhika Alkazi, Nissar Allana, Nandita Allana, Arman Alkazi, Zaarya Chaudhuri, Deepika Allana, Tariq Allana; (seated, L–R): Zuleikha Chaudhuri, Amal Allana, Simran Allana, E. Alkazi, Cyrus Allana, Feisal Alkazi, Rahaab Allana, 2016

Opening Lines: Ebrahim Alkazi Paintings and Drawings, Art Heritage, New Delhi, 2019

Courtesy: AH and AFA

Drawn from Light: Early Photography and the Indian Sub-continent, IGNCA, New Delhi, in collaboration with the Alkazi Foundation for the Arts, 2014

Courtesy: AFA

Seeking a Poetry of the Real: The Political Works of K.G. Subramanyan, Art Heritage, New Delhi, 2017

Spectatorship and Scenography in the Archives, Shridharani Gallery, 2023 ATA and ACP

PECTATORSHIP AND CENOGRAPHY
IN THE ARCHIVES

The Alkazi Collection of Photography

INDIA ART FAIR PARALLEL

Courtesy: ATA and ACP

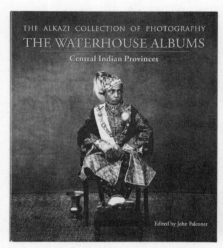 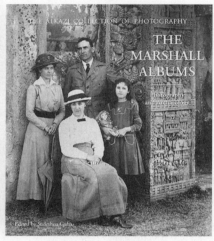  

Publications of Alkazi Collection of Photography, 2006–23

Courtesy: ACP

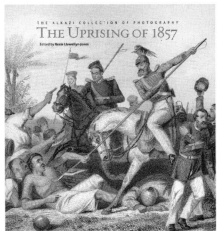
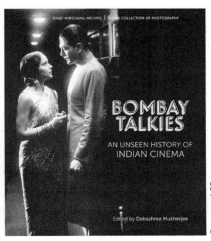

Publications of Alkazi Collection of Photography, 2006–23

ACKNOWLEDGEMENTS

Work on this book began in 2013. The one person who never failed to remind me to get this book done was my dear friend Bindu Batra. With her nudging and nagging she never let me lose sight of an unfinished promise to myself. So thank you, Bindu!

Over the last ten years I have travelled to Mumbai as well as to Kuwait, New York and London, and in each of these places where my father lived and worked, I have formally and informally spoken and/or interviewed a cross-section of people who knew him well. More often than not they provided information and insights on him that were revealing. There is no way that I can include the names of all those who have, in multiple ways, contributed towards the creation of this tapestry I have attempted to weave of my father's life. So to both those named and unnamed, I offer my thanks.

From India: Alyque Padamsee, Anupam Sud, Ayesha Sayani, Cedric and Rohini Santos, D.G. Nadkarni, Debashree Haldar, Feisal Alkazi, Gerson da Cuhna, Gieve Patel, Gulam Sheikh, Jai Zharotia, Joy Michael, Krishen Khanna, Khorshed Ezekiel, Kishori Kaul, Kusum Haidar, Manohar Singh, Minakshi Raja, Naseeruddin Shah, Naveen Kishore, Nissim Ezekiel, Pheroza Godrej, Pratibha Agarwal, Ranjeet Sabiki, Ranjit Hoskote, Roobina Karode, Roshen Alkazi, Samik Bandhopadhyaya, Salman Haidar, Shriram Lagoo, S.K. Mishra, Sudha Shivpuri, Sundari Shridharani, Surekha Sikri, Vijay Kashyap, Vijaya Mehta and Uttara Baokar.

From abroad: Alaknanda Duriaud (née Samarth), Anand Bhatia, Aruna Sultan, Candy Bhatia, Ghazi Sultan, Laila Alkazi, Lulu Alkazi, Manjari Sihare, Munira Alkazi, Richard Schechner, Salwa Alkazi, Sulaiman Alkazi, Tara Sabharwal, Vibhuti Patel and Yohan Jefferies.

Special thanks to Ritu Menon, who peer-reviewed this book, offering valuable suggestions. Thanks are also due to artist Shivlal Saroha, who gifted drawings of Alkazi to him on special occasions. These were of Alkazi rehearsing. They have been used as the beautiful end papers in this book.

For the jacket cover we used Idris Ahmed's image of Alkazi, which captures both his strength and vulnerability. Many thanks.

I am grateful to Sucharita Apte, my first assistant, who helped collate research material on my father in 1999. My current assistant, Savita Valecha, has, since 2013, been helping in all aspects of the research and production of the book. Her sheer dedication to the project is unparalleled.

From the Alkazi Foundation for the Arts and Alkazi Theatre Archives, thanks are due to Shrinjita Biswas, Ganesh Prasad and Vijay Kumar.

My children, too, helped in no small measure. Tariq provided heavy 'tech' support, day or night, across punishing time zones, with my computer deciding to quit on a regular basis; and Rahaab, with his experience of publishing, offered sound professional advice. Zuleikha was always around to soothe my anxieties, providing me with a much-needed morale boost!

Without the tremendous support of Nissar, my husband, this book would not have been possible. We have always collaborated on all projects, and this has been no exception. A good listener, Nissar has offered pertinent advice and insightful suggestions. For his unwavering commitment and patience, no amount of words can suffice.

CREDITS

There have been several institutions and individuals who have been instrumental in facilitating my research for this publication. I would like to thank them for their interest and generosity in sharing material, both written and photographic, for this book.

Institutions
Art Heritage, New Delhi
Dartington Hall Trust Archives, UK
Indian Council of World Affairs, New Delhi
Indira Gandhi National Centre for the Arts, New Delhi
Lalit Kala Akademi, New Delhi
National School of Drama (NSD), New Delhi
Natya Shodh Sansthan, Kolkata
Prime Ministers' Museum and Library, New Delhi
Royal Academy of Dramatic Art (RADA), UK
Sangeet Natak Akademi, New Delhi

Image credits
Alkazi Collection of Art (ACA)
Alkazi Collection of Photography (ACP)
Alkazi Foundation for the Arts (AFP)
Alkazi Personal Archives (APA)
Alkazi Theatre Archives (ATA)
Cedric Santos
Edward Gordon Craig Estate
Gauri Gill
Idris Ahmed
Jogen Chowdhury
Mehta Family Archives
Mitter Bedi Estate
National School of Drama, New Delhi
Nadira and Raj Babbar
Omar Khan
Pablo Bartholomew
Ram Rahman
Rama Veeresh Babu
Shivlal Saroha
Institute of Contemporary Arts (ICA)
Uma Anand
Yohan Jefferies

NOTES

PART ONE
CHAPTER 1: ESCAPE TO ANOTHER WORLD
1 Lulu Alkazi in an interview with the author, Kuwait, 2000.
2 Ibid.

CHAPTER 2: GOD SAVE THE KING!
1 Lulu Alkazi in a letter to the author, NYC, 1999.
2 E. Alkazi in an interview with the author, NYC, 1999.
3 Ibid.
4 Ibid.
5 Ibid.

CHAPTER 4: THEATRICAL PURSUITS
1 E. Alkazi in an interview with the author, NYC, 1999.
2 Ibid.
3 Father Duhr, 'Obituary for Sultan Padamsee', 1946.
4 Ibid.
5 Cedric Santos in an interview with the author, Mumbai, 2018.
6 Deryck Jefferies, biographical pamphlet for personal circulation.

CHAPTER 7: PASSING FROM TIME INTO ETERNITY
1 Prakash, G., *Mumbai Fables*, Harper Collins, 2011.
2 Cedric Santos in an interview with the author, Mumbai, 2018.

CHAPTER 8: THE HOUSE OF THE FOOLISH VIRGIN
1 Alkazi, E., *Hindustan Times*, 2007.

CHAPTER 9: TO BE OR NOT TO BE
1 Candy Bhatia in an interview with the author, USA, 2018.

2   E. Alkazi in a letter to Roshen Alkazi, New Delhi, 17 June 1963.
3   Dogramaci, Burcu, and Lee, Rachel, 'Refugee Artists, Architects and Intellectuals Beyond Europe in the 1930s and 1940s: Experiences of Exile in Istanbul and Bombay', *Architecture Beyond Europe*, ABE Journal, 14–15, 2019.
4   Ibid.
5   Rao, R. Raja, *Nissim Ezekiel: The Authorized Biography*, Viking, 2000, p. 68.

CHAPTER 10: BOMBAY DANCES WITH DEATH
1   E. Alkazi in an interview with the author, NYC, 1999.
2   Ibid.
3   Prakash, Gyan, *Mumbai Fables*, Harper Collins, 2011, pp. 142, 147–48.
4   Roshen Alkazi in an interview with the author, 2000.
5   E. Alkazi in an interview with the author, NYC, 1999.
6   Rao, R. Raja, *Nissim Ezekiel: The Authorized Biography*, Viking, 2000, p. 187.
7   E. Alkazi in an interview with the author, NYC, 1999.
8   Lulu Alkazi in an interview with the author, Kuwait, 2017.

PART TWO
CHAPTER 11: THE PARIS OF PICASSO AND THE ENGLAND OF MOORE AND SUTHERLAND BECKONS
1   F.N. Souza in a letter to Roshen Alkazi, London, 18 November 1948.
2   E. Alkazi in a letter to Nissim Ezekiel, Red Sea, 1 October 1948.
3   E. Alkazi in a letter to Roshen Alkazi, London, 18 October 1948.
4   E. Alkazi in a letter to Nissim Ezekiel, Red Sea, 1 October 1948.
5   E. Alkazi in an interview with Samik Bandyopadhyay, Natya Shodh Sansthan, Kolkata, 15 March 1988.
6   E. Alkazi in a letter to Nissim Ezekiel, Red Sea, 1 October 1948.
7   E. Alkazi in an interview with the author, NYC, 1999.
8   E. Alkazi in a letter to Roshen Alkazi, Red Sea, 1 October 1948.
9   *Alkazi Speaks*, E. Alkazi in an interview with Reeta Sondhi, *Enact*, January–March 1981, No. 169–171, NSD Issue I, Paul Press, Delhi.
10 E. Alkazi in a letter to Roshen Alkazi, Red Sea, 1 October 1948.
11 *Alkazi Speaks*, E. Alkazi in an interview with Reeta Sondhi, *Enact*, January–March 1981, No. 169–171, NSD Issue I, Paul Press, Delhi.
12 Basil Alkazi in a letter to Feisal Alkazi, 2021.

CHAPTER 12: 38, LANSDOWNE CRESCENT

1. E. Alkazi in an interview with the author, NYC, 1999.
2. E. Alkazi in a letter to Roshen Alkazi, London, 18 October 1948.
3. Ibid.
4. Ibid.
5. E. Alkazi in an interview with Samik Bandyopadhyay, Natya Shodh Sansthan, Kolkata, 15 March 1988.
6. E. Alkazi in a letter to Roshen Alkazi, London, 1 November 1948.
7. E. Alkazi in a letter to Roshen Alkazi, London, 23 October 1948.
8. E. Alkazi in a letter to Roshen Alkazi, London, 1 November 1948.

CHAPTER 13: 40,000 YEARS OF MODERN ART

1. E. Alkazi in a television interview with Karan Thapar, *Face to Face*, BBC, 15 May 2002.
2. Rao, R. Raja, *Nissim Ezekiel: The Authorized Biography*, Viking, 2000, p. 70.
3. Ibid.
4. F.N. Souza in a letter to Roshen Alkazi, 18 November 1949.
5. *Alkazi Speaks*, E. Alkazi in an interview with Reeta Sondhi, *Enact*, January–March 1981, No. 169–171, NSD Issue I, Paul Press, Delhi.
6. Paraphrased from Souza's letters in Vajpeyi, Ashok, ed., *Geysers: Letters Between Sayed Haider Raza & His Artist-Friends*, Vadehra Art Gallery, 2013, p. 21.
7. F.N. Souza exhibition catalogue, Gallery One, London, 1961.
8. F.N. Souza in a letter to Roshen Alkazi, 18 November 1949.
9. Ibid.

CHAPTER 14: THE ANATOMY OF DRAMA

1. E. Alkazi in an interview with Samik Bandyopadhyay, Natya Shodh Sansthan, Kolkata, 15 March 1988.
2. 'Ebrahim Alkazi', *Journal of South Asian Literature*, Vol. 10, No. 2/4, THEATRE IN INDIA (Winter, Spring, Summer 1975), pp. 289–325.
3. E. Alkazi in an interview with Samik Bandyopadhyay, Natya Shodh Sansthan, Kolkata, 15 March 1988.
4. Ibid.
5. *Alkazi Speaks*, E. Alkazi in an interview with Reeta Sondhi, *Enact*, January–March 1981, No. 169–171, NSD Issue I, Paul Press, Delhi.
6. Roshen Alkazi in an interview with Pratibha Agarwal, Natya Shodh Sansthan, Kolkata, 21 September 1990.

CHAPTER 15: POETRY IN PICTORIAL FORM

1. Suzuki, Sarah, in Wye, Deborah, *Artists and Prints: Masterworks from the Museum of Modern Art*, Museum of Modern Art, 2004, p. 106.
2. RADA archives, London.
3. Jacobs, Stephen, *Framing Pictures*, Edinburgh University Press, 2012.
4. Alyque Padamsee in an interview with the author, Mumbai, 2011.
5. *Alkazi Speaks*, E. Alkazi in an interview with Reeta Sondhi, *Enact*, January–March 1981, No. 169–171, NSD Issue I, Pauls Press, Delhi.
6. Ibid.
7. Saint-Denis, Michael, *Theatre: The Rediscovery of Style and Other Writings*, Routledge, 2009.
8. Ebrahim Alkazi in an interview with the author, NYC, 1999.
9. Browne, E. Martin, *Two in One*, Cambridge University Press, 1981, p. 56.

CHAPTER 16: A MEETING OF WORLD CULTURES AND AU REVOIR

1. E. Alkazi in an interview with the author, NYC, 1999.
2. Segal, Zohra, *Stages: The Art and Adventures*, Kali for Women, 1997, pp. 80–81.
3. E. Alkazi in an interview with the author, NYC, 1999.
4. E. Alkazi interviewed by Ahmad Omair, *Ebrahim Alkazi: My Native Place*, typed interview found among his personal papers, (republished in Background Colour, Outlook Web Desk, February 2022).
5. Ibid.
6. Ibid.
7. Dartington Hall Trust Archive.
8. Alkazi made it a point to support Dartington Hall with an endowment, years later when he was able. This was not only repayment for their financial help, when he needed it, but also for the remarkable work they did.

PART THREE
CHAPTER 17: 'SOCIETY NEEDS BUILDERS—NOT ONLY OF BRIDGES AND BUILDINGS, BUT OF IDEAS AND INSTITUTIONS'

1. Leyden, R.V., radio broadcast in *Bombay Diary*, AIR Bombay, 23 April 1951.
2. Postmortem after the performance of *Ghosts*. E. Alkazi addresses TG members and cast, January 1954.
3. Alkazi, E., 'Are We Too Serious?', *Theatre Group Bulletin*, June 1953, Vol. 1., No. 6.
4. Ibid.

5   E. Alkazi in an interview with the author, NYC, 1999.
6   Alkazi, E., 'The Need to Build', *Theatre Group Bulletin*, May 1953, Vol. 1., No. 5.
7   Alkazi, E., 'The Bulletin', *Theatre Group Bulletin*, December 1953–January 1954, First Anniversary Number.

CHAPTER 18: 'LIFE QUICKENS INTO ART AND IN TURN ENRICHES LIFE

1   E. Alkazi's quote from address to Theatre Group members in 1953.
2   A paraphrasing of Alkazi's essay 'Murder in the Cathedral: An Interpretation and an Approach', *Theatre Group Bulletin*, January 1956.
3   E. Alkazi in an interview with the author, NYC, 1999.
4   Roshen Alkazi in an interview with the author, August 2000.
5   Alyque Padamsee in an interview with the author, Mumbai, 2011.
6   Details of Charles Petras culled from Bernstein, Lina, 'The Great Little Lady of the Bombay Art World', *Magda Nachman: An Artist in Exile*, Academic Studies Press, 2020.
7   Rao, R. Raja, *Nissim Ezekiel: The Authorized Biography*, Viking, 2000, p. 95.
8   E. Alkazi's dialogues paraphrased from *Theatre Group Bulletin*, Editorial, December 1953–January 1954.
9   E. Alkazi's ideas paraphrased from various *Theatre Group Bulletin* editorials.
10 'Murder in the Cathedral: An Interpretation and an Approach to Its Production', *Theatre Group Bulletin*, January 1953. Alkazi made it a habit, especially in the early years, to write essays in the TGB to guide and train audiences in the new experimental means adopted by directors.
11 Rao, R. Raja, *Nissim Ezekiel: The Authorized Biography*, Viking, 2000, p. 98.

CHAPTER 19: HEADING FOR A SPLIT

1   Candy Bhatia in an interview with the author, USA, 2018.
2   *Theater Group Bulletin*, April 1953, Vol. 4.
3   Alkazi, E., 'News and Notes', *Theatre Group Bulletin*, October 1953, Vol. 1, No. 10.
4   Alkazi, E., 'The Need to Build', *Theatre Group Bulletin*, May 1953, Vol. 1, No. 5. substance of meeting and new committee discussed.
5   Alkazi, E., 'On Attending Lectures', *Theatre Group Bulletin*, April 1953, Vol. 1, No. 4.
6   Alyque Padamsee in an interview with the author, Mumbai, 2011.

CHAPTER 20: LULL BEFORE THE STORM

1. Alyque Padamsee in an interview with the author, Mumbai, 2011.
2. E. Alkazi interviewed by Ahmad Omair, *Ebrahim Alkazi: My Native Place*, typed interview found among his personal papers (republished in Background Colour, Outlook Web Desk, February 2022).
3. Grasskamp, Walter, *The Book on the Floor: André Malraux and the Imaginary Museum*, translated by Fiona Elliot, Los Angeles, California, Getty Research Institute, 2016.
4. Singh, Devika., 'Ebrahim Alkazi and Exhibition Making: Revisiting the Post-Independence Art Scene', in *Ebrahim Alkazi: Directing Art*, Mapin Publishing, 2016.
5. Alkazi, E., 'The Progressive Artist's Group Exhibition: An Evasion of Responsibility', *Theatre Group Bulletin*, March 1954, Vol. 2, No. 3.
6. Candy Bhatia in an interview with the author, USA, 2019.
7. Alyque Padamsee in an interview with the author, Mumbai, 2011.

CHAPTER 21: THE BREAK-UP

1. Text paraphrased from 'Why We Have Resigned', *TUB*, October 1954, Vol. 2, No.10. Also, responses of TG members and Alkazis's outburst recounted to the author in an interview with Alyque Padamsee, Mumbai 2011.

PART FOUR
CHAPTER 22: THEATRE AS A WAY OF LIFE

1. Abbas, K.A., 'Communism and I', *I Am Not an Island: An Experiment in Autobiography*, Vikas Publishing House, 1977.
2. Excerpt from E. Alkazi's, 'Training of the Actor', The First Drama Seminar (III), 1956, Sangeet Natak (Journal), Vol. XXXVIII, No. 4, 2004.
3. Ibid.

CHAPTER 23: HOSTING SPENDER

1. Spender, Stephen, 'Dylan Thomas', in *New Collected Poems by Stephen Spender*, Faber & Faber, 1953.
2. 'Spender at the Unit', *Theatre Unit Bulletin*, December 1954, Vol. 2, No. 12.
3. 'Poetry Reading', *Theatre Unit Bulletin*, January 1953.
4. Zecchini, Laetitia, *What Filters through the Curtain*, Vol. 22 No. 2, Routledge, 2020.

5   The Theatre Unit's First Annual Report, *Theatre Unit Bulletin*, May 1956, Vol. 4, No. 5.
6   Mehta, Vijaya, 'My Two Mentors', *Zimma*, Rajhans Prakashan, 2012, translation of passage into English by Sucharita Apte.
7   The Theatre Unit's First Annual Report, *Theatre Unit Bulletin*, May 1956, Vol. 4, No. 5.

CHAPTER 24: THE SCHOOL OF DRAMATIC ARTS: MODERNITY AND PROFESSIONALISM ON STAGE

1   Gokhale, Shanta., *The Scenes We Made: An Oral History of Experimental Theatre in Mumbai*, Speaking Tiger, 2016, p. 28.
2   Mehta, Vijaya, 'My Two Mentors', *Zimma*, Rajhans Prakashan, 2012, translation of passage into English by Sucharita Apte.
3   E. Alkazi in a letter to Roshen, Bombay, 21 January 1958.
4   Nerlekar, Anjali, *Bombay Modern: Arun Kolatkar and Bilingual Literary Culture*, Speaking Tiger, 2017.
5   Mehta, Vijaya, 'My Two Mentors', *Zimma*, Rajhans Prakashan, 2012, translation of passage into English by Sucharita Apte.
6   Bhownagary, Freny, 'Theatre Unit's Season of Plays' *Theatre Unit Bulletin*, January 1956, Vol. IV, No. 14, No. 1.
7   Alkazi, E., 'The Physician in Spite of Himself: An Experiment in the Use of Masks', *Theatre Unit Bulletin*, March 1954, Vol. 2 No. 3.
8   Ibid.
9   Alaknanda Duriaud (Née Samarth) in a letter to the author, 2016.
10 Gokhale, Shanta, ed., *The Scenes We Made: An Oral History of Experimental Theatre in Mumbai*, Speaking Tiger, 2016, p. 12.
11 The Theatre Unit's First Annual Report, *Theatre Unit Bulletin*, May 1956, Vol. 4, No. 5.

CHAPTER 25: THE THEATRIC UNIVERSE OF POST-INDEPENDENCE INDIA

1   All speeches at this seminar are verbatim and have been taken from the First Drama Seminar, 1956, Issues I–IV, Vol. XXXVIII, No. 1, 2, 3 & 4, Sangeet Natak Akademi, 2004.
2   Gerson da Cunha, 'The Nurturing Dictator', in *Icons: Men and Women Who Shaped Today's India*, ed. Anil Dharkar, Roli Books, 2008.

3   Chattopadhyay, Kamaladevi, *Inner Recesses Outer Spaces: Memoirs*, Niyogi Books, 2014, p. 341.
4   Alkazi, E., *Theatre Unit Bulletin*, June 1956, Vol. 4, No. 6.
5   Dharwadker, Aparna Bhargava, *Theatres of Independence: Drama, Theory, and Urban Performance in India Since 1947*, Oxford University Press, 2005, p. 37.
6   Canning, Charlotte, 'Anticipating Globalization: Rosamond Gilder and the International Theatre Institute', in *Staging International Feminisms: Studies in International Performance*, ed. Elaine Aston and Sue-Ellen Case, Palgrave–MacMillan, 2007, pp. 113–120.
7   Author's note: All the words in bold have been highlighted by me. As I am aware of my father's speech patterns, having both studied theatre under him and being his daughter, besides having heard him speak in public, I have tried to capture how he spoke and held the attention of the audience.

CHAPTER 26: MADRAS MOTHER: THE NEED FOR ROOTS

1   Roshen Alkazi in an interview with the author, August 2000.
2   Ibid.
3   Ibid.
4   E. Alkazi in a letter to Roshen Alkazi, Bombay, 2 July 1957.
5   Ibid.
6   E. Elkazi in a letter to Roshen Alkazi, Bombay, 25 July 1957.
7   E. Alkazi in a letter to Roshen Alkazi, Bombay, January 1958.
8   Anand, Uma, and Anand, Ketan, 'The Lone Crusader', in *Chetan Anand: The Poetics of Film*, Himalaya Films, 2007, p. 73.
9   Alkazi, E., 'Hedda Gabler in the Press', *Theatre Unit Bulletin*, July 1958, Vol. 6, No. 7.
10 Alkazi, E., 'Hedda Gabler in the Press', *Theatre Unit Bulletin*, July 1958, Vol. 6, No. 7, mentions that the press conference and the controversy had been reported in Mouj.
11 The author in a letter to Roshen Alkazi, Bombay, 31 December 1958.
12 Roshen Alkazi in a letter to the author, Madras, 6 January 1959.
13 Roshen Alkazi in a letter to E. Alkazi, Madras, 23 January 1959.
14 Ibid.

CHAPTER 27: ALKAZI'S WOMEN: AGENTS OF CHANGE

1   Alkazi, Roshen, *Seventeen Poems 1961–65*, Writers Workshop, 1965.
2   Alkazi, E., 'The Poetic Image', *Theatre Unit Bulletin*, August 1956, Vol. 4, No. 8.
3   Ibid.

4   Alkazi, E., 'Strindberg's Lady Julie, Notes for a Prospective Production', *Theatre Unit Bulletin*, August 1959, Vol. 7, No. 7.
5   Ibid.
6   Karnad, Girish, 'Theatre in India', *Daedalus*, Vol. 118, No. 4; *Another India*, Fall, 1989, pp. 330–52, published by the MIT Press on behalf of American Academy of Arts & Sciences (JSTOR).
7   Gieve Patel in an interview with the author, Mumbai, 2018.
8   Alkazi, E., 'Strindberg's Lady Julie, Notes for a Prospective Production', *Theatre Unit Bulletin*, August 1959, Vol. VII, No. 7.
9   Gieve Patel in an interview with the author, Mumbai, 2018.

CHAPTER 28: DIFFICULT DECISIONS

1   Charles Elson in a letter to E. Alkazi, 12 December 1960.
2   *Alkazi Speaks*, an interview with Reeta Sondhi, *Enact*, January–March 1981, No. 169–171, NSD Issue I, Pauls Press, Delhi.
3   E. Alkazi in an interview with the author, NYC, 1999.
4   Mehta, Vijaya, *Zimma*, Rajhans Prakashan, 2012. The establishing of small drama schools in Bombay is mentioned by the author.
5   E. Alkazi's speech on being awarded the Time and Talents Club Lifetime Achievement Award, Bombay, 1998.
6   E. Alkazi interviewed by Amit Sanyal found among his personal papers.
7   E. Alkazi in an interview with Samik Bandyopadhyay, Natya Shodh Sansthan, Kolkata, 15 March 1988.
8   E. Alkazi in an interview with the author, NYC, 1999.
9   E. Alkazi in a letter to Roshen, Amal and Feisal Alkazi, 3 August 1961.
10 Gerson da Cunha, 'The Nurturing Dictator', in *Icons: Men and Women Who Shaped Today's India*, ed. Anil Dharkar, Roli Books, 2008, p. 95.
11 Cedric Santos in an interview with the author, Mumbai, 2018.

PART FIVE

CHAPTER 30: AASHAD: PUTTING HINDI THEATRE ON THE MAP

1   Paranjpye, Sai, *Patchwork Quilt: A Collage of My Creative Life*, HarperCollins, 2020, p. 41.
2   E. Alkazi in an interview with the author, NYC, 1999.
3   *Alkazi Speaks*, interview with Reeta Sondhi, *Enact*, January–March 1981, No. 169–171, NSD Issue I, Pauls Press, Delhi.

4   For all information regarding E. Alkazi's arrival at NSD, please refer to his interview with the author in NYC, 1999, and speech on receiving the Delhi Government's Lifetime Achievement Award in 2009.
5   Ghosh, Avik, E. Alkazi interview, *Enact*, August 1969.
6   Husain, Ashfaque, 'A Cameo', *Enact*, No. 169–71, 1981.
7   E. Alkazi in an interview with the author, NYC, 1999.
8   Ibid.
9   Kumar, Kuldeep, E. Alkazi interview, *Sunday Observer*, 22 March 1987.
10 E. Alkazi in an interview with the author, NYC, 1999.
11 Ibid.
12 Speech by Alkazi on receiving the Delhi Government's Lifetime Achievement Award in 2009, and interview with the author, NYC, 1999.

CHAPTER 31: ANDHA YUG

1   *Imprint*, 1962.
2   Alkazi, E., 'Directing Andha Yug', *Enact*, 4–5, 1978.
3   Alkazi, E., 'Style in Theatre: Notes on Andha Yug and King Lear', *SNA Journal*, 1965.
4   Roshen Alkazi in an interview with Pratibha Agarwal, Natya Shodh Sansthan, Kolkata, 21 September 1990.
5   Alkazi, E., 'Style in Theatre: Notes on Andha Yug and King Lear', *SNA Journal*, 1965.
6   Ibid.
7   Sontakke, Kamlakar, 'E. Alkazi: A Dynamic Complexity', *Enact*, No. 169, 170, 171, 1981, Pauls Press, New Delhi.
8   Incident recollected by Alkazi at the illustrated talk when received the Lifetime Achievement Award conferred on him by the Delhi Government in 2009.

CHAPTER 32: THE METAMORPHOSIS OF DELHI: THE INDIA TRILOGY

1   *Alkazi Speaks*, interview with Reeta Sondhi, *Enact*, January–March 1981, No. 169–171, NSD, Issue I, Pauls Press, Delhi.
2   E. Alkazi's speech while receiving the Lifetime Achievement Award conferred by the Delhi government, 2009.
3   *Hori* brochure, National School of Drama, New Delhi, 1964.
4   Ibid.
5   Fabri, Charles, 'The Two Alkazis', *Design*, 1965.

6   E. Alkazi in an interview to the author, NYC, 1999.
7   For more material on US visit are found in E. Alkazi's personal letters to the family between March–April 1964.
8   E. Alkazi in an interview with the author, NYC, 1999.
9   E. Alkazi in a letter to Roshen Alkazi, 17 June 1963.
10 Roshen Alkazi in an interview with Pratibha Agarwal, Natya Shodh Sansthan, Kolkata, 21 September 1990.

CHAPTER 33: THE WAR CYCLE

1   Alkazi, E., Bertolt Brecht, personal papers of Alkazi, undated, probably written between 1966–1970s.
2   E. Alkazi in an interview, *Journal of South Asian Literature*, Vol. 10, No. 2/4, 1975.
3   Alkazi, E., 'Bertolt Brecht', personal papers of Alkazi, undated, probably written between 1966–1970s.
4   Alkazi, E., 'Reflections on German Theatre', *SNA Journal*, October 1966.
5   E. Alkazi in a letter to Roshen Alkazi, Germany, 9 May 1966.
6   'The Trojan Women', *Thought*, 3 September 1966.
7   E. Alkazi in an interview, *Journal of South Asian Literature*, Vol. 10, No. 2/4, 1975.
8   Nath, Rajinder, 'Paraphrasing the Superfluous', *Thought*, 8 October 1966.

CHAPTER 34: THE EAST–WEST THEATRE SEMINAR

1   'Fine Programme Presented: Reading of Eliot's Poem', *Times of India*, 14 November 1965.
2   Bandyopadhyay, Samik, 'A Tribute to Ebrahim Alkazi', Seagull Foundation for the Arts, 19 August 2020.
3   Interview with E. Alkazi, found among his papers, around 1971.
4   Nachiketa, 'Room "H": Noah's Ark of India', *Thought*, 5 November 1966.

CHAPTER 35: NEW NARRATIVE STRATEGIES: BRECHT AND FOLK THEATRE

1   Alkazi, Roshen, 'With the Theatre to the People', *Citizen*, 22 March 1968.
2   Mee, Erin, *The Theatre of Roots: Redirecting the Modern Indian Stage*, Seagull Books, 2008, p. 80.
3   Exhibition catalogue of Badal Sircar, *The Third Theatre: A Photographic Exhibition of his Work*, National School of Drama, 2009.

CHAPTER 36: REACHING OUT

1. Alkazi, E., 'A Theatre for the 5000-Year-Ago Woman: A Soliloquy', *Educational Theatre Journal*, Vol. 20, No. 2, 1968, pp. 335–39, JSTOR.
2. Prakash, Gyan, *Emergency Chronicles: Indira Gandhi and Democracy's Turning Point*, Penguin, 2018.
3. *Alkazi Speaks*, interview with Reeta Sondhi, *Enact*, January–March 1981, No. 169–171, NSD Issue I, Pauls Press, Delhi.
4. *Tughlaq*, Brochure for European Tour, NSD, 1982.
5. Ibid.
6. E. Alkazi, postcard to Uma Anand, Barcelona, 4 September 1973.

CHAPTER 37: PURANA QILA: SCALING NEW HEIGHTS

1. Deshpande, G.P., STQ, No. 6, August 1995.
2. Aparna Dhadwadkar, quoted by Erin Mee in *Theatre of Roots: Redirecting the Modern Indian Stage*, Seagull Books, 2007, p. 198.
3. *Alkazi Speaks*, E. Alkazi in an interview with Reeta Sondhi, *Enact*, January–March 1981, Issue I, NSD, Pauls Press, Delhi, 1981, No. 169–171.
4. Alkazi, E., 'NSD's 5th 5 Year Plan', *Enact*, Appendix xix, 1979, pp. 169–171.
5. *Alkazi Speaks*, E. Alkazi in an interview with Reeta Sondhi, *Enact*, January–March 1981, Issue I, NSD, Pauls Press, Delhi, 1981, No. 169–171.
6. Ibid.
7. E. Alkazi's postcard to Uma Anand, Tokyo, 23 February 1974.
8. Alkazi, Roshen, 'Style and Interpretation of Stage Costume', DADA (The Dramatic Art and Design Academy), 2002.
9. Paul, Rajinder, *Enact*, No. 93, 94, September 1974.
10. Singh, Shanta Serbjeet, 'Drama of the National School', *Economic Times*, June–July 1974.
11. Ibid.
12. Ibid.
13. Uma Anand in a letter to E. Alkazi, New Delhi, 6 August 1975.
14. Dubey, Satyadev, 'Honest to God Delhi', *Enact*, No. 89, May 1974.
15. Singh, Shanta Serbjeet, 'Drama of the National School', *Economic Times*, June–July 1974.
16. Ibid.

CHAPTER 38: ALKAZI OUSTED!

1. *Alkazi Speaks*, E. Alkazi in an interview with Reeta Sondhi, *Enact*, January–March 1981, Issue I, NSD, Pauls Press, Delhi, 1981, No. 169–171.
2. Prakash, Gyan, *Emergency Chronicles: Indira Gandhi and Democracy's Turning Point*, Penguin Viking, 2018.
3. Editorial, *Enact*, No. 131 and 132, November–December 1977.
4. *Alkazi Speaks*, E. Alkazi in an interview with Reeta Sondhi, *Enact*, January–March 1981, Issue I, NSD, Pauls Press, Delhi, 1981, No. 169–171.
5. 'National School of Drama Students Demand Public Inquiry into Functioning of the School', *India Today*, May 1977.
6. Vasudev, Uma, 'Will Alkazi Return?', *Hindustan Times*, 24 August 1986.
7. *Alkazi Speaks*, E. Alkazi in an interview with Reeta Sondhi, *Enact*, January–March 1981, Issue I, NSD, Pauls Press, Delhi, 1981, No. 169–171.

PART SIX
CHAPTER 39: OPTIONS

1. E. Alkazi in a letter to Uma Anand, Kuwait, 14 June 1977.
2. E. Alkazi in a letter to Uma Anand, Kuwait, 20 June 1977.
3. E. Alkazi in a letter to Uma Anand, Kuwait, 14 June 1977.
4. E. Alkazi in a letter to Uma Anand, Kuwait, 4 July 1977.
5. 'Culture in the Wake of the Kuwaiti Oil Boom', a conversation with Farida Al Sultan, *Bazaar*, Spring 2010.
6. Ibid.

CHAPTER 40: ART HERITAGE: UNFINISHED BUSINESS

1. Shedde, Meenakshi, 'Our Patrons Are Vulgar and They Patronize the Worst', *Sunday*, 1 January 1989.
2. Singh, Shanta Serbjeet, 'Art Heritage and Alkazi', *Economic Times*, 10 December 1978.
3. Singh, Shanta Serbjeet, 'Art Heritage Impresses', *Economic Times*, 7 November 1977.
4. Jha, Ratna Dhar, 'Review of Bulgarian Graphics', *Morning Echo*, December–January 1977–78.
5. Shedde, Meenakshi, 'Our Patrons Are Vulgar and They Patronize the Worst', *Sunday*, 1 January 1989.
6. Alkazi, E., 'Anguish in Andhra', 'The Cyclonic Silence', Art Heritage catalogue, January 1978.

7   Ibid.
8   Ibid.
9   Anupam Sud in conversation with the author, 2014.
10 Alkazi, E., Editorial, Art Heritage catalogue, 1986–87.
11 E. Alkazi in an interview with the author, NYC, 1999.
12 Pheroza Godrej in conversation with the author, September 2023.

CHAPTER 41: BRITAIN: DEVELOPING A SENSE OF HISTORY

1   E. Alkazi in letter to Uma Anand, London, 28 February 1979.
2   E. Alkazi in a letter to Uma Anand, London, 9 March 1979.
3   E. Alkazi in an interview with the author, NYC, 1999.
4   E. Alkazi interviewed by Amit Sanyal found among his personal papers.
5   Khandalwala, Karl, 'Scenes of Another Day', *Express*, London, 14 April 1985.
6   E. Alkazi interviewed by Amit Sanyal found among his personal papers.
7   E. Alkazi in an interview with the author, NYC, 1999.
8   E. Alkazi in a letter to Uma Anand, Kuwait, 12 July 1981.
9   Ibid. The Brixton racial riots caused by discrimination against the Blacks by the British police escalated in the summer of 1981.
10 Review in *City Limits*, Oxford, 23–29 July 1982.
11 David Elliott interviewed by Hilary Floe, 'Unlearning the Modern', *British Art Studies*, Issue 13, September 2019, Asia Exhibition Histories.

CHAPTER 42: THE PASSAGE OF TIME

1   E. Alkazi in a letter to Uma Anand, 9 December 1982.
2   Video interview with Nissar Allana, 1991.
3   Edited from letters written by E. Alkazi to Uma Anand between 8–20 August 1984.
4   Meenakshi Shedde in an interview, 'Our Patrons Are Vulgar and They Patronize the Worst', *Sunday*, 1 January 1989.
5   F.N. Souza in a letter to E. Alkazi, 16 October 1984.
6   F.N. Souza in a letter to E. Alkazi, 28 October 1984.
7   E. Alkazi in a letter to Uma Anand, 5 November 1984.
8   E. Alkazi in a letter to Souza, 8 November 1984.

CHAPTER 43: CICA: A GLOBAL IDENTITY

1   Ursula Bickelmann and Nissim Ezekiel, ed., *Artists Today: East–West Visual Arts Encounter*, Marg Publications, 1987.

2   Author's note: I have attempted to capture the spirit of the animated interactions between the artists at the 'East–West' encounter, inspired by its full verbatim coverage in Ursula Bickelmann and Nissim Ezekiel, ed., *Artists Today: East–West Visual Arts Encounter*, Marg Publications, 1987.
3   *Telegraph*, 25 March 1988.
4   Patel, Vibhuti, The Arts Column, *India Today*, 15 June 1990.
5   Gupta, Shubra, 'Towards Creating a National Theatre', *Sunday Mail*, 15 March 1987.
6   Raghuvanshi, Alka, 'Theatre People Cannot Survive on Fresh Air alone', *Express*, 22 February 1987.
7   Gupta, Shubra, 'Towards Creating a National Theatre', *Sunday Mail*, 15 March 1987.
8   'The Significance of a Photographic Archive', Alkazi's address to NSD students, 15 March 1987.
9   Kumar, Kuldeep, 'Alkazi Steals the Thunder', *Sunday Observer*, 15 April 1987.
10 Kumar, Kuldeep, 'Don't Play around with Traditions', *Sunday Observer*, 22 March 1987.

CHAPTER 44: THE RISE AND FALL OF CICA

1   Dhamija, Ram, 'Magnificent Mexican Mural Tradition/The Arts Panorama', *New Wave*, 3 April 1988.
2   Lloyd, Jill, 'New York; Open Frontiers for Contemporary Art', *Art International*, Autumn, 1989.
3   E. Alkazi in a letter to CICA Trustees, 7 February 1991.

CHAPTER 45: CIVILIZATIONAL CHRONICLES

1   E. Alkazi in an interview with the author, NYC, 1999.
2   Alkazi, E., 'Shadows at Sunset: Nineteenth-Century Photography in India', New Delhi, 1996. From the catalogue of exhibition held at Shridharani Gallery.
3   Alkazi attending a rehearsal of *Din Ke Andhere Mein*. Video footage of a rehearsal.
4   This entire sequence that I've described was shot by Nissar Allana and myself on video in 1991 at NSD, New Delhi.
5   Ebrahim Alkazi, 'Talk 1 Francis Newton Souza', Art Heritage, New Delhi, c. 1990s.
6   Ebrahim Alkazi, 'Talk 2 Francis Newton Souza', Art Heritage, New Delhi, c. 1990s.
7   Sunil Sethi, 'Souza and Alkazi: A Tempestuous Meeting of Titans', *Times of India*, 13 November 1996.

8 *Masterworks: The Alkazi Collection*, catalogue, 1995.
9 Directed by Ebrahim Alkazi and produced by Nissar Allana for Theatre and TV Associates, New Delhi. It consists of six segments of twenty-three minutes each.

CHAPTER 47: DISAPPEARANCE
1 E. Alkazi's speech on being awarded the Time and Talents Club Lifetime Achievement Award, Bombay, 1998.
2 E. Alkazi's speech at Osian's Cinefan Festival of Asian and Arab Cinema, Mumbai, 8 June 2007.

Scan QR code to access the
Penguin Random House India website